George IV

CHRISTOPHER HIBBERT

George IV

The Rebel Who Would Be King

GEORGE IV

First published in 2007 by
PALGRAVE MACMILLAN™
175 Fifth Avenue, New York, N.Y. 10010 and
Houndmills, Basingstoke, Hampshire, England RG21 6XS.
Companies and representatives throughout the world.

PALGRAVE MACMILLAN is the global academic imprint of the Palgrave Macmillan division of St. Martin's Press, LLC and of Palgrave Macmillan Ltd. Macmillan® is a registered trademark in the United States, United Kingdom and other countries. Palgrave is a registered trademark in the European Union and other countries.

ISBN-13: 978-1-4039-8379-4 paperback
ISBN-10: 1-4039-8379-8 paperback

Library of Congress Cataloging-in-Publication Data is available from the Library of Congress.

A catalogue record of the book is available from the British Library.

Design by Macmillan India

First published in two volumes as George IV: Prince of Wales by Longmans 1972 and George IV: Regent and King by Allen and Lane 1973.

First PALGRAVE MACMILLAN paperback edition: JUNE 2007

10 9 8 7 6 5 4 3 2 1

Printed in the United States of America.

FOR
BILL AND PAM WYNNE WILLSON
AND
DAVID AND BARBARA LAURIE

Contents

PART FOUR 1821–1830

Foreword

Christopher Hibbert once claimed to an interviewer that his sole aim was "to entertain and tell a good, accurate story." This extremely modest assessment of his own work has never been shared by reviewers or his millions of loyal readers around the world.

"One of his signal merits—it is certainly his most original," declared the *Spectator* when *George IV* was first published, "is to conceive of the interpretation of each life, once he has fully investigated and grasped it, as a breathing scale model of its own essential nature. Thus his biography of Garibaldi was appropriate solid opera, poignant and public Verdi; his life of Johnson, a cave of dark truths and imaginings shot through with rays of anarchy. A faithful submission to the subject and a narrative following exactly in its wake, that is the Hibbert recipe."

Christopher Hibbert's achievements are all the more remarkable considering he already had two successful careers behind him when he became a historian. He was born in 1924, thus making him one of the generation of boys who became either men or ghosts on the battlefield. At nineteen, Hibbert interrupted his studies at Oxford to join the Army. Within a few months he was a platoon commander in Sicily, fighting from hill top to hill top as part of the Allied invasion. He was wounded twice and received the Military Cross in 1945.

Although tempted to remain in the Army, Hibbert returned to Oxford and completed his history degree. He married and became a country real estate agent. He discovered his talent for writing almost by chance. An Oxford friend invited him to contribute a TV column for his magazine. Four years later, in 1961, Hibbert established his reputation with his award-winning *The Destruction of Lord Raglan*, a history of the Crimean War. When his next book, a biography of Mussolini, became a number one bestseller, Hibbert proved his preeminence in the field.

Since then, Hibbert has written at an astonishing rate on subjects as diverse as the history of Rome and American Revolution. More than forty of his books remain in print. However, the jewel in his crown remains *George IV*. The eighteenth century scholar, Professor J. H. Plumb, declared it to be most perceptive study ever written of the self-destructive prince.

The prevailing view of George IV was entirely negative until Hibbert's sympathetic biography revealed a gifted individual whose harsh upbringing and personal weaknesses conspired to ruin his potential. It was also the prince's misfortune to fall into the hands of the brilliant but dissolute Whigs. The Duchess of Devonshire, Charles James Fox, and Richard Brinsley

Sheridan were indeed a "School for Scandal." But while they eventually grew into sadder and wiser middle-age, the prince never matured past adolescence.

George IV's pathological self-indulgence turned him into a buffoon, blinding critics then and now to his contribution towards Britain's cultural heritage. Many of London's most beautiful buildings owe their genesis to this much maligned king. As Hibbert argues, no other monarch cared so passionately about art and architecture.

Eschewing the obvious for the nuanced, Hibbert rescued George IV from the clowns' corner to restore him to his true, tragic glory.

—Amanda Foreman

Author's Note

THIS biography of George IV is based largely upon his papers in the Royal Archives at Windsor, and I have to thank Her Majesty the Queen for graciously allowing me to make use of them. Most of the King's correspondence is now generally available in the eleven volumes comprehensively and meticulously edited by Professor Aspinall to whom all students of the period will be indebted. In addition to this correspondence, I have been granted access to those papers which could not be released at the time Professor Aspinall was compiling his edition, or which concern topics (such as accounts and Queen Caroline's affairs) outside its scope. I would also like to thank Sir Robin Mackworth-Young, Her Majesty's Librarian, and Miss Jane Langton, Registrar of the Archives, and her staff, for their generous help and advice when I was working in the Castle.

Although the Royal Archives provide by far the most vital and abundant sources for the King's life, there are numerous important manuscript sources elsewhere, and I am most grateful to the Duke of Devonshire for access to the Devonshire Collections; to the Marquess of Hertford for access to the Ragley Manuscripts; to the Earl of Halifax for use of the Hickleton Papers; to the Earl of Harewood for use of the Canning Papers; to the Earl of Crawford and Balcarres for use of the Crawford Muniments; to the Earl of Harrowby for use of the Harrowby Manuscripts; to Earl Fitzwilliam and the Trustees of the Wentworth Woodhouse Estate for allowing me to quote from the Wentworth Woodhouse Muniments; to the Earl of Denbigh for permission to quote from the Denbigh Manuscripts; to the Duke of Wellington for use of the Wellington Papers; to the Broadlands Trustees for the use of the Palmerston Papers; to the Trustees of Chequers for permission to consult manuscripts in the library at Chequers; to the Bishop and Dean of Worcester for allowing me to see the Hurd Manuscripts at Hartlebury Castle; to the Director of the Royal Pavilion, for permission to study and quote from various letters in his care; to Mrs Hervé Coatalen for letting me see the correspondence of Sir Walter Farquhar and the Hook Manuscripts; to Lieutenant-Colonel H. E. Scott for use of some material from the King's papers which are in his possession and for permission to quote from a manuscript in the Eldon Papers; to the Chairman and Secretary of Brooks's for allowing me to consult the records of the club; and to the Directors of Messrs Coutts and Company for permission to use the archives of the bank.

For helping me find the relevant papers I want to thank Mr T. S. Wragg, the Duke of Devonshire's librarian; Mr M. W. Farr, the Warwickshire County Archivist and his staff who have charge of the Ragley Papers; Major T. L. Ingram, Lord Halifax's archivist; Miss Rosamund Campbell, the Earl of Harrowby's archivist; Mr A. R. C. Grant, the Duke of Wellington's librarian; Miss Margaret Cash, Hampshire County Archivist, in whose care are the Palmerston Papers; Mr C. F. Penruddock, Secretary to the Chequers Trust; Mr L. W. Greenwood, librarian at Hartlebury Castle; Mr Derek Rogers of the Royal Pavilion; Mr J. M. Collinson of the Archives Department of Leeds City Libraries where the Canning Papers are now deposited; Mr John Bebbington who, as Sheffield City Librarian, has charge of the Wentworth Woodhouse Muniments; Miss M. V. Stokes, archivist of Coutts' Bank; and Mr N. A. Ussher, the Earl of Harewood's agent.

I have also made use of the Fremantle Collection and the Goderich Papers at Aylesbury; the Finch Manuscripts at the Bodleian, Oxford; the Pretyman Papers at Ipswich; the Waller of Woodcote Manuscripts at Warwick; the Earl Grey Papers at Durham; the Fitzwilliam Manuscripts, the Brooke Records and Lord Dover's papers and diaries at Delapre

Abbey; the Markham Papers at York; the Capell Manuscripts at Hertford; the Goulding Papers at Lincoln; and the Brougham Manuscripts in the Library of University College, London. I would, accordingly, like to express my thanks for their help to Mr E. J. Davis, the County of Buckingham Archivist; Mrs Mary Clapinson of the Department of Western Manuscripts, Bodleian Library, Oxford; Mr W. R. Serjeant and Miss Patricia James of the Ipswich and East Suffolk Record Office; Mr J. E. Fagg and Dr J. M. Fewster of the Department of Palaeography and Diplomatic in the Universit of Durham; Mr P. I. King, Chief Archivist to the Northampton and Huntingdonshire Archives Committee; Mrs N. K. M. Gurney, Archivist at the Borthwick Institute of Historical Research in the University of York; Mr Peter Walne, the Hertfordshire County Archivist; Miss J. A. Cripps of the Lincolnshire Archives Committee; and Mr Joseph W. Scott, librarian, University College, London.

I have also to acknowledge the generous help of Dr F. Taylor, librarian of the John Rylands Library, Manchester; Mr J. N. Allen and his staff at Brighton Reference Library; Miss G. M. A. Beck of the Borough of Guildford Muniment Room; Miss A. Green, the Royal County of Berkshire Archivist; the staffs of the Oxfordshire County Record Office, and of the Public Record Office of Northern Ireland; Mrs Patricia Gill, the West Sussex County Archivist, who kindly answered various questions concerning the Petworth House Archives which are in her care at Chichester; and Mrs L. M. Patterson, the secretary of the Royal Society of Literature, who showed me the Society's papers.

Mr Michael Brock, Vice-President of Wolfson College, Oxford, has been kind enough to read the book in proof and has made several valuable suggestions for its improvement. I am most grateful also to Mrs Joan St George Saunders for working for me in the British Museum and the Public Record Office, to Mrs Stewart Ryan for reading newspapers for me in the Newspaper Library at Colindale, to Miss Barbara Mason for transcribing some of the Wentworth Wood-

house Muniments at Sheffield, to Miss Mary Cosh, author of
Inverary and the Argylls, for some information concerning
Lady Augusta Campbell, to Mrs Frances Hawes, Lord
Brougham's biographer, for taking extracts from the diaries
and letters of Lady Anne Barnard at Balcarres, and to my
son, Tom, and my daughter, Kate, for transcribing various
other manuscripts. Mrs Barbro Steele has kindly helped me
to translate some of the more obscure letters which Princess
Caroline wrote to her husband in her idiosyncratic French.
Dr Kenneth Bourne has generously helped me to identify
people referred to only by disguised names in Emily Cowper's letters now among the Palmerston Papers. And Mr
Edward Miller has provided me with information about the
British Museum's acquisition of the King's Library.

For their generous and expert help in a variety of other
ways I want also to thank Sir Owen Morshead, Sir Oliver
Millar, Mr Geoffrey de Bellaigue, Lord Adam Gordon, Mr
David Higham, Mr Cuthbert Fitzherbert, Mr D. A. Hartley
Russell, Mr Shevawn Lynam, Mrs Eve Weiss, Dr Clifford
Musgrave, Mr Roger Mortimer, Mrs Alan Glendining, Mrs
John Rae, Miss Clare Pollen, Mrs Elisabeth Webb, Dr R. J.
Hetherington, Mr Anthony Berry and Mr J. R. Rudd of
Messrs Berry Brothers & Rudd of St James's Street, Mr
Brian Hill, Mr Roger Fulford, Mrs Maurice Hill, Dr A. J.
Salmon, Mrs George Onslow and Miss Jane Hoos of the
Lord Chamberlain's Office.

Finally I want to say how grateful I am to Mr George
Walker and Mr Hamish Francis for having read the proofs
and to my wife for having compiled the index.

C. H.

*Quotations from manuscript sources have been given with
the original spelling preserved. For the sake of easy reading
the punctuation has occasionally been altered, capitalization
modified and abbreviations written out in full.*

George IV

PART ONE
1762–1794

Childhood and Education
1762–1778

'An extremely promising pupil'

AT St James's Palace, during the late afternoon of 12 August 1762, Lord Cantelupe, Vice-Chairman to Queen Charlotte, was told that her Majesty was in labour; he was instructed to hold himself ready to notify the King immediately the baby was born. Towards six o'clock the Queen's pains increased, and it was clear that the birth was imminent. This was her first pregnancy, and it was a severe labour; but the hopeful, earnest little mother was a healthy girl of eighteen, and the midwife expected no complications. She 'scarce cried out at all,' the Duchess of Northumberland, a Lady of the Bedchamber, later recorded, 'and at twenty-four minutes past seven she was delivered'.

Forestalling Lord Cantelupe, the Earl of Huntingdon – the incompetent and soon to be dismissed Groom of the Stole – officiously hastened to the King's apartment to inform him that he was the father of a baby girl. Protesting that he was 'but little anxious as to the sex of the child', so long as the Queen was safe, the King immediately went to his wife's bedchamber where, soon after his arrival, he was shown as 'strong, large and pretty boy ... as ever was seen'.

Within a fortnight this large and pretty boy, created Prince of Wales and Earl of Chester and, by right of birth, Duke of Cornwall, Duke of Rothesay, Earl of Carrick and Baron of Renfrew, was placed on display at St James's Palace where, on the afternoons of Drawing-Room days, between one o'clock and three, visitors were admitted to the precincts of his cradle which were separated from the rest of the room by a Chinese lattice screen. As they awaited their turn to inspect him, they were regaled in an ante-room – as the custom of his mother's family dictated – with cake and caudle, a warm gruel spiced and sweetened and mixed with wine, a beverage much favoured in both Germany and England as a tonic for women in childbed. Drawn more perhaps by the refreshments than by the Prince, so 'vast a tumult' of people came to the Palace that £500 worth of cake was given away, and about eighty gallons of caudle consumed every day that his Royal Highness was on display.

Soon after the last of these daily receptions was concluded the little Prince was christened in the Queen's drawing-room by the Archbishop of Canterbury. The Queen, dressed in a white and silver gown with a richly jewelled stomacher, lay on her bed of state, the crimson velvet hangings of which were trimmed with gold, lined with satin, and adorned with gilded carving and plumes of white feathers. At the foot of her bed, on a table, was a large gilt baptismal bowl. The child was brought into the room on a white satin pillow, conducted by a procession of attendants under the leadership of the Lord Chamberlain, the Duke of Devonshire. His sponsors were his formidable grandmother, Augusta, the Princess Dowager of Wales, his maternal uncle, Adolphus Frederick IV, Duke of Mecklenburg-Strelitz, and his great-uncle, the Duke of Cumberland, whom he afterwards claimed dimly to remember – though the Duke died soon after his godson's third birthday – as an old man 'dressed in a snuff-coloured suit of clothes down to his knees'. 'He took me in his arms,' the Prince recalled, 'and placed me on his knee, where he held me a long time. The enormity of his bulk excited my wonder.'

The names chosen were George Augustus Frederick; and as these were bestowed upon the child – who cried 'most lustily' throughout the ceremony – his father, then aged twenty-four, was seen to be deeply moved, and to behave with the 'most affecting piety'.

Already the Prince had been provided with a considerable

establishment, including a wet-nurse, a necessary woman, a
sempstress and two rockers of the cradle who were all under
the authority of the royal governess, Lady Charlotte Finch,
daughter of the Earl of Pomfret, 'a woman of remarkable
sense and philosophy'. Lady Charlotte's chief deputy was
Mrs Henrietta Coultworth; the dry-nurse was Mrs Chapman, 'a fine active woman', affectionate and capable.

In the care of these kindly and efficient women George
Augustus Frederick, Prince of Wales, grew and prospered.
As he was taken out to enjoy the fresh air of Hyde Park, the
crowds that followed him, so Lord Bath told a friend, called
out to each other, 'God bless him, he is a lusty, jolly, young
dog truly!' His mother had him painted in her arms by
Francis Cotes and commissioned a model of him in wax
which, side by side with numerous other portraits of her
first-born baby in miniature, enamel and marble, she kept
in her room on a velvet cushion under a bell-glass.

By the age of two and a half the Prince had progressed so
well that he was able to pronounce a formal answer, 'with
great propriety and suitableness of action', to the representatives of a charitable institution to whom he handed a dona-
tion of £100. When he was four and obliged to stay in bed
with the curtains drawn after a smallpox inoculation, he
answered an inquiry from his mother's Keeper of the Robes,
Mrs Schwellenberg, as to whether he found the restriction
unpleasantly tedious, by observing with an impressively precocious gravity, 'Not at all, I lie and make reflections.' By
the age of five he had been taught to write in a neat, round
hand by Mr Bulley, the royal writing master; he had also
been taught the rudiments of English grammar by the
'quiet, patient, plodding, persevering' Miss Frederica Planta;
and at the age of six he was reported to be making good
progress with all his other lessons which began after breakfast at seven and continued till he sat down to dinner at
three. It was, indeed, generally supposed that he was a highly
promising child, healthy and intelligent, a little hot-
tempered, perhaps, and somewhat lacking in determination –

having suffered a few falls in trying to learn how to skate, he could not be induced to try again. But it was hoped that any flaws of character, or defects of physique, which might manifest themselves, would soon be eradicated by the moral and physical training to be enjoyed or endured at the Queen's House in London, and at Richmond Lodge and Kew.

In these two royal country residences the Prince spent his earliest years. They had been chosen by his father as the most suitable background for the kind of quiet, regular, domestic, country family life which he and his wife, though both so young, preferred to the glitter of St James's. The King, indeed, had little choice. Richmond Palace, which had been used as a nursery by King James II, had fallen into decay; so had Windsor Castle, neglected since the death of Queen Anne and now partially occupied by families with real or pretended claims upon royal favour. Hampton Court was in relatively good order, having been a favourite palace of the King's grandfather King George II; but, as it brought him unwelcome memories of an unhappy childhood, the King did not like it and declined to live in it.

So, there being no other country retreats convenient to London and available to him, the King was obliged to use Richmond Lodge, formerly the Keeper's Lodge in the large park to the north of Richmond Palace, which had been allotted to Queen Charlotte as part of her marriage settlement. But it was a small house, and as the Queen gave birth to new babies with seasonal regularity it became so excessively overcrowded that a larger one became essential. In 1771 the family's problems were solved by the death of the King's mother: the White House at Kew, where she had lived since the death of her husband, became vacant and the King and Queen moved in.

By then, although she was not yet twenty-eight, the Queen already had eight children, five boys and three girls. Frederick, later Duke of York, the Prince of Wales's eldest brother, had been born in 1763; Prince William in 1765; Princess Charlotte in 1766; Prince Edward in 1767; Princess

Augusta in 1768; Princess Elizabeth in 1770 and Prince Ernest in 1771.* Since the White House, commodious as it was, was not extensive enough for all these children and their various attendants, the two eldest sons, the Prince of Wales, aged eleven, and Prince Frederick, aged ten, were placed under tutors at the Dutch House nearby.

The Dutch House – now known as Kew Palace, since the White House, apart from the Kitchen Wing, was demolished in 1802 – had been built in 1631 by a rich London merchant of Dutch descent. A substantial red-brick gabled house of three storeys, with attics and a basement, it was one of a number of houses at Kew which were leased or owned by the royal family, or by various members of the Court whose numerous liveried servants could be seen on summer evenings strolling about amidst the cattle grazing on the Green.

At the Dutch House a more rigorous stage of the Prince of Wales's education began under the direction of Robert D'Arcy, fourth Earl of Holdernesse, his Governor. Holdernesse was, in Horace Walpole's opinion, a 'formal piece of dullness' who had proved himself, when in office in various administrations, 'an unthinking and unparliamentary minister'. His duties as Lord Warden of the Cinque Ports and Lord Lieutenant of the North Riding of Yorkshire, combined with increasing ill health which drove him to live abroad in 1774, did not allow him time to give much personal attention to the problems of his charges. He was obliged to leave most of the details of their education to the Princes' Sub-Governor, Leonard Smelt, and their Preceptor, Dr William Markham, Bishop of Chester.

Smelt was a talented and versatile officer in the Royal Engineers, experienced in the art of military sketching and

* There were seven further children yet to come, Prince Augustus in 1773, Prince Adolphus in 1774, Princess Mary in 1776, Princess Sophia in 1777, Octavius and Alfred in 1779 and 1780, and Amelia in 1783. Alfred died when he was a baby in 1782 and, to his father's great distress, Octavius also died the next year. 'There will be no heaven for me,' the King declared miserably, 'if Octavius is not there.'

plan drawing, yet having at the same time a deep love and knowledge of literature and art. He had served at the battles of Dettingen and Fontenoy, had been sent out to survey and report on the defences of Newfoundland, and had returned to become the friend not only of George III but of Joshua Reynolds, Fanny Burney, and several other members of Dr Johnson's circle.

William Markham was also a remarkable man. Of humble parentage, he had gained a place at Westminster School and a studentship at Christ Church, Oxford. At the age of thirty-four he had been appointed Headmaster of Westminster School; in 1767 he had been nominated Dean of Christ Church; and in 1771, two months before he became – on the recommendation of Lord Mansfield – the Prince's Preceptor, he had been consecrated Bishop of Chester. A tall and portly man, inclined to be both pompous and short-tempered, though not unkindly, he combined an 'almost martial bearing' with a deep fund of learning. Jeremy Bentham, who was a pupil at Westminster when he was headmaster, said that 'his business was rather in courting the great than in attending to the school. He had a great deal of pomp, especially when he lifted his hand, waved it, and repeated Latin verses ... We stood prodigiously in awe of him'. He had a very rich wife, the daughter of an English merchant of Rotterdam, who provided him with thirteen children. Destined one day to become Archbishop of York, at the time of his appointment as director of the 'religious and learned part of the young Prince's education', he was fifty-two years old, the same age as Leonard Smelt.

Under their watchful care, the Prince and his brother, Frederick, were kept hard at work or at some form of supervised recreation from early in the morning until eight o'clock at night, in accordance with the strict commands of the King, who strongly believed that no change for the better could be expected in the 'unprincipled days' in which they lived except by 'an early attention to the education of the rising generation'. They were instructed in the classics, of course, learned French, German and Italian; and the Prince of Wales, at least, acquired a fair grasp of all these languages, though he became fluent only in French. His hand-writing, trained by laborious transcription of the wise words of Pliny and Bacon in his copy-book, was neat and legible; he found 'great facility' in getting Greek epigrams by heart; and if his spelling was – and always remained – highly idiosyncratic, it was a good deal less eccentric than that of the Earl of Holdernesse, his Governor. Shortly after his tenth birthday, his great-aunt Amelia had cause to thank him for a 'very fine wrote letter'. 'It is far beyond what I could have expected of a prince of your age,' she told him. 'I cannot say enough, Sir, how charmed I am at seeing you so forward in every proper qualification for your rank. I hope you will not dislike a little ball about Christmas when the young gentlemen that have the honour to be liked by you have holy days.'

The Prince received constant moral guidance. His father warned him, 'little dependence can be placed on any thing in this world and the best method of continually pursuing your duty is the continually placing before your eyes that the Supreme Being has put you in an exalted station; and that you are therefore accountable to Him for your conduct'. Nothing must distract the Prince from the path of dutiful conduct nor from the way of truth.

The Earl of Holdernesse, who was, despite Horace Walpole's unfavourable opinion, conscientious and sensible, also urged the Prince of Wales to be truthful: 'Truth is the first quality of a man; the higher the rank the more to be adhered to.' Lord Holdernesse further advised him to be moderate in his diet and to beware of those who poured that species of poison in the ear which was 'the more dangerous as it is pleasing in the first sensation, tho' followed by ruin and destruction'; for the Prince, at the age of twelve, was already threatening to become excessively fond of both food and flattery.

His mother, though she seemed more concerned that his

bodily constitution should remain unimpaired, also urged him to 'disdain all flattery' and 'abhor all vice', to 'fear God', to do 'justice unto everybody and avoid partiality', above all to display 'the highest love, affection and duty towards the King'.

This last injunction the Prince of Wales found it increasingly difficult to obey. His father had seemed to love him when he was a baby – as, indeed, the King obviously loved all his children when they were babies – but the older the Prince grew the further he felt removed from his affection. It was as though his father had wanted him to remain a baby for ever and resented, even recoiled from, his progress towards puberty. He was made to wear babies' cambric frocks with hemstitched tucks and hems and Valenciennes lace cuffs long after other children of his age had been given more suitable clothes; it was said of him that he caught hold of his frilled collar one day and exclaimed in exasperation to a servant, *'See how I am treated!'*

Apart from that of his brother Frederick, he was denied the close companionship of any other children, just as he was constantly and carefully sheltered from any adult who might fill his mind with thoughts about the wonders and excitements of the outside world. That world must be veiled from him, his father repeatedly insisted, by those who 'cirrounded' him. He must be taught the virtues of rigorous simplicity, hard work, punctuality and regularity, and, at the first sign of laziness, laxness or untruthfulness, he must be beaten. And beaten he was. One of his sisters later recalled how she had seen him and Prince Frederick 'held by their tutors to be flogged like dogs with a long whip'.

Occasionally the Prince went to a concert or an opera; sometimes there were fireworks displays and country dances on family birthdays; on Thursdays, when the royal gardens were open to the public, carriages came into the drives, and boats with musicians aboard were rowed up the Thames to the little islands opposite the Dutch House; in the evenings when the Queen gave commerce parties, the Prince was allowed into her drawing-room up till ten o'clock; once or twice an artist, Zoffany or Gainsborough, came to paint his portrait. But these were rare breaks in the tedium of his days, rare glimpses of the world beyond the garden walls of Kew and of his mother's house in London.

In May 1776, when the Prince was thirteen, Lord Holdernesse resigned in consequence of a 'nursery revolution' which also led to the dismissal of the Sub-Preceptor, Cyril Jackson, whom the Governor blamed for the Princes' increasingly contemptuous treatment of him since his return from the Continent. Holdernesse's place was at first taken by Lord Bruce, 'a formal, dull man, totally ignorant of and unversed in the world'; then by Bruce's eldest brother, the Duke of Montagu, 'one of the weakest and most ignorant men living', who possessed, however, a 'formal coldness of character' that was said to make him 'uncommonly well fitted' for the post. At the same time Dr Markham, having supported the Sub-Preceptor in his quarrel with the Governor, was replaced by Richard Hurd, Bishop of Lichfield and Coventry, who was expected by the King to impose upon his eldest sons an even more exacting regime than they had already grown accustomed to.* Hurd was 'a stiff and cold, but

* The Prince of Wales, who liked Markham and considered him 'one of his best friends', had asked that he might be allowed to remain their Preceptor after Lord Holdernesse's resignation, but the King had refused the request on the grounds that the Prince 'would secretly feel a kind of victory if the Bishop remained'. After his schooldays he continued on good terms with his former Preceptor, addressing him in 1800 as 'my dear much loved friend', and signing himself 'your old and *most gratefully attached* pupil' (Markham MSS, York). He quite often dined with him when, as Archbishop of York, Markham was staying in London at his house in Bloomsbury Square and, on a visit to Yorkshire in 1806, he called upon him at Bishopsthorpe where he dutifully fell to his knees to receive his blessing (*Markham Memoir*, 42, 76–7). The Prince was less sorry to part from Cyril Jackson 'who used to have a silver pencil-case in his

correct gentleman', with a courtly, decorous manner which 'endeared him highly to devout old ladies', and which, in combination with a high, though questionable, reputation as a literary critic and philosopher, had recommended him to the King. The Bishop's chaplain, the Rev. William Arnold, replaced Jackson as Sub-Preceptor, and Lieutenant-Colonel George Hotham became Sub-Governor in place of Smelt. At the same time, to complete the 'nursery revolution', all the Prince's servants were replaced by men of sterner mettle.

Soon after his appointment, Hurd drew up his rigorous *Plans of Study for the Princes*, a programme of education covering the widespread fields of religion, morals, government and laws, mathematics and natural philosophy, history ('sacred', 'profane' and 'modern') and 'polite literature' (this being devoted mainly to Greek and Latin writers, the only three English writers considered worthy of detailed study being Shakespeare, Milton and Pope).

Strong emphasis still lay upon the classics, as it would have done, with far greater force, had the Prince attended a public school. Even on Sunday mornings his classical training was not abated, for the Greek Testament had 'to be constantly read'.

The Prince thought that Hurd was not such a good teacher as Markham who was 'a much greater, wiser, and more learned man'. When he was instructed to translate Homer and hesitated over a word, Markham had taken the trouble to explain it to him; but Hurd, as though he were not quite sure of the meaning himself, merely referred his pupil to the dictionary.

The education supervised by Hurd, however, was by no means a narrow one. The Prince was taught to play the 'cello by John Crosdill, and to sing pleasantly as well as to construe Latin; he was helped to cultivate a taste for the fine arts as well as to understand Euclid. He was taught to fence

hand while we were at our lessons,' Prince Frederick recalled, 'and he has frequently given us such knocks with it on our foreheads that the blood followed them' (*Rogers Table Talk*, 116).

and to box by Henry Angelo and to draw by Alexander Cozens. In his own garden at Kew he was instructed in the elements of agriculture, sowed and harvested his own crops and even baked his own bread.

He was much more knowledgeable and versatile at sixteen than his father had been at that age, for George III had been rather haphazardly under the direction of a Governor who was alleged to have been 'perfectly satisfied that he had done his duty so long as he was unremitting in his exhortations to his royal pupil to turn out his toes'.

At sixteen, in fact, the Prince of Wales was both accomplished and attractive. 'His countenance was of a sweetness and intelligence quite irresistible,' recalled one of the Queen's German attendants, Charlotte Albert. 'He had an elegant person, engaging and distinguished manners, added to an affectionate disposition and the cheerfulness of youth.' He was rather given to practical jokes, she added, instancing the occasion on which the oboist, Johann Christian Fischer, a greedy and nervous man, was invited to a meal by the Prince after a concert. Fischer was told that something especially delicious had been prepared for him. He sat down eagerly; the cover was lifted, and out jumped a live rabbit. But despite these thoughtless pranks, the Prince was a very likeable boy, Fräulein Albert thought, and very gifted. Miss Planta thought so, too. 'He is a fine boy,' she said, 'has an open countenance, a manly air ... he possesses the most obliging politeness, such as can only spring from goodness of heart, and by the accounts I hear he is most amiable ...'

His tutors agreed. Bishop Hurd assured a friend that he was 'an extremely promising pupil', confirming the earlier verdict of Lord Holdernesse who, when living in Switzerland, received reports of the Prince's 'accomplishments from many quarters', 'pleasing reports' which were confirmed by 'the most competant judges', his tutors.

The Prince's appearance at this time was also pleasing. It was fairly accurately described by himself in a letter to one of his sister's attendants:

[He] is now approaching the bloom of youth, he is rather above the common size, his limbs well-proportioned, and upon the whole well made, though rather too great a penchant to grow fat. The features of his countenance carry with them too much of an air of hauteur, his forehead well shaped, his eyes though none of the best, and though grey are yet passable, tolerable good eyebrows and eyelashes, un petit nez retroussé cependant assez aimé, a good mouth though rather large, with fine teeth, a tolerable good chin, but the whole of the countenance is too round. I forgot to add my uggly ears. As hair is generally looked upon as a beauty, he has more hair than usually falls to everyone's share ...

It was beautiful hair, recorded Lady Anne Lindsay a few years later, 'waved in profusion with all the glossy lustre of youth on it'. 'His eyes,' she added, 'were of a clear blue, lively full of play and intelligence ... They saw everyone, neglected no one ... His nose was a companionable one, not the haughty one of his brother, Frederick, the Duke of York ... He smiled often ...'

In the letter describing his appearance which he wrote to his sister's attendant the Prince went on to describe what he liked to consider a generally rather pleasant personality.

His sentiments and thoughts are open and generous [he wrote] above doing anything that is mean (too susceptible, even to believing people his friends, and placing too much confidence in them, from not yet having a sufficient knowledge of the world or of its practices), grateful and friendly to excess where he finds *a real friend*. His heart is good and tender if it is allowed to show its notions. ... He has a *strict notion of honour*, rather too familiar to his inferiors but will not suffer himself to be browbeaten or treated with haughtiness by his superiors. Now for his vices, or rather let us call them weaknesses – too subject to give loose or vent to his passions of every kind, too subject to be in a passion, but he never bears malice or rancour in his heart ... he is rather to fond of wine and women ...

To this modest list of weaknesses his father would have added many others, including vanity and a capricious waywardness. For accomplished as his son was admitted to be,

charming as were his manners and entertaining his conversation, in the eyes of George III his eldest son's gifts
were not such as to compensate for the manifold faults to
be found in him. Five years before, when he was twelve, the
King had complained to Holdernesse of his 'duplicity', his
'bad habit ... of not speaking the truth'. Now that he was
approaching manhood and 'some new arrangements' concerning him would soon have to be made, the King wrote to
the Prince himself to warn him about his faulty character
and misdemeanours: he had not made that progress in his
studies which, 'from the ability and assiduity' of those placed
about him for that purpose, his father had reason to expect;
his proficiency in German, in particular, was 'very moderate',
yet in Germany he would one day have possessions that
would place him 'in one of the superior stations in that great
Empire'; moreover, his reading of history had been very
cursory and, although he had 'acquired a general view of
the principal facts in ancient and modern history', he had
'no insight into the springs which caused them, or any comprehensive knowledge of the Constitution, laws, finances,
commerce, etc., ... of the other European states'.

The Prince's attitude towards his religious duties, his
father went on, had regrettably shown that he was deficient
in gratitude to 'the Great Creator', and evidently unwilling
'implicitly to obey His will as conveighed to us in the Scrip-
tures'. Above all, his 'love of dissipation' had for months,
even at his present age, been 'trumpeted in the public
papers'. It was high time that he realized that 'the good or
bad example set by those in the higher stations must have
some effect on the general conduct of those in inferior ones'.
He could certainly be of the greatest assistance to his father,
but only if he would connect himself 'with those young men
who seem to be of worthy characters and to wish to make
themselves of utility and ornament to their country'. His
chosen companions of the present did not fall into that
category.

The King's strictures on this need were certainly well justi-

fied, so Fräulein Albert said. For some time the Prince had
been contriving to mix with characters whom his father had
due cause to consider most unworthy. 'Some of those about
[him],' she wrote, 'swerved from principle, and introduced
improper company' when their Majesties believed him to be
in bed. There was, for instance, the tall and pretty wife of
one of the grooms about the Court. She was 'a great slattern,
and more low and vulgar than that class of people usually
are', but the Prince took a strong fancy to her, so it was
arranged that her husband, 'a dressed-up horror, impertinent
and disgusting', should be brought up from the stables and
given a place about the person of the Prince which would enable his wife to appear in the royal apartments without undue comment.

Two of the worst influences on the Prince, in the King's
opinion, were his uncles, the Dukes of Gloucester and Cumberland. The Duke of Gloucester was the King's eldest
brother; he had given great offence by his secret marriage
in 1766 at her house in Pall Mall to the Dowager Countess
Waldegrave who was not only the widow of the King's
detested Governor, Lord Waldegrave – a 'depraved, worthless man', in his charge's opinion – but was also an illegitimate daughter of Sir Edward Walpole, a well-known Whig.
When the marriage came to light, the Duke was banished
from Court. During the Prince of Wales's childhood, he had
spent much of his time abroad, mostly in Italy; but on his
visits to England he provided the newspapers with a great
deal of salacious gossip about his amours with various young
women of the town.

The sexual adventures of Gloucester's younger brother, the
Duke of Cumberland, whose uncle, the Prince's sponsor, had
died in 1765, were even more offensive to the rigid morality
of the King. When Cumberland was twenty-five his brothers
had had to find £10,000 to compensate the Earl of Grosvenor
whose wife had committed adultery with him. He had had a
subsequent affair with a woman named Olive Wilmot whose
daughter, insisting that her mother had been married to

him, called herself Princess Olive of Cumberland. And in 1771 he had further outraged the King by marrying a widow, Mrs Anne Horton, daughter of Lord Irnham, afterwards Earl of Carhampton, a beautiful, intelligent and amusing woman, but 'vulgar, noisy, indelicate' and much given to jokes and banter of unparalleled coarseness.

To prevent such shameful marriages in future the King had instigated the Royal Marriage Act which provided that no member of the royal family could marry without the sovereign's consent, though if that consent were refused to someone over twenty-five a year's notice could be given to the Privy Council and then the marriage could take place despite the sovereign's refusal. This Act was passed in 1772; but it was not for another eight years that the King was reconciled to either of the brothers – whose choice of wives had prompted it – and permitted them to return to Court. Even then relations between them remained strained, particularly between the King and the Duke of Cumberland who was not only a reprobate, who not only ran a faro table at his house in Pall Mall, but was also a 'great Whig'. As for his blasphemous and extravagant Duchess, the King could never reconcile himself to her, since he believed, with some justice, that she lent herself to 'facilitate or gratify the Prince of Wales's inclinations'.

[2]

Mrs Robinson and Mme von Hardenburg
1778–1782

'A certain sort of ladies'

WHEN he was sixteen the Prince – having already seduced, so it was supposed, a maid of honour to the Queen – fell in love with Mary Hamilton, the third Duke of Hamilton's twenty-three-year-old great-granddaughter, one of his sister's attendants. For weeks he wrote to her almost every day – seventy-five of his letters to her survive – assuring her of his everlasting devotion. He had first conceived his passion for her in the early spring of 1779 when he confided in her one evening that he was desperately in love without telling her who was the object of the 'most secret thoughts' of his soul. The next day he declared in a letter that his 'fair incognita' was her 'dear, dear, dear self'. 'Your manners, your sentiments, the tender feelings of your heart,' he wrote, 'so totally coincide with my ideas, not to mention the many advantages you have in person over many other ladies, that I not only highly esteem you, but even love you more than words or ideas can express.'

In subsequent letters, at once passionate and stilted, he protested that if he had been placed in a different station in life he would have had the happiness of calling her his very own. 'For after the impetuous ardor of youth, and the violent impulse of passion is passed,' he assured her, 'then it is that one wishes to find in a companion for life such sentiments and such feelings as you possess and which I have known very few women enjoy to so superior a degree as yourself.' He loved her with 'enthusiastic fondness'; he doted upon her and adored her 'beyond the idea of everything that is human'; he could not help lamenting that his rank prevented, 'at least for the present', his being united with her whom alone he could love; 'impetuosity, ardor', no word was too strong for his 'present sentiments'.

He sent her a lock of his abundant light brown hair and asked for some of hers which would be dearer to him than life itself; on the back of the locket containing it she was not to have her dear named inscribed, just the date of her birth, an event 'ever so dear' to him, and on the front was to be the motto, 'Toujours aimée'. He would give her in exchange a bracelet which would be inscribed with the date of *his* birth, and the motto, 'Gravé à jamais dans mon coeur'.

Miss Hamilton replied to his incessant messages with caution. She could, without injuring her honour, accept his 'friendship', but she could not offer him more; her virtue was more precious to her than her life. She begged him not to offend her delicacy by sending her presents. 'My God,' she replied to one particularly impassioned letter, 'what will become of you if you suffer yourself to be led away with such impetuosity.' She could never act 'so base a part as to encourage such warm declarations'.

So the Prince reluctantly agreed to address her no longer 'with the impetuous passion of a lover urging his suit', but with the endearing names of 'friend and sister'. As a brother he wrote to her asking for her frank criticisms of his conduct; and she, taking him at his word, condemned his taste for low companions and for the 'indelicate, ungentlemanlike and wicked practice' he had 'thought proper to adopt of swearing'. He acknowledged the faults, excusing himself on the grounds that he had picked up the habit of swearing from hearing 'people in the Army do so', and he had thought it necessary to show that he had now become a man by giving in 'too much to this infamous practice'. He also sought Miss Hamilton's advice about his clothes in which he already took an inordinate interest, sending her patterns and pieces of cloth and pearl-coloured silk from his tailor and asking her to put pins in the ones she liked best.

At the beginning of December 1779 the correspondence was abruptly terminated, for the Prince had fallen violently in love with someone else less virtuous, a girl of astonishing beauty and notoriously exhibitionist habits, Mary Robinson.

Mary Robinson was born in Bristol of Irish descent, the daughter of the captain of a whaler who had himself been born in America. Her father abandoned his family when she was a child to establish a whale fishery manned by Esquimaux on the coast of Labrador; and Mary was sent to school in London where her dancing-master, who was also ballet-master at Drury Lane, gained for her an introduction to David Garrick. Garrick offered her the part of Cordelia in *King Lear*; but her marriage at the age of fifteen to an articled clerk named Thomas Robinson, who was wrongly supposed by her mother to be a man of property, led to her temporarily abandoning the idea of becoming an actress. Instead, she and her husband took to leading an extravagant life which ended with their both being imprisoned for debt, together with their baby daughter. On her release she sought out Garrick who arranged her *début* as Juliet at Drury Lane in 1776. Thereafter she appeared in numerous successful productions, becoming one of the most celebrated young actresses of her day, and undoubtedly the most eccentric. She was to be seen every day, before the theatre opened, riding in her carriage on the doors of which was a device in the shape of a basket, or, as some from a distance were led to suppose, a coronet. Accompanied by her husband and by several other men who hoped to become her lovers, she dressed herself in a variety of outlandish but fetching costumes that showed her lovely face and body to best advantage.

On 3 December 1779 *The Winter's Tale* was produced at Drury Lane by royal command. Mary Robinson appeared as Perdita; and William Smith, who was also in the cast as Leontes, prophesied that she would captivate the Prince of

Wales, so lovely did she look in the part. The Prince was indeed captivated. Throughout her performance he stared at her fixedly and during one scene overwhelmed her with confusion, so she confessed, by making flattering remarks about her as she stood on the stage beneath his box. At the end of the performance he stood up and bowed to her, and 'just as the curtain was falling', she later recorded, 'my eyes met [his]; and with a look that I *never shall forget*, he gently inclined his head a second time; I felt the compliment, and blushed my gratitude'.

A few days later one of his friends, Lord Malden, called at her house in Covent Garden and, with evident embarrassment, took a letter out of his pocket and handed it to her. It was addressed to 'Perdita' and signed 'Florizel'. She supposed at first that it had been written by Malden himself, but he assured her that it came from the Prince of Wales. The next day Lord Malden called again with a second letter and a request that she should go to the oratorio on a certain evening when the Prince and the Royal Family were also to be present.

As at the Drury Lane Theatre, so at the oratorio, the Prince stared at her, bowed to her, and smiled at her with such marked insistence that 'many of the audience observed it'. He asked one of the gentlemen in attendance to fetch him a glass of water which, gazing at her earnestly, he raised towards her before drinking. 'Several persons in the pit' immediately turned round towards the balcony box in which Mrs Robinson was sitting.

During the next few weeks the Prince wrote to her almost every day, sent Lord Malden to her with fond messages, gave her a lock of his hair in an envelope on which he wrote, 'To be redeemed', and presented her with a miniature of himself by Jeremiah Meyer accompanied by two mottoes written on either side of a piece of paper cut into the shape of a heart: '*Je ne change qu'en mourant*', and 'Unalterable to my Perdita through life'. To Mary Hamilton, to whom he

had recently expressed the same sentiments, her 'very affectionate Brother' bade farewell: '*Adieu, Adieu, Adieu,
toujours chère.* Oh ! Mrs Robinson.' *

Up till now the Prince had not succeeded in meeting Mrs
Robinson who seems to have been reluctant to risk incur-
ring the wrath of his parents. He begged her, through
Malden, to come to his apartments in Buckingham House
disguised as a boy, but 'the indelicacy of such a step, as well
as the dangers of detection' made her shrink from the proposal. At length, however, provoked by the repeated infidelities
of her husband whom she found one day on returning from
a rehearsal in her bed with one of her maids, Mrs Robinson
succumbed to the Prince's entreaties and agreed to meet him
for a few minutes at Kew in the company of his brother,
Frederick.

It was agreed that she would dine with Lord Malden at the
inn on the island between Kew and Brentford. They were to
watch for the signal of a handkerchief being waved from the

---

*Miss Hamilton, having discovered some particulars about Mrs
Robinson's way of life, urgently and repeatedly warned the Prince
that a female in her line had 'too much trick and art not to be a very
dangerous object'. 'For the love of Heaven, stop, O stop my friend and
do not thus headlong plunge yourself into vice,' she ended her final
appeal. 'I conjure you to strive to conquer this unhappy infatuation
... you are preparing wretchedness for yourself ... you will repent –
but it will then be too late ... I want to raise your virtues; for you
have virtues ...' The letter was never answered. The Prince and Mary
Hamilton – who married John Dickenson in 1785 – remained on
friendly terms, however, and often met in later years. At a ball at
Carlton House in 1784 she had 'two long conversations with him ...
in the old friendly stile', and a few months later, when she saw him
from the window of her coach walking down Curzon Street, 'he
smiled, kissed his hand several times, made [her] a graceful bow – the
carriage proceeded and he walked on – presently he returned ... and
came to the coach door'. There ensued a pleasant conversation during which he held Miss Hamilton's hand 'the whole time which
greatly distressed [her] as there were many bye'. The Prince always
spoke of her with affection and respect, and she, when criticisms of
his behaviour were voiced in her presence, 'took his part' as often as
she could (*Hamilton Letters*, 190, 260).

opposite shore, then they were to take a boat for the landing place by the iron gates of the Palace. They arrived there safely and the Prince, with Frederick at his side, ran down the avenue to meet them. But there was only time for the exchange of a few words when, as the moon rose, the noise of people approaching from the Palace disturbed them and she and Lord Malden had to run back to the boat.

Other meetings soon followed, however; further love letters were exchanged; the Prince fell deeper and deeper in love; and 'Perdita', so she afterwards recorded, would never forget how charming he was to her, how graceful, how 'irresistibly sweet' was his smile, how tender his 'melodious voice'. He promised – and in writing repeated the promise – that he would give her a fortune of £20,000 immediately he came of age. On the strength of this assurance, she gave up her career on the stage to become his mistress. She was twenty-one then; he was seventeen.

He took no trouble to disguise the connection and soon it was the common talk of London. Cartoons of 'Perdita' and 'Florizel' appeared in shop windows, and Mrs Robinson was 'overwhelmed by the gazing of the multitude' whenever she appeared in public. She was 'frequently obliged to quit Ranelagh, owing to the crowd which staring curiosity had assembled' around her box; and she could scarcely venture 'to enter a shop without experiencing the greatest inconvenience'.

But the Prince's passion for 'Perdita' was soon spent. Within a few months he was said to be tired of her and to be casting longing looks in the direction of Mrs Grace Dalrymple Elliott, the divorced wife of a rich physician. And one day, after Mrs Robinson had offended him by being rude in public to a friend of his, he wrote to tell her curtly that they must 'meet no more'. Declining to accept so abrupt a dismissal, she prevailed upon him to agree to meet her once again, and the subsequent discussion appears to have been pleasant enough. 'We passed some hours in the most friendly and delightful conversation,' she informed a friend, 'and I began to flatter myself that all our differences were adjusted. But no words can express my surprise and chagrin, when, on meeting his Royal Highness *the very next day* in Hyde Park, he turned his head to avoid seeing me, and even affected *not to know me!*'

Mrs Robinson made further efforts to see him, but he declined to receive her and did not even answer the indignant, resentful letters in which she complained that he had destroyed her career and that all she now had to show for having given way to his entreaties and believed his false promises was thousands of pounds' worth of debts. The once happy intrigue had degenerated into what he described to Prince Frederick as the 'old infernal cause Robinson'.

Lord Malden, acting for Mrs Robinson, and Colonel Hotham, representing the Prince, found it extremely difficult to arrange a satisfactory settlement. When she was offered £5,000 for the return of the compromising letters which he had written to her, she angrily refused the 'insulting proposal'. She protested that she would 'quit England instantly', that 'no earthly power' would ever induce her to receive the 'smallest support' from him or to part with her valuable papers, that she hoped he would feel 'every degree of satisfaction' when reflecting upon the disgraceful way in which he had treated her. Later, when a financial settlement seemed to be all that she could hope for, she insisted that £5,000 was totally inadequate; her present debts alone amounted to £5,600. Moreover, she must have some undertaking that the Prince would give her substantially more when it was in his power to do so. But the Prince was adamant: he could not possibly bind himself for the future without the King's consent; he did not want 'anything more to do with the business'. Well then, Mrs Robinson retorted, the Prince's behaviour was 'so ungenerous and illiberal' that she felt herself justified 'in any step' that her necessities might urge her to make.

Eventually it was agreed that, in addition to the capital sum of £5,000, she should have an annuity of £500, half of which her daughter would continue to receive after her death.*

The King, who had had to approach Lord North, the Prime Minister, for the money to pay Mrs Robinson, was more dismayed by his son than ever. His own sexual urges were very strong but he had never given way to them; he had been in love with Lady Sarah Lennox when he had married, but he had never been unfaithful to the Queen. And now their son, whose duty it was to set a good example to the nation, had landed himself in this 'shameful scrape'.

* Her great inducement in agreeing to this sordid settlement, she informed Colonel Hotham, was 'to restore His Royal Highness's peace of mind'. She was so 'shocked' by the implication that she was returning the letters for money that she felt compelled to demand in writing an acknowledgement of the fact that she had not *sold* papers so dear to her, papers which she had ever valued as dearly as her very 'existance' (Capell Manuscripts FH/IX/8 M275, FH/IX/23 M295). Having collected the money, she went to live in Paris where she resisted, so she claimed, the ardent and persistent overtures of the Duke of Orleans. On her return to England in straitened circumstances she made for Brighton and, on arrival at the Ship Hotel, she wrote to inform the Prince of her sad situation. He replied that the 'scene of distress' which she so pathetically painted quite overcame him and he promised that, should it be within the compass of his means to serve her, he would certainly do so (MS letter, Chequers Library). Soon afterwards the Prince was relieved of further responsibility for her by Colonel Banastre Tarleton, Member of Parliament for Liverpool, whose mistress she remained for about sixteen years. Towards the end of her life, having become paralysed from the waist down, she devoted herself to literature, producing numerous poems and several plays. In these years the Prince, by then quite forgiven for his past treatment of her, was a regular visitor at her house in St James's Place where she received her guests elegantly reclining upon a sofa in her small drawing-room. Suffering from 'acute rheumatic disorders ... aggravated by pecuniary distress', she died at the age of forty in 1800 and was buried in the churchyard at Old Windsor (Wraxall, v, 368–9). A last request, so it was reported, was that a lock of her hair should be sent to the Prince as 'a mark of her regard' (Huish, i, 68). Her daughter, Miss Maria Elizabeth Robinson, continued to receive half her pension as had been agreed (RA Geo. IV. Box 7; RA 29859–68).

The King was now more determined than ever to keep the Prince on a tight rein. Soon after his eighteenth birthday on 12 August 1780 the Prince had been granted his own establishment, but he was still required to live with his parents at Buckingham House or in the apartments along the east front of the castle at Windsor which had now been made for him; and he was also still required to remain under the care of Bishop Hurd who was not allowed to give up the Preceptorship, of which he had felt the 'full weight', until December.

In a long letter informing him what arrangements had been made for him in 'this middle state between manhood and childhood', the King informed the Prince about the limitations to be imposed upon his future conduct:

... As you may at times be desirous of dining with some of your attendants, I shall consent when I am in town that you may have a dinner in your apartment on Sundays and Thursdays, but I cannot afford it oftener. ... You may very naturally chuse to go oftener to plays and operas than I may. I shall not object to it when I am in town, provided you give me previous notice that we may not expect you in the evening, but then you must go in your box attended by your regular attendants, as all Princes of Wales have heretofore done. Whenever you are desirous of dancing, on an intimation to the Queen or me, we shall very readily forward it, and shall have no other wish on such occasions but to make the Ball agreeable to you; but I shall not permit the going to balls or assemblies at private houses, which never has been the custom for Princes of Wales. As to masquerades, you already know my disapprobation of them in this country, and I cannot by any means agree to any of my children ever going to them. Of course you will come every Sunday to church and to the Drawing Room at St James's when I appear there, as also at the Thursday Drawing Room.

When I ride out of a morning I shall ever expect you to accompany me. On other days I shall not object to your doing it also, provided it is for exercise, not lounging about Hyde Park. Whenever you ride out or go in a carriage, one of your attendants must accompany you. ... Be but open with me and you will ever find me desirous of making you as happy as I can, but I must not forget, nor must you, that in the exalted station you are placed in, every step is of consequence, and that your future character will greatly depend in the world on the propriety of your conduct at the present period. ... I can reason more coolly on paper than in conversation, but should you at any time wish to talk on any subject, you will never find me unwilling to enter into it. Indeed, I wish more and more to have you as a friend and in that light to guide you, rather than with the authority of a parent ...

A few days after this letter was written, the Prince lost the company of his beloved brother, Frederick, who, seventeen years old and a colonel, was sent out to Hanover to improve his German and to complete his military education. So distressed was he at parting from him, 'so much affected with the misfortune of being deprived for so long a period of the sole companion of his youth', that the Prince 'stood in a state of entire insensibility, totally unable to speak ...'

Three weeks later he was forced to say good-bye to his 'best friend', Lieutenant-Colonel Gerard Lake, a man eighteen years older than himself who had recently been appointed his First Equerry and was now going out to fight in America. A talented, popular, 'sensible, worthy and gentlemanlike' man, one day to become Commander-in-Chief in India, Lake was a 'pleasing exception' to the list of 'unsuitable' companions with whom the Prince chose to spend much of his time. 'Our parting, as you may suppose,' the Prince told Frederick, 'was a very severe trial to us both, especially as we had received so great a shock in our late separation from you. You know how much I love him, and therefore will easily conceive what a loss he is to me at the present moment, more especially as I have not you, my dear brother, with me, from whom I could always meet with disinterested advice.'

Well aware of how much he was in need of their advice, both Lake and Frederick continued to offer it from their respective posts. Lake ventured to hope that the Prince's good sense ('of which no one had a greater share') would prevent his becoming the dupe of any political party, and strongly urged him 'not to write any more letters to a certain sort of ladies', adding that the trouble he had already got himself into on that account ought to be a 'sufficient warning'. Above all, Lake advised him not to allow himself, as he was inclined to do through his good nature, to be imposed upon by people who had 'not the smallest pretensions' to his 'civility or attentions' and who presumed upon that good nature to become troublesome to him. 'Believe me,' Lake assured him, offering pertinent and much-needed counsel, 'a knowledge of the world and of man is very necessary, and the most difficult to be acquired. Allow me to say it is more so for you, as the retired and private education unavoidably chalked out for a Prince has prevented you from knowing so much of them as young men who have reaped the benefit of a publick school in general do at your age; besides, your situation is such as to make people very anxious to be upon the best footing with you, and I am sorry to say that too many there are in this world who, to gain your favour, will acquiesce and encourage you in doing things that they themselves perhaps would be the first to condemn, and when they find the world disapproving your conduct, will lay the blame entirely upon yourself.'

Prince Frederick was not so well suited as Lake to offer his brother advice about 'a certain sort of ladies' since he was already deeply involved with Letitia Smith, an adventuress who was believed to have also been the mistress of the highwayman John Rann, better known as 'Sixteen-String Jack' from the sixteen silk tassels that he always wore tied to his breeches' knees. In the first letter that he wrote to his brother in Hanover, the Prince of Wales told him that he had met Mrs Smith at one of those masquerades at the Pantheon which his father had so expressly forbidden him to attend. He had beckoned to her; she had recognized him and followed him up to the gallery where their conversation was totally about Prince Frederick. She said that she could not live without him, that she had been excessively ill, and that she was resolved to set out for Hanover to be with him. 'In short,' the Prince of Wales concluded, 'I believe no woman ever loved a man more passionately than she does you. She cried very much.' Soon afterwards, she married Sir John Lade.

If Prince Frederick was not well qualified to advise his brother about women, he did think he could and should advise him to try to get on better terms with his parents. In letters asking for a variety of articles to be sent out to Hanover, from 'Huzza breeches' and dancing pumps to sabres, indian ink and books of country dances, Prince Frederick besought him

> to be upon as good a footing as possible with the King, for really it is of so much consequence to yourself that it appears to me quite ridiculous that you do not at least attempt [it]. ... For God's sake do everything which you can to keep well with him, at least upon decent terms; consider he is vexed enough in publick affairs. It is therefore your business not to make that still worse ... You know, my dearest brother, I hate *preaching* full as much as you do, and constraint if possible more, but still for both your sakes I entreat you to keep as well together as possible. I know you will. Excuse what I write to you because it comes from the heart.

But the Prince of Wales could not bring himself to follow his brother's advice to keep on good terms with his parents. It was as though their dull, domestic way of living and their constant criticism of his extravagance, incited him to further dissipation and expenditure. Certainly the Prince never tired of complaining that he was exasperated by his father's attitude towards him. He was always so 'excessively cross, ill-tempered and uncommonly grumpy', as well as being 'so stingy' that he would 'hardly allow himself three coats in a year'; while the Queen was really quite as bad, accusing her son of 'various high crimes and misdemeanours'. The 'unkind behaviour' of both of them was 'hardly bearable'. He answered his mother back, he confessed, and 'in the vulgar English phraze gave her as good as she

brought' until she fell into silence. She said that she criticized his conduct upon her own initiative, without the King's
knowledge; but the Prince felt sure, from 'the language she
used and the style she spoke in' that the King was behind it
all.

As month followed month in 1781, there were almost daily
reports of the Prince of Wales's wild behaviour, of his riding
'like a madman' in Hyde Park, of drunken brawls in the
gardens at Vauxhall and Ranelagh. And there was talk of
his successful conquest of the easily conquered Grace Dalrymple Elliott whose illegitimate daughter, Georgiana
Augusta Frederica Seymour, may have been his, as the
mother liked to suppose, though she may equally well have
been fathered by one of Mrs Elliott's other lovers, George
Selwyn, Charles William Windham or Lord Cholmondeley.
The King asked Prince Frederick, his favourite son, who was
working hard and getting on well in Hanover, to write to his
brother to remonstrate with him as forcibly as he could.
Frederick did so, entreating him for God's sake to take care
of his health: 'You cannot stand this kind of life.'

The Prince paid no attention. In vain his father complained that it was 'allmost certain that some unpleasant
mention of him' was now to be found in the newspapers each
morning. 'Draw your conclusion,' the King wrote, 'whether
you must not give me many an uneasy moment. I wish to
live with you as a friend, but then by your behaviour you
must deserve it. If I did not state these things I should not
fulfil my duty either to my God or to my country. ...
When you read this carefully over, you will find an affectionate father trying to save his son from perdition.'

The King had hoped that the payment of £5,000 on his
behalf to enable him to rid himself of Mrs Robinson might
have persuaded him to 'act in a manner worthy of approbation'. Yet his conduct had in no way improved since then;
he drank as hard as ever; he had found another unsuitable
mistress; he mixed with increasingly profligate company.
The King made it abundantly clear that he strongly dis-

approved of his going to dine with Lord Chesterfield, a man of highly questionable principles, and of his close friendship with Colonel Anthony St Leger and Charles William Windham, two young rakes whom 'all good men' despised. But the Prince continued to consort with them and was reported to have got so drunk in their company at Lord Chesterfield's house at Blackheath that he was obliged to lie down on a bed. After another drunken evening at Chesterfield's, during which a ferocious dog had savaged a footman and the host had fallen down the stairs, he had been rendered totally incapable of driving home and had had to leave the reins of his phaeton to his uncle, the Duke of Cumberland.

As he had been warned by Prince Frederick, he could not stand this kind of life. He fell seriously ill and for two days his physician, Sir Richard Jebb, felt much alarmed for him, while he himself thought that he might die. He was compelled to remain in his bedchamber for a fortnight, his face covered with red, eruptive blotches and 'dreadful to behold', without ever tasting anything but barley water 'or some damned wishy washy stuff of that sort'.

As soon as he had recovered, however, the Prince was again on his indecorous adventures. It was rumoured that, having tired of Mrs Elliott, he had brief affairs with numerous other women, nearly all of whom were older than himself. The best known of these supposed mistresses were Lady Augusta Campbell, the beautiful, wayward daughter of the fifth Duke of Argyll, who was later uphappily married to 'that most indifferent *sposo*', Colonel Clavering; Lady Melbourne, a tall, lively, handsome woman whose fourth child, George Lamb, brother of the future Prime Minister, was said to be the Prince's; the pretty, chubby singer, Elizabeth Billington, formerly the mistress, it was supposed, of the Duke of Rutland and wife of James Billington, a double-bass player in the Drury Lane orchestra; and Maria Amelia, Countess of Salisbury, a devoted foxhunter, twelve years the Prince's senior.

The Prince was also said to have made advances to the two beautiful daughters of the first Earl Spencer, Henrietta, Countess of Bessborough, and Georgiana the extravagant, intelligent wife of the fifth Duke of Devonshire.* No one seemed certain whether or not he had succeeded in making love to either of them. Perhaps he had not, for he was known to have become very sulky when they did take lovers, when Henrietta succumbed to the charms of Lord Granville Leveson Gower, and Georgiana became the mistress of the proud and handsome Charles Grey whom the Prince ever afterwards disliked.

It was certain, however, that the Prince did manage to make love to the brash and scheming Countess von Hardenburg, wife of Count Karl August von Hardenburg who had come to London in hopes of being appointed Hanoverian envoy to the Court of St James's. The Prince had been introduced to the Countess in the spring of 1781 at a concert in the Queen's apartment. Formerly the Countess Reventlow, she was an attractive, provocative woman, by

---

* The Duchess drew a candid portrait of the Prince as he appeared to her in September 1782, soon after his twentieth birthday: 'The Prince of Wales is rather tall and has a figure which though striking is not perfect. He is inclined to be too fat and looks too much like a woman in men's cloaths, but the gracefulness of his manner and his height certainly make him a pleasing figure. His face is very handsome and he is fond of dress even to a tawdry degree. ... He is goodnatured and rather extravagant.-From the usual turn of his character and some shabby traits to his mistresses one should imagine he was more inclined to extravagance than generosity, though at the same time two or three very generous things to his friends in distress do him the highest honour. ... He certainly does not want for understanding, and his jokes have the appearance of wit. He appears to have an inclination to meddle in politics, he loves being of consequence, and whether it is in intrigue of state or gallantry, he often thinks more is intended than really is. He has a great deal of quickness, and like the King has a wonderful knack at knowing all that is going forward' (Chatsworth MSS, *Georgiana*, Appendix ii, 289). 'He has his father's passion,' Betsy Sheridan confirmed, 'for knowing who and what every one is' (Sheridan, *Journal*, 168).

turns flirtatious and aloof, who, soon after Prince Frederick's arrival in Hanover, had attempted to seduce him at a dance. At their first meeting, the Prince of Wales took little notice of her; she was, he decided, 'a very devilish, agreeable, pleasant little woman, but devilish severe'. Some time later, however, when he met her again at one of the Queen's card parties at Windsor, he thought her 'devinely pretty'. It was clear that she was bored. The Prince afterwards discovered that she disliked all card games – as he did himself – unless they were games of chance and played merely for gambling. One of his sisters tried to teach her how to play, placing the cards on the table for her; but she paid little attention to the rules, repeatedly glancing up to catch the Prince's eye. From that moment, he confessed to Prince Frederick, he fell madly in love with her. 'O did you but know how I adore her,' he exclaimed, 'how I love her, how I would sacrifice every earthly thing to her; by Heavens I shall go distracted: my brain will split'.

She remained at Windsor for a fortnight during which the Prince showed her every possible attention. One day he said to her that after seeing so much of her in the country it was a pity that he could not see her as frequently in London. Could he not see her some morning after eleven o'clock when her husband was out? She affected great indignation at this improper suggestion; but when the Prince apologized with his usual grace and charm, protesting that he had not intended to give her the slightest offence, she forgave him. He seemed no nearer making love to her, however, and in his feverish anxiety to do so, he fell ill again. He became 'much emaciated', he said; he contracted a violent cough; he spat blood; Sir Richard Jebb had to be called in once again. His illness, real, imagined or contrived, had the desired effect: one morning when he called upon the Countess at her house in Old Windsor while her husband was out he complained piteously of her cruelty to him, and she replied, 'I certainly am very much attached to you, I do love you most sincerely, and it affords me great delight to think that you are attached to me, but I must tell you that I was once very much attached to another person, and did think that a woman never could love but once very sincerely during her life. If, after such a declaration, you can attach yourself to me, it will be an additional proof of your love, but should you not, for God's sake let us drop all thoughts of love and part very good friends.'

The Prince assured her that he loved her more than ever after this avowal; but two or three more days elapsed before 'she would consent to any idea of completing [his] happiness'. At last, however, she did consent; and 'O my beloved brother,' he wrote as though still 'in ecstasy', to Prince Frederick, 'I enjoyed ... the pleasures of Elyssium ... thus did our connection go forward in the most delightful manner that you can form any idea to yourself of.'

No one knew anything about the affair except his Equerry, Lieutenant-Colonel Samuel Hulse, until there appeared in the *Morning Herald* a piece of gossip to the effect that the Prince of Wales's carriage was every day to be seen outside the house of a certain German baroness in Cork Street. The story was untrue – the journalist had been misled by the Duke of Gloucester's carriage being frequently seen outside the house of a Polish countess – but when Count von Hardenburg heard about it, he demanded that his wife write to the Prince and terminate the affair immediately. Von Hardenburg himself also wrote to the Prince who 'almost fell into fits' when he received the packet and thought he 'should have run distracted' when he opened it. He replied that he was certainly very strongly attached to Madame von Hardenburg, but that she had always treated him with the 'utmost coolness'; he was the only person to blame in the whole affair. He then wrote a most passionate letter to the Countess and, thinking everything was at an end, sent an express to Lord Southampton, the Groom of the Stole and head of his Establishment, desiring him to go to the King to ask for permission for him to go abroad as 'an unfortunate affair had of late happened' which made him 'excessively

miserable'. The King replied that he could not possibly consider his going abroad for any reason whatever.

Soon after the receipt of this letter, the Prince was handed
one from the Countess, professing her attachment to him,
reminding him of all his vows, and proposing that they run
away together that night. Torn between fear of the appalling
scandal that an elopement would cause, and the desire to
possess her, the Prince as he admitted lost his senses entirely.
At first he agreed to go away with her, then he shrank from
the step, excusing himself on the grounds that, although
she was the object of all his tenderness and all his love, he
could not expose her to the possibility of her perishing for
want; his father's 'severe disposition' would hardly soften
sufficiently for him to conduct and support such a relationship.

Not knowing to whom else he could turn, he threw himself, in his own phrase, at his mother's feet. He confessed the
whole truth to her, and having done so, he fainted. She
'cried excessively', and, moved by his distress, was deeply
sympathetic. It was decided that Colonel Hulse should be
sent to the Countess to tell her that an accident prevented
the Prince going with her, and that the King must be informed of his son's latest imbroglio. The King acted
promptly; he sent for von Hardenburg who was immediately
packed off to the Continent with his wife.

On her arrival back in Hanover, the Countess quarrelled
with Prince Frederick who decided that he hated her almost
as much as he did the devil, and congratulated his brother
on having got off so lightly. The Prince of Wales could
scarcely believe that his angel could behave in the way that
his brother now described. He found it impossible to think
of her without the 'strongest love and regard'; but he had to
admit that he had entertained some doubts about her while
their connection lasted. She 'appeared to be very capricious
and very singular in some things'; 'in short it was a very
miserable, and unhappy affair altogether', and no doubt it
was all for the best that it was ended.

Carlton House and Brooks's
1782–1784

'A shameful squandering of public money'

To disentangle the Prince from the arms of designing mistresses had not proved unduly difficult, but the King was far less successful in separating his son from undesirable male companions. Protest and threaten as he would about Anthony St Leger, for example, the King could not induce the Prince to forego the company of so racy and entertaining a friend. In the spring of 1782, shortly before his twentieth birthday, the Prince went so far as to absent himself without permission from one of his Majesty's levees to dash up to Northamptonshire to hunt with St Leger. The King wrote sternly to insist on 'the like not being done again'; if his son's conduct did not amend, he would take steps that certainly would be 'disagreeable'. The Prince replied that, although his conduct in the world was 'in great measure different from the limited plan' drawn up for him, which in his youth and inexperience he had 'inconsiderately acquiesced in', he flattered himself that his behaviour, far from deserving censure, 'merited the strictest approbation'. And he carried on misbehaving and enjoying himself as before.

But although he complained about his son's misconduct with St Leger, the King's concern over this friendship was trivial compared with his anxiety about the increasing intimacy between the Prince and that abominable Whig politician, Charles James Fox.

Fox, a Member of Parliament from the age of nineteen, had come into prominence during the American war, the mismanagement of which under the Tory administration of

Lord North he roundly condemned in speeches of marvellous eloquence. To the dismay of the King, Lord North was forced to resign in March 1782, and Fox, now thirty-three, accepted office as one of the secretaries of state in the new government headed by the Whig, Lord Rockingham. The following year he became Foreign Secretary in a coalition government of which the Duke of Portland was the nominal leader; and when he went to kiss hands with the King on his appointment, it was noticed that his Majesty put back his ears like a horse bent on throwing its rider.

It was not only that Fox was politically unacceptable to the King, he was morally unacceptable too. The son of an enormously rich father who had vastly increased his fortune during eight years of office as Paymaster-General of the Forces, Charles had been sent to Eton and Oxford and on the Grand Tour, and had early developed that insatiable passion for gambling which was to lead to his being almost constantly in debt throughout the whole of his life. Walpole said that in his mid-twenties he would arrive to speak in the House of Commons after playing hazard at Almack's for more than twenty-four hours at a stretch. For the whole of the night before a debate on the Thirty-nine Articles he sat up gambling, and by five o'clock the next afternoon, a Wednesday, he had lost £11,000. 'On the Thursday he spoke in his debate; went to dinner at past eleven at night; from thence to White's, where he drank until seven the next morning; thence to Almack's where he won £6,000; and between three and four in the afternoon' he set out for the races at Newmarket.

Walpole went on to say that in three nights he and his brother lost £32,000 between them, and added, 'There being a report that Charles was going to be married, it was told to his father ... who replied: "I am glad of it, for then he will go to bed at least one night."'

When he did get married his choice of a wife was as shocking as his gambling and his drinking. For a time he became the lover of 'Perdita' Robinson after she had been

discarded by the Prince of Wales. Then, having grown tired
of her almost as quickly as the Prince had done, he took up
with Mrs Elizabeth Bridget Armistead, a delightful woman
of unknown provenance, but strong Cockney pronunciation,
who had also had a brief affair with the Prince of Wales. He
grew deeply attached to her and eventually, having lived
with her for several years, he married her in 1795, keeping
the marriage secret, however, until they made a trip abroad
together in 1802.

No one could feel in the least surprised that the friendship between such a man as Fox and the Prince was deeply
distressing to the King. It was well known that Fox's followers 'were strangely licentious in their conversation about
the King'; that at Brooks's Club, where his disciples met,
bets were taken on the duration of the present reign; and it
was equally well known that the Prince frequently went to
Brooks's and to Fox's lodgings in St James's Street where his
friend, still in his 'foul linen night-gown', unwashed and un-
shaved, with his bushy hair dishevelled and 'his shagged
breast quite open', received his morning visitors to discuss
with them the topics of the day.

But nor could anyone who knew Fox feel surprised that
the young Prince admired him so. A hard-drinking gambler
who had taken over two of the Prince's former mistresses,
paunchy, untidy, graceless, with a swarthy skin, a double
chin and black, shaggy eyebrows, he was at the same time
a man of extraordinary charm and good-nature. His smile,
like the Prince's, was delightful, his intellect brilliant, his
expression animated, his conversation entrancing. His
friendship with the Prince, thirteen years younger than himself, was not merely politically useful, it was genuinely felt.
The Prince's regard for him was near to idolatry.

As the Prince's twenty-first birthday approached, it became necessary to consider the matter of his personal income and it naturally fell to Fox, as a leading member of
the Cabinet and as an intimate friend, to play a crucial part
in the negotiations.

A previous administration had led the Prince to believe that on being granted a separate establishment, he would receive the splendid income of £100,000 a year. But when the new administration, avowedly more friendly to the Prince and unwilling to appear less generous, suggested this figure to the King, his Majesty was horrified. He drafted a letter to Colonel George Hotham, the Treasurer of the Prince's Household, to tell him that although he wished to have his son settled with comfort, £100,000 a year was the sum granted to his grandfather, who had had a wife and nine children to support, and that the weight of taxes which the people of the country laboured under made it wholly unreasonable. In a revised version of this letter sent to Hotham on 21 June, the King asked him to tell the Prince that he did not think it advisable to apply to Parliament for any further assistance than such as would enable the Prince to have £50,000, 'with the revenues of Cornwal'. This would make the Prince's income about £27,000 more than he himself had received in a similar situation. The letter ended with a sadly familiar complaint: 'The Prince of Wales on the smallest reflection must feel that I have little reason to approve of any part of his conduct for the last three years; that his neglect of every religious duty is notorious; his want of common civility to the Queen and me, not less so; besides his total disobedience of every injunction I had given and which he, in presence of his brother and the gentlemen then about them both, declared himself contented with. I must hope he will now think it behoves him to take up a fresh line of conduct more worthy of his station.'

To the Duke of Portland, the King subsequently complained of the outrageous idea of granting an income of £100,000, so long as the Prince remained unmarried. It was 'a shameful squandering of public money, besides an encouragement of extravagance'. It was impossible for the King 'to find words expressive enough' of his 'utter indignation and astonishment'. He had at least hoped that when the Duke of Portland came into office he would have thought

himself obliged to have the King's interest and 'that of the
Public at heart, and not have neglected both to gratify the
passions of an ill-advised young man'. He deemed £50,000, in
addition to the revenues of the Duchy of Cornwall, which
amounted to about £12,000 a year, perfectly adequate.

As the letters flew backwards and forwards between Downing Street and Windsor, and no hope of a compromise appeared, Fox began to fear that the dispute would bring
down the government. 'There is great reason to think our
administration will not outlive tomorrow,' he wrote on 17
June, 'or that at least it will be at an end in a very few days.'

Just at this fateful moment the King suddenly relented.
He sent for Portland and in 'an agony of tears' confessed
that he had 'gone too far', and begged the Duke to rescue
him. The Duke called in Fox who persuaded the Prince to
keep the peace within the royal family and to save the government by accepting £50,000 and the Duchy of Cornwall
revenues on the understanding that a capital sum would also
be provided. This capital sum was fixed at £60,000. It was to
be provided by Parliament – the £50,000 a year allowance
was to come from the Civil List – and half of it was to be
allocated to the liquidation of the Prince's debts. By 19 June
the storm was for the moment dissipated. The Prince, Fox
decided, had 'behaved in the handsomest manner'.

But the storm clouds were still there. The Secretary for
War felt that the government could never now gain the
King's favour. There might be a wary politeness; but there
would be 'no peerages, no marks of *real* support'. As for the
King, every morning when he woke up he wished, so he said,
that he were eighty, or ninety, or dead.

As part of the settlement it had been agreed that the
Prince should have his own house. There was no country
house available, as the King informed George Hotham, although the apartments the Prince occupied at Windsor
would 'always be kept ready to receive him'; but as for a
London residence, his Majesty was willing to grant him the
use of the house the Prince's grandmother, the Princess

Dowager of Wales, had inhabited in Pall Mall, provided he did not give any of the ground away and took upon himself 'all repairs, taxes and the keeping of the garden'.

This house was Carlton House, adjoining the Duke of Cumberland's mansion, on the southern side of Pall Mall; and the King's condition that the Prince should be responsible for the upkeep of the garden was well advised. For though the house, which had been built at the beginning of the eighteenth century, was unremarkable, the gardens were both extensive and beautiful. They had been laid out by William Kent, one of the Earl of Burlington's protégés, who had been an influential leader in the revolt against the formal gardening of the seventeenth century. They stretched down Pall Mall as far as Marlborough House, the elegant mansion built by Sir Christopher Wren for the tiresome first Duchess who had lived there until her death in 1744. As informal and natural as any town gardens could be expected to be, they were noted for some splendid elms, charming bowers and grottoes, and a number of irregularly placed statues.

Carlton House itself had never been a small house and had been considerably enlarged by the Princess Dowager of Wales who had added to it the house next door, bought from George Bubb Dodington; but it was still not large enough for the Prince who, now that he had a place of his own at last, determined that it should be as grandly imposing as possible. He instructed Henry Holland to make it so.

The son of a Fulham master builder, Holland had become the partner of the landscape gardener Lancelot ('Capability') Brown whose architectural practice he took over and whose daughter he married. Like many other eighteenth-century architects, he had turned to speculative building; and on land in Chelsea (leased from Lord Cadogan), he had built Cadogan Place, Hans Place and Sloane Street – the two last named in honour of Sir Hans Sloane, the physician and collector whose daughter, Jane, was Cadogan's wife. It was, however, Holland's work in 1776–78 as architect of Brooks's

Club – a commission which brought him into contact with
the Whig aristocracy for whom all his most important works
were executed – that gained for him the admiration of the
Prince of Wales. The subscription room in Brooks's – an
interior that still survives – was a room with which the
Prince was well acquainted and could not but have predisposed him in the architect's favour. The French influence,
particularly the influence of Louis XVI's Paris which was so
marked a feature of Holland's style and was reflected in the
French sympathies of the Whig circle, was soon to be evident in the remodelled interior of Carlton House.

Holland began work on the old-fashioned and in parts
dilapidated house in the early autumn of 1783, and by the
beginning of November the Prince was already living there
as the work went on around him. Improvements were to
continue intermittently for almost thirty years, at a cost
which the Prince himself was to admit was 'enormous'; but
within a few months of his moving into the house it had
already become magnificent.

A splendid hall, decorated with Ionic columns of brown
Siena marble, led to an octagon and a graceful double staircase. Above were the state apartments, the Prince's exotic
bow-windowed bedroom – where his friends visited him of a
morning as he lay 'in his bed, rolling about from side to side
in a state approaching to nudity' – his dressing-room and
bathroom. Beyond the music room there was a drawing-room
decorated in the Chinese taste, a taste which had had many
cultivated admirers in England since the 1750s, and which
Sir William Chambers, one of the leading architects of his
time, had encouraged by the temples and pagodas he had
built at Kew for the Prince's grandmother. An agent was
sent to China to buy furniture for this room, for which the
mercer's bill alone amounted to £6,817, and for which £441
was spent on lanterns. All the rooms at Carlton House were
as beautifully and expensively furnished, mostly with pieces
chosen by the Prince himself, often after consultation with
the Duchess of Devonshire who was not likely to have

urged economy. Below were a whole new range of servants' quarters, pantries, larders, sculleries, kitchens and cellars. Outside in the garden more statues were erected, a waterfall was constructed, a temple with an Italian marble floor was built; there was even an observatory.

Relentlessly, without regard to cost and in defiance of the King's known wishes, more and more splendours were gradually added to Carlton House. Adjoining houses were bought and demolished to make way for new wings. Craftsmen, decorators, cabinet-makers, metal-workers and wood-carvers were brought over from France and set to work in the house until it was considered finer than any other in England; worthy, in the opinion of the novelist Robert Plumer Ward, to stand comparison with Versailles; and, in that of Count Münster, with the Palace of St Petersburg which was, however, not its equal 'in elegance or richness'. To many visitors, indeed, it became altogether too rich, almost vulgar in its opulence. This was emphatically the opinion of Robert Smirke, the rather staid architect of numerous public buildings in London, who in later years observed that the apartments were 'overdone with finery'. Yet the Prince, undeterred by criticisms of either his taste or his expenditure, continued to lavish money upon it, making it more majestic than ever, buying numerous fine English and Dutch pictures, notably some beautiful van Dycks, with which to decorate its walls, building on a whole suite of new rooms, some Corinthian, others Gothic – including a magnificent fan-vaulted Gothic conservatory designed in the manner of a small cathedral – until it was quite dazzling in its magnificence.

It was furnished throughout with the most exquisite pieces, many of them from France. It was highly appropriate that a full-length portrait of the Prince's friend, the Duke of Orleans, Louis XVI's cousin, should have hung in a prominent position in one of the principal rooms – until peremptorily removed when the Duke became Philippe Egalité, supporter of the Jacobins. For, both now and later, whenever the exigencies of the Revolution and the subse-

quent wars allowed, his friends and agents went to France to
buy furniture and *objets d'art*, pictures, girandoles, clocks,
looking-glasses, bronzes, Sèvres china, Gobelin tapestries and
countless other treasures on his behalf. The sale rooms and
dealers' shops of London were similarly scoured for the most
comprehensive collection of French works of art ever
assembled by an English monarch. Cabinets, chests and
tables by Riesener, Weisweiler, Jacob and Carlin, marble
busts by Coysevox, bronzes by Keller, candelabra by
Thomire, pictures by Pater, Vernet, Greuze, Le Main and
Claude were bought for the Prince week after week, year
after year, and carefully arranged in the various rooms at
Carlton House under his discerning eye.

Although its interior was rather too ornate for some tastes,
the classical dignity of the façade, with its fine Corinthian
portico, added by Henry Holland, was almost universally
admired. Its 'august simplicity', in Horace Walpole's view,
made Robert Adam's 'gingerbread and sippets of embroi-
dery' seem decidedly meretricious. When it was finished it
would certainly be 'the most perfect' palace in Europe,
though Walpole could not conceive whence the money was
to come. 'All the tin mines in Cornwall would not pay a
quarter.'

In March 1784, when the first stages of the alteration
were more or less complete, the Prince gave a splendid,
celebratory ball in his new palace; and in May nine huge
marquees were put up in the gardens for an even more
magnificent fête during which the guests were entertained
on the newly mown grass by four bands playing triumphant
airs. This second reception was held to celebrate an event
that had given the Prince as much pleasure as the King
distress.

On 11 November the year before, the opening day of the
new session of Parliament, the Prince, exquisitely dressed in
black velvet lined with pink satin and embroidered in gold,
wearing shoes with pink heels, his hair frizzed and curled,

had taken his seat in the House of Lords. Afterwards in the House of Commons he had approvingly listened to Fox's lively speech on the treaties recently concluded with France, Spain and the United States – a speech, which 'was allowed by all those who heard it', the *Morning Chronicle* reported the next day, 'to be one of the ablest, and at the same time one of the most fair and honest ever delivered from the mouth of a Minister at the opening of a session of Parliament'.

But Fox's days of power were almost at an end. A week after the opening of the new session he introduced a Bill for reforming the government of India. The need for such reform had long been recognized; yet Fox's opponents had little difficulty in representing it not only as an attack upon the rights of the East India Company, and thus a threat to all charter companies, but also as a means of obtaining a controlling interest in Indian affairs for the Whig majority in the House of Commons. Fox was alleged to be attempting to crown himself King of Bengal; and in a celebrated caricature, which the victim thought did more than anything else to raise public opinion against his Bill, James Sayers depicted him in the opulent clothes of an Indian potentate, black-bearded and enormously fat, riding an elephant through the streets of the city – 'Carlo Khan's Triumphant Entry into Leadenhall Street'. The King, firmly persuaded that Fox was using the Bill to undermine his royal prerogative, made it known that whoever voted for it was not his friend. The warning had the required effect: the Bill passed the Commons, though many Members stayed away rather than vote for it, but it was defeated in the Lords by nineteen votes.

The next day, shortly before midnight, Fox was informed by a special messenger that the King had no further use for his services; and the following morning, 19 December 1783, it was announced in the House of Commons that William Pitt, the twenty-four-year-old second son of the Earl of Chatham, who had vehemently opposed Fox's India Bill in the Commons, had accepted office as First Lord of the Treasury and Chancellor of the Exchequer.

Yet although he had succeeded in clearing Fox out of the government, the King could not keep him out of Parliament. In the elections that followed the fall of the administration of which he had been so prominent a member, Fox was returned for Westminster. One of his most influential canvassers was the Duchess of Devonshire who tirelessly drove about the streets in her carriage, a fox's brush stuck in her hat, with her sister and other attractive young ladies. They knocked on the 'most blackguard houses in Long Acre' at eight o'clock in the morning, talking, persuading, arguing, buying votes with kisses. In the triumphal procession that escorted the candidate through London in a laurel-decked chair after his victory, the Duchess's carriage was prominent. So too was that of the Prince of Wales who – 'with Mr Fox's full concurrence' – had prudently not attended the House of Lords on the day that Fox's India Bill had been defeated, but was happy now to be seen wearing his friend's colours of buff and blue, the colours of Washington's volunteers. As the procession passed Devonshire House the Prince stood on the garden wall, the Duchess of Devonshire on one side of him, the Duchess of Portland on the other, to cheer it on its way.

He gave a breakfast for Fox the next day at Carlton House from which the guests did not depart until after six o'clock in the evening, 'the weather being uncommonly fine'. Their host then went on to a dinner party at the house of Mrs Crewe, wife of the Member for the County of Chester, where he proposed the apt toast 'Buff and Blue and Mrs Crewe!' to which his hostess brightly replied, 'Buff and Blue and All of You!'

Some days later the Prince held a second fête 'of the most expensive, magnificent and varied description, prolonged in defiance of usage, and almost of human nature, from the noon of one day to the following morning'. At the splendid banquet the ladies were waited upon by the Prince himself. 'It must be owned,' Sir Nathaniel Wraxall grudgingly allowed, 'that on these occasions, for which he seemed particularly formed, he appeared to great advantage. Louis XIV himself could scarcely have eclipsed the son of George III in a ballroom, or when doing the honours of his palace surrounded by the pomp and attributes of luxury and royal state.'

At yet another party held in celebration of Fox's victory, however, the Prince's behaviour was less admired. Indeed, according to Thomas Orde, Member for Aylesbury and a former Secretary of the Treasury, so many bumpers of wine did he drink that he fell flat on his face in the middle of a quadrille and, on being raised from the floor, was violently sick.

Sometimes, after several days of heavy drinking and excitement, the Prince was obliged to take to his bed with a high fever. As a cure, he did not hesitate to open up a vein with a lancet himself whenever his doctors decided that he had been bled enough already. Prince Frederick wrote once again to caution him about the ill effects his way of life would have upon his constitution; so, too, more than once, did his uncle the Duke of Gloucester. 'I need not ask you if you amuse yourself well,' Gloucester wrote; 'the publick papers inform us of that very largely. I only hope your health may keep pace with your spirits. ... If I was not afraid that you would call me an old gentleman, I would add that I had heard that you was not attentive enough to your health.'

But the Prince disregarded all warnings and, as soon as he had recovered, went on drinking as hard and eating as much and living as recklessly as ever.

Those who dismissed him as a gormandizing, irresponsible, extravagant drunkard and whoremonger were, his friends insisted, being unjust to him. Certainly there were occasions enough when he behaved outrageously; certainly he squandered money as though he had not the least conception of its value and was consequently cheated by dishonest tradesmen.* It was true that he drank to excess, being proud to declare that he never flinched at a bumper and was 'not even upon indifferent occasions a *shirker*'. And it was true that he had many friends unsuitable for a Prince of Wales, particularly amongst those who frequented the green-rooms of the theatres, or who, like his crony the Hon. George Hanger, a beautifully powdered dandy who always wore a rose in his buttonhole, were constantly hiding from their creditors.

He spent much of his time with Sarah Siddons's brother, John Philip Kemble, who swallowed wine by 'pailfuls', and with Richard Cosway, who was said to have turned his house into a brothel. He was frequently drunk in the company of Richard Brinsley Sheridan. But then Kemble was a great actor who, after four years' training for the priesthood at the English College at Douai, could declaim as easily in Latin as in French; Cosway was a miniaturist of genius; and Sheridan, having achieved enduring fame with *The Rivals*, *The School for Scandal* and *The Critic* had entered Parliament with the help of the Duchess of Devonshire and, as a supporter of Fox, had become Secretary of the Treasury in the Duke of Portland's administration. Moreover, the Prince had many staider friends who found his company delightful. His conversation, full of amusing anecdote and aided by an excellent memory, was nearly always entertaining when he was not drunk; and his talent for mimicry was truly remarkable. John Wilson Croker never saw 'his equal for a combination of personal imitation with the power of exhibiting the mental character'. The Duke of Wellington said that 'he had a most extraordinary talent for imitating the manner, gestures, and even the voice of other people, so much so

* Lord Charlemont gave Dr Alexander Haliday an example of this: 'The Prince who was, as he ought to have been, fond of encouraging manufacturers, visited a carpet maker who had lately discovered a new and beautiful fabric in that line. Pleased with the beauty and ingenuity of the discovery, he bespoke a carpet and was charged for it ten times as much as an ordinary gentleman might have purchased it for' (HMCR, Charlemont MSS, ii, 261).

that he could give you the exact idea of anyone however unlike they were to himself'. While George Brummell thought that his 'powers of mimicry were so extraordinary that if his lot had fallen that way, he would have been the best comic actor in Europe'.

When in more serious mood his conversation was somewhat marred by a habit of introducing classical quotations from a severely limited repertoire. Indeed, those who heard him talk often, so Lord Erskine said, discovered that he only used two, one from Homer and one from Virgil, 'which he never failed to sport when there was any opportunity of introducing them'. Yet even so intelligent and discriminating a man as Henry Brougham described his conversation as that of 'a very clever person'. He was often genuinely witty and could hold his own almost as well with the 'sprightly wits' of the Sublime Society of Beefsteaks, to whose select membership he was elected in April 1784, as with the fashionable denizens of Ranelagh, Vauxhall and the Pantheon. Lord Charlemont believed that if he could be persuaded to drink less, he might well live to be a 'blessing' to the country. And Edmund Burke went so far as to suggest that should he ever resolve to quit a course of life in which he found 'little more than disgust', he might even 'become a great king'.

His grace of manner was extraordinary: the cutler who taught him to shave, contrasting his deftness with the awkwardness of his father, said that he performed 'the operation with a facility and grace not to be described in words'. And his charm, when he chose to exercise it, most men found fascinating and women scarcely resistible. The extremely rich dilettante, William Beckford, decided after one memorable party that the 'Prince, brighter than sunshine, cast a brilliant gleam wherever he moved'; lively, kindly and 'insinuating', he was 'graciousness personified'. The young William Lamb, later to become a frequent guest at Carlton House, found him vastly entertaining, a brilliant mimic of his father's Ministers. George Canning, meeting him for the first time, was 'charmed beyond measure' and 'far beyond' his expectation with 'the elegance of his address and the gentlemanliness of his manner'. So was Charles Bannister, the good-natured actor and singer, who said that the Prince was 'always most gracious'; he would ask for a song, 'with inimitable politeness' and then compliment the performer with a 'taste peculiar to himself'.

A more fastidious observer, the mordant gossip and poet Samuel Rogers, found him 'very agreeable'. And even the Prince's ancient great-aunt Amelia, whose guttural German accents he imitated only too faithfully and whose guests were usually limited to 'Methusalems' like herself playing commerce and cribbage, welcomed him to her table. Charles Burney, the musical historian – and a man, it must be admitted, naturally predisposed in favour of royalty – was deeply impressed by him: 'I was astonished to find him amidst such constant dissipation possessed of so much learning, wit, knowledge of books in general, discrimination of character as well as original humour,' he told his daughter. 'H.R.H. took me aside and talked exclusively about music near half an hour, and as long concerning Greek literature to your brother [the classical scholar in conversation with whom he managed to introduce his quotation from Homer*] ... He may with truth be said to have as much wit as Charles II with much more learning. As to music he is an excellent critic.' After a subsequent conversation, Burney

---

* While no great scholar, the Prince's interest in the classics was not feigned. In 1800, there having been discovered a library of papyri in the recently unearthed city of Herculaneum, the Prince undertook to pay for their unrolling and copying. Since the Cambridge scholar who was chosen to supervise the work proved utterly incompetent, the Prince's scheme, as he admitted, met with only 'partial success'. However, ninety-four of the papyri were copied, and the Prince was able to present the facsimiles to Oxford University which in 1810 rewarded him with the honorary degree of Doctor of Civil Law (Hayter, *Herculanean Manuscripts*; MS. Gr Class, c 10, Bodleian, Oxford: Richardson (*George IV*), 100–103).

decided that there was no one with whom he enjoyed talking about music more than 'this most captivating Prince'.

Charles Bannister agreed with Burney that the Prince was an excellent judge of music. At the age of four he had attended a performance specially given for him at Covent Garden of the children's operetta, *The Fairy Favour*, with music by Johann Christian Bach, and ever since then music had been one taste at least that he shared with his father. He became a regular patron of operas and subscription concerts, and was himself a performer of more than average ability. He had a pleasant tenor voice, which had been trained by Sir William Parsons, the Master and Conductor of the King's Band, and he still played the 'cello with creditable skill for an amateur, 'quite tolerably' in the expert opinion of Joseph Haydn with whom he once played in a concert.

It was, however, his taste and judgement as a connoisseur of the visual arts that was more widely admired. Already he was a munificent patron; and since he enjoyed contemplating likenesses of himself and his friends and was generous with them as presents, portraitists were continuously at work on his behalf.* His mother was constantly receiving pictures of him to add to her collection; one day a miniature would come, the next a 'fine print, most generally esteemed by those who [had] seen it', which it was hoped she might consider 'not entirely unworthy' of a place in her boudoir at Frogmore, her country house in the grounds of Windsor Park. Prince Frederick was similarly favoured, once with a wax model of his brother which the Prince of Wales reckoned as being 'remarkably like, except its being too fat,

* He was always delighted to sit for a portrait. When, for instance, Lord Charlemont expressed his 'anxiety to have his portrait painted by the first of painters', the Prince could not disguise his pleasure. He immediately offered to go to Sir Joshua Reynolds's house 'whenever he was prepared to receive him' (HMCR, Charlemont MSS, ii, 116).

especially about the chin'; and on a later occasion with a half-length portrait painted by Gainsborough who was commissioned to do a similar one for Gerard Lake. Gainsborough was soon afterwards asked to paint other portraits of the Prince, of Anthony St Leger, and, for one of the rooms at Carlton House, portraits of three of the Prince's sisters. The Prince also asked Nathaniel Dance to paint his portrait, sat for Joshua Reynolds, and commissioned no less than thirty pictures from Richard Cosway. Nor were the Prince's commissions only for portraits; Gainsborough, for instance, was asked for two landscapes at a time when his work in this *genre* was not widely esteemed. The names of other artists, who then or within a year or so regularly appeared in the Prince's accounts, were W. H. Craft, Richard Collins, John Hoppner – who provided portraits of Haydn, Nelson and the Duke of Bedford – George Garrard, George Romney and George Stubbs.*

One of the earliest portraits of the Prince shows him as depicted by Stubbs trotting through a meadow with two little dogs by his horse's hooves. The Prince enjoyed riding at this time and was known to have ridden all the way from London to Brighton and back on the same day, covering a distance of 108 miles in ten hours. He often went out foxhunting and stag-hunting, too, riding as hard and long as his father, who encouraged his taste for the sport in the hope that it might distract him from more harmful pleasures. He also enjoyed shooting and considered himself 'an exceeding good shot', though he once had the misfortune to wound Lord Clermont in several places with small shot during a shooting party in Norfolk. Above all, he prided himself on his skill at four-in-hand driving, once in a phaeton-and-four covering twenty-two miles in two hours at a trot which, as he

---

* Gainsborough died in 1788, and £1,262 was still owing to his widow in 1795 when considerable sums were also outstanding to all the painters mentioned above and to several others less well known. Cosway was owed £1,631. Stubbs £1,076. All were eventually paid (R A Geo IV, Box 7).

boasted to Prince Frederick, was reckoned 'pretty good driving'.

If only, his father admonished him, he would spend more of his time in these healthy open-air pursuits instead of living so debauched a life in London, his character would be less open to censure. As it was, the King felt obliged to write frequent letters to his son, 'reprobating in each of them', observed a confidant to whom the Prince showed them, 'his extravagance and dissipated manner of living. They were void of every expression of parental kindness or affection'. It was never suggested to him that he might occupy himself in some capacity that might fit him for his future office. As though he were jealous of his heir, indeed as though he hated him *as* his heir – a common sin of rulers – the King did all he could to keep his son well clear of positions of power and influence. As the Bishop of Llandaff put it to the Duke of Queensberry, 'he was a man occupied in trifles, because he had no opportunity of displaying his talents in the conduct of great concerns'.

For want of anything more pressing to do, he spent hour after hour in the company of tailors and shoemakers, hosiers and mercers. John Rossi, the sculptor, was once kept waiting for three hours – the previous day for five hours – while the Prince tried on 'at least forty pair of boots' and conducted 'many trials of patterns and cuttings'. To one of his father's angry reproaches about his trivial life and late rising, he was alleged to have bitterly replied that he always found the day was 'long enough for doing nothing'.

The Secret Marriage
1784–1786

'Mrs Fitzherbert is arrived in London for the Season'

By the time of Fox's success in the Westminster election of 1784 relations between the Prince and his father had deteriorated so far that they seemed incapable of improvement. The King, he told Prince Frederick, was 'so excessively unkind' to him that there were moments when he felt he could 'hardly ever put up with it ... sometimes not speaking to me when he sees me for three weeks together, and hardly ever at Court, speaking to people on each side of me and then missing me, and then when he does honour me with a word, 'tis merely " 'tis very hot or very cold" ... and then sometimes when I go to his house never taking any notice of me at all, as if I was not there'. The Queen, on the contrary, was much kinder to him now than she had been in the recent past; he could not say enough of what he felt for her; they were as close to each other as they had been when he was a child; her goodness to him was such that he would 'bear anything to save her a moment's uneasiness'. But though he esteemed his father and used him with 'all possible duty, deference, and respect', he remained unalterably estranged from him. Really, he concluded on a later occasion, 'he hates me; he always did, from seven years old ... He wants to see me at variance with my brother ... He will never be reconciled to me.'

The King did not agree that he was used by his son with all possible respect. Indeed, in August 1784, when the Prince wrote to him to say that 'the very embarrassed situation' of his affairs made it necessary for him to ask permission to go abroad immediately, the King in his reply described his conduct as 'reprehensible'. Moreover, it had 'grown worse every year, and in a more glaring manner since his removal to Carlton House', upon which well over £1,000 a month had been spent upon furnishings alone since he had taken possession.

Although the Prince had told his father that he 'proposed only painting' the house and 'putting handsome furniture where necessary', in a 'very few weeks this was forgot'. 'Large additional buildings erected,' the King continued, increasingly indignant and ungrammatical, 'and, lest these should not waste enough money, the most expensive fêtes given, and at this hour considerable additional are again begun; yet the Prince of Wales chooses to term his difficulties as occasioned by necessary expenses. ... If he has deranged his affairs he ought to take a manly resolution to diminish his expenses and thus establish a sinking fund to clear those debts, which would in some measure palliate with the public for an extravagance which everyone but his flatterers have universally blamed; the Prince of Wales ought to know that every step he takes is of consequence, that if he once loses the good opinion of this nation it is not to be regained.

'I have found myself under the disagreeable necessity of showing the Prince of Wales's letter to the Queen, who is as much hurt as me, and coincides in the opinion that if his improper plan [of going abroad] was put into execution his character would be for ever blasted in this country, and also in all Europe. I therefore insist on his giving up a measure that would be a public breach with me.'

In defiance of this strongly worded warning, the following week the Prince repeated his intention of going abroad: he saw no 'fresh reason for altering his resolution of travelling' which his 'embarrassing difficulties' made absolutely necessary. He had 'an idea of residing for some time at Brunswick', an expedient that he hoped would meet with his Majesty's approbation, since he would be 'truly hurt' at a public breach. It was quite out of the question for him to

make sufficient 'retrenchments out of [his] annual expence'
to extricate himself from his difficulties. 'It would be merely
a drop of water in the sea!'

The King's reply to this was a short, firm injunction to the
Prince from 'his father and his Sovereign strictly to charge
and command him ... not to leave the realm without having
obtained particular leave'. The King was, however, prepared
to see what he could do to help the Prince out of his financial
difficulties, and he asked Lord Southampton, as head of his
Royal Highness's Household, to ascertain the exact amount
of his debts. Reluctant to leave the country against the
King's orders, though still protesting his intention of so
doing at any moment, the Prince asked Southampton to get
George Hotham, his Treasurer, to make out as accurate a
statement of his debts as he could.

Hotham was horrified by the figures which he accordingly
unearthed, even though many items were not brought to his
notice. He discovered 'with equal grief and vexation', as he
told the Prince in a letter dated 27 October 1784, that he
was totally in the hands and at the mercy of his builder, his
upholsterer, his jeweller and his tailor, the two former of
whom were carrying out works 'to an enormous amount,
without a single care or enquiry from whence money was to
arise for their discharge'. He had borrowed sums totalling
£25,000, the particulars of most of which he had 'not yet
been pleased to divulge'. Then there was the 'amazing expense' of the stables, which alone were costing no less than
£31,000 a year, although the Prince's income was no more
than £12,500 a quarter in all, excluding the 'precarious
supply' from the Duchy of Cornwall. Yet far from finding
that any economies were intended, Hotham discovered to his
'great mortification' that the cost of keeping race horses was
to go up 'beyond all kind of calculation whatever'. It was
clear that the Prince's 'torrents of expense' had run up the
total amount of his debts to an immense figure, and that it
would take months to arrive at an accurate estimate of
them.

In the meantime, it was scarcely surprising that the Prince felt wholly incapable of living on his present income and continued to express to his father his wish to live abroad to 'practice a system of economy'. This, however, was not the real reason for his wanting to leave England. He had another, more urgent, secret reason which he was anxious that his father should not discover.

In a letter informing Prince Frederick of his resolve to live abroad, the Prince had referred to this secret; but since he knew that his packets were often opened in the post, he thought it 'safest to preserve it in petto' till he had the happiness of seeing his brother again. It was a secret which, combined with bouts of excessive drinking, had brought on a 'violent and nasty fever'. He had lost so much weight that he thought his brother 'cd. not possibly know' him. The trouble was that he was once more in love and this time with a lady who composedly spurned his passionate advances.

This lady was Mrs Maria Fitzherbert, a widow six years older than himself, who had recently come to live in London after the death of her second husband at Nice. The Prince had seen her for the first time in Lady Anne Lindsay's box at the Opera; he had taken Lady Anne aside after the performance to ask her what angel it was that had sat beside her in a white hood.

Mrs Fitzherbert was the eldest of six children of Walter Smythe, and the granddaughter of Sir John Smythe, a baronet of an old Roman Catholic family from the north of England. Little is known of her childhood, except that she was educated at an English convent kept by Conceptionist nuns in Paris and that on one of her holidays she was taken to see Louis XV dine in public at Versailles. Here she was so amused to see him pull a chicken to pieces with his fingers that she broke the customary silence by bursting into laughter, a breach of etiquette which was nevertheless rewarded by the present of a box of sugar-plums handed to her, on the King's instructions, by the Duc de Soubise.

At the age of seventeen she was married to a middle-aged landowner, Edward Weld, who died within a year, after falling from his horse. Three years later she married her second husband, Thomas Fitzherbert, who also died soon afterwards, leaving her a substantial income on which she was able to live comfortably, first at Nice and then in Paris before returning to England.

On her return she rented Marble Hill at Twickenham, a lovely house of the English Palladian School built by George II for his mistress Henrietta Howard. She also had a house in London, at the Oxford Street end of Park Street, the lease of which had been left to her by her husband. She lived quietly at first, rarely going out and seeing few people beyond the circles of her own family and of those other Roman Catholic families to which her marriages had related her. Then, in March 1784, the *Morning Herald* announced, 'Mrs Fitzherbert is arrived in London for the season'.

The appearance of this charming, graceful woman in society was an immediate success. She was not particularly good-looking; her chin was too big, her nose too long, her mouth ill-shaped; but she had a pleasantly rounded figure, a fine bosom and lovely dark brown eyes, while her clear skin and golden hair were as perfect as they had been at the time of her first marriage. She had a 'very mild, benignant' expression 'without much animation', and was 'rather heavy than brilliant in conversation', though a good, encouraging listener. Everyone who knew her liked her, though those who knew her well had cause to complain of a certain haughtiness in her manner and a rather quick temper. Soon after seeing her for the first time the Prince was 'really mad for love'. In a letter Lord Wentworth received from his sister on 10 March, he was reported to be making 'fierce love to the widow Fitzherbert', and it was expected that he would succeed.

In her turn, she was attracted by him, flattered by his attentions and obvious desire for her. But there could be no question of her becoming his mistress; she was devoutly

Roman Catholic, irreproachably respectable. Yet if she could not live with him outside marriage for moral reasons, neither could she marry him for legal ones: the Royal Marriage Act stood in the way. The more firmly she resisted the Prince's advances, the more passionate, the more feverishly excitable he became. Swearing that he could not live without her, breaking into tears, throwing himself upon his bed and threatening to kill himself, he wore his friends and attendants out by his recurrent outbursts of emotion. She meant far more to him, he protested, than any other woman, any other person in the world, had ever done; he would give up anything for her, he would forfeit all rights to the throne for her. And this he would undoubtedly have to do if he married her, for the Act of Settlement provided that anyone who married a Roman Catholic could never become monarch of England. Nevertheless, since she so firmly declined to become his mistress, he was determined to marry her, despite all the provisions of the Act of Settlement and the Royal Marriage Act. The year before, he had assured Prince Frederick, who had recommended the daughter of the Hereditary Prince of Hesse-Cassel as a suitable wife, that he did not intend to marry until he was 'near the area of thirty'. But now at twenty-two – Mrs Fitzherbert was twenty-eight – he was determined to marry immediately. Less sure herself that she wanted to marry him or should marry him, and warned of his inconstancy, Mrs Fitzherbert decided to go abroad. On hearing of her intention, the Prince became more frenzied than ever; and one day in November he attempted in desperation to prevent her.

Four members of his Household arrived at her house in the 'utmost consternation' to tell her what he had done. They were Lord Southampton, Lord Onslow, the Hon. Edward Bouverie, and Thomas Keate, the Prince's surgeon. They told her that 'the life of the Prince was in imminent danger – that he had stabbed himself – and that only *her* immediate presence would save him'. At first she refused to go, 'saying that nothing would induce her to enter Carlton

House', fearing that once she went there her reputation would be irrevocably lost. They pleaded with her; she remained adamant; she would not go. At length she was persuaded to change her mind, provided that another lady went with her. The Duchess of Devonshire was selected as a suitable chaperone; and so, having called for the Duchess at Devonshire House on the way, the four men returned to Carlton House with Mrs Fitzherbert.

The Prince was lying in a downstairs room overlooking St James's Park; he was covered in blood and very pale; a glass of brandy was by his side. What exactly had happened was somewhat obscure. The Prince said that he had stabbed himself with a sword; other reports had it that he had used a dagger, or that he had tried to shoot himself, had missed, and had then seized a table knife. A later rumour was to the effect that he had not stabbed himself at all, but had torn off the bandages which Keate had placed over his side when he had been blooded to relieve his feverish tension, had thereby opened up the wound and had smeared the gushing blood all over his chest and shirt. Whatever the cause of the bleeding, Mrs Fitzherbert was so overcome by the sight of it that she almost fainted; and when the Prince assured her that 'nothing would induce him to live unless she promised to become his wife, and permitted him to put a ring round her finger', she weakly assented. The Duchess of Devonshire removed a ring from her finger, and it was placed upon her own.

As soon as she had arrived home and recovered her composure, Mrs Fitzherbert regretted what she had done. She did not afterwards blame the Prince, and always denied any suggestion that he had not been in earnest. To her relative, Lord Stourton, who said that he thought 'some trick had been practised', she upheld that this was certainly not so: she had 'frequently seen the scar'. But Mrs Fitzherbert did blame the Prince's attendants for conspiring to take advantage of her shock to make her go through the ceremony of promising to marry him. She wrote a sharp note to Lord Southampton protesting against his conduct; and in a depo-

sition written by the Duchess of Devonshire and signed by
both of them she contended that 'promises obtain'd in such
a manner are entirely void'. The next day, accompanied by
her friend, Lady Anne Lindsay, she sailed for France and
made for Aix-la-Chapelle. From there she went on to Holland, and, after visits to Antwerp, Paris and Switzerland –
where she saw a great deal of the Duke of Gloucester who
found her 'a most amiable and esteemable lady' and did all
he could to 'make her long exil as bareable' as possible – she
settled at Plombières.

The Prince, quickly recovered from his wound, longed to
follow her; and, according to Lord Holland, 'he did not conceal his passion, nor his despair at her leaving England for
the Continent'. Thus began the correspondence with the
King in which he requested, and was refused, permission to
live abroad on account of his mounting expenses and debts.

Although all reference to Mrs Fitzherbert was studi-
ously avoided in this correspondence, it cannot have been
long before his father heard of the affair which had become
the subject of conversation and speculation in every drawing-room in London, and realized that his son wanted to
leave the country for love and not for money. The fear that
the Prince would get married to the woman in some foreign
Catholic church must surely have appalled him.

Prevented by his father from following Mrs Fitzherbert
as he had wanted to do, the Prince, having despatched agents
after her to discover where she had gone, bombarded her
with a series of fierce passionate letters, beginning with one
that scrawled its way over eighteen pages and ending with
one that stretched to forty-two. He protested that ever since
that day when she had promised to marry him at Carlton
House, he had 'look'd upon [himself] as married'; he could
not live without her; he would kill himself unless they were
re-united; he had broken off connections with all other
women. He called her his *dearest and only belov'd Maria*,
his 'adored wife', his *dearest wife*, his *beloved wife*.
He besought her never to marry anyone else but him, and in

one letter (thirty-seven pages long) made the extraordinary promise that the King would 'connive' at their union. He pleaded with her to believe that he had not a single desire in life that did not 'center' on her. 'Save me, save me,' he begged, 'save me on my knees I conjure you from myself.'

'Come then, Oh! come, dearest of wives, best and most adored of women, come and for ever crown with bliss him who will through life endeavour to convince you by his love and attention of his wishes to be the best of husbands and who will ever remain until the latest moments of his existence, *unalterably thine.*' He inscribed himself *'her lover and her husband*, titles [he] would not exchange for the possessions of the whole universe'. So many letters did he write and so many couriers were needed to carry them that the ceaseless activity aroused the suspicion of the French government, and three of the couriers were at different times arrested and thrown into prison.

When he was not writing letters 'he cried by the hour', so Mrs Armistead told Lord Holland, and 'testified the sincerity and violence of his passion and his despair by the most extravagant expressions and actions, rolling on the floor, striking his forehead, tearing his hair, falling into hystericks, and swearing that he would abandon the country, forego the Crown, sell his jewels and plate, and scrape together a competence to fly with the object of his affections to America'.

In his agitated state, the Prince began to drink more heavily than ever. Mary Noel was told that he had appeared at the opera soon after Christmas hopelessly drunk with three or four companions all in the same state. If he went on like this he would kill himself, she thought; for he had already been very ill. A few months later she was further shocked to learn of his behaviour while staying at Lord Radnor's for Salisbury races. He was there with Lady Bamfylde, wife of Sir Charles Bamfylde, with whom he was seeking consolation in Mrs Fitzherbert's absence. 'He came to the ball on Wednesday last and made the town mad. He has got his present déesse, Lady Bamfylde, with him at Lady Radnor's which causes many speculations as Lady Radnor and still more my Lord was not thought to be inclined to that sort of politesse. Lady Bamfylde is the only woman in the house and the Prince opened the ball with her at Salisbury and drove her all the time the next day on the course in Mr Bouverie's phaeton. She is grown fat, old and ugly but his Royal Highness is not noted for his taste in females.'

For over a year Mrs Fitzherbert remained on the Continent wondering what to do, 'irresolute and inconsequent' in Lady Anne Lindsay's words, changing her mind from day to day, once writing a letter to the Abbess of the English convent at Liège to ask if 'a couple of English ladies could have apartments in their house', but then deciding not to send the letter after all. Lady Anne seems to have found her rather trying and irritable. She quarrelled with her French maid who accused her of treating her servants *comme des chiens*; and sometimes she quarrelled with Lady Anne. In November, tired of her self-imposed exile, she decided to return to England. 'I have told him I will be his,' she wrote to Lady Anne who had returned to England before her. 'I know I injure him and perhaps destroy for ever my own tranquillity.'

As soon as Charles James Fox heard of her return, he wrote to the Prince in an attempt to dissuade him from taking the 'very desperate step' he supposed must now be imminent. He was naturally anxious that the Prince, who had proved himself a staunch friend of his party, should do nothing to endanger his future succession to the throne; and so, in a long and concerned letter, he warned him of all the dangers and disadvantages that would attend his secret marriage, particularly in view of the nation's 'old prejudices against Catholicks' and in view also of the Duke of York being 'professedly' the King's favourite son, 'and likely to be married agreeably to [his] wishes'. In any case, the marriage could not be a real one because of the Royal Marriage Act;

any children there might be would not be legitimate. If he were Mrs Fitzherbert's father or brother, Fox contended, he 'would advise her not by any means to agree to [a marriage], and to prefer any other species of connection ... to one leading to so much misery and mischief'.

The Prince, however, could not be dissuaded from his purpose. Lady Anne Lindsay hoped that he could be induced to marry Princess Louisa of Orange, a match which had been 'much pressed on him by his family'. She was 'grieved that affections so generous and tender as his seemed to be' should be lavished on the 'lovely, but inconsequent and violent woman' that she now considered Mrs Fitzherbert to be. She had painted a miniature of Princess Louisa, a 'pretty, pleasing and good girl', while she had been in Holland; but the Prince, refusing to consider anyone other than Mrs Fitzherbert, replied that he admired the artist more than the subject. Before her flight abroad he had tried and failed to persuade Mrs Fitzherbert to become his mistress. He had therefore made up his mind to marry her, and marry her he would. But first he had to reassure Fox that he did not intend to do so. 'My dear Charles,' he wrote to him. 'Your letter of last night afforded me more satisfaction than I can find words to express; as it is an additional proof to me (which, I assure you, I did not want) of your having that true regard and affection for me which is not only the wish but the ambition of my life to merit. Make yourself easy, my dear friend. Believe me, the world will soon be convinced that there not only is, but never was, any ground for these reports, which of late have been so malevolently circulated.'

Having thus by implication denied his intention of getting married, he continued the search he had already begun for a clergyman to perform the ceremony. A clergyman of the Church of England was required, as, before the second Relief Act of 1791, marriages, even between people who were both Roman Catholics, were not legally binding if they had been solemnized only by a Roman Catholic priest. Moreover, if the details of the marriage should ever become public knowledge, the fact that it had been performed according to the rites of the Church of Rome would be regarded as an added, unforgivable offence by the more earnestly Protestant people of the country. To find an Anglican parson willing to officiate was not easy, however, since the Royal Marriage Act provided that both the witnesses and the clergyman present at a marriage that contravened it were guilty of felony. His secretary unsuccessfully approached the Rev. Philip Rosenhagen, a shady military chaplain, and he himself interviewed the Rev. S. Johnes Knight, Rector of Welwyn in Hertfordshire, a sporting parson, fond of good food and drink, who, as a close friend of Lord North, had known the Prince since he was a child. The Prince, wearing a dressing-gown and apparently having just got out of bed, spoke to Johnes Knight in his dressing-room at Carlton House, stressing his great love for Mrs Fitzherbert, lifting up his shirt to show the scar on his side where he had fallen on his sword, and speaking of his determination to repeal the Royal Marriage Act the instant he came to the throne. 'If you refuse to marry me,' he said vehemently, 'I must find out another clergyman who will.'

'This vehemence of his made me apprehensive that the Prince might get some clergyman to marry him for the chance of Church preferment, and then that this same divine for a larger bribe would betray the Prince's secret to Mr Pitt, who was then Prime Minister,' Johnes Knight, who lived to be a hundred, confessed to his daughter after the Prince's death. 'This made me unable to resist the Prince's importunity, and I could not bear to see him so miserable ... Dearest Louisa, do not blame me for this weakness; bear in mind I was young, and could not help being flattered by the attentions of a Prince, who was one of the best arguers, in his own cause, I have ever known. ... Whoever he wished to gain he talked to so frankly, and on subjects most interesting to his hearer, and his tact was so nice that he never failed in the most minute circumstance which he supposed might captivate those with whom he, for the present hour, chose to accociate.'

Having agreed that he would be walking in the street outside Mrs Fitzherbert's house on a certain day between seven and eight o'clock in the evening, Johnes Knight left Carlton House 'after thanks in abundance' had been 'showered' on him. But no sooner had he got out into the street than the Rector lost his nerve and changed his mind. Pleading as an excuse a conversation he had had with Colonel Gerard Lake, recently returned from America, in the Mount Coffee House the evening before, when he had concurred with Lake's belief that no clergyman would be found to perform the threatened ceremony, Johnes Knight wrote to the Prince to be excused from his promise.

The Prince sent him 'a very kind answer' releasing him from his engagement, and renewed his search. At length a suitably rash and ambitious clergyman was found. This was the Rev John Burt, a young curate, who was incarcerated in the Fleet Prison for debt. On the strength of a promise that he would be made one of the Prince's chaplains, that he would be created a bishop when the Prince became King, and that he would receive £500 with which to liquidate his debts, Burt agreed to undertake the service.*

At dusk on the evening of 15 December 1785 the Prince arrived at Mrs Fitzherbert's house and walked into the drawing-room, the doors of which were locked behind him. John Burt was already there; so also was Mrs Fitzherbert's uncle, Henry Errington, who had been guardian to his niece

---

* The Prince fulfilled his promise to Burt by appointing him a chaplain; but, before the larger promise of a bishopric could be fulfilled, Burt died at the age of thirty, having confessed his celebration of the marriage (*Abbot Diary* i, 68). Shortly before his death, while Vicar of Twickenham, he made application to be considered for the appointment of Dean of Peterborough, Rector of St George's, Blooms-bury, and Prebend of Rochester. The Prince supported the application which might have been successful had not the Lord Chancellor mislaid the papers (RA 5021–2, 38633–4: Asp/P, ii, 143, 212).

ever since her father, his brother-in-law, had become too ill to care for her himself. Errington had at first advised against the marriage, but recognizing that it would probably take place with or without his agreement, he had consented to give his niece away. The only other person in the room, except Mrs Fitzherbert herself, was her younger brother, John Smythe.

The ceremony was conducted without interruption – it was afterwards said that Orlando Bridgeman, a mutual friend of the Prince and the Smythe family, stood guard outside the door – and when it was concluded the Prince wrote out a certificate of marriage which he, Mrs Fitzherbert, Errington and Smythe all signed. The certificate was given to Mrs Fitzherbert for her to keep in a safe place. Immediately after the ceremony the Prince and Mrs Fitzherbert left for a short honeymoon at Ormeley Lodge on Ham Common near Richmond. The roads were deep in snow, and their carriage broke down at Hammersmith where they had supper at an inn before continuing their journey. The honeymoon was of no more than a week's duration; before Christmas they had returned to London where they already were the subject of constant inquiry and heated debate.

Apart from the witnesses, there were several people who knew for a fact that the wedding had taken place. These included the Duke and Duchess of Cumberland, Sir James Harris, British Minister at the Hague, who on a recent leave in England had acted for the government in the still-continuing negotiations over the Prince's debts and had thereby gained his friendship and confidence, and one or two members of his Household. There were several others, like the Duke of Dorset and Pitt, who did not know for sure that the marriage had taken place, but who strongly suspected it; and there were many more who, having picked up hints from friends and acquaintances, spread rumours and reports which, so Horace Walpole said, reached 'even from London to Rome'. There was no other talk in the streets than the 'hubbub' about the marriage. 'Surely there cannot be any truth in the reports of the Prince's being married to a Catholic widow?' the Earl of Denbigh asked Major Bulkeley. 'Is it believed or not? If true the consequences yet may be dreadful to our posterity.'

Lady Palmerston said the general belief was that Mrs Fitzherbert was to move into Carlton House, if she was not in fact already there; that she had been married to the Prince by a Roman Catholic priest, and that she was to be granted £6,000 a year and made a Duchess. The Duke of Rutland was informed by Robert Hobart on 27 December that the town buzzed with talk of the Prince's marriage: 'He has taken a box for Mrs Fitzherbert at the Opera, and constantly passes the greater part of the night with her. I do not hear of Prince Carnaby [Sir Carnaby Haggerston, husband of Mrs Fitzherbert's sister, Frances] being yet arrived in town. Walt Smith [Walter Smythe, her eldest brother] appears already much elated with the honour that is intended, or rather the dishonour which has already attended his family.'

Another correspondent of the Duke of Rutland, Thomas Orde, was not at all certain that the Prince and Mrs Fitzherbert were married; the reports were 'full of contradictions'; many of the people said to be present were certainly not there, and the Rev. S. Johnes Knight who was alleged to have performed the ceremony had assured Orde that he had certainly not done so. But the Marquess of Lothian told the Duke a different story: 'You ask me my opinion respecting the Prince's marriage. I think it has all the appearance of being true. I believe, when he has been spoken to about it, he has been violent, but I cannot find out he has denied it peremptorily. Most people believe it, and I confess I am one of the number. Though I dined alone with him, and you know the general topic of his conversation about women, he never mentioned *her* to me amongst others. I am very sorry for it, for it does him infinite mischief, particularly amongst the trading and lower sort of people, and if true must ruin him in every light.'

The Roman Catholic Lady Jerningham told her daughter Charlotte who was at an Ursuline convent in Paris, 'Mrs Fitzherbert has, I believe, been married to the Prince. But it is a very hazardous undertaking, as there are two Acts of Parliament against the validity of such an alliance. ... God knows how it will turn out – it may be the glory of our belief, or it may be to the great dismay and destruction of it! She has taken a box to herself at the opera, a thing which no lady but the Duchess of Cumberland ever did – a hundred guineas a year! The Prince is very assiduous in attending her in all publick places, but she lives at her own house, and he at his. Do you remember seeing her when she was the Widow Weld? She came to see me one morning in Charles Street and you found her face *too fat*.'

It was quite true, as Lady Jerningham said, that the Prince and Mrs Fitzherbert lived in separate houses, though she moved from Park Street to a mansion in St James's Square which she rented from Lord Uxbridge so as to be nearer Carlton House. When they were seen out together at the opera or a private party, he behaved with the utmost deference to her, never forgetting to go through the form of saying to her 'with the most respectful bow, "Madam, may I be allowed the honour of seeing you home in my carriage?"'.

In these early months of their marriage, they were virtually inseparable: he let it be known that where he went, she was to be asked also; if she were not asked, he would not go. Moreover, the usual rules of precedence had to be suspended: she was always to be placed at the same table as himself.

Despite the ambiguity of her position, she was welcomed almost everywhere. The families of her first two husbands behaved rather coldly towards her; so at first did the Duchess of Portland and the celebrated hostess, Lady Sefton, whose husband's family was connected with the Erringtons. But these were rare exceptions. The rest of her family remained on good terms with her, as did the Duchess of Devonshire.

whose friendly reception of her after her return to England from the Continent encouraged other leading Whig ladies to treat her in the same way. Both she and the Prince were often to be seen dining with Lord and Lady Clermont at their splendid house in Berkeley Square where the Prince had the privilege 'of commanding a dinner and naming the persons to be invited of both sexes'. Even the old-fashioned Tory, the Marchioness of Salisbury, received her at her house as she had done in the past.

But although Mrs Fitzherbert was welcomed back into society, although her gracious, unpretentious, quiet manner was universally commended, there were naturally those who felt that the exact nature of her status would have to be clarified. The caricatures of James Gillray, the finest draughtsman among London's political satirists, whose fame was by now rivalling that of James Sayers, were being sold in large numbers and were being perused and discussed in every coffee-house. One of them, which appeared in March 1786 and was 'designed by Carlo Khan', depicted the Prince and Mrs Fitzherbert being married in a French church. The officiating priest, wearing a cassock and an immense biretta, is Edmund Burke, well known for his advocacy of political concessions for Roman Catholics; the two witnesses are the Prince's disreputable friend the Hon. George Hanger, and Sheridan, who stands with a napkin under his arm and a bottle of wine in each of his coat pockets, prepared to serve the wedding breakfast. The bride is being given away by Fox, who, as the Prince's intimate friend, was wrongly supposed to have connived at the match and was accused by the Prince's first biographer of having actually attended the ceremony which was alleged to have taken place at his house in Grafton Street. The bridegroom is shown holding a ring in his right hand, with his bride's hand in his left, and looking upon her magnificent bosom with evident pleasure. A sequel to this caricature, entitled 'The Morning after Marriage', portrays Mrs Fitzherbert sitting on a bed and putting on one of her stockings as the Prince, resting on a table with garter hanging down towards slippered foot, stretches and scratches his head.

If the reports to which such caricatures gave rise were not true, the Marquess of Lothian thought it was high time they were 'publicly contradicted'. He was 'amazed that some member of Parliament has not mentioned it in the house'. No one did mention it in the House, however, until the Prince's continuing financial difficulties induced him to provoke discussion of it himself.

Happy as the Prince was with Mrs Fitzherbert, the 'most unpleasant business' of his mounting debts was a constant source of distress. The King was prepared to help him, but, as he often assured him, there were certain points which 'must be cleared up first' if the matter was to be discussed any further. 'I can as yet form no judgement of what steps can be taken,' the King complained, 'as I neither know the amount to which his debts have now arisen, nor what security there will be that his future expenses shall be confined within his income.'

In his reply the Prince confessed that his 'load of debts' had increased to nearly double what they had been two years before. In fact, when Colonel Hotham had finished doing his complicated sums a month later it appeared that the total amounted to no less a sum than £269,878 6s. 7¼d. Faced with this fearsome figure the King held it 'impossible to enter on the consideration of any means to relieve him until' he had received 'a sufficient explanation of his past expenses' and saw 'a prospect of reasonable security against a continuance of his extravagance'. It 'would be necessary to have as clear an explanation as the nature of the thing will admit, of his past expenditure, and above all to ascertain that it will be confined within proper limits in future'.

The Prince, deeming it impossible to give either the explanation or the undertaking demanded, answered loftily that his father would receive no further disturbance from him, as he was now convinced that he had 'no reason to expect either at present or in future the smallest assistance from [his] Majesty'. If the Prince chose to interpret what had passed in this way, the King briefly replied, that was his own affair and the consequences of his doing so could be 'imputed only to his own determination'.

It was hinted to the Prince that his father would prove more amenable if the Prince would marry some suitable foreign princess. But when this matter was mentioned to him, the Prince burst out vehemently, 'I will never marry. My resolution is taken on that subject. I have settled it with Frederick. No, I will never marry. ... Frederick will marry, and the crown will descend to his children ...'

It was also suggested that the King might prove less intractable if the Prince were to abandon his open support of the Whig opposition. This, however, was equally impossible. He would never 'abandon Charles' and his other friends.

So the Prince decided to make a dramatic gesture: he would shut up Carlton House, sell his carriages and his horses, and dismiss his Household with the exceptions of Hotham, Lake, Samuel Hulse, one of his equerries, and Henry Lyte, his Master of the Robes and Keeper of the Privy Purse, who were now all to be known as his Inspectors of Accounts. He took a 'firm determination not to appear again in public' till he could do so 'with that dignity and splendour' to which his rank in life entitled him.

Except for the King, who felt that the Prince was flaunting his poverty before the world merely to draw attention to his father's meanness, and for Prince Frederick, recently created Duke of York, who was 'sincerely sorry that things [had] gone so far, and that his brother had thought it necessary to take 'so very publick a step', most people commended the Prince and sympathized with his decision. The Duke of Cumberland had the 'happyness of assuring' him from Spa that his 'manly conduct' was 'universally approved'. His brother, Prince William, who was himself in acute financial embarrassment due to 'the old gentleman' keeping him 'under like a slave', wrote from his naval station at Dominique to commend him 'extreamly'. Fox cordially congratulated him on his 'manly and judicious step' which had 'united the universal opinion of all descriptions of men in his favour'. But Fox also thought it advisable to suggest that £35,000 to £40,000 a year of his allowance from the King should be assigned to trustees for the express purpose of paying it to his creditors by instalments, as otherwise the Prince's enemies would say that he was merely saving up the money to spend later upon himself.

Well-wishers, with or without hopes of future gain, offered him various sums of money. John Lethbridge, a rich Somerset landowner who was created a baronet in 1804, offered 'some few thousands' for the Prince's present use. Sir Charles Barrow, Member of Parliament for Gloucester and a leading supporter of Fox, asked him to 'condescend to accept' £2,000. Wisely, the Prince declined the money. He had determined upon total renunciation until provided with what he considered a proper allowance. It was supposed that he might leave the country until this was done, and go to live in Hanover. Instead he left for Sussex, 'an *outside passenger on the Brighton Dilly*', leaving Mrs Fitzherbert to follow him later.

5

Brighton and Westminster
1786–1787

'A subject of the greatest delicacy'

ONLY a few years before, Brighthelmstone, as it was then generally called, had been no more than a small fishing town whose cramped, squat houses were constantly threatened by the encroaching sea. In two fearful storms at the beginning of the century, much of the town had been swept away; and by the 1720s it was feared, so a visitor recorded, that the sea 'would eat up the whole town, above one hundred houses having been devoured by the water in a few years past'.

The fortunes of Brighthelmstone began slightly to improve in the next decade when it became a port of embarkation for the Continent and a packet-boat sailed weekly for Dieppe; but by 1740 there were probably no more than a thousand inhabitants living *almost underground*. It was not a place that attracted many visitors, though within the next few years there appeared one or two bathing-machines on the beach and, on occasions, a man or woman could be seen floundering in the sea – the women in long flannel gowns attended by Amazonian 'dippers', the naked men accompanied by 'bathers' whose duty it was to ensure that their charges were thoroughly immersed.

Then, in 1753, a doctor from Lewes built himself a house on the sea-front. This was Dr Richard Russell whose advocacy of bathing in sea-water – and even drinking sea-water – as a sovereign cure for various ailments had long been celebrated and whose medical treatise, *A Dissertation Concerning the Use of Sea Water in Diseases of the Glands*, originally written in Latin, had appeared in an English translation the year before. For some time Dr Russell, much impressed by the sparkling sea and invigorating air of Brighthelmstone – or Brighton as it was soon to be called – had been sending his patients there for a cure which involved bathing in the sea, drinking its water – combined with a macabre variety of preparations, from crab's eyes and burnt sponge to snails, tar, lice and viper's flesh – and, inevitably, blood-letting. The success of this cure, followed by Dr Russell's own arrival in the town and subsequent discovery nearby at Hove of a spring of chalybeate waters, whose beneficial properties rivalled those of Tunbridge Wells, ensured the future of Brighton as a popular seaside spa.

By the time Mr and Mrs Henry Thrale had become regular visitors to Brighton in the late 1760s – and occasional hosts there to Dr Johnson – the two principal inns, the Castle Tavern and the Old Ship, had been considerably enlarged. Both of them were provided with elegant Assembly Rooms, the Castle's being designed by Robert Adam's disciple, John Crunden, the architect of Boodle's Club in St James's, the Old Ship's by Robert Golden, who also designed a 'set of baths' for one of Dr Russell's successors, Dr John Awsiter. Soon the hot and cold sea-water baths near the Steine (the broad thoroughfare where the roads from London and Lewes meet) were famous all over England.

The Duke of Gloucester had visited the town in 1765, and some years later the Duke of Cumberland had spent the first of several seasons there, renting first Dr Russell's house on the front, and then Grove House, the Hon. George Windham's large, red-brick, bow-fronted mansion on the Steine. It was to Grove House that the Prince of Wales had come on a visit to his uncle and aunt, the Cumberlands, in September 1783.

It had been a Sunday, and the bells of the town had been rung in greeting. The guns of the battery had fired a royal salute; and in the evening the streets had been illuminated and a display of fireworks had been given outside Grove House. The Prince had stayed for eleven days, going for

walks, riding out with the stag hounds, attending a performance at the North Street Theatre and a ball at the Assembly
Rooms at the Castle Inn, 'the most splendid ever known at
that place'.

It was clear that he had liked Brighton very much and had
found the company of his raffish uncle far more congenial
than that of his censorious father. It had been exhilarating
to be able to escape from the restrictions of his parents' staid
Court, and the 'usual circle of old tabbies', to the lubricious
delights of Grove House.

The next summer the Prince had returned, apparently
on the advice of his physicians who had advocated sea-bath-
ing as a cure for the swollen glands in his throat, an un-
sightly affliction which distressed him deeply and which, it
was said, led to his wearing those extremely high, starched
neckcloths that became so fashionable.

On his second visit to Brighton, the Prince had stayed once
more at Grove House, and had enjoyed himself even more
than on his previous visit. He had been able to go to
Brighton Races which he had just missed the year before; he
had bathed in the sea; and on a groin on the beach one day
he had met a pretty, well-shaped girl, though 'one of the
most illiterate and ignorant of human beings', Charlotte
Fortescue. Struck again by a *coup de foudre*, the Prince had
besieged her with protestations of his love, imploring her to
abandon herself to his passion. Like Mme von Hardenburg,
she had contrived to hold him off while provoking and increasing his desire; but the desire had soon been quenched
when he found out that Miss Fortescue, while seeming so
fresh and innocent in her nervous, appealing rebuffs of his
advances, had been displaying an unseemly enthusiasm for
the rakish charms of the Hon. George Hanger. The Prince
had evidently found other, more complaisant girls, however,
for as the *Morning Post* informed its readers, 'The visit of a
certain gay, illustrious character at Brighton, has frightened
away a number of old maids, who used constantly to frequent that place. This history of [his] gallantries ... has

something in it so voluminous, and tremendous to boot, that the old tabbies shake in their boots when his R— H— is mentioned.'

Either on this visit to Brighton or on the next in the summer of 1785, the Prince had decided that he would like to have a house there of his own, and had asked Louis Weltje to find him one.

Weltje was far more to the Prince than his Comptroller and Clerk of the Kitchen and Cellars as those who recognized his untidy figure and porcine features in Gillray's cartoons well knew. He was admittedly an expert cook, despite an unpromising training as a baker of Westphalian gingerbread; but it was his keen financial sense and his adroitness as a negotiator that particularly recommended him to the Prince as a valued servant. Self-important, not to say arrogant, he had for some years worked in the Duke of Brunswick's kitchen before coming over to England, where he opened a club in St James's Street. He became a naturalized British subject in 1786; but he never learned to speak English properly, giving his orders in the kitchen and conducting his negotiations in a 'barbarous Anglo–Westphalian jargon'. This, however, had not prevented his acquiring a handsome fortune from his property speculations.

The house he chose for the Prince at Brighton was on the east side of the Steine, 'a respectable farmhouse' with a pleasant view of the seafront. It was leased from Thomas Kemp, Member of Parliament for Lewes, whose son, an indefatigable builder, was later to give his name to that part of Brighton known as Kemp Town. Although the arrangements for its lease had not yet been concluded, it was presumably to this house that the Prince, intent upon economy, retired from London in July 1786, establishing Mrs Fitzherbert in a small villa nearby.

Here on the Steine at Brighton, the Prince spent the summer and early autumn of 1786, living quietly, walking about the town and along the front, bowing and smiling to the passers-by who greeted him with friendly respect, passing the

days – though he was still only twenty-four – as any retired
gentleman on holiday might have done. He gambled a little,
though he was not now, as he said himself, really 'a gaming-
man'. He drank far less than usual and entertained but a few
of his London friends other than Sheridan, who was almost
his only contact with the gay London world of Devonshire
House and the Pantheon, of green-rooms and Brooks's, which
he utterly rejected. He seemed quite content to walk and
drive and talk with Mrs Fitzherbert who was said to be
pregnant.*

The summer passed and the autumn, and the Prince
moved from Brighton to various borrowed houses, to the

---

* Mrs Fitzherbert never denied having had children. Her relative,
Lord Stourton, wrote to Lord Albemarle in 1833 to suggest that she
might write on the back of the marriage certificate, 'No issue from
this marriage.' To this, so Lord Stourton said, 'she smilingly objected
on the score of delicacy'. The year before her death, however, she
wrote a paper which ended with the words, 'I Maria Fitzherbert
moreover testify that my union with George, Prince of Wales, was
without issue.' But although she indicated a space where the document was to be signed, she never did sign it.

Sir Shane Leslie investigated the story that a son of the marriage,
known as James Ord, was taken to America and educated by Jesuits
at Georgetown College with funds provided by the British Embassy.
He found little evidence to support the story. He did, however, believe
that it was less easy to dispose of the story that Mrs Fitzherbert's
adopted niece, Mary Anne Smythe, was in reality her daughter by
the Prince. She was supposed to have been the illegitimate daughter
of Mrs Fitzherbert's brother, John Smythe, who, according to family
information, had no children. She married the Hon. Edward Stafford
Jerningham, brother of Lord Stafford. Her grandson, the late Lord
Stafford, thought that there was 'strong circumstantial evidence' to
support the family tradition that his great-grandparents were Mrs
Fitzherbert and the Prince of Wales.

There was also talk of a boy in 1793 at Lille where Mrs Fitzherbert,
who was then thirty-seven, was alleged to have gone after a quarrel
with the Prince, and of another boy, brought up by Sir James Harris
and given his name. Her adopted daughter, Mary Seymour, intimated in later years that Mrs Fitzherbert had had more than one
child by the Prince. But although she certainly loved children and
told Lady Jerningham that she would have liked to have had 'a

Duke of Gloucester's house at Bagshot, to Lord North's mansion, Bushey Park. For six months he persevered in his determination to economize; but he found it very hard. Mrs Fitzherbert believed that the King would eventually relent and come to his help. The Prince, however, entertained no such illusion and knew that he would have to make approaches elsewhere. For a time he was tempted to borrow in France, as he was urged to do by the Duke of Orleans, but Sheridan succeeded in dissuading him from taking so compromising a step. If he could not turn to France, then, the Prince insisted, he must turn to Parliament.

Few of his Whig supporters encouraged such a move: to bring up the matter of the Prince's finances in Parliament would almost certainly lead to questions being asked about Mrs Fitzherbert whose 'Reported Marriage to the Prince of Wales' was the title of a recent, widely read ironical pamphlet by the politician and former clergyman, John Horn Tooke. In this pamphlet, it was argued that 'a most amiable and justly valued female character' was '*legally*, really, worthily, and *happily for this country*, her Royal Highness the Princess of Wales'. In view of the strength of Protestant feeling in the country, it would be disastrous for the Opposition if they were shown to be supporting the claims of a man who was married to a Roman Catholic. It was the Duke of Portland's firmly held opinion that the less said about the Prince of Wales in Parliament the better. *Quieta non movere* was his motto for the day.

The Prince, however, was not prepared to let sleeping dogs lie much longer. He must raise more money. His recent conduct could not have failed to win him a good measure of public support. If the Whigs would not raise the subject on

---

dozen of her own', it seems unlikely that the birth of babies could so successfully have been concealed from their parents' contemporaries who were constantly expecting them. No references to any children that there may have been of the marriage survived the later destruction of her papers; nor are there any references to children of hers in the Royal Archives.

his behalf in Parliament, an independent Member must be found who would. Such a Member presented himself in the form of Alderman Nathaniel Newnham, a rich and independent merchant, who sat for the City of London.

On 20 April 1787 Alderman Newnham rose in the House to ask 'whether it was the design of Ministers to bring forward any proposition to rescue the Prince of Wales from his present very embarrassed situation. For though his conduct during his difficulties had reflected greater honour and glory on his character than the most splendid diadem of Europe had upon the wearer of it, yet it must be very disagreeable to His Royal Highness to be deprived of those comforts and enjoyments which so properly belonged to his rank.' To this, Pitt replied that it was not the government's duty to bring forward such a subject except at the command of the King and they 'had not been honoured with such a command'. Undeterred by this, Newnham gave notice that he would bring forward a motion on 4 May.

Anxious to forestall the embarrassing disclosures that might ensue, Pitt, 'perceiving that the House was so full', took the opportunity on 24 April 'of alluding to a subject of the highest importance' and 'the greatest delicacy'. He wished to know 'the scope and tendency of the motion coming on next week'. After a pause, Newnham cautiously repeated that its object was 'to rescue His Royal Highness from his present embarrassed situation'; and three days later, regretting that the government had taken no steps to rescue the Prince themselves, he moved that 'an humble address be presented to His Majesty, praying him to take into his royal consideration the present embarrassed state of affairs of His Royal Highness, the Prince of Wales, and to grant him such relief as his royal wisdom should think fit'.

At this point, there rose a sturdy figure on the Tory benches, a bluff, down-to-earth Church of England squire from Devon, John Rolle, who commented in the full, thick dialect of his county that the question had extremely grave implications because it was 'a question which went immediately to affect our constitution in Church and State'. Now, as one Member put it, 'the fat was in the fire'. There could be no other question involving Church and State than that concerning the alleged marriage of the Prince and Mrs Fitzherbert.

Fox was not in the House that day and it was left to Sheridan to uphold the Prince's cause. At first he affected not to comprehend Rolle's meaning. Then, when Pitt stood up to threaten that, if Newnham persevered in his motion, he might be driven, 'though with infinite reluctance, to the disclosure of circumstances which he should otherwise think it his duty to conceal', Sheridan countered by bravely suggesting that the insinuations which had been thrown out made it quite impossible for the friends of the Prince of Wales to withdraw their motion. Fearing that he had gone too far, Pitt later that day withdrew the ineffectual threat he had made earlier: the particulars to which he had alluded, he now claimed, related 'only to the pecuniary embarrassments of the Prince of Wales' and had nothing to do with 'any extraneous circumstances'.

Sheridan had played his part in the game of bluff and counterbluff with considerable skill; but the game was not yet ended, and when he went that night to make his report at Carlton House, part of which had now been opened up again, the Prince was much agitated. They both well knew that John Rolle and his supporters would not let the matter rest in the unresolved state in which the debate had left it. It was all very well for the Prince to reply haughtily that he 'never received verbal messages except from the King' when Pitt, through Lord Southampton, made some sort of apology for the indiscreet words he had let slip in the House. But some positive action would have to be taken the next time the matter was raised. The Prince recognized by now what this action would have to be; and Sheridan, who was on good terms with Mrs Fitzherbert, was sent to call upon her to warn her that some explanation would have to be made. Without mentioning outright the possibility that the marriage might have to be denied, Sheridan urged her to consider how extremely dangerous the Prince's position was, and how the least hint from her that there was a secret hidden in their relationship might ruin them both. Mrs Fitzherbert had no intention of saying anything; her loyalty to the Prince was absolute and unshakeable. She was also aware of her own danger. She was 'like a dog with a log tied round its neck', she said to Sheridan. 'They 'must protect' her.

Sheridan certainly felt concerned to protect her. But his affection for her was not shared by Fox. Mrs Fitzherbert had made it clear to Fox that she disapproved of him. She had never forgiven him for suggesting that the Prince should make her his mistress. Consequently Fox's friendship with the Prince, though outwardly as cordial as ever, had not been the same since his young friend had fallen under her influence.

Fox was well aware of the dangerous ground on which he would be treading, but he would derive much satisfaction from formally denying the marriage in the House. He would thus floor Pitt and Rolle and the rest of his and the Prince's Tory adversaries, remove objections to an open discussion of the Prince's finances, and clear himself of the charges implicit in newspaper columns and caricatures that he had been present at a wedding which he had, in fact, strongly opposed and which, so far as he had been led to believe, had not even taken place.

He had the Prince's letter assuring him that 'there never was any grounds for these reports ... so malevolently circulated'. He had also, apparently, since then referred in the Prince's presence to the continuing and persistent rumour of his marriage but the Prince had 'contradicted the supposition at once, with "*pooh*", "nonsense", "ridiculous", etc.' To the end of his life, whenever occasion demanded, the Prince continued to deny that he had ever been married to Mrs Fitzherbert. It was as though he had actually succeeded in persuading himself that the ceremony had never taken place; or, if it had taken place, that it was illegal and therefore not a real marriage at all, and consequently one that could be denied with impunity.

In any case, Fox was prepared to deny it; and on 30 April, in a crowded and expectant House, he did deny it in unequivocal terms, referring with passionate indignation to the 'miserable calumny', the 'monstrous report of a fact which had not the smallest degree of foundation'. It was a 'low malicious falsehood', a 'tale in every particular unfounded' for which there was not 'the shadow of anything like reality'. He denied 'the calumny in question ... *in toto*, in point of fact as well as law. The fact not only never could have happened legally, but never did happen in any way whatsoever.' He had His Royal Highness's 'direct authority' for this declaration.

Although John Rolle remained unconvinced, observing that 'the House would judge for themselves of the propriety of the answer' which had been given to him, Fox was satisfied when he left the House that his conduct had been just and proper. Some time later, however, at Brooks's he met Orlando Bridgeman who came up to him and said, 'Mr Fox, I hear that you have denied in the House the Prince's marriage to Mrs Fitzherbert. You have been misinformed. I was at the marriage.'

Fox now understood that he had landed himself in a most dangerous position. Even though the deception was the Prince's and not his, he had been the means of conveying the lie to the House. Yet, if he recanted, it would mean the ruin of the Prince's reputation together with his own political hopes, for he felt sure that the Whigs would never regain power without the Prince's support. He prudently decided to say nothing more on the matter. For a year he contrived to avoid meeting the Prince, who nevertheless continued in correspondence to address him as 'my dear friend' and proposed himself as a guest at a country house where he knew Fox would be staying in the unfulfilled hopes of meeting him there.

Mrs Fitzherbert's dislike and distrust of Fox were natur-

ally deeper than ever now that he had as much as declared
that she was the Prince's mistress, the position to which he
had long before hoped to consign her. When the Prince
visited her on the morning of 1 May, he took hold of her
hand and caressed her and, according to one report, said to
her, ' "Only conceive, Maria, what Fox did yesterday. He
went down to the House and denied that you and I were
man and wife! Did you ever hear of such a thing?!" Mrs
Fitzherbert made no reply, but changed countenance and
turned pale.'

According to his own account, given years afterwards, the
Prince found Mrs Fitzherbert already 'in an agony of tears'
when he arrived. She was 'deeply afflicted and furious
against Fox'. Lady Anne Lindsay confirmed that she 'burst
into tears, said that she had indeed been shamefully used,
that the Prince had been "LIKE A MAD THING" at the liberty
Fox had taken in exceeding his commission, but that as to
herself she did not care three straws about the matter'. But
later she angrily complained to Sir Philip Francis that Fox
had 'rolled her in the kennel like a street walker; that he
knew every word was a lie, and so on, in a torrent of viru-
lence'. Francis, feeling himself incapable of damming the
torrent, gave up trying to do so and made his retreat 'as well
and as fast' as he could.

Clearly something would have to be done to pacify her,
the Prince decided. She was so angry that her character and
religion had been thus compromised that she threatened to
break off all connection with him, and for a time she refused to see him.

The Prince had felt 'more comfortable' on the night after
Fox's denial had been made in the House, but he was far
from comfortable now. He sent for Charles Grey, one of
Fox's friends, who found him very agitated, 'pacing in a
hurried manner about the room'. Somehow Fox's denial
must be modified in such a way that Mrs Fitzherbert would
be pacified, and would return to him. 'Charles certainly
went too far last night,' he complained. 'You, my dear Grey,

shall explain it.' Then he admitted 'with prodigious agitation' that a ceremony had taken place.

Grey declined to smooth the matter over, since to do so would be to 'question Mr Fox's veracity'. His Royal Highness must speak to Fox himself. 'This answer chagrined, disappointed and agitated the Prince exceedingly; and after some exclamations of annoyance he threw himself on a sofa, muttering, "Well, then, Sheridan must say something."'

Sheridan was more amenable than Grey. He immediately agreed to do what the Prince required of him, though to salvage Mrs Fitzherbert's name while implying at the same time that no marriage had taken place was no enviable task. He rose to attempt it in a speech to the Commons on 4 May.

The House settled down to listen to him in a mood of indulgence. Within the past two or three days agreement had been reached over the matter of the Prince's finances, and Alderman Newnham had been 'extremely happy' to announce that he now declined bringing his motion forward. John Rolle had caused a few moments' tension by observing 'that if it should hereafter appear that any concession had been made humiliating to the country, or dishonourable in itself, he would be the first man to stand up and stigmatize it as it deserved'. But most Members were prepared to express their satisfaction with William Drake, a Member notorious for the loudness of his speeches, who provoked a 'universal roar of laughter' when he said that he would like to declare his 'unfeigned joy in what had occurred' by joining in the general expressions of contentment with his own 'feeble voice'.

Sheridan's speech was long, conciliatory and equivocal, combining flattering remarks about the Prince of Wales's honourable behaviour in the embarrassing affair now so happily concluded with the requisite references to '*another person* ... on whose conduct truth could fix no just reproach, and whose character claimed, and was entitled to, the truest and most general respect'.

Sheridan acquitted himself as well as any Member could have expected him to do. The House murmured its approval; but it could not be supposed that Members were convinced either of the Prince's honourable conduct or of the irreproachable situation of the other person. Indeed, Daniel Pulteney, an independent Member, said that when they heard Sheridan emphasizing how 'truly respectable' was Mrs Fitzherbert's situation so soon after Fox had dragged it through the gutter, 'everyone smiled'.

Mrs Fitzherbert herself was only partially mollified. Gillray portrayed her holding a crucifix and sitting abandoned on a rock, while, in a boat named *Honour*, the Prince and Fox sail unconcernedly away, the Prince protesting, 'I never saw her in my life', and Fox supporting the denial, 'No, never in his life, damme'.

She still refused to see the Prince, who worked himself up into one of his familiar violent fevers for which he was severely bled. To offset the debilitating effects of the bleeding he drank great quantities of wine, and when wine failed to produce the desired result he tried liqueurs of 'every description'. At a ball at Lady Hopetoun's he arrived so 'stupefied' that he could do nothing but sit down and gaze about him, 'pale as ashes, with glazed eyes set in his head'. Supper and an accompanying bottle and a half of champagne were, however, only too restorative. He 'posted himself in the doorway, to the terror of everybody that went by, flung his arms round the Duchess of Ancaster's neck and kissed her with a great *smack*, threatened to pull Lord Galloway's wig off and knock out his false teeth, and played all the pranks of a drunken man upon the stage, till some of his companions called for his carriage, and almost forced him away'.

A few weeks after this ball the Prince was reported to be 'in great danger'; and, as he had done in the days when he had first fallen in love with Mrs Fitzherbert, threatened to kill himself.

Although she could not but feel that the Prince had thrown over her reputation for the sake of an increased allowance, Mrs Fitzherbert began to relax in her hard attitude towards him. She was encouraged to do so by the sympathy with which she was received and the respect with which she was treated in London society. As the Archbishop of Canterbury noticed, it was all 'very odd'; she was 'more received than ever' she had been before and stood 'more forward'. 'I do not know what rules the ladies govern themselves by,' Edmund Malone wrote to Lord Charlemont. 'She is courted and queens it as much as ever.' The Duchesses of Cumberland and Devonshire remained unwavering in their support; the Duchess of Portland warmed to her; Lord and Lady Sefton, who had been far less friendly of late, welcomed her back to their house; even the Tory Duchess of Gordon, who was on good terms with the Queen, announced her belief that Fox had lied, and invited both Mrs Fitzherbert and the Prince, now partially recovered from his illness, to a ball. They both accepted, and were seen dancing together.

So all was forgiven at last. The Prince and Mrs Fitzherbert were reconciled once more, and it was hinted that Fox had exceeded his instructions. The Prince, whose birthday that year had not been noticed at Court, was once again welcomed at Windsor. The Queen greeted him affectionately. The King spoke to him for three hours, and the Prince assured his father that he did 'most sincerely mean never to incur any future debts, which must indoubtedly be as disagreeable to the King as painful to himself'.

6

The King's Illness
1787–1788

'An agitation of spirits nearly bordering on delirium'

THE final settlement was that the Prince would receive another £10,000 a year from the King out of the Civil List, and from Parliament £161,000 with which to pay his debts, together with £60,000 towards the completion of Carlton House. His finances in order at last, he returned to Brighton on 6 July 1787 with Mrs Fitzherbert in a more contented frame of mind than he had enjoyed for many months.

The 'pretty picturesque cottage' on the Steine which Weltje had taken for him had by now disappeared and had been replaced by a far more imposing structure on which one hundred and fifty craftsmen and labourers, under the direction of Henry Holland, had been hard at work for several weeks.*

This first version of the Prince's Marine Pavilion was a long, low Graeco-Roman house faced with cream-coloured tiles, the centrepiece of which was a domed rotunda encircled by six Ionic columns bearing classical statues. The hand-

* The financial arrangements were that Weltje should lease the house at a rent of £150 with an option to purchase it, and that he should pay for its enlargement and improvement, letting it to the Prince at an agreed rent compatible with its improved condition. Weltje's total outlay, including £5,850 for the freehold of the house and grounds, and all the builders' costs, was £22,338; the rent was fixed at £1,000 a year, rising in 1799 to £1,155. The Prince eventually bought the property for £22,000; and Weltje was glad to be rid of it, for he experienced great difficulty in collecting the money due to him (RA 31467).

some, bow-fronted wings which flanked the rotunda to north and south were provided with those decorative iron-work balconies which were soon to become so distinctive a feature of the town.

The brightly-coloured interior, like the interior of Carlton House, owed much to French influences, as befitted a fashionable supporter of the Whigs. The corridors were painted 'French blue'; the library was 'fitted up in the French style' with yellow-papered walls; the dining-room was painted yellow and maroon with a pale blue ceiling. The Prince's bedroom, over the breakfast room in the southern wing, was hung with quilted chintz; and as he lay in his bed, which was curtained like a tent and draped in green and white chequered silk, he could enjoy, by means of judiciously placed looking-glasses, 'an extensive view of the sea and Steine'.

The Prince and Mrs Fitzherbert spent most of the rest of that year in Brighton. The Prince, a journalist reported, had never been seen 'in better health or more buoyant spirits'. He walked every evening in obvious contentment on the Steine; he played cricket in a white beaver hat in the Pavilion grounds; he regularly attended the performances at the theatre in North Street; each morning, if the weather was fine, he went down to bathe in the sea, attended by Brighton's famous 'bather', the tough old sailor 'Smoker Miles. Indeed, he did not like to miss his bathe even when the sea was rough; and on one occasion he came down on to the beach and walked purposefully towards his machine as the waves crashed upon the shingle with the utmost violence.

'I shall bathe this morning, "Smoker",' he said to Miles.

'No, no, Your Royal Highness, it's too dangerous.'

'But I will.'

'Come, come this won't do,' protested 'Smoker', standing in front of the Prince with his fists raised and clenched like a boxer. 'I'll be damned if you shall bathe. What do you think your royal father would think of me if you were drowned?

He would say, "This is all owing to you, 'Smoker'. If you had taken proper care of him, poor George would still be alive."'

The Prince gave way with good humour and walked back to the Marine Pavilion. His good humour this year was, in fact, proverbial, as all who knew him then agreed. His servants were devoted to him, finding him at once a generous and understanding master, who never dismissed any of them unjustly or failed to provide them on retirement with a satisfactory pension.* To the tradesmen of the town, to which his patronage was bringing such prosperity, the Prince was a very paragon, even though his bills were not always paid with the most exact promptitude. A characteristic story was told amongst them of one of their number, overwhelmed with business worries, who had tried to commit suicide. Hearing of the man's distress, the Prince – though he usually chose to give away money personally, deriving an obvious pleasure from the gratitude evoked – had immediately despatched a page to the unhappy tradesman with the contents of his pocket-book. 'Bid him make use of these,' he had

---

* The Prince's annual bill for pensions paid to former servants, servants' dependants, old friends, superannuated mistresses and their relations increased each year, until by the time of his death it amounted to £20,252. Among the pensioners listed in the Royal Archives are Charles James Fox's widow in receipt of £500 a year, Louis Weltje's widow £90, four illegitimate sons of his brother, Prince William, £200 each, and numerous retired servants granted sums ranging from £200 for a housekeeper to £30 for 'the late page Hownam's children' (RA Geo. IV. Box 7; RA 30269–30270). The Prince's generosity is also evident in his annual bill for contributions to charities. He gave £1,000 each year to the 'poor of London' and a great number of lesser sums to all manner of worthy causes and needy individuals. £10 10s, for example, went to the 'Committee appointed for bettering or abolishing the present disgraceful Trade by Chimney Sweepers' (RA 30066). £6 6s went to one Sarah West who wrote to him, 'I am one of the unfortunate women that have lived with officers – you know there is no provision for them (it would be Encouraging Vice) – I resided with Lieut. Hill of the 64th Regiment in the American War – and was the mother of four children' (RA 30306).

instructed the page. 'I may perhaps owe him something, and under the circumstances the routine of payment must appear odious.' The pocket-book was found to contain banknotes to the amount of over £700. The Prince was quite as spontaneously generous, though rather more discriminating in the amounts of his largesse, towards the various charities of the town.*

Even the most censorious could find little to complain of now in his general conduct. On 9 August the usually condemnatory *Morning Post* informed its readers that he was gaining 'many hearts by his affability and good humour'. He was also 'certainly more sober'; and his company was 'much better than it used to be'.

At the time of the Lewes races that year his company included the stately Duchess of Rutland, the Princesse de Lamballe, Lord and Lady Abergavenny and Lord Clermont, a perfectly respectable party. To be sure, the Duke and Duchess of Cumberland and the wicked little Duke of Queensberry were also members of it, but there were no stories of wild or indecent behaviour. For this Mrs Fitzherbert was given much of the credit.

Now that Fox was keeping out of the Prince's way, her influence over him was said to be complete, while his behaviour towards her was more attentive and courteous than ever. Present after present arrived for her at her house in Brighton until he had spent well over £50,000 on jewellery, silver and furniture for her. In London he took and furnished a splendid house for her near Carlton House in Pall Mall, where she lived as though she were indeed Princess of Wales. Here homage was paid to her by her numerous

---

* He did not always remember to fulfil his promises, however. Sir John Macpherson told Sir Nathaniel Wraxall that when the Prince heard that Flora Macdonald, the Jacobite heroine, was still alive and living in reduced circumstances, he displayed much concern and asked Macpherson to pay her a pension of £50 on his behalf. 'She died at the end of two years,' Macpherson added, 'but his Royal Highness entirely forgot to reimburse me, and the annuity came out of my own pocket' (Wraxall, v, 356–7).

friends and those who wished to profit – though few ever did
profit – from her intimacy with the Prince, and here she
entertained in truly regal style. Her old friend Mary Frampton was invited to one of her assemblies and found that,
although her own manners remained 'quiet, civil and un-
pretending' and no one ever accused her of using her great
influence improperly, she was surrounded with all the magnificent trappings of a princess. She was attended by a
respectable lady of impeccable antecedents, Miss Isabella
Pigot; male attendants in green and gold, 'besides the usual
livery servants, were stationed in the rooms and up the
staircase to announce the company, and carry about refreshments, etc. The house was new and beautifully furnished –
one room was hung with puckered blue satin. ... A whole
length portrait of the Prince of Wales was conspicuous in
one of the drawing-rooms and his bust and that of the Duke
of York, ornamented the dining-room.'

The Duke, after an absence of over six years, had at last
been permitted to come home and the Prince, in high excitement, had driven all through the night to Windsor to greet
him. In the early years of his stay in Hanover, the Duke had
been much annoyed that his brother, who was a very lazy
correspondent, did not write to him more often. On several
occasions he had been driven to scold him for his 'excessive
long silence', to complain that he had been quite forgotten,
that it was a 'little hard' not to receive a single line for ten
months at a stretch. Eventually he 'lost all patience'. But
now this irritation was entirely forgotten in the excitement
and pleasure of reunion. They hugged each other warmly
after gazing silently into each other's eyes, and the Prince
was moved to tears. He invited his brother down to Brighton
and gave a splendid party there to celebrate his return. He
proudly introduced him to Mrs Fitzherbert, who grew very
fond of him – as most people did – and then took him off
to London for further celebrations. It seemed, indeed, as
though the Prince had merely been waiting for the excuse
of his brother's homecoming to relapse into the dissolute

life from which Mrs Fitzherbert appeared to have saved him.

The Duke's friend and the head of his Household, Major-General Richard Grenville, a 'silent, reserved' man who had accompanied him to Hanover and had now returned with him, complained that they were 'totally guided' by the Prince of Wales and 'thoroughly initiated into all the extravagances and debaucheries of this most *virtuous* metropolis'. General James Grant, who sat in the Commons for Sutherlandshire and was notorious for his own gormandizing, confirmed that the Prince had taught his brother to '*drink* in the most liberal and copious way, and the Duke in return has been equally successful in teaching his brother to lose his money at all sorts of play – quinze, hazard, etc., to the amount, as we are told, of very large sums'. Within a few months, however, the Prince's behaviour was to provoke far stronger condemnation than this.

Early one morning in October 1788 the King sent an urgent message to his physician, Sir George Baker, asking him to come to see him 'as soon as convenient' and to bring with him 'one of the opium pills in case the pain should not have entirely subsided'.

The pain of which the King complained was 'a very acute' one 'in the pit of the stomach shooting to the back and sides, and making respiration difficult'. It had seized him so violently in the middle of the night that he had been rendered speechless for several minutes. He had suffered something of the sort in 1765 and in the summer of 1787 when he had been forced to lie down on his bed as the only tolerable posture he could find; but that painful attack had passed within a few days and he had regained his strength at Cheltenham, although his behaviour there had struck some observers as being more than a little eccentric. This new attack was considerably more severe and was attended by other unpleasant symptoms: he complained of cramp in the legs and of severe rheumatism which afflicted all his limbs and made him lame; his arms displayed the remains of a rash which he had shown the week before to his daughter, Princess Elizabeth, who had remarked how 'very red' it looked, 'and in great weals, as if it had been scourged with cords'.

Sir George gave it as his opinion that the illness was caused by the King's 'having walked on the grass several hours, and, without having changed his stockings, which were very wet, went to St James's; and that at night he ate four large pears for supper'. Castor oil and senna were prescribed; but these resulted in further 'excruciating pain' in the stomach which necessitated a dose of laudanum. The laudanum counteracting the purgatives, these were repeated which necessitated a second dose of the anodyne. 'Within twenty-four hours,' the Queen's Lady of the Bedchamber, Lady Harcourt, recorded, 'he took three doses of each.'

By the end of this period he was feverish; the whites of his eyes had turned yellow and his urine brown. The next day both his feet were swollen and painful; and by 20 October his stomach was again so agonizing that he could not attempt 'an erect posture'. With characteristic conscientiousness, he tried to attend to business by writing a letter to Pitt, and by commenting on the despatches he had received from him; but he found he could not concentrate. He made mistakes; he repeated himself; he wandered off the point; his handwriting grew big and shaky until he was forced to conclude, 'I am afraid Mr Pitt will perceive I am not quite in a situation to write at present.'

Two days later his mental distress had increased to such an extent that when Sir George Baker called upon him he found his patient 'in a most furious passion of anger'. For three hours he railed against Sir George, castigating him and his accursed remedies, threatening to forbid the importation of senna into the country, ordering that it must never be given to any member of the Royal Family, repeating himself frequently, displaying 'an agitation of spirits nearly bordering on delirium'.

In spite of his deplorable condition the King insisted, after spending a quieter night than usual, on appearing at the levee at St James's on 24 October to prove there was no cause for alarm, to 'stop further lies and any fall of the stocks'. His appearance was scarcely likely, however, to dispel worry; for his dress was disordered, his legs were wrapped in flannel, and his speech was slurred and hurried. On his return to Windsor it was clear that the effort had considerably .worsened his condition.

No one was at all sure what exactly this condition was. Sir Gilbert Elliot recognized that the King was 'certainly in a bad state of health', but he did not think that the complaint was anything too serious. The *Morning Post* assured its readers that it was a sort of dropsical disorder, 'by no means of the alarming kind'; while the *Gentleman's Magazine* announced that it was no more than 'a regular fit of the gout'.

At Windsor, though, it was obvious to all who came into contact with his Majesty that his illness was something far worse than gout or dropsy. Fanny Burney, Queen Charlotte's Keeper of the Robes, who encountered him unexpectedly on the evening of the day after the levee, found that he spoke in 'a manner so uncommon that a high fever alone could account for it; a rapidity, a hoarseness of voice, a volubility, an earnestness – a vehemence, rather – it startled me inexpressibly'. 'He is all agitation, all emotion,' Miss Burney continued in her journal the next day, 'yet all benevolence and goodness, even to a degree that makes it touching to hear him speak. He assures everybody of his health.'

He admitted, though, that he could not sleep any more; and once in the Queen's dressing-room, Miss Burney heard him tell his wife 'at least a hundred times' not to speak to him when he got to his own room next door for he was greatly in need of rest. He lost weight and began to look very frail. To Lady Effingham, one of the Queen's Ladies of the Bedchamber, he said pathetically, showing her the walking stick without which he could not get about any more, 'My dear Effy, you see me all at once an old man.'

The Queen grew 'more and more uneasy' on his behalf, and although she tried to appear calm the effort was sometimes beyond her, and alone in her room she burst into tears. She again sent for Sir George Baker, who on arrival at Windsor on Monday 27 October found the King attending a concert throughout which he talked continually, 'making frequent and sudden transitions from one subject to another ... and was continually sitting and rising'. The previous day in chapel he had stood up suddenly in the middle of the sermon, and throwing his arms round the Queen and the Princesses, had exclaimed loudly, 'You know what it is to be nervous. But was you ever as bad as this?'

He realized, before Baker did, that he was in danger of losing his reason. 'They would make me believe I have the gout,' he complained, kicking one foot against the other, 'but if it was gout, how could I kick the part without any pain?' He knew only too well that he was becoming excessively loquacious, but once he had started talking he found it almost impossible to stop. He told his attendants to keep him quiet by reading aloud to him, but he kept on talking just the same.

Music lost its power to soothe him, and he began to experience difficulty in hearing it. He also began to find it difficult to read; 'his vision was confused ... a mist floated before his eyes'. He 'likewise mentioned to me, as a cause of great distress,' Baker recorded in his diary, 'that having in the morning selected a certain prayer, he has found himself repeating a prayer which he had not proposed to make use of. Then one day, apparently, he burst into tears on the Duke of York's shoulder and cried out in anguish, 'I wish to God I may die, for I am going to be mad.'

Both the Duke and the Prince of Wales had been most attentive to their father so far. The Prince came up from Carlton House to visit the King on 30 October, and the Duke, who was at Windsor the next day, assured his brother that their father had spoken of him 'with tears in his eyes and with the greatest affection', saying how happy he had made him by coming to see him. The Prince himself, so the King said, also wept to see his father so ill. Thereafter the Duke sent regular reports upon their father's health to his brother who himself returned to his apartments in the Castle on the morning of 5 November.

That day, however, as Fanny Burney recorded in her diary, proved to be a 'dreadful' one. Looking down from the window of her room before the Prince's arrival, she had seen the King go out for a ride in his chaise with the Princess Royal. He gave orders to the postillions and got in and out of the carriage twice with such agitation that her 'fear of a great fever hanging over him grew more and more powerful'. When he returned, Miss Burney's fears were temporarily dispelled. The Princess Royal came in 'cheerfully and gave, in German, a history of the airing and one that seemed comforting'.

Soon afterwards the Prince of Wales arrived, and after a private conversation with the Queen, they went in to dinner. During the course of the meal, the King became more and more agitated until, the conversation turning to the subject of murder, he suddenly rose from the table and in a delirium of rage seized the Prince by the collar, pulled him out of his chair and hurled him against the wall. The Queen fell into violent hysterics; the Prince burst into tears, and was only prevented from fainting by his distracted sisters who rubbed his forehead with Hungary water. Later he decided, as he invariably did when excessively upset, that he must be bled.

On examining the King after this outburst, Sir George Baker decided that he was now 'under an entire alienation of mind and much more agitated than he had ever been. The pulse was very quick'; so restless were the patient's movements that he could not count the strokes. The next morning the rate was 'at least 120; but after bleeding it fell to 100'. His eyes, the Queen told Lady Harcourt, were like 'black currant jelly, the veins in his face were swelled, the sound of his voice was dreadful; he often spoke till he was exhausted ... while the foam ran out of his mouth'. He was heard to repeat, in a voice so hoarse and tired that the words were scarcely articulate, 'I am nervous. I am not ill, but I am nervous. If you would know what is the matter with me, I am nervous.'

It was decided that he must be moved out of the Queen's bedroom into a dressing-room next door. He was told that the Queen herself was ill, otherwise he would not have gone; and in the middle of the night he insisted on getting out of bed to satisfy himself that she had not been removed from the house. For half an hour he stood by her bed, staring down at her, the curtains in one hand, a candle in the other.

The next night he again insisted on getting out of bed and going into the room next door. The Queen had now been taken to an apartment further down the corridor, and in her place he found the Prince of Wales and the Duke of York, the physicians, equerries, pages and attendants sitting on chairs and sofas round the walls. He demanded to know what they were all doing there, and then began talking of his dear son Frederick, his favourite, his friend. 'Yes,' he croaked, 'Frederick is my friend.'

Sir George Baker was urged to lead his patient back to bed; but, too timid to lay hands upon him, he merely made a few hesitant suggestions which drove the King to such a fury that he penned him in a corner, upbraiding him for being nothing but 'a mere old woman' who knew nothing of his complaint. By signs and whispers, the Prince tried to get someone else to draw the King away, but no one dared approach him until Colonel Stephen Digby, the Queen's Vice-Chamberlain, who had had some experience of insanity in his own family, took him boldly by the arm and led him back to his room.

From now on the King's condition grew progressively worse. He became more violent and uncontrollable, occasionally overcome by convulsions of his arms and legs and hands. He sweated profusely and 'complained of burning'.

He still talked endlessly, one day rambling on 'for nineteen hours without scarce any intermission', and sometimes talking 'much unlike himself', that was to say 'indecently'. He gave orders to persons who did not exist; he fancied London was flooded and commanded his yacht to go there immediately; he persuaded himself he could see Hanover through Herschel's telescope; he composed despatches to foreign courts on imaginary causes; he lavished honours on all who approached him, 'elevating to the highest dignity ... any occasional attendant'. He had to be forced to have a bath and, after refusing to be shaved for a fortnight, he allowed the barber to attend to one side of his face but not the other. He grew so thin that looking-glasses were either covered with green cloth or removed altogether lest the sight of his emaciated figure should give him a fatal shock.

Sir George Baker being so obviously exhausted and so utterly bewildered by the case – as well as being 'rather afraid' of his patient – it was decided to call in other advice, despite the King's rooted aversion to all physicians. First came the ancient and highly respected Dr William Heberden who was living in retirement at Windsor. Then came Dr Richard Warren, sent by the Prince of Wales 'unknown to the Queen who', as Lady Harcourt said, 'would never have consented to the calling in a physician to whom the King had a particular objection'. It was not only that Warren was the Prince of Wales's physician, he also attended the Dukes of Devonshire and Portland, Charles James Fox and numerous other members of that fashionable society which the King so deeply distrusted. He was accepted with patent reluctance and distaste by the Queen, who was soon describing him as 'that black spirit'; while the King, a few days after his arrival, ordered him out of the room, pushed him when he would not go and, 'pale with anger and foaming with rage', turned his back on him. Warren did not take long to make up his mind that the King's life was in the 'utmost danger', that the 'seizure upon the brain was so violent, that, if he did live, there was little reason to hope that his intellects would be restored'. He informed the Prince of Wales accordingly.

Warren, whose arrival at Windsor was as eagerly welcomed by the other doctors as it was angrily condemned by the King and Queen, was soon followed by yet another consultant, Dr Henry Revell Reynolds, when it was feared that his Majesty was about to die. Ten days later when that crisis was passed, a fifth doctor was summoned, Sir Lucas Pepys.

It was sadly evident that none of them had the least idea what their patient's illness was, nor how it should be treated. Pitt, who was summoned to a conference at Windsor by the Prince of Wales in the second week of November, found them all wholly mystified, incapable of determining whether the illness was one 'locally fixed on the brain' or a 'translation of a disorder from one part to another'. They agreed that 'on the whole there was more ground to fear than to hope', but it would be at least a fortnight before they could 'venture even to pronounce' a tentative prognosis.*

* The King's malady has recently been diagnosed as a particularly virulent form of a rare hereditary metabolic disorder known as porphyria, endemic in the Stuarts and transmitted to the Hanoverians by the Electress Sophia, granddaughter of James I and mother of George I. Its victims suffer from abdominal pain, discoloured urine, weakness of the limbs, neuritis and mental derangement leading to rambling speech, hallucinations and to symptoms of hysteria, paranoia and schizophrenia which a layman might loosely term madness. (Macalpine and Hunter, 172–6). The diagnosis has been questioned (*The Times Literary Supplement* 8, 15, 22, 29 Jan. 1970) by a few historians and various experts in porphyria research, but most historians of the period have found it convincing.

7

The Regency Crisis
1788–1789

'The Prince has taken command at Windsor'

THE inability of the doctors to diagnose the patient's illness, and the equivocal reports that consequently emanated from Windsor, led to constant speculation in London. 'His recovery is hopeless,' Sir Gilbert Elliot told his wife; and others were confidently assured that his death was imminent. Captain John Willett Payne, one of the Prince's most intimate friends and a frequent visitor to Windsor, was presumed to have inside information about what was happening at the Queen's Lodge. He provided his friends in London with garbled accounts of the King's condition, told Sheridan, on the evidence of the Duke of York, that his Majesty's situation was 'every moment becoming worse', his pulse 'weaker and weaker', and said it was impossible that he could survive much longer.

Indeed, so 'extremely current' were reports of his death within the next few days that on 11 November the *Morning Chronicle* was induced to print a categoric denial. But the rumours continued to circulate as wildly as ever, and even if the King were not yet dead, it was 'a probability amounting almost to certainty', so the Marquess of Buckingham was informed, that the insanity was now 'fixed'.

This belief was reinforced by the Prince of Wales's physician, Doctor Warren, who confidentially informed Lady Spencer, the Duchess of Devonshire's mother, in Latin on 12 November that '*Rex noster insanit*'. Warren subsequently gave Pitt his opinion that there was 'every reason to believe that the disorder was no other than direct lunacy', and that the King might 'never recover'. Not all the other doctors, however, were as gloomy in their prognoses as this. Although Baker told Pitt that the patient was 'in a perfectly maniacal state', on the same day Sir Lucas Pepys reassured Fanny Burney that 'there was nothing desponding in the case', and that the King would 'certainly recover, though not immediately'. Another doctor who was called in for consultation towards the end of the month expressed himself as being 'favourable as to a possibility, and even a prospect of recovery'. This was Dr Anthony Addington, Pitt's family doctor and a former keeper of a private madhouse at Reading – a town which, he claimed, without giving his reasons for an assertion that cannot have much endeared him to its inhabitants, contained an unusually high proportion of lunatics.

Contradictory as were the opinions of the doctors as expressed in private conversations and letters, their public accounts which were sent each day to St James's were equally confusing. Well aware that their statements were not only of vital political importance but were read by the royal family at the time and would be seen by the King himself if he recovered, they could scarcely be blamed for their cautious and non-committal bulletins. Nor could they be surprised that their evasions and inconsistencies increased public unrest to such an extent that Sir Lucas Pepys feared for his life if the King did not recover. He and his colleagues received threatening letters by every post; and Sir George Baker's carriage was stopped by the mob who demanded to know what the King's present condition was. On being told it was a bad one, they cried out, 'The more shame for you!'

The widespread alarm, the rapid fall in the value of stocks, the sudden popularity of the King now it appeared that his son would succeed him, were all, as Lord Bulkeley said, 'very little flattering to the Prince'. Yet the Prince's conduct so far in the crisis had not been exceptionable. To be sure, there were stories that, being denied access to his father's room for fear lest he increase the patient's agitation, he had spied on him. Sheridan's sister said that he tiptoed into the room and peered at his father through a hole in a screen. The King looked up, saw the eye and called a page, whereupon the Prince hastily withdrew. 'I have seen my son,' the King said. They assured him he had not. 'However he persisted, and when he found they still denied it, gave no other answer but a most significant glance at the screen.'

It was also alleged by William Grenville that the Prince had taken his friend Lord Lothian into the King's room when it was darkened so that he could 'hear his ravings at a time when they were at their worst'. And Thomas Rowlandson, in an unusually offensive print entitled 'Filial Piety', depicted the Prince leading two drunken companions into the King's bedroom and calling out, 'Damme, come along. I'll see if the old Fellow's — or not.' But the Prince's sympathizers told different stories which were closer to the truth.

Sir Gilbert Elliot said that he was 'under greater restraint in his behaviour and way of life' than he had ever been since he had been his own master; he had given a most favourable impression by his attention to his father. His behaviour had been 'exemplary'.

Lord Loughborough agreed that it had gained the applause of all men, even of those who were secretly glad that he remained so unpopular. Lord Sheffield asserted that his conduct at Windsor had gained him 'great credit'. Sheridan testified to the 'universal sentiment of warm and respectful approbation of the whole' of his Royal Highness's conduct 'during this critical and arduous trial'. And Colonel William Fullerton, Member of Parliament for Haddington Burghs, fulsomely told Captain Payne that the 'general applause and admiration' which the Prince had excited 'in the mind of every man by the superior manner of his acting in such trying scenes [was] considered by the nation at large as affording the best grounded expectations and prognostications of his future government'.

This government, to which Fullerton and Payne and all their friends looked forward with such eager anticipation, seemed to draw closer and closer as the month of November

ended. There appeared so little improvement in the King's
condition that it was decided he must be removed to Kew,
where he might take exercise in the garden 'without being
overlooked or observed', and where the doctors might attend
him with less inconvenience to their various London practices. Since it was known that the King would strongly resist
being moved to Kew from his beloved Windsor, the Cabinet
was summoned to the Castle on 27 November by the Prince
of Wales to approve the move and to hear what the physicians had to say about the present state of the King's illness.

The Cabinet decided that the advice of the physicians
'ought to be followed', and it was settled that the King
should be moved to Kew on 29 November. When told of
this decision, the King 'strongly objected' to it, refusing to
get out of bed. The doctors could not persuade him, nor
could Pitt, who returned to Windsor that morning to ensure
that all went well. Nor could the King's Groom of the
Bedchamber, General the Hon. William Harcourt, nor could
his Equerry, Colonel the Hon. Robert Fulke Greville, whom
the Prince of Wales sent into his room with instructions to
urge his Majesty to prepare himself for the journey. At this
last interruption the King became 'very angry and hastily
closed the bed curtains'. The Prince himself, fearful of the
consequences, made no attempt to intervene personally;
and when Dr Warren did so, the King jumped out of bed
and had to be held back by his pages from assaulting him.

Eventually it was recognized that the King was not to be
persuaded, and he was told that, if he continued his refusal
any longer, force would be used. Reluctantly he allowed
himself to be driven off with three equerries and an escort
of cavalry.

On arrival at Kew he once more became violent when he
learned that he was not to be allowed to see the Queen and
his daughters, although he had been assured that he would
be. He attacked one of his pages, pulled another by the hair
and tried to kick a third. He continued violent the next

day, ate very little, 'refused all medicine and threw what he could away'.

From now on 'the unfavourable symptoms of his disorder' greatly increased. At nights he was 'almost unmanageable' and had to be tied to his bed, and by day he begged his pages to put an end to his miserable life. He swore, and uttered strange indecencies.

Soon after his arrival at Kew, on 3 December, the doctors were again examined on oath by the Privy Council in an attempt to ascertain the present 'situation of the King'. *The Times* that morning had complained of the 'truly ridiculous' contradictions in the reports respecting his health, yet the evidence of the doctors left the members of the Council as much in the dark as they had been before their examination. They all agreed that he was for the moment incapable of public business and that it was impossible to conjecture the likely duration of the illness. But whereas Baker, Pepys, Reynolds and Addington all gave it as their distinct opinion that the King could probably be cured, Warren was far more hesitant. In a confused, halting answer he used the word 'insane'; he mentioned an 'unknown distemper'; he said that on the data available it was impossible for anyone to judge whether or not the King would recover. At the end of the meeting Lord Camden said to the Duke of Leeds, 'Dr Warren is a damned scoundrel, tho' I believe him to be a very able physician, and I dare say you will agree with me in both.'

Able physician or not, Dr Warren was soon to have yet another colleague at Kew who entirely disagreed with both his prognosis and his methods. This was Francis Willis, an elderly clergyman who had been granted a medical degree by Oxford University and had shown exceptional skill in the treatment of symptoms of madness. One of his patients had been Lady Harcourt's mother, whose severe mental disorder he had been given the credit of curing. He was also well thought of by the Lord Chancellor, since several wards of the Court of Chancery had been entrusted to his care with satisfactory results. Not everyone was as convinced of his prowess as Lady Harcourt and Lord Thurlow, however. Lord Sheffield said that he was 'considered by some not much better than a mountebank, and not far different from some of those' that were confined in his madhouse in Lincolnshire. His colleagues at Kew, and Dr Warren in particular, were more inclined to share this opinion of him than Lady Harcourt's. Indeed, Dr Willis was considered both socially and professionally unacceptable, his qualifications, such as they were – he was not a member of the Royal College of Physicians – being considered to render him fit for a position little more important than that of head keeper.

The King, to whom he was introduced on 5 December, did not take at all kindly to this new doctor, the eighth that had been imposed on him.* He greeted him calmly enough, making a considerable effort to appear composed, assuring him that although he had been ill he was now quite well again. When Willis admitted that he was a clergyman, however, the King became agitated once more. 'I am sorry for it,' he said emotionally. 'You have quitted a profession I have always loved, and you have embraced one I most heartily detest.'

'Sir,' Willis is alleged to have replied, 'Our Saviour Himself went about healing the sick.'

'Yes, yes,' agreed the King crossly, 'but He had not £700 [a year] for it.'

Later he 'launched out in strong invective' against all his physicians and earnestly demanded that Dr Willis should take Dr Warren under his care and go back with him to his madhouse in Lincolnshire. By the end of his first day's attendance, in fact, Willis was as violently disliked by the King as ever Warren had been. When he informed his patient sternly that he was mentally deranged and required 'attention and management', the King attempted to assault

* The seventh doctor, Thomas Gisborne, a retired physician to St George's Hospital, had been called in at the end of November.

him as he had tried to assault Warren; but Willis was quite prepared for this. His method, he told Colonel Greville, was to 'break in' his patients as horses were broken. He threatened the King with 'a strait waistcoat' if he did not control himself, and went to get one from the next room to show him what it looked like.

From that day onward Dr Willis, his sons and three of his keepers who followed him to Kew, ensured that the King was kept firmly in submission. Whenever he refused his food, either because he found it difficult to swallow or had no appetite, whenever he became too restless to lie down quietly on his bed, whenever he sweated so much that he threw the bedclothes off, he was put in the straitjacket. Later, he was confined in a specially made chair – his 'coronation chair' he called it – to ensure his 'compliance with whatever [was] thought proper'. And once when he was tied in the chair to be given a severe lecture on his repetitive and improper remarks about Lady Pembroke, that beautiful and adored woman who had adorned the Court of his youth, Willis stuffed a handkerchief into his mouth to keep him quiet until the reprimand was completed.

Confined in his chair or his straitjacket when he was violent, blistered when it was considered necessary 'to divert the morbid humours' from his head, the King was also doctored with a formidable variety of medicines. He was given calomel and camphor, digitalis, quinine, and, as an emetic, tartarised antimony which made him so sick that he knelt on his chair fervently praying that he might either be restored to his senses or allowed to die.

The weeks went by and, as Fanny Burney said, the patient 'went on now better, now worse, in a most fearful manner', sometimes sweating so profusely that his clothes were drenched, 'very irritable and easily offended' and with a racing pulse, at other times in 'good humour' or 'high spirits', occasionally lying down on his bed and singing, always having to suffer confinement when he was deemed in need of either punishment or coercion. Repeatedly he said

that he could 'never more wear the crown, and desired his
eldest son might be sent for'.

The Prince of Wales, however, was not sent for. At Windsor he had assumed full responsibility and, as Fanny Burney
said, 'nothing was done but by his orders, and he was applied
to in every difficulty. The Queen interfered not in anything . . .' The Queen, indeed, was growing daily more morose
and sulky, so irritating the Prince with her sullen complaints
and grumbles that he felt driven to behave towards her in a
way that her Keeper of the Robes described as most heartless
and high-handed. He gave his orders 'without any consideration or regard for his mother's feelings', she said, knocking
his stick on the floor, condemning everything that had been
done before he took control, and retiring from her presence
without kissing her hand.

The result of this conflict was, so Lord Bulkeley told the
Marquess of Buckingham, that once the Prince took command at Windsor, there was *'no command whatsoever'*. It
was consequently resolved that the Prince should be given
no opportunity of managing the Household at Kew, a duty
which eventually therefore devolved upon the unwilling
Queen. It was bad enough, the Queen had cause to complain, to live at Kew at all, for it had never been intended to
serve as a winter residence – it was so cold and draughty
that sandbags had to be placed against the ill-fitting windows
and doors – but to be placed in the position of having to give
her consent to measures which she knew could only infuriate
the King was intolerable. It was additionally distressing that
in his agitated moments the King not only 'talked much of
Lady Pembroke' – sometimes indecently – but also 'much
against the Queen', eventually coming to the conclusion that
'all marriages would soon be dissolved by Act of Parliament'.

In her unhappiness the Queen grew increasingly resentful
at the attitude adopted by the Prince of Wales and by the
Duke of York who spent so much of his time in his brother's
company. She had been particularly annoyed with them,

and indeed had flown into a rage with them when, soon after
her arrival at Kew, they had wisely taken it upon themselves
to remove to safe-keeping the King's jewellery, money and
papers that were lying about on tables and in unlocked
drawers. The Queen, whose extreme fondness of jewellery
was well known, suspected some ulterior motive and began
to abuse her sons. They retorted with equal harshness, insisting upon handing the valuables over to the Lord Chancellor.

Even more intolerable to the Queen was the fact that both
her sons accepted the opinions of Dr Warren – who continued to insist that the King was 'in a decided state of
insanity' and who supplied them and their friends with reports in support of this belief – whereas the contradictory
reports of Dr Willis, in which she herself placed her faith,
were condemned by her sons as 'mere fabrications' concocted for a 'sinister purpose'.

The official bulletins which were sent to St James's were
certainly fabrications. The doctors could never agree on how
they should be worded and the Queen, insisting on the right
to see them before they were despatched, asked for alterations in them when she thought them insufficiently discreet.
Since they were so unreliable, Warren suggested that he and
his colleagues ought at the same time to make independent
reports of the King's mind to the Prince of Wales, who was
not allowed to see his father on the grounds that the
paient's mind would be too much disturbed by the visit. All
the other doctors agreed except Willis who informed Warren
by letter that such a procedure would be totally against his
normal practice. Warren took the letter to the Prince who
told him to assure Willis that he was not desired to sign any
paper with the other doctors unless he chose to do so, but
that the Prince would much appreciate a daily account 'in
general terms, without specifying any word or action' that
Willis thought should not be mentioned.

While the doctors squabbled at Kew, the political quarrels
intensified in bitterness in London where the government

lived in fear that the King would be declared incurably insane and that they would consequently be dismissed as soon
as his son assumed power. As early as 13 November Pitt had
recognized that he would have to introduce a Bill providing
for a Regency, and that the Regent would have to be the
Prince of Wales. As the *Morning Post* put it that day, 'the
malady with which His Majesty is afflicted is of such a
nature that the medical gentlemen have their doubts as to
future consequences, and if the King continues a few days
longer in his present situation a Regency will be appointed,
at the head of which will be His Royal Highness the Prince
of Wales'. Pitt, well aware of the Prince's dislike of him,
realized that this would probably mean the fall of his government and the installation of the Prince's Whig friends
in its place; and he reconciled himself to the prospect of returning to his career in the law.

8

The King's Recovery
1789

'The acrimony is beyond anything you can conceive'

IN expectation of enjoying the powers and privileges of a Regent, the Prince was now widely rumoured to be behaving with scandalous impropriety. It was said that at Carlton House where he gave dinner parties every Saturday and Sunday evening, all the restraint he had displayed at Windsor in the early stages of his father's illness was abandoned, that both he and the Duke of York went so far, when they were drunk, as to imitate their father's gestures and actions. Certainly the Prince could not disguise the excitement he now felt at the prospect of influence and money, and eagerly discussing with Sheridan, Lord Loughborough, Grey and others who was to have what office when the Whigs came to power, he displayed a readiness 'to go to all the lengths to which that party [was] pushing him'.

No one was yet certain, however, what the Prince intended to do when he became Regent or whose claims he favoured. It was common gossip at Brooks's that Fox, who had been on holiday in Italy with Mrs Armistead when the seriousness of the King's disorder became known, had been told to hurry home on the Prince's express instructions; but it was Anthony St Leger's opinion that the Prince's feelings towards Fox had much changed in recent years and 'that his coolness towards him was much increased by Mrs Fitzherbert who would never forgive his public declaration on her subject in the House of Commons, and had taken every opportunity of alienating the Prince's mind from him'. St Leger also thought that the Prince's opinion of Pitt was 'very much altered since the negotiations on the subject of his debts'; he was 'sure' that the Prince would send for both Pitt and Fox 'and endeavour to make his time quiet by employing them jointly'. When the Prince had seen Pitt to discuss the ordering of prayers for the King's recovery on 14 November, however, nothing was mentioned about a possible coalition. The Prince was polite enough but uncommunicative, and Pitt had reason to fear the worst.

Pitt's fears were further increased by the ambivalent attitude of the Lord Chancellor in his administration, Lord Thurlow. He and Thurlow were not on good terms, having quarrelled over the trial of Warren Hastings, and Thurlow was suspected of being so determined to remain in office that he was prepared to come to terms with the Whigs. One day at Windsor, on taking leave of some of Pitt's other Ministers, Thurlow could not find his hat; while he was looking for it a page brought it to him announcing, to his obvious embarrassment, 'My Lord, I found it in the closet of His Royal Highness the Prince of Wales.'

But although suspected of being on the point of deserting them, Thurlow managed to conceal from the government the course of his negotiations with the opposition. Indeed, the opposition themselves were not at all sure that they had secured his support in endeavouring to ensure that the Regency would be granted to the Prince without unwanted restrictions. For this support he had been offered the appointment of Lord President of the Council, but this was not enough for him; he wanted to retain the Lord Chancellorship. This was awkward, for the post had been virtually promised to Lord Loughborough. Thurlow, however, was insistent. So he was given some sort of undertaking that his claim would be preferred and Fox reluctantly agreed to break the unpalatable news to Loughborough, though even then the Prince could not be certain that Thurlow had been definitely won over.

The Times also was in the dark about this. After Loughborough had been told that he must stand aside for the sake of the party, it printed a list of what it supposed would be the new Ministers; in this list Loughborough figures as Lord Chancellor. On 28 November the *Morning Post* printed a similar list. Among the other names mentioned were the Duke of Portland as Prime Minister, Fox and Lord Stormont as Secretaries of State, Sheridan as Treasurer of the Navy and Burke as Paymaster of the Forces.

At Carlton House and Brooks's, at Devonshire House and at the Duke of Portland's mansion, Burlington House, the opposition continued their discussions, their intrigues and their feuds. Grey quarrelled with Sheridan, who had himself been a contender for the post, over who should be Chancellor of the Exchequer; Sheridan quarrelled with Portland who said that he would not serve in the same Cabinet with him; Sheridan also lost his patience with the Prince, who became so agitated over fears that his marriage to Mrs Fitzherbert might once more be raised in the House, that Sheridan burst out in irritation that he had 'the most womanish mind' he had ever come across.

The Prince of Wales told Lord Sandwich that he could be First Lord of the Admiralty, but neither Fox nor Portland would agree to this appointment. The Duke of Portland himself, although the natural choice as First Lord of the Treasury, as the *Morning Post* had indicated, was hinting that he would not agree to lead the new administration unless the Prince formally apologized to him for the 'very rough' way he had treated him during the negotiations for settlement of his debts; and the Duke was known to be further annoyed by the Prince's constant consultations with Sheridan who, with his wife, had moved into Mrs Fitzherbert's house when evicted by the bailiffs from his own. Meanwhile the Duchess of Portland was suggesting that her husband ought not to accept office unless the Prince himself asked him to do so, and that in any case the Prince, who had recently driven so wildly through the streets with his sisters and Lady Charlotte Finch that he had broken several lamps, was perhaps not quite the man to be Regent at all.

It was an opinion that pamphleteers and caricaturists did all that they could foster. Readers of the *Crisis* were reminded that the problem of the 'mysterious connection' between Mrs Fitzherbert and the Prince had never been satisfactorily resolved and that the public had a right to know if the heir apparent was 'a Papist or married to a Papist'. Subsequent pamphleteers proclaimed that the public also had a right to expect that, if he were to become Regent, the Prince would dismiss such companions as degraded his dignity, and that the 'sacred privileges of the people' would count for more in his estimation than 'the friendship of the card table or the attachments of the turf'.

The Prince's supporters, notably Sheridan and Fox, were attacked with equal force. Sheridan was a 'needy adventurer ready to bring his ability to the best market', a good enough actor, to be sure, provided he was given enough time to learn his part. Fox, whose whole life had been one of dissipation, devoted to the gaming table and the racecourse, was 'a desperado' who would have 'no remorse in tearing up the constitution by the roots to gratify the raving of his monstrous passions'. Even Louis Weltje, who was believed to be engaged in sinister attempts to bribe the Prince's adversaries, was advised by *The Times* to confine his studies to stewpans, and his influence to his patron's closet, or to go back to keeping a gingerbread stall. He was nothing but an 'itinerant German music-grinder raised from earning halfpence by the discordance of a street-walking concert'. An English Prince who showed a predilection for foreign servants such as this could not be said to love his countrymen; many a British subject of infinite merit 'was out of bread' while 'a great German toad-eater' had 'amassed an enormous fortune in the Prince of Wales's service'.

In answer to these charges, the Whigs paid large sums of money to journalists and newspaper publishers in attempts to secure their support against Pitt. Sheridan supplied a great deal of anti-government material to the *Morning Herald*, and Weltje entered into negotiations on behalf of

Carlton House supporters to buy the *Morning Post*, which had been printing items about the Prince's marriage to Mrs Fitzherbert. At the beginning of the following year he did succeed in buying it at a very much inflated price. Meanwhile Whig pamphleteers also attempted to redress the balance by issuing edited accounts of the royal physicians' evidence before the Parliamentary committees illustrative of Dr Willis's 'contradiction of himself'.

These Whig pamphlets referred to the Prince as 'a true genius', possessing 'variety and versatility of talents in the first perfection. ... Parts more lively and quick, a discernment of characters more acute and keen, and understanding more sharp and comprehensive, no man is blessed with. His conversation is unembarrassed and eloquent; his language pure without care, and flowing with fluence.' He was, in short, 'the first young man in Great Britain'.

Although even his most ardent admirers recognized that the Prince fell far short of this description, the opposition felt that his support was necessary to them and that they must enlist it at the risk of becoming tainted with his unpopularity. Consequently, a message sent by the Prince, on Sheridan's advice, to the Duke of Portland, offering to 'cancel all former discontents' was immediately accepted. The Duke agreed to forget everything that was past. He was, he said, 'properly touched' by the overture; and on 30 November, when the Prince, charming and agreeable, called on him at Burlington House, offering to shake hands and 'never again think about the dispute they had about the motion for paying his debts', the Duke thought that his manner could not have been kinder.

Other breaches in the opposition's ranks were not so easily healed; but at least, as the time approached when the Regency question would have to be debated in Parliament, all Portland's objections to becoming first minister in the new government that the Whigs hoped to form were now removed.

Parliament had reassembled on 20 November when Pitt in
the Commons and Camden in the Lords had proposed an
adjournment for two weeks so that thought might be given
to the measures which would have to be adopted if the
King's condition failed to improve. By the time of the delayed meeting of Parliament at the beginning of December,
both Dr Addington and Sir Lucas Pepys felt able to assure
the committee appointed to examine the physicians that
there were very good grounds for hope that the King would
recover, thus contradicting the far less sanguine views of
Warren, who reiterated his belief that the King was not
delirious but insane, and of Sir George Baker who was now
inclined to agree with him. None of the doctors, though, was
as certain of the case as Willis, who flatly contradicted the
evidence of Warren and Baker – henceforward known as 'the
"opposition" physicians'. Willis confidently asserted, after
twenty-eight years' experience 'of the particular species of
disorder with which His Majesty [was] afflicted', that there
was every reason to suppose that he would be restored to
health. After giving this opinion Willis reported privately to
the Queen that he felt sure that he had now 'knocked up' all
the hopes that the opposition had entertained of coming
into power with the Prince of Wales's appointment as
Regent.

The opposition, however, were far from convinced that
their hopes were dashed. In the heated debate that ensued in
the Commons on 10 December, both Sheridan and Burke
vehemently defended Warren against Pitt's accusation that,
while his 'general skill was generally known and acknowledged', he had 'comparatively little' skill in dealing with
mental disorders. Burke demanded to know how Warren,
'the first physician in this country', was 'likely to have given
a false, precipitate and ill-grounded account of his Majesty
on oath'; and Sheridan declared that it was 'ridiculous to
stand upon idle ceremonies and trifling etiquettes; he would
speak out. ... When he heard [Dr Willis] roundly declare
what every other of his Majesty's physicians pronounced it

impossible to speak to, he must assert that Dr Willis was a very hasty decider and a random speaker.'

Fox, looking ill and astonishingly thin after his exhausting rush home from Italy, cut across the argument about the credibility of the respective doctors and roundly declared that the Prince of Wales, as heir to the throne, of full age and capacity, had 'as clear, as express a right' to assume the exercise of royal power as he would have if the King were dead. This was an extravagant claim, and although it was upheld by Fox's supporters in the Commons at the time, it was afterwards felt that he had gone much too far for the opposition's good in putting forward so high a Tory doctrine. As Pitt listened to it, he is said to have smiled, slapped his thigh in triumph and proclaimed that he would '*un-Whig* the gentleman' for the rest of his life. The Prince certainly had a *claim* to the Regency, but hardly an *inherent right*. To assert such a right, Pitt argued, amounted to an unwarranted interference with parliamentary privilege. It was almost treason to the Constitution of the country.

Fox's speech was as strongly condemned outside the Commons as in it. The *St James's Chronicle*, in a characteristic commentary, observed that the once firm friend of the Constitution now appeared 'desirous by one stroke to level this most glorious fabric to the dust'. Fox, however, did not seem much concerned by the storm he had raised. As he told his 'dearest Liz', he expected that there were yet further 'hard fights' in the Commons to come and in some of them the opposition would probably be beaten; but he thought it certain that in about a fortnight the Prince would be Regent and his friends would come to power.

He was encouraged in this belief by the number of uncommitted Members who were coming over to the Whig side. Admittedly, Thurlow had shown his hand at last by emotionally declaring in the House of Lords, 'When I forget my Sovereign, may my God forget me.' But Fox was glad to be rid of that particular encumbrance and was thankful that the way now stood clear for the faithful Loughborough, although the Prince of Wales still continued to hold long discussions with Thurlow whose support Sheridan considered crucial. Of the other waverers – about thirty in the Commons and twenty, including the Duke of Northumberland and Lord Rawdon, in the Lords – several were believed to be ready to vote in the forthcoming debates with the opposition who had been lavish in their promises of honours, perquisites and titles as soon as they came to power.

The debates were long and passionate. Both Fox and Pitt spoke brilliantly, while Burke harangued the House in defence of the Constitution as he understood it, with such emotion and lack of restraint, describing Pitt as one of the Prince's competitors and his policy as nothing less than usurpation, that he had to be called to order at least four times. Dr Addington's son Henry, the Member for Devizes and soon to become Speaker, told his father that Burke 'was violent almost to madness'; and George Selwyn thought it a most lamentable affair that the King should be in a straitjacket while Burke was walking about at large.

At the end of each debate, the arguments were continued with comparable fury outside the House. 'The acrimony is beyond anything you can conceive,' Lord Sydney told Lord Cornwallis. 'The ladies are as usual at the head of all animosity and are distinguished by caps, ribands, and other such ensigns of party.' Supporters of the King and the government wore what they called 'constitutional coats'; ladies displayed their approval of the Prince and the opposition by sporting 'regency caps' decorated with three feathers and inscribed *'Ich Dien'*. Lists of future Ministers were discussed; bishops were nominated, peerages promised, and courtiers chosen. It was a foregone conclusion that the Duke of York would become Commander-in-Chief, that Mrs Fitzherbert would be made a duchess, and that something equally splendid would be done for the Duke of Cumberland who supported his nephew and the opposition – though his brother, Gloucester, did not.

At the prospect of having such patronage in his hands the

Prince became more excited than ever. Fearing that his prospects were endangered by his connection with Mrs Fitzherbert, he even began to hint that, although he was still on friendly terms with her, she had no influence over him any more for he was in love with someone else; in any event there was no reason for concern about her. Some of his letters were scarcely coherent. 'You may easily conceive I am excessively anxious in the event of the day,' he wrote to Sheridan on the eve of the debate upon 16 December. 'What are your apprehensions about numbers? For God's sake explain yourself, *who is false*, who is staunch, *who deceives us*, pray remark will you, and for Heaven's sake send me word and relieve my uneasiness. Do you think that any ... will desert us? ... Pray send word immediately. God bless you ...'

Almost as agitated as the Prince, the Duchess of Devonshire – whose husband had been invited to accept the office of Lord Privy Seal – sat up till four o'clock in the morning to hear the result of the final debate, in spite of a terrible headache. At last her brother and the Duke of Bedford came to Devonshire House 'like Priam's messengers' with the long-awaited news; by a majority of sixty-four, the opposition had been defeated.

Although most of the waverers joined forces with the Whigs, the opposition's bid failed not only on the issue of the Prince's inherent right to the Regency, but also on the questions of the restrictions to be imposed upon his powers if he *were* to be appointed. Pitt, who had clung to office with great tenacity, had conducted his delaying tactics with admirable skill; and the comfortable majorities which he was able to command were greeted with the most profound satisfaction and relief by the great majority of his countrymen.

The Prince, who had earlier told the Duchess of Devonshire that he would not agree to a restricted Regency, had now to accept that, if he were to be nominated, he would be unable to create peerages outside the royal family and would also, with a very few exceptions, be debarred from awarding any pensions, offices or honours. Nor would he have the dis-

position of the royal Household, as the King was to be entrusted to the care of the Queen.

In a letter drafted by Burke and amended by Sheridan and
Loughborough, the Prince protested to Pitt against these
restrictions. But it was unavailing. If the Prince were to be
Regent at all, he would have to be so on Pitt's terms. On 12
February the Regency Bill passed the Commons, and the
Lords were on the point of passing it also when the news
that Dr Willis had long predicted arrived from Kew.

The official bulletin on 10 February had described the
King as having passed 'the day before in a state of composure'. The next day he was said to be 'better this morning
than he was yesterday', and on the 12th he was 'in a progres-
sive state of amendment'. Two days later Sir George Baker
for the first time spoke hopefully of the case to Dr Willis,
and on 15 February even Dr Warren said that if his Majesty
continued through the day in the same state in which he
had seen him that morning, 'he might be said to be well'.
The next week the Lord Chancellor announced that the
intelligence from Kew was now so favourable that 'it would
be indecent to proceed further with the Bill when it might
become wholly unnecessary'.

Anxious to make sure for themselves that the King was as
well as the doctors claimed he was, the Prince of Wales and
the Duke of York – who had jointly informed Prince Augustus two months before that their father was now 'a com-
pleat lunatick' – arrived at Kew on 17 February. But Dr
Willis, with the prior agreement of the Chancellor, asked
them not to go into his room as 'such a step might be of the
utmost mischief to the King'.

Continuing to hear progressively better accounts of their
father, the Prince and the Duke repeatedly went to Kew and
were invariably refused admittance although, as they knew,
the Chancellor and others had been allowed to see him. At
length, on 20 February, they wrote a formal letter to their
mother asking that a day might be named on which they

might be permitted to throw themselves at the feet of their father and pour forth their 'respectful joy in his Majesty's presence'. Failing this, they asked that the physicians should give reasons for their refusal in writing. On receipt of this letter the Queen made an appointment for her sons two days ahead, as the King wanted to have the opportunity of having further discussions with the Lord Chancellor first. The date appointed for their visit was 23 February. They arrived at Kew over two hours late in a state of obvious trepidation.

The King could not at first bring himself to enter the room in the Queen's apartments where they were waiting for him, and stood hesitating on the far side of the door 'crying very much'. After some time he pulled himself together and went into the room, but at the sight of his two sons he began crying again, shedding 'tears on their faces'. They, in turn, both seemed to be 'much touched'.

When the King began to talk he avoided all mention of politics or business, telling them that he had had a chance to improve his Latin and to learn how to play piquet, speaking about horses to the Prince of Wales and about his regiment to the Duke of York. The Queen, who was plagued with toothache, was also present, Sir Gilbert Elliot said, 'walking to and fro in the room with a countenance and manner of great dissatisfaction, and the King every now and then went to her in a submissive and soothing sort of tone, for she has acquired the same sort of authority over him that Willis and his men have'.

After an hour's conversation, the Queen's dinner was announced, and the two sons took their leave. Though fully persuaded of their father's complete recovery about which they expressed their great satisfaction to Greville, it was alleged almost as a matter of course that when they got back to Brooks's 'they amused themselves with spreading a report that the King was still out of his mind, and in quoting phrases of his to which they gave that turn'.

Hearing stories like this, the Queen grew ever more resentful of her sons' collusion with the Whigs during the past miserable months. They, in turn, grew ever more exasperated by her petulant ill-temper and her unbending refusal to entertain any thoughts of reconciliation. The mutual resentment flared into a blazing quarrel in which the Prince of Wales accused the Queen of plotting with his enemies and of entering 'into plans for destroying and disgracing him'. She had, he said, 'countenanced misrepresentations of his conduct to the King and prevented the explanations which he wished to give. She was violent and lost her temper.'

When it was decided to give a concert at Windsor to celebrate the King's recovery, the sons were invited, but the Queen, grown so excessively thin that it was said her stays would go round her twice, reminded them in her invitation that the entertainment had really been arranged for those who had remained loyal to his Majesty and herself on the late occasion. The Duke of Portland told Fox that he thought the Queen's comment was 'offensive', and that the Prince and the Duke had every reason to be 'hurt and offended' by it.

Both of them, however, attended the Windsor concert at which their mother's behaviour towards them was more forbidding than ever. It seemed she was determined to make them feel that their conduct merited their being treated as unwelcome outcasts, unworthy of their parents' affection or regard. It was an overtly political occasion. The ladies of the Court wore Tory colours; the musical programme contained numerous party allusions; the elaborate confections served at supper were decorated with Tory slogans. The King behaved politely enough, but the Queen remained 'sour and glum', keeping a stern eye on her daughters to make sure that there was no unseemly fraternization between her male and female offspring. The Prince left Windsor in the most peevish of tempers.

With the help of Burke, Sheridan and others, he wrote letters to the Queen endeavouring to 'counteract the impressions' which his enemies, who had daily access to the King, gave of the part he and his brother had taken 'in the late important occurrences'. Similar letters were prepared for the King, and Sir Gilbert Elliot was asked to compose a long, detailed and thorough exculpatory memorial.*

But complain as he would that he was being treated as though he were beneath contempt, that he had only learned of his father's intention of resuming government 'by common report', the Prince could gain no satisfaction from either of his parents. As Burke said, everything possible was done 'to disgust' both him and the Duke of York and to keep them from visiting Windsor and Kew. They endured and persevered, but were made to feel wholly unwelcome. When he heard by chance that the King had suffered a bad fall from his horse, having turned abruptly in his saddle to hear something Colonel Goldsworthy said, the Prince wrote angrily to the Lord Chancellor to demand why he had been kept in 'perfect ignorance' of the circumstance. It was *'perfectly indecent'*, yet unhappily only 'too consonant to the *general system*' now adopted towards him.

This general system was clearly exemplified when the Duke of York was almost killed in a duel on Wimbledon Common with Colonel Charles Lennox, nephew of the third Duke of Richmond. Lennox, whose mother, a daughter of the Marquess of Lothian, was one of the Queen's Ladies, had publicly insulted both the Prince and the Duke of York. The

* The decision to compose this memorial was prompted by a 'most harsh and unnatural letter' which the King wrote to Prince William abusing him for associating with his brothers during his father's illness. This letter, the Prince claimed, was the 'first direct intimation' he had received that his conduct and that of the Duke of York, during his Majesty's 'lamented illness had brought on [them] the heavy misfortune of [his] Majesty's displeasure' (RA 31942-4). In fact, Prince William had been at sea during the crisis; but it was widely rumoured that he had been hoping to be appointed First Lord of the Admiralty in the event of a Regency, and *The Times* falsely alleged that he had actually returned home from America, without permission, in expectation of this appontment. In May 1789 when he was created Duke of Clarence, the King is said to have wearily remarked that he well knew that this was yet another vote 'added to the Opposition' (Wraxall, v. 171).

Duke returned the insult. Lennox issued a challenge, and the
Duke accepted it. In the consequent duel, the ball from
Lennox's pistol whistled past the Duke's ear, slicing off a curl
from his wig. But when his mother heard of his narrow
escape, she displayed not the least emotion, merely remarking that it was more likely to be Frederick's fault than
Lennox's. Later, despite the protestations of the Prince of
Wales, she insisted that Colonel Lennox should be invited
to the King's birthday party at St James's where she welcomed him warmly.

The Prince also attended the party and, noticing his
fellow-guest on the ballroom floor during a country-dance,
led his partner, the Princess Royal, out of the dance to a chair
by the side of the Queen. The Queen said, 'You seem heated,
Sir, and tired.'

'I am heated and tired, Madam,' the Prince replied, 'not
with the dance, but with dancing in such company.'

'Then, Sir, it will be better for me to retire, and put an end
to the ball.'

'It certainly will be so, for I never will countenance insults
given to my family, however they may be treated by others.'

When Fox heard of this new development in the quarrel,
he told Liz Armistead that the Queen seemed to him 'to go
beyond the worst woman we ever read of'. 'Liz would not be
such a mother if she had a son,' he continued, 'and with
such a son as the D[uke] of Y[ork] I do not believe, except
the Queen, there is another in the world that would be. ...
Friend and enemy, except only his father and mother, agree
in praising the Duke of York to the greatest degree.'

The general public, however, took a less favourable view
of the conduct of the King's two eldest sons. On 10 March
their coach was stopped by a jam of other carriages in a narrow street. 'The mob soon knew the Princes. They called
"God Save the King!", while the Prince, letting down his
glasses, joined them in calling very heartily, and hallooed,
"Long Live the King!" and so forth with the mob. But one

man called out to him to cry "Pitt for ever! or God bless Pitt!".' This was too much for the Prince who bravely responded to the demand by shouting 'Fox for ever!' At this 'a man pulled the coach-door open, and the Prince endeavoured to jump out amongst them in order to defend himself; but the Duke of York kept him back with one arm, and with the other struck the man on the head, and called to the coachman to drive on, which he did at a great pace, the coach door flapping about as they went'.

After the opera the Prince insisted on walking home to Carlton House, and, as though admiring him for his courage, the crowd along Pall Mall 'called "God bless your Highness!" which he was much pleased with. They also called "Long Live the King!" which he always joined in as loud as any of them. At St James's he fell in with a gang of butchers, with marrow-bones and cleavers, who knew him, and began immediately to play before him; and he found it impossible to get rid of them. They accordingly cleared the way for him, playing and shouting all the way up St James's Street. When they came to Brooks's they gave him three cheers; and the Prince in turn hallooed out, "Long Live the King!" and gave them three cheers himself. He then sent them ten guineas to drink.' This sort of thing, Sir Gilbert Elliot commented, 'is to the credit of his spirit and natural manners; and he is out of luck for not being extremely popular, for a tenth part of his popular qualities, and indeed of his good qualities, has made the fortune of many princes and favourites of the people'.

How far the Prince was from being a favourite of the people was demonstrated the next month, on 23 April 1789, when a service of thanksgiving for the King's recovery was held at St Paul's. Although the Whigs had their supporters in the crowds that lined the streets, it was obvious to all that the King and Pitt were the real heroes of the day. 'What pleased us most', Mary Frampton told her sister, 'was that the populace huzza'd Mr Pitt, but hooted and hissed Mr

Fox – at least, the greatest number did so. Mr Fox, in consequence, sat quite back in his coach, not to be seen.' * Pitt,
indeed, had never been 'in such high estimation'; he had
'reached the summit of human glory'. The King, too, had
never been more popular. In Datchet the month before, the
people had gone down on their knees to welcome him; and
in Windsor the military guard had been reduced to tears at
the joyful sight of his homecoming. Now in London, the
public buildings were decorated and illuminated in his
honour, and people put candles in their windows and decorated their houses with crowns, the letters 'G.R.' and the
words 'Rejoice' and 'God Save the King'. Shouting their
congratulations on the King's recovery, they abused those
'rats' who had deserted him, notably the Duke of Queensberry, the Marquess of Lothian and Lord Rawdon, and
broke the windows of houses that were not illuminated. 'The
King's recovery gave me the most heartfelt satisfaction,'
wrote Lord Cornwallis, expressing a widespread contentment. 'I rejoiced very sincerely on his own account, and I
cannot wish to see poor old England in the ravenous jaws of
the Buff and Blue Squad.'

The Prince, who was driven to the Cathedral to the accompaniment of the jeers and catcalls that now almost invariably
greeted his coach, was reported to have further antagonized
his critics by entering into a whispered conversation with
his brother and uncles during the service, by munching
biscuits during the sermon, and by making some observation to the Duke of York that made his brother laugh so
much he had to cover his face with his hands. Another
observer contradicted this by reporting that 'throughout *this*
day' the Prince behaved well. Party spirit similarly coloured
the reports of the King's behaviour during the service. The
Dean of St Paul's wrote of his 'earnest and uninterrupted

* Fox was recognized as his coach passed through Temple Bar, *The
Times* confirmed, 'and received an universal hiss which continued
with very little intermission until he alighted at St Paul's' (*The
Times*, 24 April 1789).

devotion'; and *The Times* described his demeanour as being truly religious. Sir Gilbert Elliot, on the contrary, thought that he seemed 'wholly indifferent' to the proceedings. 'He looked about with his opera-glass and spoke to the Queen during the greatest part of the service, very much as if he had been at a play.' But however the King and his son may have behaved on this particular day, it was universally agreed that the Prince's future prospects and those of the Whig party were bleak indeed.

The Bottle and the Turf
1789–1791

'A voluptuary under the horrors of digestion'

IT was partly in an effort to provide fresh encouragement to the dispirited Whigs of the north that the Prince and the Duke of York now set out on a trip to Yorkshire. It was an unexpected and undoubted success. The Prince behaved with charm and dignity, responding to his welcome with a pleasure all the deeper because of his unpopularity in London. The 'elegance and *condescension* with which he behaved upon all occasions' during his stay in York earned him, one observer ventured to hope, 'the most *zealous affection* of all its inhabitants.' He gracefully accepted the freedom of the city in a speech as well received as it was delivered. He distributed charity, and attended balls, concerts and dinners. From the portico of Lord Fitzwilliam's mansion, Wentworth House, wearing his blue, red and gold Windsor uniform, he addressed 'a delighted multitude' of twenty thousand people by the light of roaring bonfires, and held up to their admiring cheers the three-year-old Lord Milton, heir to the estates. At Castle Howard, his host decided that he was really 'very good company'. He returned to London expressing his 'uncommon satisfaction at the whole of his Yorkshire journey'.

The excursion was the 'happiest thing imaginable', Edmund Burke told Captain Payne in an enthusiastic letter, 'and the best adapted to dispel prejudices in that county which was cruelly poisoned with them. I hope his R.H. has been pleased; indeed, I ought not to doubt it, because I know the benevolence of his character, and that he could not be indifferent to the happiness he gave to so many people. I spent a good part of the evening yesterday in reading a long letter from Lord Fitzwilliam, and two others from a gentleman and a lady, relative to the Prince's Yorkshire visit. They are, with different details, all expressive of the infinite satisfaction given by his R.H. to them and to everybody who saw him. They all describe his behaviour as having the ease, grace, and pleasantness of what flowed from pure nature ... In particular, it is said that he was properly attentive and civil to those who were adverse in their politicks, so as rather to please than to offend them without losing a marked preference to his friends ...'

Even *The Times*, no friend to the Prince, gave him credit for gaining 'great affection from all ranks of people wherever he has been'. 'Those gentlemen attached to his interest will reap the benefit of it at the next general election', *The Times* added. The opposition had been 'at a very low ebb' in Yorkshire, but they seemed 'now to revive'.

Back in London the Prince found himself as unwelcome at St James's and the Queen's House as ever; and when he went to Windsor he would dine at the White Hart, spend the night in his apartments in the Castle and return to Carlton House without troubling to call on his parents who he felt sure would not want to see him. His father, whose health was improving daily, virtually ignored him; his mother, continuing to express her high opinion of Mr Pitt and, in the words of Lord Hawkesbury, President of the Board of Trade, talking 'violently and even indiscreetly against all the members of the opposition', seemed almost to hate him; his every act was 'deemed censurable'. He would have loved to be of consequence, but his ambitions were thwarted at every turn. His occasional interventions in public affairs were dismissed, even by his own political supporters, as meddling. He was condemned in the columns of *The Times* as a harddrinking, swearing, whoring man 'who at all times would prefer a girl and a bottle, to politics and a sermon'; his only states of happiness were 'gluttony, drunkenness and gambling'.

The more he was accused of being such a wastrel, the more inclined he felt to behave like one, and the more, indeed, he *did* behave like one. Deprived of the acclaim to which he had so spontaneously responded in Yorkshire, he wilfully provided his numerous enemies in London with fresh evidence of his self-indulgence. In June that year Lady Susan Leveson-Gower reported him as being 'drunk as possible' and behaving 'very ill' at Boodle's and as having to be 'dragged out' of Ranelagh.

Gillray's most frequently reproduced caricature of the Prince dates from this period. It shows him, 'a voluptuary under the horrors of digestion', picking his teeth with a fork as he recovers from the effects of an immense meal at Carlton House, his huge belly bursting from his breeches, his florid face threatening apoplexy.* Beneath his massive thighs are empty wine bottles, discarded on the carpet; beside his feet, next to an upturned dice-box, are lists of 'debts of honour unpaid' – an unfair allegation: he was no longer a gambler and 'allowed no play in his house'. At his back are more bills for which an overflowing chamberpot acts as paperweight. On a console table behind him are numerous medicines including preparations 'for the piles', 'for a stinking breath', and two famous cures for venereal disease, Veno's Vegetable Syrup and Leeke's Pills.†

To those who accepted this caricature as a true likeness of the Prince of Wales, it seemed entirely appropriate that he

---

* According to the huge scales in the Old Coffee Mill (now Messrs Berry Bros and Rudd, the wine merchants) in St James's Street, the Prince's weight in December 1797 was 17 stone 8 pounds (*Farington Diary*, iv, 98).

† The Prince was so dismayed by a subsequent Gillray print, *L'Assemblée Nationale*, which disparagingly featured Mr and Mrs Fox, Mrs Fitzherbert, Lady Bessborough and the Duchess of Devonshire, as well as himself, that he paid a large amount of money for the destruction of the plate (George, *English Political Caricature, 1793–1832*, 76). He was, however, a regular customer of Mrs Humphrey and her successor at whose shop in St James's Street Gillray's prints were displayed and sold (RA 27094–28394).

should include so many reprobates among his closest friends, and that the two most notorious dukes in England, Queensberry and Norfolk, should be frequent guests of his at Brighton.

The ninth Duke of Norfolk was sixteen years older than the Prince, the fourth Duke of Queensberry thirty-eight years his senior; and both of them had been celebrated drunkards while he was still a baby. Norfolk, an extraordinarily ill-educated man, though of considerable native intelligence, was said to be not only one of the most drunken but also one of the dirtiest gentlemen in the country, so averse to the use of soap and water that he had to be washed by his servants when too drunk to restrict them. Queensberry was cleaner, but a good deal more depraved, a 'little, sharp-looking man, very irritable, and swore like ten thousand troopers'. A dedicated whoremonger, he had made himself thoroughly detested at Court by spending his evenings during the Regency crisis drinking champagne at Carlton House although a Lord of the Bedchamber, a post from which he was immediately dismissed on the King's recovery.

In the company of Norfolk and Queensberry it was natural to find the various wild members of the Barrymore family – the seventh Earl of Barrymore himself, a young man rapidly dissipating a fortune worth over £20,000 a year, known to all and sundry as 'Hellgate'; his brother, the Hon. and Rev. Augustus Barry, a compulsive gambler ever on the verge of imprisonment and consequently known as 'Newgate'; his youngest brother who, in acknowledgement of a club foot, was called 'Cripplegate'; and his sister whose savage temper and foul language combined to render 'Billingsgate' an entirely appropriate soubriquet. Her sister-in-law, the Countess, whom the Earl had married at Gretna Green, was the daughter of a sedan-chairman and the niece of that alluring courtesan, Letitia Lade, who had numbered the Duke of York amongst her numerous lovers. Sir John Lade, Letitia's husband, an amusing, disreputable fellow, the inheritor of a large brewery fortune, who gave occasional advice in the Prince's racing stables, was another welcome guest at his table.

With the Lades and the Barrymores, with Norfolk and Queensberry, with other such dissipated companions as George Hanger and the Duke of Orleans whose inflamed, scorbutic face, rising above the dark green collar of his coat, was a familiar sight in Piccadilly and on the Steine, the Prince of Wales spent much of his time during the months that followed his father's recovery. Stories of the escapades of his friends were continually retailed in drawing-rooms and taverns and filled column after column in the newspapers. The Barrymores, in particular, were regularly in the news. Everyone had heard tales of how they raced down to Brighton in their coach, sometimes stopping to uproot or displace signposts, at other times screaming 'Murder! Rape! Unhand me, villain!' and how, when the coach was overtaken and forcibly stopped by law-abiding travellers, they jumped out to insult and lay about their would-be saviours. In Brighton, calling themselves the 'Merry Mourners', they went about at night with a coffin, knocking on the doors of middle-class citizens and tradesmen, announcing to terrified maidservants that they had come to take possession of the family corpse. One of them, 'Cripplegate', rode his horse up the staircase of Mrs Fitzherbert's house and into the garret where he left it to be brought down by two blacksmiths; another, 'Hellgate', dressed in the skirts and bodice of his cook at three o'clock in the morning, sang a serenade to Mrs Fitzherbert beneath her bedroom window.

A scurrilous publication, *The Jockey Club, or a Sketch of the Manners of the Age*, gave an audacious but not altogether inaccurate account of the activities of the 'chosen companions and confidential intimates' of the Prince of Wales, the 'very *lees* of society'. 'If a man of the most depraved, the vilest cast were, from a vicious sympathy, to choose his company, it were impossible for his choice to fix anywhere else.' When the heir to the Crown chose such company, affording such proof of his tastes and attachments, then the people had a duty 'to think seriously for themselves'.

The Prince's connection with Mrs Fitzherbert was a matter of serious national concern, *The Jockey Club* continued. His debts were equally a national disgrace. By his dissipation and extravagance he had set decency at defiance and scorned public opinion. As soon as Parliament had voted him money on his hypocritical assertion that he would in future live within his means, he had revived his turf establishment in a more ruinous style than ever and contracted fresh debts to an enormous amount. 'Had a private individual acted in like manner he would have become the outcast of his family and the whole world [would have] abandoned him.'

Nor was the Prince alone singled out for condemnation. The Barrymores, George Hanger and Sir John Lade were 'creatures with whom a man of morality or even common decency' could never associate. Lady Lade was nothing more than 'a common prostitute'; the Duke of York a lecher who spent most of his time 'amongst the nymphs of Berkeley Row'; Louis Weltje, 'a brute'; Lord Clermont, 'another brilliant ornament' of the Prince's Court, 'remarkable only for his profligacy', was 'a hardened incorrigible veteran in every species of iniquity'.

Protest as he would against this 'most infamous and shocking libellous production that ever disgraced the pen of man', demand as he would that these '*damnable doctrines* of the *hell-begotten* Jacobines' ought to be 'taken up in *a very serious manner by Government* and prosecuted', the Prince could enlist scant sympathy. Those who knew him best knew that he was a good-natured fellow at heart, far from being the vicious scoundrel depicted in pamphlets and prints, that he disapproved of the more heartless practical jokes of his companions and compensated their victims. But it could not be denied that his behaviour was frequently as irresponsible as theirs, nor that he sometimes seemed to have thought of nothing except his own pleasure.

In August 1789, on the occasion of his birthday – an event of which his parents declined to take any official notice – there were long and rowdy celebrations in Brighton. The church bells rang; the town was illuminated; various ludicrous sports including jack-ass races were held in a field outside the town; bonfires were lit; an ox was roasted whole and hunks were sliced off with a broadsword; hogsheads of ale were opened on the green; there were sailing races; and there were boxing-matches at which the Prince awarded prizes to the winning contestants.

The Prince took a particular interest in the ring, though after seeing a man killed at Brighton he settled an annuity on the bereaved widow and said that he would never watch another fight again. But his chief delight was the turf, to the pleasure of which he had been introduced by the Duke of Cumberland. Indeed, one of the grooms at Carlton House remarked that horses, of which the Prince was genuinely fond, were the one and only subject of his thoughts. He regularly attended Lewes and Brighton Races, and went racing elsewhere whenever he could. In 1786 his stud had been broken up in accordance with his proclaimed intention of leading a more economical life, but he had gradually built up a new racing establishment at Newmarket, and between 1788 and 1791 his horses won no less than one hundred and eighty-five races. On 20 October 1791, however, there was a scandal at Newmarket when his famous horse, Escape, a fine animal purchased by the Prince two years before for £1,500, was beaten by two outsiders.

Escape was ridden by Samuel Chiffney, a jockey whose high opinion of his own exceptional talents was well justified. He had won the Oaks four times, and in 1789 had won the Derby for the Duke of Bedford. In July 1790 he had been engaged as 'rider for life' by the Prince of Wales who paid him a salary of two hundred guineas a year. His failure on Escape on 20 October was followed the next day – at odds of 5 to 1 against – by an easy win which resulted in the loss of large sums of money by numerous punters and, so it was alleged, handsome profits for himself. It was also alleged that Warwick Lake, Gerard's younger brother and the Prince's racing manager who disliked and distrusted Chiffney, had made some indiscreet remarks about Escape's performance, and that the Duke of Bedford had made some equally derog- atory remarks, declaring in the course of them that Chiffney ought to be dismissed. There were further allegations that Escape had been winded just before his failure on 20 October by being given a bucketful of water.

At the subsequent Jockey Club inquiry, however, both Lake and Bedford denied the remarks attributed to them, Bedford adding that he had not even been at Newmarket that day; while Chiffney said that his bet on the second day had amounted to no more than twenty guineas. Nothing was proved against jockey, owner or trainer; but the Jockey Club was clearly not satisfied.

Outraged by the insinuations made against him, the Prince declared that he would have nothing more to do with New- market. And to demonstrate his belief that Chiffney had been quite innocent of the charges brought against him, he publicly announced his intention of continuing to pay him his two hundred guineas' salary for the rest of his life.*

Charles James Fox, an inveterate racing man, believed that although some of the Prince's people had been guilty

* The Prince's stud was accordingly sold at Tattersall's in March 1791 for prices ranging from twenty-five to 270 guineas. The prin- cipal purchasers were Lord Grosvenor, the Duke of Bedford and – to the annoyance of *The Times* which thought that he ought to have followed his brother's example and have 'seen the imprudence of keeping up a very large turf establishment' – the Duke of York. Chiffney published a spirited defence of his conduct under the char- acteristically immodest title, *Genius Genuine by Samuel Chiffney of Newmarket*. He left Newmarket for London in 1806 when he sold the Prince's annuity for £1,260. He died in poverty the following year. The Prince never patronized Newmarket again (Mortimer, *Jockey Club*, 46).

of an 'absolute cheat', the Prince himself was 'quite innocent'. Nevertheless, his behaviour was 'very injudicious'
since he did not seem displeased with his jockey, yet was
'very much so with Lake for telling him he was sorry he had
won, by which Lake only meant to say ... that he was sorry
a thing had happened which would cause disagreeable conversation to the Prince. . . . People will suspect.'

People *did* suspect; and, although there was no cause for
supposing the Prince guilty of any impropriety, Sir Charles
Bunbury, an influential member of the Jockey Club who had
once been unhappily married to the King's beloved Lady
Sarah Lennox, expressed a common view when he told him
that if he were ever to let Chiffney ride for him again, no
gentleman would allow a horse of his to start in the same
race. 'I was never more vexed in my life,' Fox concluded in a
letter to Liz Armistead, 'and I consider it as putting an end
to amusement here [at Newmarket] most completely because
there were always people enough inclined to do wrong, and
an example of this sort is sure to encourage them.'

As in sport, so in politics, this was a most unfortunate
period in the Prince's career. His perfunctory and half-
hearted attempts to form a party against the detested Pitt,
'Old Billy' as he called him, met with little success. When,
for instance, he and his brothers, the Dukes of York and
Clarence, tried to get an opposition candidate, Lawrence
Dundas, elected as one of the Members for Cambridge University they were soundly defeated. The Prince had told the
Duke of York that he and William had 'the most sanguine
hopes'; but as Pitt was one of the three candidates for the
two seats and Lord Euston, the elder son of the Chancellor
of the University, the Duke of Grafton, was the other, no one
else rated Dundas's hopes very highly. In fact, he received
no more than 207 votes against a total of 993 cast for his
opponents.

It was for the Prince a typical humiliation. He was 'little
respected', the Duke of Portland had to confess; while Sir

Gilbert Elliot was now of the opinion that if anything could make a democracy in England it was the behaviour of the Prince and his tiresome brothers. Tory supporters of the government voiced similar views in stronger terms.

The Times – whose founder, John Walter, received secret service money from the Treasury for supporting the government and for publishing items in disparagement of the opposition – ensured that this low opinion of the Prince and his brothers was kept well before the public. The insincerity of their joy at their father's recovery, *The Times* assured its readers, was quite obvious. 'Their late unfeeling conduct would ever tell against them, and contradict the artful professions they thought it prudent to make.' Although John Walter was fined and imprisoned for a subsequent libel on the Prince, a few months after its appearance he published yet another. For this he was punished by a second term of imprisonment from which he was released before completing the sentence through the generous intervention of his victim. The Prince, however, received little credit for this, and *The Times* continued to report his activities with undisguised disdain.

References to him in private correspondence were equally unflattering. He continued to give splendid levees and 'admirable dinners' at Carlton House, it had to be admitted. Lord Harrowby was assured that he still fascinated everybody there, with his 'natural ease and elegance'. Yet he consistently annoyed his guests by keeping them waiting. At one levee in February 1790, the Prince maintained 'his character for want of punctuality, and kept a vast crowd waiting in a very cold room above an hour before he admitted them. As patience and waiting are essential accomplishments at his Court, this perhaps was done by design.' At a subsequent levee he 'made people wait till near four o'clock'. 'During the interval,' James Hare, Member of Parliament for Knaresborough, told the Duchess of Devonshire, 'there were, I hear, frequent comparisons made between him and his father not much to his advantage.'

Gradually, however, despite the sorry condition of his financial affairs, relations between the Prince and his father began to improve. On 10 August 1790 he wrote to the Duke of York from Brighton asking him to find out from the King whether or not his birthday was to be celebrated, as the 'only reason' for his not having paid his respects the previous year was his not having received 'the smallest intimation on that head'. The King signified that he was at last ready to receive him once more.

He was again at Windsor for the King's birthday the following 4 June and, according to the *St James's Chronicle*, he had never made a more splendid appearance. He wore 'a bottle-green and claret-coloured striped silk coat and breeches, and silver tissue waistcoat, very richly embroidered in silver and stones, and coloured silks in curious devices and bouquets of flowers. The coat and waistcoat embroidered down the seams and spangled all over the body. The coat cuffs the same as the waistcoat. The breeches were likewise covered with spangles. Diamond buttons to the coat, waistcoat, and breeches, which with his brilliant diamond epaulette, and sword, made the whole dress form a most magnificent appearance.'

That year the Queen wrote in good time from Windsor to assure him that she and his father 'certainly' expected him in order to keep his own birthday on 12 August, 'which,' she added, 'none will do with greater pleasure than, my dearest son, than [sic] your very affectionate mother and sincere friend'. The assurances of affection and sincere friendship were to some extent formalistic, but at least the breach between mother and son which had seemed permanent eighteen months before was now evidently bridgeable.

Certainly the ball held at Windsor on 12 August 1791 was a distinct success. The following day even *The Times* praised the charming manners of the Prince, once more reconciled with his parents. 'Perhaps no heir to the Crown since the days of Edward the Black Prince', *The Times* went so far as to suggest, 'has been more generously admired for his amiable manners than the Prince of Wales; and the very happy and substantial reconciliation that has taken place between H.R.H. and his august parents, contributed in no small degree to the pleasures and festivities of the day.'

[10]

The Prince's Brothers
1792–1793

'The common cause of all the Princes of Europe'

A FEW months after that surprisingly successful ball at Windsor, *The Times* had further cause to praise the greatly improved Prince of Wales for the well-delivered maiden speech he made on 31 May 1792 in the House of Lords during a debate on the 'seditious writings' of the extreme reformers. No one knew of his intention of taking part in the debate, not even his two brothers between whom he was sitting, when he suddenly rose and spoke in so 'manly, eloquent and ... persuasive a manner' that he gained both 'the attention and the admiration of the House'. Captain Payne was overjoyed by the effect that this forceful speech had had. It was 'more, *infinitely more*' than he had dared to hope for. The 'moment lost at the Regency' was now recovered and could 'easily be maintained by constant perseverance'.

In his speech the Prince spoke fervently of his undying attachment to the principles of England's 'great and sacred' Constitution, which he had 'very early in life imbibed' and which, to the latest hour of his existence, he would 'glory in professing'.

England's 'present happy and perfect' Constitution seemed all the more precious to him now that the French Revolution had unleashed the dreadful doctrines of those hell-begotten Jacobins on an innocent world. And when, in February 1793, the French revolutionary government declared war on England, where 'in open defiance of all law and decency' infamous propagators of republican principles had long been active, the Prince recognized that his own future depended upon the successful prosecution of the war. 'THE VERY EXISTENCE OF EVERY PRINCE AT THIS MOMENT,' he wrote to the Duke of York, underlining each word with heavy strokes, 'IS CONCERNED AND DEPENDS ON THE TOTAL ANNIHILATION OF THIS BANDITTI, who are a disgrace to the human species.'

To the Duke and to others he professed an eager desire to take a personal, active part in their defeat. He badly wanted to serve abroad, Sir Gilbert Elliot said, 'and to have his share of the glory' that was going. It riled him that he was kept at home while his brothers 'and all the Princes of Europe' were 'acting personally in their common cause'. It was not that he was jealous of the Duke of York's military reputation, he insisted; indeed, he was willing to serve under him; but he did not want to be disregarded while other members of his family achieved popularity and respect.

The Duke of York, in recognition of his military training in Hanover, was, at his father's insistence, appointed commander of the British army and despatched to Flanders to co-operate with the Austrians, though he had no practical acquaintance with war and had necessarily to rely on the advice of his more experienced staff. He was to prove a less than competent military commander, and, as Gillray cruelly emphasized, he energetically embraced the pleasures and dissipations of life in the officers' mess. His bravery, however, was never questioned.

His younger brothers, Prince Ernest and Prince Adolphus, were also given opportunities to display their physical courage. And even his cousin, Prince William, the Duke of Gloucester's son, who had entered the army with the rank of Colonel in the First Foot Guards at the age of thirteen, was enthusiastically if ineffectually serving with his regiment in Flanders five years later and was a major-general before he was twenty.*

* Prince William had been born in 1776 in Rome where his father had chosen to reside following his banishment from Court as a result of his improper marriage. The marriage, which had not weathered

Prince Ernest, a handsome, very tall, well-corseted young
man, had always been destined for a military career. In
1786 he had been sent at the age of fifteen to the University
of Göttingen where military subjects formed a major part of
his curriculum; and he was still abroad, training with the
Hanoverian Army, in 1792. He was certainly not averse to a
career in the Army, but his father's rigid policy of keeping
him, and all his other five brothers, out of England and as
far away from the baneful influences of Carlton House for as
long as possible, was very irksome. 'No man ever desired
more to return to his family, to his country than I do,' he
wrote to the Prince of Wales from Hanover in February
1792. He had been kept abroad for almost six years and had
'not seen a single one out of England except Frederick'. 'I
should even be pleased if my father would permit to my
coming over to you if I even was only to stay there but a
short time. Nothing can equal the pleasure I should have of
seeing you all again; that we all should be again together
there I do not believe will ever happen again.'

It certainly was not to happen yet. The next year Prince
Ernest was serving at the front with his regiment, the 9th
Hanoverian Hussars, of which he was Colonel. And in 1794
his renewed request that he might be allowed to come over
to England on a fortnight's furlough to see his family after
an absence of eight years – and to protest at his transfer

---

well in Italy, came close to collapse when the Duke embarked on an
affair with one of his wife's attendants, Lady Almeira Carpenter.
After this the Duchess's behaviour towards her husband became so
'grossly indecent', in the words of one of his letters of complaint to
the Prince of Wales, that he considered it essential that their daughter Sophia Matilda should be provided with a governess 'to keep her
clear of the Duchess but at meals and in the evening society', and
that Prince William should be allowed to finish his education at
Cambridge. After some hesitation the King agreed to this, granting
his brother an additional pension to defray the cost. The Prince
accordingly entered Trinity College and, although his intellectual
powers were severely limited, he received the degree of M.A. in 1790
when he was fifteen (RA 54374–8, 54384, 54387).

from the dashing 9th Hussars (the 'finest' in the service, officered by 'Gentlemen, many young noblemen') to the less dangerous Heavy Dragoons (officered by 'blackguards') – was again refused by his father. A few months later, however, severe wounds, which eventually lost him the use of his left eye and almost the use of an arm, brought him home to England at last, his good looks lost forever. It was but a short stay. Before he was fully recovered he was back on the Continent once more, proving himself as talkative, opinionated and brave as ever.

Prince Adolphus had also gained a reputation for bravery. He, too, had attended the University of Göttingen and had trained with the Hanoverian Army. And he, like Ernest, had been wounded, had come over to England to convalesce and had soon afterwards returned to his regiment. He was the only one of the brothers not to become entangled in debt.

Although condemned to fight on a more remote and disagreeable front, Prince Edward also saw action in the war. At an early age he had decided on a military career, and after completing his education in Germany had been gazetted Brevet-Colonel in May 1786 when he was eighteen. The following year, having overspent his allowance in Hanover, he had been sent in disgrace to Geneva with his severe military tutor, Colonel Baron von Wangenheim.

Prince Edward had hated Geneva. It was the 'dullest and most insufferable' of all places, he had told the Prince of Wales, and he had been kept there for month after miserable month 'without a single line from the King and only one from the Queen'. He had constantly asked to be allowed to return home and for enough money to settle his debts; but receiving no answer to his petitions, he had given von Wangenheim and his other 'bear-keepers' the slip, and had returned home without leave in 1790.

The King was furious. He granted him an interview which lasted a bare five minutes and packed him off to the army in Gibraltar where he was to be 'strictly disciplined'. Prince Edward disliked Gibraltar even more than Geneva. It was fearfully hot; there was nothing to do; of his male companions some were 'stupid, others low'; and there were almost no women to be found. He carried out his duties as commanding officer of the Royal Fusiliers punctiliously, proving himself a pertinacious stickler for the rigidities of discipline and military etiquette; but the Governor felt constrained to report his wild extravagance and his 'unbounded ideas of [his] independence'. Soon he made up his mind that he could not survive the frustrations of life upon the 'solitary Rock' without a mistress. Despite the difficulties put in his way by von Wangenheim, who had kept him so short of money in Switzerland that he was scarcely able to 'enjoy those indulgences not only Princes but private gentlemen enjoy at a certain age', he had contrived in Geneva to enjoy the favours of a Mrs Rainsford with whom he had fallen in love. To find such another mistress as Mrs Rainsford in Gibraltar being impossible, he despatched a trusted friend to find him one in France. While awaiting her arrival, he lapsed further into debt by not only redecorating and refurnishing his apartments in the most expensive taste but by recruiting an orchestra and ordering four new carriages from London. When the chosen lady, Thérèse-Bernardine Mongenêt, known as Mlle de St Laurent, arrived from Marseilles he was ready to receive her in style.

She proved an excellent choice as mistress. She shared his liking for music; she was intelligent; she was good-tempered; she had 'above all, a pretty face and a handsome person'. Excellent as were her qualities, though, her arrival in Gibraltar, well publicized in the Press, frustrated any chance that there might have been of her lover's hoped-for return to England. The King would not for a moment consider it, and would not even answer his son's letters. Instead of returning to England, Prince Edward was sent to Canada. To make his exile more tolerable, Mlle de St Laurent agreed to go with him.

Even with the solace of Mlle de St Laurent's company Prince Edward found Canada worse than Geneva and Gibraltar. It was 'the most dreary and gloomy spot on the face of the earth', he wrote to the Prince of Wales from Quebec. While his brothers were 'employed on the brilliant field on the Continent', he was left to vegetate there, ignored by his parents, denied the opportunities granted to his younger brothers, Ernest and Adolphus, and kept for eight and a half years away from home without 'the most distance chance' of seeing active service upon which his *'own Regiment* of Hannoverian guards' was employed under the Duke of York in Europe.

The Prince of Wales, though he had never really been fond of Edward and was to grow to dislike him thoroughly, took pity on his plight. He exerted his influence on his behalf in London, and in January 1794 Prince Edward delightedly wrote to return his 'most hearty thanks' for his brother's help in having him promoted Major-General and placed on the staff of Sir Charles Grey, Commander-in-Chief in the West Indies. Two months later he arrived at Martinique and took an active part in the reduction both of that island and of St Lucia for which he was honourably mentioned in despatches.

Although four of his brothers – Frederick, Ernest, Adolphus and Edward – were all fighting in the war, the Prince of Wales could at least take some small comfort from the fact that the other two, William and Augustus, were not.

For years Prince William had been as distressed by his father's attitude towards him as his younger brothers had been. While he was still a child the King had decided that he should join the Navy, and in May 1779, before he was fourteen, he had been despatched aboard Captain Robert Digby's flagship with orders from his father that he was to be 'received without the smallest marks of parade' and to be treated with 'no marks of distinction'. In January 1780 he was rated midshipman and took part in the relief of Gibraltar. Thereafter for the next ten years he was, like his brothers, kept out of England, returning only for brief periods and then sent away again by the King who learned with horror of his debts and brawls, his drinking and his women. A moderately competent naval officer, as determined to maintain strict discipline in his ship as Prince Edward was in his regiment, he was promoted Captain of the frigate *Pegasus* at the early age of twenty in 1786. Nelson judged it one of the 'best disciplined' frigates he had seen, though the Prince's own officers found their captain far too rigid and obstinate, far too taken up with stringent etiquette to make service under him any sort of pleasure.

His own pleasures in the Navy would have been much enhanced had his father allowed him more money and more freedom. What could be the use of 'our worthy friend our near relation keeping us so close?' he asked the Prince of Wales in exasperation in 1786. 'Does he imagine he will make his sons his friends by this mode of conduct? If he does, he is sadly mistaken. He certainly wishes us all well and thinks he is doing his best. I am convinced he loves me by his way of receiving me last. I cannot but regard him, and would do anything to please him, but it is so difficult to satisfy.'

'I understand the old boy is exceedingly out of humour,' Prince William wrote in another characteristic letter in 1788 when he had begun to wonder if the King really did love him after all. 'I am in hourly expectation of a thunderstorm from that quarter. Fatherly admonitions at our time of life are very unpleasant and of no use; it is a pity he should expend his breath or his time in such fruitless labour. I wonder which of us two he looks upon with least eyes of affection.'

At the time that Prince Edward had been lamenting the dreary life he was made to endure at Geneva, Prince William had been complaining about the frustrations of being cooped up at Plymouth. 'Dulness rules here altogether,' he had mournfully told the Prince of Wales, 'but what is worse than all, not a woman fit to be touched with the tongs, not a house to put your head in after dark. . . . If it were not for the duty of the ship I should perhaps hang myself.'

A few months after this letter was written, however, Prince William, or the Duke of Clarence as he now was, found just the woman he was hoping to find in Dorothea Jordan, a beautiful, generous and good-natured Irish actress, who, three years younger than himself, already had four illegitimate children by two previous lovers. She was later to have ten more, five sons and five daughters, by the Duke of Clarence whose enforced retirement from active service in the Navy was rendered less unpalatable by the prospect of this pleasant domesticity. To compensate him for his early retirement from the sea, which both his limited talents and his closeness to the throne rendered advisable, he was appointed Ranger of Bushey Park; and it was in Lord North's former house at Bushey that he settled down with Mrs Jordan, much to the distress of her many admirers who resented her frequent absences from the stage which were rendered necessary by the long succession of little Fitzclarences.

The determination of the King and the Admiralty not to allow the Duke of Clarence to resume his naval command was finally fixed when he began in 1793 to make some extraordinary speeches in the House of Lords. The spirited defence of the slave trade, which he made in a long speech in April 1793 soon after breaking his arm falling down the slippery steps of Mrs Jordan's house in Somerset Street, was not widely considered objectionable – certainly not on Merseyside where it earned him the freedom of Liverpool – even though he himself felt obliged to apologize later to William Wilberforce for having suggested that he was either a fanatic or a hypocrite. Indeed, the Prince of Wales deemed it a *'most incomparable speech'*, if, perhaps, 'in the comprehension *of some people* rather too severe on Wilberforce'. But a subsequent speech delivered by the Duke in June, in which he declared to an astonished House that the objects of the war having been achieved, peace should now be concluded, was generally condemned as highly irresponsible. And what was quite as bad was his constant abuse of his Majesty's Ministers, principally Pitt, to anyone who would listen to him. The Prince of Wales, as ready to lambast Pitt as the next man, agreed that his brother went much too far; but then, as he told the Duke of York, William was not to be taken too seriously. He was as good-natured a fellow as existed; he meant no harm; but he paid 'not the smallest regard to truth'.

While the Duke of Clarence was kept out of the Navy in England, his younger brother, the delicate and artistic Augustus, was kept out of the country altogether. Prince Augustus, who had accompanied Ernest and Adolphus to the University of Göttingen, had not been able to follow them into the Hanoverian service owing to a chest complaint which necessitated his seeking the warmer climates of Switzerland and Italy. He was still in Italy in October 1792 when he wrote to the Prince of Wales from Rome to complain of his homesickness. He longed to be allowed to return home 'after an absence of so many years'. 'I have frequently wrote to his Majesty on this subject,' he said; 'the physicians have also informed the King it would be highly advantageous to my health – not a line on the subject nor even a hint. ... Perhaps a word thrown in by you on a favourable occasion might have the desired effect – the more so as he knows my wish is not to remain near the Metropolis, from which both physical and political reasons drive me. Happy in being a quiet spectator of the prosperity of my country I should be glad to retire into some quiet corner of it when I might give myself up to the recovery of my health and the forming of my mind.'

It would have been better had the King allowed Augustus to come home, for in April the next year at the age of twenty he secretly married in Rome Lady Augusta Murray. The plain and rather bossy second daughter of the fourth Earl of Dunmore, she was a woman almost ten years older than himself whose mother seems to have benignly countenanced the ceremony though well aware of its illegality.

One of the Prince's attendants informed the King of the marriage, and soon afterwards Augustus received orders to return home immediately. He took the pregnant Lady Augusta with him; and for fear lest objection might be raised against the previous ceremony on the grounds that, although it had been performed by an Anglican clergyman, it had taken place in the Papal states, he married her a second time at St George's, Hanover Square on 5 December. He signed the register as Mr Augustus Frederick and the bride signed it as Miss Augusta Murray.

As soon as the King heard of this ceremony, he ordered the marriage to be declared null and void under the provisions of the Royal Marriage Act of 1772. The Prince, who had returned to Italy soon after Christmas, was forbidden to see his wife or to correspond with his sisters. His father thereafter ignored his existence, as from time to time he had chosen to ignore the existence of others of his disobedient children. He pronounced himself bitterly disappointed in a son whose good sense he had once dared to hope would eventually 'prove conspicuous'. By the end of October 1794 Prince Augustus was miserably asking his brother to 'cast one moment of compassion on a unhappy being ... wandering among the ruins of Ancient Rome'.

While Prince Augustus had been denied the opportunity of serving his country on account of his health, and the Duke of Clarence on account of his conduct, the Prince of Wales's repeated requests to take a more active part 'in the military line' had at last been answered. In the middle of January 1793 the King agreed to appoint him Colonel Commandant of the 10th (or the Prince of Wales's Own) Regiment of (Light) Dragoons – a regiment shortly to be officered almost entirely by the Prince's personal friends and protégés.

His excitement at the prospect of getting into the splendid uniform of his regiment was boundless. In an almost in-

coherently effusive letter – for the characteristic 'prolixity' of
which he begged her indulgence – he told his mother that
his heart was overflowing so much with gratitude to his
good and gracious father' that his words and language were
too weak to express 'the most disstant idea' of his feelings.
His 'joye' was 'boundless'; his head was *almost turned*'; he
must ask her to tell the King that he was so overwhelmed
by his goodness that he was totally unfit for society but that
the next day at whatever hour would be 'the properest and
most convenient' he would come to the Queen's House to
throw himself at his father's feet. He feared he almost expressed his feelings 'in a tone of insanity'. 'The King has
already given me life, but now he has done more, for he has
not only given me life, but the *enjoyment of life* and is that
not *the greatest* of all blessings? I am not equal to meeting
you this evening overpowered with the shocking events of
France [where Louis XVI had been executed three days
before] and with the species of sentiment towards *my father*
which surpasses all discription.'

A few days later the Prince received official notification of
his appointment from the War Office, together with the
additional good news that his commission was to be dated
19 November 1782 in order that he might take rank above
all the present colonels in the Army. Filled with ideas of
military glory, he now wrote to Vienna requesting permission to serve, in the Imperial Army, *'la cause commune de
tous les Princes et Souvereins de l'Europe'*. The Emperor
raised no objection, but the King would not allow it. Nor
would he agree to the Prince of Wales being granted the
kind of rapid promotion enjoyed by his four younger
brothers in the Army, all of whom were, or were soon to
become, generals. The Prince must never aspire to become a
general himself; he must be content to be and to remain the
'first Colonel at the head of a Regiment'.

In this capacity he joined the 10th Light Dragoons in
camp near Brighton where he spent his thirty-first birthday,
his father having decided that it would be 'against all mili-

tary rules' to allow him to come to Windsor for the usual celebrations.

Denied the opportunity of distinguishing himself abroad, the Prince did not take his military duties in England too conscientiously. As *The Times* announced on 5 August, the Prince's intention was to dine in the mess every day that the Regiment was encamped ('in a delightful spot by the sea side'); but he did not intend to be separated from his comforts. His tent, an extremely elaborate construction with three separate sections for cooking, dining and sleeping, was furnished with the most elegant chairs and a superb square bed, its fringed and tasselled hangings being 'of a very delicate chintz, a white ground with a lilac and green cloud', and its four corners ornamented with the Prince's feathers and motto. Nor did he remain in camp for long. Within a month he was back living amidst the grander pleasures of Carlton House, though more concerned than ever that unless there was soon a dramatic improvement in the state of his finances those pleasures could not much longer be enjoyed.

11

Fresh Debts and New Mistresses
1793–1794

'Lady Jersey's influence'

THE Duke of York had solved his own financial problems by getting married. For a time he had entertained thoughts of marrying the rich, young and good-looking widow of the fourth Duke of Rutland who, after her husband's death, had become the mistress of Colonel John St Leger. The Duchess seemed not unwilling, but the Prince of Wales and others of the Duke's friends persuaded him, if only for St Leger's sake, to abandon the project. Far better, the Duke was advised, to consider one of those German princesses whom his father considered so eminently desirable as daughters-in-law. Fortunately there was one of these who did appeal to him. This was Princess Frederica, eldest daughter of Frederick William II of Prussia. She was very small, not at all pretty and had poor teeth; but the diplomat, Lord Malmesbury, as Sir James Harris had now become, thought that although she was indeed far from 'handsome', she was 'lively, sensible and very tractable' and that she would make him happy.

The Duke for his part had little doubt of it. He assured the Prince of Wales that – having renewed his friendship with her – he had 'grown more attracted to her' than he could possibly describe; that he was, in fact, 'over head and ears in love'. John St Leger, who had accompanied the Duke to Berlin, confirmed their fondness for each other. 'I never saw two people so compleatly in love as the Duke and Princess are,' he told the Prince of Wales. 'It is beyond anything I ever saw or heard of. I think your R.H. will like your belle sœur very much: Elle est très aimable et remplie de talents: très bonne musicienne et chantante comme un ange.'

Her parents were delighted with the match. They had not been too hopeful of arranging one as satisfactory as this for so dumpy and plain a girl, and one who was moreover nearly twenty-four. Her mother cried for joy when the marriage was announced, and her father told her contentedly that although she had had to wait a long time she had now won the great prize.

Anxious to get married as quickly as possible – both to enjoy his bride and the additional £18,000 a year which would help to solve his money problems – the Duke appealed to the Prince of Wales to do all he could to hasten the arrangements. He was to see to the ordering of carriages, and at least £20,000 worth of diamonds, to find his bride a good hairdresser, to buy her smart fans and shoes (not easily obtainable in Berlin), and to negotiate for a suitable house, preferably Melbourne House in Piccadilly.

His own house, York House in Whitehall, which he had bought in 1787, was too small; so was Cumberland House which his brother suggested. If Lord Melbourne could be persuaded to exchange his Piccadilly mansion for the smaller but elegant house in Whitehall that would be ideal.

So the Prince went on his brother's behalf to see Lord and Lady Melbourne who said that provided they were not 'any how loosers' – they were hard-pressed themselves for ready money at the time – they were prepared to do anything the Duke wished. It was accordingly agreed that 'His Royal Highness Frederick Duke of York and Albany [should] exchange with Peniston Lord Viscount Melbourne the ... premises ... at ... Whitehall and the furniture therein', and that Lord Melbourne should 'on payment of £23,571 grant and release' to the Duke of York the premises in Piccadilly.*

---

* The Piccadilly house for a time became known as York House and then, after its subsequent conversion into 'residential chambers for gentlemen', as Albany which is still its name today though it has

The Duke was further indebted to his brother for taking
the trouble to consult the royal shoemaker, Thomas Taylor,
in the matter of Princess Frederica's shoes, though the outcome of this errand, through no fault of the Prince's, was
less happy. The Duke sent the Prince one of the Princess's
shoes with instructions that Taylor make six 'very neat' new
pairs, warning him that the sample shoe 'was about a quarter of an inch too long, and too wide every way'. Taylor was
naturally apprehensive, so he told the Prince of Wales that
his shoes might not fit the Princess very well until he had
seen her foot and measured it himself. However he set to
work and soon the shoes, and the apparent delicacy of the
Princess's tiny feet, became objects of the greatest curiosity.

Their owner arrived in England, having married the Duke
in Berlin, on 19 November 1791 and was greeted with the
utmost enthusiasm. A second ceremony at the Queen's
House was all the more warmly welcomed since it was the
first acknowledged marriage in the immediate royal family
since that of the King himself. Although they were scarcely
able to eulogize the Duchess of York's beauty, newspapers
contained column after column praising her charm and
animation, her neatness and amiable manner. Copies of her
famous shoes were sold in their hundreds. Later models, of
fine purple leather five and a half inches long and studded
with diamonds, were described at length in the Press and
even depicted in engravings which, according to the *Public
Advertiser*, were acquired by the 'major part of John Bull
and his family'. It soon 'became the fashion for every one to
squeeze their feet without mercy, in order to be like her
Royal Highness, and as she wore heels to her shoes, so did
the rest of the world'. The rage for the Duchess's shoes became so excessive, in fact, that Gillray was induced to bring

---

opened its doors to married, widowed and divorced women as tenants
as well as men. The Whitehall house, built by James Paine in 1754–
58 and improved by Henry Holland in 1787, became Melbourne
House when the new occupiers moved in. Subsequently it became
Dover House and is now the Scottish Office.

the whole inflated business down to earth in a rude caricature, 'Fashionable Contrasts', which showed the Duchess's
minute feet encased in her slippers lying, heels downwards,
on the edge of the bed with the Duke's massive shoes lying,
heels upwards, between them.

The Prince of Wales welcomed his sister-in-law into the
family most warmly and appeared to be 'extremely fond of
her'. Mary Noel thought it delightful to see them dancing
together; he exerted himself 'to the very best of his power'
and behaved towards her 'more like a lover than a brother'.

Now that the Duke of York by marrying his little Princess
had raised his total income (including the revenues of the
Bishopric of Osnaburgh which his father, as ruler of Hanover, had bestowed on him when he was a child) to some
£70,000 a year, it was borne ever more strongly on the
Prince of Wales that the only solution to his own financial
chaos might well lie in the choice of a princess for himself.
To pay for the continuing improvements at Carlton House
(for which over £60,000 was still needed in 1789), for his
racing establishment (which still cost over £30,000 a year)
and his several other extravagances, he had made numerous
efforts to raise loans from all manner of sources in England
and abroad. This gave much concern not only to Pitt and
other members of the King's government but also to the
opposition who, as Sir Gilbert Elliot said, were a good deal
dissatisfied with him for 'soliciting loans in Holland and
elsewhere, on usurious terms, and to be repaid at the King's
death'. Some of his efforts to raise money were successful,
others were not. Towards the end of 1789 he and the Dukes
of York and Clarence had borrowed 350,000 guilders at 5
per cent from a Jewish banking firm at the Hague and had
ruined the firm by failing to repay the loan or even to pay
any interest. Later on negotiations were entered into with a
firm at Antwerp for raising the sum of £300,000 which became necessary when other creditors called in a loan for a
similar amount.

Appeals were also made to the English bankers, Thomas
Hammersley and William Morland, and to Thomas Coutts
who, having lent the Prince £60,000 in 1793 and after 'strain-
ing every exertion to the utmost so as to preclude all *power
of going further*', was driven sincerely to hope that his Royal
Highness would 'rigidly adhere to the system' of never asking him for any further advances of money which he would
be obliged to refuse. Appeals were then made to the Duke
of Orleans, who was induced to part with £20,000 to each
of the three brothers; to the Landgrave of Hesse-Cassel,
who indicated that he might be willing to lend £100,000 to
£150,000; and to the Duke of York's father-in-law, the King
of Prussia. 'I cannot help for all our sakes pressing you a
little bit,' the Prince wrote to the Duke of York. 'Pray do
you think that your beau père would not do a little something in the loan-way. . . . My dearest Frederick you must for
all our sakes strain every nerve. . . . I hope you will not lose
sight of this as it is of too much consequence to be neglected
and that you will prove yourself an able negotiator.' But
nothing was forthcoming from the King of Prussia. Lord
Malmesbury, who relieved the Duke of York of the embarrassing task of negotiating for a loan in Berlin, reported that
'it would not be easy for [the King] at the moment to find the
means to the extent that [was] wanted'.

So the Prince's solicitor, Charles Bicknell, and other less
reputable envoys, were despatched to Germany, to Holland,
to Belgium and, in desperation, to Ireland. And some of
these envoys, including Louis Weltje and Annesley Shee, a
man who had formerly run a lottery office near Carlton
House, expended on his behalf considerable sums which they
had difficulty in recovering. Recourse was had to all manner
of devices. Attempts were even made to raise loans from
men who were to be rewarded by titles as soon as the Prince
had power to confer them.

But the sums raised were never enough. He owed Leader,
the coachmaker, £32,777; Choppin, the horse dealer, £7,200;
White and Thomas, the breeches makers, £1,875; his various

tailors, Weston, Schweitzer and Davidson, Louis Bazalgette, and Winter & Co., a total of £31,919. He was in debt to most of his friends – more than £15,000 to the Earl of Moira – while members of his Household had not been paid for months. The Prince knew he could expect nothing from 'the Great Billy', who would certainly not risk his popularity or injure his career by advocating an increased allowance in Parliament. Nor could the Prince look for help to those who had been his supporters during the Regency crisis. The Whig opposition, severely mauled at that time, was being virtually broken up by the controversies raging over the French Revolution and the war. Fox's sympathetic attitude towards the Revolution had widened the breach between himself and the Prince – a breach which Mrs Fitzherbert was at pains to keep unbridged in the face of contrary efforts by the Duchess of Devonshire – and yet, without the support of Fox and his friends, the more moderate Whig party, which was led by the Duke of Portland and included Burke, was powerless to assist him.

Unable to enlist the help of the politicians, the Prince was also unable to turn with any hope of success to the King who was now, as Fox had to admit, 'quite master of the country'. The King's answers to his son's requests were always the same.

It was Lord Loughborough's opinion that 'in these times of democratic frenzy it was necessary to support the splendour of Courts and Princes'. The King, however, was more disposed to take the view of Lord Thurlow that 'in this painful situation' the only wise and honourable line which the Prince could pursue was 'to determine to make every practicable reduction in his expenditure, and to allot a large portion of his income to the discharge of his debts'. The Prince would be well advised, Lord Thurlow considered, to go to live quietly for a time at the country house, Kempshot House near Basingstoke in Hampshire, which he had taken for the hunting to be enjoyed there, and drastically to reduce his establishment.

The trouble with Thurlow's scheme was that the Prince now owed so much that even the most severe retrenchment would not save sufficient money to satisfy his creditors. He shut up Carlton House once again; his racing establishment was more or less dismantled; but these economies were not enough. His situation was becoming so deplorable that tradesmen began to refuse to execute his orders and even stopped him in the street to demand the settlement of their bills. The workmen laid off at Carlton House went so far as to petition the Prime Minister, who immediately passed their petition back to him. In desperation he offered enormous rates of interest to money-lenders but they would no longer help him. So many bonds had had to be dishonoured in the past that his undertakings were now thoroughly discredited. Those few friends who could have helped him were reluctant to do so since they knew that anyone to whom the Prince owed money was never welcome in his company.

So he was forced to turn once more to the solution he so much dreaded. He would have to get married.

By the time the Prince came to this unhappy decision, he was already separated from Mrs Fitzherbert. For over a year they had been growing less and less devoted to each other.

Lady Anne Lindsay recorded instances of their quarrels at the dinner-table, of the Prince parrying her accusations until at last he was provoked into making a reply that drove her from her chair with 'angry tears'. After she had left the table on one occasion, the Prince begged leave to talk to Lady Anne and 'regretted her temper, but in terms so kind, so lenient' that Lady Anne was convinced that the fault was more hers than his. 'Ah,' he said, 'if she loved and considered me as much as I love her, we should not quarrel so often as we do.' Lady Anne was 'sorry to hear it was becoming a habit, but was not surprised'. There were stories of quarrels at Brighton where Mrs Fitzherbert was ill at ease in the company of the Prince's more raffish friends. It was said that the Prince would often arrive late at night at her house with various drunken companions, and that 'she would seek a refuge from their presence even under the sofa, when the Prince, finding the drawing-room deserted, would draw his sword in joke, and searching about the room would at last draw forth the trembling victim from her place of conceal-ment'.

It was true that Mrs Fitzherbert usually forgave him for these escapades and that the Prince, for his part, came to her help so long as he could when she was in trouble with her creditors. As her allowance from him was most erratically paid, she was often in debt. On one occasion the bailiffs arrived at her house in Pall Mall with a writ for a debt of almost £2,000 and the threat that if she did not settle it by the next day she would be taken to prison. Since she had no money and the bailiffs would not allow any of her possessions to be carried out of the house to the pawnbrokers, she had to rely upon the Prince to save her. Unable to raise any money himself, he was obliged to send to Carlton House for his jewels which were, so it was said, immediately taken round to the pawnshop.

The Prince also, it was admitted, took Mrs Fitzherbert's side if she was treated slightingly by any member of his family. When the diminutive Duchess of York, who was proving to be rather more aloof and formidable than had been expected, showed that she intended to treat her with the dismissive cold civility which would have been appro-priate at the Prussian Court, the Prince strongly remon-strated with his brother. The Duke of York protested that he could not make his wife behave in a more friendly way, but the Prince argued that he ought at least to try. They fell out over the issue; the Prince talked 'coldly and unaffectionately' to Lord Malmesbury about the Duke and his wife, and it was some time before the former friendship between the two brothers was resumed. Lord Malmesbury added a note in his diary that at this time – June 1792 – the Prince 'was more attached to Mrs Fitzherbert than ever'.

Yet, as the months went by and his debts increased, their quarrels became more frequent and more lengthy. Earlier disputes had soon been settled. Edward Jerningham, the poet, had told his niece, Charlotte, that 'the tittle-tattle of the town' in the summer of 1791 had all been 'of the separation of the Prince and Mrs Fitzherbert'. But this squabble had soon been forgotten and the relationship had continued as before. Very often these early disputes had been over women. There had been an unsuccessful attempt on his part to seduce a lovely and tiresomely virtuous daughter of Lady Archer; there had been a subsequent and more rewarding attempt upon Lucy Howard whose child, George Howard, supposedly the Prince's son, died in its second year and was buried at Brighton. There had also been an affair with Mrs Anna Maria Crouch, a singer of mixed Welsh and French descent who had scored a triumph as Polly Peachum in the *Beggar's Opera*. A beautiful and fascinating woman, Mrs Crouch had been living in a *ménage à trois* with her husband, who was an impecunious naval officer, and Michael Kelly, the Irish actor and opera singer. The advent of a second lover, in the stout shape of the Prince of Wales, had been too much for Lieutenant Crouch who had taken the opportunity of leaving his wife and living more conveniently and contentedly on an allowance she made him. Her affair with the Prince had been a brief one. Indeed, some reports had it that, after making out a bond for £12,000 and settling about £400 a year on her husband to prevent his bringing an action against him, the Prince made love to her on only one occasion. Certainly Mrs Crouch soon returned to the more lasting affection of Michael Kelly, agreeing to sell back the Prince's bond. An emissary went to her house in the Haymarket to collect the bond from her, taking with him a bag containing one thousand guineas. In his coach, in the care of footmen, were two other bags containing a further thousand guineas each should the first offer not tempt her. Fortunately she settled for a thousand guineas, leaving the

Prince free to seek – and to receive – the forgiveness of Mrs Fitzherbert.

Mrs Fitzherbert had long since recognized that the Prince, in Sheridan's words, was 'too much every lady's man to be the man of any lady'. But although ready to forgive him in the past for his casual affairs, she was by now exasperated by his selfishness, his careless accusations that she no longer loved him whenever she had cause to complain of his behaviour, his absurd contentions that she was conducting a secret affair with the royalist emigré, the Comte de Noailles. The Duke of Gloucester told Lady Harcourt that the Prince had 'much consideration' for Mrs Fitzherbert, but that the offhand way in which he 'had his amusements elsewhere' led to her being 'sometimes jealous and discontented'.

Never was Mrs Fitzherbert more jealous and discontented than when she realized that the Prince was falling in love with the Countess of Jersey. She had not taken his other affairs too seriously. Indeed, John St Leger said that she had treated the Crouch affair 'with ridicule'. But Lady Jersey was a far more serious threat. Her husband, an elderly gentleman of the most courtly manners and fastidious dress, known as the 'Prince of Maccaronies', had held various appointments in the King's Household, and Lady Jersey herself was on friendly terms with several ladies about the Court, in particular with Lady Harcourt. Although there were rumours of more than one lover in the recent past, she was also on friendly terms with the Queen, who listened with pleasure to her skilful playing of the harp and who noted with satisfaction that her father, the Rt Rev. Philip Twysden, was a bishop of respected lineage. A mother of two sons and seven daughters, some of whom had already provided her with grandchildren, she was nine years older than the Prince, a woman of mature charm and undeniable beauty. Sir Nathaniel Wraxall spoke of her 'irrestible seduction and fascination'. Mary Frampton described her as 'clever, unprincipled, but beautiful and fascinating'. The Prince – on whom her allurements were exercised with the practised care of an ambitious, experienced, sensual, though controlled and rather heartless woman – was captivated. He had known her for years and had always been rather attracted by her, but it was not until now, when she was in her early forties, that he was forcibly struck by the peculiar strength of her appeal.*

So fond of her did he become that he abandoned Mrs Fitzherbert's company entirely for hers; and to the dismay of their mutual friend, Lord Hugh Seymour, wrote a letter under his new mistress's direction to say that he had now found happiness elsewhere. Lady Jersey assured him that the connection with Mrs Fitzherbert had never been wise, that her being a Roman Catholic was the cause of his unpopularity, that if it were not for her he would have no difficulty in settling his financial affairs satisfactorily, that she was not really fond of him, that she had been heard to declare that it was not so much the person of his Royal Highness that she loved but his rank.

Attracted as he was by Lady Jersey, the Prince did not find it easy to live without Mrs Fitzherbert who, as he well knew, was largely innocent of the charges brought against her. He wanted both women at once. He wrote to Mrs Fitzherbert seeking her forgiveness once more. At first she declined to give it. How could he still love her when for months he had 'given his time to another', and had behaved to her with 'the greatest cruelty'? At length, however, having received 'messages of peace in numbers', she gave way and they were friends again. But there were intermittent quarrels still, and her temper on these occasions, so Lady Harcourt alleged, was 'violent'. The Duke of York also wrote of

* Their names had been linked together in the newspapers as early as 1782, when Lady Jersey professed that she had no feelings for the boy. 'If he is in love with me I cannot help it,' she wrote. 'It is impossible for anyone to give another less encouragement than I have' (Hickleton Papers, A1.2.7).

'Mrs Fitzherbert's unfortunate temper', and advised his brother 'not to bear with it any longer'; he would be better to be 'out of her shackles'.

Threatened by the Prince's infatuation with Lady Jersey, Mrs Fitzherbert's position was further endangered by the decision of the Court of Privileges that Prince Augustus's secret marriage to Lady Augusta Murray was null and void. If Lady Augusta, a Protestant who could trace her descent from Henry VII of England and Charles VII of France, from James II of Scotland and the eleventh-century Marquis of Este, was not acceptable as the wife of a royal prince, how could she, a Roman Catholic, hope to have her own marriage judged legal in the unlikely event of it ever being acknowledged as having even taken place?

The decision of the Court of Privileges was not so unwelcome to the Prince of Wales. Although it did not alter his moral obligations to Mrs Fitzherbert, all remaining doubts about his legal obligations were thus removed. He was definitely free to marry. In June 1794, on the same day that he sent her a note explaining that he had been called away suddenly to Windsor from Brighton, addressing her as 'dear love' and declaring himself 'ever thine', he sent her a subsequent letter to tell her that he could never see her again. Not then knowing of his decision to get married, she naturally attributed this cruel letter to her rival for whom the Prince had recently built a new staircase leading to her apartments at the Marine Pavilion at Brighton. Mrs Fitzherbert endorsed the letter, 'Lady Jersey's influence'. Having done so she left home without making any reply. It was believed that she had gone abroad. The Prince, regretting having dismissed her so abruptly, tried to find out where she had gone and to persuade her to come back, but he could not find her. She did not write; and he, using her silence as an excuse to suppose that she did not truly love him, decided that there was now no longer any possible reason to delay his marriage and the consequent settlement of his bills.

In August 1794 he went to see his father who was on holiday at Weymouth and told him 'very abruptly' that he had
severed all connection with Mrs Fitzherbert and was ready
to enter 'a more creditable line of life' by getting married.

PART TWO
1794–1811

12

Princess Caroline
1794–1795

'There, dear brother, is a woman I do not recommend at all'

FOR years, so the Duchess of Brunswick said, every possible
contender for the hand of the Prince of Wales, with one exception, had been assiduously practising her English in the
Protestant Courts of Germany. The exception was her own
daughter, Caroline, whose chances of marrying the heir to
the English throne were considered negligible. In the first
place Princess Caroline was first cousin to the Prince, and
the King of England was known to disapprove of marriages
between such close relations. The Duchess of Brunswick
was his eldest and only surviving sister, Augusta; the Princess's great-grandmother, moreover, was his own great-
grandfather's sister. There were other reasons, too, why
Princess Caroline was not considered a likely candidate as a
bride for the Prince of Wales. It was rumoured that she was
a young woman of far from impeccable character, that as a
girl she had had an illicit affair with a man of low birth, that
she was exceedingly indiscreet.

Diplomats and soldiers who had been brought into contact with the Court in Brunswick agreed that the Princess
would not be a suitable choice. Arthur Paget, British envoy
extraordinary in Berlin, thought that it would be injudicious
to put down on paper a sketch of her character, but 'could
not avoid saying this much': that the proposed marriage
was far more likely to 'ensure the misery of the Prince of
Wales, than promote his happiness'. Lord St Helens, who
had spent most of his adult life on the Continent in the
diplomatic corps, wrote guardedly of a 'stain' upon her

reputation; Major Toëbingen, an immense officer in the
King's German Legion whom Mary Frampton knew very
well, wore 'a very large amethyst stud or pin, reported to
have been presented to him by the Princess Caroline'; while
Lord Holland said that any young English traveller who had
been through Germany on the Grand Tour would, if asked,
have told the Prince that the character of his intended bride
was considered 'exceedingly loose', even in that country
'where they were not at that period very nice about female
delicacy'.

When her name began to be mentioned in England, the
Queen immediately indicated that she did not approve of
it, insisting that Caroline, for reasons she did not care to
specify, was totally unacceptable. Tearfully she told Prince
Ernest that she had never liked the Duchess of Brunswick,
and, while she would treat the daughter well, she declined
to talk about her. 'Her opinions she could not give,' Prince
Ernest told the Prince of Wales, 'as she never intended to
speak about it. ... God knows what is the matter with her,
but she is sullen. I sounded her tonight about you, but no
reply soever was made.' Yet although she would not talk
about Princess Caroline's disadvantages to her family in
England, the Queen did write to her brother to confide her
fears in him.

'The fact is, my dear brother,' she wrote, 'that the King is
completely ignorant of everything concerning the Duke's
[Brunswick's] family, and that it would be unseemly to speak
to him against his niece. But it is not at all unseemly to tell
you that a relative of that family, who is indeed very
attached to the Duke, has spoken to me of Princess Caroline
with very little respect. They say that her passions are so
strong that the Duke himself said that she was not to be
allowed even to go from one room to another without her
Governess, and that when she dances, this lady is obliged to
follow her for the whole of the dance to prevent her from
making an exhibition of herself by indecent conversations
with men, and that the Duke as well as the Duchess have for-

bidden her, in the presence of this person from whom I heard all this, to speak to anyone at all except her Governess, and that all her amusements have been forbidden her because of her indecent conduct. ... There, dear brother, is a woman I do not recommend at all.'

The King, however, when told of his son's choice, was happy to accept it. Forgetting all previous prejudices against marriages between first cousins, evidently ignoring the unfortunate reports that two of her brothers were mad and that her own mother thought that their sister was not much saner herself, he expressed himself much gratified that his niece had been selected. 'Undoubtedly she is the person who naturally must be most agreeable to *me*,' he wrote to Pitt after the conversation with his son at Weymouth on 24 August 1794. 'I expressed my approbation of the idea.'

The Prince did not express any approbation himself. He was marrying, he allowed it to be supposed, because he could not get his debts settled in any other way, and because his plan of allowing the Crown to descend to the children of the Duke of York was now foiled by the Duchess's failure to bear any children and her doctors' belief that she never could have any. The Duke of Clarence appeared to have settled down permanently with Mrs Jordan; Prince Edward showed no signs of growing tired of Mlle de St Laurent; Prince Augustus was still languishing in Italy worrying about Lady Augusta Murray; Prince Adolphus, at twenty, could obviously not be expected to get married when he had no wish to do so; Prince Ernest, for the moment, appeared to take little interest in women.

So, if *he* were to provide an heir and if he were to become solvent again, he had no alternative but to marry. For this purpose he seemed to think that any German Princess would do. He made few inquiries about Caroline or any of her possible rivals. It seemed almost as though he chose the Brunswick Princess, hastily, sulkily and petulantly, as a peevish protest against having to choose any wife at all. The choice, it was said – by Lord Holland among others – was not in the

least unwelcome to Lady Jersey who actively encouraged
the Prince to make it. Being unable to marry him herself
she had no objections whatsoever to his marrying a woman
of supposedly 'indelicate manners, indifferent character, and
not very inviting appearance, from the hope that disgust for
the wife would secure constancy to the mistress'.*

The envoy chosen to go to Brunswick to make a formal
request for the hand of Princess Caroline was the tactful,
wily Lord Malmesbury who was received most cordially
by the Duchess on 28 November. It was made obvious to
Malmesbury immediately on his arrival that there was going
to be no trouble with the mother. She was rather silly and in-
quisitive, indiscreet and undignified, but 'all good nature';
she talked 'incessantly' about her daughter's future expectations. The Duke on the other hand was, 'as usual, civil,
but reserved and stiff'.

The first impression created by the Princess herself was not
altogether unfavourable, though her head seemed rather
too big for her body and her neck too dumpy. She was short,
Malmesbury noticed, 'with what the French call "des epaules
impertinentes"'; her figure was 'not graceful'; her teeth
could be described as no better than 'tolerable', and they appeared to be going bad; her eyelashes were white. But she
had 'fine' eyes and 'good' hands, and attractive fair, abundant hair. John Hoppner when painting her portrait after
her arrival in England decided that her person was 'very
bad – short – very full chested and jutting hips'. Her face,
however, with which she herself appeared to be 'very well
pleased', was not unattractive, and Malmesbury agreed that
it was quite pretty, though 'not expressive of softness'. She
was 'much embarrassed' upon being presented to the English

* 'Lady Jersey made the marriage,' the Duke of Wellington later
told Lord Salisbury, 'simply because she wished to put Mrs Fitzherbert on the same footing as herself, and deprive her of the claim
to the title of lawful wife to the Prince.' (Oman, *Gascoyne Heiress*,
207).

Lord, yet 'vastly happy' about his mission. She was twenty-four years old.

Lord Malmesbury's initial opinion of Princess Caroline improved on further acquaintance. She was 'gay and cheerful' and loved laughing; she understood a joke and could make one; she appeared to listen attentively to the advice he gave her as to how she should behave in England; she was obviously good-natured and generous, and was 'certainly not fond of money as both her parents' were. Yet it had to be admitted that with this cheerfulness and good nature went many faults. Her father, an intelligent, cautious, suspicious and evasive man, was well enough aware of them himself. He was most anxious on his daughter's behalf and much afraid of what might happen to her in England; he 'dreaded the Prince's habits' and the tactless way in which his daughter might react to them. Entreating Malmesbury to be her constant adviser, he 'hinted delicately, but very pointedly at the free and unreserved manners of the Duchess' who had never provided a good example for the girl. Caroline was not stupid, he insisted, but she had no judgement; she was always asking personal questions and expressing imprudent opinions about people and affairs in general; one needed to be strict with her; it must be impressed upon her that when the Prince took a fancy to another woman she must not show any jealousy. He had told her all this himself and written it down in German; but he urged Malmesbury to repeat it.

The next day after dinner the Duke's mistress took Malmesbury aside and confirmed all that he had been told: Caroline was not ill-disposed but very impressionable, easily led, and she had '*no tact*'. It was important that Malmesbury should speak to her as, although she respected her father, she was afraid of him and considered him 'as a severe rather than an affectionate' parent. Later Mlle Hertzfeldt added that the Princess did not have a '*cœur depravé*'; she had never done anything bad, but she always spoke before she thought. 'I repeat,' Mlle Hertzfeldt impressed upon Malmesbury, *'elle n'a jamais rien fait de mauvais, mais elle est sans jugement et on l'a jugée à l'avenant'*. It would be necessary to be extremely strict with her, to govern her by fear, *'par la terreur même'*.

The longer Malmesbury remained in Brunswick the more certain he became that the Princess was much in need of all the good advice he could offer her. She was always so talkative at supper and usually indiscreet. And after supper when playing cards – at which she was 'very *gauche'* – she was far too free and easy with the ladies about the Court, calling them *'mon cœur'*, *'ma chère'*, *'ma petite'*, even those whom she scarcely knew, gossiping with them, chattering away without a thought as to what she was saying, making 'the most improper remarks', being very 'missish' and taking pride in being able to find out about everything, whom people liked and disliked.

Frequently Malmesbury, in his firm yet delicate way, reminded her that she could not behave like this in England, that she really must learn to consider the effects of what she felt inclined to say before she spoke. He advised her that popularity in England would not be attained 'by *familiarity*, that it could only belong to respect, and was to be acquired by a just mixture of dignity and affability'. He suggested that she should follow the example of the Queen in this respect. But the Princess said she was afraid of the Queen and felt sure that her Majesty 'would be jealous of her and do her harm'. All the more reason then, said Malmesbury, to be attentive to her, holding up as a model the Duchess of York whose discretion and conduct were much admired in England. The Princess strongly disliked the Duchess, and so this piqued her – as Malmesbury intended it should.

Usually, though, she did listen carefully to what he said, particularly when he urged her 'on no account to show that she was jealous' if she detected any signs of her husband being unfaithful to her. Wisely he advised her that 'reproaches and sourness never reclaimed anybody', that he knew enough of the Prince to be quite sure that this sort of reaction 'would probably make him disagreeable and peevish, and certainly force him to be false and dissembling', whereas if she attempted to recover a 'tottering affection' by 'softness ... and caresses', he 'could not withstand such a conduct'.

The Princess had heard about Lady Jersey, for her mother, with what Malmesbury described as 'her usual indiscretion', had shown her an anonymous letter, 'evidently written by some disappointed milliner or angry maidservant', in which the writer had tried to frighten her 'with the idea [that Lady Jersey] would lead her into an affair of gallantry' and would be ready to find her a willing lover.

'This did *not* frighten the Princess, although it did the Duke and Duchess,' Malmesbury noted significantly in his diary, 'and on my perceiving this, I told her Lady [Jersey] would be more cautious than to risk such an audacious measure; and that, besides, it was *death* to presume to approach a Princess of Wales, and no man would be daring enough to think of it. She asked me whether I was in earnest. I said such was our law; that anybody who presumed to *love* her was guilty of *high treason*, and punished with *death*, if she was weak enough to listen to him: so also would *she*. This startled her.'

Princess Caroline was also shocked when her mother showed her another letter which had arrived in Brunswick. This was from her future father-in-law, who had written to express the hope that his niece would not prove to be vivacious, that she was prepared to lead in England a life both 'sedentary and retired'.

Lord Malmesbury was convinced by now that Princess Caroline's temperament was not in the least suited to such a life. He had no reason to alter his conviction that she was well-meaning and well-disposed, that she had 'great good humour and much good nature – not a grain of rancour'. But when summing up her character to himself in a series of jottings in his diary, he felt bound to conclude that she had 'no judgement! caught by the first impression, led by

the first impulse ... loving to talk, and prone to confide and
make missish friendships that last twenty-four hours. Some
natural, but no acquired morality, and no strong innate
notions of its value and necessity; warm feelings and nothing
to counterbalance them. ... Fond of gossiping, and this
strengthened greatly by the example of her mother, who is
all curiosity and inquisitiveness, and who has no notion of
not gratifying the desire at any price. In short, the Princess
in the hands of a steady and sensible man would probably
turn out well, but where it is likely she will find faults perfectly analogous to her own, she will fail.'

None of these reservations about the suitability of Princess Caroline as a wife for the Prince of Wales was made
known in his letters to England, as Lord Malmesbury's instructions had been merely to demand her hand in marriage
and to convey her to London. Indeed, the letters the Prince
received were uniformly encouraging. His aunt Augusta, his
future mother-in-law, assured him, 'Caroline is so happy
with your picture and her future situation.' His Uncle William, Duke of Gloucester, confirmed how 'much much satis-
fyed with the conduct of her daughter' his sister, Augusta,
was; and he added, 'she strongly recommends that her
daughter's cloaths should be chiefly white, as that becomes
her most: in short, she is quite delighted, as I heartily hope
you will be when you see your beautiful bride'. Lord Malmesbury wrote to say that on being introduced to the Princess she had replied in the most graceful and dignified
manner: her words had conveyed everything the Prince
could wish to hear; Lord Malmesbury would not repeat them
as he hoped his Royal Highness would soon hear them from
her own mouth; it was impossible to describe the appearance
of delight on her countenance when he had handed her his
Royal Highness's portrait. She had immediately fastened it
round her neck where it had remained ever since.

The next week Malmesbury wrote again to report that he
had been 'ordered by the Princess to say everything that is
respectful, grateful and affectionate to your Royal Highness.

She has received a box from England with English dresses and it is amazing how much they become her.'

Other reports about Princess Caroline that continued to arrive and to circulate in England were, however, more disturbing. Lord Liverpool believed that, if proper inquiries had been made, it would certainly have been discovered how 'very loose' her conduct was; and Lord Holland said that 'unfavourable reports of the person, and yet more of the manners and character of the destined bride came pouring in from Germany after the articles were signed and it was too late to recede.'

Lord Malmesbury himself discovered some additional unpleasant faults in the Princess when he was thrown into closer contact with her during the journey to England. Although the Marriage Treaty was signed on 3 December, the journey did not begin until the 30th owing to the difficulties of making safe travel arrangements in time of war; and, due to French victories and a very severe frost that prevented the British ships sailing into harbour, it was not until 28 March that Lord Malmesbury was able to get his charge safely aboard H.M.S. *Jupiter* in the River Elbe off Stade.

In those three months Lord Malmesbury's poor opinion of the character of the Duchess of Brunswick was fully confirmed. She had agreed to accompany her daughter as far as the coast, but at Osnabruck she wanted to go home to Brunswick for fear lest she be captured by the French. 'If I am taken,' she said to Malmesbury, 'I am sure the King will be angry.'

'He will be very sorry,' Malmesbury replied, 'but your Royal Highness must *not* leave your daughter till she is in the hands of her attendants.'

She argued; but Lord Malmesbury would not give way, and she was at length persuaded to remain with the party. Both Malmesbury and her daughter could have done without her company. Sometimes she was 'very disagreeable about the cold, peevish and ill-mannered ... troublesome

about choosing her apartment'. At other times she told indiscreet stories about the Queen and the Duke of York,
neither of whom she liked, and about the King with whom
she had been made to share a bed as a child. That had been
as disagreeable as possible, she said, as he used to wet it until
their 'father [the late Prince of Wales] cured him of his
fault by making him wear the blue ribbon [of the Order of
the Garter] with a piece of china attached to it which was
not the George'.

Lord Malmesbury could scarcely blame Princess Caroline
for not respecting such a mother, but he felt obliged to
reprimand her for showing her disdain so openly, for treating her rudely and actually laughing at her. He also felt
compelled to talk to her upon a more serious matter that
had become of concern to him: the delicate question of her
personal cleanliness.

The Princess did not wash often enough, and her under-
clothes – which were uniformly coarse – as well as her thread
stockings were frequently dirty and far too rarely changed.
She was actually 'offensive' from the neglect; and it seemed
remarkable to Malmesbury how 'amazingly' her education
had been neglected in this respect, 'how much her mother,
although an Englishwoman, was inattentive to it'. Malmesbury urged her to be more fastidious. The Prince himself
was 'very delicate' and expected 'a long and very careful
toilette de propreté'. What was too intimate for him to mention himself, he got one of her ladies to tell her, and this
lady executed her commission well, for the next day the
Princess appeared 'well washed *all over*'.

This was characteristic of her. There was no denying how
amenable she was, how good-natured. As he sailed down the
Elbe past Gluckstadt, Malmesbury thought that it would
be impossible to be more cheerful, more accommodating,
'more everything that is pleasant' than the Princess was –
'no difficulty, all good humour'.

Yet what could the future hold, he had due cause to wonder, for a young woman who so prided herself on the quick-

ness with which she got dressed that she neglected to wash, who cheerfully described how sick she was at sea without the least regard to the delicacy of her language, who, when she had a tooth pulled out, sent a page down with it to Lord Malmesbury for his inspection? Such conduct would never do for the bridegroom awaiting her in London.

13

The Second Wife
1795–1796

'It was like Macheath going to execution,
and he was quite drunk'

BLISSFULLY unaware of the reception likely to be accorded so unrefined a young woman, Princess Caroline walked about the deck of the *Jupiter* in happy mood, charming the sailors by her friendliness and leading the officers to declare that 'they would have had more trouble with any London lady than her Royal Highness'. She was 'always contented and always in good humour', in the words of Mrs Harcourt, who had been sent across with Captain Payne as her official chaperone, 'shewing such pleasant, unaffected joy at the idea of her prospect in life that it does one's heart good to see anybody so happy'.

Her happiness was soon overcast. On landing at Gravesend she was escorted to Greenwich, but there was no one there to meet her, other than the staff and inmates of the Hospital who poured out of the chapel 'before the service was half over' to catch a glimpse of her. There was an hour of apprehensive waiting during which the Princess made one of those silly, thoughtless, flippant jokes that were to grate upon the Prince's nerves. 'What,' she said, looking at the crippled pensioners in the Hospital grounds, 'is every Englishman without an arm or a leg?' At last there arrived at Greenwich the cause of the delay: Lady Jersey.

Lord Malmesbury had heard from Captain Payne a few days before that his charge would be subjected to the humiliation of being greeted in England by the woman who was supposed to be the Prince's mistress. Payne had told him that Lady Jersey, who with the approval of the King and

Queen had been appointed one of the Princess's Ladies of the Bedchamber, had already made a great nuisance of herself by her 'very far from proper behaviour', by her tricks to get aboard the yachts. Now not only did she keep the Princess waiting at Greenwich by not being ready at the time appointed for the coaches to set out, but when at length she did arrive with Lord Clermont and Mrs Aston, one of the Princess's other Ladies, she immediately and impertinently expressed herself 'very much dissatisfied with the Princess's mode of dress, though Mrs Harcourt had taken great pains about it'. Then, having insisted that she should take off her muslin gown and blue satin petticoat and change into a less becoming white satin dress which she had brought with her, she said that the Princess, whose cheeks were of a naturally high colour, ought to use some rouge to bring them to life. Finally, she complained that to ride in a carriage with her back to the horses would upset her, and she hoped, therefore, that she would be allowed to sit facing forwards, next to the Princess.

To this last suggestion Lord Malmesbury strongly objected and, intimating that if she really were likely to be sick when riding with her back to the horses she ought not to have accepted the appointment of Lady of the Bedchamber, he suggested that she join himself and Lord Clermont in their carriage. 'This of course settled the business,' Lord Malmesbury recorded. 'She and Mrs Harcourt, according to the King's direction, sat backwards, and the Princess sat by herself. There was very little crowd, and still less applause on the road to London, where we arrived and were set down at St James's (the Duke of Cumberland's apartments, Cleveland Row) about half past two.' On the journey Princess Caroline behaved in exactly the kind of way Lord Malmesbury had advised her not to do. Provoked by the evident disdain of the sophisticated, haughty, good-looking and well-groomed women opposite her, she began to chatter about her own experiences in the world, of her having been very much in love once with a man from whom her

high birth had made it necessary to part. This story which
was, of course, soon related to the Prince did nothing to
endear him to his bride.

Although the Prince, in a letter written at the end of
November, had *'vehemently'* urged Lord Malmesbury 'to set
out with the Princess Caroline *immediately'*, now that she
was in England he had not shown any particular anxiety to
see her; and when he did see her, he did not appear at all
taken with the sight.

He came into the room where she and Malmesbury
awaited him, approached her, and, as she tried to kneel to
him in obedience to Malmesbury's instructions, 'he raised
her (gracefully enough) and embraced her'. But, apparently,
being so close to her was most distasteful to him. He spoke
scarcely a word, turned round and, immediately withdrawing to a far corner of the apartment, called Malmesbury towards him. 'Harris, I am not well,' he said. 'Pray get me a
glass of brandy.'

Malmesbury replied, ' "Sir, had you not better have a glass
of water?" – upon which he, much out of humour, said with
an oath, "*No.* I will go directly to the Queen," and away he
went. The Princess, left during this short moment alone,
was in a state of astonishment.'

When Malmesbury joined her again, she said to him in
French – since English, despite her recent hurried lessons,
did not yet come naturally to her – 'My God! Does the
Prince always act like this? I think he's very fat and he's
nothing like as handsome as his portrait.'

Malmesbury said that his Royal Highness was naturally
'a good deal affected and flurried at this first interview, but
she certainly would find him different at dinner'. The Princess would have said more, but Malmesbury excused himself on the grounds that he must now report to the King.

His Majesty's only question was, 'Is she good-humoured?'
to which Malmesbury could honestly give a favourable
reply. But it was clear to him when the King commented,
'I am glad of it', and then fell into silence, that he had

already heard from the Queen what their son thought of the person of his bride.

At dinner that evening Princess Caroline's behaviour was as distressingly embarrassing as Lord Malmesbury had ever known it. It was 'rattling, affecting raillery and wit, and throwing out coarse vulgar hints about Lady [Jersey] who was present'. The Princess later excused herself on the grounds that it was the sight of the Prince and Lady Jersey together that made her behave like this. 'To tell you God's truth' (a favourite expression) ... 'I knew how it all was,' she told Lady Charlotte Campbell in her fractured and peculiarly accented English, 'and I said to myself, "Oh, very well!" I took my partie ... Oh, mine God, I could be the slave of a man I love; but one whom I love not and who did not love me, impossible – *c'est autre chose.*' On a subsequent occasion, she demonstrated what she meant by this when, on her husband's drinking some punch from Lady Jersey's glass, she snatched a neighbour's pipe and puffed out smoke at him.

Listening to her vulgar, impetuous, defensive chatter, while Lady Jersey remained loftily silent, the Prince, Malmesbury noticed, was 'disgusted'. This unfortunate dinner fixed his dislike of her; and the longer she persisted in her 'attempts at cleverness and coarse sarcasm' in her misguided efforts to show the Prince that she did not care about her rival, the more bitter that dislike became.

It was all the more galling to the Prince that, although the Princess had not been welcomed into London with nearly as much enthusiasm as the *Annual Register* later suggested, the people were prepared to like her, certainly to sympathize with her; for it was known that, apart from the King, who greeted her affectionately with 'tears of joy ... as if she had been born and bred his favourite child', no one in the Royal Family was in the least well-disposed towards her. The Queen was cold; the Princesses were wary; the Prince virtually ignored her. It was rumoured that Lady Jersey had gone so far as to deposit some evil-smelling substance in her hair to increase the Prince's distaste, had put Epsom salts into the pastry which she had for supper, and had dropped strong spirits into her wine to make the Queen think she was a drunkard.

An outcast, lonely and *gauche*, she enlisted the people's sympathy from the beginning. When a crowd gathered to see her she showed herself to them at a window, made a short speech in praise of the 'brave English people – the best nation upon earth', and 'bowed exceedingly ... till the Prince shut the window and made excuses of her being fatigued. Everybody speaks most favourably of her face as most pleasing,' Horace Walpole reported, 'though with too much rouge. She is plump and by no means tall.' *

The Prince, too, had his sympathizers. It was no wonder that he was disgusted by his 'sloven' of a bride, thought Lady Hester Stanhope, Pitt's niece; he had always been used to women of such perfect cleanliness and sweetness. Whereas the Princess was, so Holland said, 'utterly destitute of all female delicacy'. 'She did not know how to put on her own clothes,' Lady Hester added, '... putting on her stockings with the seam before, or one of them wrong side outwards.'

At the time of his wedding it was only natural that the Prince's thoughts should turn to that very different woman he had married nearly ten years before. When he had separated from her the previous summer he had agreed that Mrs Fitzherbert's £3,000 a year allowance should be continued as though no break had occurred; in the autumn he had requested that all his friends should continue to show her the same attention that they had done in the past; in December he had asked Lord Loughborough to obtain the King's word that her allowance should be regularly paid throughout her

* The newspapers were more flattering about the Princess: 'Teeth as white as ivory, a good complexion, a beautiful hand and arm, and may certainly be deemed a very pretty woman' (*London Chronicle*, 4–7 April 1795). The *Annual Register* described her voice, with its strong German accent, as being 'replete with melody and delicacy of tone' (*Annual Register*, 1795, 15).

lifetime in the event of his own death. Now, on the very eve of the wedding he sent her a message that she was the only woman he would ever love; and he was said to have ridden out to Richmond himself and passed by her house as though anxious to prove it. Before the ceremony he gloomily remarked to the Duke of Clarence, who had been instructed by their father not to leave his brother's side throughout the day, 'William, tell Mrs Fitzherbert she is the only woman I shall ever love.' And on his way to the chapel he said to the Earl of Moira, who was sitting opposite him in the coach: 'It's no use, Moira, I shall never love any woman but Fitzherbert.' In later years the Princess herself was to tell Jack Payne that she thought Mrs Fitzherbert was 'much more' her enemy than Lady Jersey. Certainly Mrs Fitzherbert was never to refer to her as the Princess of Wales, merely as Princess Caroline.

The wedding took place on the evening of 8 April 1795 in the Chapel Royal at St James's. The bride, whose extremely rich dress was so heavy that she almost fell over, was led into the chapel by the Duke of Clarence and attended by Lady Mary Osborne, Lady Charlotte Spencer, Lady Charlotte Legge and Lady Caroline Villiers.* She approached the altar confidently and stood there chatting away to the Duke of Clarence with characteristic gusto as she awaited the arrival of the bridegroom. When he came, supported by the unmarried Dukes of Bedford and Roxburghe, he was seen to be extremely nervous and agitated. He had obviously been

---

* They were the daughters respectively of the fifth Duke of Leeds, the third Duke of Marlborough, the second Earl of Dartmouth and, of course, the fourth Earl of Jersey. They had been selected by the Prince, and the King, so the Queen said, had approved 'greatly of [the] choice' (RA 3898, 36422: Asp/P, ii, 493). The King had not, however, approved the requests of Prince Ernest, Prince Adolphus and Prince William of Gloucester who had all asked to be allowed to come home from the Continent for the wedding as their troops were going into winter quarters. 'The Army,' the King thought, 'was the only place where an officer ought to remain, *particularly* when he commanded a regiment' (RA 36425: Asp/P, ii, 501).

drinking; and at the beginning of the ceremony the Duke of Bedford, who had seen him swallow several glasses of brandy, had difficulty in preventing him from falling over. Lord Melbourne, who was in waiting, said that 'the Prince was like a man doing a thing in desperation; it was like Macheath going to execution; and he was quite drunk'.* He scarcely glanced at his bride, though the Duke of Leeds noticed that he was 'perpetually looking at his favourite Lady Jersey'. One of his equerries told Lady Maria Stuart that he was so 'agitated during the ceremony that it was expected he would have burst out in tears'. At one point he suddenly stood in the middle of a prayer. The Archbishop of Canterbury, John Moore, paused for a moment until the King stepped forward and whispered something to his son who then knelt down again. When the Archbishop came to that part of the service in which he had to ask the question whether or not there were any impediment to lawful matrimony, he 'laid down the book and looked earnestly at the King, as well as at the bridegroom, giving unequivocal proof of his apprehension that some previous marriage had taken place. ... Not content with this tacit allusion, the Archbishop twice repeated the passage in which the Prince engages to live from that time in nuptial fidelity with his consort. ... The Prince was much affected, and shed tears.'

After the ceremony the King and Queen held a Drawing-Room in the Queen's apartments to which the Prince conducted his bride almost in silence. The Duke of Leeds, who was walking in front of them, 'could not help remarking how little conversation passed between them during the procession, and the coolness and indifference apparent in the manner of the Prince'. When the Prince appeared in the Queen's apartments, so Lady Maria Stuart said, he looked 'like death and full of confusion, as if he wished to hide himself from the looks of the whole world. I think,' she

---

* Queen Victoria, who was told this by Lord Melbourne's son, the second Viscount, was also assured that her uncle was 'extremely DRUNK' by King Leopold of the Belgians (RA Y71/63).

added, 'he is much to be pitied. The bride, on the contrary, appeared in the highest spirits when she passed by us first, smiling and nodding to everyone.... What an odd wedding!'

Towards the end of the reception, the Prince recovered his composure, and became 'very civil and gracious', though he was 'certainly unhappy' and still rather drunk. When the Earl of Harcourt came to hand back the hat which he had held for him during the ceremony, the Prince insisted on his keeping it, though it was a very valuable hat 'ornamented with a most beautiful and costly button and loop of diamonds'. The Duke of Leeds thought that this ostentatious gift confirmed the 'unfortunate suspicion' that Lady Jersey was the Prince's mistress, since the Earl of Harcourt's wife was Lady Jersey's most intimate friend.

The Prince's drunkenness increased as night approached, so his bride afterwards recounted; and when he did eventually make his way into her bedroom, he fell insensible into the fireplace where he remained all night and where she left him. In the morning he had recovered sufficiently to climb into bed with her.

The first few months of the marriage were not quite as unpleasant as this disastrous beginning led people to expect and as her biographers have suggested. Four days after the wedding the bride was seen on the Terrace at Windsor looking perfectly happy on the arm of her father-in-law who escorted her up and down with evident 'delight' and 'entire gratification'. Her sisters-in-law, although far from sharing their father's enthusiasm, seemed prepared to like her after all and to wish her well. Princess Elizabeth, to whom she spoke of her 'present happiness', praised her 'perfect good temper' and flattered herself that she would 'turn out a very comfortable little wife'. Two months later Princess Elizabeth wrote again to her brother to assure him that his wife was full of 'professions of regard and love' for her husband. The husband himself wrote to his mother from Brighton to tell her that, despite the 'execrably bad' weather, his wife was 'extremely happy' with the place which agreed with her 'most perfectly'. She was in the 'best health and spirits possible', and they were 'very comfortable'. His mother was herself happier than words could express at this unlikely and welcome news.

When she heard that her daughter-in-law was pregnant she was delighted and wrote to say that she hoped she would take 'all possible care of herself'; she was 'extremely glad' to hear that she was going 'on so well in her present situation'. As the time of the birth approached the 'sisterhood' at Frogmore were 'in a constant state of anxiety', jumping and flying to the windows whenever the house bell rang. Princess Elizabeth said that they were all sure that their brother was 'upon the *high fidgets*', walking about the room, pulling his fingers and 'very anxious'. They did not expect to see him at Windsor, being certain he would not want to leave the Princess till she was 'safe in bed'.

The Prince, indeed, was anxious. For 'two whole nights' he stayed up, 'much agitated', waiting for news of the safe delivery of the child, and was evidently much relieved when, at a quarter to ten on the morning of 7 January 1796, he was able to give the Queen the good news: 'The Princess, after a terrible hard labour for above twelve hours, is this instant brought to bed of an *immense girl*, and I assure you notwithstanding we might have wished for a boy, I receive her with all the affection possible. ... I long to see you and to press you to that affectionate heart which you never can know how much it loves you. Pray have the goodness to apologize to my dear sisters for my not writing to them, but I am so fatigued...'

Thanking God that both the mother and child were quite well 'and likely to continue so', he wrote a separate letter to his father who replied that he was 'highly pleased' and 'indeed had always wished' that the first child should be a girl: 'You are both young and I trust will have many children and this newcomer will equally call for the protection of its parents and consequently be a bond of additional union.'

That some such bond of union was now necessary the King was only too well aware. It was clear to him by now that the early hopes of a satisfactory marriage were not likely to be realized. Despite the encouraging reports received at Windsor and the Prince's evident concern during his wife's confinement, the couple were ill-matched in every way. However correctly she managed to conduct herself at Windsor, at the Queen's House and with the King, the Princess could not forbear to behave in her husband's presence in the very way that Malmesbury had warned her he would find insupportable. Incited to pert sarcasm, outrageous comment and tiresome petulance by her husband's unconcealed preference for Lady Jersey and his evident distaste for her own more flamboyant sensuality, she irritated him beyond endurance. One evening at Carlton House after she had, in Malmesbury's words, behaved 'very lightly and even improperly', the Prince demanded to know of his guest how he liked such manners and why on earth he had not been warned what she was like. Malmesbury's explanation that his orders from the King had not required him to express any opinion as to her character was gloomily accepted by the Prince; but it naturally did not please him and 'left a rankle in his mind'.

Soon the Prince's dislike turned to positive hatred, and his consequent treatment of his wife, who enjoyed the people's sympathy, became common gossip. It was said that, infuriated by the unsuitable company she entertained, he had had all the furniture removed from her dining-room with the exception of two common chairs; and that he had taken back from her a pair of pearl bracelets which had formed part of her wedding jewels and which he had given to Lady Jersey who, having 'no happiness without a rival to trouble and torment', did not hesitate to wear them in the Princess's presence. Believing that she spoke contemptuously of him to her various companions, and might already be unfaithful to him with one or other of the various men who – for reasons which to him were inconceivable – found her physic-

ally attractive, he forbade her to entertain anyone without
his approval. 'She drives always alone,' the lawyer, Charles
Abbot, noted in his journal, 'sees no company but old
people put on her list. ... She goes nowhere but airings in
Hyde Park. The Prince uses her unpardonably.'

'She is, I am afraid, a most unhappy woman,' another
sympathizer agreed. 'Her lively spirits which she brought
over with her are all gone, and they say the melancholy and.
anxiety in her countenance is quite affecting.'

'I do not know how I shall be able to bear the loneliness,'
she wrote to a friend in Germany, 'the Queen seldom visits
me, and my sisters-in-law show me the same sympathy. ...
The Countess [of Jersey] is still here. I hate her and I know
she feels the same towards me. My husband is wholly given
up to her, so you can easily imagine the rest.'

Her husband, indeed, spent as little time in her company
as he possibly could. Leaving her at Carlton House, he passed
weeks on end in the country, either at Northington Grange
near Alresford in Hampshire which, having given up Kempshot Park, he had rented for £900 a year from Henry Drummond, the banker; at the Pavilion in Brighton where
according to Lord Auckland, Lady Jersey now had her bed
in his dressing-room; or at Bognor where she was as often
seen in his company as she was on the Steine. In London
they saw each other at card parties at the Queen's House,
where, so Charles Abbot said, 'in the course of the evening
the Prince of Wales repeatedly came up to her table, and
publicly squeezed her hand'.

As Lady of the Bedchamber to the Princess she spent a
great deal of time in her company, too, and, as the Princess
knew, gave malicious reports of her behaviour to her husband and the Queen. When some indiscreet letters which
the Princess had written to Brunswick were handed to her
by a messenger who was unable to go to Germany as planned
and consequently could not deliver them, she read them,
noted the rude remarks about herself and the Royal Family
– in particular about 'Old Snuffy' or 'de old Begum' as the

Princess alternatively referred to the Queen – and immediately handed them to her Majesty whose growing dislike of a daughter-in-law she had never favoured was thus permanently confirmed.

In April the Princess decided she would stand no more. In French she wrote to her husband asking to be excused from ever dining alone again with, as she put it, 'a person whom I can neither like nor respect and who is your mistress' – a person later identified in a characteristically ungrammatical and misspelled letter as 'Lady Jerser'. 'Be as generous as your nation is,' she pleaded, 'and keep your word as every good Englishman, since such is the character of the nation. Forgive me, my dear Prince, if my expressions are too strong, believe that it is a heart wounded by the most acute pain and the most deadly sorrow which pleads for your help.'

The Prince replied angrily: 'You must allow me to answer in English your letter of this morning as you sufficiently understand the language, because it is essential for me to explain myself without any possible ambiguity upon the subject of the unwise, groundless and most injurious imputation which you have thought fit to cast upon me. ... Let me remind you, Madam, that the intimacy of my friendship with Lady Jersey ... *my mistress, as you* indecorously term her ... under all the false colour that slander has given it, was perfectly known to you before you accepted my hand, for you yourself told me so immediately on your arrival here. ... I then took the opportunity of explaining to you that Lady Jersey was one of the oldest acquaintances I had in this country and that the confidence resulting from so long a friendship had enabled her to offer advice which contributed not a little to decide me to marriage. You will recollect, Madam, that you have seven ladies in your family besides Lady Jersey, any, or everyone, of whom it is in your power to summon either for dinner or for company at any hour of the day. ... If the choice be not more extensive it is not my fault, but it is the consequence of the etiquette existing

from all times for the situation of the Princess of Wales. ...
We have unfortunately been obliged to acknowledge to each
other that we cannot find happiness in our union. ... It only
remains that we should make the situation as little uncomfortable to each other as its nature will allow. ... I have
been solicitous that you should have every gratification
which the nature of the times, the manners of this country
and the established customs of your rank would admit, with
a due regard at the same time to the pecuniary difficulties I
so cruelly and unjustly labour under. ... Let me therefore
beg you to make the best of a situation unfortunate *for us
both*, which is only to be done by not *wantonly* creating or
magnifying uncomfortable curcumstances.'

Commenting on his wife's reference to the generosity of
the English nation and the implied unfavourable contrast
with his own, the Prince expressed the fear that these references had been inserted for an ulterior motive: that the
Princess intended to use her letter – with its false insinua-
tion that she was forced to keep company alone with Lady
Jersey – as part of an appeal against the Prince to the nation
at large. He recommended her to consider exactly what result she might expect from such an appeal.

This reply elicited a further, longer and even more ungrammatical letter from the Princess in which she regretted
the 'coldness and great contempt' of his conduct towards
her, made further complaints about his intimacy with Lady
Jersey, and repudiated any idea that she was attempting to
make an appeal to the sympathies of the English people.
She had always admired the wise withdrawal of the Queen
from anything that could be called political intrigue and
would follow her example. If she could obtain her husband's friendship, it would be very precious to her; however,
she dare not ask for it at present by any other right than
that of the mother of his child.

The Prince, who felt a 'few words' of reply – 740 words –
were exacted by her letter, protested that if she wished for
more of his company she would do well not to make his own

house 'obnoxious' to him, and to consider whether 'the captious tone' she adopted towards him was calculated to make him feel at ease in her society. He hoped that, as well as following the Queen's example by not meddling in politics, she would be like her also in studying her husband's disposition and promoting his comfort; this was 'not to be effected by irritating insinuations or fretful complaints'. He hoped, finally, that this unpleasant correspondence might now cease.

The Princess, unfortunately, was not ready to put a stop to it yet. In the longest and most incoherent letter she had written to him so far, she replied that she would like the orders governing her conduct to be given to her in writing so as to avoid all misunderstanding, and that if it was right for *her* to follow the good example of the Queen towards the King there was even more reason why *he* should follow 'the 'steady and correct behaviour of the King towards the Queen'.

'I really am tired to death of this silly altercation,' the Prince complained to her Chamberlain, the Earl of Cholmondeley, on receipt of this letter. But since the Princess desired it, he would give her her orders in writing, although he had made quite clear to her already 'the latitude allowed by her situation respecting her mode of life'. If she wished to live on civil and friendly terms with him, she had only to say so.

The Princess then reiterated her request to be given in writing the exact terms upon which they were in future to live. In particular, she wanted to be assured that if they were henceforward to be man and wife in name only, he would never again, not even in the event of the death of their daughter, make any attempt to produce another heir. The Prince, accordingly, writing in French so that there should be no possibility of her misunderstanding him, gave this undertaking: 'Nature has not made us suitable to each other. Tranquil and comfortable society is, however, in our power; let our intercourse therefore be restricted to that, and

I will distinctly subscribe to the condition which you required through Lady Cholmondeley, that even in the event of any accident happening to my daughter, which I trust Providence in its mercy will avert, I shall not infringe the terms of the restriction by purposing, at any period, a connection of a more particular nature. I shall now finally close this disagreeable correspondence, trusting that as we have completely explained ourselves to each other, the rest of our lives will be passed in uninterrupted tranquility. I am, Madam, with great truth, very sincerely yours, George P.'

The Princess, however, was still not yet prepared to close the correspondence. Protesting that his letter did not make it clear that the proposal for a separation came in the first place from him and not from her, she felt it her duty to give the King, her only protector, an account of what had taken place between them. Deeply perturbed by this threat, and hoping to forestall the trouble that he felt impending, the Prince immediately wrote to his mother to say he would come down to Windsor first thing in the morning so as to be there as soon as church was over and discuss with her the best course of action.

The Queen was not encouraging. She knew the King well enough, she thought, to be fully persuaded that he would never agree to any open rupture. And this, indeed, when the Prince made a formal request for a 'final separation' in an extremely long letter on 31 May, was the King's reply: 'You seem to look on your disunion with the Princess as merely of a private nature, and totally put out of sight that as Heir Apparent of the Crown your marriage is a public act, wherein the Kingdom is concerned; that therefore a separation cannot be brought forward by the mere interference of relations.' The public would have to be informed of the whole business, and the public were 'certainly not prejudiced' in the Prince's favour. Parliament would also have to be informed, and Parliament would think itself obliged to secure out of his income the jointure settled on her in case of her husband's death. The King was 'certainly by no means inclined to think the Princess [had] been happy in the choise of conduct' she had adopted; but if the Prince had 'attempted to guide her, she might have avoided those errors that her uncommon want of experience and perhaps some defects of temper' had given rise to.

14

The Broken Marriage
1796

'The vilest wretch this world ever was cursed with'

DENIED his father's agreement to a formal separation, and tormented by the enthusiastic support which the public so readily accorded his wife, the Prince's detestation of her became more virulent than ever. It was bad enough when *The Times* took her side to condemn the vices of her unjust husband and his 'most disgraceful connexions', and when the *Morning Chronicle* reported that everyone pitied her and execrated him. It was worse when the *True Briton* lavished compliments upon 'the amiable and accomplished personage' who had been 'the object of so much unmerited ill treatment', and dismissed the Prince as 'incorrigible', a man with '*a total disregard* to the opinions of the world', whose 'conduct favoured the cause of Jacobinism and democracy in this country more than all the speeches of Horne Tooke'. It was intolerable that the Princess, on going to the opera, 'electrified the house by her presence', and that 'before she could take her seat, every hand was lifted up to greet her with the loudest plaudits, crying out Huzza! ...'*

* 'Every woman as well as man, in every part clapped incessantly,' Horace Walpole confirmed (*Walpole Correspondence*, xii, 186). And the Duke of Leeds recorded, 'I was in my box at the Opera when the Princess of Wales arrived. The pit and some of the boxes began to applaud, and the whole House almost instantly rose and joined the applause. I looked down at her box, and seeing her appear agitated, immediately went down to see her. ... After repeated curtseying to the audience she sat down. ... She said ... she supposed she could be guillotined ... for what had passed this evening' (*Leeds Memoranda*, 221). The more popular his wife became, the more disliked was his

It was all made much worse for the Prince by the fact that most of his family, unnerved by the public reaction, seemed to think that he ought to attempt some sort of public reconciliation. The Duke and Duchess of York – although the Princess, in turn, loaded them with 'cruel calumnies' – appeared inclined to sympathize with her; while his sister, Princess Elizabeth, confessed, 'We are one and all very miserable about you, and what we have suffered passes all powers of expression. ... Friends and foes are all of opinion that a *reconciliation must* take place for the sake of the *country* and the whole royal family, for if you *fall* all must fall, and then with your excellent heart how could you bear the distress and misery of your own family. I am sorry, very sorry to write these severe and cruel truths, but alas! ... if you could see the agony of mind of our poor mother and the distress she is in I am sure you would not be able to stand it and would make a sacrifice for her sake.'

Then, making the whole affair even more exasperating, there was the attitude of those of his erstwhile friends who were numbered among Lady Jersey's countless enemies, notably Lord Hugh Seymour, who referred to her as 'that bitch', Jack Payne, whose conduct towards Lady Jersey and himself since his marriage had been 'infamous', and Thomas Tyrwhitt, his Private Secretary, who, like Payne, was dismissed from his service for taking the Princess's side against her.* None of them appeared to realize what a 'very mon-

---

mistress. 'Lady St Asaph told Lady Beaumont that she was at a very large assembly at the Duchess of Gordon's to which Lady Jersey was invited – when Lady Jersey came the ladies made a line for her and let her pass unspoken to' (*Farington Diary*, i, 199–200). She was the cause of all the rage against the Prince, the Bishop of Waterford told Lord Charlemont: 'She ought to resign her office and retire; she will not. He ought to dismiss her; he will not.' Meanwhile, the Princess, on account of her supposed ill treatment, was 'the greatest favourite with the people of all ranks' (HMCR, Charlemont MSS, ii, 273).

* Some years later, after his dismissal of Lady Jersey, the Prince was equally displeased with people who continued to visit her, and worked himself up into 'a passion' with Lady Bessborough who had

ster of iniquity' his wife was. She was '*a fiend*', an 'infamous
wretch', 'a worthless wretch', the 'vilest wretch this world
ever was cursed with', the most 'unprincipled and unfeeling
person of her sex'; there was 'no end to her wickedness, her
falsity, and her designs'.

He besought the Queen to make the King realize what a
dangerous woman she was. In letters, whose language became almost hysterical, he pleaded with his 'dearest, dearest,
dearest mother', his 'most beloved mother', his 'ever best
and dearest mother', to persuade the King 'to take a firm line
in defence' of his son, otherwise the '*fiend*' would prove the
ruin of the whole royal family. 'The King must be resolute
and firm, or everything is at an end,' he begged her to believe. 'Let him recall to his mind the want of firmness of
Louis 16. This is the only opportunity for him to stemm the
torrent.... I know you will fight for me to the last, and I will
for you, and by you till the last drop of my blood, but if ever
you flinch, which I am convinced is impossible, I shall then
despair. ... My best love to all my dear sisters. I hope they

---

gone to see her son when he was very ill (*Granville Leveson Gower
Correspondence*, ii, 121). He was constantly quarrelling with those
who remained on good terms with people with whom he himself had
fallen out. As Lord Melbourne told Queen Victoria, he 'never could
bear anybody to be friends with those he disliked and consequently
my father and mother who knew Mrs Fitzherbert very well, continued her friends and [the Prince] never would see them; and then
all of a sudden, when he came back to her, there he was back at
Whitehall and came in just as if nothing had passed, and if he had
seen them just the day before' (RA Queen Victoria's Journal, entry
for 12 January 1838). Thomas Tyrwhitt was reinstated as Private
Secretary in 1797 as though the Prince had never quarrelled with
him, and remained in that office until 1804. In 1805 he became Lord
Warden of the Stannaries. A tiny, bustling, florid man, a great
favourite of Princess Elizabeth, the Prince referred to him affectionately as 'our little red dwarf', or occasionally, after he received his
knighthood in 1812, as 'The 23rd of June', he being – as he elaborately explained to his mother who might not otherwise have understood the 'ingenious pun' – the 'shortest (k)night' (RA 21295; Asp/K,
i, 384).

remain stout, for without it, we must all sink. God bless you, ever dearest mother. I am so overpowered with unhappiness that I feel quite light headed. I know not where to turn for a friend now but to you. ... I wrote at considerable length to the King yesterday to tell him that nothing but his resolution and support can bring *us all* through at this moment. ... *If I* fall *all* must fall also; but we must *all rise* victorious if the King will but take a *decided tone* to the Princess, to his Ministers and to the world in general, but if half measures are adopted there is an end of everything. Nothing can equal what I go through nor can anything paint it strong enough for your imagination. I have retained Erskine besides my own lawyers to prosecute every paragraph, every pamphlet that can be construed into a libel. By the by I see by Ernest's letter that the Princess has been at the Queen's House. For God's sake let me know everything that has past, tell me nothing, or conceal nothing from me. I suppose she has made the best of her own story and told her lies as usual. ... The thought makes me quite frantic. ...'

Appalled by the thought of what she might say about him privately, the Prince professed himself equally horrified by his wife's public conduct. When Fox, from whom he was still estranged, was re-elected for Westminster on 13 June, his supporters, headed by 'fifty bludgeon-men', carried him in procession past Carlton House where they expressed a wish to see the infant Princess. Whereupon she not only carried 'the poor little girl to the window' in order to 'make her also an instrument against her poor injured father', but 'actually afterwards drove in her carriage through the mob, to pay her devoirs to Mr Fox after such a speech too as he made, and to get herself applauded'. Surely the King must now see the Princess 'in her true colours, how false, how mischievous, how treacherous' she was, how much she was made the tool 'of the worst of parties at this moment, the democratick'.

The King, however, tended still to believe that his niece was more sinned against than sinning, and that if she re-

ceived proper guidance all would yet be well. He supposed
that if Lady Jersey retired from her service, harmony could
be restored. Certainly Princess Caroline herself led him to
believe so. For months she had been insisting that 'so long as
Lady Jersey' held the place she occupied in her Household
there could be no peace between herself and her husband;
and in this determination she had the King's sympathy.
Towards the end of June the Princess had her way. It was
agreed, as the Queen confirmed to her in writing, that the
Countess of Jersey should leave her service and should not
again be admitted to her private company. The Queen
added that the Princess ought now to show that she was
willing to have a 'complete reconciliation' with her husband
and to refrain from all reproaches.

In obedience to the wishes of her parents-in-law, the
Princess then wrote to her husband in her bad French to say
that she looked forward to the moment which would bring
him back to Carlton House and would 'finally put an end to
a misunderstanding which had ceased to exist' so far as she
was concerned. If he would do her the honour of seeking her
company in the future, she would do everything in her
power to make it agreeable to him. If she had ever displeased
him in the past, would he please be generous enough to
forgive her?

To this warm letter, the Prince delivered the curt reply:
'Madam, I have had the honour of receiving your letter this
day and propose having the pleasure of being at Carlton
House some time in the course of Monday.'

When he arrived he was as formal as this message
threatened he would be; and, as soon as he had finished
dinner, he left and went to spend the evening with Lady
Jersey.

Although forced to give up her place in the Princess's
Household to Lady Willoughby de Eresby, Lady Jersey was
determined not to give up the Prince. She wrote a rude letter
to the Princess, saying that she had only continued in a
situation 'rendered impossible' for a person of her rank, 'or

indeed for anyone possessing the honest pride and spirit of an Englishwoman', by her 'duty and attachment' to his Royal Highness, the 'same duty and attachment which she would be ever proud in possessing'.

Far from breaking with Lady Jersey, as the King had hoped he would do, the Prince saw more of her than ever. He entertained her at the new country estate, Critchell House, near Wimborne Minster, Dorset, which he had rented for £1,120 a year from Charles Sturt, having given up Northington Grange. In the late summer he went down to spend some weeks with her at Bognor; and he installed her in a house adjoining Carlton House which he had altered for Jack Payne but which was now vacant owing to Payne's disgrace. The Queen, distressed by reports of Lady Jersey's having moved into Jack Payne's former house, was reassured by her son, who wrote an extraordinarily detailed account of how the move had taken place entirely for the benefit of the Earl of Jersey, the Prince's (as yet unpaid) Master of the Horse. For Jersey 'could not be answerable to bring the whole expenditure of the stables within the sum allotted by Parliament unless he was perpetually upon the spot, which he could not be had he to run eternally two or three times a day to and from Grosvenor Square'.

Since the Prince was free to move about the country in the wake of the 'old sorceress', Lady Jersey, the Princess of Wales deeply resented the fact that her own movements and activities were so strictly regulated. When she asked permission, through Lord Cholmondeley, to spend a couple of days in the country, the Prince indignantly refused to consider the request. He warned the Queen of the *'dangerous conse-quences'* of allowing her an opportunity of *'repeating her tricks'*, especially as she still persisted 'in the line of conduct she so artfully and maliciously [had] adopted' of endeavour-ing to draw popularity to herself at his *'expense* and at the expense of the whole family'. He would not hesitate to give his *'most decided* negative' to the 'idea of a Princess of Wales travelling all over England'; but, perhaps, the Queen

would show the letter Lord Cholmondeley had received to
the King for his concurrence.

The King did not want to become involved in the matter;
but he agreed that the Prince might refuse the request on his
own responsibility. The Prince immediately did so, telling
Lord Cholmondeley that he was hurt, 'in the most sensible
way possible' that such an improper proposal should ever
even have been put to him in the first place. At the same
time he complained to Cholmondeley of the Princess's having invited company to dinner composed of others besides
her Household and of her 'having encreased her *evening
parties* beyond the list ... officially transmitted to the Ladies
of her Bedchamber'. 'And infringement of these rules I
never can nor will admit to whilst the Princess remains under
my roof, as it would lead to consequences subversive of all
order and arrangement,' he reminded Cholmondeley sharply. 'You will therefore of course write to Lady Willoughby
to explain this matter thoroughly to her.'

The Princess was 'very sorry' to receive this answer to her
request to go to the country for two days; she had not
thought it would have been a breach of Court etiquette as
the Queen sometimes went to spend a day or two with Lord
and Lady Harcourt; she was the 'more disappointed' as the
Prince had promised that she might 'enjoy uninterrupted
those innocent pleasures consistent' with her rank.

The Prince remained adamant. The Queen, he admitted,
did make occasional visits to the Earl and Countess of Harcourt at Nuneham Courtenay, but she never went *alone*;
she attended upon the King when *His* Majesty was graciously pleased to honour them with a visit. As to the innocent pleasures suitable to her rank, 'it always was and must
be understood that those pleasures can never be admitted or
thought of at the expense either of etiquette or precedent'.
The Prince hoped that in future the Princess would avoid
making such applications which were totally inconsistent
with her situation as well as with his own.

Both Lord Thurlow and the Duke of Leeds thought that

the extraordinary way in which the Prince of Wales treated his wife could be attributed only to madness; and the second Viscount Melbourne later told Queen Victoria, who loved talking about her strange uncle, that he, too, thought the Prince's conduct towards the Princess was nothing but madness. ' "George IV never was popular," Lord M. said,' so Queen Victoria recorded in her journal. 'And whatever [Princess Caroline] did, had no weight with the people, for, they said, it was all his fault at first. ... It was quite madness his (George IV) conduct to her; for if he had only separated, and let her alone, that wouldn't have signified; but he persecuted her, and "he cared as much about what she did, as if he had been very much in love with her," which certainly was very odd. ... The way in which he treated her immediately after the marriage was beyond everything wrong and foolish. Considering the way *he lived* himself, Lord M. said, he should never have attacked *her* character.'

Melbourne admitted, however, that her character was not all that the public liked to suppose it. This, indeed, was what the Prince found so unendurable. Here was the Princess spreading the most humiliating stories about him and behaving, he was convinced, in the most scandalous way; yet to the public *she* was a martyr, innocent and wronged, while *he* was considered such 'unfit company for gentlemen' that 'persons of rank (afterwards indebted to him for advancement in it)' refused to meet him at dinner at Holland House.

Princess Caroline certainly showed little restraint when talking about the Prince. She had no hesitation in making it known how drunkenly he had behaved on their wedding night, nor how, when they had gone to stay shortly afterwards at Kempshot Park, where Lady Jersey was the only other woman in the party, all the men had got drunk and had gone to sleep, snoring with their dirty boots up on the arms of sofas. The whole scene 'resembled a bad brothel' much more than a Prince's court. Her husband, she claimed, had made her smoke a pipe, and when she had discovered she was pregnant, he had announced that the child was not his.

She told Lord Minto, almost the first time she met him, that they had lived together for only two or three weeks, and 'not at all afterwards as man and wife'. 'If I can spell her hums and haws,' Lord Minto wrote to his wife after this conversation with the Princess, 'I take it that the ground of his antipathy was his own *incapacity*, and the distaste which a man feels for a woman who *knows* his defects and humiliations.'

The thought of this dreadful, mocking wife of his talking intimately to other men horrified, appalled and obsessed him. He would rather, he said, see toads and vipers crawling over his food than even so much as sit at the same table with her, so much did she revolt him, so deeply did he detest her. Yet other men, it was whispered, eagerly sought her out and contrived to be left alone with her. One of these, he believed – and had some reason to believe – was George Canning, at that time the clever young Member of Parliament for Newtown, and one of Pitt's most promising supporters. Even so, it was almost universally felt that the Prince ought either to have her back to live with him or, if they were to live apart, to give her more freedom – though people might not have thought so had they known that her own father had warned that she must be kept very strictly otherwise she would 'certainly emancipate too much'. The Prince's brother, the Duke of Clarence, while offering him sympathy in private, said to a lady at a ball at the Castle Inn, Richmond, 'My brother has behaved very foolishly. To be sure he has married a very foolish, disagreeable person, but he should not have treated her as he has done, but have made the best of a bad bargain, as my father has done. *He* married a disagreeable woman but has not behaved ill to her.'

The Prince, though, was not prepared to make the best of a bad bargain. Nor was he prepared to make any relaxation of the rules he had imposed on his wife. It was all very well, he told Lord Cholmondeley, for her to complain of the 'solitary hours' that she passed; this was 'a circumstance entirely depending upon her own pleasure'; she always had, or ought to have had, at her immediate call the two Ladies who were in waiting upon her, and besides them the other Ladies who comprised her Household ought always to be ready to obey her commands. He agreed that the Hon. Gertrude Vanneck, a huge, masculine woman, should be replaced as the Princess's Keeper of the Privy Purse by the more companionable Miss Hayman, but the Princess was not to suppose that this would entitle Miss Hayman to live in her house for this was 'quite out of the question'. No persons whatever, he repeated, could ever be received or entertained by the Princess unless they had previously been approved of by him.

When the Princess again objected to this rule and declined to obey it until she was told to do so directly by the King, the Prince appealed to his father who wrote his daughter-in-law a letter confirming that it was his opinion, too, that 'she could not receive any society but such as the Prince approved of'.

On receiving the King's letter from Lord Cholmondeley, the Princess said she would immediately go to the Prince's apartments at Carlton House and have it out with him. Lord Cholmondeley dissuaded her, saying that the Prince was too busy at the moment but that he would tell him of her wish for an interview. When the Prince heard that his wife wanted to see him '*alone*', he instantly refused the request, indicating that he would see her only in the presence of a third person and that he would, in accordance with her wish to speak to him, present himself at her apartments with Lord Cholmondeley.

Immediately he entered her room the Princess reminded him abruptly in French that in two and a half years of marriage she had been treated '*ni comme votre femme, ni comme la mère de votre enfant, ni comme la Princesse de*

Galles'. 'I give you notice here and now,' she continued, 'that
I have nothing more to say to you and that I no longer regard myself as subject to your orders or your rules.'

'The Princess then stopped,' the Prince told his father,
'upon which the Prince said, *"Est-ce-que c'est tout, Madame,
tout ce que vous à me dire?"* to which she replied, *"Oui."*
The Prince then bowed and withdrew.' He thought it 'highly
unnecessary to offer at this moment to his Majesty one single
comment on this most extraordinary conduct on the part of
the Princess'.

A few weeks later, however, he wrote to his father to say
that he had told the Princess that he 'could not help in-
ferring from her conduct that she could have no other plan
than to live in a separate house', and that, so far as he was
concerned, no objection would be raised to this. But the
King continued to refuse to consider any kind of formal
separation. She might take a small house outside London –
she did, in fact, take the Old Rectory, Charlton, near Blackheath – but she was not to give up her apartments at Carlton House.

As the Lord Chancellor said, the Prince was already so
unpopular with the people that any step which might increase that unpopularity could not be taken without danger
to 'the publick safety'. It was, therefore, of the 'utmost
moment' to preserve 'even the outward appearance of co-
habitation'; a formal separation would be 'incompatible with
the religion, laws, and government' of the Kingdom. This
was the King's view entirely, and he informed his son
accordingly.

The Prince's situation was rendered the more unendurable
by the fact that, although he had married for money, his
finances were in almost as sorry a state as ever. It had been
proposed that his income of £73,000 a year should be increased to £138,000 and that a capital sum of £52,000 should
be allowed to cover the costs of the wedding and for finishing Carlton House. But when it became known that his debts

had reached the immense sum of £630,000 in the eight years since the arrangements made in 1787, it was immediately accepted by the government that part of his increased income must be set aside for their settlement. Pitt proposed that the proportion of the Prince's income which came from the Duchy of Cornwall – about £13,000 a year – should be reserved for this purpose, and that in addition £25,000 a year should be deducted from the rest of the income. This meant, however, that the debts would not be liquidated for twenty-seven years, and the storm of protest that greeted Pitt's suggestion made it clear that the government would have to be sterner with the Prince than this.

The Prince had taken little part in politics during the past few years and now had virtually no political friends, while his unpopularity with the country at large was so great that even the King, so well liked upon his recovery in 1788, was now contaminated with it. On his way to the House of Lords in October 1795 the state coach was stoned and shouts of 'Down with George!' filled the air.

Those who had supported the Prince at the time of his earlier financial crisis were not so ready to do so now that he had shown himself to be so incurably, incontinently extravagant. Fox and Sheridan proposed the sale of various crown estates; the Earl of Lonsdale suggested that the frontages of Hyde Park, which did not form part of the Crown estates, should be sold off to builders who would readily pay two guineas a foot for it, thus realizing over £800,000. Others, including Grey, felt that in war time and at a period of so much political agitation and popular distress, the Prince should not have his income increased to anything like the amount that the government proposed. An increase to £113,000 would, in Grey's opinion, be quite sufficient.

So strong, indeed, did feelings run against Pitt's proposals that it seemed for a time that the government would have to resign; and only when the Prince himself agreed to £65,000 a year instead of £25,000 being deducted from his income for the repayment of his debts, was it saved. The Prince also had to agree to the appointment of commissioners for the future conduct of his financial affairs.

Blaming the '*infamous deceit of Pitt*' for having had to agree to a settlement that left him as badly off as ever, the Prince once more set about reducing his expenses and the numbers of his Household, expressing the hope that he would one day soon be enabled to 'resume the appearance' due to his birth.

Disappointed in his expectations of a more generous income, the Prince was disappointed, too, in his hopes of promotion in the Army. In February 1795 he was dismayed to read in the *London Gazette* that he had once again been passed over, several colonels far junior to him being promoted major-general, including his nineteen-year-old cousin, Prince William of Gloucester, with whom, and with whose father, he had been on bad terms for several years. He wrote an impassioned letter of complaint to the Queen who entered 'most sincerely' into his feelings and saw 'with great sorrow the effect' his disappointment had upon his mind; but she strongly warned him not to let his anger at it drive him once more into opposition and into the ranks of the Foxite Whigs. 'Every opposition to the Crown, headed by a branch of the Royal Family,' she wrote, '*lessens the power of the Crown!* and I am sure it cannot be your interest to assist in that. ... After all, who is the Crown to look up to for staunch supporters? Certainly the Royal Family!'

Henry Dundas, Secretary for War, gave him the same warning: 'It is impossible that your Royal Highness, after a moment's cool reflection on the subject, can put any consideration whatever in competition with those important interests which are now at stake.' The Earl of Moira wrote in similar terms, ardently hoping that the military rank he had so much set his heart on would be granted him but conjuring him 'not to let any fretfulness seduce' him into the opposition's camp if his Majesty persisted in rejecting the application.

He took their advice, but with ever greater urgency he

pleaded with the King to let him have his way, earnestly supplicating for the promotion that his younger brothers had been granted. If the country were to be invaded he might be employed, he wrote, in 'a real and important trust', professing that since there were so many other alternative heirs to the throne his own life was 'of little political importance'.

But the King refused to depart from what he had always thought right. 'My younger sons,' he repeated, 'can have no other situations in the State ... but what arise from the military lines they have been placed in. You are born to a more difficult one, and which I shall be most happy if I find you seriously turn your thoughts to; the happiness of millions depend on it as well as your own.'

The Prince, feeling that the Duke of York – who had been promoted Field Marshal on his return from the Continent in 1795 – was not doing all he might to help him, had a furious quarrel with both his brother and the Duchess, and for a time would not speak to either of them. Then, when hoping that at least he might be made Colonel of the Royal Horse Guards, an appointment upon which he had long since set his heart and which the government had indicated he might have, he was thrust into deeper gloom by a message from the Queen to the effect that the colonelcy had been given to the Duke of Richmond.*

For a time the Prince resigned himself to his disappointments until, in 1797, he renewed his application with more urgency than ever. The King, however, remained adamant. He had given the Prince command of a cavalry regiment because his son had rightly pressed him to place him in a situation in which he could 'manifest his zeal in defence of his country'; but he resisted 'every idea ... of the Prince of Wales being ... considered as a military man'.

So the Prince had to display his military virtue as a cavalry

* When the Duke of Richmond died in 1806, the Prince generously waived his claim to succeed him so that the colonelcy could pass to his friend the Duke of Northumberland (Alnwick MSS, Asp/P, v, 383).

colonel, or not at all; and when an opportunity to gain distinction seemed to present itself with a report of a French fleet sailing towards the south coast, he seized it with the utmost enthusiasm.

He was given this report as he was returning to Critchell House after a day's hunting. It was brought by an officer of his regiment who was stationed at Wareham. Immediately he announced that he was going to join the regiment and galloped off towards Dorchester in the hope that he and his men would give the enemy a warm reception. Stopping at Blandford on the way he ordered a squadron of the Bays who were in quarters there to hold themselves in readiness. Then he rode off again, arriving in Dorchester after dark. The place was quiet, and the major-general in command of the district had gone to bed. The King, who received his son's hasty message that he was 'instantly' joining his regiment early the next morning, could not credit the report of a French fleet in English waters; and soon it was, indeed, confirmed that the supposed French fleet was not a French fleet at all but an English one.

Through no fault of his own, the Prince had been made to look a fool. Inevitably he had cause to complain that his 'poor efforts to meet the danger' had been turned 'into ridicule' by the 'language of some of the Ministers and the hirelings employed by them'.

He was more than ever anxious now to obtain the promotion so long – and, as he thought, so unjustly – denied him. To remain *'a mere Colonel* of Dragoons', he bitterly complained to the Lord Chancellor, was 'wholly below the dignity' which his 'birth and station' gave him in the country. 'Only think of [Prince William of Gloucester's] being a Major-General attended by two aides-de-camp, on account of *his* rank as the *Duke* of Gloucester's son,' he exclaimed in exasperation to his mother, 'and the *Prince of Wales, eldest son* of the King only a simple Colonel, and under the command of such a dull stupid boy' as his stupendously boring cousin, 'Silly Billy'.

Yet his father would not be moved. In a final effort to persuade him to change his mind, the Prince consulted several leading lawyers who assured him that the laws and constitution of the country contained nothing which might prevent his accepting any command that his Majesty might think fit to confer upon him. The King's answer, however, was sadly familiar: 'The command I have given you of the 10th Regiment of Light Dragoons, should the enemy succeed· in their intentions of invading this island, will enable you at the head of that brave Corps to show the valour which has ever been a striking feature in the character of the House of Brunswick.'*

* The King invited William Beechey to paint a portrait of himself reviewing this 'brave Corps'. On the Queen's authority, apparently, but without the King's knowledge, Beechey included a portrait of the Prince of Wales in the picture. The King was so angry when he saw what had been done that he ordered the canvas to be thrown out of the window. Fortunately, the order was not carried out; and some time later, father and son being on rather better terms, the picture was hung at the Royal Academy. Nevertheless, when the King had a copy made to present to Henry Addington, he gave instructions that the figure of the Prince should be left out (Roberts, *Beechey*, 57–63; *Farington Diary*, i, 226; Alnwick MSS, Asp/P, v, 128–9).

15

The Return of Mrs Fitzherbert
1796–1801

'You know you are my wife, the wife of my heart and soul'

THREE days after the birth of his daughter, the Prince, feeling suddenly and alarmingly ill and protesting that he felt himself about to die, wrote out in his own hurried hand his 'last' will and testament. It as a document of extraordinary length, extending to over three thousand words. In it he mentioned, with 'the truest affection,' his friend Jack Payne, 'though, from some unfortunate misunderstandings and circumstances', he had not seen him for some time. He also mentioned his friend, the Earl of Moira, whom he appointed his executor; Mrs Fitzherbert's companion, Miss Isabella Pigot, upon whom he had already settled £500 a year; and his old and faithful servant, Santague, recommending him, together with those other domestics, who had been 'in the habit of constant attendance' upon his person, to 'the King's gracious protection' in the hope that they would not be allowed to starve. He went on to take particular notice of his 'dear parents' whose forgiveness he asked for any faults he may have ignorantly and unguardedly been guilty of, and his infant daughter whose care he entrusted, in the event of his father's death, to his 'dearest and most excellent mother', in conjunction (if she wished it) with his brothers, the Duke of Clarence, Prince Edward and Prince Ernest and his sisters, Augusta and Mary. The child's mother – though he forgave her 'the falsehood and treachery of her conduct' towards him – must in *no way either be concerned in the education or care of the child, or have possession of her person*', since it was incumbent upon him '*both as a parent and a man to pre-*

vent by all means possible the child's falling into such im-proper and bad hands as hers'.

The will, however, was principally concerned with Maria Fitzherbert, his 'beloved and adored Maria Fitzherbert', to whom he bequeathed all his estates, all his property, all his monies, all his 'personalities of whatever kind or sort', all the contents of all his houses which were listed in the most exact detail down to cabinets, girandoles and clocks, pier glasses, china, wine and liquors, jewels, plate, plans, maps, prints, drawings, trinkets, watches and boxes. He addressed her, the 'wife of his heart and soul', 'his true and real wife', his 'second self', in the most extravagant, not to say hysteri-cal, terms. She was dearer to him, even millions of times dearer to him, than that life he was now about to resign. Her person, her heart and her mind were, and had been since the first moment he had known her, 'as spotless, as unblem-ished and as perfectly pure' as anything could be that was human and mortal.

'I desire I may be buried with as little pomp as possible,' he wrote, 'that *my constant companion, the picture of my beloved wife, Maria Fitzherbert* may be interred with me suspended round my neck by a ribbon as I used to wear it when I lived and *placed right upon my heart*; I likewise will and decree and entreat of *my adored* Maria Fitzherbert to permit that whenever she quits this life and is interred, my coffin should be taken up and placed next to hers wherever she is to be buried, and if she has no objection, that the two inward sides of the two coffins should be taken out and the two coffins then to be [soldered] together. ... *To thee there-fore my Maria, my wife, my life, my soul, do I bid my last adieu; round thee shall my soul forever hover as thy guar-dian angel, for as I never ceased to adore thee whilst living, so shall I ever be watchful over thee and protect thee against every evil. Farewell, dearest angel ... think of thy* DEPARTED HUSBAND, *shed a tear o'er his memory and his grave and then recollect that no woman ever yet was so loved or adored by man as you were and are by him. ...'*

He signed his name and then, remembering something else, turned over the sheet: 'I forgot to mention that the jewels which she who is called the Princess of Wales wears *are mine, having been bought with my own money,* and therefore ... I bequeath [them] to my infant daughter as her own property and to her, who is called the Princess of Wales, I leave one shilling....' *

Despite his protestations as to how deeply he adored his beloved Maria, and despite his insistence on how greatly he longed for her to return to him, she did not respond to his blandishments. Apart from all her other reservations about the advisability of a reconciliation, she was far from convinced that the Prince's liaison with Lady Jersey was at an end; and she had good reason for holding this belief. Although the Prince did his best to avoid Lady Jersey, to whose full-blown charms he had long since grown averse, this determined lady was not easily put off. She was removed from Jack Payne's former house adjoining Carlton House in June 1799; and six months later her husband was formally dismissed from his appointment as the Prince's Master of the Horse on the grounds of economy, though he had in fact been most erratically paid. Yet she declined to be brushed aside, refusing to acknowledge any change in the former relationship, in spite of the broadest hints which were given to her by the Prince's friends and emissaries. He sent Edward Jerningham to see her and to suggest to her that the affair must be considered as finished; but she refused to accept the message. 'Damn you!' she was supposed to have said to Jerningham. 'I wish you well of your new trade.' Later the Prince sent Colonel John McMahon, soon to be appointed Vice-Treasurer of his Household, to call on her after she had met him on the stairs at the Opera House and had followed him down to talk to him. McMahon told her emphatically

---

* The relief that he felt when he had at last come to the end of this diffuse and enormously long document – so he professed four years later – 'certainly did restore one in a manner to life after a dangerous and precarious illness' (RA 50225–6: Asp/P, iv, 100).

'that it was the desire of the Prince that *she would not speak to him*'; but she refused to accept the rebuff, said that there was 'a popish combination against her', and spoke bitterly of McMahon 'for having submitted to carry such a message'.*

While the Prince was taking pains to avoid Lady Jersey, Mrs Fitzherbert was equally concerned to avoid him. She gave up going to Brighton; she sold the lease of Marble Hill, and went to live quietly in a smaller house at Castle Hill, Ealing, where she remained for several months, reluctant to consider the possibility of a reconciliation. 'The link once broken could never be rejoined,' she said, confiding in Prince Ernest; even if they were to make it up, they would 'not agree a fortnight'. The Prince, nevertheless, pursued her assiduously, sending his brothers and Miss Pigot to her with innumerable messages, assuring such mutual friends as the Duchess of Rutland that 'there *never was an instant*' in which he did not feel for her (though she 'never felt' for him) and that everything was '*finally at an end* IN ANOTHER QUARTER'. His letters to her were nearly as long as his will and even more vehement. He sent her presents which included a locket containing a miniature of one of his eyes painted by Cosway and a bracelet engraved with the words '*Rejoindre ou mourir*'. He worked himself up into such a frenzy that his family and friends feared he might be near to losing his reason.

When the Prince heard that Mrs Fitzherbert was seriously

---

* John McMahon, who became Keeper of the Prince's Privy Purse in 1804 and his Private Secretary in 1806, was a loyal and useful servant. He was said to be the illegitimate child of a chambermaid and a butler who had later kept an oyster shop in Dublin. He had been a very bright child, had become a clerk, then an actor, then a soldier in a regiment commanded by Lord Moira who recognized his talents and artful resource, helped him to buy a commission and eventually brought him to Carlton House (Huish, i, 404–8). His bustling little figure and red, spotty face were to be regularly seen in London as he hurried about upon his master's more dubious errands. From 1802 to 1812, through the influence of the Prince's friend, the Duke of Northumberland, he was Member of Parliament for Aldeburgh.

ill he became frantic, and a newspaper report that 'SHE *had died* at Bath' so overwhelmed him that he could 'neither feel, think, speak'. He thought he was going mad, he said, and became so ill that he could not hold a pen in his hand. He was afterwards convinced that if he had not been 'thus bereft of all sense' he would have killed himself. He took quantities of laudanum, and insisted on constant bleeding, losing in one three-day period no less than thirty-six ounces of blood from the arm. He grew so thin that people failed to recognize him; and Lady Holland recorded in her journal that he was 'supposed to be dying'.

'Save me, save me, on my knees I conjure you from myself,' he implored Mrs Fitzherbert in one impassioned, fervent, scarcely coherent letter in which almost every word is underlined with two or more heavy strokes. 'IF YOU WISH MY LIFE YOU SHALL HAVE IT ... OH! GOD! OH, GOD, WHO HAS SEEN THE AGONY OF MY SOUL AND KNOWEST THE PURITY OF MY INTENTIONS HAVE MERCY ON ME: TURN ONCE MORE I CONJURE THEE, THE HEART OF MY MARIA, TO ME, FOR WHOM I HAVE LIVED AND FOR WHOM I WILL DIE. ... YOU KNOW YOU ARE MY WIFE, THE WIFE OF MY HEART AND SOUL, MY WIFE IN THE PRESENCE OF MY GOD ...' He broke off in tears at two o'clock in the morning, and continued again at four: '*The wretched experiences of the last five years have* MADE LIFE ONLY DESIRABLE IN ONE SHAPE TO ME, AND THAT IS IN YOU. I AM WRAPPED UP IN YOU ENTIRELY ... NOTHING CAN ALTER ME, SHAKE ME OR CHANGE ME. ALIKE YOURS IN LIFE AND DEATH. THE CHRYSIS IS COME AND I SHALL DECIDE MY FATE, THAT IS TO SAY YOU SHALL FIX MY DOOM ...'

He threatened that if she did not return to him he would announce their secret marriage to his father and the world. 'You know not what you will drive me to FROM DISPAIR ... I WILL *prove my marriage*, RELINQUISH EVERYTHING FOR YOU, RANK, SITUATION, BIRTH, AND IF THAT IS NOT SUF-FICIENT, MY LIFE SHALL GO ALSO ... THANK GOD *my witnesses are living,* your uncle and your brother ... Oh! my heart, my heart. ...'

Frightened by this letter, Mrs Fitzherbert asked for time to consider her position; and, while she tried to make up her mind, both her own family and the Prince's urged her more strongly than ever to agree to a reunion. Princess Augusta and Princess Mary both actively encouraged it; so did Prince Ernest who assured his brother that Mrs Fitzherbert had 'a very sincere regard' for him; so did Prince Edward who, home from Canada for a time, undertook to conduct the negotiations. On 17 July 1799 Prince Edward had a 'very long tête à tête' with her. He afterwards assured his brother that if he was 'any judge at all of the business' his wishes would 'ere long be accomplished'. There was just the matter of her religious scruples to be cleared up.

This was not done without difficulty, and entailed the Rev. William Nassau of the Roman Catholic church in Warwick Street being commissioned to go to lay her case before the Pope. While waiting for his decision, she went to stay in Wales out of reach of the Prince's further importunities, and he vainly sought permission to go abroad to Lisbon or Madeira 'for a recovery of his health'.

At length the papal decision was made known. It was a favourable one. Mrs Fitzherbert might rejoin the Prince who was her lawful husband in the eyes of the Church. So, by the summer of 1800, they were 'once more inseparables', the Prince subsequently deciding that Roman Catholicism was the 'only religion for a gentleman'.

In June Mrs Fitzherbert gave a 'public breakfast' for the Prince of Wales as a way of announcing to society that a formal reconciliation had taken place.* She hardly knew

---

* According to *The Times* there were no fewer than four hundred guests, including most of the ladies of fashion in town. 'Our fashionable dames', the newspaper commented, 'continue to endeavour to outvie each other in the expence, stile or peculiarity of their entertainments.' But Mrs Fitzherbert beat all her rivals 'by the eccentri-

how she could 'summon up resolution to pass that severe ordeal', she later told a relative, Lord Stourton, 'but she thanked God she had the courage to do so'. Some of her staider friends were rather shocked by her behaviour, all the more so when it became known that she had not relinquished the generous allowance which she had accepted at the time of the Prince's marriage to Princess Caroline. Lady Jerningham, who considered the whole affair 'very incomprehensible', and revised her former opinion of Mrs Fitzherbert as 'a woman of principle', was grateful that a 'bad cold' gave her a good excuse not to attend the breakfast. A guest at a subsequent breakfast given by the Duchess of Devonshire was even more disapproving. This was Lady Jersey who coasted round the Prince as he stood by one of the bands in the garden talking to Dr Charles Burney. 'The Prince was quite annoyed with her and eyed her askance; but she is resolved to plague him; she professes it to be her resolution.' *

---

city of her entertainment and the *length* of it. . . . In the gardens three marquees were erected for the accommodation of the company who met about two o'clock and dined at seven. The entertainment did not conclude till past five o'clock yesterday morning' (*The Times*, 18 June 1800).

* Lady Jersey fulfilled her resolution, taking pride in the 'look of the utmost disdain' which she bestowed upon him when they found themselves at the same party (Rogers, *Table-Talk*, 218). She was to succeed in making trouble for the Prince with both Princess Caroline and Princess Charlotte. By 1814 the Prince was only too well acquainted with 'all the wickedness, perseverance and trick of that infernal Jezabel Lady Jersey, and of all her Jacobinal set of connexions' (RA 21560:Asp/K, i, 513). After various direct and indirect requests for a pension she was granted one (RA 20388–9, 20802–3, 21236:Asp/K, i, 216, 281, 344). Despite this she was so violent a supporter of Queen Caroline during her trial in 1820 that she was 'at daggers drawn even with the Holland family', and wore the Queen's portrait round her neck (*Lieven*, 51, 69). She grew very impatient with other 'opposition ladies' who thought it prudent to await the outcome of the trial before leaving their names at the Queen's house. She was 'longing to fly into her arms', the Countess of Harrowby told her son, 'and to pay her every possible honour and attention' (Har-

Mrs Fitzherbert, however, now confidently disregarded Lady Jersey and settled down to what she described to Lord Stourton as the happiest years of her connection with the Prince. They were 'extremely poor, but as merry as crickets'. They spent the greater part of their time in each other's company, visiting friends for long periods in the country, nearly always together in London where the Prince remained with her most evenings until midnight when he returned home to Carlton House.

'He is so much improved,' she told Lady Anne Lindsay contentedly, 'all that was boyish and troublesome before is now become respectful and considerate ... We live like brother and sister. I find no resentment though plenty of regret that I will have it on this footing and no other, but he must conform to my stipulations or I will have nothing to say to him. I did not consent to make it up with the Prince to live with him either as his wife or his mistress.'

Her poverty was more imagined than real. In January 1801, having given up her house in Pall Mall at the time of the separation, she bought the Earl of Aberdeen's handsome house at the corner of Tilney Street and Park Lane for £6,000; and, the Prince having increased her allowance from £3,000 to £4,000 a year, she sold the lease of her house in Ealing to Prince Edward and took a larger one on Parson's Green, Fulham. Her happiness was only interrupted by the Prince's 'bitter and passionate regrets, and self-accusations for his conduct, which she always met by saying, "We must look to the present and the future, and not think of the past." '

For the Prince, though, the present was not without its worries and the future did not look too promising. He was more 'comfortable' now that he had got Mrs Fitzherbert back again, even though he was apparently not allowed to

---

rowby MSS, 24 October 1820). Afterwards she went abroad. On her return she retired to her husband's seat, Middleton Park, where, so she said, she cared for the details of country life and nothing else. She died at Cheltenham in 1821.

make love to her; yet his other problems which had seemed insignificant compared with his almost demented longing for a reconciliation now returned to haunt him once more.

In the first place, there were his debts. He managed to raise yet another loan of £40,000 without interest from the Landgrave of Hesse-Cassel, but this did not go far; and soon after receiving the money he felt compelled to make further economies in his Household, abolishing the offices of Chamberlain and Master of the Horse, though Lord Cholmondeley had never received any salary for performing the duties of the one and Lord Jersey was still owed several hundred pounds for carrying out those of the other. Indeed, few of those who worked for the Prince received their salaries with any regularity. Before General Gerard Lake left for India as Commander-in-Chief, for instance, he was owed four years' salary as the Prince's Gentleman Attendant; and the allowance of the Prince's dentist, Charles Dumergue, whose skills were supposed to merit regular fees of a hundred guineas a year, was over five years in arrears by 1805. Tradesmen were kept waiting for even longer periods. Payments to numerous firms and individuals, on claims agreed in 1795, were still continuing up till October 1806. One of these creditors, the overcharging jeweller Nathaniel Jefferys, who was at one time owed over £89,000, published damaging advertisements of his alleged losses, threatened to bring his outstanding claim before the House of Commons, and in an open letter to Mrs Fitzherbert – who had offended him by not thanking him gracefully enough for helping her to pay off a pressing debt – wrote that the nation's feelings towards her were of EXTREME DISGUST'.

Ignoring his unsettled debts, the Prince continued to incur others at as fast a rate as ever, as though he were constitutionally incapable of restraint or retrenchment, spending, for example, £2,166 on new table linen, £3,419 on chandeliers. His wardrobe bills, which amounted to a total of £591 in one representative quarter, make revealing reading. A week rarely passed without one or other of his various tailors, usually Messrs Schweitzer and Davidson of 12 Cork Street or John Weston of 27 Old Bond Street, receiving a substantial order. In the course of a period of less than three weeks he was capable of placing five separate orders with John Weston for a total of twenty waistcoats of various styles, colours and shapes from 'fancy lilac double breasted' to 'brown nankeen striped Marseilles quilted', the same firm having supplied him with '18 fine Marseilles waistcoats' and '24 fine printed Marseilles waistcoats' only a month or so before. He almost invariably ordered his clothes in similar bulk. In one short summer, between 4 July and 14 September, he was supplied with seventy-four pairs of gloves; in a subsequent year, within a period of six months, he bought 'ten dozen pairs of white long gloves'. 'Superfine cambric handkerchiefs marked with coronets' came to Carlton House in batches of three dozen; 'rich gold spotted muslin handkerchiefs' arrived in smaller parcels, but they cost twelve guineas each. Everything, naturally, had to be of the highest quality, from his black silk drawers and stockings and his prime doeskin pantaloons (with corsets) to his 'superfine scarlet flannel underwaistcoats lined with firm calico', his 'fine white beaver morning gown double-breasted lined throughout with flannel with a belt made extra wide and very long', his 'black astrakhan Polish caps', and his 'fine white coating bathing suits, jackets, vests and trousers lined throughout with fine Welsh flannel'.

He spent an immense amount on fur. Pelisses, of which he had an enormous number, cost anything up to £150 each. Muffs, which he ordered scarcely less often, were almost as expensive – three 'rich muscovy sable muffs' cost a hundred guineas each. Swords were another expensive item; in eighteen months he bought four steel and gold sabres from John Prosser of Charing Cross, including 'a very superb elegant steel and gold sabre embossed with trophies and laurels' at a total cost of £236. Then there were his uniforms (a Dragoon's regimental coat alone cost £29), his costume for masquerades, his black silk masks and 'character masks made to order', his fancy-dress clothes for appearances as Henry V (£16.10s) or Leontes (£27.1s) supplied by Martin Gay, the Drury Lane theatrical costumiers, his 'tartan masquerade jackets' (£17.10s each), his 'mandarin of war's court dress' (£52.10s), his plumes (£36), his perukes (£33), and his various 'pairs of false curls'.

The Prince's perfumers, Bourgeois Amick and Son, Urania Devins, and other firms, received orders with as unfailing regularity as his tailors, bootmakers, drapers, hatters, hosiers, mercers, lace merchants and furriers. He spent over £20 a week on cold cream and almond paste, perfumed almond powder and scented bags, lavender water, rose water, elder flower water, jasmine pomatum and orange pomatum, eau de Cologne, eau Romaine, Arquebusade, essence of bergamot, vanilla, eau de miel d'Angleterre, milk of roses, huile antique and oil of jessamine. He bought them all in huge quantities – perfumed powder was delivered in amounts of up to 36 lb at a time; tooth brushes came by the three dozen. But then he bought almost everything in huge quantities: in need of a few walking sticks, he bought thirty-two in one day.

The costs of running Carlton House and of entertaining there in the grand style expected of him were, of course, enormous. Apart from the various gentlemen of the Household, the Treasurer (£500 a year), the Keeper of the Privy Purse (£500 a year), the Vice-Treasurer (£300 a year), two clerks (£150 and £100 a year), the Prince's surgeon (Thomas Keate, £150 a year) and the surgeon to the Household (John Phillips, £100 a year), apart from four Pages of the Backstairs, three Pages of the Presence, two Grooms of the Chamber, and seven musicians, there were in 1806 no less than forty indoor servants. These included a housekeeper, a wardrobe keeper, a maître d'hôtel, an inspector of Household deliveries, nine housemaids, four cooks, three watchmen, two kitchen boys and a kitchen-maid, two confectioners, two cellarmen, two coal porters, a coffee-room woman, a silver-scullery-woman, and a table decker. Their wages, which ranged from £300 a year for the maître d'hôtel down to £15 a year for the kitchen boys, came to almost £3,000, the rest of the Household adding a further £3,700 to the annual bill. In a representative month just under £500 was spent on general groceries, meat and fish, while the wine merchant's account came to £1,118, including the cost of fifty dozen bottles of vintage port.

Generous as he was with himself, the Prince was equally generous with his friends and family.* His accounts are full of bills for clothes for his sisters and his mother, for toys for children, for Brussels lace dresses and cloaks, for hats, stockings, ribbons and tippets. One day Messrs W. & G. Bicknell sent an account for '48 pairs of women's fancy white silk hose with laced clocks'; another day Messrs Beamon & Abbott requested payment of £126 for 'a superb Persian scarlet shawl'; later an account arrived for an admiral's dress

---

* The Duchess of Devonshire, who was frequently in debt owing to her passion for gambling and jewels, was one of those who had reason to be thankful for the Prince's generosity. She was constantly writing to thank her 'dearest, dearest brother', as she called him, for helping her out of one of her 'most terrible scrapes', or to ask for a further £2,000 or £3,000 'without it being known'. 'There never was anything equal' to his kindness, she assured him; she trembled to think of the sums she had cost him; it was 'quite shocking' of her to torment him as she did when she dared not approach her husband. Her 'whole heart and life' were devoted to him; she felt more than she could express. Her requests for help were often prefaced by piteous accounts of how her difficulties had brought her to a 'state of terrible weakness' and such 'nervous palpitations' that she thought she was going to die. She did not write, she once disingenuously assured him, with the 'most distant idea' of his being able to be 'of any use' to her; but she had kept her sorrows so long to herself that they preyed upon her; she relied so much on his friendship and had such confidence in him that it was a relief to open her heart to someone whose affection she had 'uniformly' cherished in her heart for many years. She never seems to have made such pleas in vain. She entreated him not to tell anyone of her financial plight – she was '*most* afraid' of Weltje, Payne and Sheridan – and he complied with her wishes. Sometimes he put money into her account without telling even her that he had done so (RA, Add. 27/71/40–41, 50, 71; Chatsworth MSS).

coat which had been made 'with rich gold epaulettes' for the Duke of Clarence at a cost to the Prince of £143.

The Prince remained on good terms with the Duke of Clarence as he did, for the moment, with his other brothers, though he had occasional differences and quarrels with all of them.

Clarence considered the Prince his 'best friend' for the support he gave him in his unavailing efforts to obtain some sort of employment. He repeatedly and vainly asked the Board of Admiralty for a command at sea; he even asked his father to appoint him First Lord of the Admiralty in succession to the ailing Lord Spencer, but – as he 'rather expected' – he was met with a firm refusal. He was also sharply rebuffed when he asked to be placed in command of the fleet in the Mediterranean, and he had to be content with the command of the militia.

The Prince's next brother, Edward, created Duke of Kent in April 1799, was also disappointed in his hopes of a higher command in the Mediterranean area. He had arrived back in England from Canada at the end of 1798 with Mlle, or, as he now called her, Mme de St Laurent, and had been received by his parents with more cordiality than he had expected; but on his return to Canada, he found that his continued liaison with Mme de St Laurent was considered to render him unsuitable for a more desirable appointment nearer home. 'I am the last person in the world to preach or to wish to meddle in your private happiness or connections,' the Duke of York admonished him, writing to him not only as an elder brother but as Commander-in-Chief at the Horse Guards, 'but at the same time I must fairly say to you you can have no idea how much the world talked of the public manner in which you went everywhere accompanied by Madame de St Laurent. I am perfectly well aware that this may be done abroad, but you may depend upon it that it cannot be done at home, and therefore I advise you as a friend to consider this subject well over. ... A great deal depends upon appearances in this world. ... Ministers would feel a delicacy in venturing to recommend to his Majesty to appoint you to [a command in England, Scotland or Ireland] under your particular circumstances at this moment.'

In May 1800, however, the Duke of Kent was obliged to return home owing to illness, and two years later he was appointed Governor of Gibraltar where it was hoped his known reverence for military discipline would help to restore order to a lax and unruly garrison.

The enthusiasm with which he set about this task, closing drink-shops, getting the troops out of bed before dawn, issuing innumerable instructions in the minutest detail about uniforms, saluting, hair-cutting and even shaving, eventually drove the garrison to a mutiny in which several men were killed. In his meticulous script, the Duke wrote long letters to the Prince justifying his conduct. He insisted that, had he met with support from his subordinates, the garrison would have been 'brought to a degree of perfection' beyond his most 'sanguine expectations', and he expressed the deepest concern that the Prince might be misled into supposing that he had had the slightest responsibility for 'those events' which had almost broken his heart and which 'cast an indelible stain upon the troops concerned in them'. The Duke's excuses, however, were wholly discounted in Whitehall. He was recalled home in disgrace, and, in a stormy interview in which both brothers lost their tempers, the Duke of York condemned his conduct 'from first to last as marked by cruelty and oppression'.

The Prince of Wales, supposing his brother to be not so much cruel and oppressive as misguided and unimaginative, offered him his sympathy as he had offered it to the Duke of Clarence, and promised that as soon as he was in a position to do so, he would see that justice was done to him. The Duke was duly grateful, thanking him in the most heartfelt terms for the 'unvaried friendship' shown to him 'through-

out life, but more especially on the present *most trying* occasion' when everything that was dear to him, his character as
a soldier and as a man, was 'at *stake*'.

The Prince's other brothers, Adolphus and Augustus, were
also in need of his sympathy. Adolphus, created Duke of
Cambridge in 1801, had fallen in love with his cousin, Princess Frederica of Mecklenburg-Strelitz, the young widow of
Prince Louis of Prussia. He asked her to marry him and
she accepted, but when he sought his father's permission the
King refused to consider it until the war was over. The Princess sought comfort in the arms of a German princeling
whom, to Prince Adolphus's bitter consternation, she secretly
married, having become pregnant.

Prince Augustus and his problems were even more of a
trial to the Prince of Wales than were those of Adolphus.
For Augustus's entanglement with Lady Augusta Murray
had now been complicated by the birth of a son which was
followed later by that of a daughter.

Prince Augustus, still languishing on the Continent where
his asthma showed no signs of improvement, was scarcely in
a position to bring up the boy; nor was Lady Augusta, whose
meagre pension was most irregularly paid. So, with characteristic generosity, the Prince undertook to take charge of
him himself, at the same time urging his brother to abandon all hope of establishing the legality of his marriage, for
the King's determination on the point remained an 'insuperable and invincible' obstacle. Prince Augustus, however, refused his brother's offer, ignored his advice and compounded
his folly by returning home to England without the King's
permission. Sent back to the Continent, he settled gloomily
in Lisbon whence he wrote the Prince miserable letters about
the 'melancholy stinking place', the falsehood of reports that
he had turned Roman Catholic, and the inadequacy of his
allowance of £8,500 a year. Meanwhile Lady Augusta, left
behind in England, also complained mournfully and at
length to the Prince about her 'distressed situation in point
of pecuniary matters'.

By the beginning of 1802, Prince Augustus, who had at last been raised to the peerage as Duke of Sussex the year before, had grown as exasperated with Lady Augusta as were the other members of his family, and as they were with him. When she came out to Lisbon to insist that he come home with her to proclaim their marriage in the face of all opposition, the Duke refused to allow her into his house; and on her return she immediately wrote an extremely long letter of protest to the Prince about the treatment she had received at his brother's hands, 'the utmost of insult and ill usage a woman could receive – never admitted to his presence – driven from his abode – the sport of his mistress and dependents'. 'Your brother, Sir,' she continued in rising anger, 'has accustomed me to hardship – has inured me to injury – has oppressed me with vexation – has steeped me in calamity – (let him remember what *was* my situation in society when we first met – and what it *is* now. This sad reverse, Sir, is his work).' As well as badgering the Prince of Wales, Lady Augusta badgered the King and the government, demanding money and a peerage, threateing to publish all the letters and documents she possessed unless justice were done, insisting upon being known as Princess Augusta, endeavouring to buy the title from the Emperor of Austria and returning, unopened, letters addressed to her as Lady Augusta Murray. The Duke decided that although his conduct had always been 'delicate' towards her, she 'certainly did not deserve it'.*

---

* It was finally agreed, in 1806, that Lady Augusta should have her debts paid and be provided with an allowance on condition that she stopped claiming to be the Duchess of Sussex. She took the name d'Ameland by royal licence. The two children were given the surname D'Este, both their mother's family and the House of Hanover being descended from the Italian House of Este, rulers in Italy in the Middle Ages. Augustus Frederick D'Este (1794–1848) joined the Army in which he achieved the rank of Colonel in 1838. He died unmarried, having failed in his protracted claims to be declared legitimate on the grounds that 'as the marriage took place in Rome it was outside the Royal Marriage Act' (Grey Papers (Durham) Box

On his return to England, the Duke of Sussex followed his brothers' example in pressing the Prince to support his application for an important military or civil appointment, preferably in Jamaica where the climate would suit him, or at the Cape, as Civil Governor. The Prince did support him, but the government were naturally reluctant to place so sickly and inexperienced a man in a position of responsibility; and their persistent refusal of his request, combined with his creditors' threats of an 'execution upon all the little property' that he possessed, dismayed Sussex to such an extent that the Duke of Kent feared it might actually 'derange his intellect'. Unless some means were found to accomplish something *'forthwith'* for their brother, Kent warned the Prince, it would be 'impossible to answer for the consequences'.

Prince Ernest, Duke of Cumberland since 1799, was another trial to the Prince of Wales, who had by now decided that he thoroughly disliked him and was constantly induced to complain of the way in which he gossiped about him behind his back. The Duke, a reactionary of the most vehement kind, accused his brother of consorting with Whigs – whose views 'threatened the very foundations' of the monarchy and the Constitution – and of all manner of radical excesses which, as the Prince complained to his mother, were 'without the shaddow of a ground' and which 'none but a *fool* would credit and none but a *scoundrel* propagate'.

The Prince's disagreements with the Duke of Cumberland were not as bitter, however, as his quarrel in 1804 with the Duke of York with whom, for many weeks, he was not on speaking terms.

The cause was the Prince's perennial disappointment at his inability to gain any sort of responsible command in the Army in which his younger brother had now reached the

---

43). His sister, Augusta Emma D'Este, married, as his second wife, Sir Thomas Wilde, who as Lord Truro became Lord Chancellor in 1850. There were no children of the marriage.

highest rank. In 1801, in the following year, and again in 1803 – when, a French invasion appearing imminent, the King announced his intention of commanding the defending army in person and of sending his wife and daughters to be cared for by Bishop Hurd at Hartlebury Castle – the Prince renewed his requests to the King, repeating his former arguments in ever more impassioned terms: 'It would therefore little become me who am the first and who stand at the very footstool of the throne to remain a tame, an idle, a lifeless spectator of the mischief which threatens us ... I am bound to adopt this line of conduct by every motive dear to me as a man and sacred to me as a prince. Ought I not to come forward in a moment of unexampled difficulty and danger? Ought I not to share in the glory of victory when I have everything to lose by defeat?'

No, the King still thought, decidedly he should not; and 'desired no further mention should be made to him on this subject'. Undeterred by the repetition of this familiar rebuke, the Prince approached his brother as Commander-in-Chief: was it not 'a degrading mockery' to be told that the only way he could display his zeal was at the head of his regiment? The Duke of York did not agree. 'Surely you must be satisfied,' he replied, 'that your not being advanced in military rank proceeds entirely from his Majesty's sentiments respecting the high rank you hold in the State, and not from any impression unfavourable to you.' The Prince was certainly not satisfied: 'I must *emphatically* repeat, "*That idle inactive rank* was never in my view," but that military rank with its consequent command was never *out of it*.' He knew he was incapable of commanding an army, he admitted to the Duke of Devonshire, but he could collect 'the best generals around him and they might in fact command and direct him'.

Everywhere he went he talked about his grievance until, as Lady Bessborough said, he could talk of nothing else. He remained for hours on end with those who felt obliged to listen to him recounting his wrongs, and became, as he al-

ways did on such occasions, exasperatingly tedious and
boring.

It was all to no avail, and in resentful desperation he decided that the whole correspondence on the subject ought
to be published. It was a decision taken against the advice of
nearly all his more responsible friends, notably the Duke of
Northumberland who thought that the Prince could do
nothing but 'submit in silence to the orders' he had received; any further step would not only be 'unbecoming his
dignity but ... unavailing'. Ignoring this advice, the Prince
allowed the correspondence to be published, on 7 December
1803, in the *Morning Chronicle*, the *Morning Herald* and
the *Sun*. *The Times* was also offered the material but declined it because of 'the delicacy of the subject'.

The Prince denied that he himself had been responsible
for the publication, assuring both the Earl of Moira and
Sheridan that he had had 'nothing to do with the business'.
But few believed him, and certainly the King did not. 'See
what he has done,' he was heard repeatedly lamenting, in a
hoarse and hurried voice, 'he has published *my* letters.' For
weeks, during which father and son did not meet and the
Prince was ostentatiously absent from his parents' Drawing-
Rooms, the King referred to him as 'the publisher of *my*
letters'.

Worse was yet to come. Some time later the Prince's regiment was withdrawn from its front-line encampment close
to the Sussex coast, where the French were expected to attempt an invasion, and sent inland to Guildford. This
humiliating withdrawal, carried out at the moment of alarm
upon instructions from the Horse Guards, was an indignity
the Prince could 'never pass by', the Duke of Clarence
assured their sister, Amelia, in his usual tactless way: it
would 'produce an irreparable breach for ever' between the
two brothers.

Goaded by the Duke's remarks, which had been reported
to him by Colonel McMahon, and infuriated by what he
took as a personal insult, the Prince threatened that he

would never again speak to the Duke of York, particularly as he himself had loyally defended him after his ignominious failure as commander of the expedition to the Helder in 1799. Once again the placatory Duke of Northumberland urged restraint, advising the Prince to behave as though not in the least provoked; he must 'endeavour to disguise his feelings'. The Prince could not disguise his feelings. He was furious with his brother and he did not mind who knew it. The Duke presented himself frequently at Carlton House to explain his reasons for the regiment's withdrawal, but the Prince refused to listen to them or even to ask him in. On making a final attempt, the Duke was handed a curt note by one of his brother's pages: 'The Prince of Wales is extremely concerned that the Duke of York has given himself the trouble of calling so frequently of late at Carlton House. But one moment's recollection and reflection must convince the Duke of York that it is impossible for the Prince of Wales, whatever may be his regret, to receive the Duke, after *all* that has so *recently* passed.'

16

The King's Relapse
1801–1804

*'We sat till past eleven and the Prince talked the
greater part of the time'*

ALTHOUGH the Prince's relations with the Duke of York
soon improved, he was never able to keep on good terms with
his father. Whenever a happier relationship between them
seemed likely, a family dispute, a political quarrel, a disagreement over money or over the Prince's employment in
the Army or the State would drive them apart again.

In 1797 the Prince had entertained hopes of being appointed Lord Lieutenant of Ireland, an idea suggested to
him by the Irish Whigs. But the King had dismissed it out
of hand; and the Prince had drawn closer once more to the
opposition, giving dinners at Carlton House for Fox, Sheridan, the Duke of Norfolk and other leading opponents of
Pitt's government.* For a time it had even seemed possible
that a new government might be formed under the aegis of
the Prince by some of these opponents and various dis-

* Some of these dinners went on until four o'clock in the morning
with the Prince's oratorical powers declining with each bottle of
wine consumed. Lord Glenbervie records William Fawkener having
told him that he 'never heard worse reasoning in better language,
that the Prince would sometimes put two or three tolerable sentences
together, but could not maintain that tone and fell into mere balder-
dash without expression or argument, but always with a sort of
emphatic speechifying manner and in tirades'. Fawkener, adds Lord
Glenbervie, 'has no high opinion of the Prince's understanding but
says the Prince thinks highly of it and that he conceives himself particularly to have great penetration into characters and great quickness and readiness in learning men's private histories and views, and
their particular passions and foibles. With this vanity he will be a
most difficult master for any Minister' (*Glenbervie Journals*, i, 343).

gruntled members of the present administration; but the Prince's widespread unpopularity, much intensified by his rejection of Princess Caroline, had stood irremovably in the way. Indeed, even if the Prince had been a far more popular figure, it was doubtful whether the Whig opposition were strong enough to form the nucleus of an acceptable government. The Prince's Private Secretary, Thomas Tyrwhitt, thought that their standing in the country had never been so low; Charles Grey agreed that they were 'without numbers or power'; and Fox considered that the old party was 'too much routed and dispersed to be rallied again'.

At the beginning of 1801, however, Pitt felt obliged to resign over his thwarted intention of bringing in a Relief Bill for the benefit of the Irish Roman Catholics, a measure to which the King – persuaded that to agree to the Irish claims would be to violate his Coronation Oath – was rigidly opposed. As Pitt's successor, the King selected Henry Addington, the Reading doctor's son who had been Speaker of the House of Commons since the outbreak of the French Revolution. Addington, a modest man of limited competence, was reluctant to accept the appointment. But the King would consider no one else: Addington was honest, reliable and, above all, his attachment to the Church of England, as his Majesty assured Bishop Hurd, was as sincere as his own. 'Lay your hand upon your heart,' the King said to him, 'and ask yourself where I am to turn for support if *you* do not stand by me.'

Addington said he would go to Pitt and try to get the Prime Minister to change his mind about the Catholic Relief Bill; but Pitt was as implacable as the King, and told him, 'I see nothing but ruin, Addington, if you hesitate.' So Addington reluctantly gave way. On 5 February he wrote accepting office, and on the 10th went to see his Majesty who embraced him as he entered the room, saying, 'My dear Addington, you have saved your country.'

That week, while out riding with one of his equerries, the King confessed to feeling unwell; he had been sleeping badly

and was 'very bilious'. Soon he was displaying all the symptoms that had characterized his former serious illness in
1788; and by the end of the month, his physical condition
having alarmingly weakened and his conduct having become 'very extravagant', the Willises – with the exception of
the father who at eighty-three had become 'rough and violent' – were once more in attendance upon their difficult
patient, helped by four 'keepers'.

It being feared that his father might even die, the Prince
of Wales summoned both Pitt and Addington to Carlton
House, Addington as *de jure* Prime Minister, Pitt, since he
still held the seals of office, as Prime Minister *de facto*.

Pitt, stiff and unaccommodating as he usually was with
the Prince, told him that it seemed a Regency might be
necessary and that, if there were to be one, he would have
to insist upon its being limited as had been proposed in 1789.
The Prince, apparently rather mortified by this suggestion,
replied that he would have to have time to think it over; but,
strongly urged by the Earl of Carlisle and Lord Egremont
amongst others to accept any restrictions that Parliament
might want to impose, he agreed to it, and seemed prepared
to abstain from the kind of reckless political intrigue in
which he had become involved at the time of his father's
previous incapacity.

He had his critics, of course. Mrs Harcourt said that, as
usual, his conduct was 'very bad'; it was no wonder that he
could not get to see the King since he always called when he
knew his father was too ill to receive him. One day he went
to the Queen's House just after his Majesty had taken his
medicine, 'and on being refused, sent word to Lord Uxbridge, with whom he was to dine, by Jack Payne, that as
the King would not see him, he really felt too much to
think of dining in company. Sad grimace.' Lord Malmesbury agreed that the Prince's conduct was most unseemly
at the beginning of his father's illness; he was 'in great agitation of mind and spirits' as he had been during the last
Regency crisis. He went about 'holding language in the

streets as would have better become a member of opposition than heir to these Kingdoms', saying his father's mind was 'completely deranged'; and on the 'second day of the King's illness ... he went in the evening to a concert at Lady Hamilton's and there told Calonne (the rascally French ex-minister), *"Savez vous, Monsieur de Calonne, que mon père est aussi fou que jamais?"'* Malmesbury admitted, though, that 'he became more decent soon after this'.

Certainly when he set about making provisional plans for a possible new administration, he did so discreetly. He cautiously approached the Duke of Devonshire, the Marquess of Buckingham and Lord Spencer; he tentatively offered the Viceroyalty of Ireland to the Duke of Norfolk with the idea of introducing a Catholic Relief Bill; he considered Shelburne (now Marquess of Lansdowne) for the office of Foreign Secretary, Grey for that of Secretary of War, Sheridan as Chancellor of the Exchequer, and Fox – though there would be difficulty with Mrs Fitzherbert over this appointment – as Home Secretary. Meanwhile there were 'great flockings of minor politicians into Carlton House'. The Dukes of Clarence and Kent hung about the Prince in the hope of better employment, though the Duke of York remained aloof at the Horse Guards, sharing his father's and the Duke of Cumberland's views on Catholic relief and supposing his future to be more secure with his father as King than with his brother as Regent.

Various names were canvassed for Prime Minister. Neither Fox nor Grey wanted so high an office at present, and, in any case, Fox could scarcely hope to attain it now that Mrs Fitzherbert had been returned to favour. Pitt was not in the running owing to the Prince's dislike of him. Addington, however, was considered a possibility; and certainly the Prince spent much of his time in private conversations with him. Subsequently the Earl of Moira emerged as a strong candidate.

But it was extremely difficult for the Prince to judge how necessary it was to consider the merits of any candidate, since he could get no reliable information about the King's condition. Even the Queen and the Princesses were not allowed to see him after 24 February, so the Prince had to rely upon what information he could glean from the doctors, Gisborne, Reynolds and the Willises. On 27 February, Dr John Willis told him that his Majesty was so confused that, if he were disposed to read, he would be unable to make out a single letter; yet later Willis and his brother expressed much more optimistic opinions and spoke of a recovery 'within three weeks'. On 1 March Reynolds reported the patient 'worse last night than ever'; and the next day he was so ill, with a pulse rate of 136, that the Prince was summoned to the Queen's House where he waited, with other members of the Royal Family, outside the sick-room expecting at any moment to be told of the King's death. But, after a strong dose of musk, his Majesty grew a little better; and although he remained for some time alternating between 'insensibility and stupor' and such 'extreme nervous irritability' that they feared a 'paralytic stroke', by 5 March he had sufficiently recovered to be able to feed himself again. A few days later the Prince was at last permitted into his room to see him, accompanied by the Rev. Thomas Willis, the doctor's brother, who had achieved considerable influence over the entire Household, and had, as the Queen put it, 'gained everybody's approbation'.

The Prince, whose conduct, even Malmesbury admitted, was 'right and proper' now, found his father pale and very thin. They had a perfectly coherent conversation; and the next week the King was well enough to receive Pitt and to accept back from him the seals of office, a ceremony which Pitt found 'particularly distressing' since it was being rumoured, notably by the Duke of Cumberland and by the Rev. Thomas Willis, that the King's illness had been induced by his agitation over the intended Catholic Relief Bill.*

---

* Cumberland took full credit for having persuaded the King to appoint Addington in Pitt's place, and was constantly urging his

Despite the King's recovery the Prince was not again admitted to his presence until 14 April, the day upon which the Willises' 'keepers' were dismissed. But on that day, so the Prince told the Earl of Carlisle, he was received with 'every mark of love and fondness'. His father 'began with the happiness he felt at being able the same day to embrace his son and dismiss Dr Willis's keepers, that being the first day since his illness that any one of his own servants had been permitted to attend him. The Prince was delighted to find that his mind was not poisoned on his account, but on the contrary [the King] did him ample justice for his correct conduct during the whole of the malady. He continually and repeatedly talked of himself as a dying man, determined to go abroad to Hanover [which no one had dared to tell him had been occupied by the Prussians at the instigation of Bonaparte, a man dismissed a few years before as 'a Corsican adventurer']. He made the Prince sit down to dinner with him, and expressed pleasure that once in his life he should have to say he dined *tête-à-tête* with his beloved son. He ate little – a small piece of mutton, a little beetroot, a small piece of cheese, and the contents of a small apple tart. He drank three glasses of wine, and all to the Prince's health. He talked of all his children in terms of the greatest affection – in terms to move to tears; but particularly so when he dwelt upon his little granddaughter. ... He insisted much on the Prince accepting a white Hanoverian horse, laying the most vehe-

---

father to stand firm against Catholic relief. While the Prince of Wales was denied access to the sick-room by the Rev. Thomas Willis, Cumberland was allowed in to play on his father's fears and prejudices. To the Duchess of Devonshire, the Prince of Wales expressed his 'disgust' at the conduct of the Duke of Cumberland 'who had broke with him during the King's illness and sided with the Duke of York' (Chatsworth MSS). His own conduct, he considered, had been exemplary. 'I have had the good approbation of the country,' he assured his friend, Arthur Paget, 'though one must always expect there will be in this world a certain number of grumblers, though there have been fewer upon this occasion than ever yet have been known upon any circumstances which has so interested the public mind' (*Paget Papers*, I, 343).

ment stress upon the Prince of Wales's right to mount such a horse, his joy, his pride; and this went to very incorrect discourse. ... He then ran off, and talked of the device he used, by some position of his wig, to make the Council believe him in better looks and health. Here [he] was very wild.'

It was clear, then, that although he was very much better, the King was still far from being cured. He went out on 18 April, having said a thankful good-bye to the Willises, to fulfil an urgent desire to see his baby granddaughter who was on a visit to Princess Caroline at Blackheath. Yet the next day Thomas Willis received a letter from Princess Elizabeth who told him how nervous she and her sisters and mother were at the prospect of being left alone with the King while he remained in such an uncertain state.

Willis and his brothers were only too eager to respond to the call, and Thomas Willis appealed to Addington for his authority to take his Majesty into their care once more. Addington said that they could do so provided the Queen agreed; but the Queen, fearful of her husband's reaction to being again put into the hands of the Willises, whom she herself had begun to find intolerably managing, refused to be responsible for giving her consent without ministerial approval. Addington, for his part, did not like to act without the agreement of Parliament. Eventually the Queen reluctantly gave way on the understanding that she would 'not be named or supposed to know anything that was intended'.

The Willises, impatient of the delay, had already decided to take action. Unwilling to forsake the task they had 'undertaken when great credit was at stake', the Rev. Thomas Willis confessed, they determined upon a 'cruel scheme', 'frightful as it was'. They planned no less than to seize the King and detain him by force.

They did so in the Prince of Wales's apartments at Kew where their erstwhile patient had gone to convalesce. When

Thomas Willis entered the room, the King attempted to escape from it, but was prevented by Willis who insisted on the necessity of his being brought 'immediately under control again'. 'Sir,' said the King, sitting down and turning very pale, 'I will never forgive you whilst I live.' He again tried to escape, but Dr John Willis and four stalwart 'keepers' barred his way.

From that moment he was kept more closely confined than ever, separated from his family, bled, cupped and purged, only occasionally being allowed out to take a few turns round Kew Green with one or other of the Willises in close attendance. His wife and daughters were permitted to see him for a short time on 19 May, but the Prince was not.

The Prince, supposing that his father had now suffered 'a severe relapse', took advice on what he should do. Lord Carlisle advised him that the first step was to remonstrate with Addington and Lord Eldon, the Lord Chancellor, for their 'supinely suffering the King's health to be tampered with by persons who [could] hardly be called physicians'. It was the King himself, however, who succeeded in getting rid of them by the simple, effective method of refusing to do any work unless he were allowed to show that their continued presence at Kew was quite unnecessary. He took 'a solemn declaration that unless he was allowed to go [on the Queen's birthday, 19 May] to the house where the Queen and his family were, no earthly consideration should induce him to sign his name to any paper or to do one act of government whatever'. The threat of a royal strike was taken seriously; and when the King walked over to the Queen's apartments on her birthday no one presumed to prevent him.

Soon afterwards the King left to continue his convalescence at Weymouth where, as he told Bishop Hurd, sea bathing 'had its usual success'. Lord Eldon urged him to retain the services of Dr Robert Willis 'at least for the present ... as a regular physician'. But the King replied that he was 'quite satisfied with Dr Gisborne', and in Gisborne's

absence he would consult Sir Francis Milman. He would not
and could not bear the idea of consulting Dr Robert Willis
or, indeed, 'any of the Willis family'.

For a time during his father's illness, as in 1788–89, the
Prince had fallen out again with his mother. The Earl of
Malmesbury said that at the Drawing-Room on 26 March,
when her Majesty looked pale and the Princesses 'as if they
had been weeping', the Prince behaved 'very rudely' to his
mother. He suspected her, not unjustly, of plotting with the
Dukes of York and Cumberland and the Rev. Thomas Willis
to ward off the threatened Regency by allowing it to be supposed that the King's illness was less severe than it was. But
the Prince was soon on as good terms as ever with the Queen
once more, and on much better terms with the King than he
had been for years. 'As Heaven's my witness,' he told Lady
Bessborough with tears running down his cheeks, 'I love my
father to my heart, and never think of his sufferings without
tears.' And she believed that he really meant it. The Prince
had 'great faults', she knew, but they were more of the head
than of the heart. She had 'never heard the Prince at any
time mention the King but with respect and affection'.

The Prince's relations with the new government were also
satisfactory, for he got on much more easily with Addington
than he had ever been able to get on with Pitt.* And once
the Preliminary Articles of the Treaty of Amiens had been

---

* The relationship between Pitt and the Prince was even more un-
friendly after Pitt's resignation. Colonel McMahon complained to the
Duke of Northumberland about Pitt's 'reprobate behaviour' in insolently neglecting the Prince while he was staying near Brighton in
the summer of 1801. 'He rode daily into town and afforded the solitary instance of being the only man of any consideration in life that
did not offer his duty and leave his name at the Pavilion' (Alnwick
MSS, Asp/P, iv, 307). The Duke of Northumberland agreed that 'the
indignities and insults offered to the Prince by that arrogant and insolent man [had] been such as [could] neither be overlooked nor
forgiven'. The Duke trusted in God that his Royal Highness would
'never consent to any coalition with Mr Pitt' (RA 40073–4: Asp/P,
iv, 489).

signed in October, Addington felt able to open negotiations
for a possible coalition with some of the Prince's Whig
'friends'.

Although these negotiations were far from universally
welcomed by members of the administration – Charles
Yorke, the Secretary of War, for one, dreaded 'a connection
with the Prince and his friends' – and although they eventually broke down, there was no doubt that the Prince was now
considered, both in government circles and at Court, as a
more responsible man than he had ever been in the
past.

At last it was possible to raise once more the delicate
question of his financial position, and to put forward a claim
to the arrears of the revenue of the Duchy of Cornwall. These
amounted, so Pitt estimated, to £234,000 which had been
withheld from him until he had reached the age of twenty-
one, although, as his lawyers undertook to prove from historical precedents, the income ought to have been his from
birth.

The Prince's claim to the Duchy arrears – which had been
appropriated by his father to settle his own debts – was due
to be raised in Parliament on 31 March 1802; but not all the
Prince's friends' felt able to vote in support of the motion.
Grey, for one, 'was not quite convinced of his right', and
when he met the Prince by chance on the street and was
greeted volubly as a sure supporter, he felt obliged to say so.
The Prince was 'evidently a good deal struck' by what Grey
said, but 'bore it very well'. The motion was defeated by 160
votes to 103.

Next year, however, a compromise was reached. In order to
re-establish the Prince in 'that splendour which belonged to
his rank', as Addington put it, it was proposed that he should
be given an additional income of £60,000 for three years to
enable him to pay off his outstanding debts. For this settlement the Prince was prepared to abandon his claims to the
Duchy's arrears, not because he did not consider himself
entitled to them, he hastened to make clear, but because he

did not want to provoke any disagreement with the King with whom he was on uneasy terms again.

Despite Pitt's contention that the government's proposal was 'highly indecent' and that 'any further vote for the Prince ought on every account to be resisted', the Annuity Bill was passed. The majority was so small, however, that the Prince, in sending a message to Parliament to thank Members for what they had voted to do for him, felt it prudent to add that he could not think of increasing the country's financial burdens now that England was once more at war with France.* Lord Malmesbury commented that there was 'general disapprobation of the way in which Addington [had] managed the Prince's business', and that the 'division ... being so near run impressed the public that his ministry was a weak one'.

Indeed, a year later, in February 1804, it seemed on the verge of collapse when the King once again fell ill with symptoms that threatened another attack of his distressing malady. Addington immediately sent for the Willises who responded promptly and, to the horror of the royal family, presented themselves at the Queen's House 'with the intention of their being introduced into the King's apartment to attend him'. The Dukes of Kent and Cumberland were fortunately there to bar their way; and faced with this firm opposition by the royal family, who had given solemn undertakings to the King never to allow any member of the Willis family near him again, Addington sent instead for the physician to St Luke's Hospital for Lunatics.

The methods of this physician, Samuel Foart Simmons, differed little from those of the Willises and he soon had his patient wrapped up in a straitjacket. As on previous occa-

* 'The Prince's business comes on again today, but I shall again be an absentee,' Lord Harrowby was informed by his son in a letter which reflected the views of many other Members. 'I cannot vote for a bill which grants £60,000 a year for no public purpose whatever; as we know the Prince will not resume his establishment at present and will probably make his debts a pretence for not resuming it at all' (Harrowby MSS, 9 March 1803).

sions, the Prince found it impossible to discover the true state of his father's condition. Simmons's reports were optimistic but qualified; his bulletins reported that the patient was 'going favourably', though 'any rapid amendment was not to be expected'. A month later it was reported that 'a short time' would 'perfect his recovery', but, as Mrs Harcourt told Lord Malmesbury, while he seemed well enough in the presence of his Ministers with whom he made great efforts to appear normal, 'towards his family and dependants his language was incoherent and harsh, quite unlike his usual character'. Mrs Harcourt added that Simmons 'did not possess, in any degree, the talents required to lead the mind from wandering to steadiness', and that the King, suspicious of the doctor and cantankerous with everyone, had made all sorts of changes in the Household, dismissing servants 'without a shadow of reason'. All this 'afflicted the royal family beyond measure; the Queen was ill and *cross*, the Princesses low, depressed and quite sinking under it'. After Mrs Harcourt had left Lord Malmesbury, Lord Pembroke was shown into his room where the two men 'dwelt on the very serious consequences to which [the King's condition] might lead, and in vain sought about for a remedy'.

The Prince of Wales had already decided that he must provide the remedy himself. Once again he set about planning a new government in agitated consultations with various advisers, including Lord Thurlow, Lord Moira and Sheridan – whom he appointed Receiver-General of the Duchy of Cornwall (on the death of Lord Elliot) forgetting that he had formerly promised the post to General Lake. He would have preferred Moira as Prime Minister; but he said that he was prepared to consider other candidates, even Pitt, who was now certainly eager to return to office and who might easily, so the Earl of Darnley assured the Prince, 'be converted into a firm and certainly a most useful friend'.

Pitt, however, shared the opinion, once expressed by Lord Thurlow, that the Prince was 'the worst anchoring ground in Europe'. He did not trust the Prince's friendship, and

doubted his sincerity in letting it be known that he was prepared to call upon men of any party or faction provided
they enjoyed the country's confidence. 'With respect to the
Prince's intentions,' Pitt warned, 'I fear no very certain dependence is to be placed on any language which he holds.'
He refused to consider the Prince as a reliable or valuable
ally, virtually disregarding his influence.

Under continued attack from Pitt, from the followers of
Grenville and Fox, and deserted by many of its former supporters amongst the county and Scottish members, the
government's majority fell in vote after vote until Addington felt obliged to resign. The King, distressed beyond
measure by his resignation, became more difficult and cantankerous than ever with his family. When he learned that
Pitt wanted to include Fox as well as Grenville in the new
coalition ministry, he refused in any circumstances to countenance Fox's appointment, all the more strongly because the
Prince, having forgiven his former friend for his attitude
towards the French Revolution and Bonaparte, was now on
good terms with him again. And without Fox, Pitt was unable to form that strong, broad-based government which he
had hoped would be able to conduct the impending war with
the spirit that Addington and his ministers had so conspicuously lacked. For it was decided on 7 May at meetings at
Lord Grenville's London house and at Carlton House that
if Fox was not to be appointed to the new government then
none of his supporters, none of Grenville's, nor any 'friend'
of the Prince's would accept office either.

Both Lord Moira and George Tierney strongly deprecated
the Prince's involvement with the Foxites and the Grenvilles,
believing that if only the Prince had rallied to Pitt he would
have become reconciled to the King, to the great benefit of
the monarchy. As it was, the King and his son were now
likely to become more estranged than ever, particularly as
the Prince – evidently much gratified to have so formidable
a body of political friends and delighted, as he told Lady
Elizabeth Foster, that he and Fox were once again so inti-

mate – took to giving large dinner parties for Pitt's opponents at Carlton House where he talked at inordinate length on all manner of subjects, political and otherwise.

'We sat till past eleven and the Prince talked the greatest part of the time,' Charles Grey told his wife after one of these Carlton House dinners. 'There was no lack of length or repetition.' It was a good thing, Grey added, that the guests met elsewhere before going on to Carlton House for 'when we meet His Royal Highness there is in general an end of everything but speeches from him'.

The Prince's loquacity was confirmed by Thomas Creevey, an enthusiastic Whig and Member of Parliament for Thetford, a pocket borough in the gift of the Duke of Norfolk. One evening at this time Creevey attended a Carlton House dinner at which were present about thirty members of the opposition including Fox, Grey, Sheridan and the Duke of Clarence. 'The only thing that made an impression upon me in favour of the Prince that day (always excepting his excellent manners and appearance of good humour)', Creevey wrote, 'was his receiving a note which he flung across the table to Fox and asked if he must not answer it, which Fox assented to; and then, without the slightest fuss, the Prince left his place, went into another room and wrote an answer, which he brought to Fox for his approval, and when the latter said it was quite right, the Prince seemed delighted, which I thought very pretty in him, and a striking proof of Fox's influence over him.

'During dinner he was very gracious, funny and agreeable, but after dinner he took to making speeches, and was very prosy as well as highly injudicious. He made a long harangue in favour of the Catholics and took occasion to tell us that his brother, William, and himself were the only two of his family who were not *Germans* – this too in a company which was, most of them, not known to him. Likewise I remember his halloaing to Sir Charles Bamfyld at the other end of the table, and asking him if he had seen Mother Windsor [a notorious procuress] lately.'

What the Prince frequently spoke about was the state of
his father's mind and the continued difficulty he experienced in getting information about it. He felt sure that he
was 'as mad as ever', but the doctors declined to say so. There
were persistent reports of the King's agitated, uncontrollable conversation, his rambling, repetitive talk about future
plans, his indecent, even obscene behaviour in front of the
servants, his writing of passionate love letters to a seventy-
year-old lady who attended his Drawing-Rooms, his rudeness to the Queen who was finding him more and more
intolerable, and who herself was becoming so insufferably
ill-tempered that the Princesses were 'rendered quite miserable' by her.

By June he was considerably better, so the Duke of Kent
reported to Carlton House. He was not entirely reconciled
to his family, particularly to the Queen whom he repeatedly
blamed for the reappearance of the 'mad doctor', Simmons,
and the 'keepers' into the house, but at least he was now
'coolly civil' to her. His behaviour to his daughters and to
Kent himself was 'particularly kind, in a proper not in an
outré way. So far for the fair side of the picture. On the
other hand' his physical health was 'unusually bad'; his face
and eyes were 'a livid yellow'; his right leg was 'much swollen and there was a tremor in his limbs'; he was very bilious
and his tongue was 'furred half an inch thick'. 'There was
also a singular catch in his throat' and 'an uncommon deficiency of sight and hearing'.

Helped by Grey, Grenville and others, the Prince wrote
letter after letter to the Lord Chancellor, Lord Eldon, complaining of the injustice of his being kept in the dark as to
the King's true condition. As his eldest son and heir to the
throne, he ought to be the first to be informed of it. If the
King were ill, why was he being burdened with 'the full
exercise of the royal functions'? If he were well, why did
'Dr Simmons and people of his appointment continue in
attendance?'

The Chancellor called on the Prince on 3 June to explain

the position in person. 'With great agitation, and occasionally with tears, he acknowledged that the King had been in a very unpleasant way at Windsor, and went on to express his readiness at all times to bear testimony to the propriety and forebearance of the Prince's conduct, and promising that if anything of the same sort recurred, the fullest information should be laid before His Royal Highness.'

The physicians had, he added, signed a document to the effect that although the King was 'sufficiently recovered to be capable of exercising his high functions', there were 'still certain symptoms remaining' that made them apprehensive of a relapse. 'Medical guidance' was, therefore, absolutely necessary. The document was signed not only by Simmons, but by Sir Francis Milman, Sir Lucas Pepys and Drs Reynolds and Heberden.

The Prince was still not satisfied. He wrote to the Chancellor again on 19 June to complain of the conduct of his Majesty's Ministers in making no communication, either with the Privy Council, Parliament or the Prince of Wales, about the medical treatment to which the King had been subjected for the past five months. He strongly criticized the manner in which Ministers 'alone [had] decided that under the British Constitution the King's Commands [might] legally be received on the highest matters of his Government, at the very time when his person and all his ordinary action[s] [were] subjected to controul. Under such circumstances [the Prince could] no longer forbear to express his entire disapprobation of *principles and measures* which he sees to be full of danger to the British Monarchy.'

But the time for formal protest had by now passed; the King's condition was improving day by day; and on 26 June the Chancellor, to his evident relief, felt able to avoid answering the Prince's charges by declaring briefly that 'in the judgement of the physicians' his Majesty was quite well.

So far recovered was he, indeed, that it was felt both by Pitt and the Queen and her children that he was capable of standing up to an interview with the Prince during which, it was hoped, a formal, public reconciliation might take place. The absence of the Prince from recent Drawing-Rooms had been conspicuous. When the King had been present, the Prince had not; when the King had not been present, the Prince had still not attended them, either because the Duke of York had been there or because the Princess of Wales had been. The King had not attended the most recent Drawing-Room held on 4 June to celebrate his birthday; but on learning that the Princess of Wales would be there the Prince drove along Pall Mall sitting prominently on the driving-box of his barouche while the guests were on their way to St James's.

It was, in fact, the King's constant and increasingly cordial attentions to Princess Caroline, to whom he had granted the profitable Rangership of Greenwich Park, that angered the Prince above all else. It was one of the principal reasons why he was so reluctant to suppose that an interview with his father could possibly improve relations between them.

Another main cause of the Prince's ill feeling towards his father was his continued failure to obtain employment in the Army. As a means of circumventing the King's determined stand on this point, Lord Moira had suggested that the Prince should be given command of a specified Military District, for which he would be directly responsible to the Commander-in-Chief. In the event of a French landing he would surrender command of this District, and present himself at the King's headquarters where he would assume the nominal responsibilities of a second-in-command. But nothing came of this curious plan which was soon forgotten; and thereafter the Prince resignedly gave up all idea 'of any military rank or command whatever'. The disappointment still rankled, though, while the Prince's anger at the King's evident attachment to the Princess of Wales burned more fiercely than ever.

Eventually, however, the Prince was persuaded to make the opening move towards a reconciliation. Fox strongly supported the idea; so did Sheridan; while the Duke of Kent wrote, 'the Queen and all my sisters *without exception,* Adolphus to a *certainty,* and Ernest, *at least to all appearances hitherto,* are full of nothing but the urgency of bringing you together *without* delay'. So, on 4 July, the Prince wrote to the Queen to say that he lamented heartily not paying his duty to the King. 'Were this allowed me,' he said, 'I should fly to throw myself at the King's feet, and offer to him the testimony of my ever-unvarying attachment. I have long grieved that misrepresentations have estranged his Majesty's mind from me.'

Despite this submission the King, insisting that no good would come of it, remained as reluctant to see the Prince as the Prince was to see him. The publication of the King's letters refusing the Prince's requests for promotion in the Army had never been forgotten nor forgiven; and there was also the Prince's more recent misfortune in becoming indirectly involved in the election as Member for Middlesex of the radical Sir Francis Burdett; at a dinner for Sir Francis the toast had been 'The Prince of Wales' rather than 'The King'.

But in the end the King gave way to the persistent pressure of Pitt and Lord Eldon, on condition that his son came to Kew and not to Windsor, that 'no explanation or excuses' were made by the Prince, and that the Queen, the Princesses and 'at least the Duke of Cambridge' were present throughout the interview. 'I will not see him at Windsor for there he will stay,' the King protested. 'I will see him at Kew for there he must go about his business when it's over. I know him. ... Yes, yes, I'll see him, and I'll be very civil to him; but I'll never forgive his publishing my letters, and I'll never correspond with him.'

As the day fixed for the interview, 22 August 1804, approached, the Prince became less and less inclined to go through with it. In addition to his earlier objections, there were now reports that the King's mind was weakening again. The Duke of Kent warned the Prince that there was 'an astonishing change for the worse, as his manner was so much more hurried, his conversation so infinitely more light and silly, his temper so much more irritable, besides a strong indication of fever on his cheek, a return of that dreadful saliva, of the strong bilious eye, and of numberless symptoms that manifested themselves last February and were the forerunners of the serious attack'. From other sources came reports that he had become so elated since the 'horrid doctor',. Simmons, had left that he gave vent 'to very improper expressions' and was 'so violent with his family that they all dread him beyond description, without having any power to restrain him'. Colonel McMahon was told on good authority that he was 'quite outrageous' with the Queen to whom he manifested the 'greatest aversion', stating publicly that he would have nothing more to do with her; that he was going to fit up the Great Lodge in Windsor Park and install Lady Pembroke there as his mistress; or if the invitation to this lady – which he had made through his surgeon, David Dundas – should not be accepted, he would have the Duchess of Rutland; failing her, he would take Lady Georgiana Buckley. McMahon was further told by one of the royal Dukes 'that on going to see the lodge the other day with two of the Princesses he accidentally met a housemaid called Sally and appeared in ecstasies at seeing her – that he desired the Princesses to stay above stairs when he came down and went into the room where she was and locked himself in with her for three quarters of an hour'.

All these 'proofs of madness and insincerity' induced the Prince to write to the Lord Chancellor saying that 'the information he had recently received' had persuaded him that it would be prudent to avoid an interview which might only 'irritate' the King's mind. Lord Eldon, however, declined to submit such an excuse to the King and urged him merely to plead illness. This the Prince, whose 'extreme agitation' at the prospect of the interview had, indeed, led to a severe attack of diarrhoea, was quite willing to do.

When the King was handed the Prince's letter, he looked at the cover and seeing that it came from Carlton House, did not immediately open it, 'evidently seeking to command himself'. After reading it, he announced, 'The Prince is ill'; then, having made some remark about the illness being probably caused by apprehension, he declared that the interview would have to be put off until his return from Weymouth.

At Weymouth the King's behaviour was alarming. On his yacht he let fly against Roman Catholics and, in the presence of the sailors, declared his hatred of all reforms. At the theatre, when he was not sound asleep, he talked as loudly as the actors. Once, being awake, he vigorously applauded some slighting reference to Members of Parliament; and on another occasion, he woke up to find the Queen was not in the box. Where was she? he wanted to know. Princess Augusta whispered where she had gone. 'The King then cried out "Why did she not take with her all the play bills?"'

He frequently threatened to keep a mistress, and several times declared that if Lady Yarmouth did not yield to his solicitations he would make love elsewhere. He even made improper suggestions 'with peculiar emphasis and strength of voice' to one of the Queen's most respectable Ladies. 'The other day he went into the markett and bought himself six mulletts, talking so incoherently at the same time to [the fishwives] that they scarcely believed they had their own senses.' His headaches were so very severe that Sir Francis Milman warned the Queen that he apprehended 'an immediate apoplexy'.

Hearing reports of the King's disconcerting behaviour at Weymouth, the Prince more and more dreaded the forthcoming interview with his father, which at length took place on 12 November.

The King, looking extremely thin and worn, and accompanied by the Queen, the Princesses and the Dukes of Cumberland, Kent and Sussex, met him at the door. 'You have come, have you!' he said, and taking out his watch expressed himself pleased that his son, who was not renowned for punctuality, had arrived five minutes early. But he did not embrace him or even take his hand, treating him 'much as he would a foreign minister'. The conversation was entirely devoted to such topics as the weather and to scandal, 'a great deal of the latter, and *as the Prince thought*, very idle and foolish in the manner and running wildly from topic to topic [dwelling a good deal upon the reports of Mrs Siddons's elopement with Thomas Lawrence], though not absolutely incoherent'. The King monopolized the conversation, scarcely waiting for and certainly not listening to the Prince's replies, and once working himself up into a formidable rage. Yet the Duke of Cumberland thought the affair went off well enough; and the Duchess of Devonshire was told that the King's conversation 'though a little hurried' was never deranged. The Queen and the Princesses all kissed the Prince affectionately, and Amelia, overcome with joy to see her 'beloved brother' again, was in tears.

It was all 'highly interesting and gratifying', the *Morning Post* commented. 'From the result of this endearing interview which has taken place, we are induced to entertain the fond hope that a most sublime display of patriotic co-operation will ere long be presented to an anxious public.'

That weekend the family were all together at Windsor. William Fremantle, who had been the Marquess of Buckingham's private secretary, was also at Windsor and thought that the King 'seemed infinitely better and less irritated'. The Prince, on the contrary, 'was evidently very much out of spirits and in ill humour – hardly spoke a word to anybody and looked very ill'. It appeared to Fremantle 'quite impossible' that the reconciliation could last. Certainly it was not likely to do so while the King continued to make his regular and lengthy visits to Blackheath to see Princess Caroline and his darling little granddaughter, nor while the quarrel over Charlotte's upbringing, which had broken out earlier on in the year, remained unresolved.*

* The King was again at Blackheath a few days after the interview with his son. When she heard that he was coming, Princess Caroline wrote a characteristic letter to him: 'I am this moment Honor'd with your Majesty gracious intention of coming to Black-Heath; and beg leave to express how much I feel myself gratified of the very distinguish'd, and condsending mark of your Majesty favour and goodness towards me and my dear Daughter. my future Conduct will I trust proof to your Majesty, my gratitude and sincere devotion with which sentimens of Dutyful Respects, Veneration and truly attachment, I have the Honor to remain my whole like Sir your Majesty most humble and obedient Servant Niece and Subject Caroline' (RA 42397).

To Lady Glenbervie, her Lady of the Bedchamber, the Princess subsequently complained that the King's behaviour to her, 'when he was represented as recovered from his insanity and used to visit her alone and dine with her at Blackheath', was far from being as agreeable to her as her letters to him suggested. 'She says [Lady Glenbervie told her husband] the freedoms he took with her were of the grossest nature, that those visits always put her in terror, that she could not refuse to see her uncle, her father-in-law and King alone in her room, without declaring that he was still mad, while the Ministers ... wished it to be understood that he was in his senses' (*Glenbervie Journals*, ii, 55).

17

The Delicate Investigation
1804–1806

'There was strange goings-on'

PRINCESS Charlotte was now eight years old. A bright, excitable girl, with blue eyes, very blonde hair, well-shaped
hands and a skin badly pitted by smallpox, she had up till
now been in the care of a Governess, the Countess of Elgin,
widow of the fifth Earl of Elgin and daughter of Thomas
White, the London banker. Lady Elgin had at first been
assisted by Frances Garth, a niece of General Thomas Garth,
a modest, retiring, young woman who had been brought up
by her grandmother 'in a very plain and solid way'. Unfortunately 'poor Miss Garth', as the Prince referred to her,
had been unable to control her spirited charge and she had
had to be replaced by Miss Hayman, 'a very lively, entertaining person', whose character was more suited to the
upbringing of a 'pepper-pot'. Miss Hayman, who had met
the Prince 'full butt in the doorway' as she was crossing the
hall at Carlton House, was delighted by the appointment,
never having, in all her life, met anyone with 'such captivating manners' as the child's father.

The King, in turn, was increasingly entranced by his pert
little granddaughter. He used to say that 'there never was
so perfect a little creature'. He talked of her endlessly and,
so Princess Elizabeth told the Prince, whenever he saw her
he was in 'extacys of joy'. The Queen, too, was charmed by
her. 'The dear little girl behaved like an angel,' she informed her son after one of Charlotte's periodic visits to
Windsor from Warwick House, the dark gloomy mansion in
a cul-de-sac near Carlton House where she lived in London.

'She delighted the King with singing Hearts of Oak, as also with her reluctance of leaving us.' She pleaded often, 'Me go again to Grandpapa'.

She was a 'remarkably firm, thriving child, very lively, intelligent and pleasant ... amazingly clever and engaging ... really one of the finest and pleasantest children I ever saw,' confirmed the Earl of Minto, who saw her one day at Blackheath where she had been taken by her Governess to see her mother. 'The ladies played on the pianoforte and the little girl danced, which she likes as well as possible. She also sang *God Save the King* and *Hearts of Oak.* I wish my girls were so accomplished.' She was also a clever mimic, like her father. 'She tears her caps,' Miss Hayman reported, 'with showing me how Mr Canning takes off his hat as he rides in the park.'

The Prince confessed that when she was little he 'doated upon her', wrote frequent letters to Lady Elgin asking her to bring the 'dear little girl' to see him, and gave her instructions as to her care and education, accompanied by perpetual warnings about the dangers of exposing the child to evil influences 'from a certain quarter'. He did not know 'what would become of the *dear* infant' if it were not for Lady Elgin's diligence in ensuring that she was spared as much as possible the '*continual bad examples*' provided at Blackheath. In the strict and elaborate rules he made governing her care he laid special emphasis on the importance of ensuring that no unauthorized persons were ever allowed into her presence.

As Princess Charlotte grew up, the Prince continued to receive favourable reports of her character and attainments. She was rather delicate it appeared, and was finding it difficult to rid herself of a slight stammer which became painfully bad when she was excited; but she was growing 'much more engaging every day' in the Queen's opinion, and her aunts agreed that she remained a 'perfect delight'. 'She is quite an angel,' Princess Amelia wrote from Weymouth, 'and I never enjoy anything so much as her being with us.'

She was taken to Weymouth each summer, staying in apartments rented for her and her extensive Household on the
Esplanade, and going out every day to bathe, to ride about
in her carriage and to pick up shells on the sands at Portland. She was, so Lady Elgin said, 'perfectly well, good and
happy'.

It could not be denied, however, that she was also excitable
and temperamental, liable to fits of sudden temper. Her
Governess recorded an account of her behaviour one day
when she had become almost hysterical with delight at the
present of a watch. 'The happiness was inconceivable, jumping and frisking like a little lamb. The letter [accompany-
ing the present] was kissed over and over and the Governess
half smothered.' Later Charlotte wanted to show the watch
to one of her tutors, Mr Watson; it was clipped on to her
dress under a fur cape, so she went to her Governess for her
cape to be taken off. 'Unfortunately, not understanding the
intention, the Governess took [the watch off] to lay it on the
table – which was sadly contrary to her meaning, and the fire
was kindled. The storm was violent – declaring her poor
governess very cruel and at last that she would never do
anything right again, etc. Mr Watson, meekness itself, was
perfectly astonished ... I stood and let her go on, and when
she stopt I said, quite calm, "Sir, I am sorry you have seen
this sad scene, you could not have supposed it". "No,
Madam, I could not and I grieve I have seen it." '

Her father, too, grieved when he heard of such scenes,
and felt more than ever determined that his daughter must
be kept out of the hands of her mother from whom, he felt
sure, she had inherited her emotional instability. Her grandfather, on the other hand, thought that the child was not
often enough with her mother; and now that Charlotte was
eight, and new arrangements for her future education
would have to be made, he hoped that she would be allowed
to see her more often.

He proposed that the child should in future live at Windsor and be brought up under his eye and protection. The

Prince agreed to this provided that the King was to have 'sole and exclusive' care, intending by this phrase to convey his wish that Princess Caroline should have nothing to do with her upbringing.

The King's intentions were different. On 18 August 1804 he wrote to his daughter-in-law from the Queen's House telling her that he could not set out for Weymouth without first seeing her and his 'ever dear granddaughter'. Would they both, therefore, meet him at Kew, the following Monday? 'I trust,' the King added, 'I shall communicate that to you that may render your situation much more happy than you have as yet been in this country, but not more so than your exemplary conduct deserves. Believe me ever with the greatest affection. ...' In her excitement at receiving the flattering and promising communication, the Princess replied with even less regard to the rules of her adopted language than usual: 'This moment I have received your Majesty most gracious letter, which the contents mak's me so happy that I am afraid at will be impossible for me to express my sentiments of gratitude upon papar....'

The meeting took place as arranged, though Lady Elgin was horrified to find when she got to Kew with her charge that the King was there quite alone. He 'was waiting to receive Princess Charlotte and took us into the dining-room,' she reported. 'Yet when he said *he* was alone, and had come merely to see the Princess of Wales and Princess Charlotte I was quite stupified. He then added he was to take Princess Charlotte to himself, as the Prince wished it, but he could say nothing yet. His Majesty was going on when the Princess of Wales came.'

Princess Caroline had driven down separately, her suggestion that her daughter should travel with her in her carriage being overruled by the Governess who had thought it better that the child should not. Princess Charlotte, she explained, was 'so nervous' that she ought to remain quiet, otherwise 'she would be agitated from her joy'.

The King took his daughter-in-law and his 'little darling'

into an inner apartment. After a moment the child came
out again, carrying the King's private key to the garden
gate, saying it was his wish that she and her Governess
should go for a walk while her mother and grandfather had
a talk. When Princess Charlotte and Lady Elgin returned,
all four of them had dinner together, the King eating his
pudding and dumplings with a good appetite, but 'over-
exerting' himself. He was '*still weak*'.

The Prince was appalled when he learned what his father
had done, and now threatened to refuse his consent to en-
trusting the child to his care. After lengthy negotiations –
which had to be conducted through the Lord Chancellor as
the King still refused to write letters to his son himself – it
was eventually agreed that Princess Charlotte should live
at Windsor from June to January and remain at Warwick
House for the remaining four months of the year. Her
mother was to be allowed to see her at regular intervals but
only as a visitor.

John Fisher, Bishop of Exeter and later of Salisbury, whose
opinions of Popery and Whiggism coincided with the King's,
was appointed Superintendent of Education at a salary of
£600 a year; Lady de Clifford, a widow of impeccable character, succeeded Lady Elgin as Governess and was also paid
£600 a year; and Mrs Alicia Campbell reluctantly accepted
the post of Sub-Governess at £400 a year, an appointment to
which the Prince agreed very sulkily as the King had made
it without consulting him. A Sub-Preceptor (the Rev. George
Frederick Nott) was to teach the Princess Latin, English,
ancient history and religion; another clergyman was to in-
struct her in French, belles lettres and modern history. German, writing, music and dancing completed the subjects on
her curriculum which was regulated by a strict and rigorous
timetable:

From 8 to 9	Prayers and Religious Instruction
From 9 to 10	Breakfast and Walk
From 10 to 11.30	French and Modern History
From 11.30 to 12	Walk

From 12 to 1.30 . . . . . English, Latin, Ancient History
From 1.30 to 2 . . . . . Dressing
From 2 to 3 . . . . . Dinner
From 3 to 5 . . . . . An airing in the Carriage
From 5 to 7 . . . . . Writing, Music, Dancing
From 7 to 8 . . . . . Amusement

A figure of £12,000 – increased to £13,000 a year in 1805 – was allotted to the expenses of the Princess's Household which, as well as the Governess, Preceptors and tutors, a dresser and an under-dresser, included a coachman and postilion, three footmen, a page, a porter, an errand-boy, a gardener and six maids.

No expense or efforts were to be spared in the education and upbringing of this girl who could hope one day to become Queen of England; and her father expected to receive, and was given, regular reports of her progress which, from the neat letters she herself wrote to him, appeared to be most satisfactory. 'If you find any alteration in my conduct,' she dutifully wrote to him soon after her tenth birthday, 'I owe it to dear Lady de Clifford ... and Mr Knott who have all laboured to bring me to a sense of my duty, which I hope I shall feel more and more as I grow up. I can but repeat the same to you again, that I shall ever feel the sincerest love, regard, respect and attachment to you, my dearest papa; and that I shall endeavour all in my power to deserve your affection and approbation more and more....'

Those who knew Princess Caroline well had little reason to feel surprised that the Prince should be so determined that she exercise no influence over their daughter's upbringing. For the reckless indiscretion of her behaviour at Blackheath was becoming notorious.

Outwardly her Household at Montague House, to which she had by now moved from The Old Rectory at Charlton, appeared to be conducted well enough. In 1801 the Prince had had cause to complain about the 'excess in her expenditure'. He had sent the Duke of Kent to remonstrate with her,

and to point out that 'she could hardly expect a larger allowance than she had while the Prince's continued so reduced'.
She accepted this 'with great good humour', readily agreed
to all requisite economies, and promised to be more 'guarded
in future' about 'the great number of company' invited to the
house and about the amount of money she spent upon alterations and decorations. It was, both Lady Charlotte Campbell and Mary Berry thought, money ill-spent, for Montague
House was 'all glitter and glare and trick ... tinsel and trum-
pery ... altogether like a bad dream', 'the dining-room, *à la
Gothique*, very pretty, but the rest of the house in abominable taste'.

By 1802 the salaries of her establishment, which had been
running at about £5,000 a year, had been reduced to just
over £4,000. She was still, however, able to live in style and
comfort. As well as a Vice-Chamberlain, a Privy Purse, a
Mistress of the Robes (the Marchioness Townshend) and
two Ladies of the Bedchamber (the Countess of Carnarvon
and the Hon. Lady Sheffield), she was attended by three
Bedchamber Women, two Pages of the Backstairs and one
Page of the Presence. The staff included a maître d'hôtel, a
chef, a coffee-room woman, a gardener, six maids, two boys, a
porter and a dairyman.

Guests at Montague House had no reason, therefore, to
complain of the service; but what did strike many of them as
eccentric, to say the least, was the Princess's conduct. They
had to agree that her conversation was 'certainly uncommonly lively, odd and clever' – but what a pity it was, one
guest lamented, that she had 'not a grain of *common* sense',
that she had a 'coarse mind without any degree of moral
taste'. They had also to agree that she was an easy, friendly
hostess, but what a shame it was, as Lady Charlotte Campbell said, that her 'low nonsense, and sometimes even gross
ribaldry' were so shockingly disconcerting. Miss Hayman,
formerly Princess Charlotte's Sub-Governess and now Privy
Purse at Montague House, had the kindness to tell her so.
She suggested to the Princess that according to the manners

and modes of English society her practice of taking some man downstairs to the Blue Room and remaining there with him for some hours after dinner, while the other gentlemen were with the ladies upstairs in the drawing-room, could be considered highly improper. The Princess 'received this hint very ill' and told Miss Hayman that she 'neither desired nor liked' advice and was not in the least improved by it.

Certainly she disregarded it. Her private life, she insisted, was her own affair. It was nothing to do with anyone else that she loved babies, and – deprived of having any more by her husband – that she adopted several orphans and found-lings and placed them in the care of local foster-mothers who regularly brought them to see her. 'It is my only amuse-ment,' she explained to Lady Townshend, 'and the only little creatures to which I can really attach myself – as I hate dogs and birds – and every body must love something in the world. I think my taste is the most natural and whoever may find fault with it may do it or not.'

Nor was it anything to do with anyone else, the Princess thought, that she liked the company of young men and entertained them in private; that she liked to sit on the floor and talk scandal to her Ladies, or go for picnics and eat raw onions and drink ale (pronounced oil), or flirt with any pre-sentable man who came to the house.

Almost every guest at Montague House had some story to tell of her arch flirtatiousness. Walter Scott, whose *The Lay of the Last Minstrel* had made him famous at thirty-three and whose politics appealed to the Princess as much as his poetry, was one of these guests. Limping behind her down a dark corridor through which she was leading him to-wards the conservatory, he had hesitated because of his lame-ness at the top of a flight of steps. 'Ah! False and faint-hearted troubadour,' she had chided him coquettishly. 'You will not trust yourself with me for fear of your neck!'

Some, including William Lamb, thought that she was more or less insane. The Prince assured Lady Bessborough that he for one believed her so. Bishop Hurd also professed himself 'a perfect convert' to the hypothesis of insanity. And Lord Holland considered that 'if not mad, she was a very worthless woman'.

For years there had been all manner of rumours and scandals about her. The repeated visits of George Canning had been widely discussed. In the autumn of 1801 and again in 1802, there had been reports that the Princess was pregnant; and some time later the Prince had told Lady Bessborough that he himself had been told that she had had a child. But he had chosen to take no public notice of all the stories, until in the summer of 1805 he felt obliged to investigate them by an extraordinary accusation levelled against the Princess by one Lady Douglas, wife of Sir John Douglas, a lieutenant-colonel in the Marines who was a Groom of the Bedchamber to the Duke of Sussex.

Lady Douglas was an attractive, socially ambitious, spiteful and 'showy bold' woman whose origins were more humble than she liked it to be supposed. She and her husband lived near the Princess at Blackheath, sharing their house at this time with the gallant and garrulous Rear-Admiral Sir Sidney Smith under whom Sir John had served in the defence of Acre against Bonaparte. It was said that Lady Douglas and the Rear-Admiral had been conducting a long-standing love affair.

The Douglases and Admiral Smith, it appeared, had once been frequent visitors at Montague House, but there had been a bitter quarrel after the Princess had discovered that Lady Douglas had been spreading malicious stories about her behind her back. She had told Lady Douglas that she would be no longer welcome at Montague House and had subsequently, so it was alleged, written her anonymous letters, followed by obscene drawings of 'Sir Sydney Smith and Lady Douglas in an amorous situation'. The Princess had also, it was further alleged, sent Sir John Douglas an anonymous letter with a picture of 'Sir Sydney Smith doing Lady Douglas your amiable wife'. The Douglases had, in turn, accused the Princess of similar offences which they detailed in written statements.

The Prince had hoped that the matter would never come to such a pass. As Lord Erskine told the King, he had taken 'no steps whatever to make it the subject of public investigation; but manifested on the contrary the greatest desire to avoid it if possible'. He now sought the advice of the Prime Minister who told him, 'I do not know, Sir, what your Royal Highness must do; but I do know what *I* must do. I must lay the whole business, Sir, before his Majesty without the smallest delay.' Lord Thurlow was of the same opinion. 'Sir,' he said, 'if you were a common man, she might sleep with the Devil; I should say, let her alone and hold your tongue. But the Prince of Wales has no right to risk his daughter's crown and his brother's claims. ... The accusation once made must be examined into.'

The King sadly agreed to be 'entirely guided by his Ministers'. And so, in the summer of 1806, a Commission of Enquiry consisting of Lords Grenville, Erskine, Spencer and Ellenborough, with Sir Samuel Romilly, the Solicitor-General, as their legal adviser, was appointed to consider the strange case of the Princess of Wales.

Lady Douglas's evidence was considered first. It appeared from this that she had first met the Princess in 1801 and had been immediately struck by what a strange woman she was. The Princess had embraced her, and had told her what nice arms she had, that she had 'the sweetest black eyes she had ever seen, that she was a charming woman'. On a subsequent visit to Montague House, where she had found the Princess in bed, consuming 'an immense quantity of fried onions and potatoes and an equal amount of ale', they had talked of Lady Douglas's approaching confinement. The Princess had never seen an *accouchement*,' she said, so she would like to be present at this one; she would bring with her a bottle of port and a tambourine to keep up her friend's spirits. She was going to have a baby of her own, she confessed. Her habit of taking unwanted babies into her protection was not as innocent as it seemed. She had started this supposedly charitable work so as to make it no cause for comment when her own baby came to be born and was introduced into the Household. People would merely suppose that it was just another destitute child like all the others she had taken care of. No one would know that she was pregnant as she knew how to manage her dress; by putting cushions under it, it would seem that she was just growing rather fat. If the worst came to the worst and she were discovered, she would 'give the Prince of Wales the credit for it, for she had slept two nights in the year she was pregnant in Carlton House'.

'I have a bedfellow whenever I like,' she added; 'nothing is more wholesome.' Her room was most convenient for the purpose as it stood at the head of a staircase leading directly into the Park. 'I wonder you can be satisfied with only Sir John,' she said to Lady Douglas more than once, urging her to 'amuse herself, with Prince William of Gloucester, who would be quite amenable. She confessed that she had herself lain with Sir Sidney Smith who liked a bedfellow better than anybody else she had ever known. As for herself, she was 'a little devil in petticoats'. Lady Douglas did not know whether or not Sir Sidney Smith was the father of the baby boy to which the Princess told her she eventually gave birth, but she 'rather suspected' that he was.

Sir John Douglas evidently also suspected this to be the case. The Princess of Wales had often been to their house, he deposed in his turn; but she came, he thought, more to see Sir Sidney than himself or his wife. 'After she had been for some time acquainted with us, she appeared to me to be with child,' Sir John said. 'One day she leaned on the sofa, and put her hand upon her stomach, and said, "Sir John, I shall never be Queen of England." I said, "Not if you don't deserve it." She seemed angry....'

Other witnesses called by the Commission deposed that Sir Sidney Smith had often been to Montague House in 1802 and had stayed very late. Robert Bidgood, who had been twenty-three years in the Prince of Wales's service before becoming a Page of the Backstairs to the Princess, said that Sir Sidney had also been seen in the house early in the morning, 'a full two hours before company was usually expected, though the footman had let no one in'. Bidgood's wife, Sarah, said that she had been told in a conversation with Frances Lloyd, the coffee-room woman, that Mary Wilson, one of the housemaids, had once gone into the Princess's bedroom to make up the fire and had found her and Sir Sidney 'in such an indecent situation that she immediately left the room, and was so shocked that she fainted away at the door'. Frances Lloyd herself, who had been nearly twelve years in the Princess's service, deposed that once when she had been in bed with a bad cold, the doctor who had been summoned to treat her had asked her if the Prince ever visited Blackheath; the doctor had been curious to know because, so he had told her, the Princess was with child. Miss Lloyd added that one morning she was called to get the Princess's breakfast ready by six o'clock, which she had never been asked to do before; and when she opened the shutters she saw the Princess and a man walking about in the garden. Sarah Lampert, a servant of the Douglases and wife of their footman, confirmed that the Princess and Sir Sidney Smith used to walk about in the garden together, and sometimes at night in the Park. She said that Sir Sidney used to creep out of the Douglases' house late at night after the master and his lady were in bed, and that in the morning his bed was found not to have been slept in. The Princess's servants had told her, Mrs Lampert added, 'what a quantity of breakfast was eaten in her Royal Highness's bedchamber and what extraordinary things she sent for, for a lady to eat in bed – meat, chicken, tongue, etc.' They were not able to get into the room to clear the meal away 'until quite late in the day'.

Sir Sidney Smith was alleged not to be the only gentleman of whose company the Princess seemed excessively fond. She also spent a great deal of time alone in the company of

Captain Thomas Manby of the Royal Navy, particularly
during a visit in 1804 to Southend where Bidgood, who grew
accustomed to the sight of water-jugs, basins and towels left
unused in the morning outside the Princess's bedroom, believed that Captain Manby was inside; for it was common
gossip among the other servants that he frequently slept in
the house. One day Bidgood, so he claimed, had seen them
reflected in a looking-glass, kissing each other on the lips.*

Lady Douglas, in a letter she wrote to the Prince after her
examination, also reported that Captain Manby had been
seen kissing the Princess. Sir Sidney Smith had told her that
he had been to dinner with Manby at Montague House
'when he observed her seek Captain Manby's foot under the
table and when she had succeeded put her foot upon Captain Manby's and sat in that manner the whole evening,
dealing out *equal attention and politeness above board to
them both*; at length she got up and went out of the door,
looking at Captain Manby who followed and went behind
the door to let him pass through and kissed him behind the
door. Sir Sidney saw it and went home immediately.'

William Cole, who had been for twenty-one years in the
Prince's service before entering that of the Princess in 1796
as a Page of the Backstairs, agreed that she was 'too familiar'
with certain gentlemen, particularly with Sir Sidney Smith
and Mr Canning.† Cole gave evidence that one evening, on

---

* Thomas Manby, at that time in command of the frigate *Africaine*, married in 1810 and had two daughters. Promoted rear-
admiral in 1824, he died nine years later in a Southampton hotel from
an overdose of opium. George Manby alleged in his *Reminiscences*
that his brother had been offered £40,000 by McMahon to support
the Douglases' case, an offer which was indignantly rejected (Manby,
127). Lady Douglas accepted an annuity of £200 which was still being
paid in 1830 at the time of George IV's death (RA 29819–55).

† More would have been heard about Canning in the 'Delicate Investigation', so the Prince suggested to a mutual friend, Lady Bessborough, had he not deleted references to him in the evidence out
of respect for herself (*Granville Leveson Gower Correspondence*, ii,
204). In fact, the witnesses made only passing references to Canning,
though the Prince's suspicions about him were shared by others. Lord

returning to the Blue Room where he had just taken some sandwiches, he found the Princess and Sir Sidney Smith sitting close together on the sofa 'in so familiar a posture as to alarm him very much'. They had both appeared confused at the sight of him. He added that on a particular occasion he had seen the figure of a man wrapped up in a great cloak enter the house from the Park, and he 'verily believed' it was Sir Sidney Smith. He also declared that the Princess and Captain Manby had been seen constantly in each other's company; and that when Thomas Lawrence was in the house, painting a portrait of the Princess, there had been similar suspicious circumstances, and whisperings in the Blue Room behind locked doors after the Ladies of the Household had all gone to bed.

Cole further deposed that he had been dismissed from the service of the Princess soon after he had disturbed her on the sofa in the Blue Room with Sir Sidney, and that on visiting his former colleagues at Montague House he had been told by Mary Wilson that 'there was strange goings-on; that Sir Sidney Smith was frequently there; and that one day, when Mary Wilson supposed the Princess to be gone

---

Boringdon, who claimed to have been Canning's earliest adherent in the House of Lords, thought that he was probably guilty; and when Canning himself asked Lady Bessborough if she had heard the stories about him and the Princess and she replied that she had done, 'he neither owned nor denied' them. Lady Bessborough was 'staggered', yet afraid that the stories were 'in great part true' (*Granville Leveson Gower Correspondence*, ii, 205–6). At the time of the separation of the Prince and Princess in 1796, Canning had apparently been with her when she had received her husband's letter agreeing never to propose 'a connexion of a more particular nature' should any accident happen to their daughter. She had asked Canning how she ought to interpret the letter – so he told the Duke of Wellington who, in turn, repeated the story to Dorothea de Lieven, the Russian ambassador's wife – and Canning had 'decided peremptorily that it was a letter giving her permission to do as they liked, and they took advantage of it on the spot' (*Lieven Letters*, 98). Whether or not they were lovers then, there is nothing to suggest that there was anything improper in their relationship after 1800 when Canning fell in love with and married Joan Scott.

into the Library, she went into the bedroom, where she
found a man at breakfast with the Princess; that there was
a great to-do about it; and that Mary Wilson was sworn to
secrecy, and threatened to be turned away if she divulged
what she had seen'.

In July 1802, Cole concluded, the Princess was 'very large',
though towards the end of the year she was her usual shape
again.

All this seemed highly damaging. Yet other servants at
Montague House were ready to declare that they had not
noticed anything particularly improper in the Princess's behaviour. One maid who had been almost ten years in her
employment had never noticed any difference in her shape
and, although Captain Manby had certainly been a frequent visitor at Southend, the Princess's bed never looked as
though two people had slept in it. Another female servant
said she was sure that the Princess, whom she had known
for eleven years, had not been pregnant in 1802; and that
although the Princess was often alone with both Captain
Manby and Sir Sidney Smith, sometimes until two o'clock
in the morning, she had never noticed any impropriety. Nor
had the footman. Nor had the maître d'hôtel who agreed
that Sir Sidney Smith was often alone with the Princess, but
then so were Canning and other gentlemen. Nor had the
Page of the Presence, Thomas Stikeman, who had been in
her service ever since her arrival in England; he had never
observed the Princess behaving improperly. Admittedly Sir
Sidney Smith was often alone with her until a very late hour,
but that did not seem to Stikeman cause for unfavourable
comment; after all, she was consulting him about the decora-
tion of some of her rooms which were being 'altered in the
Turkish style'. To be sure he had been rather uneasy about
Captain Manby staying so late when they had been on holiday at Ramsgate; but he had himself observed nothing
improper, even though other servants had seen the Captain
in the house earlier than nine o'clock in the morning, and a
watchman had once found him 'concealing himself in a dark

passage leading to the Princess's apartments'. 'The Princess,' Stikeman said, 'is of that lively vivacity, that she makes herself familiar with gentlemen. ... Nothing led me from the appearance of the Princess to suppose she was with child, but from her shape it is difficult to judge when she is with child. When she was with child of the Princess Charlotte I should not have known it when she was far advanced in her time if I had not been told it.'

The Hon. Mrs Lisle, a sister of Lord Cholmondeley and one of the Princess's Bedchamber Women, was rather more severe. She did not think the Princess had been pregnant at the time in question. But she had certainly spent hours alone with Captain Manby and other gentlemen, including the Hon. Henry Hood, son of Admiral Lord Hood, the Governor of the nearby Greenwich Hospital, with whom she went out for rides in a little whisky. It was in the Princess's nature to do so; she preferred men's company to that of her Ladies. She behaved with them, Mrs Lisle disapprovingly observed, 'as any woman would who likes flirting'. Mrs Lisle could 'not have thought that any married woman would have behaved as her Royal Highness did to Captain Manby'.

The doctor who had attended at Montague House in 1802 and had treated the coffee-room woman's cold, denied he had made any remarks about the Princess's pregnancy. Sir Francis Milman who had also attended the Princess in 1802 said that if she had been pregnant he could not have helped noticing it. Sir Sidney Smith firmly rejected all suggestions that he had not acted with propriety. Captain Manby declared that the story of his having kissed the Princess was a 'vile and wicked invention', nor had he ever slept in a house occupied by her. He assured Lady Townshend that his conversations with her had been devoted to discussions 'relative to the equipment of her protégés who were going as midshipmen' with him. Thomas Lawrence admitted to having slept in the same house as the Princess, but he had never been alone with her behind locked doors and nothing had ever passed between them which he could 'have had the least objection for all the world to have seen and heard'.

This conflict of evidence obviously disturbed the Commission. Most of the hearsay evidence was, of course, valueless; and all the condemnatory evidence that came from the servants who had been in the employment of the Prince before his marriage was, to some extent, suspect. But there was other evidence that could not be ignored. Witnesses who could 'not be suspected of any unfavourable bias and whose veracity in this respect' there was 'no ground to question' had 'positively sworn' to conduct 'such as must, especially considering her Royal Highness's exalted rank and station, necessarily give occasion to very unfortunate interpretations'. The 'circumstances ... stated to have passed between her Royal Highness and Captain Manby must be credited'. There were far too many stories like the ones Lord Glenbervie told of the Princess – of her having sat next to Captain Manby at dinner, and after dinner on a sofa, of her having 'directed all her *looks*, words, and *attentions* to him', of her having stood up almost immediately he left the room, with the excuse that she had heard a baby crying, and of her going into an adjoining room to which she had a private key and in which she remained for about three-quarters of an hour.

The Commissioners were, however, happy to announce their 'perfect conviction' that there was 'no foundation whatever for declaring that the child now with the Princess [was] the child of her Royal Highness or that she was delivered of any child in the year 1802'.

This child, they decided, was born in Brownlow Street Hospital on 11 July 1802, the son of Samuel and Sophia Austin. The parents had come to London from Somerset to find work some years before; but the father, who suffered severely from rheumatism, had found it difficult to keep any job for long, and at the time of the baby's birth had recently been discharged from his employment at Deptford dockyard. The mother, who knew that poor women were given food in the kitchens of Montague House, went there herself in the hope of charity, taking her baby with her. The footman, Stikeman, suggested that the Princess might adopt the child if the mother could bear to part with it, and advised her to come back another day when her Royal Highness was there to see it. Mrs Austin took the advice, returned to Blackheath some days later, and was shown into the Blue Room. The Princess came in, touched the baby, whose name was William, under the chin, and exclaimed, 'Oh! What a nice one! How old is it?' The mother said, 'Six months.'

The Princess then turned away and spoke in French to one of her Ladies who told Mrs Austin that, if she could bring herself to part with the baby, he would be '*brought up and treated as a young prince*'. After a brief discussion the mother agreed, and when all arrangements had been made she was told to go into the coffee-room for some refreshments before she went home. The coffee-room woman was rather grumpy and disillusioning. 'I don't suppose the child will be kept in the house,' she said. 'I don't know what we shall do with it here; we have enough to do to wait on her Royal Highness.' It would probably be put out to nurse with the Steward's wife who looked after other children who were in the Princess's care.

Worried by these remarks, Mrs Austin returned to Montague House some time afterwards to make sure her baby was being properly cared for. She was invited into the house and told to look through a keyhole into a room where she saw the Princess walking up and down, nursing the baby and talking to him. Since then she had been back to Blackheath to see the child regularly, and to collect an allowance for the education of a younger child. She was quite satisfied that William was being well cared for, and deeply grateful for all the Princess had done for her and for her husband, who had now been found regular employment as a locker in the docks through the Princess's influence.*

*

* William Austin, or 'Willikin' as the Princess called him, was educated first at Blackheath, then at a school at Greenwich run by Dr

The Commissioners who had conducted 'the Delicate Investigation' confirmed that Princess Caroline was a kind-
hearted and generous woman; they had also declared that
she was not the mother of the child who lived in her house.
But their report had done nothing to abate her reputation
as a woman of inveterately rash behaviour. It may well be
that Lady Douglas was a mischief-maker and a liar, driven
by jealousy and malice to invent the charges she had made
in her statement; but it was just as likely that the Princess
had, in fact, told her that she was pregnant and made all the
remarks about bedfellows which she was alleged to have
made. Samuel Lysons, the antiquary, was one of many who
held the opinion 'that she endeavoured to make Lady
Douglas believe she was with child, and that though Lady
Douglas gave some of her evidence apparently inconsiderately yet that what she swore to was her belief'. Her husband, in the opinion of the Rev. Robert Finch, was certainly
a 'very honourable man'.

Charles Burney, the son of the musical historian. The Princess later
took him on her travels on the Continent, bringing him back to England in 1820. After her death he returned to Italy where his behaviour
became increasingly wild and strange until he was placed in a public
lunatic asylum in Milan in April 1830. Later he was removed to a
private asylum outside the town; and here he was maintained out of
the proceeds of a trust, which had been executed in his adoptive
mother's lifetime, amounting to about £150 a year – she left him
nearly everything in her will but her estate was insolvent. He was
brought home in 1845 to an asylum in England, Blacklands House,
Chelsea, where he was periodically examined and found to be 'so
lost and imbecile in mind that he requires the attention paid to a
child. He occasionally appears cheerful, and attempts to sing, but
never enters into conversation.' To the end he remained in 'the same
lost and fatuous condition as when admitted' (R A Geo. Box 13). He
died in 1849. The Princess paid for one of his two younger brothers
to be apprenticed to a firm of piano manufacturers and arranged for
the other to be found employment in a solicitor's office where he had
hopes of being articled at her expense. She died before his hopes
were realized, however; and by 1846, having lost eight of his thirteen
children after 'long and expensive illnesses', he had remained an ill-
paid clerk for thirty-one years (R A Geo. Box 13).

It was possible, too, of course, that the Princess had had a child in 1802; there were rumours enough to this effect, it being evidently 'common talk upon the Heath that year that the Princess was with child'. The Earl of Westmorland, who had been the Lord Privy Seal in his friend Pitt's administration, thought it worth while to write to Henry Addingon (by this time Lord Sidmouth) to tell him that a friend of his had been told by a reputable attorney that proof existed of such a birth. The proof was in the hands of Richard Edwards of Crane Court, Fleet Street, printer of a book about 'the Delicate Investigation'. Indeed, it was the opinion of that relentless gossip, Lord Glenbervie, that William Austin was certainly the Princess's illegitimate child – this was Mary Berry's opinion, too – and that he was not the only one she had had.

The Princess herself, though she also liked to say that the only '*faux pas*' she had ever committed was going to bed with Mrs Fitzherbert's husband, took pleasure in fostering such rumours. Her daughter believed that one of the foster-children in her care, Edwardina Kent – who was named, 'by way of a good joke', after the Duke of Kent – was her child by Sir Sidney Smith; and during a conversation one evening with Lady Glenbervie, a Lady of the Bedchamber, the Princess murmured in a 'kind of reverie', gazing at William Austin, 'It is a long time since I brought you to bed, Willy.' But another of her Ladies, Lady Charlotte Campbell, was assured that 'Willikin' was not her son. 'No,' the Princess said, 'I would tell you if he was. No, if such little accident had happened, I would not hide it from you. He is not William Austin, though; but, *avouez moi*, it was very well managed that nobody should know who he really is, nor shall they till after my death.'

In later years the Princess decided to elaborate this story: she confided in Henry Brougham's brother, James, that she had humbugged 'the whole set' of people involved in 'the Delicate Investigation'. William Austin, she now said, was the natural son of Prince Louis Ferdinand of Prussia, a

nephew of Frederick the Great, and had been brought over
to England 'by a German woman'. She had obtained a child
of a similar age and appearance from the Austins, and this
baby had been 'taken God knows where but sent away'; the
baby from Germany had been substituted in its place and
the Princess had contrived to ensure that Mrs Austin did not
see it for some time: 'She never knew or suspected that it
had been changed' and, of course, 'believed to that hour'
that the child was her son. In 1805 or 1806 Captain Manby
brought Prince Louis over to England and the Princess had
seen as much of him as she could. She insinuated that he had
been in love with her all his life until, courting death, he had
been killed at Jena. She, for her part, had always been attached to him and, as her heart was 'engaged to him', she had
never been able to love the Prince of Wales, though she
would have respected him if he had treated her well. She assured Brougham that her mind was much easier after telling
him this; he was the only person she ever had told. Subsequently she often asked him whether he thought Austin
really looked like a labourer's son, 'whether he did not betray
his blood by looking so like a German, and things of that
sort'.*

---

* This story has been generally discredited; but on her deathbed
she repeated the substance of it to Dr Stephen Lushington, one of her
counsel during the proceedings in the House of Lords in 1820. Towards the end of his long life, in September 1858, Lushington put the
story on record in response to a request by Lord Brougham.
  'I will tell you all I know as to W. Austin,' Lushington wrote. 'The
Queen on her deathbed informed me that W. Austin was not the person he purported to be, that he was in truth a son of a brother or
friend of Brunswick who was dead and that he had been clandestinely brought over from the continent. She then explicitly declared
that W. Austin was not her own child. She did mention who the
mother was but indistinctly.
  'When attending the funeral I was on board a vessel in the Elbe
commanded by Capt. Fisher, W. Austin being with him, a German
nobleman or General (I do not remember which) asked for permission
to see W. Austin; he immediately said you know his history and to
my great surprize repeated in substance what the Queen had said to

To those who knew the Princess well, these reckless statements seemed perfectly in character. She was constantly making such assertions, repeatedly blurting out remarks that were either incredible or offensive and often both, though sometimes vividly pertinent: 'Prince William of Gloucester would likely to marry me ... he is the grandson of a washerwoman.' 'The Duke of Kent is a disagreeable man and not to be trusted.' '[The royal dukes] all have pudding faces which I cannot bear.' 'The Duke of Cambridge looks like a sergeant, and so vulgar with his ears full of powder.' The Prince of Wales 'lives in eternal hot water and delights in it. If he can but have his slippers under an old dowager's table and sit there scribbling notes that's his whole delight. ... He has offered me 60,000 if I'll go and live at Hannover, but I never will; this is the only country in the world to live in. ... [I] ought to have been the man and *he the woman to wear the petticoats*. ... He understands how a shoe should be made or a coat cut, or a dinner dressed and would make an excellent tailor, or shoemaker or hairdresser but nothing else.'

But if the Duke of Cambridge was vulgar, it was generally agreed that the Princess of Wales herself was even more so. To Lady Hester Stanhope she was 'an impudent woman ... a downright whore ... she danced about exposing herself like an opera girl ... she gartered below the knee: – she was so low, so vulgar'. Others might be amused by her parties at Blackheath where a mechanical doll performed obscene antics, and her adopted, pampered child, 'Willikin', was dangled over the dining-room table to snatch his favourite sweetmeats from the dishes, knocking over the wine in the process. But Lady Hester was disgusted by the child. 'Once he cried for a spider on the ceiling,' she recalled, 'and, though

---

me respecting W. Austin's birth and parentage and he then added that Austin bore a great resemblance to his reputed father.

'I have no recollection of the name of this Consul or General. The enquiries made for him afterwards by order of Lord Liverpool produced no result' (Brougham MSS, 10, 268).

they gave him all sorts of playthings to divert his attention, he would have nothing but the spider. Then there was such a calling of footmen, and long sticks, and such a to-do! He was a little, nasty, vulgar, brat ... and so ugly. ... The P[rince]ss used to say to Mr Pitt, "Don't you think he is a nice boy?" To which Pitt would reply, "I don't understand anything about children." '

Lady Bessborough thought the Princess's levity was 'inconceivable'; Lady Sarah Spencer and her mother were so distressed to receive an invitation to Blackheath that they fled from Spencer House pleading a 'pre-engagement' with the Dowager Countess Spencer at her country house in Hertfordshire; while Mary Berry, who was presented to her at a ball at Henry Hope's house, wrote of her, 'Such an exhibition! But that she did not at all feel for herself, one should have felt for her. Such an overdressed, bare-bosomed, painted-eye-browed figure, one never saw. G. Robinson said she was the only true friend the Prince of Wales had, as she went about justifying his conduct.'

Having read the report of the Commission, the Prince discussed it with his elderly, cantankerous friend, Lord Thurlow, who persuaded him that the Commissioners had shown 'too great a degree of lenity to the Princess'. Although, he said, there 'might not be quite sufficient' evidence to 'commence an action for High Treason, still, from the circumstances of her imprudence, amounting nearly to positive proof ... they ought to follow it up by a recommendation to the King (which he ought instantly to sanction) of bringing in an Act of Parliament to dissolve the marriage'.

The Commissioners, of course, were not prepared to make any such recommendation. They had already gone further than in justice they ought to have done when they declared that the allegations of misconduct ought to be credited until they received some 'decisive contradiction' – which was to say that the Princess was to be presumed guilty until proved innocent, whereas her guilt was very far from being established. Lady Bessborough and Lord Boringdon might well have been right in supposing that Canning was her lover; there might well have been good grounds for the rumours which Richard Ryder, Member of Parliament for Tiverton, heard to the effect that, not content with Canning, she had seduced both the Duke of Cumberland and Sir William Scott; Lord Eldon might well have had reason to believe that Thomas Lawrence had also made love to her; her footman, Roberts, might well have been justified in declaring that the Princess was 'very fond of fucking'. But there was no actual proof of adultery; and the King accepted that there was not.

He did recognize, though, that his niece had been guilty of much 'levity and profligacy' and that he could not protect her from the consequences even had he wished to do so. He told the Queen that the Princess could no longer be received as an intimate of the family, 'and no nearer intercourse [could be] admitted in future than outward marks of civility'. It was not only that she had been shown to be morally unstable, but that she was, what was in his eyes quite as bad, 'a female politician'.

This was undeniably true, although her supporters continued to insist that it was all the Prince's doing.

18

Foxites and Pittites
1806–1809

'At the head of the Whig Party'

EVER since the innovation of the Prince's grand political
dinners at Carlton House, and the fall of Addington's government the Prince had begun to be 'a very great politician',
in the words of Thomas Creevey, and 'considered himself at
the head of the Whig Party'. He had become even more influential at the beginning of 1806 when Pitt died at the age
of forty-six, worn out by his exertions to win the war and to
stay in office. For Pitt's death opened the way for what
became known as the 'Ministry of all the Talents', a government less broadbased than its name implied, its most powerful members being friends of Fox. When Lord Grenville,
Pitt's successor as Prime Minister, insisted on Fox being included in the Cabinet as Foreign Secretary, the King resignedly remarked, 'I thought so.' But Fox's reception at the
Queen's House when he went to kiss hands on his appointment was not the ordeal that he had expected. The Queen's
civility, in fact, was 'quite marked', especially as she hadn't
spoken to him since 1788.

Two of Fox's closest colleagues, Earl Spencer and William
Windham, who had now returned to his side from the Portland group, became respectively Home Secretary and Secretary for War and the Colonies. Charles Grey, who was to
become Viscount Howick in April and, on his father's death
in 1807, the second Earl Grey, was appointed First Lord of
the Admiralty; the Earl of Shelburne's son, Lord Henry
Petty (later Marquess of Lansdowne) became Chancellor of
the Exchequer; Earl Fitzwilliam was appointed Lord Presi-

dent of the Council; Lord Erskine replaced Lord Eldon as Lord Chancellor; and the Earl of Moira came into the Cabinet as Master General of the Ordnance.

Although Moira was the only personal representative of Carlton House in the Cabinet – and although the Prince complained that he had been insufficiently consulted about the ministerial appointments – now that so many of his 'friends' were in office his influence was more considerable than it had ever been before. Indeed, Lord Melville thought it paramount; the power of the Crown had passed from St James's to Carlton House, and the Prince was now 'looked up to as the fountain of office, honour and emoluments'. Certainly both the Prince and Moira made numerous demands on the new government's patronage; and their recommendations, as Lord Holland said, 'were greatly attended to'. More peerages and honours were conferred at the Prince's instigation 'than at that of any other individual, Lord Grenville and Mr Fox alone excepted', though these honours 'were all more calculated to display his influence in procuring favours than to promote the interests of the party, or even his own. They were given to men who never professed attachment to the Whigs or to him, and who, it was foreseen, would take (as most of them subsequently did) the first opportunity of deserting both.'

The Prince was undoubtedly extravagant in his offers of patronage and showed great determination in ensuring that his promises were fulfilled. In the first list of recommendations for baronetcies sent to the King, every name that was not submitted by Fox was put forward either by Moira or the Prince. The Prince pressed one of his claims 'with uncommon earnestness', Grenville said, 'and had, I fear, actually committed himself by a written promise on the subject'.

While the Prince had been enjoying the new-found influence which the formation of the 'Ministry of all the Talents' had brought him, Princess Caroline had been drawing ever closer towards her husband's political opponents, declaring

that she was 'proud to name herself a Pittite'. Not only
Canning and Brougham, but such figures as Lord Castlereagh, Pitt's Secretary of State for War, Lord Eldon, the
dismissed Lord Chancellor, Eldon's friend and fellow arch-
conservative, the Duke of Cumberland, and Spencer Perceval, who had resigned as Attorney-General on Pitt's death,
were now regular visitors at Montague House, where they
provided the Princess with their encouragement and advice.

Perceval, Eldon, Canning and Castlereagh all dined with
the Princess at Montague House on 15 June 1806 and discussed the action to be taken now that the Commissioners,
who had undertaken 'the Delicate Investigation', had condemned her conduct without inviting her to defend it. It
was eventually decided that copies of the evidence should be
sent to the King together with a long and detailed defence
prepared under the direction of Spencer Perceval, who, convinced that the Princess was 'a much injured lady', went
about declaring that he would go 'to the Tower or to the
scaffold in such a cause'.

The King, as Lord Holland said, 'adroitly' referred Perceval's defence to the Cabinet, saying that he would be
guided by their advice. There was then a prolonged delay,
the Princess complaining of the 'long weeks of daily expectation and expense' having brought her 'nothing but disappointment', the Prince upbraiding the government for
displaying a 'total want of energy and good-will' towards
him and for not acting with vigour in his support which,
from 'the peculiar formation' of the ministry, he felt himself
'entitled to expect'.

It was not, however, until two days before Christmas that
the Cabinet gave their reply, and then it was an indeter-
minate one. In a dissenting minute the Secretary for War,
William Windham, expressed the opinion that the charge
originally brought against the Princess was 'as to part
directly disproved, and as to the remainder' rested on evidence that could not entitle it to the 'smallest credit'. But the
other members of the Cabinet said that they concurred with

the conclusion of the Commissioners and humbly submitted that the Princess's request to be once again received by the King and to be assured of his 'satisfactory conviction of her innocence' was a matter 'depending solely' on his Majesty's 'own feelings and persuasion'.

The King, dissatisfied with this vague reply, insisted on a more definite answer. So the Cabinet discussed the case again. They discussed it in Downing Street; they discussed it at the Foreign Office; they argued at length; they broke up and met again. On occasions their ponderous deliberations wandered far from the point at issue and entered into such subjects as the improbable contents of a box which, so Lord Moira had learned, had been entrusted by the Princess of Wales to a gentleman to deliver to Captain Manby. The gentleman, Admiral Nugent, notoriously absent-minded, had left this box in a hackney-coach, and had subsequently asked a friend, Moira's informant, who lived near the hackney-coach stand, to make inquiries about it and to recover it by offering, if necessary, a reward of two hundred guineas. The friend did manage to recover the box and, intrigued by the generous reward he had been authorized to offer, opened it.

Inside were many letters to Captain Manby, several trinkets, ornaments and 'souvenirs'. These last included a letter bag containing several hairs which Moira's informant had been 'married too long not to know came from no woman's *head*'. It being objected that this information could not very well weigh with the Cabinet at this stage of the business and that, in any case, the hairs were 'not of a nature to be produced as evidence even if the examination were to be instituted anew', Lord Ellenborough, the Lord Chief Justice, pleasantly observed that these exhibits *might* be admitted as evidence if the larger 'record to which they were originally attached' were also to be 'examined and compared in the court'.

All this, as the Lord Privy Seal observed, was 'laughable enough', but it did add considerably to the length of the

Cabinet's deliberations; and it was not until the end of January 1807 that they reached their conclusion. This was that there was no longer any justification for the Princess of Wales not being received into his Majesty's presence, but that the 'result of the whole case' did 'render it indispensable' that a 'serious admonition' should be conveyed to her Royal Highness. With their advice, the Cabinet enclosed a draft letter which they suggested the King should send to the Princess, telling her that although it was no longer necessary for him to decline receiving her, at the same time he was compelled to express his 'concern and disapprobation' of her conduct.

The King accepted the Cabinet's advice and despatched the letter to his daughter-in-law, merely striking out the words 'concern' and 'disapprobation' in the draft and substituting 'serious concern'. Immediately on receipt of the King's letter, the Princess replied saying that she would come to Windsor on the following Monday. Ever since the beginning of 'the Delicate Investigation' she had been bombarding the King with letters, begging for his 'gracious protection', appealing to his 'sound judgement and great clemency', pleading with him to be restored to his favour, assuring him that the evidence brought against her by 'strong and powerful enemies' was 'most malicious, atrocious and false', longing for 'that happy moment' when she might be allowed to appear again before his Majesty's eyes and to receive once more the assurance from his own mouth that she had his protection.

On receipt of this last letter, announcing that she would come to Windsor on Monday, the King hastened to acquaint her that he would prefer to see her in London and would let her know what day, 'subsequent to the ensuing week', would be convenient for him.

Here the matter ended for the moment, as in March 1807 the so-called 'Ministry of all the Talents' fell. Fox had proved himself an excellent Minister and his authority had been unquestioned; but in the summer of 1806 he had become seriously ill and by September he was dead. Grenville, in hope of gaining greater strength for the government in Parliament, had called a general election. And although over forty more Members believed to be in general sympathy with the ministry had been returned, Grenville's power, now that Fox had gone, had soon been shown to be severely weakened. The new ministry managed to abolish the slave trade, but, falling out with the King over the Roman Catholic Militia Bill, it collapsed in ruins.

The Prince did nothing to try to save it. Annoyed with Grenville for declining to take up the still burning question of his debts, for not supporting him more strongly in his quarrel with the Princess, and for treating him with 'the most marked neglect', failing to consult him in any one important instance, he stood aside, an idle spectator of its dissolution. In any case, as he told Moira, since the death of poor Fox he had 'ceased to be a party man'. In his dear friend's lifetime it had been the pride of his like to acknowledge himself in alliance with him; now that he was dead, he himself was politically 'neutral'. So the Whigs were out of office once more.

The government that succeeded the 'Talents', under the uncertain and reluctant leadership of the Duke of Portland, was a sadly divided one. But it included many of the Princess's friends: Canning became Foreign Secretary, Spencer Perceval, Chancellor of the Exchequer, Lord Eldon, Lord Chancellor, and Lord Castlereagh, Secretary for War. And one of the Cabinet's earliest acts was to confirm their predecessors' view that there was no longer any need for the King to decline receiving the Princess of Wales into his presence. The Cabinet suggested that, since the evidence produced against her was 'undeserving of credit', she should be admitted with 'as little delay as possible' and should be 'received in a manner due to her rank and station'. It also noticed in a separate minute dated the same day, 21 April 1807, the Princess's request to be allotted 'some apartments in one of the royal palaces' more convenient to Court.

The King agreed to this request, allowing her apartments at Kensington Palace which the Princess accepted 'under the full confidence' that when an apartment at St James's could be 'made vacant' it would be allotted to her. But, as the King replied to the Home Secretary, Lord Hawkesbury, who sent him the Cabinet's minutes, he felt some little time was necessary for him to prepare for an interview with the Princess which he had not expected to take place so soon and which could not 'in its nature be very pleasant'.

The Prince, for his part, was continuing to insist that the interview ought not to take place at all, and that the only hope of removing 'all chance of future discord' was a formal separation. Despite these protests the Princess was received at Court on 4 June. The Prince, who was also there, did not speak to her, talking to his sisters with his back to his wife so that they could not speak to her either, even if they had wanted to. As the Prince and Princess left, Lady Bessborough noticed that they 'both looked contrary ways, like the print of the spread eagle'.

More than ever determined to have as little to do with her as possible, the Prince went out of his way to ensure that they never met by chance. For fear lest he should see her, he did not make a courtesy call on her mother, his aunt, the Duchess of Brunswick, when she arrived in England in the summer. And when it became so hot that he thought it advisable for Princess Charlotte to leave London earlier than usual, he did not want to send her to Windsor in case her mother should use it as an excuse for frequent visits there, making it impossible for him to visit his family without the risk of meeting his wife. The King and Queen agreed, considering that until all 'unpleasant matters' were past and 'quiet restored', it would be far better to find a house for Princess Charlotte 'near the seaside'.

Although the Princess's behaviour seems to have become

rather less open to reproach after 'the Delicate Investigation', it was still far from discreet. She continued to 'dress very ill, shewing too much of her naked person'; she still continued happily to flirt with a varied assortment of men of all ages from the elderly pot-bellied lawyer, Sir William Scott, to the much younger Lord Henry Fitzgerald; she encouraged the advances of both John William Ward, afterwards Earl of Dudley, and William Henry Lyttelton, afterwards third Lord Lyttelton of Frankley – though Ward, for one, declared that he had no wish to take advantage of her fondness for him. 'When Ward and Lyttelton first began to frequent Kensington, Ward said to the other, he thought the Princess had cast a favourable eye upon him. Lyttelton replied, "No, I only fan the flame which you have kindled." On which Ward rejoined with one of his arch and malicious looks, "I had much rather be the bellows than the poker." '

William Eliot, a young Lord of the Treasury, described a 'long, long Friday, Saturday and Sunday' he spent in the Princess's company a few months after she had been received at Court again. As the only other man present was the Princess's Vice-Chamberlain, 'all the whispers, all the glances, all the nods, all the endless etceteras' were directed towards him. 'I certainly never saw nor heard anything at all like the style of proceeding,' he wrote. 'Indeed I was perfectly convinced ... that the poor woman is downright mad. It is quite out of the question giving you any sample of the conversation. ... One night I had the honour to play at chess with her till 2 o'clock in the morning with [three of her Ladies] gaping in attendance, and all the rest of the world gone to bed.' Another night, Eliot was taken out for a walk alone in the dark with her for he knew not how long; another evening, also for a seemingly endless time, he wheeled her about the grounds in a garden chair. 'Being thus persuaded as I am still that she was quite mad, and that a raving fit might break out from one minute to another,' he concluded, 'I leave you to guess the extent of my misery.'

To the Prince, what was above all else intolerable about

his wife was her continuing popularity. This was much increased by the sympathy felt for her on news of her father's
death from wounds received at the battle of Auerstädt.
Also, the Prince had been virulently condemned for bringing her to face charges which, it was suggested, he had himself concocted. The *Morning Post*, no longer his supporter,
expressed its sympathy for 'a truly *virtuous* and *illustrious*
female' who had for many months been 'the object of the·
most foul and infamous calumny ever advanced by the most
unprincipled of men'. She no sooner entered a theatre than
the audience broke out into tumultuous applause which
clearly delighted her as much as it distressed the Prince
who was, as Lord Fitzwilliam said, more susceptible to adverse expressions of public opinion than any other man
alive.

Those who knew her more intimately than most of the
members of theatre audiences, however, had to agree with
Lord Minto who regretted that one could never feel sure
that she would 'act prudently or honestly for any time'. At
this stage in her career, for instance, she quarrelled with the
men who had previously supported her and were now in
power. Spencer Perceval, who no longer had any cause to
publish the defence that he had compiled for her when in
opposition, and who destroyed all the printed copies he could
get hold of, was 'a presumptuous, foolish lawyer'; Lord
Eldon was 'a vulgar bore'; all their colleagues were 'drivel-
lers'. On the other hand, the previous Prime Minister, Lord
Grenville, who had also been a driveller when supported by
the Prince of Wales, was a paragon to her now that he had
incurred her husband's displeasure. She was, as Canning
observed, naturally given to opposition.

She was also still naturally given to extravagance, if not
on the same dramatic scale as her husband. The economies
to which she had agreed in 1801 had long since been forgotten. Although she received an allowance of £12,000 a
year from the Prince, together with an additional £5,000
from Parliament which had also put up £34,000 for the cost

of her house, her admitted debts amounted to £49,000. By 1808 her unpaid tradesmen had become so exasperated that, after an unavailing appeal to Spencer Perceval as Chancellor of the Exchequer, they had threatened to stop all supplies to Montague House.

The government's view was that it was not the public's responsibility to settle the Princess's debts, but that of the Prince, who had an income of the most generous size. The Prince argued that, even if he were willing to settle the debts of so unworthy a woman, he could not possibly do so. Ministers countered with the unpalatable truth that if the Prince did not make it possible for her to pay her creditors, the public's hostility would fall on him not on her, and he was already so disliked that the probability of increased unpopularity would scarcely bear contemplation. To this argument the Prince felt bound to give way. He agreed to pay off her debts by quarterly instalments – though he still could not discharge all his own – and to increase her income of £17,000 a year on condition that any future debts she might incur would be borne by herself.

Even this sacrifice seemed to the Prince not too high a price to pay for the sake of averting further unpopularity. He persevered, as best he could, in his determination to remain aloof from politics, though he could not forbear despatching a two-line reply to Spencer Perceval's rather fulsome letter informing him that he had accepted office as Prime Minister on the Duke of Portland's death. Lord Moira thought he saw 'the very curl' of the Prince's lip when his fancy was 'tickled at giving so civil a rebuff to the advances of the tiny Premier'. He abandoned his open support of Catholic relief, in case, so he said, his continued advocacy might provoke a return of the King's insanity for which his family and the country would blame him. And for fear of becoming involved in the calumny, he even continued in a 'state of neutrality' when his brother, the Duke of York, fell so drastically in the public esteem on being accused of appalling misdemeanours at the Horse Guards.

The charge brought against the Duke by Colonel Gwyl-
lym Lloyd Wardle, the radical Member of Parliament for
Okehampton, was that he had used the patronage at his
disposal as Commander-in-Chief at the Horse Guards for
the benefit of his former mistress, Mrs Mary Anne Clarke,
a flamboyant and extravagant actress. It was alleged that
Mrs Clarke had accepted money from officers who wanted
promotion or employment, and that the Duke not only
knew of her activities and agreed to her recommendations
but actually shared in the proceeds.

Wardle's charges were eagerly supported by other radicals,
including Samuel Whitbread, one of the Members for Bedford. The Prince, seeing in them an attack on the whole
royal family, at first declared that he would stand by his
brother. As more and more witnesses gave evidence, however, and as the charges against the Duke appeared to be
hardening, the Prince gradually began to withdraw his support. There were many who urged him to do so and thought
him wise to do so. Lord Temple, later Duke of Buckingham
and Chandos, who had been a junior Minister in his uncle
Lord Grenville's administration, strongly advised him not to
interfere as he might otherwise become identified with the
Duke's disgrace. George Tierney, who had also served as a
junior Minister under Grenville, agreed that the Prince
would be well advised to remain aloof; and so did Thomas
Tyrwhitt, now Member for Plymouth.

The Prince obviously felt uneasy in his neutrality, and
several times wavered towards his original position of open
support. The King sent a message to him asking him to
make it clear that he stood behind his brother and the government who supported him, while the Queen pleaded with
him to do so for the sake of his father who was beside himself with worry. But the Prince still hesitated. He had never
been on cordial terms with the Duke since his failure to gain
promotion in the Army and what he took to be the Duke's
shifty behaviour during their father's illness in 1804. They
were civil to each other when they met, but observers noticed

that the Prince's attitude was formal and stiff. As the Duke of Kent said, the Duke of York had always been his father's favourite, the Prince being his mother's, and this pronounced preference, combined with 'various events' which had taken place since the Prince had adopted his early line of opposition in politics, had widened the breach between the two. There was '*apparent* good standing' between them, but it went 'no further than *that*'.

As though to excuse himself for his disobliging attitude over the Clarke scandal, the Prince complained that his brother had never consulted him about the matter, nor had the government, so why should he interfere to save them now? In any case, even if the Duke were not guilty of all the charges, he had not paid the allowance to Mrs Clarke that he had promised her, and this was shabby of him. Nevertheless, the Duke was his brother after all, and he did not want to appear actually hostile. He therefore told McMahon, who was now Member of Parliament for Aldeburgh, to vote for the Duke when the time came, though he refrained from making similar requests of the Dukes of Northumberland and Norfolk who between them controlled the votes of many other Members. 'This,' Fremantle observed disdainfully, 'is only another proof of his great weakness and indecision.' As it happened, these additional votes were not needed. The House decided by a majority of eighty-two that the Duke was not guilty of corruption or of conniving at his mistress's corruption. Since he had obviously discussed his official business with her, though, he was dismissed as Commander-in-Chief.

The Prince emerged from the sad affair with his reputation more tarnished than ever.

19

Princess Charlotte and Minny Seymour
1806–1809

*'How aimably polite and fascinating his manners
are on his own ground'*

IN such unhappy times as these the Prince was thankful to
escape to Brighton where he was so much better liked than
he was in London.

Brighton had grown and flourished to an extraordinary
degree since the Prince's first visit there in 1783; and had
become, according to the proud if somewhat ambiguous
boast of the *Brighton Directory* of 1800, 'the most frequented
[and] without exception one of the most fashionable towns
in the Kingdom'. The population had risen to over 7,000 and
handsome houses were still being built on every side. The
graceful Royal Crescent, begun in 1798, was finished, at last,
nine years later, and its builder in celebration of the event
had erected a vast statue of the Prince of Wales on the grass
in front of it. It represented the Prince in his colonel's uniform making a suitably heroic gesture; but the soft stone
from which it was carved was not strong enough to withstand the salt sea breezes, and one of its arms consequently
fell off, misleading visitors into supposing that it represented
the great Lord Nelson.

West of the Royal Crescent, on the Steine, stood Mrs Fitz-
herbert's attractive new house – built for her by William
Porden at a cost of £6,300 – next door to the rather larger
one in which, during his occasional visits, the Duke of
Marlborough was cared for by a staff of forty servants.
Nearby was the Prince's Marine Pavilion, slightly altered
in recent years by Holland's nephew and assistant, Peter
Frederick Robinson, who had made it appear less classically

austere by removing the statues from beneath the cupola and adding green, tent-shaped metal canopies to the balconies. Robinson had also added two oval rooms, one a dining-room, the other a drawing-room, as wings projecting at angles from the eastern front.

Some years before, the Prince had entertained the idea of altering the appearance of the Pavilion in a far more drastic way. In 1801 Henry Holland had made some sketches for a new exterior in the Chinese style which it was estimated would cost £9,500; and in 1805 William Porden, Holland's successor as the Prince's architect, had also made some Chinese sketches. These were never put into effect, however. Porden, who had once been a pupil of Samuel Pepys Cockerell, Surveyor to the East India Company, was deeply interested in the Indian movement in architecture which his master, Cockerell, had applied at Sezincote in Gloucestershire, a large house that he had designed for his brother, the nabob, Sir Charles Cockerell. The Prince also admired Sezincote; and, after seeing it, seems to have discarded the idea of a Chinese pavilion in favour of an Indian one. He asked Humphry Repton, who had laid out the gardens at Sezincote, to come to Brighton 'to deliver his opinion concerning what style of architecture would be most suitable for the Pavilion'. Repton's views coincided with those of the Prince and by 1807 he had finished designs for an Indian pavilion which his patron found 'perfect'.

But although the Prince announced his intention of carrying the work into 'immediate execution', he had for the moment to be content with building stables and a riding house, an immense structure in the Indian style, which was finished at a cost of over £55,000 in 1808 and provided, under a huge central cupola, eighty-five feet wide, stabling for fifty-four horses as well as living accommodation for the ostlers and grooms.*

* The stables and riding house took over three years to build, partly owing to the difficulty of obtaining timber of sufficient size for the vast dome during the French blockade of continental ports,

A great deal of money had also been spent on remodelling and redecorating the interior of the Pavilion itself. Here in 1802 a Chinese gallery had been made for some lovely Chinese wall-papers that had been given to the Prince, and a Chinese corridor had been formed 'of stained glass, of an oriental character, and exhibiting the peculiar insects, fruit, flowers, etc. of China'.

The taste for *Chinoiserie* had become rather less fashionable in England since the Emperor Ch'ien-lung's rebuff of Lord McCartney's mission in 1794; but the Prince's own enthusiasm was unimpaired. He dismantled his Chinese Room at Carlton House and brought its contents to Brighton, together with all manner of Chinese porcelain and furniture, bamboo sofas and lacquered cabinets, weapons and curios, ivory junks and pagodas, lanterns and uniforms. In the Chinese corridor there were even larger-than-life-size figures of Chinese fishermen in flowing silk robes dangling lanterns from their rods.

Lady Bessborough – who was told by the Prince that he had chosen to decorate the Pavilion in the Chinese taste 'because at the time there was such a cry against French things, etc. that he was afraid of his furniture being accused of jacobinism' – thought it all 'really beautiful in its way'. She had no idea that the 'strange Chinese shapes and columns could have looked so well'. It was in 'outré and false

---

but more particularly because the Prince could not afford to pay the tradesmen at work on it. 'I am harassed with letters from the tradesmen at Brighton,' Porden complained to the Prince's Vice-Treasurer on 22 January 1807. 'The distress of many of these creditors is I believe very great and the clamour against his Royal Highness will be in proportion. ... The stoppage of money at this quarter has been particularly distressing to me ... the naked timbers of the roof of the riding house stand exposed to all weathers, a monument of disgrace to his Royal Highness and all concerned' (RA 33593–4). In June Porden felt obliged to renew his complaint: 'My workmen complain heavily that they are not paid while the tradesmen employed at Carleton House regularly receive their money; a complaint that I know not how to answer' (RA 33595).

taste', of course, but 'for the kind of thing as perfect' as could be. Mary Berry would not agree with her. The effect, she thought, was 'more like a china shop ... than the abode of a Prince. All is gaudy without looking gay,' she recorded in her journal; 'and all is crowded with ornaments without being magnificent ... all is Chinese, quite overloaded with china of all sorts and of all possible forms, many beautiful in themselves, but so overloaded one upon the other.'

In the exotic surroundings of the Marine Pavilion the Prince was to be seen at his most happy, charming and re-laxed. Thomas Creevey who was a frequent visitor through-out the autumn of 1805 said that the Prince behaved with the greatest good humour as well as kindness to everyone; 'he was always merry and full of his jokes, and any one would have said he was really a very happy man'. He said repeatedly himself that he would never be as happy when he was King as he was then. Lady Jerningham, who also saw a good deal of him at this time, agreed that he was full of 'affability and good humour'. 'Your father sat by him some time on a couch,' she told her daughter, 'and they were mak-ing jokes and laughing most heartily. ... It is really not to be described how aimably polite and fascinating his manners are on his own ground – the most finished civility, joined to the utmost degree of good-natured affability.'

He had put on weight again, despite the use of a 'vapour bath' which he had bought 'with full equipment' that sum-mer; but he had lost little of his grace, and his charm was as captivating as ever – at least to those who did not pre-sume to become over-familiar with him: as Lord Thomond remarked, he observed 'with nice attention any encroach-ment upon his importance'.* He still drank a good deal, and

---

* It was owing to such 'encroachment' that the Prince, many years before, had fallen out with his uncle, the Duke of Cumberland, whose 'style was so low that, alluding to the Principality of Wales, the Duke called his nephew *Taffy*. The Prince was offended at such indecent familiarity and begged it might not be repeated – but in vain' (Walpole, *Last Journals*, ii, 405).

liked to get his guests drunk when he could; but he was rarely now drunk himself, though sometimes he appeared a little unsteady when he went after dinner to the Assembly Rooms at the Castle Inn. Here the other guests clambered up on to benches to get a look at him. Sometimes in his own house he had to make excuses to his partner and leave the floor when the wine he had drunk made him too dizzy to dance; and once he was taken violently ill with 'an inflammation on his stomach' which the Duke of Cumberland attributed to his 'drinking hard three days successively' with his guests at the Pavilion. But, under the benign influence of Mrs Fitzherbert, his days of regular, habitual drunkenness were past. He now took trouble to avoid most of those inveterate drunkards who in the past had looked to him for toping company. When the Duke of Norfolk came on his annual visit from Arundel, the Prince made excuses not to drink with him after dinner, pleading that he had important letters to answer, and leaving Norfolk to go on drinking with the Duke of Clarence. Norfolk did not take too kindly to this treatment and showed that he was affronted. So one evening the Prince took another of his guests, Thomas Creevey, aside and said to him 'stay after everyone is gone tonight. The Jockey's got sulky, and I must give him a broiled bone to get him in good humour again.' So Creevey stayed; but, the drink overcoming him, he fell asleep. He woke to find Norfolk snoring contentedly, while the Prince and the Duke of Clarence were deep in an animated discussion as to 'the particular shape and make of the wig worn by George II'.

Occasionally the Prince was sulky himself; but he could soon be brought round, as the Duke of Norfolk could. To one young lady who had given some slight offence he showed that he was displeased by bowing to her curtly as she arrived and giving her no more than a 'little parting shake of the hand' when she left. The next morning when she arrived she made him a curtsey 'perhaps rather more grave, more low and humble than usual (meaning – "I beg your pardon

dear foolish, beautiful Prinny for making you take the pet")'.
Immediately he held out his hand, and all was forgiven.
One of Sir Philip Francis's daughters recorded an equally
characteristic story of the Prince's essential good humour.
Her brother, Philip, with whom he often sang at the Pavilion, was rendering with him one evening an Italian hunting
song when Francis 'suddenly found the full face of the Prince,
somewhat heated by the eagerness of his performance, in
immediate contact with his own; and this circumstance,
combined with that of the loud bass tones in which his
Royal Highness was singing the words, *"Ritornoremo a
Clori, al tromontar del dì"*, striking him in some ludicrous
point of view, he became absolutely unable to resist the
effect on his nerves, and burst out laughing. The Prince
evidently perceived that his own singing had produced the
unreasonable laughter, but, instead of showing his displeasure at a rudeness which, however involuntary, would
have been resented by many far less illustrious persons, he
only called the offender to order with the words, "Come,
come, Philip!" his countenance betraying at the same time
a strong inclination to join in the laugh himself.'

A friend of Francis's sister, Sarah – whose little daughter
could often be seen at Brighton sitting on the Prince's knee
and eating sugar plums – was entranced by evenings spent
at the Pavilion. 'The Prince's talents for conversation and
powers of entertainment' were, she thought, 'truly extraordinary and delightful'. She shared to the full the Francis
girls' 'extreme admiration of all his amiable qualities, fascinating manners and uncommon accomplishments', and
she, like them, had to acknowledge her *'weakness'* for him.

Dinner at the Pavilion was served pretty punctually at six
o'clock, and it was a meal of surpassing excellence. 'The like
I never saw, and the like I probably shall not see again,'
wrote a highly contented clergyman, who had been flattered
to be asked to say grace 'in the best way that ever such an injunction was given'. 'A more cheerful meeting never passed,
there was as much decorum as if we had been dining at the

table of the most correct among our bishops. Such music, such brilliant conversation, such a profusion of luxuries – the Master of the feast so condescending, and gracious.' A more fastidious guest, Lady Bessborough, agreed that dinner at the Pavilion was always excellent, though she had cause to complain that the dining-room, like the other rooms in the Pavilion, was appallingly hot. There were usually about fifteen guests, one of whom was always Mrs Fitzherbert, who was 'very fat' now, according to Mrs Calvert, though still attractive despite a set of 'not good false teeth'. After dinner Mrs Fitzherbert and one or two others played cards; while the Prince talked to those who – like himself – did not enjoy cards; or listened to his band; or got out his maps to discuss the progress of the war, to find the site of the most recent battle and to display his 'vast powers of recollection in military information', the accuracy of which, so Sir Nathaniel Wraxall said, 'excited astonishment' even amongst experienced soldiers.

Sometimes, having had a little practice shooting with an air-gun at a target fixed at the far end of the room, the Prince would introduce a performance on the organ by his Organist in Ordinary, Charles Wesley; or a pianist would be invited to play upon the 'curious fine-toned six octave grand piano in black ebony case' which he had bought for £680 in 1808.

The band stopped playing punctually at midnight when servants came in with sandwiches and wine.

The Prince went to bed late and got up very late. Most mornings he could be seen sitting on the balcony of Mrs Fitzherbert's house – to which, it was believed, there was an underground passage from the Pavilion – or promenading along the Steine, bowing with varying degrees of elaboration and with a grace 'universally admired' to friends and acquaintances, or greeting a favoured and favourite friend with 'literally open arms'.

The friends were remarkably varied. Sir Philip Francis was so frequently a guest at the Pavilion that the set of rooms he occupied there were named after him. A room was also always available for Sheridan, once again one of the Prince's closest and most indulged companions. Despite his age – he was fifty-five in 1806 – Sheridan still behaved like the wild young man he had once rejoiced in being. He would come into the drawing-room disguised as a police officer and arrest the Dowager Lady Sefton for playing some unlawful game; he would creep amongst the guests during an exhibition of phantasmagoria, and in the darkness sit upon the lap of the haughtiest lady in the room; he would go into the kitchen at any hour that he felt hungry and, by cajoling the servants – making them laugh by telling them that if he were Prince of Wales they would all have much better accommodation than *this* – he would soon have everyone waiting upon him.

Late one night he went to see if he could find a bit of supper, was soon provided with what he wanted, 'ate away and drank a bottle of claret in a minute', then returned to the ballroom where he was still dancing between three and four o'clock in the morning. The Prince continued to regard him, for all his follies and debaucheries, as 'a man that any prince might be proud of as his friend'.

In marked contrast to Sheridan were the exquisite, meticulous George Brummell and the gruff old Lord Thurlow, both often to be seen in the Prince's company. 'Beau' Brummell, sixteen years younger than the Prince, had established his reputation for social elegance, wit and meticulous appearance while still a schoolboy at Eton and an undergraduate at Oriel College, Oxford. Struck by his manners, his dress and pert self-confidence, the Prince presented him with a cornetcy in his regiment when he was only fifteen, and thereafter their friendship became firm. Occasionally the Prince was put out by some peculiarly sardonic remark of his protégé, whose reputation was such that he was commonly supposed to have disdainfully jilted a woman on discovering that she ate cabbage. The Prince was also offended sometimes by the deep reverence with which Brummell's views on fashion in dress were treated, as if *he* rather than the Prince himself were the arbiter of taste in such matters. However, the Prince's admiration for his young friend was unfeigned. He went to watch him dress and stayed on to dinner. It was said that his graceful way of opening a snuff-box with one hand was copied from Brummell, though the Prince did not really like the snuff which he bought in such large quantities from Fribourg and Treyer (and kept in an astonishing variety of valuable snuff boxes), either brushing his nose slightly with the pinch or dropping it altogether before it reached his nose. It was even alleged that he 'began to blubber when told that Brummell did not like the cut of his coat'.

Thurlow was a man of utterly different cast from Brummell. He was always dressed in bulky, old-fashioned clothes, huge cuffs and buttons, long ruffles and a vast wig. He had the biggest, bushiest black eyebrows that Creevey had ever seen and a voice like 'rolling, murmuring thunder'. The Prince always behaved towards him with the 'most marked deference and attention'; and he had good reason for doing so, for although Thurlow was 'the politest man in the world to ladies', he was very rough with men. When he caught them out in some unfortunate slip or ridiculous observation he never let go of them. Creevey, who took care to keep clear of him, had seen 'the sweat run down their faces from the scrapes they had got into'. He did not, of course, mix very well with some of the other guests at the Pavilion. One day during the race week he found himself invited to dinner at the same time as Sir John Lade. 'I have, Sir,' he told the Prince gruffly when informed of this unfortunate juxtaposition, 'no objection to Sir John Lade in his proper place, which I take to be your Royal Highness's coach-box, and not your table.'

A far more appealing person to be seen from time to time at the Pavilion was a little girl, Mary Seymour, whose eighth birthday was celebrated on 23 November 1806. She was the youngest of the seven children of Lord Hugh Seymour, a son of the first Marquess of Hertford, and of Lady Horatia Seymour, a daughter of Earl Waldegrave. Lord Hugh, a naval officer, had been appointed Master of the Robes and Keeper of the Privy Purse to the Prince in 1787, and both he and his wife had thereafter become friendly with Mrs Fitzherbert. Knowing of her marriage to the Prince, Lord Hugh had refused to continue to serve in the Prince's Household after the second marriage to Princess Caroline. His wife, however, had remained on intimate terms with Mrs Fitzherbert, who offered to take care of any of her children when Lady Horatia's declining health led her doctors to insist that she should go to live in a warmer climate. The offer had been accepted and after Lady Horatia's departure for Madeira, her baby girl, who was considered too delicate to undergo the long sea voyage, had been entrusted to Mrs Fitzherbert's care. The mother had died in July 1801 shortly after her return to England, and the father had died in Jamaica a few weeks later. In his will he appointed the Earl of Euston, whose wife was Lady Horatia's sister, and Lord Henry Seymour, his brother, as his executors and his children's guardians. The children were all mentioned by name with the exception of Mary who had not been born when the will was drafted. But both executors thought that Mary, or Minny as she was called, ought to be considered as coming within the terms of the will, and they wrote to Mrs Fitzherbert asking her to give the child up to her aunt, Lady Waldegrave. They recognized that it would come as 'an unpleasant proposal' to Mrs Fitzherbert who, they 'really believed', was 'much attached to the child'; but there were good reasons for removing her 'from what hereafter might be thought an *improper* education'.

Mrs Fitzherbert, who had become devoted to Minny, was deeply distressed when she received the letter. She could not bear the thought of parting with the child. She told Lord Thurlow that she would never give her up, saying that if the worst came to the worst she would run away with her.

'The misery I have at the thoughts of having her taken from me is more than I can express,' she protested to Lord Robert Seymour. 'She is now past four years old. I am perfectly certain no person can feel for her as I do. ... I fairly own to you that I am so totally wrapped up and devoted to that dear child that if I lose her it will almost breake my heart. ... The child was placed with me by both the parents in confidence that I should treat it as my own. This confidence I accepted and had occasion to renew the promise to her poor mother whilst she was sinking fast into the grave...'

She explained how, 'with a heavy heart', she had offered to deliver Mary up to her mother on Lady Horatia's return from Madeira, and how Lady Horatia had replied, 'Don't think I could be so unfeeling as to take her from you. *You are* more her mother than *I am*.' She explained, too, how Lady Horatia had called her back as she was about to leave the room and begged her 'to request the Prince to call upon her as she wished to speake to him'.

'I delivered her message,' Mrs Fitzherbert continued, 'and the Prince accordingly went to her. The next day I saw her and she repeated to me the conversation that passed between them, a great deal relative to Lord Hugh's and her own concerns, and then said "I have been recommending my little Mary to him and have received his promise to be her friend and protector through life."'

According to Lady Euston, Lady Horatia's feelings about the Prince were more ambivalent than Mrs Fitzherbert's letter implied. She recognized that he loved Minny, but she doubted that his reputation and character were those of a suitable guardian. As she told Lady Euston, she wanted him to be kind to her children, yet she could not help feeling that to be too much in '*that* society' might be dangerous for them. She had tried to avoid seeing the Prince, Lady Euston maintained, as such a visit would be 'extremely unpleasant' for her: she had not spoken to him for many years, as their former friendship – broken when he had rejected Mrs Fitzherbert for Lady Jersey and had married Princess Caroline – had never been resumed. She knew that he would attempt to justify his conduct and his subsequent quarrel with Lord Hugh, so she asked her maid to say that she was lying down and could not see him should he call.

But the Prince was undeterred. One day, while Lady Euston was sitting with her, Lady Horatia's door flew open and there he was, walking into the room as though 'visiting an old friend'. He 'started and changed colour' at the sight of her, for she looked so ill; while she was too overcome to speak. 'He took her by the hand,' Lady Euston reported, 'and began to talk as fast as possible, and she once or twice looked at me as if she was quite overcome by his talking. ... She did not speak to him at all, and as she sat with her head turned towards me she once or twice in a low voice expressed a degree of vexation on his volubility – she grew more and more faint.' Yet, after he had gone and she had recovered, she smiled at Lady Euston and asked her 'whether it did not put [her] in mind of former times when he used to *go off* upon some favourite subject till he *talked himself into believing that all he said was true*'.

That evening she decided that, after all, she was glad that the Prince had been. He had spoken of Lord Hugh and of Minny and their other children with such obvious affection that she could not help but be pleased by it. Lord Hugh would have been pleased as well, for he 'had always been very sincerely attached to the Prince', and, despite their quarrel, was still 'certainly more attached to him than he now liked to acknowledge'.

After his visit to Lady Horatia, the Prince wrote to the executors offering to settle £10,000 on Minny – payable, with interest, when she reached the age of twenty-one or when she married or he himself died – provided that she were allowed to remain with Mrs Fitzherbert who could not, he said, be more attached to her if she had been her own child. The Prince declared 'his ultimate view to be to raise her up as a companion and as he [hoped] a bosom friend of his own

daughter', who was about three years older. But Lord Henry
was adamant: Minny was perfectly well provided for already; she must be brought up by her aunt.*

The Prince consulted Lord Thurlow, who suggested that
he should employ Samuel Romilly to fight the case for him.
The resultant court hearing was an extremely long one.
Lord Eldon, who appeared for the executors, argued strongly
that 'whatever amiable qualities' Mrs Fitzherbert might
possess, 'the religion she professed excluded her from the
right to retain the custody of a Protestant child'. Romilly
and Thomas Erskine, who appeared with him, pointed out
that the child was already being given religious instruction
by an Anglican clergyman under the direction of the Bishop
of Winchester. In an affidavit 'Maria Fitzherbert, widow'
swore 'That although she was bred in the Roman Catholic
faith she always entertained and expressed the opinion that
a child ought to be educated in the religion professed by its
parents. ... That Mrs Fitzherbert had in fact educated a
child of inferior condition born in her own house, in that
religion. ... That the Appellant was of a delicate constitution and of a very tender and affectionate disposition, and
having no other mother than Mrs Fitzherbert, she was
bound to her by as strong ties of affection as she could possibly have been to her natural mother.'

The Prince of Wales also made an affidavit in which he
swore that he had called on Lady Horatia a few weeks before
she died; that she had told him how fond of him her child
was, and how fortunate she was to have such a dear friend as
Mrs Fitzherbert to look after her for her; and that she had
said to him, 'I have something more, Prince of Wales, to say
to you; recollect that it is the last request of a dying mother,

* The financial provision was made, all the same. In 1815 the
Prince asked that the bond, setting forth the terms of the gift, should
be lodged with Coutts's Bank, 'in *confidential* trust for Miss Seymour', who was then sixteen. He stipulated that Mrs Fitzherbert,
from whom he had by then finally parted, should not be told whence
the money came, merely that the deposit had been made (Archives of
Coutts & Co.; R A Geo. IV, Box 7).

and that is that you will take on oath and swear most solemnly that you will be the father and protector through life, of this dear child. ... Whereupon, his Royal Highness accordingly, without the smallest hesitation, gave his most solemn engagement to her to fulfil to his utmost this request.'

The Master in Chancery considered that the executors had the better case; so did a higher court, presided over by Lord Eldon, who had become Lord Chancellor once more since the case began. Thomas Erskine, Mrs Fitzherbert's counsel, advocated an appeal to the House of Lords; and by the time the appeal was heard by the Lords, Erskine had replaced Eldon as Lord Chancellor, so Mrs Fitzherbert's chances of winning appeared more promising.

Both she and the Prince determined that no opportunity should be lost of ensuring success. They enlisted the support of the Marquess of Hertford, Minny's eldest uncle, who agreed to say in the House that it was painful to have a family matter discussed in front of strangers, and that if their Lordships agreed, he and Lady Hertford would take upon themselves the guardianship of their niece on the understanding that they would be free to deal with her as they thought best.

The Prince then went about energetically from one peer to the next urging them to vote for this solution, even going so far as to hint that he himself was the father of the child to whose care he was bound by 'a promise exacted by her dying mother'. When he heard that Spencer Perceval strongly objected to this behaviour, referring to him as a liar and a cheat, he burst out vehemently 'with most offensive personal abuse, and an oath which cannot be recited, that he felt he could jump on [Perceval] and stamp out his life with his feet'. Many Members of the House of Lords deprecated this interference in their judicial duties as strongly as Perceval did; and Romilly urged Colonel McMahon to endeavour to put a stop to the Prince's unseemly activities which would do his cause more harm than good. But, as it happened, despite the resentment aroused by the Prince's canvassing, the Lords decided by a large majority that the child should be given up to the Hertfords. Only thirteen votes, including that of Lord Eldon, were cast against the proposition. As soon as the result of the voting was known, Lady Hertford asked Mrs Fitzherbert to continue to care for their niece; so the matter was finally settled.

The Prince was overjoyed. Romilly said that he could not have been more anxious that Mrs Fitzherbert should keep the child, if Minny had, in fact, been their own daughter. And naturally it was whispered that she *was* their daughter – the Prince's concern to ensure that she remained with her adoptive mother, Mrs Fitzherbert, being contrasted with his determination that Princess Charlotte should *not* be brought up by *her* real mother.

There could indeed, be little doubt that his love for Minny Seymour was far deeper than the affection he bore his own daughter, whose provenance he could not bear to contemplate. He spent as much time with Minny as he could, gave her regular presents, wrote to her on her birthday and watched her grow into a pretty, delightful young woman. He sent her gold charms and almanacs, cakes and money, scent and bracelets and earrings; and she wrote back to her 'dear Prinny' – or 'dear Priney' as she spelled the name when she was little – with natural affection, drawing hearts and crosses for kisses at the bottom of her neat little letters, thanking him for 'making us all so happy'. 'Dear Prinny,' she wrote when she was twelve, 'I am much obliged to you for your nice letter and very pretty presents. I soon poked the ten pound note out of the essence box and was very much delighted with it [money was always 'very acceptable', she assured him in a subsequent letter, since sometimes she was 'rather an extravagant personage']. What a naughty personage you are dear Prinny to send me such new years gifts. I opened the parcel very cautiously.'

Lady de Clifford's little grandson, the Hon. George Keppel, who was about the same age as Minny, was often taken to play with her, and in later years he confirmed how fond she and the Prince appeared to be of each other. The Prince struck the little boy as 'a merry, good-humoured man', tall and fat, 'with laughing eyes, pouting lips' and a rather turned-up nose. He liked him, as children did, for he was fond of them, took notice of them and knew how to talk to them. 'He wore a well-powdered wig,' Keppel remembered, 'adorned with a profusion of curls, which in my innocence I believed to be his own hair, as I did a very large pigtail appended thereto. His clothes fitted him like a glove; his coat was single-breasted and buttoned up to the chin. ... Round his throat was a huge white neckcloth of many folds, out of which his chin seemed to be always struggling to emerge.'

As soon as the Prince sat down, Minny would jump up on to his knee, sitting on his leather pantaloons, her little feet dangling by his Hessian boots. Immediately there began an animated talk between them. Sometimes George Keppel was invited to sit on the spare knee 'and to share in the conversation, if conversation it could be called in which all were talkers and none listeners'.*

There were no such displays of fond affection between the Prince and his daughter, Charlotte, admittedly a less appealing child than Minny. Hot-tempered, cheeky and acquisitive, she had, as Lady de Clifford had discovered, a very high opinion of herself, 'an unfortunate vanity', which was, her eldest aunt, Charlotte, commented, 'a little in her blood'. Her preceptors and tutors found her a rather tiresome, over-excitable pupil, though shrewd and innately affectionate. She did not much care for her Governess, Lady de Clifford, George Keppel's 'snuffy old grandmother', who had cause repeatedly to reprimand her for her ill manners

---

* Mary Seymour continued to live with Mrs Fitzherbert until her marriage in 1825 to Colonel the Hon. George Dawson (later Dawson-Damer), a son of the first Earl of Portarlington. She had five children, and died in 1847 at the age of forty-nine.

and lack of consideration, as when she rushed into a room, leaving the door wide open. To her Governess's reprimand, 'My dear Princess, that is not civil; you should always shut the door after you when you come into a room,' she riposted rudely, 'Not I, indeed. If you want the door shut, ring the bell'; and she flounced out again, leaving it open.

Although she was very fond of Mrs Campbell, and was kindly disposed to the Rev. George Nott, she heartily disliked her other Governess, Mrs Udney, 'a great goose', and positively detested Bishop Fisher, a pompous, self-important busybody whose interfering fussiness equally exasperated Lady de Clifford. One day, in a sudden access of rage, Princess Charlotte snatched the wig from the opinionated Bishop's head and threw it into the fire. Another day, after she had hit a maidservant who had offended her, the Bishop asked her why she had failed to follow his advice of always saying the Lord's Prayer when she was angry to calm her temper. 'I did, my Lord Bishop,' she replied saucily, 'or I should almost have killed her.' When she was taken into a house she ran as fast as she could to the top of the stairs and down again; when visitors came to see her at Warwick House, she marched them round her father's rooms pulling off the covers and leaving them on the floor; when George Keppel's sisters came to play she was very rough with them, pushing them into beds of nettles and giving them presents if they neither cried nor complained to their governess. Dr Fisher found her quite as tiresome as she found him, complaining of her appalling ill manners, noticing with profound distaste that 'her nose requiring to be wiped, she did not apply her handkerchief, but wiped her nose with her sleeve as vulgar people do'.

Her hoydenish behaviour, her loud and ready laugh, her brash impudence profoundly distressed her father, who was painfully reminded of her mother. He believed that she ought to be controlled more strictly and was very insistent that her visits to Blackheath and Kensington should be severely limited and meticulously supervised by her Governess, who was never to let the child out of her sight for an in-stant. 'The boy whom the Princess of Wales has brought up and who is certainly not fit company for my daughter,' he instructed Lady de Clifford, sending a copy of the letter to the Princess, 'is not to be brought in Charlotte's society, as I have learned he has been too often produced on these occa-sions. These regulations I hold to be absolutely necessary, and I depend upon you for their being strictly adhered to.'

The Prince wrote in similar terms to the King, adding, 'the Princess of Wales must never be under the same roof with me. My daughter's present residence cannot but be re-garded the same as my own house, there being a commu-nication between that house and mine and a consequent possibility of my meeting the Princess were she to come here.'

The Prince was also concerned that the teaching staff at Warwick House, who were always squabbling with each other, were not fulfilling their duties properly. He suspected that his daughter was herself responsible for many of their disagreements. Mrs Campbell, whom he had never trusted anyway, being a woman of Tory connections nominated by the King, had had to be reprimanded for allowing her charge – indeed for 'encouraging' her – to make out a will in which the Princess bequeathed to her her 'three watches' and 'half [her] jewels'. Mrs Campbell, whom the Princess had referred to as her 'adopted mother', had subsequently resigned on the grounds of 'ill health'.

The Rev. George Nott, the Princess's Sub-Preceptor, whose 'dutiful daughter by adoption' the Princess liked to consider herself, was also mentioned favourably in this innocent docu-ment which decreed that he should be left all her 'best books' and 'papers', together with all her money 'to distri-bute to the poor'. The Princess trusted that, after her death, the King would make Mr Nott a bishop.

Already the Prince had had occasion to rebuke his daugh-ter's Sub-Preceptor for subscribing himself the Princess's 'most faithful friend' in a letter which he had written to her reproving her for her unpunctuality. Mr Nott, the Prince had sharply reminded Bishop Fisher, was her 'instructor', most certainly *not* 'her faithful friend', 'a footing of intimacy ... never authorised' and the assumption of which must, of course, be prevented in future. The Prince was all the more concerned because the Bishop – whom he disliked as much as his daughter did – had suggested that his daughter might be allowed to 'pass the evenings' with Mr Nott. This was a suggestion that could not possibly be entertained. The Princess's day was fully occupied from the hour of 'rising till the time of her dinner', so it was only natural that 'the resumption of study instantaneously after dinner' would be 'peculiarly irksome to the child and unprofitable from the impossibility of commanding her attention'. But the Bishop's concern that if she were left 'entirely idle' she would 'fall into a state of listlessness' showed that he was unacquainted with the manner in which her evenings were employed. She was always pleasantly occupied with ladies and governesses, in music, in dancing or in being 'read to out of some amusing but instructive author'. There was, therefore, no reason whatsoever for the singular request that Mr Nott should be allowed into the Princess's society in the evenings. She was now eleven years old. 'I must make it a rule not to be infringed,' the Prince concluded, 'that my daughter shall never be left alone with any of her masters. ... I repeat to your Lordship that no man is to be of my daughter's private society.'

Soon after this letter was written Mr Nott was the cause of further trouble. It was alleged, supposedly by Mrs Udney, that he had influenced the Princess in unfilial feelings towards her father, and had failed to check the Princess's unfortunate disposition for idle and even malevolent gossip. In consequence of this report, and despite a warm defence of his subordinate by Bishop Fisher, Nott was suspended. Then, in a counter-attack on Mrs Udney – who had been dismissed in Princess Charlotte's will in six words: 'Nothing to Mrs Udney for reasons' – the Bishop accused her of allowing the

Princess to read a highly unsuitable book without his permission, an English translation of Ovid's *Metamorphoses*, and even worse, of showing her an obscene caricature of Nelson's mistress, Lady Hamilton, and explaining its meaning to her.

No one ever did discover the truth behind the squabbles at Warwick House. Mrs Udney was apparently not considered blameworthy, for she continued in her appointment, as did Lady de Clifford. But then Mr Nott was evidently not held to have disgraced himself either, for although suspended – to be succeeded eventually by the Rev. William Short – he was later appointed a Prebend of Winchester, an appointment that led to Mrs Campbell's asking for 'some mark of royal favour' which would show that she, too, had not forfeited the King's good opinion of her. She had to wait some time for this approbation, but was eventually appointed one of Princess Charlotte's attendants.

While her instructors bickered amongst themselves, and her father appeared to take the side of those strict ones she did not like, Princess Charlotte felt increasingly less fond of him as the months went by, and also less fond of her aunts whose 'compagny', she said, 'I hate and detest'. Her letters were outwardly dutiful and suitably affectionate. 'O my dearest papa,' she wrote to him on his forty-fifth birthday in her remarkably neat, round script, 'may I become every year more worthy of so kind a father and be a comfort to him when grown up. ... I assure you, my dear papa, I will struggle to get the better of my lessons and of all my learning and to do everything I can do to please you.' But she felt constrained to add, 'I am ashamed to say but I hope you will forgive me, that I did not always feel the attachment I ought to have felt. I was ungrateful to a father who, tho' he had a great deal of business, I am sure never had me out of his mind, but I was sufficiently punished, for you could not bear your daughter ungrateful and therefore you would not see her.' 'O how I wish I could see more of you!' she wrote in another letter. 'But I hope I shall in time. I am sensible

how irksome it must be to you to see me, feeling I can be no
companion to you to amuse you when in health; and am too
young to soothe you when in affliction. Believe me that I am
always truly happy when I do see you.'

His mother and his sisters urged him to try to go to see
her more often, for she badly needed, as Princess Elizabeth
said, the 'affection and attention of her father'. 'She is very
sensible of any the smallest attention shown to her,' the
Queen wrote, 'and also, which is very natural, seems to
feel very strongly any apparent neglect. ... She is blessed
with an uncommon share of good sense, she has talents and
facility to learn any thing, is easily led to follow good advice
when treated with gentleness, desirous to oblige when an
opportunity offers, and capable of very strong attachment....
As to her manners I will not deny they are a little brusque,
but more society will correct that. ... From the bottom of
my heart do I wish that she should connect with her filial
duty a sincere friendship for you which may be gained
by seeing a little more of her, and by making her look upon
you as the source of every amusement and pleasure granted
to her. In another quarter every possible pains are taken to
make her visits the most agreeable and every amusement
thought of to gain her affection.'

If the Prince did not go to see Charlotte as often as he
could, particularly when he thought there might be a possibility of meeting her mother; if he now summoned Lady de
Clifford to bring her to him at most irregular intervals, he
always appeared to find time to go to see Minny Seymour.
He also found it possible to spend a great deal of time in
the company of Minny's aunt, the Marchioness of Hertford,
at her house in Manchester Square.

20

The Advent of Lady Hertford
1806–1809

'His father's malady extends to him,
only takes another turn'

ISABELLA, Lady Hertford, the daughter of the ninth Viscount Irvine, was a very rich, beautifully dressed, handsome,
formal and stately woman of ample, though well-corseted
proportions. At first no one had considered the Prince's close
friendship with her family particularly remarkable, even
though they were the most dedicated of Tories. The Marquess, who had married Isabella as his second wife when he
was thirty-three in 1776, was a pleasant, easy-going man,
moderately successful as a politician and later as Ambassador in Berlin. He had been appointed Master of the Horse
in 1804. Their only son, the Earl of Yarmouth, who – though
possibly it is his father – appears as the Marquess of Steyne
in Thackeray's *Vanity Fair*, was married to the heiress Maria
Fagniani, daughter of the Marchesa Fagniani and of either
George Selwyn or the Duke of Queensberry, each of whom,
claiming the honour of paternity, left her large sums of
money. Both Lord Yarmouth and his father were on excellent terms with the Prince, sharing with him that collector's
passion for French furniture which filled Hertford House
with the treasures that can still be seen there.

It soon became clear, however, that it was the company
of Lady Hertford that principally attracted the Prince to
Manchester Square and to Ragley, the Hertfords' country
seat in Warwickshire. It was said that the Prince's new-found
preference of Cheltenham to Brighton, which he now
claimed was 'too cold' for him, was due to Cheltenham's
propinquity to Ragley; and that the Marchioness, an ambi-

tious and rather masterful woman, was highly gratified by the Prince's attentions and the opportunities for political influence which they presented. No one for a moment supposed, though, that however hard he might press his suit she would give way to him and become his mistress. She was celebrated for her staid, unresponsive nature; 'stately, formal and insipid', Lord Holland thought her; and now that she was getting on for fifty it was not considered likely that she would suddenly change for the better. Mrs Calvert, while allowing that she was still beautiful, thought her 'the most forbidding, haughty, unpleasant-looking woman' she had ever met. Lord Glenbervie was wholly mystified by the Prince's motives, not understanding his need to be dominated by an authoritarian woman older than himself. The Prince visited her every morning when she was in London, wrote to her every morning when she was not, and often dined 'en famille with her and Lord Hertford'. Yet what could he find to write about? She had been a grandmother for 'more than twelve or fourteen years'. Lord Hertford had an income of over £70,000 a year, so he could not be said to be conniving at the intimacy between his wife and the Prince for commercial reasons. Also she looked her age; but then, as Lady Stafford commented, 'elderly dames' seemed 'to be to his taste'.

The more firmly she held to her virtue – and Robert Plumer Ward was told by one of the Prince's doctors that she succeeded in keeping it intact – the more emotional were the Prince's feelings for her. He wrote to her more frequently than ever, sitting up all night to do so, Lady Elizabeth Foster said; he fell silent at the thought of her and his eyes filled with tears. A mature, ample, protective, enclosing woman, she could offer him so much, yet stood aloof from him, until he became, as Lady Bessborough said, 'really distracted' and could think of nothing other than '*la bella e grassa Donna che lo signoreggia ora*'. He fell ill; he was feverish; he demanded to be blooded; he lost his appetite; he grew thin. Soon he was seriously ill.

All his life the Prince had been subject to such violent and sudden attacks of illness, especially when emotionally disturbed. His usual symptoms, accompanied by 'great agitation of spirits', were high fever, a racing pulse, weakness in the arms and legs, severe abdominal colic and what he himself referred to as 'violent bilious attacks', 'a violent stoppage in the bowels', 'severe spasms on the neck of the bladder', and 'violent inflammatory attacks' on the lungs. From an early age he seems also to have suffered from gout and 'some degree of rheumatism' and these complaints appear to have been exacerbated in times of stress, as in 1789 when, worried to distraction about his debts, his pulse rate was so rapid that Warren could not count it – 'it resembled a machine completely disorganized'. So, too, was the case in 1792 when, distraught by his father's refusal to give him an Army command, he was reported as having been 'threatened with apoplectic symptoms' and as having no more than two more years to live. He insisted upon being blooded with alarming frequency – continuing his practice of opening the vein himself when his doctors would not do so – took a great deal of laudanum accompanied by medicines to make him sweat, and tried cures at Bath and Cheltenham. But he discovered no satisfactory treatment. Every attack was followed by a period of 'extreme weakness and lassitude'. It is possible that, like his father, he was a victim of porphyria.

He himself recognized that his 'mind' was the 'main spring' of his illnesses. In 1791 'numberless causes of vexation' made him 'very seriously ill indeed', and although, as he told the Duke of York, he did all he could to master himself, he 'could not hold up any longer, and sank under feelings which are not easy to be described'. For this 'violent complaint' he had himself blooded five times, yet even so his nerves felt 'but in a shattered state'. Mary Berry said that, having spat blood, he 'fainted away after his levée' in April. 'He is supposed to have ulcers on his lungs, like the late Duke of Cumberland,' Sir James Bland Burges told his sister in May, 'and was actually blooded four times last week. His physicians have ordered him to live upon French beans and barley-water. He, however, dined on Friday with three hundred officers, made great havoc of sundry savoury meats and much champagne, claret, and burgundy.'

Two years later when war broke out with France he once again, so he informed Sir John Lade, fell 'very ill *indeed*'. And in 1799, when he was in a fever of agitation about Mrs Fitzherbert's application to the Pope for permission to return to him, he became so seriously ill that his doctors decided that the only cure would be to send him to Bath. From there he replied to a letter from Dr John Turton who had written to him because the Queen was worried that he would take the waters 'improperly': 'I have certainly been very unwell since I have been here. ... *Mine is a very nervous* and so far a *delicate* fibre, consequently the disorders of the body in general *with me* owe their source to the mind. (This God knows has for some time, and a long time too, been too much the case with me, and then any little addition, such as a casual cold, or even any indisposition, no matter how trifling, contributes much to the unhinging the whole system.)'

As though nervously aware that his periodic attacks were similar to his father's, he did not like detailed accounts of them to be generally known. 'I have been between ourselves *very ill indeed*,' he once wrote to the Countess of Elgin, 'and it is little known *how ill*.' Of a later attack his daughter wrote that news of it had been kept 'profoundly' secret until 'all shadow of alarm was over'. More than once he admitted to being 'very unwell', but the admission was made '*confidentially*' and was not to be talked about. He even went so far as to cause it to be known that his symptoms were other than they were, for fear lest some sinister interpretation might be put upon them. The precaution seemed well justified when he learned that during one of his attacks, when he lay '*constantly on his stomach* in bed', complaining 'of violent pain' and 'spasmodic affection', and taking 'a hundred drops of laudanum every three hours', the Duke of Cumberland, making trouble as usual, was going about saying it was 'all sham', that the illness was really *'no other* than that he *was mad'*.

There was no doubt that his agitation was sometimes so extreme that he did, indeed, appear to be in danger of losing his reason. In 1804, when he was so disturbed both about his failure to get on in the Army and about the possibility of a regency due to the King's illness, he was reported to be in 'a fever of uneasiness', to be talking 'all day without ceasing to Mrs Fitzherbert'. At the same time Sheridan told his wife that the Prince, 'just recovered from an illness in which his life was despaired of for two days', was 'so nervous and anxious' that it was 'not easy to thwart him, though he [ran] a great risk of making himself ill again'. He kept Sheridan in his bedroom, talking to him continually till four o'clock in the morning.

Two years later when the Prince was making a tour of the north of England – staying at Doncaster, Aske, Bligh and Ledstone Hall, with Lord Darlington at Raby Castle in County Durham, with the Staffords at Trentham, with Lord Derby at Knowsley, Lord Fitzwilliam at Wentworth Woodhouse, and at Castle Howard, Lord Carlisle's seat in Yorkshire – he fell seriously ill again. This time the attack was attributed to his great distress at the death of Fox.

He was said to have been overcome with grief at Nelson's death. Certainly he mourned Nelson as 'the greatest character England could ever boast of', and claimed to have 'loved him as a friend'. Yet the loss was not really a personal one. Although Lady Hamilton told Alexander Davison, his prize-agent, that Nelson had 'adored' the Prince, this was no more than flattery intended for his Royal Highness's ears. In fact, when Nelson had learned that the Prince was to be invited to the Hamiltons' house he protested in most vehement terms. 'Does Sir William want you to be a whore to the rascal?' he demanded. It was 'shocking conduct' to have asked him. If Sir William knew as much of the Prince's character as the world did, he would rather have let the lowest wretch that walked the streets dine at his table than that 'unprincipalled lyar'. Lady Hamilton's 'hitherto unimpeached character' would be ruined; 'no modest woman would suffer it'. The Prince was 'permitted to visit only people of *notorious ill fame*'; it had been reported that he had said he would make her his mistress; he was 'a false lying scoundrel'.*

If the Prince mourned the loss of Nelson as a national rather than personal tragedy, he felt the death of Fox as both. When he heard of it, though he had long been expecting it, he flung himself on a sofa and burst into passionate tears. He professed himself 'overwhelmed with grief'; and as he wrote to Lord Holland from Trentham, where he was staying when the news reached him, his tears still fell so thick that he could not see what he wrote. For days he could not bring himself to speak to anyone except his hostess, Lady Stafford. Both Lord Fitzwilliam and Lord Carlisle reported to Charles Grey that he had utterly lost his appetite and could not sleep, that his strength had quite failed him. He ate little but fish and salad, and drank only barley-water, warm milk and soda-water; he looked pale and old and wrinkled in the black clothes he wore for months. 'The Prince is here and very unwell,' Lord Fitzwilliam told Lord Grenville on 24 September 1806. 'He has been so during the whole of this tour. He has lost all appetite and even has he for wine. He was deeply affected with the death of Fox, and has never recovered his spirits since. When first I saw him it was very manifest how much he felt on the occasion. But to return to his health. We got Walker, formerly his apothe-

---

* The King, who strongly disapproved of Nelson's liaison with Lady Hamilton, did not deem it appropriate that the Prince should attend the funeral as chief mourner, as he had wanted to do. This privilege was accorded to Admiral Sir Peter Parker, the Prince attending in a private capacity. To his obvious dismay, he was refused permission by his father to attend Fox's funeral in any capacity at all. He contributed £500 towards its cost (RA 40784:Asp/P, v, 499; BM Add. MSS 51520).

cary in London, but now retired in Yorkshire, to see him. From a strong pulse, he found it quite thin, low and weak. He thinks him seriously unwell and that he requires much attention and repose. Whether he will be persuaded to manage himself as he ought to do is more than I feel confidence of.'

Although the King refused him permission to attend Fox's funeral for reasons of 'propriety', the Prince interrupted his northern tour to be in London while 'the melancholy ceremony' was taking place. Lord Fitzwilliam was gratified to find him rather better on his return to Wentworth House, still 'wonderfully abstemious both in eating and drinking', but in a 'wonderful degree of agitation on a variety of subjects'. He had got over the first shock of grief at Fox's death, but he was now 'in the figgets' about the war, the elections and, above all, Princess Caroline.

By the beginning of December it was being suggested in London that he did not have much longer to live, the Duke of Clarence, with characteristic bluntness, putting forward the view that three months would see him out. Joseph Farington, the diarist, heard that 'an eminent medical man' had given it as his opinion that he could 'never recover' from the state he was in; he was drinking the strongest, iced tea to 'allay the internal heat'. Three months later one of his tailors, John Weston of Old Bond Street, confided to a friend of Farington's that he had become so thin that his clothes hung like greatcoats upon him and were 'obliged to be taken in greatly'. Since the death of Fox he had worn nothing but black and within the past three months had ordered only two new suits to add to the 'some hundred suits' he had in his wardrobe. His temper was 'not so good as it was'; he was 'hasty about trifles, about the placing of a button, and peevish'. His servants were much concerned, 'fearing for their situations'. Edward Jerningham found it quite painful to look at him, so greatly had his countenance altered, 'not so much from the reduction of his embonpoint as from a sallowness and an expression in his eye as if he suffered mental

and corporeal pain. He assumed a cheerfulness, but it was
visibly put on from his good humour and a desire to please.'
On 2 May, when he attended the Royal Academy dinner,
everyone noticed how 'very ill he looked'. Farington, concerned to see him eat nothing but fish and salad, a little pudding and one or two radishes, noticed that he had lost all his
'joy and gaiety, and spirit of address'. When the President of
the Royal Academy, Benjamin West, proposed a toast to the
Prince's health there 'was much *clapping*, which expressed
the general feeling that *he wanted it*'.

Towards the end of the year he recovered once more; but
by the late autumn of 1807 he was in a more agitated state
than ever over Lady Hertford. Neither McMahon nor
Lieutenant-Colonel Benjamin Bloomfield – who had only
recently entered his service as one of the Prince's Gentleman
Attendants but had known him for some time as a horse-
artillery officer doing duty with the Prince's regiment at
Brighton – had ever seen him 'in such a state of lowness and
depression'. By the middle of December, sunk in melancholy, he was 'immovable' from his room, so Bloomfield told
Lord Hertford, 'plunged into a state of apathy and indifference towards himself' which was indescribably alarming.
One evening, Bloomfield found him agitated 'beyond all former example. He clasped his hands and, in quick steps,
walked up and down his room as if rouzed by some dreadful
event, when he exclaimed, "Oh, my dear Bloomfield, a
terrible catastrophe was near happening ..." and in the
greatest agony continued, "If Lord and Lady Hertford were
but here, the only persons to whom I can talk and confide. ... What is now to become of me, of wretched me in
this moment of accumulating difficulties and distress, is
more than I can support."'

A few weeks before he had tried to regain his health by
a course of the waters at Cheltenham, then by a short tour
of the West Country and visits to the Hertfords at Ragley
and to Berkeley Castle; but he had gained no relief. Indeed
his visit to Berkeley Castle was made a 'martyrdom', so he

told Lady Hertford, by 'the mistaken over-attentions and the bourgeois and insufferable vulgarity and ill-breeding of the Maestra del la Casa', Lady Berkeley, a butcher's daughter. His behaviour was certainly very tiresome there and his hostess was thankful when he had gone. 'Having dined there at six o'clock, Lady Berkeley did not ask him to fix an hour the following day but ordered the dinner to be ready at six, and at that hour the Prince was informed that dinner was ready. He sent word that he could not then dine, and the dinner was taken off the table, and they waited till eight o'clock before he made his appearance. He was there on a Sunday and Lady Berkeley asked him whether he proposed to go to Church? To which he answered "That if she desired it, or it would oblige her, he would go." To this she made no reply, and he did not go. At Bristol, at Gloucester and wherever he went the people were dissatisfied with his behaviour.' *

He returned home looking 'most wretchedly' and, in Fre-

---

* When he was well the Prince was normally a far less troublesome guest. Lord Lonsdale said 'that wherever the Prince went, and under all circumstances, he expects to see such preparation, and such attention and respect as he thinks due to him, but that when this has been shewn, he dispenses with such a continuation of it as would at all affect the comfort of those about him, with whom he lives easily and pleasantly. It is not so with some others of the family, particularly [Prince William of] Gloucester, who subjects people where he visits to a tedious attention to ceremonious personal respect to him' (*Farington Diary*, v, 216). At Lord Crewe's, Gloucester 'made them very weary of him by his fastidious pride and the trouble he gave', refusing to allow the port to be passed in front of him at table and insisting on hot suppers every night. 'Miss Crewe and her young friends would sometimes retire from the general apartment to another sitting room and there set down familiarly to work. [Prince William] would come into the room and they according to etiquette would *stand up*, from which he would not relieve them' (*Farington Diary*, iv, 51). Prince William never even 'allowed a gentleman to be seated in his presence', so Lady Shelley said, 'and he expected the ladies of the party to hand him his coffee on a salver – to stand up while he drank it, and then to remove the cup' (*Shelley Diary*, i, 29).

mantle's opinion, 'very little mended'. At the beginning of
1808 he was so affected by the sight of his old friend, Lord
Lake, on his deathbed that he fainted and was 'not restored
until a quantity of cold water was sprinkled over his face'.
Some months later Joseph Farington's brother, Robert, who
saw him at Weymouth, was shocked by his altered appearance, the strongly marked lines in his sallow face; he had a
'shattered look'.

'More or less ever since I quitted you at Ragley,' he wrote
in anguish to Lady Hertford, 'I have been persecuted by the
most horrible and spasmodick attacks in my head. ... The
agony I suffer is hardly to be credited.' If only she would
write to him all would be better.

To unsympathetic observers the Prince's plight seemed
only too familiar. 'His health was reported to be bad, and
his appearance confirmed the report,' wrote Lord Holland.
'Those, however, who had made a study of his gallantries,
recognized his usual system of love-making in these symptoms. He generally, it seems, assailed the heart which he
wished to carry by exciting their commiseration for his sufferings and their apprehensions for his health. With this
view he actually submitted to be bled two or three times in
the course of a night, when there was so little necessity for it
that different surgeons were introduced for the purpose, unknown to each other, lest they should object to so unusual
a loss of blood.'

'I really believe his father's malady extends to him, only
takes another turn,' concluded Lady Bessborough, who told
her lover, Lord Granville Leveson Gower, that the Prince,
driven wild by Lady Hertford's rejection of his advances,
had thrown himself upon her instead. 'Such a scene I never
went through,' Lady Bessborough said. He 'threw himself on
his knees, and clasping me round, kissed my neck before I
was aware of what he was doing. I screamed with vexation
and fright; he continued, sometimes struggling with me,
sometimes sobbing and crying. ... Then mixing abuse of
you, vows of eternal love, entreaties and promises of what he

would do – he would break with Mrs F. and Lady H., I should *make my own terms*!! I should be his sole confidant, sole adviser – private or public – I should guide his politics, Mr Canning should be Prime Minister (whether in this reign or the next did not appear); ... then over and over and over again the same round of complaint, despair, entreaties and promises, and always Mr Canning ... and whenever he mentioned him it was in the tenderest accent and attempting some liberty, that really, G., had not my heart been breaking I must have laughed out at the comicality of having [Canning] so coupled and made use of – and then that immense, grotesque figure flouncing about half on the couch, half on the ground.'

But, as Lady Bessborough knew, it was not really herself but Lady Hertford that the Prince wanted. 'He writes day and night almost, and frets himself into a fever, and all to persuade la sua bella *Donnone to live with him – publickly*!! ... I should not be surprised if he and the ci devant [Mrs Fitzherbert] were to quarrel quite during their meeting at Brighton.... She has got irritated, and he bored.'

This was only too true.

For a long time now, it had been noticed, both at Carlton House and at the Pavilion, that Mrs Fitzherbert was being pushed into the background, and that Lady Hertford was gradually taking her place. Lady Hertford, so correct in her conduct and manners, declined to dine at either house unless Mrs Fitzherbert were there too; her reputation might thus be protected while her rival was humiliated. And humiliated Mrs Fitzherbert certainly was. The Prince still spent part of his mornings at Brighton with her, but in the evenings when she came to the Pavilion 'he did not even notice her in the slightest manner'. She 'afterwards understood that such attentions would have been reported to her rival'.

She had had many other rivals in the recent past. The Prince was believed to have had brief affairs with the dancer, Louise Hillisberg, with the notorious Harriette Wilson who admitted in her *Memoirs* to having offered herself to him, and with Marie Anne, the French wife of the second Earl of Massereene; and in 1805 he had apparently established another Frenchwoman, Mme de Meyer, in apartments in Duke Street, Manchester Square, where he used to visit her late at night, leaving his carriage in a corner of the Square and walking to her door muffled up in a large greatcoat.*

Mrs Fitzherbert had sensibly disregarded these brief affairs and peccadilloes. But she could not ignore his passion for Lady Hertford. Often she threatened to leave him, yet hesitated to do so for fear lest she might lose Lady Hertford's niece, her beloved Minny. Also, she still loved him. In the summer of 1808 she made up her mind to see no more of him, at least for a time. Her 'sudden and unexpected departure' went to his 'very soul', he wrote in a distraught letter to her companion, Miss Pigot. The tears flowed from his heart; he would take no notice of the letter Mrs Fitzherbert had written to him, as otherwise he would 'verify

---

* The Prince, it seems, declined to accept the paternity of a daughter of a Mrs Mary Lewis, a boarding-house keeper whom he had met at Weymouth. He did, however, apparently accept the paternity of three other children. One of these was the son of a Mrs Crowe who lived in Charles Street, St James's Square under the name of Seymour, with an allowance from the Prince of £1,000 a year. The boy was christened George and known as 'Prince' to his mother and his school friends; he was said to be twenty-two in 1820 and to have been provided for in the army (RA Geo. IV, Box 10; RA 39524-6). Another of these children was William Francis, son of a Mrs Davies, who was modestly provided for on his mother's death when he was eleven and at school at Parson's Green (RA 29957-73). The third child was the son of Eliza Crole, who, as Major G. S. Crole, decided to sell his commission in 1832 being 'heartily tired of the service' and never having had 'much partiality for it'. He trusted, in a letter addressed to the King's Private Secretary, that the purchase price for the lieutenant-colonelcy for which he was tired of waiting, would nevertheless be made available to him (RA 29974-97). Mrs Crole herself received a pension of £500 a year (RA 30370). In discussing the provisions of his will with Lord Eldon in 1823 King George IV 'mentioned that he had a natural son, an officer in the East Indies, to whom he thought himself bound to give a legacy of £30,000' (RA Eldon MSS, quoted in Asp/P, viii, 483).

the very kind accusation which amongst many others' she had laid at his door, namely of his 'always acting a part, and playing to the galleries'. But if she returned to him, he would receive her 'with open arms'. To Mrs Fitzherbert herself he wrote incoherently, 'As it is, my only, only only love, quite out of my calculation by being able to sleep, I may as well employ myself in that what to me is the only pleasant, as well as the only interesting occupation of my life, which is the writing to thee; and though this alas! is but poor consolation, still as I fancy to myself that it is in some degree, or at any rate, a convincing proof ... I cannot resist the temptation as it affords me not inconsiderable relief of applying to my pen to endeavour ... to establish within my bosom at least a species of requiem. ... I am a different animal a different being from any other in the whole creation. ... Every thought and every idea of my existance and of my life never leave and never quit thee, for the smallest particle of an instant.'

To such repetitive appeals Mrs Fitzherbert gave way. But she went back to him only to find that he was still as infatuated as ever with Lady Hertford. At length, driven beyond endurance, she wrote to tell him that she could no longer bear to let the present miserable situation continue. 'It has quite destroyed the entire comfort and happiness of both our lives; it has so completely destroyed mine, that neither my health nor my spirits can bear it any longer. What am I to think of the inconsistency of your conduct, when, scarcely three weeks ago, you voluntarily declared to me that *this sad affair* was quite at an end, and in less than a week afterwards the whole business was begun all over again? The purport of my writing to you is to implore you to come to a resolution. ... You must decide, and that decision must be done immediately, that I may know what line to pursue. I beg your answer may be a written one, to avoid all unpleasant conversations upon a subject so heart-rending to one whose life has been dedicated to you, and whose affection for you none can surpass.'

Unwilling to lose her, yet besotted by longing for Lady Hertford, the Prince made a placatory reply and continued to ask her to the Pavilion. But on 18 December 1809 she gave a firm and final refusal. She could 'not possibly accept the honour' of his invitation; the 'very great incivilities' she had received these past two years had been too keenly felt by her to admit of her putting herself 'in a situation of being again treated with such indignity'. 'For whatever may be thought of me by some individuals,' she continued, 'it is well known your Royal Highness four-and-twenty years ago placed me in a situation so nearly connected with your own that I have a claim upon you for protection. I feel I owe it to myself not to be insulted under your roof with impunity.'

The Prince replied that he would 'never forget those affectionate feelings' he had ever entertained for Mrs Fitzherbert, and signed himself, 'Always with every possible kindness and good wishes towards you I remain, my very dear Maria, ever very sincerely'.

Mrs Fitzherbert knew now that the separation was complete.

21

The Windsor Nunnery
1797–1810

*'They were secluded from the world, mixing
with few people'*

No one was more upset by the Prince's treatment of Mrs
Fitzherbert than were his sisters, with whom she had been
upon the best of terms. All of them, with the single exception of Charlotte, the Princess Royal, were still living at
home, longing for the day when they would be allowed to
escape into marriage, growing older and thickset, less good-
natured, ever more frustrated by the enclosed life they were
required to lead in what they described to each other as
'The Nunnery'.

Throughout their lives their parents had watched over
their growth and development with the most attentive concern. In their childhood this had been tolerable and had
gone unquestioned. To be constantly chaperoned, to have
a governess standing by whenever a man, even a trusted
schoolroom instructor, was present, to have every hour of
the day rigidly planned, to be unable to pursue any activity
outside the normal curriculum without permission, never to
be allowed to read a book that had not previously been
approved by their mother, all these conditions, rules and
regulations seemed acceptable. No other way of life had
been known to them.

They had, without undue complaint, got up early, learned
their lessons with varying degrees of success, been taken
for drives in the country, gone for walks, sometimes with
their governesses or ladies, sometimes with their parents
also, walking two by two in schoolgirls' crocodile formation.
At Windsor, in the summer evenings, they had gone

'terracing', as they called it, promenading up and down beneath the Castle walls with their parents' attendants and guests while the band played appropriate tunes. In their leisure moments they had taken up their knitting needles or their spinning-wheels or drawing-boards, while their mother, who could never bear to see anyone idle, listened to one of her ladies reading from some improving work as she stitched away at her needlework. When it was time for bed they would, one by one, kiss their mother's hand, curtsey to her companions, and, accompanied by a female attendant, leave the room.

Occasionally there was a ball or a concert; sometimes there was a visit to the theatre to see an approved or specially censored play; often there was a birthday party when they all had new clothes. But they rarely saw any men other than their father, his pages, equerries and attendants; and even these they did not see at mealtimes, etiquette forbidding any man to sit down in the Queen's presence. The Princesses, in fact, were shown very little of the world beyond the walls of the Queen's House, the gardens at Kew and the slopes of the Castle at Windsor. Once or twice a year they went *en famille* to stay for a few days with such friends of their parents as the Harcourts at Nuneham Courtenay; or they were taken to the races at Ascot. Once they, or at least the three oldest of them, were taken with their mother and father on a formal visit to Oxford University; and once they were conducted round Whitbread's brewery.

Although so constricted a life, it was not an unhappy one when they were young. They were often seen laughing together, and the healthy good looks and pleasant, easy manners which they all possessed were universally admired. Gainsborough, on being commissioned to paint them, confessed that he went 'all but raving mad with ecstasy in beholding such a constellation of youthful beauty'.

The older they grew, however, the more irksome the restrictions imposed on them were naturally felt to be. They had no personal income other than that allowed them by their mother; they were never permitted to go away for a holiday by themselves, even suitably and heavily chaperoned, but were expected to accompany their father to Weymouth, where the Queen usually felt ill and they always felt bored.

Since the King got up at five, so did they; they walked down with their attendants to the bathing-machines; they rode round the grounds of Gloucester House in a donkey-chaise; they walked on the sands; they went to the Assembly Rooms and to public breakfasts given by the local gentry and dignitaries. Night after night they went to the play-house to see the same piece performed by '*a very bad sort of actors*', because the King enjoyed it and they had, as Princess Mary complained bitterly to the Prince, 'nothing to do but submit and admire his being so *easily pleased*'. Weymouth, in fact, as Mary had to admit in another letter, was 'more *dull* and stupid' than she could find words to express, 'a *perfect stand*-still of *every*thing and everybody except every ten days a very long review'. The review, she was assured, was 'very fine', but as she was '*perfectly unknowing* in those sort of things' she did not find it in the least amusing. Her sisters found life at Weymouth quite as tedious as she did, and Princess Elizabeth added another complaint when she said that whenever she was there she wished 'to lose the sense of smelling'.

In 1797 when she was thirty-one the oldest of the sisters, Charlotte, had managed to find a husband at last. She was an attractive young woman, though clumsier and less self-confident than the younger girls. At her first Court ball one of her shoes fell off as she was curtseying to the Queen; and although her partner, the Prince of Wales, held her hand in his usual 'most graceful' manner while it was being replaced, so that not everyone noticed the accident, others did notice it and it was remarked that the 'Princess was never elegant in exhibition'. Her shyness made her seem on occasions rather arrogant and aloof; and she was, in fact, inclined to be managing by nature. She felt sure, with some justification, that her mother did not love her as she should, and kept her subdued in the background as though she were a little girl.

One day, in her mother's presence, the Prince had made some good-natured jokes about her which she had taken very badly. Afterwards she had asked her brother never to joke with her about the smallest trifle in front of the Queen as he did not know how much she suffered for it later. The Prince had been most contrite and most affectionate, saying it had always been 'the principal object' of his life to do everything he could to make everyone in the family happy; and Charlotte, encouraged by his kindness, had gone on to say that her parents obviously loved all her other sisters better than herself, that they constantly restrained her, 'just like an infant', and made no attempt to find her a husband abroad or give her an establishment of her own at home. In fact, they made her lead a 'perpetual tiresome and confined life' as though she were not a daughter but a slave.

She begged her brother to see what he could do to find her a husband and mentioned as a possibility his friend, the Duke of Bedford. Knowing that their father would never consent to such a match, the Prince wrote a very long letter to the Duke of York, who was at that time in Germany, to ask his advice about the likelihood of a foreign match.

The Duke of York replied that the Prince of Prussia was hoping to marry one of their sisters; but he was not likely to be interested in Charlotte, who was then twenty-five, since he was only twenty-one. The Prince then interested the middle-aged widower, Prince Peter of Oldenburg, in marrying his anxious sister; and Charlotte was seen to blush whenever his name was mentioned; but although her sisters began teasingly to refer to her as 'the Duchess of Oldenburg', nothing came of this suggestion either. And it was not until the Hereditary Prince of Württemberg came to England in 1797 that Charlotte's long spinsterhood was over.

The Prince was very fat – so fat, indeed, that Bonaparte

said that God had created him merely to demonstrate how far the human skin could be stretched without bursting – and very plain. Charlotte appeared to be 'almost dead with terror and agitation' at her first sight of him, which was not surprising as there were strong rumours that he had connived at the murder of his first wife. 'Timid and distressed' as she went into the chapel to be married, she was 'a good deal affected on her return'. Her sisters and father all cried; 'everyone kissed her hand and bowed to the Duke of Württemberg without being spoke to by either'.

Charlotte settled down happily in Germany, however, writing regularly to the Prince, giving unsolicited advice on the education of her little namesake, having good cause to complain – as had all his brothers when they were abroad – that he did not reply to her letters as often as he might, but remaining 'ever most sincerely attached' to him and always grateful for the 'many proofs of friendship' he had shown her.

At the time of the Princess Royal's marriage, Princess Augusta was twenty-nine, Princess Elizabeth twenty-seven, Mary twenty-one, Sophia twenty and Amelia fourteen. Princess Augusta was more self-confident than her elder sister, a lively, cheerful, affectionate woman, amusing and boisterous. In her younger days she had played cricket and even football with her brothers; she was studious, though, as well as energetic, and Fanny Burney was astonished by the range of her knowledge and the sharpness of her insight. Her hopes of marrying had been dashed by the King, who had found fault with the various suitors proposed for her, and in any case had been unwilling to grant permission for her to marry while the Princess Royal remained unattached. Denied the companionship of any suitable young men of her own age, she had at first formed a romantic admiration for one of her father's doctors, the courtly Henry Vaughan (who changed his name to Halford on inheriting the large estate of an elderly cousin), and then had conceived an enduring passion for one of her father's equerries, a dashing Irish soldier,

Major-General Sir Brent Spencer. She confided in the Prince of Wales how much she loved the General, and felt relieved when she had done so; but there could be no thought of a recognized marriage so long as the King was capable of preventing it; and by the time that he was not, she was nearly forty-five. She died unmarried.

Her sister Elizabeth's long struggle for a husband was eventually more successful, though for many years it had seemed that she was the least likely of all the girls to get married. She had been very fat as a child and for years had been an invalid. Artistic and emotional, she was, like her eldest sister, rather managing and interfering; she was also, like Charlotte and all the others, strongly sensual. There had been rumours years before of an illicit affair with one of the King's pages and, less believably, of a pregnancy; and at the time of Charlotte's marriage to the Prince of Württemberg she had written to the Prince in the hope that now one of the girls at least had been settled, the turn of the others would follow. Sympathetic as always to his sisters in their plight, he renewed his efforts to help. The possibility of a match with Louis Philippe, Duke of Orleans, was suggested, only to be condemned out of hand by the Queen, who understandably refused even to consult the King knowing perfectly well what his reaction would be to his daughter's marriage to a Roman Catholic, a penniless one at that, and a man whose likelihood of ever becoming King of France – which, in fact, he did do against all the odds in 1830 – seemed then peculiarly remote. Princess Elizabeth then turned once again to her brother, whose promises of future complaisance, when in a position to fulfil them, were evidently so reassuring that she fell 'on her knees with *gratitude*'. The promises he had made would be '*secreted*' in her '*own breast*'; 'volumes would not suffice' to express half of what she felt towards him for his 'unbounded goodness'.

For the moment, though, she understood that she would have to 'go on vegetating' as she and her sisters had been forced to do 'for the last twenty years' of their lives. When she mentioned marriage to her mother she was told that that was a subject not to be raised at the moment. So Princess Elizabeth sublimated her longing for babies of her own by looking after other peoples', and in charitable works for orphans. She was, as her mother wished, never idle; she wrote letters for the Queen, and she produced numerous creditable engravings; she amassed an admirable collection of porcelain; she took up farming and kept a set of Chinese pigs in one of the fields at Frogmore. Anxious not to have become undesirable by the time it became possible for her to marry, she drank sugar melted in water at night to keep her temper sweet, and went for long walks at eight in the morning so as not to become more stout than she already was. She told the Prince that all she wanted in the winter of her life were good friends, warmth, a comfortable chair, a book and 'a good fireside with a *kind brother*'. But the Prince knew that what she was really hoping for was something far more exciting than that. In the meantime, what she sardonically described as the *'lively, cheerful* and *gay life'* which she and her sisters led was, he realized, sadly tedious to them all.

Mary, the fourth sister and the Prince's favourite, troubled him less with her problems. She was a kind, affectionate girl, but more self-contained than the others, more remote, more critical. Discreet in her behaviour, she was quite outspoken in her remarks. She offended the Duke of York by drawing attention to his growing corpulence, and excused herself by observing, 'It is so *very visible* that I could not help *making the* remark'. It was tacitly supposed that she would one day marry her cousin, the boring, pompous and conceited Prince William of Gloucester of whom, unaccountably, she seemed quite fond.

No such opportunity offered itself for either of the two youngest Princesses, Sophia and Amelia, both of whom, being denied acceptable suitors, had affairs with gentlemen about the Court much older than themselves. Sophia was generally considered a delightful girl, very pretty, rather

unruly, passionate, moody and delicate. Both the Duke of
Clarence and the Duke of Kent admitted to the Prince that
she was their favourite; and the Duke of Cumberland's deep
affection for her was felt to be not altogether healthy. In
fact, Cumberland was reported by the Princess of Wales to
have fathered a child to which Sophia seems to have given
birth in secret at Weymouth in August 1800 when she was
twenty-two. It was a report which the Duke of Kent for one
seems to have both believed and propagated. The child was
more likely, however, to have been fathered by one of the
King's equerries, Major-General Garth, uncle of Miss
Frances Garth, Princess Charlotte's former Sub-Governess.

General Garth might almost have been selected by the
King for service at Court on the grounds of his appearance.
It could hardly have been expected that so unprepossessing
a man could have appealed to any of his daughters, impressionable and frustrated though they were. He was very small,
and his undistinguished face was badly disfigured by a
purple birthmark that covered part of his forehead and surrounded one eye. Charles Greville, the future clerk to the
Privy Council, went so far as to describe him as a 'hideous old
devil'; but then 'women fall in love with anything – and
opportunity and the accidents of the passions are of more
importance than any positive merits of mind or of body. ...
They [the Princesses] were secluded from the world, mixing
with few people – their passions boiling over and ready to fall
into the hands of the first man whom circumstances enabled
to get at them.'

Garth, who was thirty-three years older than Princess
Sophia and had been in the King's service since she was a
young girl, found himself alone with her, apart from the servants, one summer's evening at Windsor when her parents
were in London. She had been ill for some time and had been
taken from the Lower Lodge to Queen's Lodge where she was
put in a bedroom beneath General Garth's. Nine months
later she was 'brought to bed', so Lady Bath told Greville on
the authority of Lady Caroline Thynne, at that time Mis-

tress of the Robes to the Queen, a 'very simple, natural and true' woman with 'ample means of information'. The King was told that the Princess was dropsical and he evidently believed it, or at least chose to believe it. In any case, it was easy to deceive him now for he was almost blind.

Princess Sophia, the Duke of Kent's 'poor little Barnacles', his 'dear little angel', never fully recovered her health, though she was to survive all her sisters, except Mary, and to live on well into the reign of her as yet unborn niece Victoria. Her invalidism seems, indeed, almost to have become a form of self-indulgence which was pampered by repeated visits and constant presents from her eldest brother, her 'dear love' for whose affectionate attentions she thanked him in letter after fond and tender letter. Occasionally, so Lord Glenbervie said, she saw her son, who had been christened Thomas and left at Weymouth at the home of Major Herbert Taylor, the Private Secretary to the Duke of York and afterwards to the King.* She may conceivably have married the child's father in a secret ceremony, for he remained in favour at Court, being promoted Lieutenant-General and then General and appointed to a responsible position in the Household of Princess Charlotte. But Princess Sophia seems not to have much enjoyed her life for all her family's kindness. '*Poor old wretches* as we are,' she wrote to the Prince in her tiny writing, lamenting the lot of her unmarried sisters and herself and thanking him for his kindness to the '*four old cats*' at Windsor, '*poor old wretches*, a *dead weight*

* There is nothing in the Royal Archives either to confirm or to repudiate Glenbervie's story – which he had from that unreliable source, the Princess of Wales – but the young Thomas Garth, as portrayed by Barraud, certainly bears a strong resemblance to Princess Sophia's portrait by Beechey. In 1824 he filed an affidavit in Chancery maintaining that he had come into possession of certain documents which Sir Herbert Taylor had agreed to buy from him in exchange for an agreement to settle all his debts and an annuity of £3,000 a year. Taylor, so Garth contended, was attempting to get these documents removed from the bank where they were deposited without fulfilling his part of the bargain (*Greville Memoirs*, i, 270–71).

upon you, *old lumber* to the *country*, like *old clothes*. I wonder you do not vote for putting us in a *sack* and *drowning us*
in the *Thames*.'

By the time she wrote this letter, Princess Sophia's younger
sister, Amelia, had died. At the age of fifteen she had contracted tuberculosis. Three years later she was also suffering
from erysipelas, and for much of the rest of her life she was
in pain. In vain efforts to cure her, the royal doctors bled her,
purged her and blistered her; applied leeches to her skin
and quills beneath it; immersed her in hot sea-water baths,
prescribed beef-tea, calomel and madeira; poured emetics
and laudanum down her throat accompanied by a variety of
powders, medicines, restoratives and stimulants. Her sufferings, and the patient resignation with which she bore them,
aroused the sympathy of all her brothers and sisters whose
letters to each other are replete with references to 'poor dear
Amelia', the pretty baby of the family, her present condition
and the likelihood of its amendment.

The Prince was a constant visitor. She was his godchild,
and next to Mary, who nursed her devotedly during her
periodic attacks, he loved her perhaps even more than any
of his other sisters. In 1798 when she was sent to Worthing
to spend the summer in a house by the sea, he rode over to
see her almost every morning from Brighton. He suggested
that she should be brought to stay with him in the Pavilion,
where he would make her comfortable in a pleasant little
apartment, but her parents thought it better that she should
stay where she was. When he could not visit her, he wrote to
her and sent her presents.

She adored him. He was her 'dear angelic brother', her
'dear angel', her 'beloved eau de miel'; she inscribed herself
his '*own child*'; she had always loved him, she confessed,
better than any of the younger brothers; a new dictionary
would have to be invented for her to be able to say just how
much she did love him. She longed for his visits which were
her 'greatest happiness', and always felt 'as if in a dream'

after he had gone. To see him was 'really and truly a cordial', more good to her than any medicine. He was all the more dear to her, for, as her illness progressed, she fancied that the rest of the family were less than affectionate in their attitude towards her, particularly the Queen and Princess Elizabeth, known by her as 'Fatima', whom she believed to be under their mother's influence. Repeatedly Amelia complained of 'the Queen's *ill and cross* looks'; she could 'not feel any pleasure in seeing *her*'; she didn't expect 'much *feeling or pity* in that *quarter*'; her cruelty was 'not *new*' but now she could not stand it; as for Elizabeth, one day or another she should hear her '*mind*'.

On Christmas Eve 1809 she wrote angrily to the Prince, 'to describe *her* [the Queen's] *feelings*, her manner and her visit to me yesterday, *all* I can say till we meet is it was the STRONGEST CONTRAST to the dear King POSSIBLE, but I am too much used to it to feel *hurt* by *it*. But I pity her.' A few days after Christmas she added, 'I hear Gl. F.R. is returned and the Queen *was particularly* cross to *him*'.

This was the trouble. The 'Gl. F.R.' to whom Amelia referred was Major-General the Hon. Charles Fitzroy, one of the King's equerries and a man with whom she was passionately in love. He was better-looking than Princess Sophia's lover, General Garth; but whereas Garth had some charm and wit, Fitzroy was generally reckoned to be a dull, sedate, reserved soldier, interested in little apart from his profession, and not likely to be attractive to women, particularly to those, like Amelia, who were over twenty years younger than himself. He was a son of the first Lord Southampton, who had been a Groom of the Bedchamber to the King, and was descended from one of the illegitimate sons of Charles II. The King was devoted to him, so much so that he was referred to at Court as Prince Charles.

The Queen, who had learned of the affair as early as 1803, kept it secret from the King for fear of the consequences, but she repeatedly remonstrated with her daughter about 'this unpleasant business', 'this unfortunate indulgence'. To refer to the love of her life in these dismissive terms was, for Amelia, unforgivable; and her mother never was forgiven. The Queen's 'ill and cross looks' made her ever more determined to marry her 'blessed and beloved angel', her 'precious darling' as soon as she could. She gloried in her attachment to him, she told him. 'O, Good God, why not be together?' she asked him imploringly. 'I pine after my dear Charles more and more every instant.... I really must marry you, though inwardly united, and in reality that is much more than the ceremony, yet that ceremony would be a protection.' She liked to suppose that he was, in fact, her husband already, and she assured the Duke of York that she 'considered herself married'. She signed herself dear Charles's 'affectionate and devoted wife and darling'.

Like Princess Elizabeth in similar circumstances, Princess Amelia pleaded with the Prince to help her; and he seems to have made a promise to do so as soon as he could; but nothing could be done while the King was alive. And this knowledge of her father's stubborn intractability gradually eroded the love that once she had felt for him; but out of duty and kindness she hid her feelings from him.

In her last illness in the summer of 1810, when, as Princess Sophia said, her suffering was 'VERY GREAT INDEED', the King came to her room frequently, holding her hand, peering down at her, trying to discern with his failing eyes the features of his favourite child. She gave him a ring into which she asked Rundell, Bridge & Co., the Court jewellers, to set one of her jewels and a lock of her hair pressed under a little crystal window with the inscription *Remember Me*. She put it on his finger herself, and as she did so he burst into tears.

Her last thoughts were of General Fitzroy. 'Tell Charles,' she murmured at the end, 'I die blessing him.' In her will she bequeathed him everything she had with the exception of a few tokens to the Prince of Wales, to the Duke of Cambridge, whom the Prince had asked her to appoint joint executor with himself, to Princess Mary and, as an afterthought in a codicil, 'something belonging' to her, to her other sisters and 'the dear King'.

In fact, Princess Amelia had little to leave but jewellery and debts. She had been an extravagant young woman, and had borrowed money from both Mary and Sophia, and from her brother, who had once lent her £4,000. The Prince had the jewels valued and presented them to Princess Mary, giving their purchase price to the fund for the settlement of the debts. The unfortunate General Fitzroy, cajoled by the Prince into renouncing his claim, was obliged to content himself with a monetary compensation and a few boxes of worthless effects. Lord Holland thought that, in the circumstances, the Prince could not very well have dealt with the problem of Amelia's will in any other way; throughout the business he had behaved 'with great delicacy and good nature'. Lady Holland thought so, too: 'The Prince behaved throughout with the greatest tenderness ... with the utmost circumspection and decorum.' Even the King, when his doctors believed him well enough to hear the contents of the will and the action that his son had taken, was said to have commented, 'Quite right, just like the Prince of Wales.' But afterwards the Prince's conscience was much troubled. Three years later, on Amelia's name being mentioned, he 'burst into tears ... seemed embarrassed and excessively overcome ... and regretted he could not more fully comply with her last wishes'. So deeply affected was he by her death that after the funeral he was never again able to sleep in a room that was not lit by several wax candles.

22

Approach to the Regency
1810–1811

'Mr Perceval has seen the King'

AT the time of Princess Amelia's death on 2 November 1810, the King was seventy-two. His past few years had been troubled by a series of national and family misfortunes and calamities that had worried him to excess. The scandal over the Duke of York and Mrs Clarke had been immediately preceded by the retreat of Britain's army in Spain to Corunna and the death there of its commander, Sir John Moore; it had been shortly followed by the disastrous expedition to the island of Walcheren, an attempt to open up a second front in the west against Napoleon, which had also ended in a British retreat and the loss of thousands of British troops. Then, in the summer of 1810, the Duke of Cumberland became involved in an even more unsavoury scandal than the one that had led to the resignation of the Duke of York.

Cumberland, 'alias the *Black Sheep*' as his brother the Duke of Kent referred to him, had become increasingly embittered, increasingly reactionary and increasingly strange ever since his return home from the war in 1796. Granted a most generous allowance of £18,000 a year by Parliament, he had also received some highly lucrative military appointments in England; but his hopes of a command in the Peninsula had been thwarted, and his criticisms of those whom he felt stood in the way of his ambitions grew ever more outspoken and vituperative. He was an intelligent man with a cruel, sardonic humour, 'very sarcastick', as the Prince said, 'very comical though very impudent'. As another of his brothers, the Duke of Clarence observed, if anyone had a corn he was sure to tread on it. The Prince of Wales's feeling for him alternated between the deepest distrust and the closest intimacy. In 1808 the Prince was reported to be constantly in his company, yet he could never forget that the Duke, as an inveterate Tory, espoused the cause of the Princess of Wales; and he could never forbear to warn his sisters against allowing themselves to be left alone in their rooms with him.

His reputation was such that when, in the early morning of 31 May 1810, his Corsican valet, Joseph Sellis, was found dead in bed with his throat cut, it was immediately rumoured that the Duke – who was supposed either to have been caught in bed with his wife or to have been blackmailed by him after making homosexual advances – had murdered him.

At the subsequent inquiry the Duke himself claimed that he had been asleep in bed in his apartments at St James's Palace when he had been woken by a light blow on the head which he had supposed had been caused by a bat attracted into the room by a candle burning by his bedside. He sat up and his eyes caught the flash of a sabre blade which he attempted to grab, almost severing his right thumb. He jumped out of bed, and ran for help to the adjoining room of his English valet, Cornelius Neall, crying out 'Neall! Neall! I am murdered!' His assailant pursued him, cutting him superficially on his buttocks and thigh and more seriously on his head, and would have killed him had it not been for the thickness of his night-cap. His cries for help caused the assailant to flee, dropping the sabre on the floor. Neall, wielding a poker, rushed into the room, followed by other servants who later found a pair of slippers belonging to Sellis in a closet. Shortly afterwards 'a guggling noise' was heard coming from Sellis's room; and the valet was found by a Sergeant of the Coldstream Guards, on duty at St James's, lying on the bed with his hands 'straight down and the blood all in a froth running from his neck'. A razor with a white handle lay on the floor about two feet from the bed; Sellis's blood-stained coat lay hanging over a chair; a basinful of blood-stained water stood nearby.

It seemed clear that, after making his attempt upon the Duke's life, Sellis had returned to his room and was endeavouring to remove the evidence of his guilt when the guards appeared in the corridor outside and, rather than submit to arrest, he had killed himself. This was the view taken by the jury at the inquest; and since the foreman of the jury was the honest Radical reformer, Francis Place, there seemed no cause for dissent.

Yet the motive for the attempted murder remained a mystery. Witnesses at the inquest gave evidence to the effect that Sellis and Neall had been on very bad terms, that Sellis had threatened to leave the Duke's service unless he received better wages and the same perquisites as Neall, that Sellis had been heard to express republican sentiments, 'to damn the King and the royal family', and to say it was 'a pity they were not done away with'. Cornelius Neall testified that some months before, Sellis had accused him of theft, an accusation which was investigated and found to be untrue; and afterwards, discovering 'an evil disposition' from Sellis towards him, he 'thought it right to hang a pistol at the head of the bed' for his protection.

Neall's wife, who had known Sellis for almost twelve years, confirmed that he was very obstinate and quarrelsome and would not bear contradiction, that he lived 'very much to himself' and was 'very distant' with all the other servants.

Mrs Sellis said that her husband had 'frequently complained of a giddiness in the head', but she had never heard him make any criticism of the Duke's conduct towards him. A letter from her husband to the Duke was produced in which Sellis complained of the 'unconfortable and most unpleasant way' in which he was made to travel, being placed upon the carriage box, 'the most disagreeable of all grievances', whereas the Prince of Wales's servants were allowed inside the carriage or provided with a post-chaise.

It appeared, however, that Sellis was in general treated

well by the Duke who was 'very partial' to him, and that if he had any grievances against him they were more imaginary than real. It was the opinion of Colonel Henry Norton Willis, the well-informed Comptroller of Princess Charlotte's Household, that Sellis, his mind deranged by his illness, had been goaded into fury by the Duke who 'in his violent, coarse manner' taunted him for being a Roman Catholic.*

Following so soon on this unpleasant scandal, and on the humiliating retreats of the armies from Spain and the Low Countries, the fatal illness of Princess Amelia was too much for the King to bear. During the last week of her life, he shocked the Queen's tall, plain and prim companion, Miss Cornelia Knight, by the 'dreadful excitement in his count-

* There is a curious document in the Royal Archives (Asp/P, vii, 373–8), a 'memoir' by Charles Jones, for several years the Duke's private secretary, who 'compelled by some irrisistable power' which seemed to be calling to him from the grave, set down in 1827, when he feared that he was dying, an account of a conversation he had had with the Duke on Christmas Eve, 1815. Having locked the door and sworn Jones to secrecy, the Duke confessed, 'You know that miserable business of Sellis's, that wretch, I was forced to destroy him in self-defence, the villain threatened to propagate a report, and I had no alternative.' This document – found amongst the papers of a descendant of Captain Jones which were purchased by a Manchester bookseller who presented it to the Royal Library in 1899 – appears to be genuine, but whether Jones misunderstood the Duke's meaning or intentionally wished to harm him it is, of course, impossible to say. The Duke may for some strange reason, in keeping with his mysterious character, have wanted to mislead or shock his secretary or to impose some burdensome secret upon him. What at least seems clear enough is that, whatever he might or might not have said, he did not murder Sellis. According to a confidential report sent to Lord Henry Seymour by one of the Duke's pages 'the drapery of the Duke's bed over his head was very much cut which saved his life. His bed was also covered with blood. The Duke received four blows on his head ... and as he was escaping into Neall's room, the assassin made a desperate lunge which took off a large splinter off the edge of the door. No traces of blood were found from the Duke's room to Sellis's. The razor was found close to Sellis's bed. The body and bed completely covered with blood' (Seymour of Ragley MSS, CR 114A/277).

enance' when he came into the drawing-room. As he could
not distinguish faces any more, 'it was the custom to speak
to him as he approached' so that he could recognize people
by their voices. Miss Knight forgot what she said to him but
could never forget what he said to her: 'You are not uneasy,
I am sure about Amelia. You are not to be deceived, but you
know that she is in no danger.' While speaking he squeezed
Miss Knight's hand with such force that she could scarcely
help crying out with the pain. 'The Queen, however, dragged
him away,' Miss Knight recorded in her memoirs. 'When tea
was served I perceived how much alarmed I had been, for my
hand shook so that I could hardly take the cup.'

On 29 October when Perceval saw the King, his conversation was 'prodigiously hurried ... extremely diffuse ... and
indiscreet' and it seemed that another lapse into insanity
was imminent. The next day he was slightly less hurried and
irritable, but his conversation remained 'unconnected'; that
evening he was 'extremely violent', breaking out, 'as in
former instances, in most unfit language to the Princesses'.
By the morning of 1 November he was quieter again, but his
mind was quite vacant, and his doctors felt that they would
once again have to enlist the expert help of Dr Simmons.
When Simmons, accompanied by his son and four assistants,
arrived at Windsor, however, he insisted that he must be
given full charge of the case; and since the 'ordinary physicians' refused to agree to this, he marched off 'with his troop
immediately'. The next day Dr Heberden summoned the
medical officer of St Luke's Hospital and the keeper of a
private madhouse in Kensington Gore.

By now it was becoming clear that a new regency crisis was
approaching. On 2 November Canning told his wife, on the
information of Lord Wellesley, the Foreign Secretary, that,
although tractable, 'poor old Knobbs' was 'just as mad as
ever he was in his life'. Wellesley described 'the sight, but
still more the *hearing* of him before he went into the room,
as most dreadful – a sort of wailing, most horrible and heart-
rending to hear'. In a lucid moment he exclaimed that this

was the fourth time he had been ill, giving his reasons for the three previous attacks and adding: 'And now it is poor Amelia.' The violence of his disorder had reached so 'horrible a height' by 3 November, the day after Princess Amelia's death, that it was necessary to place him in a straitjacket. For a short time after that he showed signs of improvement, accepted the fact of his daughter's death which he had previously been unable to comprehend, began to sleep better, to grow calmer and to eat with evident pleasure his simple meals of bread and cheese and mutton broth with turnips. But then he relapsed once more into his former feverish restlessness and incessant rambling, interrupted by intervals of quiet in which he corrected himself frequently and allowed 'others to correct him'.

The doctors were all obviously puzzled by his case, agreeing that he was without doubt incapable for the moment of attending to government, but varying in their opinions as to when he would be likely to recover. Dr Reynolds, who agreed with his patient in attributing the illness to anxiety on account of Princess Amelia, had seen the King recover from his three previous attacks and saw no reason at all why he should not recover from this one. But the others were less sanguine: the King was an old man now, almost totally blind.

As in 1788, the government held fast to hopes of the King's early recovery, trusting that he would be better before a Regency Bill became necessary, fearing that such a Bill would result in their dismissal in favour of the Prince's Whig friends. Parliament was adjourned for a fortnight on 1 November, and for a further fortnight on 15 November; but Ministers recognized that with Napoleon's armies so dangerously rampaging on the Continent a decision could not much longer be delayed. On 18 December, following an indecisive examination of the doctors by select Committees of the Commons and Lords, Perceval, while continuing to assure the House of Commons that the King would probably soon be better, felt obliged to write to the Prince to inform

him that he intended to introduce a Regency Bill, with restrictions on the lines of Pitt's proposed Bill of 1789.

The Prince, remaining faithful to his resolution not to
interfere in politics, had so far done nothing to cause offence
either to Ministers or the Queen. He had gone down to
Windsor immediately on hearing of the onset of his father's
malady, had then retired into the seclusion of his apartments in the Lower Lodge and had not only declined to discuss the King's condition with the opposition but had also
said nothing of any significance to the members of the
government who came down to Windsor to find out from
the doctors how their patient was progressing. The Prince's
conduct was 'perfectly proper, correct, most dignified', the
Duke of Bedford said. Whenever Ministers approached him,
the only answer he made to them was that they themselves
'must be the best judges of the line of conduct they ought to
pursue'. Any observer could see, 'even with the most prying
eye', Colonel McMahon told the Duke of Northumberland,
that the Prince gave 'no audience or access to any description
of politician whatever'. Lord Holland confirmed that his behaviour had been exemplary, that he had 'conducted himself
... with great caution, great dignity and great feeling'. There
was no doubt, Holland added, that this could 'in some
measure' be attributed to his being 'deeply affected' by Princess Amelia's illness and death.

When Perceval elaborated his proposals for the Regency
Bill, however, the Prince took strong exception to them.
For the Regent's powers were to be severely limited for about
twelve months. He was not to have powers to create peers,
except in the cases of military or naval commanders who
might not survive to enjoy the honour; he was to be allowed
to grant pensions and make appointments to public offices
only for the duration of the Regency 'and subject, as to their
further continuance, to the subsequent pleasure of his
Majesty' upon his recovery. Moreover, 'the management of
the whole of his Majesty's Household, and the power of

appointing the officers and servants of that establishment' were to be entrusted to the Queen.

Immediately on receipt of Perceval's letter, the Prince replied by reminding him of the answer he had given to Pitt's similar letter in December 1788; and he had 'only to declare' that the sentiments expressed in that letter 'admitted of no change'. The Prince then called all his six brothers and his cousin, William, now Duke of Gloucester, to a meeting at Carlton House. They all arrived within a few hours, and at midnight they signed a letter, written by the Duke of York, in which they entered their 'solemn protest' against measures which they considered 'perfectly unconstitutional', as well as being 'contrary to and subversive of the principles which seated [their] family upon the throne of these realms'.

While the interference of the Royal Dukes was widely resented, there was a good deal of sympathy for the Prince in his demand for a regency without restriction. A limited regency might well have been considered appropriate in 1788 when he was only twenty-six and scarcely to be described as circumspect: but he was now over fifty and had recently displayed a far more responsible attitude. Besides the country was at war and a strong government was essential. This view was forcibly expressed by Lord Grey, who contended that 'under the pretence of preserving the rights and providing for the restoration of a King' who could now never possibly be a king in anything but name, Perceval's administration were merely endeavouring to 'secure the Government in their own hands'.

But Perceval remained, in Whitbread's phrase, 'as bold as brass', 'in great vigour of speaking', determined not to give way. To Plumer Ward it seemed 'amazing' how he fought. He gained his point. Voting on an amendment to remove the restrictions on the proposed regency was close; but the amendment was defeated, and by 8 January 1811 the principle of a restricted regency had been accepted by both Houses.

The next day Lord Grey arrived in London from his home in Northumberland and went to Carlton House to confer with the Prince about the formation of a new Whig government. The Prince had already talked his problem over with Lords Grenville and Moira and had discussed the implications of turning the Tory Ministers out. He had recognized that a strong administration was essential and that it might, therefore, be necessary to bring in Canning, despite his association with the Princess of Wales. He had also made clear his wish to reinstate the Duke of York, with whom he was now on good terms again, as Commander-in-Chief at the Horse Guards.

As Grey lamented sadly, the difficulties in making the necessary arrangements were so great as to drive anyone as mad as the King. He himself heartily disliked Canning and did not wish to serve with him though Grenville thought it would be impossible to command enough support in the House of Commons without his help. Grenville wanted to be First Lord of the Treasury, but said that he could not afford to give up his profitable sinecure as Auditor of the Exchequer, though Grey, Holland and Whitbread thought the two offices quite incompatible. When it was suggested to him that he might become Home Secretary instead of First Lord of the Treasury, he said that he could only forego the office normally associated with the Premiership if he were to be responsible for the Treasury patronage. He also wanted his brother, Thomas, to be First Lord of the Admiralty, though Lord Grey had promised this appointment to his own brother-in-law, Whitbread.

The Prince asked that Sheridan should be given the Irish Secretaryship, but Grey objected to 'sending a man with a lighted torch into a magazine of gunpowder'. The Prince also wanted his friend, the Duke of Northumberland, in the Cabinet; but Grey disliked Northumberland almost as much as he did Canning; while the Duke of Norfolk's request to the Prince to be appointed Lord Privy Seal was frowned upon by Grenville. The Marquess of Buckingham, who threatened not to support the new government if Whitbread went to the Admiralty, hoped to see his son, Lord Temple, as Secretary of War, an office provisionally allocated to Grey's friend, Sir James Willoughby Gordon. The Duke of Gloucester and the Duke of Kent pressed rival claims to the Master Generalship of the Ordnance, to the dismay of those Whigs who were already opposing the reinstatement of the Duke of York as Commander-in-Chief.

Towards the end of January 1811 it was more or less settled that Grenville would become First Lord of the Treasury, agreeing for the moment to forego the salary of the Auditorship of the Exchequer while retaining the sinecure for his future security. Grey was to be Foreign Secretary; Holland, Home Secretary; Tierney, Chancellor of the Exchequer; Erskine, Lord Chancellor; and Whitbread, First Lord of the Admiralty. But when these names were submitted to the Prince, he seemed unwilling to commit himself to a change of government at all. So long as there was a possibility of the King's recovery he was reluctant to take the drastic step of dismissing his Ministers. Both Grey and Grenville agreed that if the King's recovery really were to be expected within the near future, then it might be better to leave matters as they stood; and they advised the Prince to go down to Windsor straight away to interview the doctors.

The Prince, though evidently very reluctant to do so and, as Grey noticed, very nervous at the prospect, consented to go, saying that he would leave the next morning. When the time came, however, the Prince could not bring himself to go, excusing himself on grounds of illness. 'I do not believe he will have nerves to take the manly and decisive measures which alone can enable him to conduct the Government with effect,' Grey commented resignedly, 'and I am persuaded, if the present reports of the King's improved state continue, that he will not dare to make any change in the Administration.'

The Prince's hesitation was understandable, for the King was daily getting better. Indeed, on the very day that the

Prince had intended going down to Windsor, his Majesty
was able to conduct a relatively coherent interview with
Perceval in which he learned of the progress of the Regency
Bill, expressed himself pleased with the favourable reports of
the Prince's conduct during his illness, and said that he was
ready to take up the reins of government again if that was
required of him. Perceval replied that the doctors did not
think he was quite ready for that yet; but it seemed that one
day soon he might well have recovered sufficiently to resume
his duties.

The Queen implied as much in a letter to the Prince on
29 January in which she wrote, 'You will be glad to hear, my
dearest son, that Mr Perceval has seen the King and communicated the state of public business pending in the two
Houses of Parliament. His Majesty gave perfect attention to
his report, and was particularly desirous to know how you
had conducted yourself, which Mr Perceval answered to have
been in the most respectful, most prudent, and affectionate
manner.'

The Prince felt convinced that this letter had actually
been drafted by Perceval and the Queen had merely copied
it out, for what woman, he asked, ever used such a phrase as
'the state of public business pending'? It was an artifice, 'too
gross to escape detection'. Grey was also sure that the letter
was written 'in concert with Perceval'; it evidently, he told
his wife, was 'part of a plan in which I think there can be no
doubt that that greatest of all villains, the Duke of Cumberland, has had an active part, to intimidate the Prince by the
expectations of the King's immediate recovery, from changing the Administration. So bare-faced a plot, and so much
of the same character as the proceedings in 1804, ought to
have a directly contrary effect. But *I believe it will be successful.*'

There was certainly no doubt that the Duke of Cumberland, very anxious to keep the Tories in office, was extremely
grateful to Sir Henry Halford – who had, he said, '*behaved
nobly*' – for impressing upon the Prince the delicate balance

of the King's mind and the possibly fatal effects of a sudden change of government. There was certainly no doubt, either, that since the Princess of Wales had quarrelled with the Duke of Cumberland over his advice to her not to 'treat little Billy as fit to be brought up with her daughter', the Prince and his brother were almost inseparable.* As Glenbervie wrote, 'the intimacy between the Prince of Wales and the Duke of Cumberland since the rupture between the Duke and the Princess and more particularly since he went to reside at Carlton House, after the attempt on his life, has been a matter of as general notoriety as the Prince's undisguised hatred of him before that time. The Princess says he now entirely governs the Prince and that it is by his persuasion (others say by Lord and Lady Hertford's) that he has determined to make no changes, except probably giving the presidency of the Council or some other great office to Lord Moira.'

Swayed by contrary advice from his family and friends, the Prince appeared to change his mind from day to day. When it was hinted that only timidity and nervousness prevented him from turning to the Whigs, he 'launched out in his eloquent, rhodomontading manner', accusing them of 'treating him worse than his avowed enemies' when they had been in office before, and adding 'that he knew they now complained of his not sending for them, but that he would

* The Prince had provided a sickroom for his brother at Carlton House while the Duke's apartments at St James's were thrown open to the public who entertained themselves by inspecting the splashes of dried blood on the walls. Dr William Cookson had visited the Duke at Carlton House where he had found him in 'a very nervous state, supposed to be owing to the large quantities of laudanum' which he took. 'He suffers much pain,' Cookson had told Joseph Farington, 'and is much afflicted with spasms. One of the servants at Carlton House [said] that the Prince is much affected by the Duke's illness, "more so", he had added, "than either his mother or his sisters appear to be".' The servant had gone on to say, 'whenever any of the Prince's family are indisposed he feels for them' (*Farington Diary*, v, 70).

be damned if he did; they accused him of being timid and nervous, but that by God they and the world should see that he was *un homme de nerf*; that he would not be dictated to by the haughty freaks and caprices of any man'. Yet when Lord Holland called at Carlton House he gained the impression – the Prince was always 'very dexterous in conveying an impression ... without saying anything positive' – that 'he would place his government in the hands of the Whigs, but that he would take his own time and way of doing it, and that he had been nettled at the observations to which his delay had given rise, or in which their impatience had indulged'.

Fearful of the consequences of committing himself to the Whigs, the Prince consulted the King's doctors at Carlton House on 30 January. Dr Robert Willis confessed that he could not 'look with any degree of confidence to his Majesty's complete recovery within any limited time', but his hopes of an eventual recovery had 'rather been increased of late' and the King's present progress towards that recovery was upon the whole as favourable as Willis had expected.

Sir Henry Halford went further than this by stating that he thought it 'highly probable' that the King would recover 'within three months'; and Dr Heberden, though giving his opinion 'without any considerable degree of confidence', agreed that it was more likely than not that the patient would recover within three months.

The doctors reports left the Prince in a more indecisive state than ever; while the anxiety of his mother and sisters about the King's reactions to a change of Ministers weighed heavily with him. Also, neither Grey nor Grenville was particularly anxious for office in the difficult circumstances in which they would be placed by accepting it. 'What has passed,' Grey told his wife, 'has given me such an insight into the probable state of things under a new Government that I much doubt whether any circumstances could ever induce me to take a share in it.'

So, with the female members of his family opposed to a

change, with the Whig leaders now reluctant to take office, with the doctors hinting at his father's recovery within three months, and with the Hertfords and the Duke of Cumberland, as well as the Duke of York, urging him to keep the Tories in office, the Prince felt obliged to disappoint those friends who had so eagerly been looking forward to the enjoyment of power, and had been tiresomely pressing their claims.

On 4 February the Prince wrote to Perceval to inform him of his 'intention not to remove from their stations ... his Majesty's official servants.

'At the same time,' he continued verbosely, in the sanctimonious tone with which he was inclined to burden such communications as this, 'the Prince owes it to the truth and sincerity of character which he trusts will appear in every action of his life, in whatever situation placed, explicitly to declare that the irresistible impulse of filial duty and affection to his beloved and afflicted father leads him to dread that any act of the Regent might in the smallest degree have the effect of interfering with the progress of his Majesty's recovery. This consideration alone dictates the decision now communicated to Mr Perceval.'

Although Grenville was profoundly relieved by the Prince's decision and 'went down to Dropmore lightsome as a bird', the rank and file of the party were furious. 'Shoals' of angry men went down to Carlton House, Plumer Ward reported, and 'the whole of Pall Mall was crowded with knots of opposition'. Moira and Sheridan both warned the Prince 'that his character would be wholly gone ... Young Lord Devonshire spoke to him very strongly'; and Lord Thanet told him that his decision 'was the greatest calamity that had happened to the country since the death of Mr Fox'. In his reply the Prince implied to Thanet that he had but to wait a few weeks when the whole situation might well be changed.

At twelve o'clock on the morning of 5 February 1811, the bandsmen of the Grenadier Guards, bearing their regi-

mental colours, marched into the courtyard of Carlton
House. They pitched the colours in the centre of the grand
entrance and then struck up 'God Save the King' as the first
of the Privy Councillors arrived for the ceremony of swearing in the Prince as Regent.

Inside the palace, Yeomen of the Guard, soldiers of the
Life Guards and the Prince's liveried servants lined the staircase and the grand hall.

Soon after half past two, preceded by the officers of his
Household and accompanied by all the royal Dukes, the
Prince – 'grown enormously large' again since recovering
from his illness in 1809 – made his way through the circular
drawing-room into the grand saloon where he sat down at
the head of an immensely long table which was 'covered
with crimson velvet with massy silver inkstands originally
belonging to Queen Anne'. One by one the Privy Councillors, all in full dress, entered the room, the Archbishop of
Canterbury, the Lord Chancellor, the Archbishop of York,
the Lord Privy Seal and almost a hundred others. As each
one came through the doorway in correct order of precedence he bowed to the Prince who acknowledged the courtesy with his accustomed grace. When all were seated in
their respective places, the Prince stood up to make his oath
of loyalty to the King and to swear that he would 'truly and
faithfully execute the office of Regent of the United Kingdom of Great Britain and Ireland ... and ... consult and
maintain the safety, honour, and dignity of his Majesty,
and the welfare of his people ...'

The oaths and declarations, the signings and countersign-
ings all being completed, the Councillors approached the
Regent to kneel before him and to kiss his hand. Although
none of them could have failed to notice the marble bust of
Charles James Fox which had been removed from the
Prince's private apartments to its present ostentatiously
prominent position 'at the head of the room', and although
some observers thought that he turned his head away rather
abruptly when those whom he did not like knelt before him,

it was generally agreed that he maintained throughout the long ceremony 'the most dignified and graceful deportment'.

So, with appropriate stateliness and splendour, while the band continued to play triumphant airs in the courtyard and while Princess Charlotte, riding her horse up and down in the garden, peered inquisitively through the windows, the Regency began.

PART THREE
1811–1820

23

Whigs or Tories?
1811–1812

'The Prince is excessively nervous'

FOR months the Prince of Wales had been eagerly looking forward to celebrating the inauguration of his Regency by holding a grand fête at Carlton House. He would have liked to do so immediately after the swearing-in ceremony; yet as long as his father's physicians at Windsor continued to hint that his Majesty's mind might yet be 'roused from its disordered actions', a celebration of his own accession to power would clearly be premature. When the spring of 1811 gave way to summer, however, and his father's condition deteriorated, he decided to wait no longer. Twice he fixed a date for the party, but on both occasions was obliged to postpone it because of disturbing reports from Windsor. Then came more reassuring news, and he announced that on 19 June the fête would definitely be given, ostensibly in honour of the exiled royal family of France. Two thousand invitations were hastily despatched, some to people no longer living.

By eight o'clock on the appointed day, Pall Mall, St James's Street and the Haymarket were blocked with carriages, though the guests were not due to arrive until nine. Above the shouts of the coachmen, the crack of whips and the screech of iron-rimmed wheels could be heard the band of the Guards playing in the courtyard of Carlton House beneath Henry Holland's fine Corinthian portico. Beyond the wall that divided the gardens of the house from the Mall, matting had been laid over the smooth grass of the lawns; and covered walks, decorated with painted trellises, flowers and looking-glasses, had been specially built as promenades and supper galleries. The Prince's servants in their dark blue liveries, trimmed with gold lace, hurried about attending to their final duties.

The guests were received in the hall by various members of the Regent's Household and then wandered through the magnificent rooms on the ground floor which few of them had ever seen before.* The Regent himself appeared at a quarter past nine and stood waiting in a room, hung with blue silk and decorated with gold fleur-de-lis, to welcome the Comtes de Lisle and d'Artois, the Ducs de Berri, de Bourbon and d'Angoulême, the Prince de Condé, and Louis XVI's only surviving child, the Duchesse d'Angoulême. He was wearing the richly embroidered and idiosyncratically designed uniform of a field-marshal, a rank to which he had long aspired and from which his father had steadfastly debarred him. He was also wearing the glittering star of the Order of the Garter and a splendid aigrette.

He was forty-eight years old, but looked as though he might well have been several years older. His features, though still quite handsome, were overblown and heavy, and the expensive oils, ointments, creams, pastes and unguents which he bought in such immense quantities from his perfumers and which were applied so assiduously to his almost copper-coloured skin made it look waxlike rather than youthful. He had lost some weight since he had turned the scales at over seventeen and a half stone in 1797, but his well-corseted pantaloons could not disguise the fact that he was still extremely fat. His grey eyes were rather watery;

---

* Even those who had seen the rooms before had not seen all the furniture, pictures and ornaments in them. For the Regent was continually improving his collections, selling items, acquiring others, exchanging pictures that he no longer liked for ones he preferred, bringing out of store or down from the attics works which had not yet been displayed or which deserved a reappraisal. 'He changes the furniture so very often,' Lady Sarah Spencer commented, 'that one can scarcely find time to catch a glimpse at each transient arrangement before it is all turned out for some other' (*Lyttelton Correspondence*, 103–4).

the flesh beneath his chin tended to sag into the folds of his immensely high neckcloth; and artificial pieces were required to maintain the luxuriant appearance of the thick brown whiskers that adorned his cheeks. But he was as graceful as ever; his manner was still wonderfully easy and courteous, his charm irresistible. As he walked amongst his guests, affable, amusing and urbane, it was difficult not to agree with William Beckford that he was indeed 'graciousness personified'.

The entire entertainment, so Thomas Moore told his mother, was truly 'worthy of a Prince'. 'The extraordinary part of it was, that so large a number should have been served in such a style,' another guest thought; 'tureens, dishes, plates, even soup plates, were everywhere of silver with as many changes as were wanted. There were hot soups and roasts, all besides cold, but of excellent and fresh cookery. Peaches, grapes, pine apples, and every other minor fruit in and out of season were in profusion. Iced champagne at every three or four persons, all the other wines also excellent. There was no crowding, hurry or bustle in waiting; everything was done as in a private house.'

'Nothing was ever half so magnificent,' Moore continued rapturously. 'It was in *reality* all that they try to imitate in the gorgeous scenery of the theatre ... assemblage of beauty, splendour, and profuse magnificence ... women outblazing each other in the richness of their dress. ... I really sat for three quarters of an hour in the Prince's room after supper, silently looking at the spectacle ... the Prince spoke to me, as he always does, with the cordial familiarity of an old acquaintance.'

At half past two the Regent himself sat down to dinner; the long table was set for two hundred of his most honoured guests beneath ornate lanterns fixed to the fan-vaulted ceiling of the Gothic conservatory. Above him was an illuminated crown with the letters GR; behind him were crimson-draped stands – piled high with silver-gilt plate – and sixty attendants, one of whom stood '*in a complete suit of ancient armour'*. On the table in front of him was a miniature fountain whose waters flowed in a silver-bedded stream to right and left of him. The stream was bounded by mossy banks, water plants and flowers; tiny gold and silver fish swam through the arches of miniature bridges or, sadly, lay dead, floating on top of the water. A model lake was surrounded by miniature urns from which rose breaths of fragrant smoke.

The Duchesse d'Angoulême sat on the Regent's right; the wife of his eldest brother, the Duchess of York, on his left. His mother was not there as she thought it unseemly to hold such a party while the King remained so ill, and had strongly advised her son not to do so during this 'great calamity'. His sisters were also absent, in accordance with their mother's strict orders. Princess Caroline, the Regent's detested wife, had not been invited and had not expected to be invited. Ever since she and her husband had separated she had been 'like an archbishop's wife', she said with characteristic exaggeration and equally characteristic good humour: she did not 'partake of her husband's honours'. But she had not the least objection to the ladies of her Household accepting the invitations they had received, and she even bought them new dresses and ostrich feathers for the occasion.

To her extreme annoyance and disappointment, the Regent's daughter, Princess Charlotte, had not been invited either. She had been longing to go, as she confessed to her former Governess, Miss Hayman; it was her 'duty to go'; it was 'proper' that she should go; she thought it 'very hard' that her father had not asked her. She was no longer a child; she was fifteen, tall and well developed for her age. Others, too, thought it hard on the girl. She was admittedly still rather rowdy and gauche; her laugh was sometimes still far too loud and, as John Sanders, the architect, noticed disapprovingly, she had an 'extreme, awkward, neglected manner, lolling and lounging about without any self control'. She was also 'very talkative', Miss Berry thought, and very ill-bred; she did not 'walk any better', and had 'not dignified manners'. Yet she was 'very quick and very lively', and certainly no longer the tiresomely exuberant and ill-mannered, pert little girl who had so exasperated her tutors. And she was, after all, heir to the throne. But the Prince had his reasons, as events were to show, for keeping the girl on a tight rein and as much as possible out of the public eye. As the time for the fête approached, he had sent her down to Windsor to stay with her grandmother.

So neither his wife nor his daughter nor his mother nor any of his sisters were at Carlton House that evening. Nor was Mrs Fitzherbert. She had received an invitation, but when she learned that Lady Hertford – the woman who had usurped her place in the Regent's affections – was to sit at the royal supper-table, she decided to ask him personally whether or not she too would be given a place there. For months past at Brighton she had been humiliated by the Prince's devoted attentions to Lady Hertford at the Pavilion where her own presence had been virtually ignored. Would she be given a place at the Regent's table at Carlton House? she had asked him bluntly. In the past, 'to avoid etiquette in circumstances of such delicacy as regarded her own position with reference to the Prince, it had been customary to sit at table regardless of rank'. Would the same rule now apply? Repeatedly since their secret and illegal marriage in her drawing-room in 1785, the Prince had promised formally to establish her position in society as soon as it was in his power to do so. But that was before the advent of Lady Hertford. 'You know, Madam, you have no place,' he had replied.

'None, Sir, but such as you choose to give me.'

Though pressed by the Duke of York to admit her to the table, he firmly declined to do so, maintaining that the special privileges accorded to her when he was merely Prince of Wales could no longer apply now that he was Regent; so she had refused to go to the fête at all. They never spoke to each other again.

The Prince was not sorry to see Mrs Fitzherbert go out of

his life. She had become increasingly cantankerous of late; at fifty-five she no longer had the resilience to bear his selfishness patiently. In the past she had overlooked or forgiven his waywardness, his faithlessness, his repeated slights, for she had loved him.

Indeed, although she was sorely tried by the silence with which her subsequent letters to him were greeted, she was never entirely to outgrow her love for him. But she knew now that they could never be happy in each other's company again. She demanded a formal separation, and the Regent readily granted it, agreeing without demur to the continuation of her annuity of £6,000. This, having been rather ungraciously accepted, was soon afterwards deemed utterly insufficient. All her pecuniary difficulties, she crossly reminded the Regent, 'originated from ... the old debts of former times ... and the very scanty allowance' which he made her. £6,000 was 'not now worth as much as £3,000 was about nine or ten years ago'. The Regent obligingly agreed to increase the pension to £8,000 and then to £10,000, and hoped that with that she would be satisfied and bother him no more. All his thoughts were now centred on Lady Hertford; when parted from her, he confessed, he could only think of presenting her with his 'uggly phizz' once again.

Although the Carlton House fête was universally admitted to have been a triumphant success by those who had attended it, it naturally came in for much criticism from those who had not. 'What think you of the bubbling *brooks* and *mossy banks* at Carlton House?' Shelley asked, expressing a widespread indignation. 'It is said that this entertainment will cost £120,000. Nor will it be the last bauble which the nation must buy to amuse this overgrown bantling of Regency.' Many others were equally critical, both of the cost of the fête and of the opulent palace in which it had been held – a palace occupied by a man whose debts, though they were gradually being paid off, still amounted to over half a million pounds. His Household there was reputed to be enormous, as indeed it was. Apart from his Treasurer (Sir Samuel Hulse), his Private Secretary (Colonel John McMahon), his Assistant Private Secretary (General Sir Tomkyns Turner), a Vice-Treasurer and a Vice-Chamberlain, a Keeper of the Wardrobe and a Gentleman Porter, there were, in 1811, two clerks, five Pages of the Presence, five Pages of the Backstairs, a housekeeper, an inspector of the Household, a maître d'hôtel, a *tapissier*, a butler, a table decker, and two surgeons to the Household. The forty-three indoor servants included a silver-scullery-woman, a laundress, two cellarmen, three confectioners, four watchmen, six cooks and ten housemaids.*

The sumptuous interior of the palace in which these people worked came in for even more adverse criticism than the cost of maintaining it. There was 'not a spot without some finery upon it, gold upon gold'. For some it was 'really all too much', 'overdone', 'superfluous', 'vulgar in its opulence'. Yet everyone wanted to see it, of course; and as many as could took the opportunity to do so afforded by the Regent's opening it to the public for three days after the fête. On the third day no less than 30,000 people tried to get in; and, despite the efforts of the Duke of Clarence who stood on top of the garden wall endeavouring to control the crowds in his best quarterdeck manner, there was a stampede in which several distraught women visitors were stripped nearly naked. 'They were to be seen all round the gardens, most of them without shoes or gowns; and many almost completely undressed, and their hair hanging about their shoulders.'

* As was shown in an earlier chapter of this biography, the Prince was and always remained, a kind and considerate master. The Bishop of Lincoln's wife, with whom the Prince was to stay in 1814, was assured by his servants, 'There never was a man more easily pleased than the Prince Regent. Everything is right and he is kind and good to all.' 'How different,' the Bishop's wife commented, 'is all this authentic history to public rumours!' (Pretyman Papers, Ipswich, HA 11a).

The Regent was reported to be 'exceedingly upset' by the mismanagement, and to have relapsed into that mood of strange, unaccustomed withdrawal which observers had noticed during the earlier months of the year. At that time, as though worrying about the political problems with which he would soon inevitably be faced, he had seemed un-wontedly distant at private parties and public functions, speaking 'much less, both to men and women than he did'. In March 1811, at a reception at Lady Hertford's, Miss Berry had seen him arrive about midnight from a dinner party at Lord Cholmondeley's. He looked wretched, she had thought, 'with a muddied complexion, and was besides extremely tipsy'. But he was 'gravely and cautiously so', gave her a 'formal grave bow', and spoke little to anyone. It had even been reported, so one of his physicians told Plumer Ward, that he was 'engaged with religion' and was reading a chap-ter of the Bible every day in the earnestly Protestant company of Lady Hertford. Under her influence, it was sup-posed, he was now 'affected by Methodistical notions, and Rowland Hill, the Methodist preacher, [had] been with him a second time'.

In the company of those whom he took to be his suppor-ters he had been able momentarily to relax. At the Royal Academy dinner on 27 April, for example, he had appeared at his most attractive; and in one of the best royal speeches that Wilberforce had ever heard, he had, with obvious sin-cerity, declared that although 'others might be more able to judge the excellence of works of art, [they] could not ex-ceed him in his love of the arts, or in wishes for their pros-perity'.

Yet for most of that year he had seemed worried and pre-occupied, daunted by the amount of papers to which he was now expected to attend. One day Lord Dundas saw him sit-ting at a table at Carlton House between his Secretary, Colonel McMahon, and McMahon's assistant, General Tur-ner, 'the one placing a paper before him for his signature, the other drawing it away'. Having dealt with what Dundas believed to be as many as 14,000 papers, the Regent said wearily, 'playing at King is no sinecure'.

'The Prince is very nervous, as well he may be at the prospect before him,' reported George Tierney on 20 July, 'and frequent in the course of the day in the applications to the liquor chest. I much doubt, however, whether all the alcohol, as they call it, in the world under whatever name administered, will be able to brace his nerves up to the mark of facing the difficulties he will soon have to encounter.' The more he drank, indeed, the less decisive he became; and he certainly drank a great deal that summer. According to Lord Hampden he was quite capable of getting through three bottles of wine at dinner, 'besides maraschino, punch and eau de Garuche' which he liked 'excessively strong and hot'.

One of his worst trials was his arch-conservative brother, the Duke of Cumberland, who appeared to follow him wherever he went, warning him against Whigs, against reform, against Catholic emancipation. Princess Charlotte said that her uncle, 'Prince Wiskerandos', whom she heartily disliked, was her father's 'right hand'. In fact, the Regent, who could not bear being pestered, was by now quite exasperated by the Duke – who had been convalescing at Carlton House ever since his valet had tried to murder him at St James's Palace the year before – and he went so far as to move to Stable Yard solely to shake him off. The Duke's society 'is becoming excessively irksome to him,' Lady Holland accurately informed Lord Lansdowne, 'but it denotes a lamentable lack of energy that he can only get rid of a troublesome inmate by flying his own home. The other day when he went to Windsor he took Tommy Tyrwhitt [his former Private Secretary] in his chaise and bid him keep close to the door when they were to come back in order to escape the Duke of Cumberland's importunities, but he had a more dextrous foe than he calculated upon, for the Duke, after the Prince was seated, got up upon the steps upon the pretence of whispering, and instead of getting down, hollowed out to Mr Tyrwhitt that he had better follow in his chaise. The Prince was either too timid or too much confounded to remonstrate.'

In the autumn the Regent escaped to Brighton and there he appeared far happier than he had been in London, charming his guests with his easy, friendly manner, his 'animated and varied conversation', and the delightful way in which, when he went to bed, he would bid them all good night with a graceful wave of his hand and a favourite farewell, 'God bless you all!'

Sir Philip Francis, the reputed author of the *Letters of Junius*, reported him as being 'very gay' at a dinner party at the Pavilion on 30 October, and Thomas Creevey, who was there the following day, enjoyed a 'very pleasant evening. About half past nine, which might be a quarter of an hour after we arrived, the Prince came out of the dining-room,' Creevey recorded in his journal. 'He was in the best humour, bowed and spoke to all of us, and looked uncommonly well, though very fat. He was in his full field marshal's uniform. He remained quite as cheerful and full of fun to the last – half past twelve – asked after Mrs Creevey's health, and nodded and spoke when he passed us. ... He looked much happier and more unembarrassed by care than I have seen him since this time six years. This time five years ago, when he was first in love with Lady Hertford, I have seen the tears run down his cheeks at dinner, and he has been dumb for hours, but now that he has the weight of the Empire upon him, he is quite alive.'

The next evening he was in the same 'high good humour' as he sat in the Music Room, between Giovanni Battista Viotti, the violinist, and Lady Jane Houston, beating his thighs in accompaniment to the band, 'singing out loud, and looking about for accompaniment from Viotti and Lady Jane'. Creevey, a dedicated Whig, listened for some political pronouncement, some indication as to how much longer the Regent intended to keep in power the Tory government which he had inherited from his father. Creevey had hoped that upon assuming the Regency the Prince would have immediately cast out the Tory Prime Minister, Spencer Perceval, whom, as a former supporter of the Princess of Wales, he did not much like, and call into office those Whigs with whom he had once been on such friendly terms. This was certainly what most Tory Ministers, including Lord Liverpool, had expected. 'We are all, I think,' wrote Palmerston, Secretary at War, to his sister, 'on the *kick and the go.*'

Yet the Prince had not dismissed them, and the Whigs had begun to doubt that he ever would do so. Several Whigs had dined with him at Carlton House on 1 July; but on the 11th he dined with Lord Camden, Lord President of the Council, and on the 24th with the Secretary for War, Lord Liverpool. Also that month, upon passing the windows of Perceval's kitchen, Creevey had been appalled to see 'four man cooks and twice as many maids preparing dinner for the Regent'. He had supposed that the ground was being prepared for maintaining the existing government in office. The Whig leaders, Lords Grey and Grenville, it was by then generally expected, would be 'passed over and the present Ministers continued with the addition of some of the Prince's private friends, such as Lords Moira and Hutchinson and [Lady Hertford's son] Lord Yarmouth, and old Sheridan'. It was certainly Perceval's own view that his government was to be kept in office, though Lord Bathurst, President of the Board of Trade, rather doubted it. Lord Moira agreed with Perceval: the Regent was becoming used to his Ministers; he did not like change anyway and was too lazy to provoke it. Besides, he was finding it extremely difficult to persuade his close friends to serve with the present Ministers. It was the Prince's view that 'his friends ought to come forward whenever he [chose] to call upon them, *without regard to who [was] his [Prime] Minister*'. It was a 'strange fancy', to be sure, but it existed and '*very strongly too*'.

This was one fundamental problem. Another was that the Whigs in general knew that the Prince was far from reli-

able, and were not at all sure that they could trust him even
if they were to negotiate with him. 'I know there are difficulties all round,' said Grenville, 'but I know of none greater
than a confidential intercourse where you cannot place confidence.' Even the Prince's personal friends shared this view.
As Hutchinson said, there was with him 'a close connection
between promise and retraction'.

So the summer passed and no changes were made, while
the Regent displayed a rash determination to make the most
of the still considerable powers of the monarch and to exercise his patronage by granting preferment to his friends,
sometimes without consulting Perceval, at others in direct
opposition to his wishes. He insisted, for instance, that his
faithful servant, Colonel McMahon, should be appointed
Paymaster of the Royal Bounty to Officers' Widows, a sinecure worth about £2,700 a year, which was about to be
abolished and which the Commons refused to sustain. He
was equally insistent that his brother, the Duke of York,
who had been forced to retire as Commander-in-Chief in
1809, should be reappointed though the Cabinet warned him
against it. He assured his friend the Duke of Northumberland that 'one of the first acts' of his 'emancipation' would be
to call up his son, Lord Percy, to the House of Lords, and he
promised an appointment in his Household to the Duke's
son-in-law, Lord James Murray. He overruled Charles
Yorke, First Lord of the Admiralty, in nominating his own
candidate to be a Marshal of the Admiralty in place of the
Minister's. And he later told Perceval that he was absolutely
determined that the brother of his old tutor, Dr Cyril Jackson, should be granted the vacant bishopric of Oxford.
'Perceval then put on one of his little cynical smiles,' so the
Regent related, 'and observed, "Your Royal Highness perhaps does not know Dr William Jackson's *character*. He
is a notorious *bon vivant*."'

'Oh, as to that,' the Regent replied, 'I know him very well.
I have known him all my life. He has drunk a bottle of port

in this house before now and I hope that, when he has got his mitre on, that he will drink another.'

At Brighton, however, neither politics nor patronage was discussed, and no members of the government were invited to the Pavilion. Nor were Hutchinson or Moira. Lord Yarmouth was often there with his mother, and so was the persistent and tiresome Duke of Cumberland, looking 'really hideous', in the regimentals of his own German hussar regiment, with 'everybody trying to be rude to him and not standing when he came near them'. Yet although these two, Cumberland and Yarmouth, were suspected to be his 'real advisers', in public at least they were mute. There was 'no intercouse between the Regent and them'.

Reluctant as he was to commit himself, the Regent's political decision could not be delayed much longer. The restrictions on his powers, which had been imposed for a year, were due to expire in February 1812; after that there could be no further delay. The Whigs had reluctantly accepted the fact that it was difficult for the Regent to bring them into office so long as his father's recovery seemed possible; but the reports from Windsor suggested that an early recovery was now highly unlikely. In the middle of July the Duke of Cumberland had written, 'the King has taken 4 jellies, some coco and tea, is totally lost as to mind, conversing with imaginary persons, as he is constantly addressing himself to *Eliza*. ... 'Tis a most melancholy prospect.' Since then, the prospect had not brightened in the least.

On 17 September the doctors reported that 'His Majesty showed clearly his incapability of maintaining any steadiness in his ideas and conversation for more than an instant. ... He never failed to decline into some wild unnatural frame of thought after a sentence or two.' They had 'the mortification of hearing him speak of new arrangements which the *late King* was *now* making – and detail accounts of strange and horrible events which he himself was convinced had occurred in the course of the last night'. He was convinced that his sons were also dead, 'or sent away to a distant part of the globe. He was engrossed by the wildest and most extravagant fancies', sometimes imagining that he could call from the dead anyone he chose, at other times that he was an animal in Noah's Ark. In short, he appeared to be 'living in another world', and had lost 'almost all interest in the concerns of this'.

Even so, the Regent hesitated. He did not altogether trust the Whigs any more. Their ideals and aspirations, as exemplified by the stout, uncouth figure of the delightful and sadly missed hero of his youth Charles James Fox, had held a strong appeal for him in earlier years as an unruly son of a disapproving father. But the case was altogether different now. The loyalty of the Whigs to the Crown he thought questionable, their would-be policies of emancipation and reform too radical. Moreover, as a party they were in disarray, at odds with the radicals, suspicious of one another, without true leaders. Grey, whom the King disliked as much as ever, was unwell and sulky; Holland was also ill; Grenville seemed indifferent to the prospect of office; Lansdowne was considered too inexperienced, Brougham too insincere, Tierney too devious, Whitbread too emotional, Sheridan too profligate. No one thought of George Ponsonby, the official leader of the opposition in the House of Commons, as more than a temporary compromise until some more effective spokesman could be found. Above all, in the Prince's mind, was the knowledge that the Whigs were certainly incapable of continuing the war in any state of unity. Many of them were in favour of ending it altogether and of coming to terms with Napoleon. Creevey, for one, was delighted when he thought he detected signs of the Regent's enthusiasm for Portugal and Wellington 'going down', and when Sir Philip Francis assured him, upon the evidence of 'equerries and understrappers', that the Peninsular campaign was now 'out of fashion'. Both Creevey and Francis hoped that the concern that the Regent expressed upon reading the returns of the army's casualties in the Peninsula would make him 'think of peace'. The Regent was not thinking of peace, though. On the contrary, the idea of a negotiated settlement appeared to him absurd when, after years of sacrifice and struggle, the fortunes of the war seemed to be turning, when Wellington was making headway, and Napoleon was withdrawing troops from the Peninsula to send across the Dnieper into the wastes of Russia.

Difficult as the decision facing him was, the Regent affected not to be unduly concerned about it so long as he remained at Brighton. On 9 November he was still 'very merry and seemed very well'. Three weeks later, however, he was far from merry and very ill indeed.

He had gone to Oatlands, the Duke and Duchess of York's country house, to attend a ball held in honour of Princess Charlotte. He had given his daughter a lively demonstration of the Highland fling, had slipped, strained his ankle against the leg of a sofa, and retired to bed. Soon it was clear that he was not merely suffering from a twisted ankle; he 'complained of violent pain' from which he could only obtain relief by lying on his stomach and by taking 'a hundred drops of laudanum every three hours'. Some people talked of gout, but others, better informed, knew that the complaint was far more serious than that. 'The Prince is, I believe, extremely ill,' Lady Bessborough told her lover, Lord Granville Leveson Gower. '[One of his several doctors, Sir Walter] Farquhar says he suffers such agony of pain all over him it produces a degree of irritation on his nerves nearly approaching to delirium. What will become of us, if as well as our King our Regent goes mad? It will be a new case in the annals of history.' Ready as always to make trouble, the Duke of Cumberland, so William Fremantle reported, went about saying that his brother was mad already, that the complaint about his ankle was 'all sham', that he could get up perfectly well if he had a mind to, that the malady 'was higher than the foot, and that a blister on the head might be more efficacious than a poultice on the ankle'. The illness was nothing but insanity.

Cumberland with great vehemence denied having made these remarks, reports of which led to his brother refusing to see him alone any more. Sir Benjamin Bloomfield, who had been the Regent's Gentleman Attendant since 1808, described to Princess Charlotte a dreadful journey with Cumberland at the beginning of December. He '*never had* passed so *unpleasant* a journey in all his life', Bloomfield avowed, 'as [the Duke] was *vociferating oaths* against the *person* (whoever it was) that *could* set afoot such a lie ... declared that if he could discover the person he would *destroy him* with his own hands, used the most solemn oaths to declare *his innocence*, in short worked himself up into a sort of frenzy that [I] hardly knew what [I] would do next, as there were firearms in the carriage – and this conduct the whole way up to town'.

Whether or not the Duke had said his brother was mad, Fremantle was himself inclined to suppose that the Regent's brain was indeed sadly affected, and he told the Marquess of Buckingham that he thought that this was because he was so desperately 'worried and perplexed' by the problems of the now imminent unrestricted Regency. These had harassed 'his mind and rendered him totally incapable, for want of nerves, of doing anything'.

For several weeks he continued 'very ill' with agonizing 'pains in his arms and fingers' and 'the loss of all power in them'. On 23 November he complained to Lady Hertford that he had passed a night so bad that 'it surpassed in every respect everything' that she could form herself 'the smallest idea of'; the day before he had been 'incapable of moving a single joint' in his 'whole frame'. One of his doctors, Sir Everard Howe, told Thomas Lawrence that he was now taking as many as 250 drops of laudanum a day, and even so could get only three hours' sleep.

By 1 December Princess Charlotte found him looking much better, but obviously 'suffering a great deal of pain still'. For two hours he 'talked entirely of the King and gave a *most distressing* and lamentable *account*'; nevertheless he was '*more easy in his manner*' which the Princess thought was '*a step*' at least. A fortnight later he was suddenly and unexpectedly back in London, still 'nervous to the greatest degree', so George Tierney thought, as he was bound to be if the stories about the quantities of laudanum he took were true. According to Princess Charlotte he was also taking 'a great quantity' of hemlock which was now his only means of getting any sleep. However, Sir Walter Farquhar assured her on 18 December that the danger was over, though he could not declare when his patient would be '*quite recovered* as he had retarded his recovery himself so much owing to his playing with his constitution', disobeying the doctors' instructions, dosing and treating himself as he thought fit. He was still excessively nervous, and when he heard accounts of the murders in Ratcliffe Highway, he was 'so much alarmed' that he gave orders that no strangers should be admitted to Carlton House after eight o'clock at night, to the great disappointment of his servants, 'who had made preparations for entertaining their friends at Christmas'.

It was 'much believed' that the attack in the arm was 'paralytic'; and, according to Princess Charlotte, he himself attributed the weakness and twitching in his hands to paralysis. This was a likely enough diagnosis, Princess Charlotte thought, since huge quantities of opium were 'liable to cause that'. He could hardly write on account of three 'of his fingers being compleatly numbed and useless', which made his friend and physician, Sir Henry Halford, think that the Regent might be suffering from palsy. A year later he was still complaining that his 'poor right paw' could still hardly hold a pen, and that he had the '*greatest pain and difficulty in writing, having the gout all over him but particularly in both his hands*'.*

* As was suggested in Part Two, the Regent may have been suffering from porphyria, that rare hereditary metabolic disorder which, in a far more severe form, afflicted his father and which, endemic in the Stuarts, was transmitted to the Hanoverians by the Electress Sophia, granddaughter of James I and mother of George I. The Prince's

symptoms seem consistent with such a diagnosis, though he was
never subject to the extreme mental derangement which characterized his father's case (Macalpine and Hunter, 229–46). He always
took great trouble to conceal his illnesses when he feared that they
might be reported as hereditary afflictions of the brain; and an article
in the *Sunday Times* which guardedly made this suggestion drove
him to demand that the Attorney-General should lose no time in
attending to the 'infamous attack' made upon him. He also wrote to
the Home Secretary, 'Why not treble the duty upon all Sunday
newspapers?' He read everything of this kind, feeling it 'a duty to
do so', hence he could 'well judge of the mischief resulting from this
abused liberty of the press'. His observations equally applied 'to
obscene prints in the form of caricatures'. There was scarcely a shop
in London dealing in such trash in which he was 'not exposed in
some indecent ridiculous manner'; and it was 'high time' that a stop
was put to it (Parker, i, 336–7). During this illness in 1811–12, and
all subsequent illnesses, he was extremely reluctant to allow any
bulletins to be issued since, he insisted, they only led to gossip.
During a severe illness in 1824, when for three days he never spoke
and his life was despaired of, Sir Henry Halford was desired to travel
to Windsor by night and to go back to his London patients in the
morning, so that all might be 'kept in the most profound secrecy'
(Buckingham, *Memoirs of the Court of George IV*, ii, 77).

24

An Adonis of Loveliness
1812–1814

'This (or else my eyesight fails),
This should be the Prince of Whales'

THE Regent's general recovery was slow, and was rendered all the more prolonged by the political problems he was now urgently called upon to settle. He had postponed his decision as long as he possibly could, seeking advice from every quarter, then discussing the advice with yet other advisers, keeping all contenders for office in the dark as to what he intended to do, hoping that after wearisome, exhausting negotiations a strong government acceptable to himself would eventually emerge. Ideally this government would 'unite as many persons of talent ... as possible'. It would include moderate men of both parties, as well as his personal friends; it would carry on the war in the Peninsula with renewed energy; and it would postpone the problem of Catholic emancipation.

In the past, during Fox's lifetime, the Regent had always looked upon Catholic relief with sympathy, as his friends Lord Moira, Lord Hutchinson and Lord Hutchinson's brother, Lord Donoughmore, still did. But now – due largely to the influence of the Hertford family, it was supposed – the Prince was more inclined to agree with the Duke of Cumberland that it would be a most dangerous innovation. Not wanting to be accused of having broken faith, he maintained that he still favoured relief, yet he could not see his way to granting it so long as the King was alive. After all, his argument ran, he was only acting as Regent in the King's name; the King had had strong feelings that to give way to the Catholic claims would be to violate his coronation oath; the King's feelings must be respected.

As Prime Minister in his ideal government the Prince favoured the claims of the Duke of Wellington's brother, Lord Wellesley, the Foreign Secretary, that 'Spanish grandee grafted on an Irish potato', in the Regent's characteristically acute description. Lord Wellesley himself had no doubts as to his own suitability for the post; and on 16 January he tendered his resignation on the grounds that Perceval was incompetent and that neither he nor the rest of the Cabinet were pursuing the war with sufficient vigour. The Regent persuaded him to remain for the time being, holding out the hope that he might soon find himself at the head of a coalition government; and the next month the Regent sat down to write a letter to the Duke of York – an intermediary known to be strongly against Catholic emancipation – who was to take it to Lord Grey who was, in turn, to make its contents known to Lord Grenville.

Neither Grey nor Grenville was in the least disposed to consider the coalition which the letter, in a calculatedly wounding way, proposed. The Regent was merely offering the Whigs a few ministries in return for their acknowledgement that the Tories deserved to remain in office in recognition of their 'honourably distinguished' conduct of the war in the Peninsula. In their rather haughty reply, Grey and Grenville pointed out that they differed from the present administration on 'almost all the leading features of the present policy of the empire', particularly Ireland, and they refused to consider joining it unless there were to be a clear understanding that Catholic relief would be granted. In any case, neither Grey nor Grenville was convinced that it would be wise to accept office even if it were to be definitely and unreservedly offered them, irrespective of the differences over Catholic emancipation. As Grenville said, there was a 'total want of confidence in the Prince's steadiness and good faith'.

Having thus skilfully broken with the Whigs without actually refusing to offer them office, the Regent turned back to Perceval whose government was confirmed in power, to the profound satisfaction of the Duke of Cumberland to whom his brother was now reconciled. The Regent's difficulties, however, were far from over. Lord Wellesley, disappointed in his hopes of succeeding Perceval, reiterated his determination not to serve under him any longer, and advised the Regent to strengthen the government by bringing in both Lord Castlereagh and George Canning.

When this advice was passed on to the Cabinet, they unanimously decided to resign unless Wellesley did so. His ambitions frustrated, Wellesley did resign, proceeding to Carlton House 'in the highest style, state liveries and full dress', to deliver up the seals to the Regent who 'was, or appeared to be, *deeply* affected and almost unable to speak'. Then, to the Regent's further chagrin, he was asked to accept the admission to the government of Lord Sidmouth as Lord President of the Council. 'Is it possible Mr Perceval, that you are ignorant of my feeling and sentiments towards that person?' he exclaimed angrily when the Prime Minister explained the necessity of bringing Lord Sidmouth in. 'I now tell you, I will never have confidence in him, or in any person who forces him upon me.' The Regent thoroughly disliked Sidmouth, his father's conscientious and prudish former Prime Minister, whom he blamed for his past failure to obtain the military promotion upon which he had set his heart. 'If you choose to employ him, be it so,' he went on. 'But I warn you that you must take all the responsibility of the measure upon yourself.' In the end, however, the Regent was forced to give way.

While the Cabinet, thus strengthened, were far from satisfied that they had the Regent's confidence, the Whigs were outraged by his treatment of them. Even Lord Moira, who for years had been one of his most intimate friends – and had, in consequence, become almost bankrupt – was for a time estranged from him, unable to reconcile his personal friendship with loyalty to Whig principles. Lords Hutchinson and Donoughmore were also estranged; so was the

Duke of Norfolk. 'It grieves me to the soul to tell you, Sir,' Moira wrote to him on 28 February, 'that the general astonishment at the step which you have taken is only equalled by a dreadful augury for your future security. It is not the dissatisfaction of disappointed expectants to which I allude. A disinterested public views with wonder your unqualified and unexplained departure from all those principles which you have so long professed. It observes with a still more uneasy sensation your abandonment of all those persons for whom you had hitherto proclaimed esteem, whose adherence you had spontaneously solicited, and of whose services (rendered at the expense of foregoing their private advantages) you had for years availed yourself.'

At the St Patrick's Day dinner at the Freemasons' Tavern on 17 March, when the Prince was normally the 'reigning and rapturous toast', his name was loudly hissed. Sheridan loyally stood up to defend it; but, as was so often the case now, Sheridan was drunk, and his speech was received with shouts of protest and hisses louder than ever.

Very few other Whigs remained faithful to the Regent. Lord Forbes, his aide-de-camp, thinking that his political opinions did not 'in the least degree accord with those of the Ministers, in whom his Royal Highness the Prince Regent thought it expedient to repose his confidence', felt it his duty to submit his resignation from the Household. The Regent declined to accept it; but Creevey, who attended a dinner party at Michael Angelo Taylor's house in White-hall, a favourite rendezvous of the Whigs, recorded that Lord Forbes came to the table 'with the yellow lining and the Prince's buttons taken away from his coat. He said never again would he carry about with him so degrading a badge of servitude to such a master.' *

---

* Lord Forbes's host, Michael Angelo Taylor, had formerly been a close friend of the Regent. They had recently fallen out because – so it was said – the Regent had tried to seduce Mrs Taylor. Her husband had discovered him in the process and knocked him down (*The Rising Sun*, ii, 157–9; BM *Sat*, viii, 481).

Forbes's indignation was common throughout the Whig party. Deprived of the pleasures, power and perquisites of office, its members rounded on the Regent and on the Hertfords, the Duke of Cumberland and the Queen, whom they believed chiefly responsible for turning the Regent's mind against them. Creevey was vehement in his condemnation of 'this madman', 'this most singular man ... doomed, from his personal character alone, to shake the throne'. Brougham attacked him in even stronger terms; so, too, did Whitbread. As Lord Holland later observed, they all 'charged his Royal Highness with ingratitude and perfidy', encouraging 'every species of satire against him and his mistress'. Indeed, Lady Hertford, 'the old lady of Manchester Square', was quite as savagely attacked as he was himself. Lord Grey, who declared that he would never take office until 'this destructive influence' had been abolished, referred in the House of Lords to an 'unseen and separate influence which lurked behind the throne ... an influence of [an] odious character, leading to consequences the most pestilent and disgusting'. Another Member of the House described a similarly pestilential figure 'issuing forth from the inmost recesses of the gaming house or brothel and presuming to place itself near the royal ear'.

Enraged, the Regent retaliated. At a banquet at Carlton House he launched 'a furious and unmeasured attack' upon his erstwhile political friends by whom he persuaded himself, as he so often did persuade himself, that he had been monstrously ill used. So angry with the Whigs did he become, in fact, that Princess Charlotte burst into tears and had to be led out of the room by Sheridan. It had once been her father's proud boast that he had 'bred up his daughter in the principles of Mr Fox'. Now it had come to this.

Worse was yet to come. On 11 May Perceval was shot through the heart in the lobby of the House of Commons by John Bellingham, a deranged commercial agent ruined by the war; and the Regent had another ministerial crisis on his hands. Lord Liverpool, formerly Secretary for War, succeeded Perceval as Prime Minister; and Lord Castlereagh became Leader of the House of Commons as well as Foreign Secretary. The Regent tried to give the government further strength by asking Wellesley and Canning to rejoin it. Canning, however, refused to work with Castlereagh, and declared that he would not join a government which was not committed to Catholic emancipation. Wellesley, his eye still on the leadership, also refused; and, in any case, Liverpool and his colleagues made it clear that they would refuse to have either him or Canning back.

An exasperated backbencher now proposed a motion of 'no confidence' in the present administration; the motion was carried, and Lord Liverpool's government resigned on 22 May. Once again the Regent turned to Wellesley and through him halfheartedly approached the Whigs with renewed proposals for a coalition; but this time, too, as he surely hoped they would, the negotiations came to nothing. Then, professing to be desperately in need of the reassurance and advice of his old, estranged friend, Lord Moira, he sent for him and 'flung himself upon his mercy'. When Moira dutifully called at Carlton House, the Regent 'hung round his neck in tears' and 'seems to have been very nearly in convulsions'. Moira said that perhaps it would be better if he called another day to discuss the situation when the Regent was 'more composed'. The next day, however, he was just as agitated as ever; but, after a long discussion, Moira agreed to attempt yet another approach to Grey and Grenville. He was no more successful with them, though, than Wellesley had been. They demanded the resignation of the Regent's Household, including, of course, Lord Hertford, and his son, Lord Yarmouth; and this the Regent loyally refused to consider. Lord Moira then set about composing a government with the help of the Tories; yet although a brave soldier he was 'the greatest political coward in the world', and in the end his nerve failed him. The Regent, having used him as he had used Wellesley to get rid of the Whigs, now decided that the time had come to 'fall back upon his old government' and to reappoint Lord Liverpool as Prime Minister. At last, by a combination of wearying procrastination and cunning manoeuvre, he had got the government he had all along been endeavouring to establish: Perceval's government without Perceval, a government that would pursue the war with vigour, and leave the Catholic question alone.

Throughout the protracted negotiations which had taken place since Perceval's murder, the Regent had appeared to be in 'a state of agitation beyond description'. Sheridan 'described the Prince's state of perturbation of mind as beyond anything he had ever seen'. He sought relief in drink as well as in laudanum. As Princess Charlotte commented disapprovingly, 'too much oil was put into the lamp'. It was not only the harassing negotiations with government and opposition that had bothered him. There had also been a series of anonymous letters, signed 'Vox Populi' and 'An enemy of the damned Royal Family', which threatened him with 'the same fate as Mr Perceval' if he did not see to it that bread was cheaper and that Bellingham was reprieved. In the north, where anger over what was felt to be his betrayal of the Whigs was particularly strong, walls and doors had been placarded with notices offering a hundred guineas as a reward for the Regent's head. In addition, there had been angry scenes in Parliament over his continuing to employ Colonel McMahon as his Private Secretary at a salary of £2,000 a year, an office which the opposition condemned as unconstitutional, since no British sovereign, except King George III when he was nearly blind, had ever had a Private Secretary before. There had above all been the constant importunity of numerous claimants who looked to him, now that his powers were unfettered, to fulfil old promises, not to mention the worry of his debts.

At the end of 1811 his debts amounted to £552,000; and he had wanted the Cabinet to appeal to Parliament to settle them. He had also asked for £150,000 for what he termed

'Regency services'. The Cabinet had insisted that he must be
content with £100,000 for 'Regency services'; and as for his
debts, it had been suggested to him that Parliament would
never agree to pay off so immense a sum; he must endeavour
to do so himself by means of his own economies. This had
been the 'decided and unanimous opinion' of the Cabinet,
'most reluctantly and unwillingly adopted'.

There had also been strong opposition to the Regent's
requests for £196,000 a year for the establishments of the
King, the Queen and the Princesses. And the Regent had
not only had serious differences with the government about
this, he had also had to contend with the objections of his
increasingly ill-tempered mother. If the Princesses were to
have their own establishments – which she was very much
opposed to their having – the Queen wanted to know why
she herself could not have a 'separate and distinct establishment'. It was all very well to argue that, in the event of the
King's recovery, he would want to find 'his government, his
family and his everything exactly *eo ipso* as he left them'; in
the meantime she had to confess that she was 'very uneasy'.
She wanted 'a certain sum' stipulated for herself alone so
that she could never 'be either suspected or accused of
incroaching upon the King'.

She was 'voracious', the Regent's former Secretary, Tyrwhitt, complained, 'and had tormented the Prince in his
worst illness, at Oatlands, with a visit to prevent his giving
the Princesses an independent establishment'. However, she
was not able to prevent it. He remained firm in support of
his sisters' cause; and although the Queen was eventually
promised her own establishment, so, too, were the Princesses.
They were to receive £9,000 a year each, in addition to
£4,000 a year from the Civil List, and were thus to become
independent of their parents at last. They had had to wait
an inordinately long time. Since the eldest, Princess Charlotte had married the Hereditary Prince (now King) of
Württemberg in 1797, not one of the other sisters had found
a husband. Augusta was now forty-four, Elizabeth forty-two,

Mary thirty-six and Sophia thirty-five. They all looked to their eldest brother for his future help, and all wrote affectionate letters to thank him for the great kindness he had always shown them in the past. He was still, and was ever to remain, their '*dearest, dearest* brother' whose 'angelic behaviour' towards them would always be remembered.

It was rarely that anyone else referred to him in such terms. He was as unpopular with the people as a whole as he had ever been. The Marquess of Buckingham was informed by William Fremantle, that when he went to the Queen's Drawing-Room at the end of April 1812, there were 'upwards of ten thousand people in Pall Mall through which he passed, but there was not one single token of applause. It was a dead silence throughout.' 'At the play the other night,' Fremantle continued, 'when *Henry V* was acted, all the allusions to his breach of promise when Prince of Wales were thundered with applause and in the new play which is now acting at the Lyceum there are some allusions to female influence in government which are constantly met by clapping and applause'.

After the St Patrick's Day dinner at the Freemasons' Tavern, where the drunken Sheridan's amphibological remarks in defence of the Regent's name were drowned in the general hissing, the *Morning Post*, which had been purchased on behalf of Carlton House some years before, wishing to make amends for this 'ungenerous conduct', referred to the Prince in ludicrous hyperbole as 'the Glory of the People', 'the Maecenas of the Age', an 'Adonis of Loveliness'.

These 'astounding eulogies' were altogether too much for the *Examiner* which briskly responded with the assertion that this so-called 'Glory of the People' was, in fact, 'the subject of millions of shrugs and reproaches', that 'this Adonis of Loveliness was *a corpulent gentleman* of fifty! In short, that this delightful, blissful, wise, pleasurable, honourable, virtuous, true *and* immortal PRINCE [was] *a violator of his word, a libertine over head and ears in debt and dis-*

*grace, a despiser of domestic ties, the companion of gamblers
and demireps, a man who has just closed half a century
without one single claim on the gratitude of his country or
the respect of posterity'.*

The author of this attack, Leigh Hunt, and his brother
John, editor of the *Examiner*, were arrested and charged
'with intention to traduce and vilify his Royal Highness, the
Prince of Wales, Regent of the United Kingdom'; and,
despite a spirited defence by Henry Brougham who, enthusiastically welcoming the case as an excellent opportunity for
damaging the Regent, 'fired for two hours very close and
hard into [him] on all points, public and private', they were
found guilty, fined £500 each and sentenced to two years'
imprisonment.

The sentence caused widespread indignation and made
the Prince more unpopular than ever. Shelley, who visited
Leigh Hunt at Horsemonger Lane Gaol, and proposed a
subscription for the 'brave and enlightened man', furiously
condemned the Regent as a 'crowned coward and villain',
an 'infernal wretch', constantly demanding more money –
and for what? 'For supplying the Augean stable ... with
filth which no second Hercules could cleanse.' Keats
lamented that 'kind Hunt was shut in prison'; and Charles
Lamb's anonymous verses on 'The Prince of Whales' were
repeated with renewed conviction:

> Not a fatter fish than he
> Flounders round the polar sea.
> See his blubbers – at his gills
> What a world of drink he swills ...
> Every fish of generous kind
> Scuds aside or shrinks behind;
> But about his presence keep
> All the monsters of the deep ...
> Name or title what has he? ...
> Is he Regent of the sea?
> By his bulk and by his size,
> By his oily qualities,

> This (or else my eyesight fails),
> This should be the Prince of Whales.

Benjamin Haydon expressed the general view when he commented that although Hunt's libel was impudent enough, the 'debauched Prince ... amply deserved it'. And although writers were inclined to be more circumspect thereafter, the number of attacks upon the Regent were by no means diminished. A few weeks after the Hunts were sentenced, Thomas Moore, lending his pen to the Whigs' attack, published anonymously *Intercepted Letters or the Two-penny Post-Bag* in which the 'R–G–T' was held up to a ridicule even more wounding than Hunt's savagery.

It was at this time that the Prince had the mortification of quarrelling finally with Beau Brummell whose elegance and caustic wit he had for so long, if rather jealously, admired. There had been numerous petty quarrels in the past, since Brummell had always declined to mark his friendship with the Regent with that deference expected of the intimate Carlton House circle. The rule was that the Regent might treat his friends familiarly, but that they must not presume upon this to be familiar in return, either with him or with distinguished guests in his presence. It was a rule that Brummell had often broken. Captain Gronow recorded one particular occasion when Brummell, dining at the Marine Pavilion at Brighton, 'incurred his master's heavy displeasure in the following manner. The then Bishop of Winchester, perceiving Brummell's snuff-box within his reach, very naturally took it up and supplied himself with a pinch; upon which Brummell told his servant, who was standing behind his chair, to throw the rest of the snuff into the fire or on the floor. The Prince [who had a great reverence for bishops] all the while looked daggers: he gave Master Brummell a good wigging the following day, and never forgot the insult offered to the Bishop.'

Soon afterwards there came that fatal day when the Regent, arriving at a ball at the Argyle Rooms, spoke to their mutual friend, Lord Alvanley, but ignored Brummell.

'Alvanley,' Brummell called out, 'who is your fat friend?'
That question – there are conflicting reports as to the circumstances in which it was asked – marked the end of their
friendship.

Brummell was later asked to a dinner at Carlton House
but merely, so General Sir Arthur Upton, one of the other
guests, thought, in order that the Regent – who could never
forgive ridicule of his personal appearance – might take his
revenge. Brummell, elated at not having been cut off the
Prince's invitation list after all, drank too much wine at
dinner. His host, turning to the Duke of York, said that
perhaps it would be as well to ring the bell and ask for Mr
Brummell's carriage before he became quite drunk. Brummell stood up, left the room, and never spoke to the Regent
again.

Twice more at least they saw each other, once when the
Regent's carriage stopped outside the picture gallery in
Pall Mall. Brummell was standing in the doorway. He raised
his hat to the sentries, pretending that their salute had been
intended for him, then turned his back as the Regent stepped
out of his coach. Some time later they were forced together
by a crush outside the opera as they were waiting for their
carriages. They looked straight into each other's eyes, but
neither spoke. Brummell backed away when he could do so,
coolly staring into the Prince's angry face.

Although he found it only too easy to make enemies, the
Regent had not lost the art of making friends, both with
men of his own age, such as the rich art patron, Sir John
Fleming Leicester, and with men much older, like the Rus-
sian-born merchant and philanthropist, John Julius Angerstein, whose collection of pictures was to form the nucleus
of the National Gallery. He could be as charming as ever
when he chose. Maria Edgeworth once saw him at Mrs
Hope's, talking with most attractive animation, 'one third of
the night', in the centre of the room to Lady Elizabeth

Monk. On another occasion he had a conversation almost as long and quite as intense with Mme de Staël who thought that no one could have been more *'aimable'*, and who thereafter lost no opportunity of 'saying flattering things' about him. John Constable who met him at a dinner before the opening of the Reynolds exhibition at the British Institution found his easy friendly manner most agreeable. Lord Byron, whose *Childe Harold's Pilgrimage* was published in March 1812, the same month as Leigh Hunt's libel in the *Examiner*, was introduced to him at a ball and was delighted to find 'a finished gentleman from top to toe ... with fascination in his very bow'. They spoke together for more than half an hour about 'poetry and poets'. Byron reported the conversation to his publisher, John Murray, who in turn wrote to another of his authors, Walter Scott, to tell him that the Regent had displayed 'an intimacy and critical taste which at once surprised and delighted Lord Byron. But the Prince's great delight was Walter Scott, whose name and writings he dwelled upon and recurred to incessantly. He preferred him far beyond any other poet of the time, repeated several passages with fervour, and criticized them faithfully. He spoke chiefly of *The Lay of the Last Minstrel* which he expressed himself as admiring most of the three poems. He quoted Homer, and even some of the obscurer French poets, and appeared, as Lord Byron supposes, to have read more poetry than any Prince in Europe. He paid, of course, many compliments to Lord Byron, but the greatest was "that he ought to be offended with Lord Byron, for that he had thought it impossible for any poet to equal Walter Scott, and that he had made him find himself mistaken".'

Impressed as he was by the Regent's charm of manner, and flattered as he was by his gratifying taste in literature, Byron did not hesitate to join in the general vilification. He was the author of 'To a Lady Weeping' which appeared anonymously in the *Morning Chronicle* in the month that *Childe Harold's Pilgrimage* was published. Sympathizing

with Princess Charlotte's distress at her father's outburst
against the Whigs during the dinner party at Carlton House,
it bids her

> Weep, daughter of a royal line,
>   A sire's disgrace, a realm's decay:
> Ah, happy! if each tear of thine
>   Could wash a father's fault away!
>
> Weep – for thy tears are virtue's tears –
>   Auspicious to these suffering isles;
> And be each drop in future years
>   Repaid thee by thy people's smiles.

Two years later, when opposition to the Regent was even
more vehement than it was in 1812, Byron had these lines
republished over his name. Both then and on their first appearance they reflected the public mood towards the Regent
far more accurately than the portrait of the gracious, cultivated 'Prince of Princes' in *Don Juan*.

For a time at the beginning of 1814 the Regent had enjoyed a brief spell of popularity when it transpired that
Andrew James Cochrane Johnstone, an unscrupulous Member of Parliament who had been insisting in the House of
Commons that the evidence given against the Princess of
Wales in 'the Delicate Investigation' of 1806 was perjured,
was himself a perjurer. But the tide had soon turned against
the Regent once again. Indeed, throughout 1814 discredit-
able stories about him circulated widely in London society,
and many were true enough, for he was drinking more
heavily than ever. In January much was made of his visit to
Belvoir Castle where he had stood as godfather to the Duke
of Rutland's heir and where he had helped himself far too
generously from the fifty-gallon cistern of punch which the
Duke had provided for his guests.

Yet the picture so often drawn of a constant sot was grossly
distorted. On his way back from Belvoir Castle to London
the Regent sayed for the night in Huntingdon at Buckden

Palace, the episcopal residence of the Bishop of Lincoln, where both the Bishop and his wife were entranced by his friendly and gracious behaviour. Mrs Tomline had taken the greatest pains to ensure that her distinguished guest should be properly welcomed and correctly treated. She had written to a knowledgeable friend, Princess Charlotte's Lady Companion, for advice; and she had been told exactly how to receive him, how to light him to his room, what to wear, and whom to invite to dinner. 'You need not attend him to his room more than once,' she had been informed. 'The best thing would be for him to choose his place at table. ... You might write to Lord Lowther [who was to be in attendance] say what company there is in the neighbourhood and ask whom the Prince would like to meet. I think he likes to meet company. ... The Prince has no water (or finger) glasses at his table, neither has any royal personage here, except the Princess of Wales. ... The more you are dressed the better, certainly with diamonds. ... A handsome morning dress for breakfast is quite sufficient. ... *No* livery servants must wait, except his own ... His valet, Dupaquier, must have a bed in a room as near him as possible. ... He will make all easy to you; he is so well bred.'

So that there should be no mistakes or misunderstandings, Mrs Tomline wrote down the most precise instructions for her own servants and for those she was to borrow for the occasion from her neighbours. They were told exactly where to stand during dinner and given instructions, as detailed as those in a military drill book, as to how to serve the dishes and the wine. 'The Prince's own two pages stand behind his chair and do not move,' they were informed. 'But whatever the Prince asks for is handed to them to give to him, and his plates are taken from their hands. ... The Prince to be served before the ladies on all occasions.' They were told when to remove the upper of the two table-cloths – 'after the cheese has been handed around and the epergne taken away' – when to leave the room – 'after the ices are taken off and the dessert plates changed and the wine set upon the table' –

and when to bring the coffee, tea and liqueurs into the drawing-room – 'after the Prince is served, coffee is to be brought
as usual for the company, tea $\frac{1}{2}$ an hour afterwards, liqueurs
$\frac{1}{2}$ an hour after that'.

In an immensely long letter to her sister, Mrs Tomline
described how she stood at the bottom of the staircase waiting for the Prince to arrive, 'dressed in diamonds, according
to the custom'. It was dark outside, and servants were posted
with flambeaux on either side of the entrance gates, on top
of the main gateway, beside the entrance porch and on the
porch roof. Ten more servants were stationed at strategic
points within the house, where forty-four people, including
the Prince's two pages, his valet and four footmen, were to
sleep that night.

At the sound of carriages in the drive, the Bishop, who
had once been Pitt's tutor, and his eldest son, who had come
down from Cambridge for the night, walked down the porch
steps. The Prince alighted, shook the Bishop and his son by
the hand, apologized for being late, and approached Mrs
Tomline who made 'a very *profound* courtsey which HRH
returned with a very "beautiful and respectful bow", as it was
said to be by bystanders'.

'I then took one candle from a servant in waiting,' Mrs
Tomline continued, 'and the Bishop took another to light
HRH upstairs (according to *ceremony*, not *necessary*, for I
had procured *plenty* of lamps for all the passages and appart-
ments). ... The Prince said something *very graciously* and
took my hand, begged I would not trouble myself and said a
something about the weather. At the Drawing Room door I
stopped for him to enter first which he did with a sort of
apologizing bow, and walked to the fire as people usually do.
By this time his attendants [Lord Lowther, General Turner
and Sir Carnaby Haggerston] were come into the room, and
the usual sort of introductions took place, in the most
familiar, easy way possible on his part. He made me sit down
almost immediately, but he and everyone else continued
standing ... I was exceedingly delighted by the Prince's

inimitable manner – such mingled condescension and dignity I had no idea of before. ...

'When the Prince went from the Drawing Room to dress, the Bishop and I conducted him to his room. He begged I would not give myself this trouble, but in a way that showed it was proper I should go, and then said, "If it must be so, allow me your hand." On the landing at the dressing room door he turned to stop my proceeding any more, and in the most obliging manner possible thanked me for my most flattering attentions. ... He expressed himself instantly delighted with the room, and the Bishop left him to dress. It is singular that he *never* uses a dressing room *anywhere*, but always dresses in his bedroom which he likes to be *very* warm. ... He brings his own sheets everywhere ... Instead of the *ten* blankets you heard of he sleeps even *this* weather with *only* two and no counterpane or quilt. What can possess people to frame such fibs for no purpose?'

Having dressed for dinner, the Prince returned to the drawing-room where the other fifteen guests were now assembled. He offered Mrs Tomline his arm on dinner being announced, asked her where she usually sat and took the chair on her right. He talked to her about her family, about the recent festivities at Belvoir, 'a good deal about the present state of Europe', and told her an anecdote concerning Napoleon, repeating in French 'with a sort of shudder', an exceptionally vainglorious remark the Emperor was alleged to have made. Mrs Tomline confessed that she was utterly captivated by him and felt completely at ease in his company.

'I was not at all nervous, somehow or other,' she told her sister, 'though I hardly know how to account for not being so on such a great occasion. I do not think I ever felt more *self-possessed* than I was during the whole visit. ... The Prince's manner was so very gracious and encouraging as to set me at ease. ... Strange as it may appear, the Bishop was more nervous than I was.'

When the dinner – a 'most capital' one, the hostess was

proud to say – was over and the ladies had retired, the Prince asked the Bishop to come to sit next to him, talked to him of 'parliamentary subjects' and of the problems of Catholic emancipation to which the Bishop was rigidly opposed. 'Nothing could equal the grace and kindness of his manner to the Bishop,' reported Mrs Tomline, who was proud 'yes, *properly proud* of the honour done' to her 'beloved husband'.

The Prince retired to bed at half past twelve – he usually went about one o'clock – and the Bishop lighted him to his room once more. 'I offered to go also,' Mrs Tomline said, 'but he took hold of both my hands with a grace which is quite indescribable, saying this could not be permitted and that he must be allowed to wish me good-night *here* with many thanks for my most obliging attentions to him in every way. ... When he got to the door of the Drawing Room he turned round and made a *grand* bow of leave to the company that seemed to excel in grace and dignity and condescension. ... Really the Prince Regent's manners are most *fascinating*! And his correctness here was perfect. ... You can scarcely conceive the impression made by him.'

On his return to London, however, he began to drink heavily again and the impression he gave was far less favourable. Within three weeks of his return, one of his doctors, Sir Henry Halford, had never seen him so ill 'in all his life before', and confided in Princess Charlotte that another 'such attack' would be '*fatal*'. Sir Henry attributed the attack to excessive drinking, of which the Regent had been doing a 'vast deal'. A few weeks later, Charles Greville recorded a characteristic story in his diary: 'The Regent was very near dying in consequence of a disgraceful debauch, about ten days ago. He sent for Mr Colman [George Colman, the dramatist and theatrical manager] of the Little Theatre, from the King's Bench [debtors' prison] and sat up the whole night with him, and others of his friends, drinking, until he was literally dead drunk. He was saved with some difficulty by Sir W[alter] Farquhar.'

Neither the British victories in Spain, nor even the end of

the war and Napoleon's abdication in April affected the Regent's unpopularity to any noticeable degree. When, on the day that Napoleon left for Elba, he escorted the cumbersome figure of Louis XVIII into London after his long exile in Buckinghamshire, he aroused no marked enthusiasm; and though the white flags of the Bourbon dynasty and fleurs-de-lis fluttered from hundreds of windows, beside the national flag of Britain, though there were scattered cheers as the impressively escorted procession made its way down Piccadilly to Grillon's Hotel in Albemarle Street where the French King was to stay, no one could pretend that either of the two stout gouty gentlemen in the state carriage drawn by eight white horses was being acclaimed as a hero. Despite his army's victories the Regent was still no more than a 'graceful *en-bon-point* Adonis, Prince of modern Macaronis'. Whenever his yellow carriage with its maroon blinds swung through the park, pulled by superb bay horses and escorted by galloping Life Guards, it was watched by the people in pointed silence, and sometimes even actually booed. One day as it drove into the City, which it was never to do again, it was surrounded by a hissing mob who called out threateningly, 'Where's your wife?'

'Prinny is exactly in the state one would wish,' Creevey commented vindictively. 'Nothing can equal the execrations of the people who recognize him. *She*, the Princess, on the contrary, carries everything before her. ... All agree that [he] will die or go mad. He is worn out with fuss, fatigue and *rage*. He came to Lady Salisbury on Sunday from his own dinner beastly drunk, while her guests were all perfectly sober.'

But still, whether the people wanted him to or not, the Regent could not avoid taking a leading part in the victory celebrations, as it was not only his taste but his duty to do so, and a duty, it was grudgingly allowed, that he did perform well. 'Our Prince Regent is never so happy as in show and state,' commented Lady Vernon, 'and there he shines incomparably.'

Having invested the new French King with the Order of the Garter and buckled the Garter round Louis's elephantine knee – it felt just like 'fastening a sash round a young man's waist' – the Regent wished him well on his journey from Dover. Standing at the end of the pier, he bowed as the *Royal Sovereign* headed for the French coast and Louis XVIII rested his vast unsteady legs in his cabin.

Returning to London, the Regent prepared himself to receive the Tsar Alexander I and Frederick William III, King of Prussia, who, with Prince Metternich, representing the Emperor of Austria, were due to arrive on 7 June. The Regent was not looking forward to their coming. He had already met the Tsar's recently widowed sister, Catherine, the Grand Duchess of Oldenburg, whom he heartily disliked. The Grand Duchess, an ugly, vivacious, clever, mischievous and self-important little woman, had arrived at the end of March and had been installed in the Pulteney Hotel in Piccadilly, which had been taken over for her by the Russian ambassador at a cost of 210 guineas a week. The Regent had arrived to welcome her to England before she had had time to change out of her travelling clothes; they had met on the staircase and had taken an instant dislike to one another.

During the next month the Prince's dislike had grown more intense from day to day. The Grand Duchess had done all she could to annoy the Prince by receiving the leaders of the opposition, and by announcing that she would go to see the Princess of Wales, which she no doubt would have done had not the Russian ambassador prevented her by threatening to resign. She had also welcomed Princess Charlotte and had spent hours alone with her in her room.

A dinner given for her at Carlton House had been a lamentable disaster. She had begun by demanding that the band be sent away as music made her feel sick; and when her host, in an attempt to smooth over this embarrassment, had ventured to hope that a woman of her charm would not continue to wear mourning for long, she had 'answered by an astonished silence and looks full of haughtiness'. She had then made some criticisms of the Regent's treatment of his daughter to which he had unwisely responded, 'When she is married, Madam, she will do as her husband pleases. For the present she does as I wish.' This reply had given the Grand Duchess the opportunity of observing with a smile, 'Your Highness is right. Between wife and husband there can only be one will.' The Regent had turned to Countess Lieven, the Russian ambassador's wife, and whispered in her ear, 'This is intolerable.'

'Handsome as he is,' the Grand Duchess had subsequently reported to her brother, 'he is a man visibly used up by dissipation and rather disgusting. His much boasted affability is the most licentious, I may even say obscene, strain I have ever listened to. You know I am far from being puritanical or prudish; but I avow that with him ... I do not know what to do with my eyes and ears – a brazen way of looking where eyes should not go.'

The situation became even more strained and embarrassing when the Tsar himself arrived. He was far from being predisposed in the Regent's favour. He had read with extreme annoyance of the reception that had been accorded in London to Louis XVIII who, ignoring Alexander's own contribution to the downfall of Napoleon, had had the effrontery to reply to the Regent's congratulations by declaring, 'It is to the counsels of Your Royal Highness, to this glorious country, and to the steadfastness of its inhabitants, that I attribute, after the will of Providence, the re-establishment of my House upon the throne of my ancestors.'

Declining to stay in the Duke of Cumberland's apartments at St James's Palace, which had been prepared for him, the Tsar accepted the advice of his sister, who had great influence over him, and put up instead with her at the Pulteney Hotel. Immediately on his arrival there he stepped out onto the balcony to acknowledge the rapturous cheers of the crowds who had gathered in Piccadilly to acclaim him. This was particularly galling to the Regent who, having ridden out to Shooter's Hill to welcome his guest, would now be obliged to drive all the way through the crowds to the Pulteney Hotel to see him, instead of being able, as he had planned, to slip quietly down the Mall to St James's. Eventually he decided not to risk exposing himself to the insults of the crowd, and sent a message to the Tsar that he could not come to his hotel. The Grand Duchess, who had been waiting for hours with her brother to receive him, angrily exclaimed, 'This is what the man is like.'

Over the next few days the relationship between the Regent and the Tsar rapidly deteriorated. They kept each other waiting; they scarcely looked at each other when they did meet. Fancying himself as a despot upon whom the rays of enlightenment had descended, the Tsar went out of his way to talk to the Whig leaders as well as the Tory Ministers, and actually went to see Jeremy Bentham. He caused yet further offence when he showed himself to be rather attracted by Lady Jersey, with whom he waltzed energetically around Lady Cholmondeley's ball-room, and when he refused to enter the Regent's coach unless the Grand Duchess accompanied them, though the Regent carefully explained to him 'that no woman ever went into the same carriage as the Sovereign when he appeared in public as such'.

The blunt, reserved, down-to-earth King of Prussia did not antagonize the Regent in the same way as the mystically ruminating, liberal-minded Tsar; but he, too, was a difficult guest, insisting on sleeping on a rough camp bed instead of the state bed that had been provided for him at Clarence House, and behaving generally like 'a sulky bear'.

Overlooking these slights, the Regent commissioned portraits of both his guests from Thomas Lawrence – whose great gifts demanded an indulgent attitude towards his former escapades with Princess Caroline at her house at Blackheath – and accompanied them on various visits to the sights of London and to Oxford where they were to receive the honorary degree of Doctor of Civil Law and where the honorary degree of Doctor of Laws was to be bestowed upon Metternich.

The Regent, who had himself been honoured with the degree of D.C.L. in 1810, following his gift to the University of the fruits of the Herculaneum Mission, arrived at Magdalen Bridge wearing his scarlet robes and was met there by the Mayor and the Chancellor. He and his fellow sovereigns were escorted to the Sheldonian Theatre, the Divinity School, the Clarendon Press, the Bodleian Library, and then to dinner in the Radcliffe Camera where spectators were admitted to the gallery to watch the feast, at which the King of Prussia's celebrated General, the bluff Prince von Blücher, got extremely drunk on strong beer and cognac. On the last day of the visit, at dinner at Christ Church where the Regent was staying, Blücher was guilty of similar misbehaviour, and when his health was drunk he mumbled a response in his guttural German. 'The Prince, perceiving the indecorum of this, at once rose,' an undergraduate recalled, 'and announced that so excellent a speech should not be lost upon the greater part of the company, who could not be expected to understand German, and that, therefore, in the absence of a better interpreter, he would volunteer for that office himself. ... He then delivered an extremely neat and tactful address of thanks to the University.' The undergraduate considered this behaviour characteristic of the Prince's 'peculiar grace and elegance' which had 'shown in its best lustre during the whole visit'. Maria Edgeworth confirmed that the Prince's visit to Oxford had been a great success and that he had entered the Sheldonian Theatre to 'loud applause'.

In London, though, the rude behaviour of the people towards him sometimes made it impossible for him to remain pleasant and composed. Carlton House was illuminated during the celebrations with green and yellow flares placed between palm trees in painted tubs; yet it was outside the windows of the Tsar and the Prussian King that the crowds gathered. The cheers that greeted the visitors when the Regent accompanied them in public were not too hard to bear for he could flatter himself that he had a share in them, though the Tsar's hail-fellow-well-met response to the acclamations was 'mighty irritating'. But he could not hide from the fact that he was more likely to be hissed than cheered when he went out alone.

Towards the end of the visit there was a splendid banquet, costing £20,000, at the Guildhall. On proceeding to his place on the dais through an aisle between the seven hundred standing guests, the Regent had to wait while the Tsar stopped to chat with Lord Holland and Lord Grey. He then had to suffer the further embarrassment of hearing the Grand Duchess insist that the singers from the Italian Opera stop their performance since they, like the Carlton House band, made her feel sick. It was only with the most sulky reluctance that she agreed to 'God Save the King' being played softly after the loyal toast.

By this time Ministers and opposition alike had grown decidedly tired of both her and her brother. 'When folks don't know how to behave,' Lord Liverpool murmured to Countess Lieven, 'they would do better to stay at home.' Lord Grey decided that the Tsar was a 'vain, silly fellow', after all.

What had been most intolerable of all to the Regent during these weeks, when London had been celebrating the end of the war with such enthusiasm, had been the rapturous applause invariably accorded to his wife. He had debarred her from attending all official functions but he could not prevent her going to Covent Garden, where she was greeted with loud clapping, with shouts of 'Three hearty cheers for an *injured woman*,' and with demands that the orchestra should strike up God Save the King, the 'good King, the protector of outraged innocence'. The Regent turned pale when he saw the artfully timed entrance of the Princess, who contrived to arrive in a black wig and many diamonds just as the applause for the Regent's royal guests was subsiding. A friend of Thomas Moore had never seen 'anything so pointed as the manner in which the entire audience turned to her and cheered her'.

After the performance her carriage was cheered more wildly than ever as it made its way through crowds who shouted to ask her if she would like them to burn down Carlton House.

25

Princess Caroline
1812–1814

'The poor Princess is going on headlong to her ruin'

FOR all the public's support of her, the Princess of Wales was now a lonely and dispirited woman. She was 'very large and coarse', in Joseph Farington's opinion, 'exhibiting nothing of feminine grace or dignity, nor was there any taste shown in her manner or in her dress'. For a time after her formal separation from the Prince she had lived happily enough at Kensington Palace, which the Regent was rumoured to be anxious to close down as a hotbed of Jacobinism. She had given dinner parties and dances which had been attended by guests whom any ambitious hostess would have been proud to have at her table. Writers came and politicians, musicians and scholars; and if she really preferred the racy gossip of such guests as Lady Oxford, whose children by a variety of fathers were known as the Harleian Miscellany, she could nevertheless enjoy the conversation of Charles Burney, Lord Byron, William Lamb, Samuel Rogers and George Canning. Nor was she entirely neglected by the royal family. To the Regent's profound annoyance the Dukes of Kent, Sussex and Gloucester accepted her invitations; the Duchess of York called upon her regularly; even the Queen, disapproving and distant as she was, asked her to the Queen's House when her mother, the Duchess of Brunswick, was also to be of the company. But as time went on she grew increasingly bored by the life she was forced to lead and the limitations imposed upon her conduct. She was 'always seeking amusement,' Lady Charlotte Campbell commented, 'and unfortunately often at the expense of prudence and propriety'. After unwillingly suffering the company of some tiresome guest she would exclaim – though in less fractured English than that in which Lady Charlotte chose to record her remarks – 'Mine Gott, dat is de dullest person Gott Almighty ever did born!' Sometimes she would suddenly get up in the middle of a particularly boring party, and leave for the theatre where a box had been provisionally booked for her. On other occasions, fancying a drive might relieve the tedium, she would step into her carriage and, without telling the coachman where she wanted to go, would point in the appropriate direction. At other times she would give a ball and would bounce up and down crying out *'Vite! Vite!'* if her partner, though exerting himself to the utmost, did not dance quickly enough for her satisfaction; or she would lead her guests all over her apartments in a dance of her own invention. She did these extraordinary things, Lady Charlotte Campbell thought, for no other purpose than to make people stare.

Occasionally she would make a tour of Bayswater, knocking on doors and asking if there were rooms inside to let. She did in fact take a cottage in Bayswater where she spent whole days pretending to be an ordinary private person, as Marie Antoinette had done at her Hameau at Versailles. In the evenings she made up extravagant fantasies about her past life with which she regaled her astounded ladies, or she sang – and sang very badly – to the accompaniment of a weird and grasping family of Italian musicians, named Sapio. 'The poor princess is going on headlong to her ruin,' wrote Lady Charlotte Campbell. 'Every day she becomes more imprudent in her conduct, more heedless of society. ... The society she is now surrounded by is disgraceful.' Lady Charlotte, much alarmed by a 'change in the shape' of the Princess's figure, thought that she might be pregnant until reassured that the change was due to her Royal Highness 'having left off stays – a custom which she [was] very fond of'.

The dreadful Sapio, whom Lady Charlotte called the

'Ourang-Outang', was one of the worst of the Princess's new
friends. He came to dinner one evening when the 'music
mania' was at its 'highest pitch' and was 'more free and easy
and detestable than ever. ... Then her Royal Highness sang
– Squall – Squall ...' During a subsequent musical evening
the 'horrible din of their music hardly ever stopped the
whole evening, except when it was interrupted by the disgusting nonsense of praise that passed between the parties'.

Lady Elizabeth Foster, who had married her lover, the
Duke of Devonshire, after Georgiana's death, thought that
no one now had any 'doubt of the Princess having had
attachments and even intrigues'. For the past 'seven or ten
years' everybody was in agreement as to her 'imprudence of
conduct, indelicacy of manner and conversation, and criminal attachments'.

'I daresay they think me mad!' Princess Caroline commented carelessly; and her mother certainly thought her so.
'She has this excuse,' the old Duchess confided to Lord
Redesdale, touching her head and bursting into tears. 'She is
not quite right *here*.'

Unbalanced she may have been, but she was still astute.
And when the clever and ambitious lawyer, Henry
Brougham, and Samuel Whitbread, the enthusiastic, impetuous and eloquent champion of reform, took up her
cause, she realized that they had other motives than her own
defence. Whitbread, the hero of the Whig left in the House
of Commons, was undoubtedly more sincere in his cham-
pionship than was Brougham, who did not even like her any
more; but both of them, as she well knew, saw in her an
invaluable weapon with which to beat the Regent and the
Tories. Brougham had seen and seized his opportunity in
June 1812 when the Regent had used his now unshackled
powers to restrict even further the number of visits his
daughter was allowed to make to her mother. Ever since the
1806 'Delicate Investigation' into the Princess's strange conduct at Blackheath, Princess Charlotte, with the King's approval, had been forbidden to see her mother more than

once a week. In 1812 the Regent decided that she was not in future to be allowed to see her more than once a fortnight.

The Regent had sound reasons for imposing this restriction on his daughter, far better reasons than all but a few people knew. Even those who disregarded the evidence against the Princess submitted to the King's Commissioners in 1806, or who believed she had since reformed her life, could not convincingly argue that the Princess of Wales was an ideal parent for a high-spirited, impressionable sixteen-year-old girl. The conversations at her dinner-table were notorious – at least amongst those who had first-hand knowledge of them; and the Regent knew that no attempts had been made to curb them when Charlotte was a member of the party. It was not only society scandals and illicit amours, such as Mrs Clarke's affair with the Duke of York, that were openly discussed in her presence; she was also introduced to the company of men like Sir William Drummond, the diplomat, who assured her that the Christian view of the Bible was all nonsense, that priests had always been the 'most corrupt and contemptible of mankind'. Moreover, the Princess knew all about her mother's supposed lovers, past and present and was encouraged to be friendly with those loose young men who were often to be found strutting about her rooms at Kensington and Blackheath.

The King himself had attempted to put a stop to his granddaughter ever paying a visit to the Princess of Wales unless suitably chaperoned; but as Princess Charlotte herself confessed, 'notwithstanding that order, she generally saw her mother alone and had witnessed many things in her mother's room which she could not repeat'. Later the King had ordered that she 'should never meet any society whatever there'; but this injunction had also been flouted.

It was not that Princess Charlotte was particularly devoted to her mother. Indeed, Lady Charlotte Campbell said that Princess Caroline was 'too quick-sighted' not to be perfectly aware 'that her daughter did not care three straws for her'. In letters to her best friend, Margaret Mercer

Elphinstone, Princess Charlotte wrote of her '*duty*' calling
her to Kensington, of her having to go to 'a very disagreeable dinner' where she would be 'most horribly tired'. 'I shall
be ... just in time', she told Miss Elphinstone in a characteristic note on 6 January, 'to set off for dinner [with my mother]
which shall be *humdrum* enough.' Although she did not see
him very often, and was never entirely at ease with him
when she did, Princess Charlotte appears, indeed, to have
preferred the company of her father, more and more so as
she grew older. He was '*very kind*' when he went to see her
one day while she was staying at Bognor, and she drove him
out 'by his *own desire* in the phaeton'. She would have enjoyed his visits to her much more, she confessed, if her fearful uncle, Cumberland, had not always accompanied him
and spoiled it all with his rude banter and indecent jokes,
his way of bullying her. When her father had been due to
dine with her at Warwick House on 24 September 1811, for
example, 'the *charming* D. of Cum' who had been to see her
the day before and had been 'as disagreeable as usual' had
told her that he would come too, and this she was sure would
'spoil it'.

   If Princess Charlotte was never very anxious to visit her
mother, the mother did not display any marked affection for
the daughter. Princess Caroline made a great fuss when the
Regent forbade their meeting more than once a fortnight.
She protested to her 'ever beloved Charlotte' that she was
being deprived of 'the only happiness' which was left to her
'to enjoy upon this earthly world'; she told her that she
would never relinquish the right to see her; she said that her
pen was too feeble to express her 'deep felt regret'. But her
protests were made largely because Brougham advised her
to make them and because, as she confessed to her intelligent and amusing Lady-in-Waiting, Lady Charlotte Lindsay, a confidante of Brougham's, she derived great 'fun'
from her 'warfare with the royal family', keeping them 'in
hot water', 'teazing and worrying them'.

This 'warfare' entailed several visits to Windsor, where she followed Princess Charlotte, insisting that she must see her there if she were not allowed to see her once a week at Kensington. Charlotte herself dreaded these visits to Windsor where she felt 'banished and in prison'. Her ill-tempered grandmother, constantly sniffing snuff, was so fearfully disapproving; and though the 'old girls', her aunts, were always 'very happy' to see her and *'in their different ways'* to *'do them justice'* were always as 'attentive or endeavouring to be *civil'* as they could possibly be, their life was so 'dreadfully dull' that they had become dull too. The noisy visits of her flamboyant mother – who was never dull whatever else she was – might, therefore, have been welcome in the staid and tedious atmosphere of the Windsor Lodges. But her mother was never admitted.

Princess Caroline protested to her mother-in-law about her husband's cruel rules, and asked if they could not be modified on her instructions; but Queen Charlotte, entirely unsympathetic, refused to interfere and told her son what his wife had done. He expressed himself most gratified by the 'very kind and considerate and well judged and most prudent method' that she had adopted to 'baffle this not only extraordinary ... but most impudent fresh attempt on the part of this most mischievous and intriguing infernale' to affect a fondness for her daughter 'which she never did feel and [was] totally incapable of feeling to create a discord or confusion in the family under the pretence of seeing her'.

Undeterred by rebuffs, the Princess and Brougham decided to make a formal protest in writing to the Regent. Brougham drafted the letter; she signed it and sent it off. It was returned to her unopened, since the Regent, having 'some years ago declared that he never would receive any letter or paper from the Princess, intended to adhere to that determination'. She then despatched it to Lord Liverpool who also sent it back: no direct communication from her to the Prince could be received under any circumstances.

Eventually she prevailed on Lord Liverpool to read it to the
Prince who was 'not pleased to signify any commands upon
it'.

Ultimately, though, he did relent; and gave permission for
the Princess to see her daughter on 11 February, less than a
fortnight after her previous visit. This did not suit Brougham's book at all. The more intractable the Regent was
made to appear the better. So, before Princess Charlotte's
next visit to her mother took place he arranged for the letter
of protest to be published in the leading Whig newspaper,
the *Morning Chronicle*, with the Princess of Wales's entire
approval.*

* For several years past, both the Regent and the Princess had been
conducting their feud with each other through the Press and had
been doing all they could to win over journalists and newspapers to
their respective sides. The Princess, who was supported by the
Morning Chronicle, the *Pilot* and the *Star*, gave occasional sums of
money to the *Sunday Review*; while her friend, Lady Perceval, supplied the *News* with forged letters (Aspinall, *Politics and the Press*,
306–11). McMahon and Charles Arbuthnot were both active on the
Regent's behalf. In 1812 McMahon supplied the *Morning Chronicle*
with copies of documents damaging to the Princess's reputation; and
in 1813, so Lady Charlotte Lindsay told Brougham, the proprietor of
the *Evening Star* was offered £300 a year if he would turn against the
Princess; but championing the Princess was far more profitable than
supporting the Regent, and the offer was declined (Brougham MSS,
March 1813: Aspinall, ibid., 93). Peter Stuart, a former proprietor of
the *Morning Post*, claimed 'some permanent situation under government' on the grounds that he had been promised that his small annuity 'would be doubled or tripled as a permanency whenever His Royal
Highness by the accession of power was enabled to do so'. The
egregious Rev. Henry Bate Dudley also demanded a reward for services in the past when he had defended the Regent in the pages of
the *Morning Herald*. He was granted a baronetcy and a stall in Ely
Cathedral, and, although his claims to further church preferment
were refused, he obtained by blackmail an annuity of £300 (Aspinall,
ibid., 168). Another journalist, Thomas Ashe, claimed to have
been 'seduced, at a time of dire distress, to abandon the
services of the Princess of Wales' and to have thereafter received
'upwards of 1,000 guineas' for elevating 'the husband at the expense
of the wife' (RA Geo. IV, Box 12:Asp/K. ii, 36). This Thomas Ashe

The Prince's immediate reaction was to submit to the Privy Council, the Archbishops, the Speaker, the Master of the Rolls and other lawyers, the evidence collected during the 'Delicate Investigation' of 1806, together with the question 'whether it is fit and proper that the intercourse between her Royal Highness, the Princess Charlotte and the Princess of Wales should continue under restriction and regulation'. The Regent went to Warwick House to tell Princess Charlotte what he had decided to do. It was 'a very serious investigation', he warned her, but that 'whatever way it ended', his treatment of her 'would be equally kind and considerate, as he should not consider her accountable for the faults of her mother'. As she listened to her father's words, Charlotte, standing by the fireplace, appeared to be 'dreadfully overcome'; she 'looked penetrated with grief and spoke not a word'.

Towards the end of February the Privy Council reported that 'after a full examination of all the documents' before them, they were of the opinion 'that under all the circumstances of the case' it was 'highly fit and proper ... that the intercourse between her Royal Highness, the Princess of Wales, and her Royal Highness the Princess Charlotte should continue to be subject to regulation and restraint'.

As soon as he could, Whitbread leapt to the Princess of Wales's defence in the House of Commons, pointing out that in 1807 the Cabinet had virtually cleared her of the charges made the year before. The Regent thereupon riposted by publishing the evidence that her servants had brought against the Princess, to which Brougham then responded by republishing *The Book*, Spencer Perceval's defence of the Princess which had been printed in 1806. By this time, so Lady Melbourne said, it had become the 'fashion amongst

---

was imprisoned as a debtor in 1814 in the King's Bench from which he was evidently released by an official from the Home Department who paid off his debts for him (RA Geo. IV, Box 12, 1 November 1820).

ladies to burn their newspapers that the servants may not
read such improprieties'.

Newspaper proprietors themselves were delighted to have
such material to publish. Although the Whig *Morning
Chronicle* had printed the Princess of Wales's letter of
complaint to the Regent, it did not support Brougham and
the Princess unquestioningly since to do so was not in keeping with the general party line. Other papers, however, found
it highly profitable to support them. *The Times* had not
done so at first; but a bad fall in circulation suggested a
change of policy. After the change the circulation was
rapidly made up again. The *News*, a strong supporter of the
Princess, had increased its circulation by over a quarter by
the end of the first four weeks of Brougham's campaign.

But if newspaper readers, while taking delight in all the
scandal, were generally not prepared to have the Princess presented in a bad light, Princess Charlotte was deeply disturbed
by all the stories which were spread abroad about her mother
and which she knew were far from groundless. She liked
Brougham, who was fond of her in turn; and she shared his
hatred of the Tories; but she could not feel as he did about
his war with them over the restrictions imposed upon her
mother's visits to her. One day, after the restrictions had
been imposed, she met her mother in the Park. And as soon
as she got home she wrote to her father to explain to him
that the Princess, who was on her way to visit the dying
Duchess of Brunswick, had stopped her carriage and spoken
to her for five minutes. 'I trust this circumstance will not
happen again,' she told him, 'but as it was entirely unexpected by me I wished to give you the earliest intelligence,
as I make it a point *never* to have *any concealments* from
you. I hope you will soon come to me.'

Relations between mother and daughter had grown progressively worse throughout 1813 and by the spring of 1814,
so Lady Charlotte Lindsay told Brougham, Princess Charlotte 'seemed to be in despair about any possibility of recon-

ciliation'. She knew that her mother 'found very great fault with her to everybody, and said that "she could not think she was her daughter, as she showed such want of character", and that "she had no spirit or steadiness" '. Princess Charlotte also knew that her mother, tired of the campaign that was still being waged on her behalf, was thinking of leaving the country, but *she* had not been consulted; and it was a matter, as Brougham apprehensively advised her, that concerned her intimately. If her mother went to live on the Continent, the Regent might well find grounds upon which to divorce her. He would then be free to marry again, perhaps have a son, and Princess Charlotte would no longer be heir to the throne. Yet Princess Caroline's desire to live abroad, despite all the appeals that were made to her, was growing stronger month by month; and by the time the visit of the Tsar and the King of Prussia to England was over she felt that she should delay no longer.

The Princess of Wales had been outraged to receive from the Queen notification of the Regent's command that she must not attend the Drawing-Rooms to be held in honour of the foreign sovereigns as he himself would be present. She had been told that it must be 'distinctly understood, for reasons of which he alone [could] be the judge', that it was the 'fixed and unalterable determination' of the Regent 'never to meet the Princess of Wales upon any occasion, either public or private'. The Princess had protested; she had reminded the Queen of how she had been treated 'up to the period of his Majesty's indisposition'; she had declined to surrender her 'right to appear at any publick drawing-room' to be held by her Majesty. She had also written to the Regent declaring that she would 'not submit to be treated as guilty' having 'been declared innocent'. 'Can your Royal Highness have contemplated the full extent of your declaration?' she asked him. 'Has your Royal Highness forgotten the approaching ... possibility of our coronation?' But in the

end, for all her indignation, she felt obliged to give way and
to 'yield in the present circumstances to the will of his Royal
Highness'.

Forbidden to attend official functions, care had also been
taken to ensure that she did not see the foreign sovereigns in
private. Every possible obstacle had been placed in her way;
even the Duchess of York, the King of Prussia's sister, had
been prevailed upon to suspend her visits to her during King
Frederick's visit. So, while everyone else was enjoying themselves, she was left at home frustrated, making wax models
of her detested husband, sticking horns in their heads and
pins in their bodies, and gloomily watching them melt in
front of the fire.

At the opera, which Brougham had urged her to attend,
the supremely tactless Tsar, who had repeatedly asked if he
could go to see the King, had peered at her through his
binoculars, and had said that he would call upon her
whether the Prince liked it or not. She had waited in for him
all afternoon, wearing her best dress, anxious to talk to him
about her father who had died fighting in the Tsar's cause;
but he had never come.

It was the final disappointment. Foreign kings and em-
perors ignored her; her husband hounded her; most of his
family avoided her; her former friend and protector, the
King, her uncle, though even he had been less indulgent of
late, was now unable to help her; her mother had died; and,
as for her supporters, the Whigs, why all they did was 'for
the gratification of the *party*' not for *her* gratification! They
ordered her about, told her where to go and what time to
arrive, tormenting her with their selfish advice. 'No child was
ever more thwarted and controlled than she.' As for all this
cheering by the people in the streets and the audience at the
opera, it was 'of no consequence' to her 'but to Mr Whitbread. And that's the way things always go and always will
go until I can leave this vile country,' she concluded sadly.
She did not know who plagued her more, her friends or her
enemies.

Anxious that every inducement should be given to his wife to fulfil her intention of going abroad, the Prince agreed that Lord Castlereagh should assure her that an annuity of £50,000 would be made available to her immediately, in place of her present income of £22,000 a year. Whitbread and Brougham were strongly against her accepting the 'insidious offer' of so large a sum lest it should appear that, by doing so, she was abandoning her claims and grievances for money. They drafted a letter which was to be sent by the Princess to the Speaker of the House of Commons refusing it; but before Whitbread had had time to take the draft to her, she had already, to his 'infinite surprise', written to Castlereagh accepting the offer – as Canning, almost alone among her advisers, had hoped she would – adding that she did so 'in order to prove to Parliament' that she was 'never averse to any proposal coming from the Crown to replace her in the proper splendour adequate to her situation, and to throw no unnecessary obstacles in the way to obstruct the tranquility or impair the peace of mind of the Prince Regent'.

Whitbread, 'much chagrined and disappointed' by these comments, told the Princess that he 'exceedingly' disapproved of them, that she had 'surrendered everything' by them, that they would be used against her 'whenever she wished to assert the rights of her station'.

She replied that 'she meant to relinquish nothing, and particularly that she meant to go to St Paul's' to the thanksgiving service at which, it had been made clear to her, she would not be welcome. She demanded a seat in the Cathedral 'upon the same level with the seats of the rest of the royal family'; but she was curtly informed by the Lord Chamberlain that her request could not be granted without the authority of the Regent, and his Royal Highness had not 'been pleased to give his authority for this purpose'.

Lady Charlotte Lindsay, who had burst into tears when told that the Princess had accepted the offer of £50,000 a year, told Brougham that she seemed quite unaware of her folly and of her having forfeited all claim to his 'advice and assistance'. Brougham, indeed, felt 'fully justified in giving her up'. 'I suppose you have heard of Mother P. bitching the thing so completely in snapping eagerly at the cash, and concluding with a civil observation about unwillingness to "impair the Regent's tranquility"!! etc.' he wrote to Creevey. 'This was all done on the spot and in a moment, and communicated to Sam and me next day ... However, tho she deserves death, yet we must not abandon her, in case P. gets a victory after all.'

The next week Brougham saw and seized his opportunity to deprive the Regent of his victory. 'Mrs Prinny's' request for a seat in St Paul's for the thanksgiving service had been refused and all was 'alive' once more: now a letter could be written complaining of her continued ill-treatment, pointing out that her acceptance of the offer of £50,000 a year was 'wholly misconstrued', and that she now spurned it.

But although Whitbread easily persuaded her to inform the government that she did not need £50,000 – £35,000 would be sufficient – Brougham found it a much more difficult task to persuade her to change her mind about leaving England where she was proving so valuable a weapon in his war with the Regent and his Tory ministers. 'Depend upon it, Madam,' he warned her, 'that there are many persons who now begin to see a chance of divorcing your Royal Highness from the Prince. ... As long as you remain in this country I will answer for it that no plot can succeed against you. But if you are living abroad and surrounded by base spies and tools who will be always planted about you, ready to invent and swear as they may be directed, who can pretend to say what may happen?'

Margaret Mercer Elphinstone added her pleas to those of Brougham. 'Let me entreat you to use every exertion of your influence for Princess Charlotte's sake,' she urged Lady Charlotte Lindsay, 'to induce the Princess not to make a long absence, which would be ruinous, both to the interest of mother and daughter.'

26

Princess Charlotte
1812–1814

'If she were mine, I would lock her up'

FOR many months now Henry Brougham had been assiduously fostering the idea that the Regent thoroughly disliked his daughter, that he was jealous of her, that he would be glad to have her out of his way. 'He is jealous of her to a degree of insanity, and has been for some time,' Brougham had assured Lord Grey at the beginning of 1813. 'I believe the Duke of Cumberland and Yarmouth have actually been feeding him with hopes of getting rid of her by divorcing his wife, and this he is fool enough to believe. It seems too absurd, but you may rely on it some such thing has been broached.'

It was true, of course, that the Regent could not fail to be exasperated by those enthusiastic shouts which almost invariably greeted her carriage – 'God bless you! Never forsake your mother!' – that, detesting Princess Caroline as he did, he could not but find distasteful in their daughter all that reminded him of his wife. Charlotte was better looking than her mother, but she was already rather showily full-blown. She was talkative and on occasions rather coarse. Her Governess had had to remonstrate with her about the immodest way she wore her clothes and showed her drawers and her legs as she got in and out of carriages. 'I don't care if I do,' she had responded, proud of her legs which were certainly very pretty. Her conversation had been 'forward and dogmatical on all subjects, buckish about horses, and full of expressions very like swearing'. In short, as Miss Berry had observed, she had been 'very ill brought up'. Her man-

ners were 'so odd', the Grand Duchess of Oldenburg told the
Tsar, that they took your breath away. She looked like a
plump boy, 'or rather like a young rascal, dressed as a girl',
the Grand Duchess thought. But she had 'much wit and dog-
gedness in her nature', 'a will of bronze in the least things, a
searching reasoning power'; she had 'great intelligent eyes of
pale blue' which, unfortunately, sometimes had 'the fixed
look of the House of Brunswick'.

She was also warm-hearted and emotional, and obviously
attracted to men. The Regent conceived it his 'duty as a
father' to ensure that she was kept firmly in hand, that she
was closely watched from morning to night by those who
had been appointed to supervise her upbringing. He repeatedly reminded her Governess, Lady de Clifford, of her
duties in this respect and on one occasion at least felt obliged
to give 'her ladyship a severe lecture'. Eventually Lady de
Clifford resigned. It was given out that she had done so on
the grounds of ill-health, but the real reason was a quarrel
over her charge's association with Captain Charles Hesse of
the 18th Hussars, a handsome womanizer who was said to be
an illegitimate son of the Duke of York. The Prince, who
was always extremely well-informed about Princess Charlotte's friends and behaviour, had heard disturbing rumours
about Hesse which Lady de Clifford herself partially confirmed. It was not until after Lady de Clifford's resignation,
however, that Princess Charlotte confessed the full story to
her father. Her aunt, Princess Mary, was present when the
confession was made and she afterwards made a record of
what her niece had said.

Princess Charlotte had made the acquaintance of Captain
Hesse one day when she was out riding at Windsor where
his regiment was quartered, Princess Mary wrote. 'Lady de
Clifford had allowed him to ride by the side of the open
carriage morning and evening for six weeks before she repri-
manded her for it. ... And after the regiment moved from
Windsor and was quartered at Portsmouth and Lewes, the
Princess Charlotte confessed to her father she always met

him at her mother's at Kensington, and had private interviews with him ... with the Princess of Wales's knowledge and connivance. ... The Princess of Wales used to let him into her own apartment by a door that opens into Kensington Gardens, and then left them together in her own bedroom, and turned the key upon them saying, "*A present je vous laisse, amusez vous.*"'

'I can tell you what is more,' the Princess continued as her father stood 'horror struck' by this revelation that his wife had virtually invited their daughter, then aged sixteen, to make love with Captain Hesse. 'My mother carried on a correspondence for us, and all the letters backwards and forwards went through her hands.' Presents had also been exchanged, and Princess Caroline, without her daughter's knowledge, had given him a portrait of her. 'God knows what would have become of me if he had not behaved with so much respect to me,' Princess Charlotte concluded. She had never really been able to make out whether Captain Hesse was her mother's lover all the time, but she supposed Princess Caroline's 'object was to draw her into this scrape to bring the boy [her adopted son, William Austin] forward as heir to the throne'. She added that her uncle, the Duke of Brunswick, who had often put her on her 'guard on the subject of [her] mother's conduct', told her that he was sure that the boy was her mother's own child.

The Prince, who was relieved to learn that no promise of marriage had ever been given to Hesse but dismayed that he had not so far returned her indiscreet letters or presents as he had promised to do, told her how appalled he was by the 'dreadful situation in which she had been placed'. But if she concealed nothing from him he would not reproach her; on the contrary 'his object must be to save her' and to 'prevent the possibility of such a thing happening again'.

He was kind to her and she was grateful. That evening after dinner she went to Princess Mary's room 'and said that her mind was greatly relieved since she had *told all* she had in her *mind* to her father, that she had been miserable and never had courage before this to do so'.

This was Christmas Day, 1814; but at the time of Lady de Clifford's resignation in 1812, when her father suspected, though did not know for sure, what was happening between Hesse, herself and her mother, Princess Charlotte had been far less amenable and not in the least contrite.

She had, in fact, been excessively cross when she learned that Lady de Clifford was to be replaced by another Governess, the Dowager Duchess of Leeds. The last thing she wanted was another governess. Now that she was nearly seventeen she felt entitled to her own Household with Ladies-in-Waiting, and on 10 January 1813 she wrote to her father accordingly. He replied that she could not possibly have a Household of her own until she got married. Undeterred by this refusal, she repeated her request to Lord Liverpool.

The Prince was furious by this '*deceit* and duplicity', by her having gone behind his back to his Prime Minister. He drove down to Windsor with Lord Eldon, the Lord Chancellor, a particularly unfortunate choice in his daughter's opinion, since Eldon was not only a pompous man of extremely humble parentage – risen from the coal wharfs of Newcastle-upon-Tyne and known in the royal family as Old Bags' – but, of all the members of the Cabinet, the most unlikely to have any sympathy with her case.

How could she be so impertinent as to demand her own Household at her age? her father wanted to know when she had been called down into the Queen's room to confront him. He told her that he knew 'all that passed in Windsor Park' and it was, therefore, utterly out of the question for so 'stiff-necked, stubborn and silly' a girl to have her own establishment. Lord Eldon then reminded her what the English law had to say about the Sovereign's power over members of his family and, upon being asked what *he* would do if he had such a daughter, he maintained, 'If she were mine, I would lock her up.' The Princess listened to all this in silence; but later on in the room of one of her aunts, she burst into tears and sobbed, 'What would the King say if he could know that his granddaughter had been compared to the granddaughter of a collier?'

'Things were in a most uncomfortable state after this scene,' commented Cornelia Knight, the Queen's tall, touchy, and humourless companion who had been asked to chaperone Princess Charlotte, and never to let her 'go out of her sight for one moment', pending the arrival of the Duchess of Leeds. The Princess fell ill with a heavy cold and a 'little nervous fever, occasioned by all she had gone through'. But at least she could comfort herself with the reflection that, although she would have to accept the Duchess of Leeds as her Governess, the Duchess's principal assistants were not to be known as Sub-Governesses but as Lady Companions. The appointment of Lady Companion was offered to Miss Knight who badly wanted to accept it since she found life at Windsor 'every year more and more confined', and had grown unutterably bored with having to listen to all 'the complaints and private quarrels' of the royal family. Life at Warwick House – 'miserably out of repair and almost falling into ruins', as she was to discover it to be – would have its disadvantages, yet it would certainly be less tedious than life with the Queen.

Her Majesty, however, did not want to lose Miss Knight's company, though she would not actually commit herself to saying so, wishing her companion 'to take the refusal' on herself so that the Queen might thus avoid offending the Prince. Eventually Miss Knight had 'an hysterical fit', and then barred herself in her room having aroused the Queen's fury by attempting to buy herself out of her employment. She had tried to do this with the offer of a loan of £1,000, which she 'knew the Queen was very desirous to procure', and which, added to the salary Miss Knight was to give up, would have 'set her Majesty completely at ease in respect' of the expense of various improvements she wanted to make at her retreat at Frogmore. It was not until the Regent had written to his mother and she, in turn, had commanded Miss Knight to leave her employment for Princess Charlotte's, that the matter was resolved.

If Miss Knight was anxious to move to Warwick House, the Duchess of Leeds was certainly not, and was very unhappy when she arrived there. She found her charge quite as difficult as Lady de Clifford had done, and she was so upset by the prospect of having to scold her that she cried in her sleep. Charlotte's petticoats were too short; she nodded at people instead of bowing to them; she whispered to the maids of honour at Chapel between the prayers and the sermon; she bought her friends expensive jewellery which she could not afford. The Duchess knew that she ought to reprimand the girl for these offences; but she 'did not like to venture on anything herself unless driven to the last extremity'. Above all, the Duchess was harassed by the Prince's strict instructions about her supervision of the Princess's correspondence, since she found it impossible to ensure that her charge was not in touch with proscribed friends and relations. Indeed, the Princess, an inveterate letter-writer, sent and received numerous communications without her Governess's knowledge, a selection of them being passed to her on one occasion in the Duchess's presence by her mother who had concealed them in a parting present of a pair of shoes.

Once the Regent had won his point that visits between mother and daughter must continue to be subject to restrictions, his rules governing Princess Charlotte's conduct were somewhat relaxed. 'What is passed is passed and gone by,' he assured her, 'and therefore let us think no more of it; and pray do not let it give you any further uneasiness. ... God bless you, my dearest child.' To show her that all disagreements between them were now truly in the past, he invited her to a dinner at which he was as kind as she could have wished.

The dinner was given on the day that an unidentified coffin had been opened in St George's Chapel at Windsor and had been found to contain the remains of King Charles I. Having elaborately demonstrated upon Miss Knight's tense neck the way in which King Charles had been beheaded, the Regent presented to his daughter the centre sapphire from the Stuart crown, which he had received from Paris together with some Stuart papers. Soon afterwards he asked his daughter for a portrait of her for which she gave several sittings to George Sanders. Then came another invitation to dinner and the Prince was once again in excellent humour, though before Miss Knight left he said to her, tapping her on the shoulder, 'Remember, however, my dear Chevalier, that Charlotte must lay aside the idle nonsense of thinking that she has a will of her own; while I live she must be subject to me as she is at present.'

So, indeed, she was; and at the least sign of insubordination there was trouble. It was clear to Miss Knight that the Regent was determined to keep her 'as long as possible *a child*'. Whenever he suspected that there was the possibility of a scandal such as the Hesse incident had threatened to become, he renewed all his orders, made complaints to her attendants, and declined to see her for weeks on end. First of all there was a fuss over her supposed interest in the Duke of Gloucester, a particular *bête noire* of the Regent, who knew that he had been in the habit of attending Princess Caroline's parties with his cousins the Dukes of Kent and Sussex. One evening at the Duke of York's, when the Regent saw his daughter and Gloucester sitting next to each other on a sofa, he told Lady Liverpool to go over to her and ask her to change places with Lady Bathurst. Charlotte declined to do any such thing. She got up, left the room and returned home 'indignant and hurt at having been watched and worried'.

After this there was a fuss about the Princess going to Sanders's house for her sittings instead of giving them at Warwick House. Warwick House was too dark, it was explained; but that was a most unsatisfactory excuse: the Prince knew that she was likely to meet the most unsuit-

able people in the artist's studio. Then there was trouble
over the Princess's supposed attraction to the Duke of
Devonshire. The Duchess of Leeds assured the Regent that
the Princess had never 'written a line to the Duke of Devonshire or stopped at Chiswick in her life or sent any message
there'. But the Regent thought that the Duchess was not
taking her duties conscientiously enough, and he sent Sir
Henry Halford over to Warwick House to reprimand her
and Miss Knight for having driven twice in one day down
the Chiswick Road when the Duke was giving a 'great breakfast' at Chiswick House, an outing suggested by Miss Knight
who had been concerned to find some sort of amusement for
the Princess whose 'life was so monstrous, that any other
young person must have felt it excessively dull'.

'Young P. and her father have had frequent rows of late,
but one pretty serious one,' Brougham contentedly informed
Creevey. 'He was angry with her for flirting with the D. of
Devonshire, and suspected she was talking politics. ... P. will
put on his dignified air on which he piques himself, and then
say, "Your Grace will be pleased to recollect the differences
between you and my daughter."'

Frustrated and unhappy, Princess Charlotte was reported
to be 'in a bad state of health', with a fixed pain in her side
for which she wore 'a perpetual blister'; she was also putting
on weight. At a big party at the new Military College at
Sandhurst her father did not even talk to her, and she in
turn turned her back on her grandmother to show her
general distaste for the entire proceedings which ended with
her father, the Duke of York and the Sovereign Prince of
Orange collapsing drunkenly under the dining-room table.

The Prince of Orange's son was soon to be the cause of
the worst row that she and her father had yet endured.

Prince William of Orange was not a prepossessing young
man. Endeavouring to compensate for an unhealthy, sallow
appearance and a frail physique he adopted an excessively
hearty manner, drank too much and shook people by the

hand with intemperate vigour. Brougham referred to him as 'Young Frog'. He had spent two years at Oxford, had served on the Duke of Wellington's staff in Spain, and was shortly, at the age of twenty-two, to be given a command at Waterloo which he was to execute with notable incompetence. But despite his many faults he was not an entirely unattractive young man. Princess Charlotte was for a time to feel for him a kind of affection, and to decide that her father's obvious wish that she should marry him was not as unacceptable as she had at first declared it to be.

'I think him so ugly,' she commented soon after first meeting him, 'that I am sometimes obliged to turn my head away in disgust when he is speaking to me. Marry I will, and that directly, in order to enjoy my liberty; but not the Prince of Orange.'

Since there was no question of her being allowed to marry the Duke of Devonshire, she would have preferred the Duke of Gloucester although he was so tiresomely self-satisfied and getting on for forty. It was 'perfectly true', she admitted, that she did not particularly care for him; but she could never expect 'to marry from inclination', anyway; and at least the Duke was good-natured: she 'might reasonably look forward to being treated with kindness'. She discussed the matter with her father's chosen messenger, Sir Henry Halford. Sir Henry reported her preferences to the Regent who did not care for the idea at all, replying that he would have to go down to Windsor to talk to the Princess himself. When he arrived he was in a better mood than had been expected, and Charlotte, whose stammer usually grew much worse during her painful interviews with her father, had reason to feel thankful after this one that he had not been cross with her. He began by saying that he would be 'very calm and very affectionate' and that although he could never consent to her marrying the Duke of Gloucester he would not bring any pressure to bear on her with regard to anyone else. He could not forbear making a few favourable remarks about the Prince of Orange, but he made it clear that he would not force her hand in that direction. All the same, his wishes were unmistakable.

In her predicament Princess Charlotte turned for advice to Lord Grey. After complaining that she was 'secluded from all society almost entirely' and felt 'threatened with more restrictions if possible from the few friends' that she did see, she went on to tell him of Sir Henry Halford's frequent visits to her. These visits were not welcome, but as Sir Henry came 'from the Prince and by his orders' she could not always refuse seeing him, though sometimes she had done so when she thought that she could without causing offence. Miss Knight had tried to put a stop to his coming and his endeavouring to influence the Princess in lengthy private interviews; but the Regent had declared that Sir Henry was 'the friend of the family'; he had no objection to his daughter being left alone with him. Since, therefore, Halford could not be prevented from coming to Warwick House with his messages and orders from the Regent, how should she answer him? She was 'decidedly against the Prince of Orange'; but how long could she go on maintaining her resolution not to marry him?

Lord Grey replied that while no law, human or divine, gave her father the right to coerce her into marriage, she ought to 'avoid, by all proper means, the appearance of a public opposition to his pleasure, and that she should dispose herself as much as possible to a compliance with it'. This was not the advice for which she had been looking, and she wrote to Lord Grey again, evidently hoping for stronger support. Grey contented himself with the observation that he had always felt sure she would not be pressed to a marriage against her inclinations, and the Regent's assurances to her had made it clear that he would never require of her 'so painful a sacrifice'.

There the matter was left for a time; but as 1813 drew to a close, further hints were dropped at Warwick House about the advantages of a marriage to Prince William. One day the persistent and persuasive Sir Henry Halford called and had 'a long interview' with the Princess on the subject; and gradually she came to view Prince William in a different light. Looking at a print of him, she decided that perhaps he was not so ugly after all; he was 'certainly adored in the army'. Invitations to Carlton House followed; and, as Brougham told Lord Grey, the Princess was once more 'on perfectly good terms' with her father. 'She has completely altered her language as to the Prince of Orange, and I am quite clear she will take him if they offer him to her. ... I always thought that the best ... part of her character was the spice of the mother's spirit and temper; but I fear she has a considerable mixture of the father's weakness and fickleness. Indeed what can you expect? Her behaviour to Lady de Clifford [was] such as I almost defy her father to surpass, accomplished as he is in such walks.'

At one dinner-party the Regent, in the brightest of good humours, presented his daughter with a diamond-studded belt which he had been sent from Turkey and to which he had added a diamond clasp. At a subsequent Carlton House party the Prince of Orange was present and after dinner the Regent took him and Princess Charlotte into the conservatory where they walked up and down together, the Regent doing most of the talking, Princess Charlotte looking pale in an unbecoming violet satin dress trimmed with black lace. She confessed to a friend afterwards that she was 'more agitated' than she could express. Having marched them up and down for some time, the Regent took Charlotte to one side and said to her enquiringly, 'Well, it will not do, I suppose.'

'I do not say that,' she replied. 'I like his manner very well, as much as I have ever seen of it.'

Taking this as a declaration of consent, the Regent, 'overcome with joy', took her back to the Prince of Orange and 'joined their hands immediately'. Prince William was 'so much affected, but so happy', Charlotte thought; and as for herself it all appeared 'like a dream'. Back at Carlton House after midnight, she told Miss Knight what had happened, that she was engaged. Prince William had turned out to be 'by no means as disagreeable' as she had expected.

Two days later, accompanied by her father, Prince William arrived at Warwick House and they were left alone together for the first time. He was 'naturally dying of shyness and fear', and was even more perturbed when his talking of their having a home together in Holland as well as in England reduced the Princess to tears.

She had not before considered this aspect of her marriage, and after the Regent had tactfully hurried the Prince of Orange away to another engagement the thought of living abroad with him preyed on her mind. Shortly before Christmas she went to Windsor where she was to be confirmed on Christmas Eve, and there the congratulations, the 'little jokes and witty sayings', the expressions of pleasure that could not conceal the '*sorrow*' of her maiden aunts, all increased her disquiet. When she returned to London she was 'quite ill for some days afterwards'.

The day after her eighteenth birthday, on 8 January 1814, Lady Charlotte Campbell came to visit her at Warwick House and found the Princess 'very gracious', yet she had talked in a most desultory way, and it would be difficult to say of what. 'Her hands and arms are beautiful,' Lady Charlotte decided, 'but I think her figure is already gone, and will soon be precisely like her mother's: in short it is the very picture of her, and *not in miniature*.'

Lady Charlotte was a rare visitor. 'We scarcely saw anyone,' Miss Knight said, 'the days passed quietly ...' The Duchess of Leeds's daughter lived in the House, but she was younger than the Princess who, in any case, did not like her. Charlotte grew more and more depressed. Her father had not been able to come to see her on her birthday as he had gone up to Belvoir Castle to stay with the Duke of Rutland for the christening of his godson. And she was conscious that he was once again displeased with her. Miss Knight certainly found him so when, at his request, she called at Carlton House one morning after his return from

Belvoir Castle. He was ill in bed, having celebrated the Rutland baby's christening with such excessive enthusiasm that his doctors had felt obliged to exhaust him by bleeding him and keeping him 'low for several days'. He complained first of all that Princess Charlotte was having an exceptionally fine carriage built for herself by a man called Birch instead of by his own coachbuilder, that she had consulted the Duke of Kent about this instead of himself, that she was having it painted green and not, as it should have been, yellow, like his own. He went on to complain that his daughter spent too much on jewellery, and that it was shameful of 'young ladies of immense fortunes', like Mrs Thrale's granddaughter, Margaret Mercer Elphinstone, to accept valuable presents from her.

Miss Knight, anxious to exculpate herself from any possible blame in this, assured him that she herself had made an agreement with the Princess to accept no presents from her, as she had also done with Princess Amelia. The mention of his beloved dead sister was too much for the Prince to bear in his weakened condition, and he burst into tears. Recovering himself, he enjoined Miss Knight to ensure that Princess Charlotte did 'not now think of frivolity'. 'She was to be married, and must think of the duties of a wife.'

The more Princess Charlotte thought about becoming a wife, however, the less the idea appealed to her since it seemed to entail her living abroad. It was far from her wish to retract her consent to the marriage, she told Lord Grey; but she was 'too much an Englishwoman' not to feel most reluctant at leaving this country, 'both from affection and a sense of duty'.

Lord Grey agreed that it was 'unquestionably of the utmost moment' that she should not be pressed to leave against her inclinations; it was 'no less important to the public' that her 'habits should be formed amongst the people she was to govern'. However, everything that he had heard of the Prince of Orange, particularly from officers who by living with him had the best means of forming an opinion

about him, justified the choice which her Royal Highness
had 'so happily made'.

In her next letter, Princess Charlotte enclosed one she had
received from the Prince at The Hague which had made
her even more apprehensive. The Prince told her that he
was 'daily more tired' of Holland and wished himself 'a
thousand times back to England' since the formalities and
etiquette that had to be observed at the Dutch court were
quite against his nature. Yet it was clear from his letter that
he would be expected to spend six months every year in
Holland, where they were to have a nice summer house
outside The Hague as well as a town house in the capital. He
had 'nothing more at heart' than to make her happy, so he
hoped that she would bring English ladies of honour with
her. After all, every place was 'almost alike if one lived with
friends'.

Princess Charlotte did not mention her reluctance to live
abroad to her father when he summoned her to Carlton
House on 2 March. With a gouty leg resting on the seat of
a nearby chair, he handed her a letter from Holland in
which a formal proposal of marriage had been made. But to
her friend, Priscilla Burghersh, she strongly objected: 'As
to going abroad, I believe and hope it to be quite out of the
question, as I find by high and low that, naturally, it is a
very unpopular measure in England, and as such of course
(as my inclinations do not lead me either) I could not go
against it, and besides which, I have now no manner of doubt
that it is decidedly *an object and wish of more than one* to
get rid of me if possible in that way. ... You are far too
sensible not to know that this [marriage] is only *de conven-
ance*, and it is as much brought about by *force* as anything,
and by deceit and hurry; though I grant you that, were
such a thing absolutely necessary, no one could be found so
unexceptionable as he is. I am much more *triste* at it than I
have ever chosen to write; can you be surprised?'

She was strongly urged to stand firm against living abroad
not only by her sympathetic girl friends, but also by Henry

Brougham and by the Duke of Sussex, who approved of the marriage but thought the question of her going to Holland ought to be discussed by Parliament. Lord Liverpool believed that the representatives of the Russian Court were also intriguing against the threatened close alliance between the House of Orange and the English royal family which did not suit Russian policy. 'She has been induced to insist upon conditions being inserted in the contract of marriage of which she never thought until recently, and which (to the extent to which she is desirous of pushing them) cannot be admitted,' Liverpool told Castlereagh. 'The object is to break off the marriage with the Prince of Orange and to form a connection between the Princess and one of the Grand Dukes of Russia.' Liverpool had 'the strongest reason to believe' that Mme de Tatischeff, wife of a Russian diplomat and a woman often in Princess Charlotte's company, was engaged in this intrigue. It was furthermore supposed that the Emperor of Russia's sister, the Grand Duchess of Oldenburg, had also been involved in the intrigue, an additional cause of the Regent's dislike of her family.

Princess Charlotte's visit to the Grand Duchess at the Pulteney Hotel had so disturbed the Regent that he had sent Sir Henry Halford to Warwick House with instructions to Miss Knight not to let the Princess and the Grand Duchess meet so often. The Regent's concern was understandable, for the Grand Duchess was 'a great favourite of Princess Charlotte'. Their conversations had been quite uninhibited, the Grand Duchess always having spoken with the utmost candour, telling Charlotte how vulgar she found the Duke of Clarence and that, having now seen the Prince Regent, she could 'never think of marrying *him*'.

At the suggestion of Lord Grey, Princess Charlotte wrote to her father on 15 April politely requesting to see the marriage contract, which she heard from the Prince of Orange had been shown to him and the terms of which he found 'most liberal'. Begging that she, too, might see the contract, she asked at the same time for an article to be inserted in it preventing her being taken or kept out of England against her inclinations. She felt, she said, a 'decided repugnance to a removal from this country'.

On receipt of the Princess's letter, the Regent immediately sent for Miss Knight who was to present herself at Carlton House at twenty minutes past eleven on 17 April. According to Miss Knight's long account of this interview, it was an extremely painful one. 'The Prince was very angry,' Miss Knight wrote. 'He asked me whether I knew of the letter he had received from Princess Charlotte on Friday, which I answered in the affirmative: he said it was an impertinent letter from a daughter to a father, that she had no right to ask to see the contract; that a sketch of it had been sent over to the father of the Hereditary Prince of Orange, not to himself – that I must tell Princess Charlotte that the marriage was her own choice, and her own proposal and that when he had told her of the probability of her going to Holland she had made no objections.'

The Regent went on to say that he would forgive his daughter if she would withdraw the letter; but if she would not do so it would have to be laid before the Cabinet and Privy Council as the House of Orange would naturally insist on the marriage treaty being broken if she persisted in her determination not to leave England. As to her demand for a house for herself and the Prince in England, 'he said, with much displeasure that he could not find one to purchase in a moment, and that perhaps he must build one; and that I might quiet her mind by assuring her that she would not be an exile from England, that she would not have to stay more than 7 or 8 months at a time in Holland, though perhaps if she were in a family way it might be imprudent for her to remove from The Hague, but that provision would be made in the contract that her eldest son, (as intended for the throne of England) should be brought up here from the age of three or four, and the second in Holland. ... That they had fitted up a splendid residence for her at The Hague and in the country, that he would visit her there, and she and her husband might be his guests in England. He said she had already more liberty than was prudent and should have less if she broke off the marriage by persisting in not going to Holland. He said she might be popular for a short time by obtruding that reason on the publick, but that her popularity would not last.'

The next day Princess Charlotte replied that it gave her the 'very deepest concern' to have incurred her father's displeasure. 'But I cannot with all that respect and affection retract one word of my determination,' she continued. 'I was astonished to hear from Miss Knight you thought the marriage was first proposed by me, and that it was to gratify my wishes you gave your consent.'

Although Lord Grey supported the Princess in her determination that there should be an article in the marriage treaty preventing her being taken out of the country against her will, he was alarmed by reports that, even if it were to be conceded, she would break the engagement anyway. 'I would earnestly dissuade the Princess from [taking this step], except in the last and most unavoidable necessity,' Grey wrote to Margaret Mercer Elphinstone. 'The connection is much approved of by the country ... its failure would create general disappointment, and if it could be presented as arising from levity or capriciousness in the Princess would injure her in the public estimation.'

This was the Regent's view entirely; and, knowing that Charlotte was being encouraged to make difficulties and that she had 'legal advisers', he was very cross to receive his daughter's demands for what he considered to be wholly unnecessary and unreasonable stipulations in the marriage contract. Feeling that he could do no more himself, he asked the Duke of York to go to Warwick House to reason with her. The Duke wrote to tell his niece that he was coming, but she desired him not to come 'as she did not wish to have any unpleasant discussion with him'. Undeterred, the Duke called at the house, where he told Miss Knight that he wanted to see the Princess. She declined to come down, and the Duke was forced to go away without seeing her, express-ing the regret 'that she had ill advisers from amongst those who were not well disposed towards government'.

When he had gone the Princess wrote him a letter explain-ing her objections to the marriage, objections which she once more repeated on 22 April, saying that she was 'per-fectly ready to communicate' them to the Prince's Ministers if he deemed it requisite to send them to her. She would not see the Lord Chancellor, however, as they were 'not on speaking terms'.

'If these have ever been your sentiments, dearest Char-lotte,' the Duke of York replied sternly, 'it is much to be lamented that you did not make them known sooner, and that you allowed the most formal publick acts to take place, and every preparation to be made, when in your own mind, or at least after a moment's consideration, you must have been aware that the whole was nugatory on this determina-tion.' The Princess denied that she had allowed any public acts to take place, whereupon the Duke reminded her of her having granted an audience to a representative of the Dutch government to whom she confirmed her acceptance of a for-mal offer of marriage, and of her having ordered diamonds with money transmitted to her by the Prince of Orange. This elicited another long letter from Princess Charlotte in which she reiterated her denial that the marriage had been first proposed by her and her determination that, if it were to take place, she would not leave England.

Three days after this letter was written, early on the morn-ing of 30 April, there arrived at Warwick House a young man who gave his name as Colonel St George. Miss Knight came down the rickety black staircase to be confronted by the Prince of Orange who asked to see the Princess. He was told she was still in bed; he said he would wait; he was then informed that she could not see him before three o'clock; he begged to be allowed to see her earlier than that; very well, she would see him at two.

He then wrote her a note which was sent up to her bed-

room: 'Dearest Charlotte, I am extremely disturbed at your
not wishing to see me; but I ask it once more as a particular
favour that you will allow me to wait till you are up. If you
insist upon a refusal I must follow your wish and return
at two o'clock. I am most desirous and anxious to be able to
speak to you freely.'

Having read this note, Princess Charlotte got up at last
and came down to see the Prince. He asked her if he had
offended her in any way and was assured that he had not.
But there was still the problem of where they were to live.
So the Prince said he would go to see the Regent.

He left immediately, then hurried back within an hour or
two to announce excitedly that the Regent wanted them
both to go over to Carlton House to see him; there had never
been any intention that she should live 'chiefly abroad'; all
past differences would be forgotten. But Charlotte declined
to go. Her spirits were so much overcome, she said, and her
nerves so shaken. And when the Prince had left she wrote to
tell him that she trusted they would not meet again until she
had 'every possible assurance and satisfaction' that her conditions to the marriage were 'fully agreed to'. She must be
'complete mistress' of her own actions, she wrote in a subsequent letter after the Prince had asked her categorically
what her conditions were, whether she was 'determined
never to leave England' or whether she meant 'occasionally
to visit Holland and other parts of the Continent' with him.

So the inconclusive discussions went on, Princess Charlotte
insisting that she must never be required to leave England
without her consent, Lord Liverpool, now a frequent caller at
Warwick House, endeavouring to persuade her – since The
Hague was 'not as far from London as Edinburgh or Dublin'
– to give some indication that she would be prepared to
gratify the Prince of Orange's family by visiting Holland.

But it was all to no avail. Princess Charlotte was intractable; and her Whig advisers were evidently anxious that she
should remain so, thus causing as much embarrassment to
the government as she could.

The Duke of Sussex was one of these advisers who encouraged her not to give way. During a long conversation with
Lord Grey about the marriage, Sussex said that the Princess
was 'much irritated against the Duke of York' who, so she
had been warned, 'aimed at the Regency in the event of the
Prince's death'. Princess Charlotte had also got it into her
head that the Duke of York was trying to prove 'the Prince's
marriage with Mrs Fitzherbert which had been solemnized
twice, i.e. by clergymen of both churches'. The Duke of
Sussex professed that he could not conceive how Charlotte
had come to believe such things; but in a memorandum of
his conversation Lord Grey noted that he had 'reason to
believe' that Sussex himself was responsible.

As well as receiving advice from Lord Grey and mischievous warnings from the Duke of Sussex, Princess Charlotte
was also constantly in touch with Brougham and with her
mother, though her mother seemed more concerned that
she should display her disapproval over her own exclusion
from the Queen's court at the time of the visit of the foreign
princes to London than that she should put an end to the
marriage proposals by declining to leave the country. 'It is
not for me to give you my advice upon such a delicate subject,' her mother wrote to her; 'but all those friends as Lord
Grey, Lansdowne, Mr Whitbread, Brougham and Co. are
particularly anxious that you should manifest your feelings
very publicly at the great insult your mother has received
from the Queen and that you ought to refuse your attendance at Court which would raise you very much in the
estimation of the world to take publicly the part of your
oppressed and persecuted mother. However you are perfectly
at liberty to act after your own judgement.'

Princess Charlotte, much annoyed that she herself had
been invited to so few of the great functions that summer,
was quite prepared to take her mother's side over this; and
when her father, hoping that his daughter would soon be
persuaded to come round to his view, sent to Warwick House
a list of wedding guests among which Princess Caroline's

name was not included, she immediately returned it to him.

At the same time Princess Charlotte informed the Prince of Orange that her mind was unalterably made up on the point: she would not go to Holland after marriage, and she would never leave England at all unless she wanted to. If Prince William could not convince the Dutch government that these were essential conditions she would call the marriage off altogether.

Ultimately, towards the end of May, the Prince of Orange told Princess Charlotte confidentially that his father would consent to everything 'for the sake of his happiness'; and on 5 June 1814 she was informed that *her* father and the government were also prepared to give way. It was agreed that she should never leave the country without her own consent and that whenever she did consent to go abroad she could always come home 'at her own pleasure'. On 10 June she wrote to Lord Liverpool to accept these terms.

The matter did not rest there, however. Soon after this stipulation in the marriage contract had been approved, the Regent, 'greatly out of humour', arrived at Warwick House with the Bishop of Salisbury. He hoped and trusted that his daughter would give up the stipulation 'as a mark of civility to the House of Orange'. Politely but firmly Princess Charlotte declined to give way. Brougham had successfully impressed on her the vital necessity of her remaining in England immediately after the marriage, for if she went abroad her mother would no doubt go too; and this might well result in that dreaded sequence of events: a divorce, the Regent's remarriage, a new heir and her loss of the thone. Moreover, the nearer the marriage approached the less disposed she felt to go through with it at all. She and the Prince of Orange had not been 'on comfortable terms for some time'. It continued to rankle with her that during the visit of the foreign sovereigns to England he had gone everywhere, regardless of the fact that she had been invited scarcely anywhere. She had gone to a boring reception given by her grandmother and to a dinner at Carlton House, and that was all. All the foreign sovereigns and most of the princes had called on her at Warwick House but none of them had stayed even to take tea with her. She had been left to drive about in her carriage to look at the crowds and the decorations, the arrivals and departures, the guards of honour and the escorts, staring at everything and everyone 'with perfect sang-froid'.

To make matters worse, when the Prince of Orange found time to call on her their differences seemed deeper at each succeeding visit. One day, for instance, she said that at their future house both her mother and father must be equally welcome; but, knowing well what the Regent would have to say to this arrangement, Prince William replied that he thought it ought to be open only to her father. Then there was the unpleasant business of Prince William's heavy drinking at the parties to which he went and she was not invited. Brougham reported him as having been made 'remarkably drunk' by her cousin, the wild young Prince Paul of Württemberg for whose behaviour his stepmother, the Regent's oldest sister, was obliged to apologize. The Prince of Orange was again very drunk on 10 June at Ascot Races and had returned to London clinging to the outside of a stage-coach. Princess Charlotte, already 'quite enraged' at not being allowed to go to the Races herself, was disgusted at the reports of his condition.

She felt the time had come for a 'thorough explanation' with him. Although no arrangement had been made for a house for them in England, preparations for the wedding were going on apace: the Queen was already making fussy arrangements about the trousseau; the Regent, so she learned from her aunt, Princess Mary, was intending to ask the Orange family over to England as soon as the other royal guests had gone home. Princess Charlotte told the Prince that she would like to see him immediately he returned from the celebrations in Oxford. He accordingly presented himself at Warwick House on 16 June.

Lady Charlotte Lindsay was there at the time and immediately afterwards submitted one of her lengthy reports to Henry Brougham: 'While we were talking the Prince of Orange was announced: she went to him, and desired that I should remain where I was to hear the result of their conference, which has ended in her *positive declaration* that she *will not leave England now*, but will avail herself of the discretionary power promised her in the contract; and gave as her reason the situation of the Princess of Wales, whom she thought herself bound in duty not to leave under her present circumstances. He appeared to be very unhappy, but seemed to admit that if Princess Charlotte adhered to this resolution the marriage must be off. He begged her to reconsider it, and left the house in much agitation.'

That same evening Princess Charlotte wrote to him to tell him that she now considered their engagement '*to be totally and for ever at an end*'. Until he received this final letter he had continued to believe that she might repent; but he had to recognize now that his hopes of marrying her and of becoming Prince Consort of England were not to be fulfilled. He replied that he had informed his family of her decision but that he was not prepared to tell her father, an unpleasant duty which she must perform herself.

The night before he left England he attended a ball at Devonshire House; he went up to Lord Castlereagh's niece, Lady Emma Edgcumbe, wrung her hand with his customary force, and said, 'Goodbye, God bless you, Lady Emma. I am off tomorrow.' There were tears in his eyes, she said. 'He appeared miserable.'

At Warwick House, Princess Charlotte awaited her father's reactions to the information she had had to impart to him. So far, all he had done was to write to tell her that he had received her letter with 'astonishment, grief and concern'; but she could not be in any doubt that there was bound to be a far more violent reaction than this.

27

The Warwick House Affair
1814

'Like a bird let loose from its cage'

CREEVEY, for one, looked forward to the next instalment of the drama with anticipatory delight. 'Well, my pretty,' he told his wife. 'We have now a new game for Master Prinny. ... Whitbread has shown me Princess Charlotte's letter to the Prince of Orange. By God! It is capital. ... The marriage is broken off and ... the reasons are – first, her attachment to this country which she cannot and will not leave; and, above all, her attachment to her mother, whom in her present distressed situation she likewise cannot leave. ... What think you of the effect of this upon the British publick? ... And what do you suppose has produced this sudden attachment to her mother? It arises from the profound resources of old Brougham.'

There was a further reason which Creevey did not know but which the Regent suspected, and that was that Princess Charlotte's eye had lighted upon other Princes who were in London at that time and were more attractive than Prince William of Orange. There was Prince Augustus of Prussia, there was Prince Frederick of Prussia, and there was Prince Paul of Württemberg, all of whom, the Regent sourly noted, had called at Warwick House and none of whom was notably virtuous. After Prince Paul's call, the Regent demanded a full report from the Duchess of Leeds who replied that both herself and Miss Knight had been present during the interview and added, 'I am extremely concerned and surprised at your Royal Highness not condescending to take the slightest notice of me last night at Lady Hampden's for I can with truth assure you, Sir, I have served your Royal Highness most honestly and faithfully in the most difficult situation in which human being ever was placed. My resignation is always ready to be laid at your feet.'

Another caller at Warwick House was the bland and good-looking Prince Leopold, third son of the Duke of Saxe-Coburg-Saalfeld, who had come over to England in the suite of the Tsar and who had served with the Russian army against Napoleon. Princess Charlotte invited him to breakfast; and it was thereafter rumoured in London, so Mrs Tomline, the Bishop of Lincoln's wife, was assured, that it was this 'new fancy' which was the 'real cause for the breaking off of the marriage' to the Prince of Orange. The Regent, who was not informed of the invitation to breakfast, did not believe that Prince Leopold would be guilty of any impropriety: he was 'a most honourable young man' and had written him a letter perfectly justifying himself. But the Regent did not trust Prince Paul or either of the Prussian princes, particularly the handsome, disreputable Prince Augustus who, as the Duke of Kent said, was the 'black sheep in his family'. The Regent had good reason not to trust the assured and experienced Prince Augustus, for between 11 June and the end of the month there had been at least two clandestine meetings between him and Princess Charlotte at Warwick House. On one of these occasions when the Princess's astute and managing friend, Margaret Mercer Elphinstone, called she was told by a thoroughly alarmed Miss Knight that the two of them were alone together in the Princess's room. Miss Elphinstone said that they must be interrupted, and when Miss Knight refused to interfere she went upstairs to disturb them herself.*

* Throughout this period, so Mrs Tomline was reliably told by one of her London correspondents who was well informed about the activities at Warwick House, Miss Knight behaved 'very indiscreetly'. There was 'no intrigue' on her part to break off the marriage to the Prince of Orange; but she had little control over her charge and was certainly guilty of an 'improper yielding' to the Princess's strong will (Pretyman Papers, Ipswich, HA 119).

Hearing rumours of what was going on, the Bishop of Salisbury, the Princess's former preceptor, whom she had never liked, went to Warwick House to suggest that she should write a submissive letter to her father holding out a hope that she might, even now, be prepared to marry the Prince of Orange within a few months. If she did not do so 'arrangements would be made by no means agreeable to her inclinations'. She wrote a submissive letter couched in affectionate terms; but it contained no suggestion that she was prepared to reconsider marriage to the Prince.

Two days later she and Miss Knight received a summons to Carlton House. The Princess asked to be excused, on the grounds that she had not been well for some days and was still suffering from intermittent excruciating pain in her knee. So Miss Knight went to see the Regent by herself. Miss Knight, whom he knew to have connived at Charlotte's meetings with Prince Augustus, found him 'very cold, very bitter and very silent'. On her return to Warwick House she told the Princess how angry her father was about the Prussian Princes. Believing that the hateful old Bishop had spread the suspicions at Carlton House, Charlotte seems to have supposed that the best response would be a display of outraged innocence. She wrote an angry letter to the Bishop in which she boldly declared the *'whole allegation to be false* and *a base lie'* and assured him that 'no such violent accusation or measures' would have any effect on her. Fearing that this defiant letter would doubtless provoke a furious reaction at Carlton House, the Princess warned her page after she had sent it that 'it was possible all the servants might be sent away, but that she would never forget them whenever it was in her power'.

Her fears were fully justified. At six o'clock the next evening, 12 July, the Regent was seen emerging from Carlton House. He marched across the courtyard with the Bishop of Salisbury and four ladies and entered Warwick House. Leaving the Bishop and the ladies downstairs, he walked up the staircase and into Charlotte's room where he found her lying on a sofa. It was clear that this latest rebellion of his daughter's, following so soon on the numerous frustrations and humiliations he had undergone that summer, was more than he could bear with any pretence to composure. To be hissed in the streets while his foreign guests were cheered was bad enough; to know that his wife, despite all her gross misbehaviour, was the heroine of street mobs and theatre audiences while he was their villain – this was worse; but now to have an insubordinate daughter, manipulated by his political enemies, flirting with a most undesirable young man and rejecting a highly desirable marriage which she had formerly welcomed and which would remove her from the evil influence of her mother – this was intolerable.

He told her that her servants were all to be dismissed, that the ladies he had brought with him were to take over Warwick House, that she herself was to be confined at Carlton House for five days and then taken to Cranbourne Lodge in Windsor Forest where she was to see no one but her grandmother once a week, and that she was to leave immediately.

He was with her alone for three-quarters of an hour, then called in the Bishop of Salisbury who remained with them for a further quarter of an hour. Already, before her father's arrival, so Miss Knight told Mrs Tomline, Princess Charlotte was 'so agitated and wretched, and her eyes so swelled with crying' that she was quite unfit to leave the house. By the time the interview was over she was more distraught than ever. She ran from the room 'in great distress', fell on her knees before Miss Knight and cried out, 'God Almighty! Give me patience!'

But she did not remain kneeling long. Suddenly she made up her mind: she would run away. She dashed into her bedroom, asked her maid for her bonnet and shawl, and rushed down the backstairs, across the courtyard, past the sentries at the gate and out towards Charing Cross. At Charing Cross she jumped into a hackney coach and told the driver that she would give him a guinea to drive her as fast as he could to her mother's house in Connaught Place.

Her mother was not there. She had gone to Blackheath for the day and had not yet arrived home. Fully in command of the situation and of herself, indeed evidently relishing the drama which she had called into being, she sent a groom to fetch her mother back, despatched another messenger to bring Brougham to Connaught Place immediately, and scribbled a scarcely legible note to her uncle, the Duke of Sussex. This note she handed to a third servant, then asked a fourth to serve her dinner.

While Charlotte was waiting for the meal to be brought up to the drawing-room, Brougham arrived in answer to her summons. He had been at a dinner party at Michael Angelo Taylor's and, having spent most of the previous night working on a brief, was tired out; he had fallen asleep in the carriage and was 'still half-asleep' as he stumbled upstairs to the drawing-room. Princess Charlotte ran up to him, and said, 'I have just run off.' Before he had had time to find out why, Princess Caroline and Lady Charlotte Lindsay came into the room, followed by the servants with a meal. Princess Charlotte asked Brougham to sit down with them, but he declined the invitation, explaining that her message had arrived just as he was finishing dinner at a friend's house.

'You may eat a little bit with us,' Charlotte said. 'And at any rate you can carve.'

She was in excellent spirits, Brougham noticed, 'like a bird let loose from its cage'. She talked away cheerfully, laughed a great deal and was obviously enjoying herself enormously.

During the meal Miss Elphinstone arrived in a hackney coach with the Bishop of Salisbury. Charlotte sent the Bishop back to Carlton House with a message stating her terms for submission: the reinstatement of Miss Knight and her maids and no restrictions to be placed upon visits to her by Miss Elphinstone who, for the moment, remained at Connaught Place to join the merry party in the drawing-room.

From time to time various of the Regent's representatives were announced as being at the door. Their names were

greeted with shouts of amusement and they were not invited in. The Lord Chancellor, Lord Eldon, arrived, and it
was decided that he should be left to wait in his carriage
outside in the street. Then Lord Ellenborough came, bringing with him a writ of habeas corpus. Brougham put in a
word for him as his chief; but the ladies decreed that he
must remain outside 'as well as Old Bags'. Ellenborough
was followed by John Leach, a pernickety and affected
King's Counsel whose name evinced cries of 'Little Bags!'
'Reticule!' 'Ridicule!' Even the Duke of York was kept waiting downstairs, though Princess Caroline did go down after
dinner to have a word with him.

The Duke of Sussex, as a known sympathizer, was asked
upstairs immediately, fell into conversation, in German,
with Princess Caroline and was then introduced to
Brougham whom he had not previously met.

'Pray, Sir,' the Duke asked him directly. 'Supposing the
Prince Regent, acting in the name and on behalf of His
Majesty, were to send a sufficient force to break the doors
of the house and carry away the Princess, would any resistance in such case be lawful?'

'It would not.'

'Then, my dear,' he said turning to Charlotte, 'you hear
what the law is. I can only advise you to return with as much
speed and as little noise as possible.'

This was not at all the kind of advice that Charlotte was
hoping to receive; and her father's reply to her message,
which the Bishop of Salisbury now brought her and which
required her to 'submit unconditionally', made her more
than ever determined not to do so. She believed that if she
were to submit, she would be forced to go through with the
marriage to the Prince of Orange, though Brougham repeated the assurance he had often given her, that it could
never take place 'without her consent truly given'.

'They may wear me out by ill-treatment,' she protested,
'and may represent that I have changed my mind and consented.' She could only be sure of remaining safe, if she

held to her determination to remain with her mother. But
her mother – though she did not say so – was apparently not
so taken with that idea as her daughter was: she had made
up her mind to leave England and did not want her daughter to interfere with her plans.

What should she do? Princess Charlotte asked Brougham.
She was now growing rather nervous, not so sure of herself.
Brougham replied that she really ought to go back to Warwick House or Carlton House. At this she began to cry. Did
he too, she asked him pitifully, refuse to stand by her? Quite
the contrary, Brougham assured her. As to the marriage she
'must follow her own inclination entirely', but 'her returning
home was absolutely necessary'. Yet she would not give
way: she would never go back, she said; nothing and nobody would induce her to do so. The discussion went fitfully
on; and it grew late; the night passed, and dawn came.
Brougham wearily took the Princess to the window and
asked her to look out into the Park. 'Look there, Madam,'
he said. 'In a few hours all the streets and the Park, now
empty, will be crowded with tens of thousands. I have only
to take you to that window, and show you to the multitude,
and tell them your grievances, and they will all rise on your
behalf.'

Brougham could not remember exactly what she said in
reply to this, but it was something like, 'And why should
they not?'

'The commotion will be excessive,' he told her. 'Carlton
House will be attacked – perhaps pulled down; the soldiers
will be ordered out, blood will be shed; and if your Royal
Highness were to live a hundred years, it never would be
forgotten that your running away from your father's house
was the cause of the mischief; and you may depend upon it,
such is the English people's horror of bloodshed, you never
would get over it.'

This was an argument to which she could not fail to respond. She looked at Brougham with an expression he could
only describe as one of 'stupefaction'. But before she sub-

mitted she insisted that he should prepare a document
which declared that she was 'firmly resolved' that the proposed marriage between herself and the Prince of Orange
should 'never take place', 'that *this* was her voluntary
avowal, and to be considered as such, whatever she might
afterwards be represented to have said, she being now at
liberty and about to be taken back to Carlton House'. If
ever there should be an announcement of the marriage 'it
must be understood to be without her consent and against
her will'. Brougham did as she wished; he then made six
copies of the document which her mother, Lady Charlotte
Lindsay, the Duke of Sussex, and himself all signed. Then,
towards five o'clock in the morning, she drove back with the
Duke of York to Carlton House.

She was delivered into the charge of her four new ladies,
Lady Ilchester, Lady Rosslyn and two of Lady Rosslyn's
nieces, who in due course accompanied her to Cranbourne
Lodge where they were joined by her former Governess, Mrs
Alicia Campbell. At Cranbourne Lodge she felt 'quite hopeless and spiritless'. It was as though she had been cast into
prison. She was closely watched all day; and at night one
or other of her ladies slept in her room or in an adjoining
room with the connecting door left open. She was forbidden
to receive or to send letters; her only permitted visitor was
Margaret Mercer Elphinstone, who her father believed
would prevent her from doing anything stupid. Miss Elphinstone was a convinced Whig but, as Lady Charlotte Lindsay
knew, did not encourage her to support her mother. And, as
far as the Regent was concerned, that was all important.

The only parties Princess Charlotte was allowed to attend
were her grandmother's tiresome musical evenings at Frogmore; the only change to which she could look forward was a
visit to Weymouth for the recruitment of her health.

It was during this miserable time in Windsor Forest that
she received a letter from her mother which caused her so
much 'distress and agitation' that Miss Elphinstone had
never seen her so 'deeply affected and apparently mortified'

in her life. Miss Elphinstone felt she would never forget the 'dreadful effect' this letter had had upon the Princess. 'Even when I left her two days after,' she said, 'her pulse continued at 98.' For her mother had written to say that she was definitely going abroad. She had indicated that she might return one day, but she did not say when that day might be. 'She decidedly deserts me,' Princess Charlotte complained to Miss Elphinstone. 'After all if a *mother* has not *feeling* for her child or children are they to *teach it to her* or can they *expect to be listened to* with any *hopes of success*?'

All that Brougham had foretold now seemed likely to transpire: there would be a divorce, a second marriage, a new heir, and her title to the throne would be gone.

For days past, Brougham had been doing his utmost to make Princess Caroline change her mind; but at length he had had to accept the fact that she would be deterred no longer. Nothing could stop her now, he was informed by Lady Charlotte Lindsay, who had never seen 'so fixed a determination'. Declaring that since she was deprived of the honour of being Princess of Wales, she would be plain Caroline, 'a happy, merry soul', she made the final preparations for her departure.

At the end of the first week in August she rode down to the Sussex coast where she presented herself at Worthing in a satin pelisse with huge golden clasps, and one of those tall military-style hats which she so unfortunately favoured, a great construction of violet and green satin surmounted by a plume of green feathers. She drove along the front with Lady Charlotte Lindsay and William Austin, a brash, though rather vacant-looking boy, now fourteen years old. Also in attendance were Lady Elizabeth Forbes, as Lady-in-Waiting, and, as her three Chamberlains, Colonel John St Leger's younger brother, Anthony Butler St Leger, Keppel Craven, and the odd, good-natured, gregarious archaeologist and traveller, Sir William Gell, known as 'Topographical Gell', 'a coxcombe', in Thomas Moore's opinion, 'but rather amusing'. Her equerry was Captain Charles Hesse; and her doctor was Henry Holland, a young man of twenty-five whose taste was for travel rather than medicine, whose favourite prescription was 'the frequent half-hour of genial conversation', and whose reputation in later life, having married the witty daughter of the Rev. Sydney Smith, was that he was 'unfit to attend a sick cat'.

With these ill-assorted attendants and a train of servants, stewards and couriers, the Princess, who had assumed the name of the Countess of Wolfenbüttel for the duration of her journey, stepped aboard the frigate *Jason*, characteristically creating an air of mystery about her by displaying peculiar concern for the contents of a certain metal case, on which was painted in large white letters, '*Her Royal Highness the Princess of Wales, to be always with her*'. As the *Jason* sailed out to sea it was noticed that she was crying.

With his loathed wife out of the country at last, and his unruly daughter safely restrained at Cranbourne Lodge, the Regent, during the late summer of 1814, might reasonably have looked forward to an easier and happier life. But his enemies declined to leave him in peace. When his daughter's flight from Warwick House to Connaught Place became public knowledge, Francis Horner, the Whig Member of Parliament for St Mawes, declared that he thought the Regent's conduct was that of a Prussian corporal; and Henry Brougham wanted to know whether 'anything so barbarous' as the Regent's treatment of his daughter could be found outside Turkey. To be sure the *Morning Post* blamed the daughter rather than the father for her 'unnatural rebellion', and castigated Miss Knight as one of Princess Charlotte's 'obnoxious associates'; but Brougham was quite right when he wrote contentedly that the affair was 'buzzed over town, of course', and that all were 'against the Prince'.

Brougham wrote out five questions for the Duke of Sussex to ask in the House of Lords. Was the Princess enjoying the same freedom of communication with her friends which

she had had at Warwick House? Was she allowed to send
and receive letters as before? Was she 'in that state of liberty
which persons considered not in confinement ought to be
in'? Was she to be allowed to undergo that course of sea-
bathing which her physicians had prescribed for her? And
was she to have an establishment suitable to her rank?

The Whig party as a whole, however, would not give
Brougham and Sussex the support they needed, and Lord
Grey came to the conclusion that it would be better if the
matter were dropped. Lord Liverpool assured the House of
Lords that Princess Charlotte was being given all the freedom that was reasonable and compatible with an education
pleasing to 'God, nature and the laws of the country'; and
although many Members doubted that this was so, no further steps were taken to free her from the Regent's strict
control.

28

Impresario, Collector and Patron
1814–1815

'The country will have cause to be grateful'

HAVING temporarily settled the problem of Princess Charlotte without undue embarrassment, the Regent now turned his attention to the more congenial task of arranging a fête at Carlton House as a personal tribute to the Duke of Wellington, the signing of the warrant for whose pension he had been pleased to make 'the first act of his unrestricted regency'. For this fête he had a special polygonal building put up in the garden. It was a solid structure, one hundred and twenty feet in diameter, built of brick with a leaded roof; but the interior was to give the impression of summer light, airiness and festivity. This effect was achieved by painting the umbrella-shaped ceiling to resemble muslin and by decorating it with gilt cords, by fixing looking-glass to the walls and hanging them with muslin draperies, and by the sparkling illumination of twelve chandeliers. On the day of the fête huge banks of artificial flowers were arranged on the floor in the shape of a temple behind whose walls of petals and foliage were concealed two bands.

A covered promenade, its interior decorated with draperies and rose-coloured cords, led to a Corinthian temple where the guests could admire a marble bust by Turnerelli of the great Duke placed on a column in front of a large mirror engraved with a star and the letter W. The walls of a second enclosed walk, decorated in green calico, were covered with transparencies representing such appropriate subjects as 'Overthrow of Tyranny by the Allied Powers' and 'Military Glory'. Elsewhere in the garden were supper tents and refreshment rooms hung with white and rose curtains, and with regimental colours printed on silk.

The first of the two thousand guests began to arrive at nine o'clock in the evening and were received at the grand entrance by equerries who conducted them to the fanciful rooms and tents and corridors on the garden front. The Regent himself appeared in his field-marshal's full-dress uniform, wearing his English, Russian, Prussian and French orders, looking extremely content and welcoming.

The fête was all that he could have hoped for. Even the Queen, who did not sit down to supper until two o'clock, stayed on until half-past four; and there were many guests still there at dawn.

While the Regent had been planning this fête at Carlton House, he had also been supervising the preparations for a most elaborate gala in the London parks to celebrate the anniversary of the Battle of the Nile and the centenary of the accession to the English throne of the House of Hanover. For weeks past the newspapers had been reporting on the strange and exotic buildings which were appearing in the parks – in St James's Park, a Chinese pagoda and a picturesque yellow bridge ornamented with black lines and a bright blue roof; in Green Park, an embattled Gothic castle over a hundred feet square; in Hyde Park, ornamental booths and stalls, arcades and kiosks, swings and roundabouts. The trees were hung with coloured lamps; lanterns lined Birdcage Walk and the Mall; railings and dwarf walls were torn down to widen the entrances. The *Sun* reported that five hundred men had been at work for a month to produce the 'most brilliant fireworks ever seen in this country'. The *Morning Post* promised spectacles of unparalleled splendour. Only *The Times* struck a gloomy note, remarking that the public would 'first gape at the mummery, then laugh at the authors of it and lastly grumble at the expense'. *The Times*, having piously complained of the preparations continuing on a Sunday, also condemned the gingerbread stalls, the facilities for selling ale and gin, and the scanty precautions against the intrusion of a violent mob. 'Was there not something in the shape of a promise given that no fair should take place?' an editorial demanded. 'And was not the just outcry against its debauchery, drunkenness, and mingled and various abominations silenced only by the distinct pledge that nothing of their cause should be permitted?'

It seemed on the morning of the appointed day, 1 August, that *The Times*'s peevish prophecies of disaster were about to be fulfilled when a heavy rain began to fall. Between ten and eleven, however, the sun came out and the celebrations began.

First there was a spectacular ascent from Green Park when Windham Sadler's colourful balloon 'sprang into the air with its usual velocity and Mr Sadley, who had taken up with him 'a vast number of programmes of the jubilee ... flung them down again from the sky with much industry and profusion'. Then there was a regatta on the Serpentine, followed by a splendid naumachia representing the Battle of the Nile which ended with the French fleet being destroyed by fireships. This was followed by a display of fireworks even more magnificent than the *Sun* had predicted. From the battlements of the Gothic castle in Green Park there blazed an amazing array of maroons and serpents, Roman candles and Catherine wheels, fire-pots and girandoles. Rocket after rocket shot into the sky, each one containing 'a world of smaller rockets'. And when the dense clouds of smoke, which hid the sombre canvas castle from view for a minute or two, had blown away there was seen standing in its place, as though 'placed there by magic', a brightly illuminated Temple of Concord, its walls displaying allegorical pictures prominent amongst which was *The Triumph of England under the Regency*.

The crowds cheered; the Japanese lanterns shone gaily against the yellow and black walls of the Pagoda; the gas jets spluttered on its blue roof; and when at ten o'clock the whole building burst into flames and fell into the waters of

the lake, killing a lamplighter and injuring five other workmen, this was supposed by most of the crowd to be yet
another brilliantly contrived spectacle. The royal family
looked on approvingly from the windows and lawns of Buckingham House where the Queen had invited three hundred
guests to a banquet.

The proceedings were universally agreed to have been an
enormous success. There had been no riots; the crowds were
in excellent humour; the few troops on duty were not required; and even *The Times* agreed that the celebrations
had gone off very well, that 'it was an indisputable fact that
so immense a number of the people had never before been
brought together by any description of public rejoicings or
any of the great events which have so often gilded the pages
of British history'.

The Regent could congratulate himself upon being personally responsible for this particular 'description of public
rejoicings' which had proved so successful and so enjoyable.
For a time, indeed, now that Princess Caroline was safely
out of the country and Princess Charlotte was secluded from
the public eye, now that he had proved himself so inspired
an impresario, he began to lose some of his unpopularity.
Two days after the great gala in the parks, the *Courier*,
always a strong supporter of the royal family and the government, fulsomely reported: 'Among the many instances
which have come to our knowledge, so honourable to the
character of the Prince Regent as a man of feeling, one
occurred at the levee on Thursday last' when a man, who
had lost a leg, stooped to kneel before him. 'No, no,' the
Regent protested, knowing of the man's disability from
having met him previously at Brighton, 'No, no, you will
hurt yourself.' 'It is in these little traits of character,' the
Courier commented, 'that one discerns the goodness of his
heart and it is our greatest pride, whenever we meet with
them, to be the humble instrument of recording them.'

This sort of unctuous compliment was scarcely to the
taste of the readers of *The Times*, but it did reflect a gradual,

if shortlived, change in the public attitude towards the Regent which became noticeable at this time. To the Regent's own taste no compliment seemed too outrageous; and if the public were reluctant to give him the full credit to which he felt entitled, he was never sparing of praise himself. Indeed, it later became one of his rather engaging idiosyncrasies to suggest that he was personally responsible for the military and naval triumphs which were being celebrated that summer, and were to be celebrated the next. The Duke of Wellington usually listened to such tales in silence, though once, after hearing the Regent relate how he had made a body of troops charge down a particular sharp declivity, the Duke was heard to observe, 'Very steep, sir'.

An extremely vain man, the Regent had always endeavoured to evade the painful realization of his own unpopularity by pretending that it did not exist; and sometimes he seems actually to have succeeded in persuading himself that it did not exist, for he had extraordinary powers of self-deception. He once, for instance, solemnly assured Lady Cowper that he had visited her mother, Lady Melbourne, every day as she lay dying and that she had expired in his arms, when Lady Cowper knew perfectly well that he had never been near the house. To his doctors, when suffering from an exceptionally severe hangover, he would explain, 'By God, it is very extraordinary ... for I live very abstemiously and went to bed in good time,' though they knew as well as he did that he had been drinking maraschino until two o'clock that morning.

He had once, at the height of the public outcry against his supposed ill-treatment of Princess Caroline, astounded Lord Moira by remarking with evident self-satisfaction that 'no prince was ever idolized by the people of this country as himself'. Sir Philip Francis gave an example of this remarkable self-deceiving vanity when recounting an after-dinner conversation at the Pavilion one evening during the early days of the restricted Regency, when the Prince had not been free to make peers as he wished. The guests, following the Prince's complaint about this restriction, had amused themselves by inventing titles and testimonials for each other. Sir Philip suggested as an appropriate citation for Sheridan, at that time in more than usually straitened circumstances, 'The Man Who Extends England's Credit'.

Everyone laughed, but the Prince, noticing how upset Sheridan was, said to him, 'Don't mind him, old fellow! His penalty shall be to find a name for *me*, and woe betide him if I'm not content with it.'

'Name, name,' everybody shouted.

'*The* Man,' proposed Sir Philip with heavy emphasis on the first word.

'Go on,' said Sheridan.

'I've done,' said Sir Philip.

The Regent said, 'I'm content' and bowed 'gracefully round'.

The compliment, he clearly thought, was not overdone. When the news of Napoleon's abdication arrived in London he wrote to his mother to tell her that he was 'really quite bereft of the means of expressing' himself, or of giving vent to feelings which surpassed 'all description'. And he added, 'I trust my dearest mother that you will think that I have fulfilled and done my duty at least, and perhaps I may be vain enough to hope that you may feel a little proud of *your son*.' For, after all, as he put it in another letter, the victory could not have been won without his own 'original and indefatigable endeavours'. The boast, of course, was not altogether unjustified. His decision to keep the Tories in office in 1812 and his support of them since certainly did give him good reason to feel entitled to share the credit of victory. But to arrogate to himself the lion's share seemed to his critics absurd.

His 'indefatigable endeavours', he liked it to be supposed, were largely responsible for the final overthrow of Napoleon who, having landed in France from Elba in February 1815, was defeated by the armies of Wellington and Blücher in June at Waterloo; and he used to say with pride of his achievements, 'I set them all to work'. Of course, he did not always expect to be taken seriously. When he heard that after Waterloo the country's revenue exceeded by 'many, many, many millions, that of any former year, ever yet known', he 'could not help telling the Chancellor of the Exchequer that the balance should be transferred to his "private coffer" in consideration of his exertions' and all that he had done for the country 'as well as the whole world'.

The Regent was at a party at Mrs Boehm's in St James's Square when Major the Hon. Henry Percy, bloodstained and dusty, arrived to announce the victory and to lay the eagles of the French army at his feet. His hostess was 'much annoyed with the battle of Waterloo as it spoilt her party'; but the Prince delighted in the scene. He asked the ladies to leave the room while Lord Liverpool read out the despatch which Major Percy had brought with him. When Lord Liverpool had finished reading, the Regent turned to Major Percy and in his most good-natured, gracious manner said to him, 'I congratulate you, *Colonel* Percy.'

Soon afterwards, however, reflecting upon the great number of men who had been killed, tears began to run down his cheeks. 'It is a glorious victory,' he said, 'and we must rejoice at it, but the loss of life has been fearful, and *I* have lost many friends.' *

*

* The Allies declared that Napoleon was their prisoner and England was made responsible for selecting his place of confinement. Napoleon himself asked if he could live in England, a request which Lord Holland and the Duke of Sussex publicly urged should be granted. But the Regent agreed with the government that there could be no question of his living in England where, as Lord Liverpool said, 'he would become an object of curiosity immediately, and possibly of compassion in the course of a few months'. So the request made in a personal letter to the Regent was refused with the agreement of the other Allied powers. The Regent, however, noting that Napoleon had referred to him as 'the most powerful, the most constant and the most generous of [his] enemies', declared approvingly, 'Upon my word, a very proper letter: much more so, I must say, than any I ever received from Louis XVIII' (Holland, *Further Memoirs*, 220).

Waterloo *was* a glorious victory, the people agreed; but
they declined to acknowledge that the Regent had had any
part in it. In any case, military triumphs on the Continent
were of less concern to them than the price of bread at home
during the post-war slump. The Corn Law of 1815, which
aimed to restore agricultural prosperity at the expense of
the consumer, enraged the London poor. Members of Parliament known to be in favour of it were attacked on their way
to the House; and, in the mistaken belief that the Regent
himself was an active supporter of the Bill, a crowd of
demonstrators deposited a blood-stained loaf on the parapet
of Carlton House which had to be protected by troops from
a threatened assault by the mob.

Nor was it, of course, only the poor who were bitterly
offended by the contrast between the squalor in which tens
of thousands of people in the slums of London had to live
and the ever increasing splendours to be seen behind the
Corinthian portico and garden wall of the Regent's palace.
George Tierney, one of the more extreme Whigs, complained
in 1815 that the furniture for Carlton House had cost the
nation £260,000; charges for upholstery were £49,000 in a
single year; plate and jewels cost about £23,000 each year.
Yet Carlton House was constantly being improved, re-
furnished and redecorated; and it was the tax-paying middle
classes who had to bear most of the cost. A new Gothic
dining-room, divided into five compartments with walls of
varnished wood decorated with the arms of the Kings of England, was added at the east end to complement the conservatory; a second Gothic library was installed as well as several
new Corinthian rooms including a golden drawing-room;
and if some of the buildings that appeared from time to
time in the gardens were found to have other uses – like the
polygonal structure erected for the Wellington fête, which
was moved to Woolwich to serve as a weapons museum and
armoury – there were many others that were merely demolished and carted away. Five days after the Wellington fête
it was announced in *The Times* that the Regent would

shortly take possession of the Duke of Cumberland's apartments at St James's Palace, which had been prepared for the Emperor of Russia, 'previous to the commencement of grand alterations at Carlton House'.

The Regent's reckless expenditure would have been considered rather less censurable had he been content with his London palace; but he continued to lavish money on other equally extravagant enterprises elsewhere, though his debts, while gradually being reduced, still amounted in May 1814 to £339,000. At the beginning of 1815 work had begun on rebuilding the Marine Pavilion at Brighton, the existing structure by Henry Holland being now considered rather humdrum; and the Regent's Treasurer dreaded to think what the ultimate cost of this new work would be.

Some years before, James Wyatt had submitted an estimate which suggested a likely figure of £200,000. Wyatt was the architect of the Pantheon in Oxford Street, described by Horace Walpole as 'the most beautiful edifice in England', and of Fonthill Abbey, William Beckford's fantastic mansion in Wiltshire. He had done a good deal of work for George III and, for the Regent, had designed the second library at Carlton House. But before any work on the new Pavilion could be begun, he was killed in a carriage accident; and the Regent, 'very much affected ... even to shedding tears', had to find another architect to fulfil his plans. He soon found one in John Nash.

He already knew Nash well. It was he who had been responsible for the new Corinthian rooms at Carlton House, as well as the buildings in the gardens for the Wellington fête in 1814 and the pagoda and bridge in St James's Park that same year. The Regent had also been closely involved with Nash's plans for a massive redevelopment scheme which was eventually to transform the face of central London. In fact, it was widely believed that the relationship between Nash and the Regent was something more than that of architect and patron. For Nash, the son of an impoverished Lambeth millwright, had risen with remarkable

speed in the architectural profession. Trained in the office of
Sir Robert Taylor, he had launched out and bankrupted
himself as a speculative builder before going into partner-
ship with Humphry Repton. But in 1798 he had married a
woman much younger than himself, a woman who was
supposed to have been one of the Prince's mistresses. And
thereafter he became much more successful and much
richer, arousing a good deal of dislike by his self-satisfaction
and display, his snobberies and affectations. 'A great coxcomb', Robert Finch recorded in his diary. 'He is very fond
of women ... attempted even Mrs Parker, his wife's sister.
He lives in Dover Street, has a charming place on the Isle
of Wight and drives four horses.'

Coxcomb or not, Nash was an architect of exceptional
talent whose emergence as the Regent's favourite architect
was fully justified by his performance. The Regent eagerly
discussed with him the plans for an extensive development
in Marylebone Park – an expanse of open land north of
Portland Place which had just reverted to the Crown from
the noble families to whom it had formerly been let – and
for a new road that was to sweep up to this new development from Pall Mall. The development in Marylebone
Park was to be known as Regent's Park: the road that led
to it as Regent's Street. These were both impressive schemes
for the improvement of the capital that remained, throughout their gradual realization, close to the Regent's heart.
Indeed, without the Regent's support and his influence
over the apathetic and hidebound Commissioners for
Crown Lands they could never have been realized at
all.

At the time many people wished that it had not been
possible to realize them. The stucco and cast-iron terraces
were widely condemned as meretricious. Prince Pückler-
Muskau described Nash's architecture as 'monstrous'; Maria
Edgeworth was 'properly surprised by the new town ...
built in Regent's Park – and indignant at plaister statues
and horrid useless *domes* and pediments crowded with

mock sculpture figures which damp and smoke must destroy in a season or two'.

The charges were understandable. There was much in Nash's work that was grandiose, extravagant and showily exuberant; but for all their audacious – sometimes even outrageous – panache, his buildings were eventually seen to be as delightful as the Regent had found them from the beginning. Their influence spread all over England, from seaside resorts on the south coast, to inland spas such as Cheltenham, from the outer suburbs of London to the market towns of the country.

Admiring Nash's gifts and sharing his panache, the Regent had no hesitation in asking him to work with him on the designs for yet another architectural adventure, a romantic country house in Windsor Great Park. This new residence was known at first as The Cottage; and then, since this seemed scarcely appropriate for the large building it eventually became, as the Royal Lodge, or, as his enemies preferred, 'The Thatched Palace'.

The Royal Lodge, originally a modest house occupied by the Deputy-Ranger, was converted by Nash into an enchanting and imposing Gothic *cottage orné*. Its roof was thatched and its windows mullioned; its brick walls were rendered in coloured plaster; a thatched verandah, supported by rustic columns entwined with ivy and honeysuckle, extended along the south front at the western end of which there was a large glass conservatory. Tall, elegantly shaped chimneys rose above the reeds of the roof; the larch trees and pines that encircled the lawns secluded the house without keeping the sunlight from its windows. By the end of 1814 over £52,000 had been spent upon it, including £17,000 for furniture. It was to be constantly altered, renovated and enlarged; and a new dining-room – the only part of the rambling house to survive *in situ* today – was still not completed at the time of its owner's death.

Robert Smirke, a practical, methodical, rather staid architect, examples of whose work were soon to be seen all over
London, was highly critical of the Regent's fanciful taste
and extravagant expenditure. He condemned the apartments
at Carlton House, for instance, as being 'so overdone with
finery, and superfluous as, supposing the owner not to be
known, would give an unfavourable idea of the kind of mind
he must have'. Yet even Smirke conceded that the Regent's
patronage of the arts and artists, of scientists and scholars,
was to be commended as compensation for his many faults
and follies, and that he was a truly discerning connoisseur
as well as a generous patron. Richard Westmacott, the sculptor, gave evidence of this when he unpacked, for the Regent's
inspection at Carlton House, some fine casts of the group
of Niobe which had been sent to London by the Grand Duke
of Tuscany. The Regent commented that one of the statues
did not belong to the group. 'I was pleased at the Prince
making this remark without any observation from me,'
Westmacott reported to Lawrence. 'The Prince's remarks . . .
were not only judicious but expressed with a feeling and in a
language of art that I was not aware he was master of.'
When Thomas Lawrence was knighted in April 1815, having
fulfilled the Regent's commission to paint the various allied
sovereigns, ministers and generals who had contributed to
Napoleon's downfall, Smirke wrote that 'no act of our
Regent Sovereign was ever more just', and that if he kept up
to that, the country would have 'cause to be grateful'. The
Regent himself assured Sir Thomas that he was proud in
conferring a mark of his favour on one who had raised the
character of British art in the estimation of all Europe.

Lawrence had been in France when the Regent recalled
him to London to begin painting those portraits of the allied
leaders which now hang in the Waterloo Chamber at Windsor. He had gone over to Paris to see the works of art which
Napoleon had brought together in the Louvre from
all over the Empire. These works of art included the Apollo
Belvedere and various other statues which had been taken

from Rome and which the Pope now offered to the Regent on the grounds that the expense of bringing them back would be too heavy for the Papacy to bear. Much as he would have liked to possess 'these inestimable productions', the Regent replied that he could not take advantage of their owner's necessity, and he offered to pay for their return to Rome himself.

The generosity did not go unrewarded. The Regent was sent in return a number of casts from marbles in the Vatican museum which were immediately offered to the Royal Academy, whose President was informed that 'if casts from any other of the fine antiques in Rome should be considered desirable for the School of the Royal Academy, His Royal Highness would, on their being specified, use his influence to obtain them'. This offer was followed by the loan to the Royal Academy school of the Raphael cartoons, 'one at a time for a few months each', and of *Rembrandt and Saskia about to go out*. The Rembrandt was a picture he had recently acquired as a companion piece to Rembrandt's *Shipbuilder and his Wife* which Lord Yarmouth had bought for him some years before.

While Lawrence was working for the Regent in London, Antonio Canova was at work on his behalf in Rome. Canova had been sent to Paris by the Pope to superintend the return of various Italian treasures, and after his work there was completed he had gratified a long-felt wish to visit London. The Regent had greeted him warmly, presented him with a valuable snuffbox and commissioned from him various works, including a group of Mars and Venus, a statue of a nymph, and later, to the horror of the Whigs, an expensive statue in Rome to the memory of the exiled Stuarts whom the Regent profoundly revered.*

---

* When part of James II's remains were discovered during the rebuilding of the parish church at St Germain-en-Laye in 1824, they were removed in great state on the express instruction of George IV and placed beneath the altar before being solemnly reinterred in the newly completed church (Campana de Cavelli, *Les derniers Stuarts à*

The Regent's 'fine taste, sound judgement, and extensive information' made a deep impression on Canova who used to say that of all the sovereigns he had met in the course of his career – and he had talked to almost all the crowned heads of Europe – there was not one 'in whose address were more happily combined, the suavity of the amiable man, and the dignity of the great monarch'. He particularly respected the Regent for the support which he had given to the nation's purchase of the marble friezes from the neglected Parthenon brought back from Greece by the seventh Earl of Elgin. These friezes, the Elgin marbles, had been subjected to much ignorant criticism from the kind of self-professed connoisseur satirized by James Gillray; but Canova confirmed their supreme merit and welcomed the Regent's interest in their purchase.*

St Germain-en-Laye, Paris, 1871, i, 99). The marble group of Mars and Venus was completed in 1817 and placed, rather inappropriately, in the Gothic conservatory at Carlton House in 1824. Together with another group by Canova of a girl and cherub which reached Carlton House in 1819, the Mars and Venus group is now at Buckingham Palace (*Buckingham Palace*, 183).

   * Canova's colossal marble statue of Napoleon, in the pose of a naked Roman emperor, 11 feet 4 inches in height, also came to England at this time. Canova had been commissioned by Napoleon to execute the work in 1802 and had completed it in 1810. Napoleon did not like it, however, since the winged figure of Victory in the statue's right hand does not return his stern gaze but seems about to fly away from him. The statue was consequently packed away out of sight. It was bought in 1816 for less than £3,000, a figure which nevertheless enabled the Louvre to complete the installation of the Salle des Antiques. The Regent presented it to the Duke of Wellington, and it now stands in the staircase vestibule at Apsley House (Archives Nationales o³ 1430: *The Wellington Museum*, HMSO, 1964, 37). After Canova's death in 1822, George IV bought his last two works for 5,000 guineas. The King's agent, W. R. Hamilton, Minister at the Court of Naples, could not say that Canova's brother was '*perfectly* satisfied' that the sum paid represented 'the full amount' which the sculptures were worth, nor what the artist would have expected for them; but Hamilton was fully persuaded that the

As in art, so in the sciences, the Regent's patronage was eagerly sought and gratefully welcomed. He was President of the Royal Institution, which consequently became 'more the *ton* than anything' and attracted 'ladies of all ages' to its lectures. He bestowed an unsolicited knighthood on the chemist, Humphry Davy, subsequent inventor of the safety lamp; he also knighted William Herschel, the astronomer; he endowed readerships in mineralogy and geology at Oxford; he championed William Congreve, inventor of the Congreve rocket, at a time when he was being much ridiculed, made him one of his equerries, and would no doubt have knighted him too had he not succeeded to his father's baronetcy.

He also professed himself anxious to promote the cause of literature. He was a patron of the Literary Fund, regularly subscribed to it, and obtained for it a Charter of Incorporation. He was particularly anxious to give his personal encouragement to the work of Jane Austen. He frequently read her novels, so she was told by her brother's doctor who was also one of the Regent's physicians, and he kept a set 'in every one of his residences'. One day in 1815 she was invited to Carlton House where she was conducted round the library by Stanier Clarke, the Regent's librarian, who told her that his master had 'read and admired' all her publications, and that she was free to dedicate a novel to him if she wished to do so. She did wish to do so, and told her publishers that her next novel, *Emma*, which was already advertised for publication, was to be 'dedicated by permission to HRH the Prince Regent', and that it was her 'particular wish that one set should be completed and sent to HRH two or three days before the work [was] generally public'.

'Abbato Canova was highly flattered that these his brother's latest finished works should be deposited in the palace of the King of Great Britain' (R A 27064, 12 August 1825).

29

Cranbourne Lodge and Claremont Park
1814–1817

'Is there any danger?'

WHILE Jane Austen had been at work on *Emma*, Princess Charlotte had been languishing in her close confinement at Warwick House, Cranbourne Lodge and Weymouth. The people she was allowed to see were limited to the names on a list drawn up by her father who insisted that though she was permitted to go to the theatre once or twice a week she must not sit at the front of the box or stay till the very end of the performance. 'Nothing can be so wretchedly uncertain and uncomfortable as my situation,' she complained miserably to Priscilla Burghersh. 'I am grown thin, sleep ill and eat but little. Bailly [Dr Matthew Baillie] says my complaints are all nervous, and that bathing and sailing will brace me; but I say *Oh no!* no good can be done whilst the mind and the soul are on the rack constantly, and the spirits forced and screwed up to a certain pitch.' It was not that she missed her mother. Indeed, she told her aunt Mary that she thought the best thing that Princess Caroline could do would be to stay abroad, and that she did not mind if she never saw her again. What she complained of most, so Margaret Mercer Elphinstone informed Brougham, was that one of the ladies was 'obliged either to sleep in the room with her, or in the next with the door open, and that many of her letters have been kept back'.

In a long letter to Lord Grey, Miss Elphinstone had given a worrying account of the Princess's health at Weymouth during the late summer of 1814. She had become 'worse daily', and the pains in her knee had been so severe that she had been unable to sleep for nights on end. 'To make her sejour at the seaside as disagreeable as possible,' Miss Elphinstone had continued, 'the Prince has positively refused to allow her to drive her ponies there, as he says it would collect a mob at the door every time she went out. He has also prevented her Sub Tutors from going with her, though she asked to have them as a favor, so that she will be literally deprived of every amusement and occupation that could for a moment divert her thoughts from her present melancholy situation. ... Her allowance, which used to be paid regularly (every month I believe) has been withheld from her, ever since she left Warwick House. A tradesman sent in his bill to her a few days ago, begging to be paid as he was in great distress for money – to accomplish this, and to pay some little pensions that were due to poor people, she protests she was obliged to part with some of her diamonds – surely this tyranny cannot last long.'

So far as the Princess's allowance was concerned, Miss Elphinstone did not know the full facts. On the day after she had written to Lord Grey, the Regent had written to his mother from Ragley asking her to let Charlotte have £200 which he would pay the Queen back as soon as he returned to London. He had added that, 'strange as it may appear', he had never in his life known what the amount of her allowance was. He had presumed the King had made adequate provision for her, and had told Lady de Clifford that he 'wished that Charlotte should at all times be liberally supplied with money, and not stinted in the least, and that the allowance should be proportioned to her years, increasing of course as she grew more advanced in her years; and that if hereafter the sum thus allowed by the King was not sufficient for affording what was proper for Charlotte for her pocket', Lady Clifford had but to apply to him and he would do 'all that was necessary' so far as his means would admit.

In fact, the amount of the pocket money was £10 a month. In addition she was allowed £1,000 a year for her other expenses, excluding the house and stable accounts. But this

had proved far from enough for her. By the end of 1814 she
had become involved in debt to Colnaghi for nearly £600 for
prints, and to various dressmakers and jewellers to the
astonishing amount of over £20,000. This had been largely
due to her excessive generosity to her friends, all of whom
had received expensive presents of jewellery from her at the
time of her engagement to the Prince of Orange; she had
hoped that the bills would be paid out of the sum which she
expected to receive from Parliament on the occasion of her
marriage.

His knowledge of the great amount of her debts had not
prevented a happy reconciliation of the Regent and his
daughter five months after her flight from Warwick House
when she had confessed to him for the first time the full
story of her association with Captain Hesse and her mother's
active encouragement of the affair. Her father's kindness
and understanding about all this had impressed her deeply.
She had told the Duke of York 'with great glee' of the
happiness she felt 'at being upon so cordial and affectionate
a footing' with her father once again.

But the narrow escape she had had with Captain Hesse
and the other unsuitable young men who had been allowed
to be alone with her made her father all the more certain
that she ought to get married as soon as possible. Her recent
capricious behaviour had, he felt sure, done much harm to
her reputation abroad; and if she were left unattached much
longer it might be difficult to arrange a suitable match for
her at all.

Princess Charlotte agreed with him about the desirability
of an early marriage. 'My character, my dear father, you
must believe is no matter of indifference to me. ... Having
entered upon this subject I cannot conclude it without begging you to take into consideration how much a matrimonial
connection would be likely to remove me and my reputation
from all this present distress.' Yet Princess Charlotte could
not agree that a renewal of the engagement to the Prince
of Orange, as her father proposed, was at all acceptable.

The Regent still considered that Prince William would prove a highly suitable husband. He believed that she had been prejudiced against him by Lady Jersey and Brougham, by the Duchess of Oldenburg and Whitbread, and that he was far from being the wastrel that they said he was. To be sure he drank rather a lot; but that was understandable in his present distress. It was not an incurable fault. The British Minister at The Hague had always entertained a good opinion of him.

The Regent invited Margaret Mercer Elphinstone to the Pavilion where, as she admitted, he was 'more than gracious' to her; but she 'soon discovered the motive of all this mummery'. 'I was catechised and sermonised for two hours,' Miss Elphinstone reported to Lord Grey. 'His grand plan is still to bring about the Orange marriage to which he wished to make me instrumental. ... I at once declined, stating that it was a subject so disagreeable to the Princess that I dare not venture to touch upon it. ... [Only a few days ago she said that] so far from repenting of the step she had taken in refusing the Prince of Orange she would rather continue to suffer all the privations and restraints she had [recently undergone]. "Well," said the Prince, "it is just as I thought. When she once takes a thing into her head she is as obstinate as the devil. However, as this is the case I desire you will not repeat any part of this conversation to her. At all events it is a subject *I* can never again mention to my daughter after what has passed – it can only come from her own good sense or the counsel or influence of her friends."'

Soon afterwards Princess Charlotte raised the matter herself. She wrote to her father from Cranbourne Lodge to tell him that she understood it was still his wish to secure her marriage with the Prince of Orange: 'Pardon me if I say *that* information greatly pained me. ... There is no act of obedience, no sacrifice you could wish me to make that I am not ready for, if it is necessary to prove my sense of duty. But where the future (and I may add) the whole happiness of my life is concerned ... I think I cannot be too plain in humbly stating my strong and fixed aversion to a match with a man for whom I can never feel those sentiments of regard which surely are so necessary in a matrimonial connection. ... I hope you will not love me less for thus laying open the sentiments of my heart, as you told me you would never urge any union that would make me miserable.'

Undeterred by this letter, the Regent replied that he did, indeed, want her to reconsider the House of Orange match which, he reminded her with some exaggeration, she had formerly 'so earnestly and so ardently' asked him to approve. As she herself had admitted, she was not free to choose a husband as the rest of the world did. Was it not then extremely fortunate to find 'youth, character, power, rank, consequence, national interests and actual national alliance, all united in one', as they happily were in the Prince of Orange?

Princess Charlotte did not think this fortunate in the least. She had no such high opinion of the character of the Prince of Orange whom she 'could not esteem, regard, or look up to as a wife should her husband'. So, the Regent at last accepted that there was nothing more that could be done. He told her that her precipitate reply to his letter, written before 'there was time for reason to operate on the representations' which he had made, had given him 'no inconsiderable degree of pain', yet she could rest assured that he would not press 'the matter further'.

Relieved and thankful, Princess Charlotte grew more and more cheerful as the weeks went by. Her health improved; her knee 'benefited much from fomentations of hot salt water'. At Weymouth, aboard the Queen's yacht, she could be heard laughing again and calling out with familiar gusto for a luncheon of 'cold beef, with plenty of mustard'. At Cranbourne Lodge, Lady Ilchester noticed 'an air of happiness' about her which she had not seen before. As her friends knew, this happiness was due to the fact that she had found a man she wanted to marry and who wanted to marry her.

Prince Leopold of Saxe-Coburg-Saalfeld was good-looking and charming in a rather solemn kind of way. Talented and respected, he was as smart as the Prince of Orange was slovenly, though some people found him a little unctuous and shifty, noticing, as Lady Charlotte Campbell did, that he never looked at the person to whom he was talking. His virtues had been extolled to the Princess by the Duchess of Oldenburg, whose Russian relatives would be delighted to see her married to the son of a petty German princeling rather than to the future King of the Netherlands on whom they had designs themselves and to whom they eventually succeeded in marrying the Tsar's sister, the Grand Duchess Anna Paulowna.

Princess Charlotte had not at first been unduly excited at the prospect of marrying Prince Leopold, except as a means of escape from her present seclusion. If she did so it would be 'with the most calm and perfect indifference', though she admitted to Margaret Mercer Elphinstone that he had 'the highest and best character possible in every way', and was 'extremely prepossessing in his figure and appearance'. Of the men available to her, he would be her first choice if the choice were left to her. Certainly he was most attentive and made it flatteringly clear to her how much he liked her. 'At all events,' she said, 'I know that *worse off* ... I *cannot* be than I am *now*, and after all if I end by marrying Prince L., I marry the best of all those *I have seen*, and that is some satisfaction.'

Her father was not at all taken with the idea of having him as a son-in-law. It was not only that he was of no importance whatsoever in European politics, that he was so poor he had had to rent lodgings over a grocer's shop in Marylebone High Street, but there was something in the ingratiating suavity of his manner which was decidedly distasteful. He was gifted admittedly; his service in the Russian army as a very young cavalry general had been quite distinguished; he would no doubt treat Charlotte well, but it was difficult to regard him as other than a calculating careerist. The Regent, who was extremely adept in choosing nicknames, called him *le Marquis peu à peu*. The less inventive Lord Frederick Fitzclarence dismissed him as a 'damned humbug'.

In the end, however, the Regent allowed himself to be persuaded. It was no recommendation to him that the Duke of Kent – through whose hands the correspondence between Prince Leopold and Princess Charlotte had passed – advocated the match. But the Duke of York was also in favour of it; so was Lord Castlereagh, on whom Prince Leopold had made a good impression at the Congress of Vienna; and Princess Charlotte assured him that no one would be 'more steady and consistent in this ... engagement' than herself. So it was settled; and in January 1816 both Charlotte and Leopold were invited to Brighton.

It was a very happy time. Her grandmother, much better tempered than usual, was there; so were her aunts; and they all 'seemed delighted to have her under her father's roof. It certainly was a gratification to the [Regent] to find it really gave so much pleasure to the Princess,' Lady Ilchester reported, 'for he had been led to suspect that she did not like to come, which was a complete mistake, and of which he [was] now convinced.'

He could not have been kinder, Charlotte herself thought, although he was suffering so badly from gout that he had to wheel himself about in a Merlin chair in which he sat the whole evening talking to Lady Hertford, his sisters and selected friends, or listening to the band. The Queen played cards and others of the guests played backgammon or strolled up and down between the cast-iron and bamboo staircases at either end of the Chinese gallery, their brilliant suits and dresses illuminated by the coloured lanterns and reflected in the panels of looking-glass on the doors.

'The Chinese scene is gay beyond description, and I am sure you would admire it, as well as the manner of living at the Pavilion,' Lady Ilchester told a friend, 'though the extreme warmth of it might, perhaps, be too much for you.

Everyone was free in the morning of all Court restraint, and only met at six o'clock punctually for dinner to the number of between thirty and forty, and in the evening as many more were generally invited; a delightful band of music played till half-past eleven, when the Royal Family took their leave, and the rest of the company also, after partaking of sandwiches. The evenings were not in the least formal.'

Throughout her visit the Regent was in 'high spirits and good humour', Charlotte wrote contentedly; and she told her aunt Mary that his kindness towards her made her 'as happy as possible'. 'He is grown thinner and his legs considerably reduced.... There is not a soul that is not in extacies at my fate and choice.'

She was obviously so herself. For in the comforting atmosphere of her family's friendliness and her father's evident affection, she had fallen in love. Her previous indifference was quite forgotten. She had 'not one anxious wish left'; she was now 'thoroughly persuaded' that Prince Leopold would 'do all and everything' he could to please her and make her happy. A Council was held at the Pavilion and the Regent gave his formal consent to the marriage.

Soon afterwards Princess Charlotte went to visit the Queen at Windsor 'with the happiest face imaginable'. She 'talked of the event in a very quiet and reasonable way', looking forward to 'more real happiness in this expected union than in the former choice she had made'. 'In my humble opinion I believe she truly means what she says,' the Queen reported to the Regent, 'and if it is possible to make her feel before marriage that though the Prince becomes an object of consequence by marrying her, he must be the head of the family and she submit to him as his wife, all will do well. And on his side, he must be careful not to give her too great an idea of her own consequence, nor be drawn in to make promises before marriage which he might (being ignorant of the customs and manners of the country) find difficulty to fulfil afterwards.'

Having delivered herself of this advice, the Queen entered eagerly into the arrangements for the marriage, offering advice about the trousseau, about a country house for the bride and bridegroom, suggesting that Cranbourne Lodge should be given to Princess Augusta, and proposing that Princess Charlotte's Ladies should have £400 a year, not £500 as the Regent had suggested, since 'the Queen's Ladys [had] only five' and they might claim more. Above all, the Queen busied herself about the Princess's jewels, having a passion for jewels herself. She ordered Bridge, the jeweller, to come to Windsor with those the Princess had ordered – which far exceeded in price the sum that Parliament had voted for them – so that the girl could be given proper guidance in choosing the best.

It had been agreed that Charlotte and Leopold should be allowed £60,000 a year 'to maintain an establishment which without being either extravagant or profuse' would be 'suitable to their rank and station', and that they should, in addition, be granted a capital sum of the same amount, '£40,000 for furniture, plate, etc., £10,000 for personal equipment and £10,000 for jewells'. It was also agreed that, in addition to a London home, Marlborough House, they should be provided with a house in the country. So Claremont Park at Esher in Surrey, which had been built by Lord Clive, was bought for them from Charles Ellis, the rich Member of Parliament for Seaford, for £69,000. The Regent would have liked to bestow a further favour by creating Prince Leopold Duke of Kendal; but he was dissuaded from doing so on the grounds that 'nothing could be more inconvenient, *personally*, to the Consort of the future Queen, and also to the public, than his having a seat in the House of Lords'.

On the day of the wedding, 2 May 1816, Princess Charlotte dined at the Queen's House with her grandmother and aunts. After dinner she put on her shimmering silver wedding dress and the wreath of diamond roses which the Queen had helped her to select from the ample stock of Messrs

Rundell, Bridge & Co. She was ready just before eight o'clock when she came down the staircase with Princess Augusta and stepped into the carriage that was to take her to Carlton House.

Looking out of the window as she drove through the Park she saw the hundreds of people who had spent the afternoon cheering and clapping outside Clarence House, calling for the bridegroom to show himself on the balcony. 'Bless me!' Charlotte exclaimed. 'What a crowd!'

The wedding was conducted at Carlton House with the splendour associated with all the functions that were held there. The bride and bridegroom knelt on crimson velvet cushions, beneath candlesticks six feet high; and when the ceremony was over, the Princess knelt to her father for his blessing which he gave her with such a 'good hearty paternal hug' that Lady Liverpool was delighted. During the ceremony there was one unfortunate incident, so Lady Charlotte Campbell was told: when Prince Leopold repeated the words, 'With all my worldly goods I thee endow', 'the royal bride was observed to laugh'. After the ceremony there was another embarrassing moment: the Queen, insisting that it would be 'so improper' for the bride and bridegroom to drive away together, asked Mrs Campbell, Princess Charlotte's former Governess, to sit between them in the carriage. Mrs Campbell was brave enough to refuse.

From the beginning, Princess Charlotte was ideally contented with her husband, though naturally there were occasional differences, as when, for instance, he wanted to go to bed but she did not choose to do so, and he had to wait until she was ready. 'We lead a very quiet and retired life here,' she wrote from Claremont, 'but a very *very* happy one.' They spent nearly all their time together, walking arm in arm through the gardens, driving out side by side, close to each other, their heads almost touching, singing duets in the drawing-room after dinner, reading to each other. Only when he went out shooting were they apart, and when he

returned she would brush his hair. For the first time in her
life she took criticism without resentment. '*Doucement, ma
chère, doucement*,' he would say to her, endeavouring to
cure her of her natural impetuosity and rough ungainliness,
and she would smile and try to please him. When he corrected her in his meticulous, pedantic way, she would listen
patiently; when he scolded her for lightheartedly making
fun of someone, she tearfully promised not to offend him in
such a way again.

One of his suite, a young German doctor of Swedish
descent, Christian Stockmar, thought that his master was
quite right to correct her, for she had 'most peculiar manners, her hands generally folded behind her, her body always
pushed forward, never standing quiet, from time to time
stamping her foot, laughing a great deal, and talking still
more'. She was 'astonishingly impressionable and nervously
sensitive', and she could be very rude: on Stockmar's being
presented to her for the first time she examined him intently
'from head to foot'. His own first impressions of her were 'not
favourable'. Yet he soon grew deeply fond of her and she of
him. She took to calling him 'Stocky' and to confiding in
him the unhappiness of her past. 'My mother was bad,' she
once told him, 'but she would not have become as bad as
she was if my father had not been infinitely worse.'

But all that unhappiness, all those quarrels with her father
were now truly in the past. 'Harmony, peace and love'
reigned at Claremont, Stockmar said, and on her visits to
Carlton House and the Pavilion she and her father were perfectly at ease. 'Happily for me,' she had assured her father
not long before her marriage, 'we are now upon the most
comfortable and confidential terms possible'; and so they
still remained. She contentedly told Dr Baillie how 'affectionate and tender' her father had been to her of late. He visited
her at Claremont on 16 October, and it was a happy day.
'You must be well soon for my sake,' she wrote to him that
autumn, hearing he was unwell again. 'Pray don't forget me

and believe me a devoted child, my dearest Father, your very affectionate Charlotte.'

Princess Charlotte's one concern seemed to be her difficulty in having a baby. She conceived twice, but on both occasions she miscarried; and when she became pregnant for a third time it was considered that Dr Baillie should have the benefit of the advice of a specialist, in the tall, thin, elegant shape of Sir Richard Croft.

Croft, as the leading and most fashionable *accoucheur* of his day, was a highly self-confident, though far from skilful physician. He took upon himself the sole responsibility for his patient's care, bleeding her regularly and imposing on her a thin, weak and most unappetising diet, mainly composed of liquids. He believed this treatment necessary because of her 'morbid excess of animal spirits'.

The pregnancy, however, continued satisfactorily; and on 9 October it was announced that a baby would be born in nine or ten days' time. No complications were expected, though to the Queen's experienced eye her granddaughter's figure appeared so unnaturally immense that she could not help being 'uneasy to a considerable degree'. By 21 October she was still 'well'; and in spite of her suffering the next day a 'little from headache', as a cure for which 'blood was ... several times ... drawn from a vein at the back of the hand', the doctors thought there remained no cause for alarm.

Princess Charlotte did not share their confidence. Moods of excessive excitement alternated with periods of deep despondency. On 10 October she wrote a gloomy letter to her 'dearest mother', though before her marriage she had promised her father never to do so again and had, in fact, told Princess Mary that she hoped all intercourse would '*entirely cease*'. 'Why is not my mother allowed to pour cheerfulness into the sinking heart of her inexperienced and trembling child?' she asked miserably. 'I have but one mother and no variation of place or circumstance can remove her from my mind. ... Should it be the pleasure of Providence that I survive the hour of approaching danger, I may at some future period be endued with power to restore you to that situation you were formed to embellish. But if an all wise decree should summon me from this sphere of anxious apprehension, not for myself but for my mother a pang of terror shoots across my bewildered brain. ... Believe me, my adored mother, I fear less to die than to live, the prospect of protracted existence is so blended with dangers and difficulties, so shadowed with clouds and uncertainties, so replete with anxieties and apprehensions that I must shrink from the contemplation of it, and fly for refuge even to the probability of my removal from so joyless an inheritance.'

On 3 November her labour began. It continued for fifty hours. She was in great pain; but she said to one of the nurses, 'I will neither bawl nor shriek,' and she did not do so. She bore 'all without a murmur'. Sir Richard Croft remained with her, allowing into the room neither Dr Baillie nor an assistant *accoucheur*, Dr John Sims. He advised his patient not to eat anything.

'Nothing can be going on better,' he announced at three o'clock on the afternoon of 4 November to General Sir Robert Gardiner, Prince Leopold's principal equerry. And at a quarter to eight the next morning he reported to the Cabinet Ministers, who had been summoned to Claremont so as to be present when the child was born, that his patient had made 'a considerable, though very gradual progress throughout the night'. The labour was 'so very slow' that he could not determine when it would be accomplished. Nevertheless, her 'pulse and general appearance' were good.

She continued in labour throughout the day, the pains 'in some degree relaxed'; and it was not until nine o'clock that night that she was at last delivered. The baby, 'a beautiful fine boy ... very large', was dead.

The mother, however, continued to do 'extremely well', though there seemed something strange about her 'unnatural composure, not to say cheerfulness', and the way in which she had accepted her suffering almost as if she had been too elated to feel it. Yet 'no unfavourable symptoms' had occurred; there was 'no apparent danger'. The Ministers left the house and returned to London. Prince Leopold and the doctors went to bed.

At midnight Princess Charlotte complained to her nurse of a singing in her head and of feeling suddenly cold. She tried to drink some gruel, but she could not swallow it and was sick. Then she felt a sudden, agonizing pain. 'Oh what pain,' she cried, clasping her hands to her stomach, 'it is all here.'

Croft and Sims, who were hurriedly summoned from their beds, found her pulse alarmingly rapid and irregular. They put bottles of hot water and warm flannels in her bed, poured brandy, hot water and wine down her throat until she scarcely knew what was happening any more. 'They have made me tipsy,' she complained pathetically to Dr Stockmar. She had a pain in her chest now as well as in her stomach and could scarcely breathe. 'Is there any danger?' she asked and was told to compose herself. She then went into convulsions. Afterwards 'she could not articulate, but sunk into a calm composure, until ... with a gentle sigh, she expired'.*

The Prince Regent himself had been seriously ill again in September. 'We have been near losing him,' Lady Holland

---

* The mysterious causes of Princess Charlotte's death have been long debated. It has been recently suggested that she may have inherited porphyria. 'Cases have been observed where a fulminating attack of porphyria set in a few hours after confinement with signs of cerebral irritation, spreading paralysis, convulsions and finally respiratory failure' (Macalpine and Hunter, 246). At the time the doctors were blamed, and in particular, of course, Sir Richard Croft, who had taken upon himself so much of the responsibility for the case. In subsequent generations Princess Charlotte's case was cited as a classic example of the danger of not using instruments soon enough, thought Croft's reluctance to use 'artificial assistance' was strictly in accordance with contemporary obstetric practice. Croft never recovered from the disgrace and from the cruel attacks that were subsequently made on him. The Regent kindly tried to make amends for

reported, 'and as the physicians mistook his disorder, they have probably curtailed his length of life, for the disease was treated as inflammatory and they took 60 ounces of blood. When Baillie saw him he declared it to be spasm, and gave laudanum and cordials. The consequences are likely to produce dropsy.'

He was convalescing at a shooting party at Sudbourne in Suffolk with the Hertfords when he heard from Sir Robert Gardiner that his daughter had been in labour for twenty-seven hours, that the exertions of the womb were 'less vigorous than they ought to be', and that some 'artificial assistance' might become necessary. He left for London immediately, refusing to wait for fresh horses to be put into the post-chaise, and asking every time the carriage stopped whether there was any further news. Once he was told that the Princess continued in labour. A messenger with a letter informing him that his grandson was stillborn passed him on the road.

He arrived at Carlton House between three and four o'clock in the morning, and having ascertained that although the baby was dead, his daughter was 'doing extremely well', he went exhausted to bed. Soon afterwards he was roused by the Duke of York and Lord Bathurst who told him that Princess Charlotte also was dead. He 'struck his forehead violently with both hands, and fell forward into the arms of the Duke of York'. His doctors were called and thought it

---

these attacks by thanking him publicly for the 'zealous care and indefatigable attention manifested by Sir Richard towards his beloved daughter', and by assuring him that he was entirely satisfied with the 'medical skill and ability which he displayed, during the arduous and protracted labour, whereof the issue, under the will of Divine Providence, had overwhelmed His Royal Highness with such deep affliction' (Asp/K ii, 212–13). Few of Croft's former patients shared this professed confidence. And on 13 February 1818, while attending a woman whose difficulties in labour resembled those he had witnessed at Claremont, he took a pistol from the wall and shot himself in her house (*Gentleman's Magazine*, lxxxviii, i, 277).

necessary to bleed him with their customary immoderation.

He recovered sufficiently to drive over to Claremont where Prince Leopold, overwhelmed with grief, did not feel up to seeing him. He drove over again five days later, all the blinds of his carriage drawn, and saw Leopold and the bodies of his daughter and grandson, both of which, to Prince Leopold's 'surprise and sorrow', had been embalmed. Leopold was still very distressed. But, so the Queen said, much was to be 'expected from the mildness of his character to contribute towards the recovery of his spirits'. And as Princess Mary observed, though evidently 'much affected', he remained 'completely calm and composed'. The Regent asked him if he would like to come to stay at Carlton House where he might feel less unhappy; but he preferred to stay where he was, protesting that he would live for the rest of his life at Claremont, forbidding anybody to remove the Princess's watch from her mantelpiece or her cloak and bonnet from the screen in the sitting-parlour on which she had placed it after their last walk together.

In contrast to the unhappy yet composed Prince Leopold, the Regent was so overcome with emotion that it was 'impossible to attempt to describe' the condition into which he worked himself; it could 'scarcely be imagined'. His shock was 'so intense as to excite great apprehension and alarm'.

On leaving Claremont he drove over to see his mother, who had returned to Windsor from Bath where, since Princess Charlotte had not wanted her fussing about at Claremont, she had gone, on Sir Henry Halford's advice, to take the waters. Seriously ill and very tired, she had broken out into a fit of compulsive sobbing when told of her granddaughter's death, for she had grown fond of her in recent months; and as soon as she felt able to do so she had taken up her pen to tell her son how deeply she felt for him in his present loss and misery, how fully she shared his grief. She had tried to comfort him by telling him that he had done all he possibly could to make his 'child completely happy by granting her to marry the man she liked and wished to be united to', and by giving her a house where she had enjoyed 'to the very last almost complete felicity'.

Yet the Regent seemed beyond the reach of sympathy. When his sister Mary went to visit him at Carlton House she was so upset by his condition that she was obliged to go into an anteroom to regain her composure before leaving the house. She later acceded to his urgent entreaties to go down and keep him company at Brighton where he hoped to recover his spirits.

His recovery was very slow. 'All his thoughts and conversation turn upon the late sad event,' Croker told Lord Whitworth on 14 November. 'He never stirs out of his room, and goes to bed sometimes at eight or nine o'clock, wearied out, and yet not composed enough for sleep.' He was 'still very much and very truly indisposed', he confessed to his 'dearest mother' on 16 December when explaining to her why he had not written to her for some time past. 'I do not know under what denomination to class the attack,' he told her, 'or by what name regularly to define it and call it, for it seems to me to have been a sort of mishmash, Solomon-grundy, Olla podrida kind of business in itself that is quite anomalous; a good deal of rheumatism, as much of cold, with a little touch of bile to boot, not a very pleasant mixture on the whole, and composed of as unpleasant ingredients, as can well be thought of or imagined. In short all this potpourri has rendered me both bodily as well as mentally very unfit.'

A fortnight later he was feeling somewhat better, at least his 'poor stomach' did, which he attributed to his taking Brandish's medicine twice a day, a medicine strongly recommended to him by Sir Henry Halford. It agreed with him perfectly and alleviated 'in great measure all those dreadful sufferings' he had 'experienced for some time past'. He was still, however, far from well in the summer; and on 27 July his speech to Parliament had to be read by commission as it contained references to his daughter's death and he could not bear to read these out himself.*

*Prince Leopold, who rarely missed an opportunity of blackening the Regent's character in the eyes of their niece, Queen Victoria, assured her in 1839 that 'it was observed that for years he had not been in such good spirits than by the loss of his daughter. She was more popular than himself. That, since her marriage, was her only crime' (RA Y65/60917, 18 January 1839).

30

Royal Marriages
1815–1818

'The damnedest millstone about the necks of any
government that can be imagined'

PRINCESS Charlotte's sudden death had stunned the country 'as if by an earthquake at dead of night', Henry Brougham recorded. 'This most melancholy event produced
throughout the Kingdom feelings of the deepest sorrow and
most bitter disappointment. It is scarcely possible to exag-
gerate, and it is difficult for persons not living at the time to
believe how universal and how genuine those feelings were.
It really was as if every household throughout Great Britain
had lost a favourite child.' This was not quite true. In the
opinion, for example, of the Duke of Wellington, whom
Princess Charlotte annoyed by calling 'Arthur', *tout court*,
'her death was a blessing to the country'. She 'would have
turned out quite as her mother. ... In addition to her
mother's inclinations she had an exceeding bad manner.'
Nor had Lord Holland entertained a very favourable
opinion of her. 'Little had appeared in this young lady,' he
thought, 'to justify the inordinate grief at her death ... she
had shown even in the nursery, and still more in the months
preceeding her marriage, that she inherited, together with
the Prince Regent's quickness of apprehension and feeling,
some of his greatest defects, *viz.*, a love of exaggeration, if
not a disregard of truth. ... a passion for talebearers and
favourites, and all those petty failings and practices which
lead to what the French call *tracasseries*.'
But certainly in the country at large the death of Princess
Charlotte was looked upon as a tragedy.
For a long time before her death the public had been in an

irritable, restless humour. 'The general spirit of the country,' wrote Robert Peel, Chief Secretary for Ireland, 'is worse, I apprehend, than we understand it to be.' At the beginning of the year the Regent was reported to have been so much hissed by the mob as to be 'quite disgusted'. He had driven to Parliament through a crowd which was 'animated by a very bad spirit', and which was 'amazingly increased both in numbers and violence' upon his return to Carlton House. As he passed down Pall Mall, his carriage window was shattered and he felt a missile of some sort fly past his face. The Duke of Sussex reported the incident with a kind of malicious pleasure to Lord Holland, adding in a significant whisper, 'He himself *pretends* he was shot at.' According to Lord James Murray it was not pretence at all. Lord James, who had accompanied the Regent in the carriage as Lord in Waiting, 'spoke distinctly [of] two small holes ... within one inch of each other through an uncommonly thick plate glass window; and the space between the two holes was not broken'. He believed that 'the holes spoken of were made by bullets from an air-gun'.

There were many people who would have been glad enough if the missile, whatever it was, had killed the Regent who was widely held responsible for the repressive measures which the government adopted in their efforts to quell the national disturbances. 'At present we have a starving population,' Mrs Leadbeater was told by a friend in March, 'an overwhelming debt, impoverished landholders, bankrupt or needy traders; but we have fine balls at the Regent's.' In June he opened Waterloo Bridge, on the second anniversary of Napoleon's defeat. It was a lovely sunny day, and a 'glorious, beautiful, gratifying spectacle'; but the cheers were for Wellington, not for him, not for that 'uncommonly huge mass' which, so Cobbett estimated, weighed 'perhaps a quarter of a ton'. He had let loose his stomach now, so Lord Folkestone observed, and it reached his knees.

For a time the attitude of the public towards the Regent was shocked into change by Princess Charlotte's death, though it was widely reported that he did not share the general grief, that his neglect of her was in some way responsible for her death, even that he and the Queen had poisoned her. But by the end of November, as Croker told Peel, the grief was wearing off and the public was returning to its 'sulky humour, waiting for any fair or unfair excuse to fly into a passion. ... If there should arise any division in the Royal Family, it will be the match to fire the gunpowder. *Apropos* of royal matches, I hear that Ministers have been a little puzzled how to deal with the avowed readiness of the Duke of Kent to sacrifice himself and jump into the matrimonial gulf for the good of his country, but they have hit upon a scheme which seems politic. They propose to marry the Duke of Clarence, as the eldest unmarried Prince, and he who has a right to the first chance; and also to marry the Duke of Cambridge, the youngest unmarried Prince, from whom the country has the best chance; and having thus resolved to burn the candle at both ends, Vansittart [the Chancellor of the Exchequer] discovers that he cannot afford to burn it in the middle too, and therefore Kent and Sussex cannot have the wedding establishments etc., suited to their rank.'

It was certainly true that Vansittart – having been compelled to abolish the property tax, which was considered in Parliament appropriate only to a time of war, and to discontinue the war malt tax, which was no longer acceptable to the country Members – was loath to provide expensive households for those various members of the Royal Family who were now taking it into their heads to get married. 'My God!' exclaimed Wellington when Creevey mentioned to him 'the proposals to augment the establishments' of the royal dukes, 'they are the damnedest millstone about the necks of any government that can be imagined. They have insulted – *personally* insulted – two thirds of the gentlemen of England, and how can it be wondered at that they take their revenge upon them when they get them in the House of Commons? It is their only opportunity, and I think, by God, they are quite right to use it.'

Within the Royal Family there were far deeper divisions than Croker supposed. The Prince and his sisters were on those happy, close, affectionate terms that they had always enjoyed. They took it in turns to write to him to send him what little news there was ever worth conveying from Windsor, to give him bulletins on their father's condition, on their mother's and their own varying states of health, to thank him for presents and for being so kind to them during their holidays at Brighton to which they looked forward with such eagerness. In her tiny writing Princess Sophia would report on the 'dear King's occasional bursts of passion', or his favourite sister, Princess Mary, a more regular correspondent, would reassure him that his Majesty's days were generally 'very quiet' and 'composed', though he was sometimes 'rather high at dinner time'. Mary would also send frequent reports about her sisters, particularly Sophia, whose frequent illnesses distressed them all, for it was 'a sad house to be ill in'. Princess Elizabeth would tell him about a cricket match which had been arranged 'for the Eatonians', or of a rare, enjoyable evening party: 'I wish you had been here with us to-night for we have laughed in a manner we rarely do now unless occasioned by you. Dundas's manner of speaking French is beyond everything ridiculous and in telling my mother a story in which he was to mention Soissons he pronounced it with such an English accent that it was enough to kill me. He said, "in the town of *So is son*"; and my mother's quiet way of answering "Soissons" was so ridiculous that when she was gone we all of us were in fits.'

It was very rarely that their mother reduced them to laughter; more often she drove them to tears. She had grown very fat, so enormous, indeed, that one cruel observer said that she looked as though she were bearing all her fifteen children at once; she suffered from occasional attacks of erysipelas which not only reddened her face but made it swell to a distressing size. And, correspondingly, she grew ever more cantankerous and difficult until, as Lord Glenbervie said, her irritability became so 'intolerable' that her daughters were driven 'quite miserable' by it. She refused to see the King alone, finding him frightening as well as embarrassing, and Princess Mary said that when she did go to see him, taking one or other of her children with her, her manner towards him as he rambled on was to say the least 'unfortunate'. This manner, Princess Mary thought, was attributable partly to 'extream timidity', partly to an innate deficiency in 'warmth, tenderness, affec'.

In protest against their mother's treatment of them, the Princesses constantly appealed to the Regent, who did all he could to help them. The first of his sisters' appeals had been addressed to him almost as soon as the restrictions imposed upon his Regency had expired. Princess Augusta, then aged forty-three, had written to him to ask him to grant her her heart's desire by consenting to her marriage to the man whom she had now loved for nine years, Lieutenant-General Sir Brent Spencer, one of her father's equerries, a brave Irish soldier eight years older than herself. She had confided in the Prince her love for him several years before and he had been kind and understanding; but there was nothing at that time that he had been able to do to help her, for their father would never have consented to the match. Now that the King no longer had the power to prevent it, she had approached her brother again: 'I now beseech you my dearest to consider *our situation*. If it is in your power to *make us happy I know you will*. Of course it will be necessary to keep it a secret and it must be quite a *private marriage*. ... No consideration in the world ... shall make me take such a step unknown to *her*. I owe it to her as my mother, though I am too honest to affect asking for *her consent as it is not necessary*. ... I am certain the Queen *cannot approve* if she *merely* thinks of my birth and station, but that is *the only reason* she can object to it. ... But when she considers the character of the man, the faithfulness and length of our attachment, and the struggles I have been compelled to make, never retracting from any of my duties, though suffering martyrdom from *anxiety of mind* and *deprivation* of happiness. ...'

The Queen, as all who knew of Princess Augusta's secret might have expected, had been appalled when she had heard of it. She had refused to talk about it; she would not hear of her daughter's marriage to such a man. Over the next few months the atmosphere at Windsor had become so strained and insupportable that the Princesses had threatened to quit 'the paternal roof' unless their mother gave them more freedom.

The crisis had been reached in December 1812 when the Queen had sulkily grumbled that her daughters' wish to go to London more often than they did at present displayed a want of 'delicacy and affection towards the King'. There had been a 'dreadfull scene', Princess Augusta reported. 'Upon my honor my sisters [Elizabeth, then aged forty-two, and Sophia, thirty-five, and Mary, thirty-six] were perfectly respectful both in manner and words, though she was too violent to allow it and even when she told them that she would never forgive them, Eliza said, "*May God* forgive you for saying so." She won't allow that *any of us* feel for the King's unhappy state of mind. ... She has declared that after to-night the subject is *never* to be *mentioned again* and that she COMMANDS us to be silent upon it. I am ashamed to have written so much on so *painfull* a subject because I love the Queen with all my heart; but I *feel* the *injustice most deeply* with which she treats *us all four*. It is undeserved – and our lives have not been *too* happy. ... Never was a daughter more faithfully attached than Eliza to the Queen – and she really has sacrificed every comfort in life to prove it, and sad and cruel is the abuse she has met with. I am miserable that you my dearest brother that you should have so much vexation on our account. We are all gratitude to you.'

Princess Elizabeth wrote by the same post to tell her
brother how deeply she had been hurt by the Queen's words,
how it quite broke her heart to be told that she was wanting
in delicacy and affection towards the King after all the
sacrifices she had made and all the sacrifices she was still
prepared to make to ease her mother's mind and try to give
her some happiness. The blow of being thought unfeeling
haunted her. It was quite impossible for her to go to London
now with a heart so ill at ease.

The Queen also wrote that same night to excuse herself, to
say that she quite understood that her daughters might
want to go to London 'sometimes', but not every week, as if
they were to do so she would be 'almost left quite alone'.
She went on to complain that she had been 'amazingly
offended' by the 'easy manner' in which Lord Liverpool had
disposed 'of the royal family appearing in public'. 'As to the
representation your sisters have made of what did pass on
Sunday night before they left Windsor I am ignorant of,'
the Queen continued in rising anger. 'But ... when Elizabeth, by defending her own conduct, struck in a most violent
manner upon a Holy Book, saying she would have an oath
that she had done all in her power to please, it so provoked
me that I did say after that violence I should not be surprised at her giving me a box at the ear, which gave her an
hysterick fit, and they left me determined to report it the
moment they came to town. ... Whether this conduct is
what a mother ought to expect from her children I leave to
the judgements of those who have any. In short this last
journey of theirs has given me a blow which can not be
easily effaced, for the coming to ask my advice and hearing
my objections and not following is treating me like a fool.
The telling me that the living with me here in my distress
is disagreeable, and to repeat to anybody what concerns the
interior of a family is more than imprudent. ... The Dukes
of York and Cambridge's impertinent behaviour to me on a
former occasion I can never forget, and as to Ministers they

can have nothing to do with it. At least if they do, I shall stop them short.'

The Regent immediately went to see the indignant Queen and, having soothed her ruffled feelings, persuaded her to accompany her daughters to Carlton House. Before Christmas he had managed to bring peace once more to the squabbling family, and Princess Augusta thanked him warmly for the 'very kind part' he had taken on their behalf. 'I am very certain that it is to *your good offices* that we are indebted for her assurances that she had misunderstood us,' Augusta wrote, 'and I only hope that we shall not have any occasion to plague you with our applications for redress.' It was a hope that was not to be realized.

Scarcely had the Regent temporarily patched over the differences between his mother and his sisters, than he was called upon to settle a quarrel between the Queen and the Duke of Cumberland who, in 1815, selected as his bride her niece, Princess Frederica of Mecklenburg-Strelitz. The Regent might well have felt some reluctance in helping his brother for he had heard from Princess Elizabeth who had had 'volumes from Royal' – their eldest sister, Princess Charlotte, Queen of Württemberg – about Ernest's characteristic mischief-making while he was in Germany where he had spoken 'so improperly' of the Regent that it was 'quite abominable'. Charlotte, who detested their brother Ernest, had said, 'If it was one person that told me I would not believe it, but all say the same.' The Regent, however, chose to disregard the reports of his brother's indiscreet gossiping. He had thought it advisable to supersede him by appointing their more tractable younger brother, the Duke of Cambridge, Governor of Hanover, a disappointment which had reduced Cumberland to tears. And he was now anxious to make amends by helping him, even though he did not consider Princess Frederica a very suitable choice. She had been married twice before, first to Prince Frederick of Prussia and

then, when she was engaged to the Duke of Cambridge, hurriedly to Prince Frederick of Solms-Braunfels by whom she
had discovered herself pregnant.

The Queen at first approved the match, but after learning
more from her daughter, Charlotte, in Württemberg, she
decided that Princess Frederica was, after all, a most unfortunate choice. So did the House of Commons, which
rejected the government's Bill to increase the Duke of Cumberland's allowance from £18,000 to £24,000 a year. Despite
his mother's opposition and Parliament's disapproval, the
Duke married Princess Frederica at Strelitz, but when he
proposed to bring her over to England the Queen warned
the Regent that she would on no account receive her.

The Regent drove over to Windsor in the hope of inducing
her to change her mind; but she was obdurate. This had
made the Duke's blood boil in his veins, so he said, and his
mother would soon find out that he was 'pretty *decided*'
when he resolved 'on any thing'. He brought his bride over
to England on 27 August 1815 and their marriage was
solemnized according to the rites of the Anglican Church
two days later at Carlton House in the Regent's presence,
and in the conspicuous absence of the Queen and her daughters. The bride was enchanted by the Regent's kindness. He
embraced her warmly, gave her, 'in a way that was simply
lovable', a present of his portrait in enamel, mounted in
'beautiful large stones', and held her left hand 'throughout
the entire ceremony'. His consent to the marriage earned
the Duke and Duchess's 'heartfelt gratitude'; but it led to
serious trouble with the Queen and with the government.

The Queen's anger was much increased when she received from the bride's brother, her eldest nephew, Prince
George of Mecklenburg-Strelitz, a letter '*couched in terms
so offensive and so insulting*' that she could not '*with any
regard to decency shew it to any individual*'. 'I have too frequently experienced proofs of your kindness and affection,'
she wrote to the Regent, 'to allow myself to believe upon this
occasion that you could ever have invited or encouraged any

proposal for bringing my nephew to this country if you could have foreseen that he was to be brought here for the purpose of *bullying* and *insulting* your mother. ... But I cannot deny that I have felt most acutely the want of support which I might have expected.'

The Regent wrote a long, pained reply in which he denied the unreasonable accusations, saying that he had hoped that his conduct through life would have protected him from the suspicion that he was 'capable of tamely submitting to an offer of insult or disrespect' to his mother.

But the Queen was not to be placated. She was more determined than ever now not to receive her niece; and, in a subsequent letter, reiterated the impossibility of ever doing so. So overwrought did she become, indeed, that she fell seriously ill; and Lord Bathurst, on behalf of the government, thought it advisable to suggest that Cumberland should take his wife back to Germany, for if the Queen's malady were to 'end fatally' the people would attribute it to the Duke's continuing in England. 'Mischievous persons' would then 'be able so to work on the public feelings as to expose her Royal Highness most unmeritedly to personal insult and reproach'.

The Regent agreed that it would be advisable for his brother to leave the country before more harm was done; and when the Duke protested that he could not afford to do so, money was offered him for the purpose. The Regent asked the Duke to call on him at Carlton House where, 'in the most emphatic manner', he told him that 'his decided opinion was that he should, with his Duchess, immediately leave England – that the Prince Regent could not separate himself from the Queen, that time might yet heal their distresses, and circumstances might arise which might enable him to receive them in the manner all must wish'.

Yet the Duke remained as obstinate as his mother. Alternately protesting that the Duchess's health was 'very precarious', that he could not leave by himself for 'such an act would be a desertion of the Dutchess whom he was resolved at all hazards to protect', and that 'a departure would be immediately held forth as a *proof of conscious guilt and fear of shewing'* themselves, he refused to leave. And the Queen, despite a letter of protest from the King of Prussia to the Regent, still refused to receive his wife.

The Regent told the King of Prussia that he wished to God he could shake his mother's 'unfortunate determination', but 'by the laws and customs' of the country she was 'wholly independant' of him and he could not oblige her to 'receive any person, whether of the Royal Family or otherwise, against her own inclination'. The Regent patiently continued in his efforts to change his mother's mind, while at the same time endeavouring to persuade his brother to go back to Germany should he not be successful. He even considered giving him the Governorship of Hanover in place of the Duke of Cambridge; but Count Münster, the Hanoverian Minister, was rigidly opposed to the idea.

Once again the Regent and his brother fell out. The Duke called at Carlton House and for five minutes the two men sat in studied silence without looking at each other. The Duchess, forgetting all her brother-in-law's past kindness, refused to believe that he could not insist on her being received by the Queen. 'Oh, really, sire,' she exclaimed in irritation when he tried to explain the situation to her. 'The coal-heaver is master *in his* own house.' He endeavoured to make amends by inviting her to dinner at Carlton House with all the most fashionable ladies in London; but when Lady Stafford told her that the Regent hoped that after this grand dinner she would find it easier to leave the country with honour, she was more indignant than ever.

As late as April 1818 the Regent was still strongly urging his mother to receive the Duchess. But the Queen remained adamant: she would not in any circumstances receive her, and expressed 'an anxious wish that she would not again be urged upon this painful subject'.

The Duke of Cumberland stubbornly stayed on in England until the end of July 1818 when he and the Duchess

returned at last to Germany. The Regent came to say good-
bye, and the Duchess thought that his guilty conscience
would not allow him to look her straight in the eye. But
although the Duke was deeply disgruntled with the rest of
his family he was in the end prepared to recognize that his
eldest brother had done all he could to help him, and he
wrote to tell him so, from the York Hotel, Dover, on the
morning of his departure: 'I cannot leave my native shore
without ... expressing to you my sincerest and most heartfelt gratitude for all your brotherly kindness to me during
my stay in England which believe me will never be effaced
from my recollection. In short you ALONE among eleven
brothers and *sisters* have proved to me that you are really a
brother and *friend*. God bless you for it.'

To everyone's surprise the Queen raised no objection to
the next marriage in her family, that of her daughter, Mary,
to the Duke of Gloucester, whose mother, the illegitimate
daughter of Sir Edward Walpole, had also been denied
entrance to the Queen's court. But if his mother approved of
this match, the Regent did not. He had never liked his
cousin Gloucester, and he had grown to like him even less
since he had, with the Duke of Sussex, openly sympathized
with Princess Caroline and taken it upon himself to champion Princess Charlotte at the time of her rebellion over the
proposed match with the Prince of Orange. He had not taken
seriously the stories he had heard about his daughter's considering Gloucester as a husband for herself, stories which
were characteristically spread about by the Duke of Cumberland who said it looked as though she were going to
choose the Cheese instead of the Orange. For who could
really want to marry the Cheese? Princess Mary can have
wanted to do so, he supposed, only as a means of escape from
'the Nunnery', where her painfully restricted life was made
all the more unbearable in winter by 'dreadful chilblains'.
She had never been attracted by men in the way that
her sisters were; and the idea of anyone falling in love

with the Duke of Gloucester seemed to the Regent absurd.

Prince Leopold's friend Stockmar shared the Prince's distaste, and described Gloucester as being 'large and stout, but with weak, helpless legs ... prominent meaningless eyes; without being actually ugly, a very unpleasant face with an animal expression'. But if she did not love him, Princess Mary had, unaccountably, always been quite fond of him; and since she was the Regent's favourite sister, 'the most of an angel he ever knew', he gave his consent to the marriage when she asked him for it, and took great trouble to negotiate satisfactory terms.

The wedding, which ultimately took place at the Queen's House on 23 July 1816, was a most disorderly affair. The room was excessively hot and overcrowded; the seating so badly arranged that only a few people in it could see what was happening; the congregation so restless and talkative that the Lord Chief Justice called out jocularly, 'Do not make a noise in that corner of the room. If you do, you shall be married yourselves.'

The bride looked as though she were about to faint; her sisters and her ladies could not stop crying; nor could Lady Eldon. The Regent, who was giving his sister away, 'several times had recourse to his pocket handkerchief'. The Queen seems to have been almost alone in remaining dry-eyed throughout the lengthy and disorganized proceedings.

While the Duke and Duchess of Gloucester settled down to a quiet country life at Bagshot Park, the Duke of Clarence continued his erratic search for a suitable wife for himself. He had separated from Mrs Jordan, the mother of his ten illegitimate children, in 1811; but he had not yet succeeded in finding anyone to take her place. The Regent had once told him that he doubted that anyone *would* marry him; but debts of £56,000 made a wife an urgent necessity.

He had considered numerous heiresses, both foreign and domestic, only to have his overtures rejected. He had first wanted to marry Catherine Tylney-Long, a 'lovely nice little angel' worth over £40,000 a year; but she had preferred the more obvious charms of Wellington's nephew, William Wellesley-Pole. He had then proposed to the equally rich Margaret Mercer Elphinstone, 'who, in the most decided and peremptory terms, rejected him'. He had then offered himself to Lady Charlotte Lindsay who had turned him down with similar promptitude. Unsuccessful overtures to the Dowager Lady Downshire were followed by a firm decision to marry the Earl of Berkeley's widow. But the Regent had declined to accept a butcher's daughter, whom he considered decidedly vulgar, as a sister-in-law; and she herself had considered the proposal 'impossible'; so the search went on. The next quarry was the Tsar's sister, the Grand Duchess of Oldenburg. He asked the government for his travelling expenses to pay court to her; the government declined to pay them; so, generous as ever, the Regent gave his brother £1,000. He might have saved his money. The Grand Duchess found him quite as vulgar as the Regent thought Lady Berkeley. He was 'awkward, not without wit, but definitely unpleasant', and wholly wanting in 'delicacy'. The Duke had then turned his attention to Princess Sophia, the Duke of Gloucester's sister, who married neither him nor anybody else. After that match was ruled out he announced to the Regent that he was indefatigably 'ready and happy to set out for the Continent' as he had 'not any doubt that the eldest daughter of Landgrave Frederick of Hesse [was] a lady in every respect fit for [his] wife provided pecuniary matters [could] be arranged and the lady's consent obtained'. The lady's consent was not obtained, however; and a few weeks later the Duke had transferred his attention to Caroline, the eldest daughter of the Electoral Prince of Hesse-Cassel, whose youngest daughter, Augusta, was to be married in 1818 to the Duke of Cambridge. Nothing came of this proposal either; and the Regent suggested to his brother that he might care to consider 'the only daughter of the King of Denmark'. In fact there were two daughters; but neither of them became the Duchess of Clarence.

By this time the Duke's protracted and capricious search had long since led Lord Auckland to suppose that the King's 'mad doctors', the Willises, had another patient in need of their attentions. The search, however, was now nearly over. At the beginning of 1818 the Regent learned from his sister, Princess Mary, that their mother was half 'distracted' by a letter from the Duke in which he announced that he had proposed to and been accepted by Miss Wyckham, a 'fine vulgar miss', heiress to the Oxfordshire estate of Lord Wenman. 'On this being told to the Regent, his Royal Highness *groaned*,' Lady Jerningham reported, 'which is, it seems, his way of disapproving.'

The Duke had informed Princess Mary that whatever his mother or brother might think about the match, he was determined to go through with it. '*Nobody* could *prevent* his having Miss Wyckham if he *chose it*, he had but to apply to Parliament. He was in perfect good humour but most decided on the *subject*. ... He said ... the Prince's consent will be *rung from him* at last, so he better give it at once. ...' 'I told him it would break the Queen's heart,' Princess Mary informed the Regent. 'He said I love her very much but a man must judge for himself in this world ... and then wanted to convince me in *your* heart you approved of it *now*, only that Ministers would not let you approve.'

The Ministers, indeed, were unanimous in their condemnation. When the Regent handed the Cabinet his brother's petition, they replied that it was 'their indispensable duty' to declare that it would not be in 'the best interests of the State' to accede to the Duke's request. To their surprised relief, the Duke gave way without further ado, merely asking that a barony should be conferred upon Miss Wyckham, though this, as Lord Liverpool pointed out when declining the request, would lay her open to the accusation that she had purchased a peerage by releasing the Duke from his obligation to her.

At last a bride was found in the small and far from prepossessing person of Princess Adelaide, the eldest daughter of the Duke of Saxe-Coburg-Meiningen. She was 'frightful', Charles Greville thought, 'very ugly with a horrid complexion'. But the Queen knew her to be a good-natured woman, and her own widowed mother was happy enough to find a husband for a daughter who would soon be twenty-six and who might be considered to have made a good match with a man, admittedly a man in late middle age, with some prospects of becoming King of England.

There was some little difficulty over the Duke's increased income on his marriage. He wanted an additional £10,000 a year at least, as well as a town house, extensive repairs to his house at Bushey, his debts paid and handsome provision for his illegitimate children. But Parliament declined to grant so large an addition to his present income of £18,000 a year; whereupon the Duke said that if he could not have the income he would not take the wife. The problem was eventually settled, however, and on 11 July 1818 the marriage took place at Kew. On the same day the Duke of Kent was also married at Kew.

The Duke of Kent had experienced almost as much difficulty in finding a suitable bride as the Duke of Clarence. He had been looking about for one since 1816 when, still in company with Mme de St Laurent, he was living modestly in Brussels, having made an assignment of most of his property in favour of his creditors. He had managed to obtain a loan of a thousand guineas from the Tsar to pay for a journey of inspection to eastern Europe, but the excursion had been fruitless. The Duke did not particularly want to marry. He was perfectly happy with Mme de St Laurent, who choked convulsively over her breakfast one morning soon after Princess Charlotte's death, when she read an article in the *Morning Chronicle* on the subject of her lover's duty to marry and to provide an heir, which the Duke and Duchess of York had not succeeded in doing and the Duke of Clarence might also fail to do.

'Before anything is proceeded with in this matter,' the

Duke confided in Thomas Creevey one day in December
1817 in Brussels, 'I shall hope and expect to see justice done
by the nation and the Ministers to Mme St Laurent. She is
of very good family and has never been an actress, and I am
the first and only person who ever lived with her. ... As to
my own settlement, as I shall marry (if I marry at all) for the
succession, I shall expect the Duke of York's marriage to be
considered the precedent. That was a marriage for the succession and £25,000 for income was settled, in addition to all
his other income, purely on that account. I shall be contented with the same arrangement. ... You have heard
the names of the Princess of Baden and the Princess of Saxe-
Cobourg mentioned. The latter connection would perhaps
be the better of the two, from the circumstances of Prince
Leopold being so popular with the nation.'

So, in this businesslike way Prince Leopold's sister, Victoria, the thirty-one-year-old widow of the Prince of Leinin-
gen-Dachsburg-Hardenburg, was chosen. The marriage took
place at Coburg in May 1818; and after it had been solemnized by the Anglican church at Kew in July, the Duke and
Duchess returned to Germany. They came back to England
the following spring for the Duchess's confinement. Her
baby girl, her only child, the future Queen Victoria, was
born at Kensington Palace on 24 May 1819.*

---

* The Duke of Kent, claiming that he did not have enough money
for the journey, borrowed £5,000 from Lords Fitzwilliam and Dundas
for the purpose of bringing his wife home so that their baby could
be born in England. He also received assistance from Lord Darnley
and Alderman Matthew Wood, whose baronetcy was the first conferred by Queen Victoria. The Prime Minister did not think there
was any reason for the Duchess of Kent or any of the other royal
Duchesses who happened to be abroad at the time to come home for
their confinements. 'It would be a most severe burden upon the royal
family', he considered, and an unnecessary one, though it might be
advisable for 'some British subject' to be in the house at the time of
the delivery (Twiss, ii, 319). Prince Leopold, when King of the Belgians, assured his niece, Queen Victoria, more than once that her
uncle the Regent had done all he could to prevent her being born in

While the Dukes of Clarence and Kent had been preparing for their marriages, so also, at the age of forty-seven, had their sister, Princess Elizabeth.

The Princess had dreaded telling her mother of her plans, for the Queen was seriously ill now as well as cantankerous.

England. 'Arrived in London, we were very unkindly treated by George the 4th *whose great wish was to get you and your mama out of the country*,' he told her emphatically. 'And I must say without my assistance, you could not have remained. You know now sufficient of the value of money to be aware that no royal Duchess with child can live on £6,000 a year, particularly when she had not a spoon or napkin of her own.' King Leopold – who was always assuring Queen Victoria how unpleasant was her uncle's character, how strongly marked it was by 'extreme selfishness, a great spirit of revenge and intrigue, and a complete absence of anything manful' – told her in subsequent letters that he did not know what would have become of her had he not been alive to protect her after her father's death: 'I know not what would have become of you and your mama, if I then had existed no longer. George the IVth hated your father. ... He did all to prevent *your being born in England*' (RA Y67/30, 22 January 1841; RA Y71/63, 17 May 1845; RA 74/69, 2 September 1848). This was not strictly true. Certainly the Regent disliked both the Duke and the Duchess of Kent and curtly refused to comply with the Duke's long list of demands, including 'pecuniary assistance', for the satisfactory accomplishment of the Duchess's confinement in England. He agreed with the Prime Minister that there was no necessity for the Kents to come home, despite the Duke's protestations that there was 'a total want of convenience' at his house at Amorbach, and that it would be too expensive to spend the period of the Duchess's confinement at Brussels. But once the Duke had made arrangements to pay his own expenses he withdrew his objections, sending the royal yacht to wait for the Duke and Duchess at Calais and making arrangements for apartments to be prepared for them at Kensington Palace (RA 22293, 6 April 1819; Woodham-Smith, 21–5). The Duke, however, had never forgiven his brother for not insisting that he should be reappointed to his military command in 1811, though he had done everything he could for the Duke of York (RA 46504–5, 31 July 1811; RA 46519–20: Asp/P, viii, 371–3). He now felt he had further grounds for resentment. He declared that his brother had been extremely selfish, and he was most indignant about being told that he must not, in the circumstances, expect to meet 'a *cordial* reception' on returning home. Before his return he wrote a long

Her treatment at Bath in November 1817 had not done her much good; and on her return to Windsor she was 'dreadfully low' and found such difficulty in getting her breath that Princess Elizabeth was really frightened to be with her. 'I cannot possibly stand it,' Elizabeth told the Regent on 25 January 1818; 'thank God, she cannot bear me with her, though I entreat her to cry as I am sure when her spirits are in that state it is better to give vent to tears than choke herself by swallowing them.'

Two days later, however, the Queen was so much better that she felt able to take a long drive; and on the 29th Princess Elizabeth plucked up courage to tell her of the offer that had been made to her by the Hereditary Prince of Hesse-Homburg. At first the Queen had seemed resigned to it. 'You always wished to settle,' she had said to her daughter encouragingly on being told of her intentions, 'and have always said that you thought a woman might be happier and more comfortable in having a home.'

But that very evening, as her mind dwelled on the unpleasant prospect of being deprived of her daughter's company on which she had been able to rely for so many years, she began to be difficult, 'flurried and vexed'. When Count Münster called at the Castle to discuss the arrangements for the proposed marriage she refused to see him: he had come to see her daughter not her. She grumpily refused to go in to dinner or to play cards; she said she did not care what Elizabeth did. 'Do as you please,' she told her, 'you are of age.'

'I have done everything that can be done to make her happy,' Princess Elizabeth complained sadly to the Regent, 'but I am hardly used.' 'Believe me I am nearly distracted,' she continued the next day. 'My mother is so angry that it frightens me. ... [She] says she is so incensed by my conduct

---

letter from Cologne setting out his complaints which, so he informed his correspondent, he did not 'wish to be concealed from the world'. 'You have therefore my sanction,' his letter concluded, 'subject to your usual prudence and discretion, to make what use you please of the information I have given you' (RA M3/1, 5 April 1819).

that she cannot bear to see me.' Princess Augusta tried to comfort her sister by telling her that their mother was a 'spoilt child'; their father had spoilt her 'from the hour she came' to England; and they themselves had continued doing so from the hour of their birth. She was just vexed that she could not manage this her own way. Elizabeth told her brother all that Augusta had said, and added that she felt sure he would soothe it all out and 'soften' their mother.

The Regent went down to Windsor to try to do so. He spoke to her for a long time, and before leaving assured Elizabeth that everything would now be all right.

'Alas! Good humour and all our prospect of bringing the Queen round vanished as your carriage drove off,' Princess Sophia told him the next morning. 'The irritation in her mind continues very great, and now will be greater as I verily believe that until yesterday she still had hopes that Eliza had not made her final irrevocable decision. ... I cannot say that I perceive any material difference in the symptoms of the Queen's disorder, but it is impossible not to suppose that this violent agitation must be productive of some ill effects. ... I find from our friend Sir Henry [Halford] who saw her this morning that her suppressed anger made it difficult for him to judge correctly of her pulse and her breathing.' As for Elizabeth she had by now decided that her mother was not nearly so ill as she liked her daughters to suppose: 'She has been very comfortable with others when I am away, before me she tries to be worse.'

The day after the Regent's visit, the clouds at Windsor were 'as thick if not thicker' than ever; and by 9 February Princess Elizabeth could scarcely write to him for her eyes were 'completely blinded for tears'. After a second visit, however, their mother was induced to behave less unreasonably on condition that she was not deprived of her daughter's companionship immediately after the marriage. She sent Elizabeth a diamond necklace by way of truce; and at a subsequent interview, though 'some things of course' hurt the Princess's feelings, 'upon the whole' the conversation went off well. On leaving her mother's room, Elizabeth sat down to write to her brother to thank him for all he had done: she could 'never express how deeply' she felt his affection which had supported her more than she could say.

A week later *The Times* announced that the marriage was 'at length finally determined upon', and that it had been 'definitely fixed, that, instead of leaving this country immediately, as was originally proposed', her Royal Highness would remain in England for some time. This arrangement had 'been brought about for the satisfaction of her Majesty to whom her illustrious daughter [had] in a peculiar degree, endeared herself by a long series of filial attentions, and from whom the Queen, in her declining years, felt it impossible to endure the pang of separation'.

The marriage took place on 7 April at the Queen's House; and some of those who saw the bridegroom there for the first time were surprised by Princess Elizabeth's anxiety to marry him. For the Hereditary Prince of Hesse-Homburg, who had vainly proposed himself as a husband for Princess Augusta in 1804, was now forty-nine and far from attractive. A much-decorated soldier, with those flamboyant whiskers favoured by German generals and the Duke of Cumberland, he was immensely fat, was reputed to wash at the most infrequent intervals and smelled of garlic and tobacco. Yet Princess Elizabeth disregarded his personal appearance, and grew increasingly fond of her 'kind and affectionate better half'. She had every reason to be grateful, she assured her brother, for the prize she had drawn. There was, indeed, something rather endearing about him. He was known to the public as 'Humbug', but his wife referred to him more affectionately as her 'beloved Bluff'. It was as touching as ridiculous that on bending down to pick up a fan which the Queen had dropped at her levee, his stout bottom rent the seat of his trousers.

The wedding was free of such incident, though on their way to the Royal Lodge at Windsor, which the Regent had lent them for their honeymoon, the bridegroom was sick and was obliged to spend the rest of the journey sitting outside in the dicky. The Princess had ordered a new carriage, but the journeymen employed in its manufacture had gone on strike, and she had had to make use of her old bumpy landaulet.

During the honeymoon the Prince spent a good deal of his time smoking in the conservatory. But his wife was ideally happy. Before leaving for her new home in Germany, she wrote a letter of thanks to the Regent. He had been prevented from attending the wedding by an attack of gout so severe that he could not walk; the *Morning Post* declared that he would not have attended it anyway, 'owing to a similar scene having been fresh in his recollection in the marriage of his beloved daughter, the Princess Charlotte'. His sister thanked him effusively for making it possible for her to marry 'so excellent a being' whose 'one thought' was to make her happy. As always her brother's conduct had been 'so delicate, so angelic, so like himself'. He was, and was to remain, her 'beloved and dearest angel'.

31

Repasts and Riots
1818–1820

'The pomp and magnificence of a Persian satrap'

WITH the Queen also the Prince was now on the best of terms. Past quarrels had been quite forgiven; and his mother recognized that her eldest son was 'all goodness and ever ready to forward the happiness of his family'. Towards herself in her declining years he could not have been more considerate, more understanding. He knew only too well how much his sisters had had to endure because of her selfishness and increasing ill temper; but in taking their side when necessary he had always behaved with the greatest kindness, gentleness and tact. Guests at Carlton House and at Brighton noticed with what affectionate deference he treated his mother, waiting upon her himself, making sure she was comfortable and had everything she wanted. She was duly grateful, and always thanked him most warmly for his 'really unbounded kindness' towards herself and his sisters during their visits. In her turn she took special pains to make each year's celebration of his birthday at Frogmore the kind of event which he would appreciate. Once she had had a collection of splendid tents, which had been presented to her by the Sultan of Mysore, erected for him in the gardens; she had had Chinese lanterns hung from the trees and, while a band played in a shrubbery, she had walked up and down on the lawn with him, holding his arm. On another occasion she had invited him to a party at the Queen's House. It would not be 'à la manière de Carlton House', she had warned him, 'but about 150 or 200 people, and if you should like to take a quiet dinner with me en famille I will order it at six that we may have a little time to breathe before the company comes.'

On the plain sheets of cheap paper which all the Royal Family at Windsor used, she had written to him regularly to give him advice about Princess Charlotte, to congratulate him upon the 'good news from the Continent', to keep him informed about the health of the King and the rest of the family, to offer her sympathy when he was ill, to warn him against taking insufficient care of himself and of taking too much laudanum, to urge him to consult Sir Henry Halford of whom she had a much higher opinion than she had of his other doctors. She had given him news about the activities of the Court at Windsor; she had sent him occasional presents – 'four of the finest smoked geese' she had ever seen, 'to be eaten raw', or the 'March of a Cossack Division', 'painted in gouache therefore requiring glass to prevent its pealing off'. She had suggested days of national thanksgiving for such events as the restoration of Hanover, and had made her wide knowledge of etiquette available to him when, for instance, the Duchess of Brunswick died: 'As one of the Royal Family you will of course have her buried in one of the royal vaults, either Westminster or Windsor, the latter place, Colonel Taylor [Herbert Taylor, her trusted private secretary since the establishment of the Regency] thinks was the King's desire she should be deposited. Your mourning of course must be that for a mother, and Charlotte's the same with bombazine. The public places must be shut, as she is one of the family, until the interment and of course you will have no levee during that time. ... I advise this the more as every little trifle in the conduct of the Royal Family is at present so severely censured.'

The Queen attended her daughter's marriage to the Hereditary Prince of Hesse-Homburg; but it was her last public appearance. She was seventy-three, frail and doddering, and it was clear that she did not have long to live. After Elizabeth's departure for Germany in July she became subject to

fits of uncontrollable weeping in which she found it difficult to get her breath and, therefore, grew 'alarmed about
herself'. According to Charles Greville, these spasms of
breathlessness could also be induced by fits of anger as, for
instance, when she heard that the Duchess of Cambridge
had met the Duchess of Cumberland in Kew Gardens and
had actually embraced her. 'She was in such a rage that the
spasm was brought on and she was very near dying.'

In the autumn of 1818 she was moved to Kew where she
was looked after by Princess Augusta and by Princess Mary
whose husband, the Duke of Gloucester, had had to agree
that she should not forsake her filial duties just because she
was his wife.

From Kew, Princess Augusta wrote to the Regent to prepare him for her approaching death. Augusta had told their
mother that the doctors had given warning that she was
very ill. The Queen had murmured, 'So!' and laying her
head on the pillow had 'cried very much indeed'. 'I wish to
God I could see *your brothers,*' she had said to Augusta when
recovered. 'Tell them I love them, but I am too ill. I can only
see you and Mary.' 'She then said, "I pray from night till
morning and from morning till night. I think a great deal,
I assure you, I wish I was near the dear King where I ought
to be at dear, dear Windsor."' She put her head on the
pillow and Augusta thought that she had gone to sleep, but
her hands kept moving up and down gently as if she were
praying.

She told Sir Herbert Taylor, who saw her on 31 October,
that she was praying constantly when people thought that
she was asleep. Her sufferings were 'very great', she said, and
their influence on her mind was 'very distressing'. Sir Francis
Milman, who was assisting Sir Henry Halford in the case,
considered that she was 'in a state of such nervousness and
agitation' that it was absolutely essential 'to hold no unnecessary language' to her concerning her condition or the
possibilities of a cure. Yet, when Taylor went to see her a
fortnight later to discuss her will, she was calm and col-

lected. Taylor suggested that Frogmore should be left to
Princess Augusta and the Lower Lodge to Sophia and she
said, 'Yes, Sir. I think that would be very right. You will put
it so.'

Taylor went to see her on 16 November with the will ready
for signing. When he arrived at the door he was told that
Halford had informed her of her 'immediate danger'. Halford was kneeling beside her, holding her left hand and
feeling her pulse, 'with a most anxious expression of countenance. ... The perspiration was running down her face, her
eyes were moist, she breathed quick and appeared to be in
great suffering.' She recognized Taylor, gave him her right
hand 'with a most affectionate look and a painful smile', and
pressing his hand, continued to hold it in hers. He asked
her if she was ready to sign the will, but being deaf in the
right ear, she did not hear him and had to ask Halford what
he said. Halford told her and, when she had signed the will,
he asked Taylor, speaking in Latin, to send immediately for
the Regent.

The Regent drove down to Kew post-haste, and he was
there, sitting by her bed and holding her hand, when she
died the next day, 17 November 1818.

He was 'extremely affected' by her death, Croker said; and
Lady Jerningham heard that he was so distressed that it was
feared he would not be able to 'go through with the outward
pageantry' of the funeral. For several days he did not move
from Carlton House. 'There is no one who will feel [the
Queen's death] more than you, who was ever so devotedly
and tenderly attached to her,' Princess Elizabeth wrote to
him, 'and with reason for no parent was ever more wrapt
up in a child than she was in you, and I firmly believe that
she would with pleasure have sacrificed her life for you.'

His doctors advised him to go to Brighton to recuperate.
But he could not bring himself to move; and it was not until
the beginning of December that he left London. Even then,
so he told his brother, William, he could not describe what
his feelings still were; they existed 'to the utmost extent of

the bitterest anguish in the deepest recesses' of his heart. Ever since their mother's death he had not been able to hold up his head in the least; in short he had been 'incapacitated for everything'.

The Pavilion to which the Regent returned in December 1818 was no longer the long, low cream-coloured Graeco-Roman house which Henry Holland had designed in the 1780s. The designs for a new Pavilion in the Indian style, which Humphry Repton had presented to the Prince in 1807, had been temporarily set aside; but the idea of a Moghul palace had never been completely abandoned, and in 1815 John Nash had borrowed from the Regent's library at Carlton House various books containing plates of Indian scenes painted by Thomas Daniell and his nephew William.

Inspired by these scenes, Nash had prepared drawings and plans for the Regent which had gradually been put into effect. The transformation had been very slow. By the middle of 1816 little work, other than the enlargement of the Chinese corridor, had been completed; for the Regent's finances were in an even more precarious state than normal. In March he had received a strong warning, signed jointly by Liverpool, the Prime Minister, Castlereagh, the Foreign Secretary, and Vansittart, the Chancellor of the Exchequer. These Ministers had warned him of the 'unprecedented difficulties' which were thrown upon the government 'in all financial discussions in the House of Commons at the present moment in consequence of the temper of the times, and more particularly of the distress' which was 'so severely felt by most classes of His Majesty's subjects'. They had been 'fully persuaded' that no government which did not 'enforce a system of economy and retrenchment' and which did not abstain from every expense not 'indispensably necessary', could hope to continue in existence. No subject was 'viewed with more jealousy and suspicion than the personal expenses of the Sovereign or his representative at a time when most of the landed gentlemen of the country

[were] obliged to submit to losses and privations as well as to retrenchment'. 'Your Royal Highness's servants humbly submit', the ominous letter had concluded, 'that the only means by which [there] can be a prospect of weathering the impending storm is by stating on the direct authority of your Royal Highness and by your command, if it should be necessary, that all new expenses for additions or alterations at Brighton or elsewhere will, under the present circumstances, be abandoned. Your Royal Highness's servants are perfectly convinced that Parliament will never vote one shilling for defraying such expenses, if unfortunately they were to be persevered in.'

Of this there could be no doubt. Whig Members had long been complaining in the strongest terms about the expensive alterations begun and contemplated at Brighton. One of them had expressed the hope that Parliament would hear 'no more of that squanderous and lavish profusion which in a certain quarter resembled more the pomp and magnificence of a Persian satrap, seated in the splendour of Oriental state, than the sober dignity of a British Prince, seated in the bosom of his subjects'. Henry Brougham went even further and in what Castlereagh termed 'a most violent speech' condemned the Regent's 'profligacy' and 'extravagance' in terms which would not have been too strong, in Samuel Romilly's opinion, to have used in describing the days of the Emperor Tiberius.

Faced with such criticism, the Regent had been obliged to call a halt to the work at Brighton; and it was not until a year later, after the Queen had 'most graciously and liberally contributed to the promotion of the splendid improvements of the Palace by a grant of £50,000 from her private purse', that the labourers and craftsmen had taken up their tools again. Thereafter the work had continued steadily and the Regent's vision of an Indian palace had gradually taken shape. At first two big wings had appeared at north and south with oriental windows and sharply pointed battlements, topped by tall pagodas and minarets; then, between

these wings, a huge new onion-shaped dome built on a cast-
iron frame had been lifted into position where once Holland's low classical dome had stood. Other oriental domes
had appeared; then screens of Indian columns, graceful
colonnades, pierced stone lattice work, delicate cornices,
cast-iron pillars wreathed with iron serpents, overhanging
eaves and fretted battlements had taken shape until the
splendid edifice that so astonished the Regent's contemporaries was complete.

Inside, the Chinese decorations remained, though they
were continually being altered and refined, made less exuberant, more stately. Under the direction of Robert Jones
and the Craces, father and son, new wallpapers went up,
ceilings and domes were freshly painted, chandeliers were
hung, rich curtains cascaded from bamboo pelmets, Chinese
and Japanese lacquered cabinets and tables were arranged
in the rooms, Chinese banners were fixed to the walls. And
all the while the Regent came and went, offering advice,
making criticisms, demanding alterations: in one single
six-month period the decorations of the southern wing were
changed four times. The bills mounted year after year.
Nearly £9,000 was spent in 1814, over £22,000 in 1815, almost
£10,000 in 1816, £15,000 in 1817, £33,000 in 1818, over £40,000
in 1819 – the year in which £30,000 was raised on mortgage
through Coutts's Bank – and over £25,000 in 1820, a total of
more than £155,000 in seven years.

Nash's two great new apartments were the Music Room
and the Banqueting Room, both with huge chandeliers like
waterlilies and enormous wall-paintings, Chinese landscapes
of scarlet, gold and yellow lacquer in the Music Room,
Chinese figures in the Banqueting Room. The domed ceilings of both rooms were elaborately painted, the Music
Room with green and gold shells, the Banqueting Room
with a spreading and fruiting palm tree, a silver dragon
appearing among the leaves.

Croker, who visited the transformed Pavilion in December
1818, was not much impressed by it all. Nash's two new

rooms were 'both too handsome for Brighton', though he later admitted that the Banqueting Room, when lighted up at night, was 'really beautiful'. The outside was 'said to be taken from the Kremlin at Moscow'; but it seemed to him to be 'copied from its own stables, which, perhaps were borrowed from the Kremlin'. Anyway, it was 'an absurd waste of money' and would be 'a ruin in half a century or sooner'.

Dorothea de Lieven, wife of the Russian ambassador, was not much impressed either when she went over 'the Kremlin' with the Duke of York. 'We were shown a chandelier which cost eleven thousand pounds sterling,' she told Prince Metternich, who had become her lover during the Congress of Aix. 'I write it out in full because it is really incredible. The chandelier is in the form of a tulip held by a dragon. ... How can one describe such a piece of architecture [as] the King's palace here? The style is a mixture of Moorish, Tartar, Gothic and Chinese, and all in stone and iron. It is a whim which has already cost £700,000; and it is still not fit to live in.'

However the kitchens and larders, which were under the expert direction of Jean Baptiste Watier, were 'admirable – such contrivances for roasting, boiling, baking, stewing, frying, steaming and heating; hot plates, hot closets, hot air, and hot hearths, with all manner of cocks for hot water and cold water, and warm water and steam, and twenty saucepans all ticketed and labelled, placed up to their necks in a vapour bath'.

The Regent, a dedicated gourmet and gastronome, was a frequent visitor to these kitchens which he had had ornamented with fanciful cast-iron columns in the guise of palm trees, and with elaborate bronze smoke canopies and hexagonal lanterns. Occasionally he would give informal parties here; and once, during the Christmas holidays in 1817, he gave a supper party for the servants. A scarlet cloth was thrown over the stone floor; 'a splendid repast was provided, and the good-humoured Prince sat down with a select party of his friends, and spent a joyous hour. The whole of the

servants, particularly the *female portion*, was delighted with
this mark of royal condescension.'

For eight months, until homesickness drove him back to
France, the great chef, Antonin Carême, worked here; and
one evening in January 1817 he provided a menu of thirty-
six *entrées*, as well as four soups, four *relevés de poissons*,
four *grosses pièces pour les contre-flancs*, ten *assiettes
volantes de friture*, eight *grosses pièces de pâtisserie*, thirty-
two *entremets* and four *plats de rotis* – *les coqs de Bruyères,
les canards sauvages, les poulets gras bardés, les gelinottes.*

Life at the Pavilion followed much the same pattern as it
had done in the past. About twice a week there was a dinner
party to which twenty or so guests were invited, many of
them complaining, as guests at the Pavilion had always had
cause to complain, of the excessive heat of the rooms. They
assembled just before 6.30, and the Regent on entering the
room walked round to shake hands and exchange a few
words with them all. He then led the lady or ladies of
highest rank to the dining-table.

After the meal the band struck up as usual; the Regent
occasionally played patience, and Croker was 'rather amused'
one evening 'to hear him exclaim loudly when one of the
kings had turned up vexatiously, "Damn the King".' 'The
supper,' Croker added critically, 'is only a tray with sandwiches, and wine and water handed about.'

In fact, Croker did not think the evening entertainments
at the Pavilion were as agreeable now as they had been. 'The
dinners are dull enough,' he recorded on 15 December 1818.
'They are too large for society and not quite crowded enough
for freedom, so that one is on a sort of tiresome good behaviour. How much pleasanter it used to be with a dozen at
a circular table in the old dining-room. His Royal Highness
not looking well today. The fineness of the weather does not
tempt him abroad; his great size and weight make him nervous, and he is afraid to ride – I am not surprised at it. I
begin to fear that he will never ride again. He says, "Why
should I? I never had betters spirits, appetite, and health

than when I stay within, and I am not so well when I go abroad." He seems as kind and gracious as usual to everybody.' In the company of the Duke of Wellington, though, he affected an air of excessive bonhomie which the Duke found most distasteful. 'By God, you never saw such a fellow in your life as he is,' Wellington exclaimed to Creevey in response to a question about him. 'Then he speaks and swears so like old Falstaff, that damn me if I was not ashamed to walk into a room with him.' When the earnest-minded William Wilberforce was a guest, however, the Regent took care to be more delicate. Wilberforce had heard rumours that the talk at the Pavilion was commonly such as he would dislike to hear. But he found *the direct contrary was the fact. ...* The Prince [was] quite the English gentleman at the head of his own table.'

Although, as he told Croker, the Regent spent most of his time indoors, sleeping late and sitting quietly in the afternon with Lady Hertford, he had not given up riding altogether. Sometimes in the mornings he could be seen trotting about the Pavilion lawn or more often in the Riding House, having mounted his horse by means of a complicated mechanism described by a *Times* correspondent: 'An inclined plane was constructed, rising about the height of two feet and a half, at the upper end of which was a platform. His Royal Highness was placed in a chair on rollers, and so moved up the ascent, and placed on the platform, which was then raised by screws, high enough to pass the horse under; and finally, his Royal Highness was let gently down into the saddle.' This was, of course a most tiresome process, so complicated a manoeuvre that the Regent could rarely be troubled to go through it merely to get astride a horse. And when the caricaturists took to ridiculing the method he was obliged to adopt, he instantly abandoned it, declining to ride at all except when he was sufficiently recovered from his gout to mount his horse unaided. Then he could be seen, as Lord William Gordon saw him, in January 1819, riding out 'almost every day'. For the rest of the time he con-

tented himself with driving about in the yellow Berlin which
Thomas Moore used to see on its way to Lady Hertford's
house in Manchester Square, or in a tilbury, a small two-
wheeled gig, which he drove with his groom sitting beside
him. This riding in a gig with a groom, however, was considered as vulgar as being cranked into the saddle was
ludicrous. 'Grave men,' Charles Greville commented, 'are
shocked at this undignified practice.'

In June 1819 the Regent left Brighton for London to
attend the christening at Kensington Palace of the daughter
of the Duke and Duchess of Kent. He had been asked to
stand as godfather and, without much relish, he had agreed
to do so. He was much displeased to learn that the other
godfather was to be the Tsar Alexander. The names her
parents had suggested for the child were Victoire Georgina
Alexandrina Charlotte Augusta, and these did not please
him either. He told his brother that the name of Georgina
could certainly not be used, 'as he did not chuse to place the
name before the Emperor of Russia's – and he could not
allow it to follow'. He added that he would discuss the other
names with him at the ceremony which he had decided must
be a private family affair so that the Kents could not make a
grand occasion of it.

But, according to the Duchess, no satisfactory discussion
took place. The Archbishop of Canterbury had the child in
his arms before the Regent pronounced the name he had
selected from those offered for his consideration – 'Alexandrina'. There was a long pause while the parents and the
Archbishop waited for him to give another name. The
father reminded him that, after Georgina which he would
not allow them to use, they had suggested Charlotte. The
Regent firmly shook his head. The Duke then proposed the
name Augusta; but his brother did not approve of this
either. Nor did he approve of Elizabeth which the father
finally put forward. There was now only one name left of the
five the parents had proposed. Looking at the Duchess, who

had been reduced to tears, he said, 'Give her the mother's name also then, but it cannot precede that of the Emperor.' So she was baptized Alexandrina Victoria.

Thankful to escape from the company of the tiresome Kents – whose self-importance as parents of the heir to the throne was profoundly irritating – the Regent now set out for Cowes where in August he was seen to be in 'excellent health' enjoying his first visit to the Regatta aboard the *Royal George*. A sailor's life suited him 'admirably', and he was 'received everywhere with enthusiasm'.

While the Regent was enjoying himself at Cowes, between 50,000 and 60,000 people assembled in St Peter's Field, an open space near the centre of Manchester, to hear the radical orator, Henry Hunt, voice their demands for parliamentary reform. News of this proposed meeting had deeply disturbed the Cabinet in London. All over the country, ever since the Corn Law riots of 1815, there had been intermittent outbreaks of violence, revolutionary gatherings, fierce threats against the established order. At a huge meeting in Spa Fields, London, a tricolor flag and a revolutionary cap had been paraded before the cheering crowds who had later broken into a gunsmith's shop and marched towards the City. The French Revolution was too recent in men's memories for such disturbances not to cause the greatest alarm. Throughout 1816 isolated disturbances had seemed to threaten national revolution. On many occasions troops of Yeomanry were attacked by the mobs which they had been called out to disperse. In Devon and Cornwall they had to be rescued by Dragoons; at Norwich they were stoned and attacked by fireballs; in Essex they were thrown back by rioters who took shelter behind tombstones and pelted them with rocks.

The Cabinet had earlier refused the demands of Lord Sidmouth, the Home Secretary, to prohibit all public meetings; but after these and other riots, they had felt compelled to act decisively and to suspend the Habeas Corpus Act. Protest

against the Goverment's measures led to further disturbances and to a march towards London from Lancashire of
hundreds of petitioners, known as 'The Blanketeers' from
the coverings they carried with them for their night shelter.

In 1817 a good harvest and a revival of trade had helped
to restore the country to a relative quiet. But in 1819 the
troubles had started again; and when on 16 August both
Yeomanry and Hussars were used against the largely peace-
ful crowd in St Peter's Field, Manchester, and several people,
including two women, were killed, revolution appeared to
threaten once more. Lord Sidmouth had little doubt that the
'clouds in the north' would soon burst, and he wrote to
Lord Eldon, the Lord Chancellor, to tell him that he wished
he could persuade himself of the 'sufficiency of the means
either in law or force', to curb the spirit of the revolt and
'crush its impending and too probable effects'.

Lord Grey felt sure that 'the leaders of the popular party'
wanted revolution rather than mere reform; and that, 'inflamed' as they were by distress, the people were ready to
support them. The Regent shared this view. At Lord Sidmouth's request he wrote a letter approving the action of
the Manchester magistrates in St Peter's Field and com-
mending the 'forbearance' of the commander of the regular
troops. He approved the measures known as the Six Acts by
which the government endeavoured to curb the activities of
the revolutionaries, and read with approval letters from the
Duke of Cambridge who protested that 'nothing but firmness' could quell the 'abominable revolutionary spirit now
prevalent in England'. On his return to London from Cowes,
the Regent was made only too well aware of the strength
of this revolutionary spirit. He was 'hissed by an immense
mob' around his front door; and Lady Hertford was all but
tipped out of her chair into the street and had to be rescued
by Bow Street Runners.

It was at this time that Arthur Thistlewood, a former
estate agent who had been arrested after the trial of the Spa
Fields rioters, conceived in his disordered brain the bizarre

and monstrous plan of assassinating the entire Cabinet. He and thirty-odd followers planned to execute their murders at Lord Harrowby's house in Grosvenor Square, where the intended victims were due to dine on 23 February 1820. They were to be slaughtered in the dining-room and the heads of Lord Sidmouth and Lord Castlereagh, one of the Home Secretary's strongest supporters, were to be carried off in a bag. Having been told about the plot by an informer, the government were able to have Thistlewood and his associates arrested at their headquarters in a ruined stable in Cato Street on 23 February 1820. Lord Sidmouth, who had personally supervised the operation with his habitual calm and courage, was praised by the Regent as the 'Duke of Wellington on home service'.

'The Ministers have had a narrow escape,' Lord Althorp wrote to Lord Milton two days after Thistlewood's arrest, 'for nothing would have been more easy than to have murdered them in the way it was intended.' Both Althorp and Milton had opposed the more repressive of the government's Six Acts on the grounds that 'if you prevent the people from meeting in the open you will drive them to plots and assassinations'; and they feared that further disorders were inevitable.

Their fears were justified. The Cato Street Conspiracy was followed by a number of alarming incidents, particularly in the north. Accounts of insurrectionary movements were received from Barnsley and Sheffield; over a thousand armed men assembled at four different points around Huddersfield intending to attack the town on the night of 31 March; and artillery was ordered to Wakefield in April. But as in 1817, so now as the spring of 1820 advanced, the disturbances died down with the general improvement of the economic situation, and a revulsion amongst the more moderate reformers against the savage plans of the extremists.

Before the summer was over, however, the government were threatened from a new and unexpected quarter; and the Regent was to face an adversary far more destructive of his peace of mind than either Hunt or Thistlewood.

32

The Milan Commission
1814–1820

'Two young and hot lovers could not have done as much'

EVER since her arrival in Brunswick in August 1814, Princess Caroline had been providing Europe with scandalous stories about her astonishing behaviour. She had exhausted her hosts and her attendants by her restless energy, by going to balls and masquerades, to supper parties and gambling parties night after night, by refusing to go to her bed and by having the musicians dragged from theirs to play on until dawn. She had provided her Gentlemen with a startling new livery of gaudily embroidered coats and plumed hats. At Geneva she had appeared at a ball 'dressed *en Venus*, or rather not dressed, further than the waist'; at Baden, at the Opera, she had pranced into the box of the mourning, widowed Margravine, shouting with laughter and wearing an outlandish peasant headdress ornamented with spangles and fluttering ribbons; later at Baden, so Miss Wynne was told by Lord Redesdale, 'when a *partie de chasse* had been made for her, she appeared with a half pumpkin on her head', explaining to the astonished Grand Duke that it was the 'coolest sort of coiffure'. At Genoa she was drawn through the streets in a gilt and mother-of-pearl phaeton dressed in pink and white, like a little girl, though exhibiting a large expanse of middle-aged bosom and showing two stout legs in pink top boots; at Naples where she went in defiance of the urgent advice of Lord Liverpool, she had been so obviously captivated by the virile, arrogant swagger of Napoleon's hirsute brother-in-law, Joachim Murat, that men said she had induced him to make love to her; and at a

ball there she was alleged to have appeared 'in the most indecent manner, her breast and her arms being entirely
naked'. At Athens she had 'dressed almost naked and danced
with her servants'; on Elba she had made a flamboyant pilgrimage to the house where Napoleon had lived in exile.*

The Hon. J. W. Ward imagined in November 1815 'that
"Injured Innocence" which made such a run two years ago
would now be hissed off the stage'. On a visit to Milan,
Robert Southey heard that the Princess was reported to be
insane. And Walter Savage Landor repeated stories of indecent paintings on the walls of her villa, of orgiastic balls that
were given there, of the 'Deptford boy' (William Austin)
spitting in the face of his tutor. Landor himself had seen
Austin at a theatre in Italy, 'and all the time he was there
he was employed in scratching his head and examining the
success of the operation'.

'I cannot tell you how sorry and ashamed I felt as an
Englishwoman,' Lady Bessborough, who saw the Princess at
a ball, told Granville Leveson Gower. 'In the room, [danc-
ing,] was a short, very fat elderly woman, with an extremely
red face (owing I suppose to the heat) in a girl's white frock-
looking dress, but with shoulder, back and neck, quite low
(disgustingly so) down to the middle of her stomach; very
black hair [in fact, a black wig] and eyebrows, which gave
her a fierce look, and a wreath of light pink roses on her
head. ... I was staring at her from the oddity of her appear-

* Count Münster, the Hanoverian Minister, whose agents were
employed to watch her movements and activities, thought that 'her
predilection for everything connected with the Bonaparte family'
deserved 'as much and even more notice as her love affair'. The
Marchese Circello reported to Prince Castelcicala, in the year of
Waterloo, that the Princess had examined the house in which Napoleon had lived on Elba 'with the utmost attention and minuteness,
expressing her admiration of every corner of it, especially those
rooms which Napoleon had been reported to have preferred'. Before
his portrait she had announced, 'Napoleon, I salute you, I always had
and have now the greatest esteem for you.' She asked if she might
keep his ebony billiard cue as a 'precious memento' (RA Geo. IV,
Box 8, 9 December 1815).

ance, when suddenly she nodded and smiled at me, and not
recollecting her, I was convinced she was mad, till William
Bentinck [the British envoy], pushed me and said, "Do you
not see the Princess of Wales nodding to you?" ... I could
not bear the sort of whispering and talking all round about
the Principessa d'Inghilterra.'

But the Principessa seemed not to care, nor even to notice
it. It was as though she were revelling in her freedom to behave as badly as she felt inclined to behave, and, in so doing,
to insult and infuriate her husband.

One by one her English attendants had left her, first
Colonel St Leger, then Lady Charlotte Lindsay and Lady
Elizabeth Forbes, then Sir William Gell and Keppel Craven,
finally Captain Hesse and Dr Holland.* Their places were
taken by an extraordinary collection of retainers including
French chambermaids and French cooks, Arab footboys,
Austrian postilions and Italian footmen, whose 'overbearing
insolence' was 'beyond description' and whose 'entrance into
any territory [was] as much dreaded as the incursion of
freebooters'. Over them all presided the swarthy, robust and
handsome figure of Bartolommeo Bergami. Bergami – or
Pergami as he preferred the name to be spelled – was thirty-
two at the time of his appointment, and separated from a
sullen, silent wife whose dialect was difficult to understand
even in the very few sentences which ever escaped her. He
had formerly been a soldier, a quartermaster in a regiment
of Hussars, and afterwards a courier on the personal staff of
General Pino; he had served in the Russian campaign of
1812, and in the subsequent wars of 1813 and 1814. His
family, so he claimed – and so it was afterwards confirmed –
was an old and respectable one which had fallen on hard

* Captain Samuel George Pechell, R.N., who was later to be a
witness against the Queen at the enquiry into her conduct in the
House of Lords, said that Lady Charlotte Campbell had 'made no
scruple of giving as her reason for leaving [the Princess] that she had
daughters and would not allow them to stay where there was such an
example' (Journal of J. A. Powell, 5 August 1818–3 July 1820, RA
Geo. IV, Box 23).

times through the extravagance of his father, the son and grandson of well-to-do physicians. Certainly Bartolommeo Pergami himself, English observers agreed, though a man of no education and little talent, had the manners of a gentleman. It had not, therefore, seemed inappropriate when Princess Caroline had appointed him her *valet de place*. What had seemed wholly objectionable was Pergami's rapid promotion to Chamberlain, the appointment of numerous friends and relations of his to her Royal Highness's staff, his evidently welcome presence at her dinner-table – where his former fellow-servants waited on them both. With the Princess's help, her handsome, sturdy Chamberlain acquired a country estate near Milan, assuming the title of Baron della Francina; also with the Princess's help he was created a Knight of Malta. His little daughter, Victorine, often slept in her bedroom and called her 'Mamma'.

It was in the company of this attractively vigorous and attentive companion that the Princess, by now an intrepid and resourceful traveller, set out upon her famous pilgrimage to the Holy Land. Since she had already sailed to Sicily and drunk tea with the Dey in his seraglio at Algiers, had explored the Greek islands and the mosques of Syria, had driven through Constantinople and inspected the defences of Acre, no one in London was unduly surprised when it was learned that, accompanied by a horde of attendants and hangers-on which now numbered over two hundred persons, she had ridden into Jerusalem on an ass. Nor was any great surprise evinced by the report that the increasingly eccentric Princess had there established the Order of St Caroline of Jerusalem whose Grand Master was 'the Colonel Bartholomew Pergami, Baron of Francina, Knight of Malta and of the Holy Sepulchre of Jerusalem', whose most honoured Knight was William Austin, and whose motto was 'Honi soit qui mal y pense'.

On her return to Europe, via Jericho, the Princess moved into a villa on Lake Como which she greatly enlarged and named the Villa d'Este after the distinguished family from

which she was descended. From there she moved to the Villa
Cassielli on the Adriatic near Pesaro where she was told that
her daughter was dead. She realized then that her husband
would have no further compunction in initiating proceedings
against her in order to secure a divorce. So long as her 'ever
beloved daughter was still alive,' she wrote to Henry Brough-
ham, 'such proceedings would never have taken place to
make such false and foul accusations upon my character'.
But now that Charlotte was dead, she supposed that the
Prince would do all he could to rid himself of her.

For months past, indeed, the Regent had been closely following his wife's wild progress with intentness and disgust.
Foreign rulers had been made aware that any favours
granted her would cause grave displeasure in London. British
diplomats had been asked to watch and report on her movements; and the letters that were consequently received in
London tended to confirm all that the gossipmongers said.
From Hanover came reports of her 'very incongruous conduct' which 'created general astonishment and justly merited
indignation': those with opportunities of observing her
closely 'fully confirmed whatever [had] been generally circulated about the indecorous public and private conduct of
the Princess', mentioning particularly her 'glaring very intimate connection with a certain Bergamo'. Similar reports
came from Vienna; and from Florence came letters about
her continuing 'exceedingly prodigal behaviour', her 'intimacy' with Pergami which was 'the subject of conversation
everywhere', her carrying about a baby in her arms, the
belief that she was insane.

Faced by such reports as these and encouraged by his
friend Sir John Leach, now Vice-Chancellor, the Regent felt
that he had no alternative but to ask the government to
authorize an official enquiry into the Princess's conduct. The
government agreed to pay the costs of such an enquiry on
condition that 'whatever might be the nature of the evidence
obtained, however decisive as to criminality, the question of

the expediency of any proceedings must always be considered as an open question'.

The three men chosen to undertake the investigations were William Cooke, of Lincoln's Inn, 'one of His Majesty's Counsel learned in law', Major Thomas Henry Browne, an Italian-speaking officer who had served in Spain under Wellington, and John Allan Powell, a solicitor, also of Lincoln's Inn. They were sent out to Milan – at that time under the rule of Austria – with instructions 'to engage all such assistance either legal or otherwise' as they considered expedient and to place themselves 'in communication with the governments of several countries' to which their enquiries might lead them.

They left for Italy in the summer of 1818, and before the end of the year had examined and taken down the 'voluntary answers' of numerous servants, sailors, innkeepers, gamekeepers, fishermen, postilions and gardeners, who all seemed in general agreement about the Princess's unbecoming conduct. The evidence was not always easy to collect. The Austrian authorities in Milan afforded Powell and his colleagues 'every possible protection and countenance'; but when they moved south into the Papal States they had cause to complain that officials there were 'very lukewarm', not to say 'inimical'.

'I fear the police and authorities near you are too much disposed to favour the person in question', Thomas (recently promoted Colonel) Browne wrote to Baron Ompteda, Hanoverian Minister at the Vatican, who had attempted to collect evidence upon the Regent's behalf before the arrival of the 'Milan Commission'. 'The Papal Government would appear to be more inclined to withhold than to assist in discovering the truth, which is rather singular when it is no secret how much devotion to the Prince Regent is always expressed by Cardinal Gonsalvi [the Papal Secretary of State]. Were we to require what is unreasonable, or to seek for evidence or facts which had never existed, the case would be different and we should justly meet with difficulties from the Roman authorities but as this is not the case we are not a little astonished to find that all the authorities civil and military are at her disposal.' It had also required 'much management to induce' the witnesses to give their evidence without the promise of reward, the Italian character being 'keenly alive to interest'. Moreover, their dread of assassination was great. 'The Princess', Browne went on, 'is at this moment so completely surrounded by the family of Pergami, and they are such a determined set of Ruffianos that they would not scruple at any act, however desperate, against those whom they might suspect of acting to their prejudice.'

Nevertheless, before the end of November 1818, Browne had 'no doubt of everything being completely proved'; he had 'collected sufficient evidence to warrant a public enquiry', and felt that the case was 'already made out'. By July of the following year, when a total of eighty-five persons had been examined, William Cooke felt able to report: 'From this comparison of evidence and from the cool, clear, and distinct manner in which these persons delivered their testimony, we should give credit to the truth of what they have said. We are under the necessity, therefore, of humbly stating that in our opinion this great body of evidence established the fact of a continued adulterous intercourse' between the Princess and Pergami.*

---

* The charges of wholesale bribery later to be levelled at the Milan Commission were unjustified. Indeed, the papers in the Royal Archives show how careful the members of the Commission were to follow the orders they had received from Sir John Leach, who had ordered Cooke to conduct the enquiry with the utmost caution and impartiality and 'to assimilate the examination of the witnesses as nearly as might be to the principles of a British Court of Justice'. Leach had 'in the strongest terms impressed upon the Commissioners that not only were they not to offer or promise bribe or reward but were to forego the most important testimony rather than hold out any expectation of benefit to the witness'. These instructions appear to have been carried out. Care was taken to enquire into the character of possible witnesses; and the testimony of those who were discovered to be of bad character was not accepted. The evidence of thirty witnesses was rejected on the grounds that their accounts were improbable or their characters were suspicious. Of the £10,000 allowed to

One of the earliest witnesses to be examined was Giuseppe Sacchi, a former cavalry captain, for nine months courier to the Princess and for three subsequent months her equerry, who had entered her service at the Villa d'Este in November 1816 and had left it at Pesaro at the end of November 1817. He was later to swear that he had often seen the Princess and Pergami walking about arm in arm and kissing each other, and that the balls which were given at Pergami's villa near Milan – and of which several other witnesses were to speak in similar terms – were 'quite brothels', attended by women of 'very low condition'. Male servants in the Princess's employment would frequently leave the ballroom with these women 'according to their pleasure and will'; and the Princess once jokingly chided Sacchi, 'I know, you rogue, that you have gone to bed with three of them and how many times you have had intercourse with them.' Pergami, 'who was present, began to laugh and cry aloud, "It is true! It is true! It is true!".'

Sacchi went on to depose that he had seen Pergami more than once enter the Princess's room late at night and that he had heard her call him, 'mon ange', 'mon amour', 'mon cœur'. They travelled by night in the same carriage where 'two or three times' Sacchi found them in the morning 'both asleep and having their respective hands upon one another. Her Royal Highness had her hand upon a particular part of Mr Bergami and Bergami had his own upon that of Her Royal Highness ... Once Bergami had his breeches loosened and the Princess's hand was upon that part.'

---

the Commission, not more than £120 was paid out 'as a recompence for their loss of time and trouble' to the eighty-five witnesses whose evidence was considered worth recording. Having rejected the evidence of an untrustworthy sailor, Browne reported to London that it had 'been the uniform practice of the Commission to reject everything which did not bear decided marks of unimpaired recollection and sincerity'. It cannot be doubted that the Milan Commissioners were far more scrupulous than the Queen's agents nor that their witnesses were generally much more reliable (RA Geo. IV, Boxes 8, 9, 10, 11, 13, 23).

References to the festivities at Pergami's villa near Milan and at the Villa d'Este were also made by numerous other witnesses including Teodoro Majocchi who had entered the Princess's service in December 1817 after having been first postilion to General Pino. Majocchi described in particular the obscene dances performed for the Princess on these occasions by one of her servants, a mulatto from Jaffa named Mahomet. Like Sacchi, Majocci had seen Pergami enter the Princess's bedroom, and he described how intimate they were; how he held her round the waist when lifting her onto her ass and held her hand while she was riding it; how, when they travelled together, they shared the same carriage in which Pergami kept a bottle 'to make water in'; how they took great care to have rooms as close as possible to each other in all the inns where they stopped for the night, and alternately wore the the same blue silk bedgown.

Majocchi, who had accompanied the Princess on her pilgrimage to Jerusalem, gave an account of the sleeping and bathing arrangements on board the polacca which were later to become a subject of heated discussion at diningtables all over Europe, and were to give rise in London to the much quoted verse about Pergami:

> The Grand Master of St Caroline
> has found promotion's path.
> He is made both Night Companion
> and Commander of the Bath.

According to Majocchi, the Princess found it so hot on the polacca that she had a tent fitted up for her on deck, and in this tent she used to sleep with Pergami. She also had him in her cabin when she was having a bath for which Majocchi was in the habit of supplying the water; 'then the door was shut, and Bergami and the Princess remained alone in the cabin.'

Vincenzo Gargiullo, the captain of the polacca, confirmed that the Princess and Pergami had slept together under the tent and that he was present when she had her bath. Indeed, he accompanied her 'for anything she did, for any other thing she did', even when she went below to go to the water-closet. Gargiullo recalled how Pergami had made the Princess laugh by 'putting some pillows or cushions under his Grecian robe' to make himself look pregnant. And both he and his mate, Gaetano Paturzo, had seen Pergami sitting on a gun on deck, kissing the Princess who sat on his knee.

Other members of the crew and the Princess's entourage claimed to have been witnesses of these and worse improprieties; but the most damning evidence of blatant intimacy came from Louisa Demont, the Princess's smartly dressed, sly-looking *femme de chambre* who was also aboard the polacca.

Mlle Demont testified that Pergami was usually present when the Princess was at her toilet, when she was almost entirely undressed with her breasts quite bare, and that he would often go into her room at night scantily clothed, once presenting himself in nothing but his shirt and slippers. Sometimes in the night Mlle Demont would hear the Princess's door open and close; and, in the morning, when she went into her mistress's room to make the bed she would find that it had not been slept in. The Princess had herself painted as a penitent Magdalen with her hair disordered, her eyes heavenward, naked to the waist. She gave the finished portrait to Pergami.

So the evidence accumulated and was elaborated. Outdoor servants and workmen who had had opportunities to see Pergami and the Princess at the Villa d'Este and elsewhere, waiters and maids who had observed them on their travels were found to provide more and more evidence of her Royal Highness's guilt. They had been seen kissing and 'caressing each other with their hands', lying together in a boat on Lake Como; Pergami had been observed with his hands on her naked breasts and on her thigh; he had been surprised coming out of her room 'with only his drawers on'. Month by month, as the piles of depositions mounted, the three commissioners felt increasingly confident not only of the

Princess's guilt but of their being able to offer enough un-
shakable evidence for it to be proved in an English court of
law. The Regent could not have felt other than satisfied by
the results of their unpleasant work, yet he had cause also
to feel concerned by the enquiries at the same time being
undertaken by the Princess's advisers.

Although she had so dismissively spurned his urgent advice to her not to go abroad in 1814, Henry Brougham had
ever since been keeping a careful watch on the Princess's
activities, expecting the time would surely come when she
would feel obliged to call once more on his services. When
reports of her scandalous conduct made it clear that the
Regent would be induced to take action against her, Brougham had asked his brother James to go out to Italy to help
her sort out her financial problems and, at the same time, to
provide him with a first-hand report about the Princess's
behaviour and intentions.

James Brougham arrived at Pesaro in the spring of 1819
and was received by the Princess with the 'greatest attention
and kindness'. In two long letters to his brother, written towards the end of March, he first of all described the Princess's establishment. This consisted of eighty people in all,
over sixty of whom lived in the villa. She had '48 horses and
God knows how many carriages of different sorts', Brougham
reported, '– some of the horses the finest Arabians I ever
saw – and all *good*. A ship with a captain and eight men.' It
was all very '*hospitable* and *plentiful*'; indeed, it was very
surprising that the Princess was not more deeply in debt
than she was, particularly as she had even less idea of the
value of money than her husband had. She had added two
large wings to the Villa Cassielli, which she had bought and
given to Pergami, yet 'she *says* the addition wont cost more
than £500!!' She had paid £7,500 for the Villa d'Este 'and
laid out upon it in building and furniture upwards of
£20,000, and above £2,000 in making a road, you may say
altogether £30,000'.

She was very generous, and well enough liked. But she was full of complaints. She said that her English servants had cheated her outrageously, and the general behaviour of English people towards her had been abominable. The Royal Family, under the Regent's influence, had cut all connection with her. 'Leopold never wrote to her *at all.* The courier who went round Europe came here on his way to Naples, with a common circular letter telling her of Princess Charlotte's death. The Queen's death was never announced to her *at all.* The Duke of Gloucester was near, and never took the smallest notice of her. And all her old friends cut her in the same way.' The Regent's Milan Commission annoyed her 'most terribly', especially the evidence of her maid, Louisa Demont, who was 'a great Whore'. She insisted that people had been paid to poison her and the kitchens were watched accordingly; two servants paraded the hall at night; Baron Ompteda, who had been in the district trying to get people to bear witness against her, was not only the Regent's spy, but was also at the bottom of this plot to poison her.

As to the stories about her conduct with Pergami, Brougham was sorry to have to say that there was certainly enough 'to justify reports'. '*Le Baron*' admittedly appeared to be a '*remarkably good sort of man* . . . very active – quite a different man' from what he had expected. But their relationship was undeniably most irregular. Pictures of Pergami were in every room of the villa and all the plate in the dining-room, except for a few things which she had brought over from England with her, bore his arms. 'Nothing can appear more revolting to propriety than the Princess of Wales, with her large fortune using another person's plate,' Brougham thought. 'Certainly the whole thing tells badly. *His* house and grounds, *his* plate, his ordering everything, he even buys her bonnets, this I saw, and all his family quartered upon her!!!' His brother, Louis, was first equerry; his sister, an ill-bred woman known as Countess Oldi, was 'Lady in Waiting', his old mother superintended the linen, his daughter called the Princess 'Mamma'. 'In fact, they are to all appearances man

and wife, never was anything so obvious. *His room* is close
to hers, and his *bed room* the only one in that part of the
house. The whole thing is apparent to everyone, though
perhaps there might be difficulty in proving the fact to find
her guilty of high treason, yet I should think all the circumstances being stated would completely ruin her in the
opinion of the people of England. That once done, the
Prince might get divorce, or at any rate prevent her being
Queen if she wished it.'

For this reason James Brougham strongly recommended
that some sort of settlement should be made with the Princess so that a public enquiry into her conduct could be
avoided. 'I should propose that she write a letter to the
Prince stating her reasons for wishing a divorce or Parliamentary separation. ... You must give me the style of this
letter, because she will ask me to write it for her, and it must
be well done, as there is no saying what may be made of it
hereafter. She should begin by asserting innocence ... high
toned in the style of Mary Queen of Scots ... accusing the
Regent of plaguing her by these inquisitions, and concluding
by saying as her daughter is dead, and there is no hopes of
her having any pleasure in England she thinks it better for
both to separate. I am quite convinced that it is the very best
thing that can be done on every account, and the sooner the
better, before she loses more character, or in fact before
England knows more of the matter.'

Brougham felt sure that the Princess would be happy to
settle for a divorce. She told him that long before Princess
Charlotte's death she had resolved never to go to England
again; she had no ambition to be Queen *'and never had'*.
The only thing that might have induced her to return
would be to pay the Duke and Duchess of York a visit as she
liked them both. She would be quite content, she said, to
settle for £100,000 and to 'give up her annuity and everything', and although this 'would be madness – *not three
years income!'* Brougham was confident that he and his
brother between them could arrange a satisfactory figure for

her with the Regent's advisers; and the more she got the more she would be obliged to them both.

But the matter could not be settled so simply. Henry Brougham accepted his brother's advice and formally proposed that, provided her present annuity were guaranteed to her for life, she would agree to the ratification by Parliament of the terms of a separation and would renounce her right to become Queen, taking some other title after the Regent's coronation, such as Duchess of Cornwall.

This solution was not considered practical, however. In the first place Brougham was advised by Lord Lauderdale, a shrewd if eccentric Scotsman trained in the law, that Parliament could not pass an Act ratifying the separation unless the Princess were proved guilty of infidelity or confessed to it. And for her to confess was, she insisted, 'impossible'. Nor would she agree to a less formal separation by mutual consent: that was 'doing nothing'. Moreover, the Regent would not agree to separation by mutual consent either. He wanted to be more securely rid of the woman: there must be a divorce. It was Lord Lauderdale's opinion that he was actually contemplating getting married again. Certainly Prince Alexander of Soms wrote to him to suggest that it might be a good idea for him to marry a daughter of Victor Emmanuel, King of Sardinia, who was a great-grandson of Anne of Orleans, the granddaughter of Charles I, and thus the Stuart claimant to the throne of England. Also, a story later got abroad, so W. H. Fremantle told the Marquess of Buckingham, 'that they are trying to cook up a match for the King with a Princess of Tours and Taxis (I believe a sister of the Duchess of Cumberland) and a sister of the Princess Esterhazy. Metternick is at the bottom of it.' But the Regent never spoke of marriage himself; he wanted a divorce merely to be free of that 'vilest wretch this world ever was cursed with'.

The Cabinet were very reluctant to agree to a divorce, which could not be obtained 'except upon proof of adultery, to be substantiated by evidence before some tribunal in this country – and such a proceeding could not ... be instituted without serious hazard to the interests and peace of the Kingdom'. Moreover, the Cabinet doubted that the evidence collected by the Milan Commission, damning though it was, was strong enough to prove the Princess's adultery. The body of it consisted 'almost exclusively of the evidence of foreigners most of them not above the rank of menial servants and that of masters and attendants in hotels wholly unacquainted with the English language'. The Cabinet also feared that the Regent's marriage to Mrs Fitzherbert would be raised again and that the further damaging gossip about his past mistresses and present companions would be spread about by his enemies to increase his unpopularity. Above all, it was feared that the Princess's legal advisers would produce equally damning recriminatory evidence against the Prince; they even suggested that to air so much dirty linen in public would have a serious effect upon public morals.

While the Cabinet hesitated and held back, taking 'the whole case', as Castlereagh put it, 'into their mature consideration', the Regent became more anxious for a divorce than ever, dreading what the Princess might do unless action were taken against her while she still *was* a Princess and had no claim to be Queen. And in his anxiety, as so often in times of stress, he once more fell seriously ill.

33

The Queen on Trial
1820

'No other subject is ever talked of'

THE Regent's anxiety was much increased by the disturbing bulletins which the Duke of York had for some time past been sending him from Windsor. His father, now in his eighty-second year and 'greatly emaciated', though still finding 'amusement in the inexhaustible resources of his distempered imagination', was slowly dying. Scarcely had the doctors been summoned to the Prince's own bedside than he was given the news, which he received 'with a burst of grief', that 'his Majesty expired at 32 minutes past 8 o'clock p.m., 29 January 1820'. At the age of fifty-seven, he was King himself at last. The proclamation of his accession was delayed for a day, however, as 30 January was the anniversary of the execution of King Charles I; and it was not until Monday, the 31st, that, accompanied by the royal Dukes and by Prince Leopold, he emerged from Carlton House to stand in the cold air while the aged Garter King of Arms read out the traditional formula in a slow and quavering voice.

The next day the new King was attacked by an inflammation on the lungs, and a bulletin was issued with the grave news that his Majesty was 'severely indisposed'. He could not sleep; he had a racing pulse and pains in the chest; he experienced great difficulty in breathing. It was feared that he might be suffering from pneumonia or pleurisy; but whatever the disorder was, he came close to death. Wellington told Lady Shelley that he thought the King might slip through their fingers. 'Heavens, if he should die!' Princess Lieven wrote to Metternich. 'Shakespeare's tragedies pale before such a catastrophe. Father and son, in the past, have been buried together. But two Kings! I hope this one will recover.' Thomas Creevey for one did not think that he would. 'He is, I apprehend, rapidly approaching death,' Creevey told Elizabeth Ord – 'and then for the Queen and Bruffam!'

Brougham, in fact, was praying heartily for the King's recovery, for he dreaded the idea of his successor, King Frederick I, who would turn out to be a 'shady Tory-professional King' and would never give 'these villains', the present Tory Ministers, 'the least annoyance'. Frederick I would not long survive, nor would 'that Prince of Black-guards, "Brother William",' so, 'in the course of nature', the Whigs would live only 'to be *assassinated* by King Ernest I or Regent Ernest'. Even if Regent Ernest were not to survive, the Whigs could hope for little from other members of the family.

The Duke of Kent had adopted Whig opinions late in life but only in opposition to the King; and Kent had died a few days previously. The Duke of Sussex's political opinions were more sincerely held, but as the Hon. H. G. Bennet said, Sussex was in the habit of talking 'very sad stuff'; and, as Creevey decided, though Sussex never said anything that made you think him foolish, and was 'civil and obliging, there was a *nothingness* in him that [was] to the last degree fatiguing'. In any case, the likelihood of a King Augustus I was very remote indeed.

While the Whigs discussed the possible consequences of the King's death, he began slowly to recover, despite the loss of a total of 150 ounces of blood at the hands of Sir Henry Halford and Sir Matthew Tierney.

He felt himself sufficiently recovered by 14 February to wish to attend his father's funeral the following day; but his physicians, 'scarcely yet relieved from that state of anxiety and alarm' which his 'dangerous illness had given rise to', viewed his expressed intention with 'absolute dis-may' and most strongly urged him 'to forego that satisfaction' to his feelings that he naturally attached to 'a performance of the last act of filial piety to the late King'.

The King gave way to their entreaties and remained indoors, 'terribly' worried about the woman he declined to call the Queen. The previous week, despite his debilitated condition, he had spent a whole evening in 'very serious agitation', studying all the prayer-books in the Carlton House library, hoping to find a precedent that would support his determination not to allow Church congregations to pray for the well-being of Queen Caroline and to exclude her name and title entirely from the Liturgy.

He could not find a precedent, but he was determined that they should be excluded anyway. Although not all the members of the Cabinet concurred, and the Archbishop of Canterbury was also opposed to their exclusion, the government agreed after lengthy deliberations that she should not be mentioned in the Liturgy and that she ought not to be crowned Queen. They went on to say in a memorandum of extraordinary length that, while they deprecated her conduct, they could not recommend the King to proceed to a divorce. They suggested instead that 'the Princess', as they were careful still to refer to her, should be given an allowance on condition that she remained abroad, which they confidently expected she would do rather than return to face the accumulating evidence of the Milan Commission.

The King read this memorandum with 'some surprise and much regret'. He recognized perfectly well that the Princess's counsel would rake up 'recriminations of every kind', but he was prepared to face this if only he could once and for all rid himself of his unspeakable wife. He believed that the evidence against her was entirely convincing, and was struck by 'the extraordinary coincidence of testimony of different witnesses who [had] been separated from each other for years'. The general tendency of the evidence was confirmed 'by several English persons'. Having made up his mind 'to all the discomfort to which' he could be exposed, he was determined on a divorce, even if he had to go to Hanover to obtain one, and, encouraged by Sir John Leach, who had carefully studied the Commission's evidence, he threatened to dismiss Lord Liverpool's government. 'The King has declared his determination to look for other servants if we do not agree to bring forward a Bill for Divorce,' Canning, President of the Board of Control, noted in his diary on 10 February. 'Be it so!'

In acrimonious discussions with his Ministers he ordered the Prime Minister out of the room; he commanded Wellington 'to hold his tongue'; and in a subsequent quarrel with the Lord Chancellor he said to him insultingly, 'My Lord, I know your conscience always interferes except where your interest is concerned.' When Canning, 'after two sleepless nights trying to make up [his] mind', offered his resignation on the grounds of his former friendship with the Queen – 'no doubt one of the *many favoured*', Castlereagh rudely commented – the King declined to accept it, so Canning withdrew to France and resigned later.*

Nor was the divorce the only question which divided the King and his Ministers; for he was thoroughly dissatisfied with their refusal to sanction a Bill providing for an enlarged Civil List .'He has been pretty well disposed to part with us all because we would not make additions to his revenue,' Eldon noted in a memorandum on 26 April. And part with them he certainly would have done had he been able to do so. But to find an alternative government proved impossible. He asked Sidmouth, now his most favoured Minister, to replace Lord Liverpool; but Sidmouth declined even to consider the proposition and advised the King to stick to his

---

* As suggested earlier, if Canning had been Princess Caroline's lover before his marriage, the affair was evidently a brief one. Canning met the Princess for the first time on 22 June 1799. He found her 'most extraordinary and most delightful'; he was 'charmed with her beyond measure'. Just over a year later, on 8 July 1800, he married the heiress, Joan Scott. After the marriage he was a frequent guest at Blackheath, sometimes alone but often with his wife. The Princess was also a frequent guest of Mr and Mrs Canning at their country house (Canning's MS diaries in the Canning Papers, 29d, 29di).

present administration. No responsible potential minister could be persuaded to form or to join a government brought about in these conditions. So the King was obliged to give way. He sent for Lord Liverpool, apologized to him for his hastiness, and took what comfort he could from the Cabinet's promise to institute proceedings for a divorce should 'the Princess' return to England. As for his disappointment at being refused an increased Civil List, he wrote to the Prime Minister: 'The King is fully sensible of the importance of publick economy and is desirous to make every personal sacrifice on his part for that object, and the King will never require that the intended arrangement shall be disturbed unless it shall be found to be inconsistent with the dignity and splendour of the Crown which the King considers to be inseparable from the public interest.'

James Brougham had believed Princess Caroline to be quite sincere the year before in her protestations that she had no wish to return to England, but since then she had begun to change her mind. When she had learned that her father-in-law was likely to die she had written to Henry Brougham to say that she *might* return if the country would protect her. Excited by the possibilities of this, the Duke of Sussex woke Henry Brougham at two o'clock on the morning of 30 January to tell him that the King indeed was dead.

Soon after dawn a courier was despatched to Italy to advise the Queen to come north to Brussels or Paris, or even to Calais, and to demand a yacht to bring her to England. It seems unlikely that Brougham really wanted her to come all the way to England, even though her presence would prove a useful weapon with which to overthrow the Tories and so bring the Whigs and himself to power. In August he had written to the King's friend, Lord Hutchinson, to say, 'Her coming would be pregnant with every sort of mischief (not to mention the infernal personal annoyance of having such a devil to plague me for six months). I think it would expose things to the risk of clamour and violence which no one can hope to estimate, far less to direct, or, in case of necessity, disarm. ... Therefore I am disposed to prevent her coming by every means in my power.'

Since this letter had been written, George III's death had admittedly transformed the situation. The risk of 'clamour and violence' was just as great, perhaps even greater: memories of Peterloo might be fading, yet the unrest and discontent in the country were as threatening as ever. But Princess Caroline was now Queen, and her uses as a threat to the Tories were incalculably more valuable.

Yet it was probably only as a threat that Brougham envisaged her. 'It would be *frightfully dangerous* for her to come here all at once,' he warned Lady Charlotte Lindsay on 18 February. 'All now depends on her coming to Brussels or some near and handy spot. If she arrives plump on you at Paris, make her either stay there or at Calais till I come out to her.'

For the moment the Queen herself did not appear to be particularly inclined to hurry home. She had been in Leghorn when the news of the King's death reached her; but despite Brougham's summons to 'Brussels or Calais', she was unfortunately 'absolute obliged' to turn her back on 'dear old England', so she told her former physician, Walter Farquhar. She had to 'go first to Rome to Mr Torlonia, my banker, which usual received my letter of credit from Coutts House in London'. She would return to England eventually, though. 'Any merchant ship or frigate' would be 'quite sufficient' for her, she assured Farquhar; and she told Brougham that she would reside at 'the old Queen's palace in the Green Park without any alterations and expence for the nation'.

While the Queen remained in Rome, the King and the government discussed the terms that should be offered to her to induce her to stay on the Continent. It was felt that almost no sum would be too great provided that she could be prevented from returning to England. Eventually it was agreed that she should be offered £50,000 a year if she would relinquish the title of Queen or any other title indicating her relationship with the English Royal Family, and if she would undertake not to come into 'any part of the British dominions'.

Before this offer was made to her, however, she left Rome for France by way of Geneva. Exasperated on the journey by news of her omission from the Liturgy and by her treatment at the hands of the representatives of the foreign courts who, in deference to the known wishes of King George IV, declined to accord her the recognition to which she felt entitled, she entered France quite fixed in her determination to return to England and demand to be accorded her rights. She was accompanied by Alderman Matthew Wood, an extreme radical Member of Parliament for the City of London and twice its Lord Mayor, who had sailed out to meet her and to offer her the doubtful benefit of his far from disinterested advice.

The son of a Devonshire serge-maker, Wood had left Exeter to seek his fortune in London where he was now in a thriving way of business as a chemist and hop merchant. A consistent supporter of the more advanced Whigs, he saw in what he no doubt took to be the sad case of Princess Caroline those political opportunities that had appealed to Henry Brougham. Unlike Brougham, though, he knew little of the evidence that was mounting against the Queen whom he vehemently urged to return to London where she would receive the welcome due to an injured heroine.

Brougham, accompanied by Lord Hutchinson, left for France on 1 June and, on the afternoon of the 3rd, arrived at St Omer, where the Queen had agreed to meet him. It was immediately clear that she was not in the least disposed to listen to the government's proposals, and she informed Brougham of her intention of proceeding straight to England. 'I entreat your Majesty once more earnestly and patiently to reflect upon the step about to be taken,' Brougham implored her the day after his arrival at St Omer. It would be far better, he advised her, to accept the generous

annuity that was offered her on the understanding that it
would be granted 'without any renunciation of rank or title
or right' and with a pledge on the part of the government
that she should be 'acknowledged and received abroad by
all diplomatic agents' according to her 'rank and station'. If
she *did* return to England she ought to do so secretly, and
to dispense with 'such marks of popular favour' as were
more suitably displayed towards a parliamentary candidate
at an election than towards a Queen of England. 'My duty
to your Majesty binds me to say very plainly,' he continued,
'that I shall consider every such exhibition as both hurtful
to your Majesty's real dignity and full of danger in its probable consequences.' When this plea proved ineffective he
sent another at seven o'clock the same evening. 'I earnestly
implore you to refrain from rushing into certain trouble
and possible danger.'

But it was all to no avail. The Queen sent Brougham a
curt note commanding him to inform Lord Hutchinson that
it was 'quite impossible' for her to consider the government's
proposals. Then, without waiting to consult Brougham further or waiting for Hutchinson's reply, in which he said that
he would send a courier to London for further instructions,
she got into her carriage and left for Calais. In fact, she had
already written to Lord Liverpool from Villeneuve-le-Roi on
29 May, to inform him that she intended arriving in London 'next Saturday the 3thd of Juin'. She had asked for one
of the royal yachts to be ordered to take her across the
channel, and had ended her letter with the ominous words,
'I desire ... also to be informed of his Majeste's intentions
what residence should be alloted to me, either phermenent
or temprory: I trust that his Majeste is recovered from his
severe illness. Caroline Queen of England.'

'It is impossible for me to paint the insolence, the violence and the precipitation of this woman's conduct,' Hutchinson reported in exasperation to Bloomfield. 'I never saw
anything so outrageous, so undignified as a queen, or so
unamiable as a woman. ... She has really assumed a tone

and hauteur which is quite insufferable, and which nothing but the most pure and unimpeached innocence could justify. .... We have at length come to a final and ultimate issue with this outrageous woman. She has set the King's authority at defiance, and it is now time for her to feel his vengeance and his power. Patience, forebearance and moderation have had no effect upon her. I must now implore His Majesty to exert all his firmness and resolution: retreat is impossible. The Queen has thrown down the gauntlet of defiance. The King must take it up.'

Hutchinson was convinced that Brougham possessed 'no real authority or power over the mind or decisions' of the Queen. 'I do not think that he ever made the slightest impression upon her or that she ever listened to him for a moment with the serious intention of following his advice,' Hutchinson reported. 'Before our arrival she had organized everything for stage effect: her chief informer was that enlightened mountebank, Alderman Wood.'

Her demand for a yacht to convey her across the Channel having been ignored, she arrived at Dover on 5 June in the ordinary packet. 'This brave woman', as *The Times* referred to her, was clamorously welcomed by a royal salute from the Castle and by a crowd even larger than Alderman Wood had promised her. To the triumphant strains of a raucous band, she was escorted to her hotel by tradesmen and fishermen carrying banners and shouting suitable slogans. The next day she left for London by way of Canterbury and Greenwich, collecting ever larger and more enthusiastic crowds of supporters as she approached the capital. She drove over Westminster Bridge in an open carriage, the purple silk pelisse she had worn on landing having now been changed for a more sombre mourning dress with an Elizabethan ruff, donned in respect for her late father-in-law and uncle, George III. Next to her, so delighted by the cheers that he occasionally stood up to return them at the top of his voice, sat Alderman Wood; opposite was her Lady-in-Waiting, Lady Anne Hamilton, and an Italian servant;

behind, in a second carriage, rode William Austin, accompanied by Alderman Wood's son; a third carriage contained
an assortment of Italian attendants. 'Her progress was slow
through the countless populace,' reported Thomas Denman,
the handsome, sociable and eloquent lawyer who had been
appointed her Solicitor-General, 'her travelling equipage
mean and miserable, her attendants appeared ill-calculated
to conciliate good-will in this country. Hardly a well-dressed
person was to be seen in the crowd. Two or three men on
horseback assumed a rather more respectable appearance,
but one of these was my bankrupt cousin.'

There was no gainsaying, though, the general enthusiasm
with which she was greeted. Charles Greville, who rode out
to watch her enter London, found 'the road thronged with
an immense multitude the whole way from Westminster
Bridge to Greenwich. Carriages, carts and horsemen followed, preceded, and surrounded her coach the whole way.
She was everywhere received with the greatest enthusiasm.
Women waved pocket handkerchiefs, and men shouted
wherever she passed.'

The cavalcade proceeded unsteadily up St James's Street,
where she 'bowed and smiled to the men who were in the
windows' of White's Club, and then on to Alderman Wood's
house in South Audley Street where she showed herself to
a wildly excited mob that 'streamed through the streets all
night with torches, making passers-by shout, "Long Live the
Queen!"', and roaring their support of 'Queen Caroline and
her son, King Austin'. For two days the mob surged round
the house, occasionally retiring to demand illuminations in
her honour or to break the windows of people deemed less
than enthusiastic in her support. Lord Sidmouth, going
'home from Cabinet with the Duke of Wellington, could not
get into his own house,' Croker reported, 'and the mob broke
the windows of the Duke's carriage'. Lady Hertford's house
was assaulted and her windows broken; the mob also stoned
Sidmouth's house from which Admiral Lord Exmouth
rushed out armed with sword and pistol and drove them

away. 'The fermentation encreases much,' Sir Thomas Tyrwhitt told Coutts, the banker. 'It has got amongst the sol-
diery, who skirmish in their barracks.' The Marquess of
Buckingham's correspondents shared Tyrwhitt's apprehensions. Thomas Grenville told him that the rumours about
the military were increasing 'daily and frightfully'; while
W. H. Fremantle wrote, 'I have great doubts if the troops
are not infected. The Press is paid abundantly [to support
the Queen] and there are some ale-houses open where the
soldiers may go and drink and eat for nothing provided they
will drink, "Prosperity and health for the Queen!" ... The
City is completely with her. ... The King grows daily more
unpopular.' Lady Jerningham decided that the spirit of the
times was most alarming; the country was nearer to disaster
than it had ever been since the time of King Charles I. Lord
Grey had already informed Holland that they would see, if
they lived, 'a Jacobin Revolution more bloody than that of
France'.

On 8 June the Queen moved to a quieter house in Portland
Place, before establishing herself at Brandenburg House in
Hammersmith, a mansion built for one of his mistresses by
Charles I's nephew, Prince Rupert. Meanwhile the King,
bitterly castigating her disgraceful entry into London sitting
next to 'that beast Wood', was forced to conclude that he
had never been more disliked. To his surprise and obvious
elation he was fitfully cheered when he went to the Chapel
Royal on Sunday 18 June, and allowed himself to be persuaded by his companions that the shouts indicated a significant change in public opinion. The Cabinet, therefore
'thought it highly necessary, in consequence of the feeling
betrayed by the Guards, the known bias of the lower orders
of the metropolis, particularly of the women, in favour of
the Queen, and the cry of "No Queen, no King!" which had
been heard in the country as well as in London, that the
King should be undeceived on this point, and deputed Lord
Sidmouth to wait on his Majesty for this purpose.' Soon
afterwards, insulted by mobs shouting 'Nero!' beneath the

windows of Carlton House, the King retired to the Royal Lodge in Windsor Park, a move which heightened the feeling against him for, as Lord Liverpool said, he was condemned as 'a coward afraid of showing himself'.

Before his departure he had sent messages to both the House of Commons and the House of Lords recommending to their 'immediate and serious' attention the contents of a certain green bag. This bag, soon to become a favourite subject of almost every caricaturist and lampoonist in London, contained the most important of the Milan Commission's papers. The King trusted that, having examined these papers, Parliament would 'adopt that course of proceedings which the justice of the case, and the honour and dignity of His Majesty's crown' required.

A Secret Committee of the House of Lords was accordingly appointed to study the documents in the green bag; and in due course this Committee, which included the Archbishop of Canterbury, the Lord Chancellor and various other members of the Cabinet, came to the conclusion that the papers, containing as they did allegations 'of the most licentious' conduct on the part of the Queen, regrettably called for 'a solemn enquiry'.

Since Pergami was Italian and not subject to English law, and since the alleged offences had not taken place in England, it was impossible to institute a trial for high treason which would have otherwise been the appropriate procedure. It was therefore considered necessary to introduce a Bill of Pains and Penalties, a parliamentary method of punishing a person without resort to a trial in a court of law. The Bill, which was technically a private Bill, the Law Officers acting for an unnamed person whom everyone knew to be the King, was read for the first time in the House of Lords on 5 July. It accused the Queen of having conducted herself towards Bartolommeo Pergami with 'indecent and offensive familiarity and freedom', and of having carried on 'a licentious, disgraceful, and adulterous intercourse' with him; it sought to 'deprive her Majesty Caroline Amelia Elizabeth of the title, prerogatives, rights, privileges, and pretensions of Queen Consort of this realm, and to dissolve the marriage between his Majesty and the said Queen'.

Rather than proceed to these lengths, and to the scandal of a public enquiry, Members of both Houses endeavoured to arrange a settlement. Brougham and Denman, representing the Queen, and Wellington and Castlereagh, on behalf of the King, met to discuss this possibility; but from the outset their talks had been unpromising: the Queen – 'the most impudent devil that ever existed', in Wellington's opinion – had been insistent that her name should be restored to the Liturgy, and on this point, as Castlereagh remarked, the King 'was immovable as Carlton House itself'. Eventually a deputation from Parliament, led by William Wilberforce, who sympathized with both the King and the Queen, had begged her Majesty to yield, on the understanding that she did so not because she feared the results of a public enquiry, but because she had the interests of the country at heart. She had agreed to consider this petition, yet on 24 June – influenced by Wood, so Denman thought – she had rejected it, to the evident satisfaction of the mob who abused Wilberforce as 'Dr Cantwill' for ever having put it forward.

As they waited for the public enquiry to begin, people throughout the country lost no opportunity of displaying where their sympathies lay, toasting the Queen in taverns and ale-houses with such vigorous thumping on the tables that half the glasses were smashed. An exhibition – 'through the channel of optical illusions' – of 'the grandest display of LIKENESS OF EMINENT CHARACTERS (forty in number) ever introduced to the public' went on show in various towns and was an immense success. King George the Third – 'God bless him!' – was the first figure displayed, 'accompanied by a figure of Fame'. He was followed by 'a small full length study of his present Majesty', preceded by 'Henry 8th of England, whose Queen he caused to be beheaded', and succeeded by 'Witch of Endor'. Then came 'Her Present Most

Gracious Majesty QUEEN CAROLINE; God bless her!!!'; and
she in turn was followed by 'an Italian Female Wretch, an
Accuser of the Innocent Queen Caroline', 'No friend to the
Queen – THE POPE!!', 'A Turkish Bribed Accuser of Royal
Female Innocence', and various other villains intent upon
her destruction. A fine finale included 'The SPIRIT of the
basely persecuted, innocent, injured Queen Caroline, ascend-
ing in glory to Heaven for PROTECTION!!', 'The Angel of
Innocence', 'A heavenly Messenger', 'Mr Brougham', and,
last of all Queen Caroline once more, this time 'magnani-
mously, gracefully, condescendingly saluting her good subjects'.

Although the Queen had her detractors in all classes and
even in Whig families like the Hollands, where Lady Holland was very far from agreeing with her husband's support
of her, there were many more people in the country at
large who shared Lord Holland's view rather than his wife's.
Even those who agreed with Byron that there was 'not the
slightest doubt about the Queen and Bergami', agreed also
with Brougham that after 'the treatment she had received
ever since she came to England, her husband [had] no right
to ... the punishment sought against her'. As Cobbett put it,
'the people, as far as related to the question of guilt or innocence, did not care a straw'. They were prepared to champion her anyway. 'The common people, and I fear the soldiers, are all in her favour and I believe the latter more than
is owned,' Emily Cowper told her brother. 'As for her virtue,
I don't think they care much about it, for tho they call her
innocent, the Mob before her door have repeatedly called out
"A cheer for Prince Austin".' Lord Carlisle testified that 'the
infatuation for the Queen prevails equally in the most
secluded valleys of our moors as at Hampstead and
Highgate'; and Sir James Mackintosh went so far as to
say, 'All the world is with her'. The 'military in London'
were now showing more and more 'alarming symptoms of
dissatisfaction', Charles Greville recorded, 'so much so' that
it was doubtful how far even the Guards could be trusted.

A battalion of the 3rd Guards refused to give up their ball cartridges when coming off duty and were hastily marched out of the capital. On their way through Brentford they were heard drunkenly crying out, 'God save the Queen!' Henry Luttrell said to Greville, 'The extinguisher is taking fire.'

Sir Thomas Williams told Grey-Bennett that he, too, had heard the 3rd Guards shouting 'God save the Queen!' and 'The Queen for ever!' as they marched out of London. 'As usual all this was denied by the Government and the officers,' Grey-Bennett recorded in his diary; 'but it is true. ... Even the 10th Hussars, the King's Own Regiment showed ... a strong feeling of compassion for the Queen; and a person of credit told me that he walked into the Toy Tavern, Hampton Court, where the Regiment was quartered, and passing by the tap saw twelve or fourteen soldiers sitting in it, where, one of them taking up a pot of porter said, "Come, lads, the Queen!" when they all rose and drank her health.'

Those who had known the Queen personally in the past had little doubt that she was guilty. Thomas Lawrence wrote of her 'daring profligacy', and Scott of her 'shockingly irregular' conduct. But these were views which most people thought it prudent not to express in public. Even in the King's stronghold of Brighton the manager of a theatre told Lord Darlington that he dared not permit the singing of 'God Save the King' any more for fear of provoking a riot; and Brighton ladies were apt to say to each other, 'Well, if my husband had used me as hers has done, I should have thought myself entitled to act as she has done.' Apart from the crowds at Ascot who always cheered the King when he drove to and from the races, it seemed to Croker that it was only a few 'people of fashion at the west end' of London who did not support the Queen against her husband, and they, like everyone else, talked of nothing else. 'No other subject is ever talked of,' Charles Greville wrote. 'If you meet a man in the street, he immediately asks you, "Have you heard anything new about the Queen?" All people express themselves bored with the subject, yet none talk or think of any other. ... Since I have been in the world I never remember any question which so exclusively occupied everybody's attention, and so completely absorbed men's thoughts.'

An unprecedented number of caricatures and satirical pamphlets appeared in the shops and were sold in the streets. William Hone, George Cruikshank and a host of other satirists and artists championed the Queen and ridiculed the King; while only one printseller ventured to produce loyalist prints. 'The most remarkable aspect of this fierce encounter', wrote Richard Rush, the American Minister in London, 'was the boundless rage of the Press and liberty of speech. Every day produced its thousand fiery libels against the King and his adherents, and as many caricatures, that were hawked in all the streets. This tempest of abuse ... was borne for several months without the slightest attempt to check or punish it.' *

On 17 August the public enquiry began in the House of Lords. The Queen, who had for convenience taken Lady Francis's house in St James's Square, near to Castlereagh's, 'presented herself at the window' in response to the shouts

---

* In fact, the King, excessively sensitive as he was to all forms of ridicule, made many attempts to check the abuse. William Hone claimed to have been offered 'up to £500' for the suppression of 'The Queen's Matrimonial Ladder', a pamphlet which depicted the King in the worst possible light (Rickword, *Radical Squibs and Loyal Ripostes*, 27). Certainly, through Bloomfield, the King bought up the plates and copyrights of particularly offensive prints, and obtained undertakings from artists and dealers not to publish anything else on the same subject. For example he paid George Cruikshank £100 'in consideration of a pledge not to caricature His Majesty in any immoral situation' (RA, 19 June 1820). When it became known that Carlton House was prepared to pay for the suppression of offensive caricatures, however, the number of them naturally increased. Moreover, the pledges were observed more in the letter than in the spirit (BM *Sat*, x, xii, xi–xlvii). Cruikshank's work for William Hone in 1821 displayed the King, if not in an 'immoral situation', as a water scorpion, 'an offensive insect' living 'in stagnant waters, continually watching for prey' and sallying forth 'in search of a companion of the other sex and soon [begetting] an useless generation' (*The Political Showman – at Home!*).

of 'The Queen! The Queen!' from the people in the Square. 'Her appearance called forth from the surrounding multitude the most unbounded marks of applause,' *The Times* reported. 'A short interval only had repassed before the multitude again expressed their wish to see her.' She willingly responded to the calls and appeared once more 'with her wonted dignity'. Soon afterwards she left for the House of Lords in a state carriage drawn by six bays, attended by liveried footmen, cheered by shouts of 'God bless you!' and by protestations of loyalty unto death. 'Alderman Wood preceded her in a carriage and four horses,' the Duke of Wellington noted, 'and his carriage was preceded by a fellow on horseback carrying a *Green Bag*!'

The crowds in the Square that morning and on each subsequent day of the 'trial' – as most people referred to the proceedings in the House – were both noisy and immense. People clambered onto the roofs of carriages and rented standing room in carters' wagons for a shilling a day to catch a glimpse of the Queen as her postilions whipped the horses out of the Square, down King Street, into Pall Mall, and past Carlton House where, to the delight of the mob, the guard presented arms. She was not an appealing sight, though *The Times* loyally reported her as looking 'extremely well': she had grown very fat during her years of exile, and she wore more rouge than ever upon her naturally ruddy cheeks. Her eyebrows were painted black, and long black curls hung down on either side of her face from her wig. Observers noticed that she had taken to adopting a stern and resolute expression which suited her as ill as her favourite hat, a huge, high-crowned black concoction, banded and bowed, and surmounted by an enormous spray of ostrich feathers. In the House she wisely set this hat aside in favour of a big white veil which almost concealed her face and, falling down from her shoulders, disguised the true proportions of the ample bosom in the bodice of her black dress.

As she entered the chamber of the House, where tem-

porary balconies had been erected above the benches to
accommodate the great number of Members who were present, all the peers stood up. Attendance was compulsory
except for Roman Catholics, minors, invalids and those peers
who were either absent from the country or who could
satisfy the Lord Chancellor that a family bereavement entitled them to leave of absence. Despite the recent death of
his Duchess, the Duke of York was there, insisting that he
would be 'ashamed' not to be present to do his duty, 'painful
as it might be'. His brother, the Duke of Sussex, however,
evaded the likelihood of his giving further offence to his
brother by failing to condemn the conduct of his cousin, and
excused himself from attendance on the grounds of his con-
sanguinity to them both.

The proceedings were opened by the Duke of Leinster
who rose 'and said in a purely Irish tone that, without
making an elaborate speech, and for the purpose of bringing his business to a conclusion, he should move' that the
order for the second reading of the Bill of Pains and Penalties should be rescinded. Only forty-one peers out of the 247
present agreed with him, and even these, nearly all of them
Whigs, mostly voted so not out of any conviction as to the
Queen's innocence but as a protest against the government's
ineptitude in endeavouring to prove her guilt. A majority
of the leading Whig peers, including Lansdowne, Derby,
Spencer, Erskine, Grey and Fox's lifelong friend, Fitzwilliam, voted against Leinster's motion; and subsequently
Grey, the most influential of these – presumably in the hope
that the Queen might be encouraged to negotiate if made to
stand trial on such a charge – asked for a legal opinion as to
whether the Queen might be held guilty of high treason
notwithstanding the circumstances of her alleged adultery.
After a brief deliberation the judges declared that 'there
was no statute law or law of the land touching the Queen's
case', and so the way now lay open for Brougham to contend that the Bill of Pains and Penalties was quite as repug-
nant as a trial for high treason.

Within the past few weeks, Brougham had had no reason
to change his private opinion that his client, whom he found
increasingly dislikeable, was guilty; and the Queen seemed
to suspect this. Certainly she did not trust him. He had been
to see her upon the evening of her return to London, and he
had not impressed her with any confidence in his ability
to prove her innocence. After he had left her, she had commented disapprovingly to Denman, who still doubted that
she was guilty, 'He is afraid.' She tried to persuade Sir
James Scarlett, reputedly the best advocate in England, to
join her list of counsel; but Scarlett tactfully declined her
offer.

Whatever Brougham's apprehensions may have been, however, and despite the disparaging way in which he talked
about her outside the House – 'she is pure *in-no-sense*,' he
said when asked his opinion of her in private – as her Attorney-General before the Lords, he performed his task brilliantly. Even Mme de Lieven – whose sense of propriety was
offended by a 'little attorney', a mere lawyer 'sprung from
the lowest ranks of society', presuming to ridicule the government – had to admit that he had an 'astonishing facility'.
His opening speech was generally considered a masterpiece.
There were those, even amongst dedicated Whigs at
Brooks's, who thought that it was rather tasteless at such a
time to suggest that a Bill of Pains and Penalties ought to
have been brought against the Duke of York in consequence
of his adultery with Mrs Clarke eleven years before; and
there were others who regretted his oblique references to the
King's own 'criminal intercourse'; but most of those who
heard his speech 'allowed it to have been excellent'. Lord
Fitzwilliam deemed it 'a most strong and powerful speech',
though he wondered whether, 'its object being to deprecate
any proceedings', it did not carry too much 'the appearance
of fearing enquiry'.

Fitzwilliam also thought the speech of the Queen's Solicitor-General, Thomas Denman, who supported Brougham

the next day, was equally excellent, 'indeed it was even better', and this in spite of the fact that Denman was suffering from jaundice. It was, in fact, as 'argumentative, impressive and convincing' as could be; 'it made a deep impression on the *whole* House'. Such, in Fitzwilliam's opinion, could not be said of the speeches of either the Attorney-General, Sir Robert Gifford, a plain, shrewd, practical West Countryman, or of the Solicitor-General, John Singleton Copley, the convivial son of the American portrait painter. Indeed, Gifford's speech struck Fitzwilliam as no better than 'a sort of scold', while Copley's was 'a display of theatrical eloquence' which 'produced little effect'.

Fitzwilliam was, of course, listening to the speeches as a confirmed Whig, and his comments did justice neither to Gifford's sound common sense, nor to Copley's effective replies to the Queen's Counsel's eloquent jibes against the King and the royal dukes. But there was no doubt that many supporters of the government as well as most of its Whig opponents agreed with Creevey who wrote from Brooks's on the evening of 18 August, 'The truth is the Law Officers of the Crown are damnably overweighted by Brougham and Denman. ... Nothing can be more triumphant for the Queen than this day altogether.'

The Queen was clearly enjoying to the full her initial triumphs and growing popularity, although the long legal arguments in the House naturally bored her. In the early days of the proceedings she attended quite regularly, sitting on the special chair provided for her within the bar of the House, accompanied by Lady Anne Hamilton who was wearing the thickest and heaviest of veils. But she soon took to spending the greater part of her time in the retiring room which had been provided for her, a room normally reserved for the chairman of committees, where she played backgammon with Alderman Wood. Once she was observed in the House to fall asleep which led to this epigram by Lord Holland:

Her conduct at present no censure affords
She sins not with couriers but sleeps with the Lords.*

While she had been staying at Hammersmith, loyal addresses, presented to her by delegations of earnest supporters, had poured into Brandenburg House from all over the country, from Bath and Bristol, from Nottingham and Norwich, from Leeds and Liverpool; and she replied to them all, under the guidance of Alderman Wood, William Cobbett, and her other advisers, in terms calculated to encourage her admirers to further demonstrations in her support. Now that her trial had begun, she was more popular than ever. Creevey was astonished by the numbers of people who came out into the streets to watch her pass by; where the devil they all came from he could not imagine; by 19 August they were 'prodigiously encreased since the first day'. Mme de Lieven estimated that there were twenty or thirty thousand of them, all of them radicals.

They greeted Ministers with cat-calls and abuse. Wellington was hissed and booed with exceptional vehemence as he rode his horse through the gap in the fence that had been erected around the approaches to the House. 'They look upon him particularly as the Queen's enemy,' Emily Cowper observed. 'I suppose they think he is against everybody's wife as well as his own.' One day upon his return to Apsley House a gang of roadmenders stopped his horse in Grosvenor Place and demanded that he repeat, 'God Save the Queen!' 'Well gentlemen,' he – or some reports say the equally abused Lord Anglesey, or Lord Londonderry or Theodore Hook – replied with characteristic aplomb, 'since you will have it so, God save the Queen – and may all your

---

* She was, of course, irresistible as a butt for such jokes. Lord Norbury, when asked how she had enjoyed herself in Algiers, replied, 'She was as happy as the Dey was long'. When someone wondered what newspaper she read, Norbury said that she 'took in the Courier' (*Greville Diary*, i, 115).

wives be like her.' Castlereagh felt obliged to board up his house in St James's Square and to have his bed installed in the Foreign Office. Mme de Lieven told Metternich that curiosity induced her to drive towards the House where the crowds stopped her, told her to shout the by now obligatory formula, 'Long live the Queen!' and ordered her servants to take off their hats. 'I was in an open carriage,' she wrote. 'My heart beat quickly for a moment; but I put a bold face on it and I did not shout. I had forbidden my servants to take off their hats. The Russian cockade, which has three colours, gave me a certain constitutional look, which was a good thing in the circumstances. A smart touch of the whip set the horses bounding, and I got out of it. ... Five men were killed by the soldiers the day before yesterday in front of the Houses of Parliament. The newspapers say nothing of this; for the Jacobin papers do not want the occurrence, should it become known, to discourage the mob from going to the House, and the Ministerial papers themselves are not anxious to boast about it. The Duke of York told me about it yesterday; he had got it from the military reports. The Duke is the idol of the mob; they are all for the Queen and for him. He frowns and does not bow, because they cheer him by the title of King.' * Fitzwilliam confirmed that the Duke's

---

* According to Emily Cowper, however, the Duke of York was delighted by his reception. She told her brother, Frederick Lamb, 'He is so pleased at [the calls of] "Long live Frederick the 1st" – he bows and bows and rides along with his hat in his hand. I was told the scene was droll yesterday at leaving the House. The Duke of Richmond came out with Anglesey but managed to shrink back before they reached the barrier in Palace Yard. The Duke of York was setting off from the House; the Duke of Wellington hurried after him to go through the mob in his company. The Duke of York, unwilling to lose his cheers, spurred his horse to avoid his joining him – so much for the little vanities of mankind! ... The Duke of Wellington and Anglesey are violently hissed which makes them very angry. The latter made a speech yesterday to the mob, saying if all their mouths were bayonets planted at his heart he should do his duty. This got him a few cheers which I hope will not last, it would make him so elated' (Palmerston Papers, CIV/4/3, 24 August 1820).

popularity had never been higher. He was 'huzzaed every step he took'. So, too, with quite as much enthusiasm, was the Duke of Sussex, while squads of soldiers on parade had been heard to shout to the Duke of Gloucester, 'You ought to be our King!'

Vigorous support for the Queen was now far from being limited to the 'radicals', 'mechanicks', 'artisans' and 'hooligans' whom most observers described as constituting the greater part of the mob that surged around the Houses of Parliament. Thomas Babington Macaulay, then a Cambridge undergraduate, was a passionate Queenite; so, too, to almost wild excess, was General Sir Robert Wilson; so was Coleridge. Byron, too, though much less vehemently, continued to hope that the Queen would win, for she had always been 'very civil' to him. Lady Jersey, of course, was 'absolutely in a raging fever', 'quite frenzied', so 'violent' that she was 'at daggers drawn even with the Holland family' and inveighed 'bitterly against the moderate tone adopted by Lord Grey'.

Nobody could have been more displeased than Lady Jersey by the proceedings in the House of Lords on the day that the first witness, Teodoro Majocchi, gave his evidence. Majocchi was a respectable-looking, well-dressed man – 'very shrewd and cautious', Lord Fitzwilliam thought – and his damning account of the Queen's behaviour caused the deepest dismay to her friends. The Queen herself, indeed, as though only too well aware of the effect his evidence would have, rose to her feet 'with the rapidity of lightening' at the sight of him, raised her veil, and looking fiercely at him as she took a few steps towards him, cried out in a furious tone of voice something that sounded like 'Theodore! Theodore! Oh, no! no!' Others thought that she screamed 'Traditore! Traditore! Oh, no! no!' But George Keppel, who was close to her, could not distinguish any words at all. The exclamation seemed to him 'a paroxysm of madness'. Having made her frenzied objection, whatever it was, she then rushed out of the chamber; she was taken so ill that night that she had to be 'copiously bled'.*

'She was thunderstruck at seeing him,' Mme de Lieven commented. 'It made a very bad impression. She explains it as a start of indignation, at the sight of a witness on whose gratitude she thought she could count. But nobody is deceived about the cause of the start. ... Lord Liverpool immediately sent a messenger to inform the King, treating "Oh Theodore" as a fact of the greatest importance. ... I have not had the heart to read the evidence; it is too disgusting. It the Queen really a woman? And how can the House of Lords, uniting as it does all that is most dignified and most exalted in the greatest nation in the world, lower itself by listening to such vile trash? Was there no other way of treating her as she deserves? Worst of all, how could statesmen have allowed things to come to such a pass? One of the Queen's lawyers put the trial in a nutshell when he called it a solemn farce. ... At Lady Jersey's ... I heard [Brougham] say of some fantastic action ascribed to the Queen: "I can believe in any folly on the part of that woman. We know quite well she is capable of it." ... I am certain [the Bill] will not be passed. Anyway, the Queen is quite mad, and what surprises me is that they don't question the witnesses about that, or at least ask her doctor. If they pronounced her mad they would avoid all this scandal and be nearer the truth besides.'

Two of Brougham's fellow-counsel, Nicholas Tindal and Thomas Wilde, were so disturbed by Majocchi's evidence about the Queen's visits to Pergami's bedroom, her kissing him, his helping her with her bath and the sleeping arrangements aboard the polacca that they both woke him up in the

---

* Enquiries conducted by the Milan Commission had satisfied its members that Majocchi was 'honest' and 'trustworthy' (RA Geo. IV, Box 8, Envelope 8). A letter addressed to the Queen after her death and purporting to be a confession that he had accepted a bribe of '£1,000 English money' to swear falsely against her, a crime for which he was now 'artely sorry', is an obvious forgery (RA Geo. IV, Box 11, 8 November 1821).

middle of the night to offer him their advice as to his conduct of the man's cross-examination the next day. They need not have troubled. Brougham was a brilliant cross-examiner, and his treatment of Majocchi was masterly. By the time he had finished with him, the poor man was so muddled, nervous and unconvincing – 'frightened out of his wits', according to one report – that he seemed capable of giving no other answer than ' I do not remember' to every question that Brougham asked him. '*Questo non mi ricordo.*' '*Non mi ricordo.*' '*Questo non mi ricordo.*' '*Non mi ricordo*', '*Non mi ricordo.*' The answer became a kind of refrain. In the printed record of Majocchi's cross-examination it occurs eighty-seven times. For months afterwards the phrase, *Non mi ricordo*, was just as popular with satirists and caption-writers as ever the green bag had been with caricaturists; and even in mid-Victorian London it was a catchphrase that had not lost its peculiar meaning.

The principal witnesses who immediately followed Majocchi – Gaetano Paturzo, the mate of the vessel on which the Queen had sailed to the Holy Land; Vincenzo Gargiullo, the vessel's master; Meidge Barbara Kress, a chambermaid at one of the inns where the Queen had stayed on her travels; Paolo Raggazzoni, a master mason at Villa d'Este; and Paolo Oggioni, a kitchen help – all provided the Lords with much of the evidence that they had given the Milan Commission, and were, as Lord Fitzwilliam noted, not unduly damaged in cross-examination. Fitzwilliam was convinced that unless the evidence so far given could be contradicted, 'the inference must be adultery'. Lady Cowper thought so too. On 24 August, after the Lords had heard the evidence of Gaetano Paturzo – 'a very good witness' whom '*every* body' thought 'fair and honest and above board' – she decided that the Queen's friends had 'no leg left to stand on'.

After the Italian sailors had been cross-examined, an English naval officer, Thomas Briggs, whose evidence carried more weight with most Members than all the Italians put together, testified that he had taken the Queen from Genoa to Sicily aboard the *Leviathan*, and that she had altered the sleeping arrangements which he had made so that Pergami was provided with a cabin near her own. Briggs's evidence also remained largely undisturbed by the various questions that were put to him.*

When it came to the turn of Louisa Demont, however, the case was quite different. Her examination by the Solicitor-General was convincing enough: she repeated most of her stories about the Queen and Pergami and their presumed love-making, the Queen's abandoned behaviour, and her prurient enjoyment of Pergami's obscene anecdotes. She raised the 'strongest suspicions', so Lord Fitzwilliam told his son, and 'proved the undeniable opportunities for adultery'. But when she was cross-examined by one of Brougham's colleagues, John Williams, her replies were almost as evasive as Majocchi's; one of them, often repeated, was, 'I will not swear it, but I do not recollect it.' It was suggested to her, for instance, that while she was living in London she had passed herself off as Countess Colombiera or Colombrère, which certainly seems to have been the case. But she could not swear to that; she did not recollect it. She did admit, however, that she had been dismissed from the Queen's service for 'saying something about her' – that she was in love with Giuseppi Sacchi – which she afterwards 'confessed to be false'. It also appeared that, after her dismissal, she had written to the Queen asking for 'that forgiveness which alone [could] restore [her] to life', and that she had also written to her half-sister, who was still in the Queen's service,

* In a conversation with Admiral Lord Keith in 1818, Captain Briggs had said that the Princess had objected to his arrangement of the cabins with the words, 'You are a very good captain of a ship but do not understand ladies.' Having rearranged the accommodation so that Pergami's cabin was next to her own, she spent much of the day with him, and, for all Briggs knew, the night as well. He begged Lord Keith not to let his conversation with him go any further; but Keith felt he could not withhold it from Bloomfield to whom he communicated these 'facts so extraordinary' (RA Geo. IV, Box 8, 13 April 1818).

in praise of her Majesty's virtues. When asked if she had used such phrases as 'august Princess' and 'generous bene-factress' which were contained in these letters, she replied, again, 'I will not swear because I am not sure of it ... I do not recollect whether I have made use of them; I wrote fre-quently to my sister; and I do not recollect the expressions.' She was also unable to say with any certainty that the hand-writing was hers.

Thomas Creevey was delighted by this evidence from the *chienne* Demont who was 'fifty times nearer the devil' on the second day of her cross-examination than she had been on the first; she had turned out to be everything that one could have wished for; it was all 'most infernally damaging for the prosecution'.

The witnesses who followed Mlle Demont, however, were far more damaging to the Queen than to the prosecution. There was a mason to tell of his seeing Pergami sitting with his arm round the Queen when she was bare to the waist; there was a gardener to tell of their kissing; there was Sacchi to swear what he had seen the Queen and Pergami doing behind the curtains of their carriage. There was, in fact, as Creevey was forced to conclude with regret on the evening of 4 September, after eleven witnesses had been examined in a single day, 'much *dirt* and some *damage* certainly'.

A good deal of further damage was promised by the Attorney-General when the next batch of his witnesses arrived; but on 7 September he felt obliged to close his evi-dence as there was strong doubt that they ever would arrive. Terrified by reports of what had happened to previous wit-nesses on their landing at Dover, they had refused to con-tinue their journey beyond Beauvais and had scurried back to Italy where reports of the 'Dover massacre' were spread far and wide by the Pergami family and their friends. It was said that Italians had been set upon and severely wounded by the wild Englishmen of Dover, that Sacchi had been assassinated, Demont imprisoned for life, and that Queen Caroline, now placed upon the throne, had given orders for the arrest of all those who had given evidence against her.

It was true that witnesses against the Queen had been abused by the people of Dover and that some of them had been stoned on the road; yet this had been interpreted in Italy, so Colonel Browne complained, 'as the decided execration of a whole nation'. The King's advisers had therefore considered it necessary to ask Giuseppe Rastelli, the Milan Commission's courier, to return to Italy to assure the worried families of the witnesses that no harm would come to them in England. His efforts had not so far been successful.

Among the witnesses who refused to go to England was one who might well have proved to be the most damaging of all. This was Jacinto Greco, a Calabrian who had worked as cook in the Princess's household during her stay in Sicily. According to a former employer, interviewed by the Milan Commission, he had an 'excellent character'; and one Innocenza Biancha, 'a most respectable merchant of Syracuse', also spoke very highly of him.

In the statement he gave to the Commission, Greco claimed to have seen the Princess and Pergami *in flagrante delicto* on a sofa in the saloon of their Sicilian palazzo. But when asked to go to England to repeat this story Greco firmly refused. His wife had been told that if he did so his head would be cut off by the English mob, and he appeared to believe it. In no circumstances was he prepared to leave Italy.

34

'The Queen For Ever!'
1820

'The town is literally drunk with joy'

WHILE Rastelli was endeavouring to persuade the reluctant witnesses to return with him to England, the Queen's agents in Italy were busily trying to collect evidence with which to refute their testimony. These agents had found several people willing to testify to the effect that they had seen nothing in the Queen's behaviour to suggest impropriety; but one of the agents, Samuel Fyson, was 'very worried', so he confessed to the Queen's solicitor, Henry Vizard, about the witnesses' 'quality'. Most of them were no more credible than the worst of the witnesses that the King's agents had managed to produce. The prosecution had got up their evidence 'badly', but he feared that the defence's would be *worse*. Nor did Fyson think that his colleague, Jabez Henry, had examined the witnesses carefully enough. Admittedly everything had had to be done in a great hurry, as so little time had been allowed for the preparation of the defence, but Henry had made only the briefest enquiries into the characters of the people whom he had examined and passed as suitable candidates to stand as witnesses. Worse than this, he had paid out huge sums of money which the prosecution, if they discovered them, could easily represent as bribes. There had been much talk of bribes being offered to prosecution witnesses; but the defence were much more open to criticism on that head. 'It is undoubtedly necessary sometimes to bribe a man (if I may use that term) to leave his country,' Tyson concluded in his frank letter to

Vizard. 'But I hear of very large sums having been given and I dread the exposure.'

In fact, the King's agents were well aware of the large sums being offered to potential defence witnesses. £10,000 had been made available to Vizard by the Treasury; and a further £20,000 was paid to him in December 1820. But it was believed that the Queen's friends had many other sources of supply. Colonel Browne reported to Powell that 1,600 louis d'or had been offered to Cardinal Albani by Torlonia, the Roman banker, to persuade him to go to England to speak for the Queen. 'There is some *strong secret fund* at work somewhere or another,' Powell believed. Money was being 'thrown about in abundance'. Jabez Henry was living in an apartment costing fifty louis d'or a month, and his courtyard was constantly full of servants, agents and couriers. Despite this he had not 'so far got any persons except bad characters to agree to give evidence in England', Browne reported to Joseph Planta, an official at the Foreign Office, 'a bad lot, of the same class as ours. . . . I fear however that they will make much use of certain difficulties still thrown in their way as to passports, vexations to us in fact and not to them.' *

James Brougham (who was himself paid £2,500 for his expenses while in Italy) agreed that Jabez Henry was paying too much to too many witnesses. 'I did all in my power to prevent this new shoal of witnesses from being sent,' he

* As soon as the government heard of these complaints by the Queen's agents and of 'the obstacles interposed in Italy to the departure of witnesses', Castlereagh wrote to Lord Stewart, British Ambassador in Vienna: 'I lost no time in representing to Prince Metternich the propriety and indeed the necessity of regarding every application which Mr Henry, Her Majesty's acknowledged law agent, may have made or may make to the Austrian Government in the same light and in the same force as if it were made by Mr Brougham or by the Queen herself: His Majesty's Government being extremely anxious that every possible facility should be afforded to Her Majesty for procuring all the evidence she may think necessary during the progress of these proceedings' (RA Geo. IV, Boxes, 11, 11 September 1820 and 13, 15 September 1820).

reported to Vizard on 28 October, 'but the fear of displeasing the Queen who asked them to go operated on Mr Henry's mind as to let them. ... They are totally useless. ... Allow me to hint to you privately that Pergami has been spending money among people of no earthly use at Pesaro.' One of these people, in particular, was a woman of notorious character, and what on earth was the good of having a 'woman from Italy speaking to character when she herself is the very worst in every way?' Moreover, his brother had 'very strongly impressed upon him' the danger of there being any imputation of bribery. 'He says nothing could be more fatal to the defence than its coming out that the slightest bribery had been employed,' Brougham warned Jabez Henry, 'and both Pergami and his brother may from unwise zeal have done this – caution them for the future. ... I need not say that bribing people to keep away from the other side is equally bad. This cannot be too strongly impressed on all concerned.'

Undeterred by criticism, Jabez Henry continued to assemble his 'shoals of witnesses' in accordance with the Queen's instructions. He got former servants of hers to depose that they had never seen the Queen and Pergami in each other's arms, that they had never observed any familiarity in the Queen's bedroom nor any indecent behaviour at the Queen's balls, that the mulatto servant was thrown out of the room when he began his obscene dance, that the Queen and Pergami never sat next to each other in her carriage but always face to face. Jabez Henry found fishermen and gardeners, carpenters and masons who were all prepared to swear that, so far as they had been able to observe, the Queen was – as Thomas Denman, in his opening address, had said she was – 'as pure as unsunned snow'. Giovanni Battista dell' Orto, a young man of twenty-two, living with his father, a baker, provided this characteristic testimony: 'Without hope of gain he is ready to prove: That going two or three times a day (being the baker's son) to her Majesty's Palace [at Como] he never saw anything that would injure her reputation, but she was always dignified in her manner and decently dressed, whether walking, riding on a donkey or in her carriage.'

But James Brougham had to confess that he was not in the least convinced by all these witnesses. 'The more I have examined the case,' he reported to Vizard, 'the less I think our answer to it will depend on any evidence we can hope to have even if one had a year – but it is very strong indeed on theirs.'

It was all very well for Lady Charlotte Lindsay's brother, Lord Guilford, who had seen a good deal of the Queen when she first arrived in Italy, to say that there was 'nothing unusual' in the behaviour of the Queen towards Pergami, 'except the advancement of the individual'. For there were quite as many English witnesses who said exactly the opposite, Lord de Clifford and Lady Clavering amongst them. And it was all very well for the Queen's agents to produce men who claimed that attempts had been made to bribe them to give evidence against her. For there was just as much evidence on the other side – most of it equally unreliable – purporting to show that attempts had been made to bribe witnesses in the Queen's defence.

Admittedly the Queen's representatives were constantly receiving letters disparaging the prosecution witnesses. One William Hughes, a bank clerk in Gloucester, who had known Teodoro Majocchi when he had been in service there, wrote to say that Majocchi had always maintained that the Queen was 'most respectable'. A certain Harvey Warburton informed Vizard that both the Captain and mate of the polacca were 'well known for their roguery to the House of Claude Scott', importers of grain; and Captain Gargiullo's roguery was confirmed in a letter to Alderman Wood by Benedetto Salomone, a former captain in the Italian legion. But then, the King's representatives received quite as many letters in disparagement of the defence witnesses, and many more from people who claimed to be able to prove the Queen's 'indecent familiarity' or 'disgraceful intimacy' with Pergami, yet did not wish to come forward in person 'in the present state of public feeling'.

James Brougham was particularly disillusioned with Pergami. Far from being the *remarkably good sort of man* he had at first supposed him to be, he was, in fact, 'a very great liar', almost as bad as his brother, Louis, who was 'the greatest rascal unhung'. Both Samuel Fyson and Jabez Henry were inclined to agree with this estimate. Fyson advised Vizard that Pergami was certainly 'not a *gentleman*' who ought to be produced as a witness: 'He is naturally of a hasty and thoughtless disposition, at the same time that he is extremely impatient. In several instances he has made statements inconsistent with what have proved to be the facts ... I should not be inclined to make him a witness unless it became indispensably necessary. ... He is loose-headed and impetuous and would certainly lose his temper.' As for his brother 'his *very looks* would damn the whole family'.

Assured by the blithely confident Jabez Henry that the witnesses he was so cursorily examining were going to 'expose the machinations' of her enemies, the Queen remained the heroine of the London mob, who raced after her every morning as she drove to the House, shouting for joy when 'she directed the barouche to be thrown open' so that they could see her better. The evidence presented in the Lords had not in the least diminished her popularity, although, as Lord Liverpool confided to Canning, the case as now proved against her was in 'certainty a very strong one'.

On the day that the Attorney-General had closed his evidence for the prosecution, she sailed triumphantly down the Thames in her state barge. Lord Erskine, who watched the procession from Blackfriars Bridge, estimated that as many as 200,000 people had collected to see her. There was not a single vessel in the river that did not hoist its colours and man its yards in her honour; and the watermen, who were 'all her partisans', were with the greatest difficulty prevented

from destroying the hulk which had been anchored near
Parliament Stairs as an added protection for the Italian witnesses who had been herded together for their safety in a
guarded house in Cotton Garden.

A few days later, while writing a letter to Miss Ord at
Brooks's, Thomas Creevey heard 'a noise of hurraing and
shouting in the street'. He 'ran out to see the *Navy of England* marching to Brandenburg House with an address to
the Queen'. 'I have seen nothing like this before – nothing
approaching to it,' he continued. 'There were thousands of
seamen, all well dressed, all sober – the best looking, the
finest men you could imagine. Every man had a new white
silk or satin cockade in his hat. They had a hundred colours,
at least, or pieces of silk, with sentiments upon them such as
"Protection to the Innocent".'

Soon after this the Queen 'received eleven more addresses,
accompanied in each case by a deputation of several thousand people carrying banners with the most subversive inscription', Mme de Lieven recorded. 'With all one hears and
reads, it is difficult to believe that there are still a King and
a Government in this country. Just now, as I was passing by
our stables, I read, written in large letters on the wall: "The
Queen for ever, the King in the river!" All the walls in town
are scrawled over with nice things of this kind. I can't tell
you what horrible faces one sees nowadays in the streets and
the main roads and how insolently they come up and bawl in
one's ear, "The Queen for ever!"' But, as Creevey said, it
was not only the poorer classes who demonstrated their support of the Queen and their antagonism towards the Bill:
'The entire middle order of people are against it.' Indeed her
cause was warmly adopted by everyone who was in opposition to the King and the government. 'Well, Robinson, you
are a Queenite, I hope?' Coleridge asked his friend, Henry
Crabb Robinson. 'Indeed, I am not,' Robinson replied. 'How
is that possible?' 'I am only an anti-Kingite.' 'That's just
what I mean.' 'There is no denying it, the feeling of the
people is almost everywhere in favour of the Queen,' Lady

Cowper confirmed, 'not merely the rabble, but the respectable middle ranks. All their prejudices are in her favour.
They hate the King, disapprove of his moral conduct and
think all foreigners are liars and villains.'

As though intoxicated by the partisan adulation accorded
her and by the prospects before her, the Queen became more
and more provocative in her declarations and in her answers
to the addresses that came pouring into Brandenburg House.
She was 'as full of revenge as careless of crime', Plumer
Ward was assured; she was going the way of Catherine the
Great, a favourite heroine of hers, who 'by means of the
Guards, murdered her husband and usurped the throne'. She
herself announced that that was her exact intention. By God,
she said, she 'would blow him off his throne'. It was a possibility that Henry Brougham, for one, did not consider at all
unlikely.

Brougham opened his defence on 3 October with a speech
which Creevey concluded was 'a most magnificent address,
nothing but perfection', and which Charles Greville
thought 'the most magnificent display of argument and ora-
tory that had been heard for years'. It does not read so well
now: its rhetoric seems strained, its sincerity suspect, but
there was no doubt of its success with his contemporaries.
Lord Fitzwilliam, for one, was convinced that Brougham
had 'shewn incontestibly' that 'one and all of the Italian witnesses' were perjured. 'The *monde* at Brooks's talked of nothing but Brougham and his fame, and the comers-in from
White's said the same feeling was equally strong there.' His
speech had 'not only astonished' but had 'shaken the aristocracy'. Denman considered it 'one of the most powerful
orations that ever proceeded from human lips'. Lord Erskine
was so overcome by it that he burst into tears.

Brougham's initial triumph was somewhat overcast, however, when his witnesses appeared. Lord Guilford, the first
of these, struck Creevey as 'the most ramshackle fellow you
ever saw', 'a kind of *non mi ricordo* likewise'; the next was

that boring old gossip, Lord Glenbervie; the third was Lady Charlotte Lindsay. The evidence of both Glenbervie and Lady Charlotte was favourable enough, but neither was able to convey any personal affection for the Queen whom – as their diaries made clear when published years later – they did not, in fact, much like. On examination, Lady Charlotte was obliged to disclose that she had spent no more than twenty-four days with the Queen at the beginning of her stay in Italy; and on cross-examination by the Solicitor-General, who used her, in Lord Fitzwilliam's words, as he would 'a shoplifter at the Old Bailey', she admitted that she might have said that she would have quitted the Queen's service far sooner even than this had she not badly needed the salary. Eventually she burst into tears. The King protested that he never thought he 'should have lived to witness so much prevarication, so much lying, and so much wilful and convenient forgetfulness' as Lady Charlotte had displayed in her examination. And it is certainly true that her evidence gave a very different impression from the private letters she wrote home when on the Continent.

The next witnesses, however, were much more confident and convincing than these early ones. Keppel Craven was 'as distinct and favourable as possible', Sir William Gell 'still more so'. Indeed, by the time Gell stood down, having sworn that upon his honour he never once saw the Queen speak to Pergami except on matters of business in all the three months he spent with them, Lord Fitzwilliam felt bound to conclude that he did not see how Ministers could now proceed with the Bill. 'But if they do, and carry it through the House of Lords,' he told his son, Lord Milton, in one of a long series of letters which were written regularly throughout the proceedings and which accurately reflect the almost daily changes of mood in the House, as witnesses came and went, contradicting each other, swaying opinion now this way, now that, 'I do seriously believe that they will pull down the House of Lords about our ears. In short the tenor of this day's evidence goes far to make me doubt of any crime: it is a foul conspiracy hatched under the wing of an ambitious lawyer, and brooded over by a wicked commission in Milan.'

Fitzwilliam's fellow Whig, Thomas Creevey, agreed with him: 'Gell, cross-examined and examined by the Lords, left everything still more triumphant for the Queen; so much so that Pelham [a friend of the King, and Bishop of Exeter] and a few other bishops are gone home to cut their throats. Lord Enniskillen has just said in my hearing that the Ministers ought to be damned for coming out with such a case. ... The town is literally drunk with joy at this unparalleled triumph of the Queen. There is no doubt now in any man's mind, except Lauderdale's, that the whole thing has been a conspiracy for money.'

The supporters of the Bill naturally took a different view. 'The opposition affect to consider the Bill as completely defeated,' Mrs Arbuthnot wrote. 'But *we*, on the contrary, feel that no real way has been made as the witnesses as yet have not contradicted any of ours. The Duke of Wellington called on me and told me he thought he had got a clue for exposing the perjuries of Sir William Gell who swore he had never seen any improper conduct in the Queen. The Duke had been sitting for our picture to Lawrence who told him that [Sir Thomas Freeman] Heathcote (the former member for Hampshire) had said that Sir William Gell's evidence was so disgraceful and so in direct opposition to the abusive language he had always held about the Queen that he for one, though a former friend, would never speak to him again.'

By the evening of the next day it certainly appeared that the evidence given by Gell and Keppel Craven was far from reliable. The witness responsible for this change of feeling in the House was an Anglo-Irishman, Lieutenant Flynn RN, known to the Queen – never unduly concerned with the niceties of rank or nomenclature – as Captain Fling and Captain Flint. Great store had been set by this man's evidence: as the Prime Minister told the King, if he should deny the facts to which the prosecution witnesses had deposed 'whether truly or falsely (provided it was done with constancy)' it would be impossible to answer for the consequences.

Lieutenant Flynn had been in command of the polacca of which Vincenzo Gargiullo had been the 'working' captain. He denied most of what Gargiullo and the mate had said, both about the tent on deck and the bath in the cabin; but in cross-examination he floundered so much – maintaining that, although he did not think Pergami slept under the tent with the Princess, he did not know where he did sleep – that it was difficult to credit any part of his evidence. At one point during his cross-examination Copley felt sure he was lying. He stared at him so hard that 'he fainted away and was taken out of court'.

Flynn 'is mad', Creevey decided after this lamentable performance. 'He has perjured himself three or four times over, and his evidence and himself are both gone to the devil. He is evidently a crack-brained sailor.'

'Undoubtedly the whole of his evidence' would have to be thrown overboard, Fitzwilliam told his son. But an even worse witness was yet to come. This was another Lieutenant in the Royal Navy, Joseph Robert Hownam, the son of a royal page, and a young man to whom the Queen had taken a fancy when he was a boy, paying for his education, having him to stay with her at Kensington Palace and supplying him with money 'all along very liberally'. She had arranged for him to join the Navy in which he had served in the *Africaine* under Captain Manby, the officer with whom the Queen was alleged to have had an affair at the time of the 'Delicate Investigation' in 1806. Hownam had been asked to join the Queen in Genoa in 1815 when she was thinking of going to Africa, and had been of her party when she sailed to the Holy Land.

He had hoped to help his patroness by coming over from France, where he was then living, but his answers to questions put to him during his examination and cross-examination damaged her cause severely:

'Where did her Royal Highness sleep on the voyage from Jaffa homewards?'

'Under the tent on deck.'

'By whose direction was the tent put up?'

'By direction of the Princess.'

'What was the occasion of her Royal Highness sleeping under the tent during the return voyage?'

'In consequence of the excessive heat, and the [smell of the] animals on board [in the hold].'

'You have said that you did not know where Pergami slept; upon your oath do you not believe he slept under the tent?'

'I have heard he did sleep under the tent.'

'I do not wish to know what you have heard.'

'And I believe he did sleep under the tent.'

'As you are a married man, would you have any objection, or conceive it improper that Mrs Hownam should so sleep in a tent in the dark with a male person?'

'I trust that every man looks upon his wife without making any comparison or exception; I never made the comparison.'

'Do you say that you see no impropriety ... in a male and female sleeping so placed in such a tent?'

'I do not conceive there was any impropriety in the thing, because I must have felt it, and I did not feel it; I have seen so many situations that her Royal Highness has been placed in, in the course of her travels, that I do not look upon it as improper.'

By the time that Copley and Gifford had finished with Lieutenant Hownam, 'all unprejudiced men' seemed to think, so Charles Greville said, that the evidence was 'sufficiently proved'. Both the Duke of Portland and Lord Harewood declared themselves satisfied that the case against the Queen had been 'made out'. The fact had been 'proved', and all further proceedings were useless. Lord Lonsdale was 'vehement as to the *proved* guilt of the Queen'.

Within the next few days, however, opinion began to change once again. The defence were able to cast grave, though unfounded, suspicion upon the methods used by the Milan Commission in collecting their evidence and to persuade many Members to believe that Giuseppe Rastelli, the Commission's courier, had been guilty of suborning witnesses for the prosecution. Demands were made for Rastelli to be re-examined on this point; and the defence were able to make much of the fact that he was not available, having been sent back to Italy to allay the fears of the witnesses who had fled from Beauvais.

In the absence of Rastelli, John Allan Powell, the Lincoln's Inn solicitor who had been a member of the Milan Commission, was summoned to the bar of the House. He explained his reasons for sending Rastelli back to Italy: 'I learned that various reports were propagated in Italy of the dangers which the witnesses for the Bill ran, by coming over to this country. I had heard that reports were propagated in Italy that they had received great personal injuries. I had heard that the families of those persons who were here were exceedingly anxious upon the subject of their relations who were in this country. I had understood Rastelli to be acquainted with the greater part of the families of those persons, and I considered that it would be an act of humanity to those relations and friends, that [he] ... should report to [them] what their situation really was.'

When the Chancellor asked counsel if they had any questions to ask Mr Powell, Brougham suddenly stood up and said intently, 'My Lords, I wish to ask the witness one question. "Who is your client or employer in this case?"'

To cries of 'Order! Order!' the witness was directed to withdraw. So far the King's name had not been mentioned in this connection. But Brougham was determined to bring it in by implication. He insisted that he had a right to know whose agent Powell was, to be informed against whom he was contending, against the government or against some 'shadowy figure' standing behind them. Not knowing who the party was against whom he appeared, he could not 'fix him with any character', Brougham complained; he could not 'trace his lineaments'. 'I know nothing about this shrouded, this mysterious being – this retiring phantom, this uncertain shape,' he continued to the obvious amusement of many peers in the Chamber, and then, in a quotation from *Paradise Lost* suggested to him by Spencer Perceval's son, he drew a malevolent parallel between the King and the powers of darkness:

> If shape it might be called that shape had none
> Distinguishable in member, joint or limb;
> Or substance might be called that shadow seemed,
> For each seemed either ...
> ... What seemed his head
> The likeness of a Kingly crown had on.

The King found the insult impossible to forgive. 'He said that I might at least have spared him the attack on his shape,' Brougham recorded. 'He thought that everybody allowed that whatever faults he might have, his legs were not as I had described them.' It was several years before the King could bring himself to allow Brougham – to whom he afterwards refused to speak – to progress in his profession and to admit him to the ranks of King's Counsel.

The case was now nearing its close. Further attempts were made to show that people had been bribed to appear against the Queen, further witnesses appeared to suggest that, after all, the Queen's behaviour had been 'most regular'. And, although it was difficult to overcome the bad impression left by Flynn and Hownam, some ground was made up. By 19 October Lord Fitzwilliam was firmly of the opinion that a majority of his fellow peers agreed with him in thinking that the Bill ought not to pass. There had been a meeting of the government's supporters, including Lord Harewood, two nights before, 'when they came to a resolution of not supporting the Bill, and several have given Lord Liverpool intimation that he must not expect their support on this occasion. ... Nevertheless, don't imagine,' Fitzwilliam warned Lord Milton, 'that all, or that a majority of our House are ready to put an end to the Bill: the very contrary, they still adhere to the Ministers, and however ill

they think of the measure, their first consideration is the pre-
servation of the Ministers, and by this feeling they regulate
their conduct.'

On 24 October Denman began to sum up the evidence on
the Queen's behalf in a speech which Lady Harrowby considered was 'in a higher and more *creditable* style than
Brougham's'. It was an excellent speech, Fitzwilliam agreed,
illustrated 'with beautiful remarks; his conclusion was beyond all description fine'. This opinion of Denman's conclusion was not, however, widely shared; and Denman himself
afterwards profoundly regretted it. For having declared that
he knew of no example of a *Christian* King who had thought
himself at liberty to divorce his wife for misconduct when
his own misconduct in the first instance was the occasion of
her fall, but that he found a parallel in the history of Imperial Rome in the case of Nero, Denman went on to quote
in Greek the reply of one of Octavia's servants to someone
who had tried to suborn her on behalf of the Emperor: 'My
mistress's vagina is purer than your mouth.'

This angered the King even more than Brougham's references to Satan; and Denman felt obliged to submit a most
humble apology explaining his distress that a quotation
which he had intended to apply to Giuseppe Rastelli should
have been taken to apply to the King. The King accepted
the apology, and eventually agreed to Denman's elevation
in his profession but, as in the case of Brougham, he refused
ever to speak to him again.

If this misguided quotation of Denman's temporarily
harmed his own future, his final quotation harmed the
Queen. For having insisted that she was quite innocent of
the charges brought against her, he concluded with Christ's
words to the adulterous woman: 'If no accuser can come
forward to condemn thee, neither do I condemn thee: go,
and sin no more.'

This was, of course, too good an opportunity for the
Queen's enemies to miss, and it was not long before these
lines were quoted everywhere:

> Most gracious Queen, we thee implore
> To go away and sin no more;
> Or if that effort be too great,
> To go away at any rate.

In his reply to the Queen's counsel, the Attorney-General was shrewd and matter-of-fact rather than emotive. He could not enliven his speech 'with the eloquence of his learned friends, nor scatter over it those flowers of imagination in which they had indulged'. But his speech was, perhaps, all the more effective for that; and he was content to leave it to Copley to reply to Denman in Denman's manner.

Copley made much of the defence's failure to call as a witness Pergami's sister, a lady described by one of their witnesses, Lord Guilford, as 'very modest, not particularly vulgar' – 'the precise shades of distinction could not be accurately marked'. For, if anyone could swear to the Queen's innocence, surely she could? *

Copley also took trouble to ridicule the 'very singular' argument that because no one had seen her aboard the polacca with her dress taken off, 'it was to be concluded that there had been no criminality. Was a proposition so monstrous ever urged before any tribunal, more especially before such a tribunal as this?' The Queen had been seen looking out of her tent in a morning-gown, and it appeared that the dress of the other party was a loose Tunisian robe. If such obstructions as these were effectual, 'what,' Copley wanted to know, 'was to become of population? Formerly it

---

* All Brougham's colleagues had wanted to call Countess Oldi, realizing how much the prosecution would make of their failure to do so. But Brougham, knowing her to be as inveterate a liar as her brother, dared not do so. He feared that 'she would lie without scruple'. Brougham also feared that Mariette Brun, Louisa Demont's half-sister, would be an unreliable witness, and he dared not call her either. In his letter to the Queen telling her that he had decided not to call them, he did not mention the real reasons for his decision but said merely that he had thought it better to close the case 'at a very favourable opportunity' (R A Geo. IV, Box 11, 23 October 1820).

had been said that a hooped and whale-boned petticoat was insufficient. ... Was it credible that the Queen's morning-gown had made a stouter resistance?'

On 2 November the proceedings entered their final phase with a summing up by the Lord Chancellor, Lord Eldon, who was himself satisfied that adultery had taken place aboard the polacca, or at least that 'there were sufficient cir-cumstances to lead a plain man to infer it'. Eldon went on to condemn Brougham, who had throughout the progress of the case treated their Lordships with undisguised disdain, for having suggested in his opening speech for the defence that if their judgement went against the Queen, it would be an act that 'would return to them upon their own heads'. 'Whether an advocate be right in using such language or not,' Eldon said, 'you will allow me to observe, my Lords, that it ought to have no effect upon you. ... For myself, if I had not a minute longer to live, I would say to your Lord-ships, "Be just and fear not".'

Eldon was followed by Lord Erskine who, despite his close friendship with the King, was a strong opponent of the Bill, and voiced his disapproval with a vigour too extreme for his age and health. After some minutes 'his voice suddenly ceased ... and he fell forward senseless on the table'. On his recovery he returned to his attack on the Bill with more vehemence than ever, maintaining that it was supported by 'perjury, and perjury alone', and that the 'character of that perjury proved the perfect innocence of her Majesty'.

Lord Grey, in a much less impassioned speech, agreed that the Queen ought to be declared not guilty. 'He fairly avowed that in the outset his prejudices and feelings were unfavour-able to the Queen: he did think it possible that a case would be made out that would compel him to vote, however reluc-tantly, in support of the Bill; but as it now stood, viewing it first as a question of guilt or innocence, and, next, as a matter of political expediency, he was bound to declare that he could never lay down his head in tranquillity in future if

he did not do his utmost to resist its progress.' When Grey
had finished several peers went down to the bench where he
was sitting, 'squeezed his arm and said, "beautiful"'.

It was this matter of 'political expediency' to which Grey
referred that seemed uppermost in the mind of most peers
who subsequently spoke in opposition to the Bill. Lord
Ellenborough, for example, said that he would vote against
it because of 'the strong and almost universal feeling which
existed against it'; but he could not pass over the Queen's
conduct 'without censure'; in her duty of setting the kind of
example expected of a Queen of England she had 'utterly
failed'. It was a view which was widely shared by Whigs and
Tories alike. Grantham spoke for many of them when he
declared that he felt bound to vote against the Bill, but he
could not put his hand on his heart and say, 'Not Guilty'. In
letters to Lord Milton, Lord Althorpe expressed a similar
view: 'I have no respect for the Queen whatever. ... She is a
woman of the most infamous character. ... I believe her to
be guilty, though I do not think it has been anything like
proved. ... My father and mother [Earl and Countess Spen-
cer] are stout anti-Queenites, and indeed my mother seems
almost to forget she is in opposition. ... I myself should have
very little satisfaction in voting the Queen innocent ... I
most fervently wish that the Bill will be thrown out.'

While the Lords continued to discuss her conduct in the
House, the Queen was greeted with shouts as enthusiastic
as ever when she appeared outside it. On the day that
Brougham had brought her defence to a close there was an
enormous procession through the streets, 'made up of some
thousands of men on foot and in carriages, the pedestrians
marching gravely two by two, carrying inscribed banners:
"Virtue triumphs!", "Down with the conspirators!", "Non
mi ricordo" and shouting "Hurrah!" Next came the guild of
workers in crystal. Two hundred masters and apprentices
were each carrying in procession on the end of a fork some
specimen of their handiwork – a crown, a sceptre, vases, urns

... all of the very finest workmanship. In the distance, the effect produced was that of walking diamonds; the sun glittered on it; it was really beautiful. Next came the bakers displaying samples of their trade; [then came] the Quakers, accompanied by their wives and daughters – the most moral people in England.'

Almost every day there was a procession such as this. On 25 October, Sir Willoughly Gordon was 'quite sure he saw 40,000 people, with banners, pass through Piccadilly on their way to the Queen'. On 30 October there was a magnificent display by the brassfounders, and Thomas Creevey had 'no notion there had been so many beautiful brass ornaments in all the world. Their men in armour, both horse and foot, were capital; nor was their humour amiss. The procession closed with a very handsome crown borne in state as a present to the Queen, preceded by a flag with the words – "The Queen's Guard are Men of Metal".' Creevey was 'quite sure there must have been 100,000 people in Piccadilly, all in the most perfect order'. He was thankful that they *were* in perfect order. He would not like anyone to tell him, he admitted, what would happen next if these 'organised armies' that marched through the streets four or five abreast should ever lose their temper.

The Queen was still just as eagerly supported by the 'solid middle classes' as by the mob, Mme de Lieven assured Prince Metternich. 'You have to see for yourself what the Queen's escort is like to get an accurate notion of the cheering and the people who cheer. The streets are full of well-dressed men and respectable women, all waving their hats and their handkerchiefs. You see the real mob, too ... but they are certainly not in the majority. All this shows only too clearly how unpopular the King is and what the people think of his behaviour, and how convinced they are that any woman who was protected and proclaimed guiltless by the venerable George III is bound to be the victim of calumny and vile persecution under George IV. You have to take this into account in trying to understand the inexplicable things that are taking place. ... Yesterday, the Queen received thirty addresses; meanwhile, she is on trial, and the King is in hiding.'

Towards the end of the month, Whig ladies began to call on the Queen, to the appalled dismay of Mrs Arbuthnot who could not believe that any woman of good conduct would 'condescend to notice a person who [had] been proved to have slept for five weeks with her menial servant'. For the past month Lord Fitzwilliam had been attempting 'to prepare people for the step, even *before* the overthrow of the Bill'. 'We ought all, ladies as well as men,' he told his son, 'to write our names at the Queen's door.' His wife, 'a great lady of the most impeccable reputation', was the first to go, and cleared the way for others to follow her. Lady Jersey, not content with a mere courtesy call, went about 'wearing the Queen's portrait round her neck', and was, as Lady Harrowby said, 'longing to fly into her arms and to pay her every possible honour and attention'. Prince Leopold also called on her, though, in his case, it was felt that he had been driven to it by 'mere cowardice'. 'He ought to have made this gesture on the day of her arrival in England, or not at all,' Mme de Lieven thought. 'No doubt he is afraid of the mob. If he had gone at once, he would perhaps have been wrong as regards his relation with the King; but it would have been to show courage and act on principle; for, after all, the Queen is the mother of his wife. ... She sent him away without seeing him, and quite right too.'

The redoubtable Mme de Lieven herself certainly did not lack courage in facing the mob. 'I was driving to Bond Street,' she recorded, 'when I met the Queen in a state coach with six horses, being led at a walking pace, and escorted as usual by some hundreds of scallywags. As soon as they saw my carriage, they stopped it and ordered my servants to take off their hats, and me to let the window down. Neither I nor my servants obeyed. I was surrounded by people shouting abuse, whistling and booing. Meanwhile, the Queen passed by throwing me a withering glance. I saw two enor-

mous black eyebrows, as big as two of my fingers put together: the contents of two pots of rouge on her cheeks: and
a veil over everything. She looks completely brazen.'

The speeches in the House were at last concluded on the
afternoon of 6 November, and the voting on the Bill of
Pains and Penalties took place. Each peer was asked to say
'Content' or 'Not content'. Ninety-five peers voted 'Not content'; 123 were 'Content'. The usually large government
majority was cut to twenty-eight, and such a majority on a
matter of state, as Grey commented, was 'tantamount to a
defeat'. Grenville thought that the Bill would now have to be
abandoned; Liverpool was inclined to agree; other members
of the Cabinet, including Lord Sidmouth, objected; and it
was eventually decided that if the majority fell below ten,
then the Bill would be withdrawn. The rejoicing that night
in the streets was wilder than ever; the mob bore Brougham
in triumph to Brooks's.

The next day the House considered the question whether
or not the divorce clause should be deleted from the Bill.
On this the division was a curious one. Ministers hoped that
by dropping the divorce clause they might push the Bill
through more comfortably; and most of the bishops also
wanted to drop the clause as it sidetracked the jurisdiction
of the ecclesiastical courts. All the Whig peers, on the other
hand, were prepared to vote for its retention, believing that
the Bill was far more vulnerable with the clause remaining;
and many Tories were prepared to vote with them, since they
wanted the Bill to pass as it was originally drafted. So the
motion was defeated by a large majority; and the divorce
clause was retained.

On 10 November the voting on the third reading of the
Bill took place. When his name was called the Duke of
Clarence 'leaned over the rail of the gallery as far into the
House as he could, and then halloed – "Content!" with a
yell that would quite have become a savage. The Duke of
York followed with his "Content" delivered with singular

propriety'. The majority that agreed with them was an extremely narrow one: 108 members voted for the Bill, 99
against it. As Lady Harrowby had forecast, the majority was
'so trifling' that it created 'more *embarras* than if the Bill
had been thrown out altogether'.

The government were forced to recognize now that there
was virtually no chance whatsoever of getting the Bill
through the Commons. Indeed, they dreaded the thought
of its even being debated in the Commons; Sir Thomas
Tyrwhitt had already decided at the beginning of September that there would be a mutiny in the House if the thing
went on much longer. Brougham had got hold of a copy of
the will which the King had made and in which he referred
to Mrs Fitzherbert as his 'dear wife', and he was threatening
to produce it as an argument that the King had forfeited
his legal right to the throne. The government also knew that
Brougham intended to bring direct recrimination against
the King. He had found numerous witnesses to swear to the
King's sexual escapades with the daughters of a turnpike
man named Hyfield, and to his liaisons with a French courtesan, Mme de Meyer, with a Mrs Crowe whom he kept in
a house in Charles II Street, St James's Square, and by whom
he had had a child, with a Weymouth boarding-house
keeper, Mrs Mary Lewis, and even with a common prostitute.

The Duke of Wellington expressed himself as being quite
unimpressed by this recriminatory evidence; he told the
Duke of Portland that 'the King was degraded as low as he
could be already'. But Ministers, for the most part, feared
the dangers of further opprobrium. Rather than expose the
King to this damning evidence in the Commons, and accepting the fact that even if no such evidence were to be offered
the Bill would not pass there, the government decided to
take the matter no further. So Lord Liverpool announced
his 'intention to move that the Bill do pass this day six
months' – a parliamentary phrase meaning that he would
abandon it. At least he could prevent an acquittal by the

Commons, having just scraped together a majority to affirm her guilt in the Lords.

The King was profoundly upset when told that the Bill would have to be abandoned, and claimed to have 'serious thoughts of retiring to Hanover, and leaving this Kingdom to the Duke of York'. For weeks past he had been complaining about the progress of the Bill, and the government's handling of it, and in his anxiety he had been venting his ill humour in abuse of his Ministers, his 'language and manner', according to Charles Arbuthnot, being 'those of a Bedlamite'. Lord Castlereagh 'lamented very much the King's indiscretion in talking of those he still retained as his Ministers in so indecorous a manner, and said that such conduct and feelings entirely destroyed any pleasure there might be in serving him. He did not, however, seem to believe that the King had any fixed plan for getting rid of [the government].' Nor did Wellington think the King had 'any settled purpose of changing his government'. He had heard from his sister-in-law, Mrs Wellesley-Pole, one of his Majesty's guests at Brighton, that the King's language was 'beyond anything indiscreet and improper, that the language there now [was] not whether the Ministers [would] be changed but only as to the time'. But Wellington considered it was all just talk: the King liked people to imagine that his Prime Minister was a sort of maître d'hôtel whom he might dismiss any moment it happened to suit him. The King discussed the problem with Lord Lauderdale and with his friend Lord Donoughmore; and to the consternation of Lord Liverpool, who thought that he was certainly about to enter into an intrigue with the Whigs, he sent for Lord Grenville to show him the documents about Princess Charlotte and Captain Hesse and to ask him if, in Grenville's opinion, they ought to be published. Grenville declined to commit himself, but he did offer the opinion that, in any case, the Queen ought still to be excluded from the Liturgy.

After Grenville's departure the King went to dine with

Princess Augusta at Frogmore. W. H. Fremantle was also there and the King called him aside to tell him 'how much satisfied he had been with Lord Grenville'. Fremantle gained the impression, however, that 'the interview was more for the purpose of consulting and asking his advice' than for any object of changing the government.

The King 'looked dreadfully dejected and thoughtful', Fremantle thought; 'but when he had dined (professing to have no appetite) and ate as much as would serve me for three days ... together with a bottle of strong punch, he was in much better spirits and vastly agreeable. ... He did not sit a quarter of an hour after [the ladies] left us, and ... not a word was said of politics. He remained till twelve o'clock, and he and Princess Augusta and myself sang glees.'

The government, relieved to learn that the interview with Grenville had not set in motion any negotiation with the Whigs, still held to the view that the Queen's name ought to excluded from the Liturgy, although they did not expect to carry the point in the Commons. For most of the rest of the year they gloomily anticipated defeat, while the King prepared memoranda which he entitled, 'Advantages supposed to be gained by a new government' and 'The Evils attendant upon a change of government'.

The Queen, for her part, appeared overcome by emotion when she was told the news of the Bill's abandonment. She had 'a *dazed* look more tragical than consternation ... evidently all shuddering'. As she entered her carriage to be taken away to Brandenburg House she was observed to be in tears. It was as though she already realized that the celebrations now reaching their climax would soon die away and she would be forgotten.

For three days and nights the celebrations continued, with fireworks and bonfires, dances and parades. Church bells were rung and apprentices ran wild. In Peterborough, as in several other provincial towns, the magistrates called in the troops to quell the disturbance. Lady Milton was not alone in complaining of the 'rebellious, licentious, disgrace-

ful and revolutionary spirit' that had manifested itself. All
the large cities in the country were illuminated; and the
state of London, so Creevey recorded, was 'beyond everything'. There had never been such rejoicing since Waterloo;
there was to be nothing like it again until the passing of
the Reform Bill. The people, so Mme de Lieven said, never
stopped cheering in the streets on the night that the Bill
was thrown out of the Lords. Two days later, after terrific
bursts of cannon and musket fire – the 'English way of rejoicing' – the people were 'still mad with enthusiasm for
the Queen, and here and there indulged in looting and all
kinds of brutality'. At the head of the tallest mast of the
decorated ships in the river was an effigy of a bishop, between twenty and thirty feet in height, hanging by his heels.
Wellington was booed more loudly than ever; Castlereagh
got 'roughly handled at Covent Garden'. And Brougham
was the great hero of the entire country. He was presented
with the freedom of numerous cities; public houses were
named after him; attorneys loaded him with briefs if only
for the honour of talking to him.

In the general enthusiasm, all parties congratulated
themselves 'on no longer being faced with the prospect of a
revolution'. The trial had been a cathartic experience; in
the excitement it engendered, everything else had been forgotten, even Peterloo and the Cato Street Conspiracy. It
mattered little that, at the end of it, the government obtained strong support for their motion that the Queen's
name should remain excluded from the Liturgy, that she
was not to be crowned, nor to live in one of the royal palaces.
The people congratulated themselves on having won a great
victory; and so, in a sense, they had. They had been on the
side of the Whigs and the Whigs had won. After the trial the
liberal Whigs were firmly in control of the party; and the
Tories had to recognize that they could not very well survive another period of such unpopularity unless they as a
party became more liberal too. An age was dawning in
which the Reform Bill could become a reality.

PART FOUR
1821–1830

35

Coronation
1821

'Of the splendour of the whole spectacle it is impossible
for me to give you the *slightest* idea'

FOR months past, carpenters and painters, upholsterers and
joiners had been hard at work in both Westminster Abbey
and Westminster Hall. In the Abbey, tiers of crimson cloth-
covered benches, boxes and galleries had been ranged beneath the western windows looking down upon the nave.
Further seats had been provided in the choir and in the
north and south transepts. Boxes for the Royal Family, the
Press and foreign Ministers had been built in the sanctuary.
The interior of Westminster Hall, where the coronation banquet was to be held, had been even more drastically transformed. A new wooden floor, covered in blue cloth, had been
laid above the stone flags; tiers of seats rose above it against
the cloth-draped walls. At one end a Gothic triumphal arch
soared towards the gallery where the King's band was to
play. Facing this arch at the far end of the Hall was the
dais for the King and the royal dukes. Between dais and
arch, across the whole length of the Hall, were the diningtables for the privileged and distinguished guests; the backs
of the chairs were in the shape of Gothic arches and covered
with scarlet cloth. A raised and covered walk, spread with
a vivid blue carpet, led from the Abbey to the Hall and was
overlooked by decorated stands, seats in which were being
offered for sale at prices ranging up to twenty guineas.

At Carlton House the King studied the arrangements, following the precedents for the coronation of King James II
but making such alterations and improvements as he considered advisable, 'perfectly absorbed in all the petty ar-

rangements'. Visitors were taken to see the coronation robes, on which over £24,000 had been spent, the ermine alone costing £855. One of these visitors was Count Joseph Boruwlaski, the 2ft 4ins tall Polish dwarf, who came to present a copy of his memoirs and who received in exchange a beautiful miniature watch and seals which the King presented to him with the words, 'My dear friend, I shall read and preserve this book as long as I live for *your* sake; and in return, I request you will wear and keep this watch for mine.' The robes which the dwarf was then taken to see were of an astonishing splendour. The King's crimson velvet train, ornamented with golden stars, was 27 feet long; his huge black Spanish hat was surmounted by sprays of ostrich feathers and a heron's plume.

His Majesty appeared to be on edge. He had set his heart on a splendid ceremony, lavish, dignified and memorable, for which Parliament had voted no less than £243,000; but he was haunted by the fear that his wife would spoil it, and the apprehension led to sudden outbursts of exasperation. There were reports that when contradicted one day by Sir Benjamin Bloomfield, now his Keeper of the Privy Purse, he 'seized him by the collar and gave him a good hearty shake'.

His apprehension was well founded. The Queen no longer commanded the general sympathy that she had done before and during her trial; but she still had supporters enough among the mob – so many, indeed, thought Lady Sarah Lyttelton, that the ceremony might have to be postponed. 'The mob are rather too cross, and too fond of the Queen to [permit] a ceremony in which she is not to take part,' Lady Sarah told Captain Spencer. 'They will make some bustle on the occasion. We are all in a fright about it. As it is they make bustle enough; every day there is a gathering on some account or other. And her Gracious Majesty takes care to keep it up, by showing herself all about London in a shabby post-chaise and pair of *post-horses* and living in the scruffiest house she could think of, to *shew* she is kept out of the palace.' Lord Temple reported that fears of riots were making it difficult to sell seats in the stands along the processional route.

On 18 July 1821 the King's robes were carefully packed and transported to the Speaker's House at Westminster, not far from the church of St Margaret's whose bells, sometimes drowned by the boom of cannon firing across the river, were pealed every half hour from midnight until dawn.

Just before half past ten on the morning of the 19th, while rockets exploded in the sky, the King entered Westminster Hall. He was almost half an hour late as Lord Gwydyr, the acting Lord Great Chamberlain, had torn his clothes while dressing; but his Majesty's entrance was none the less impressive for being delayed. 'Something rustles, and a being buried in satin, feathers and diamonds rolls gracefully into his seat,' Benjamin Robert Haydon recorded. 'The room rises with a sort of feathered, silken thunder. Plumes wave, eyes sparkle, glasses are out, mouths smile and one man becomes the prime object of attraction to thousands. The way in which the King bowed was really royal. As he looked towards the peeresses and foreign ambassadors, he showed like some gorgeous bird of the east.' He was 'in full robes of great size and richness', and wore a brown wig, the thick curls of which fell low over his forehead and over the nape of his neck. He had by now – though many caricaturists were unaware of the fact – discarded the russet whiskers which had until recently bristled on his cheeks, giving his face a rather choleric, bucolic look, and he appeared surprisingly young for a man in his fifty-ninth year. There were many who had expected him to present a slightly ridiculous appearance; and there were some, including Mrs Arbuthnot, who thought that he *did* look ridiculous. But most people were impressed by his magnificent dignity. 'The young people in particular' who had gone 'merely with the expectation of a show', were 'taken by surprise and found themselves affected in a manner they never dreamt of'.

Indeed, the whole scene impressed the spectators with its

dignity and splendour. Even the white and blue satin Elizabethan costumes which were worn by those Privy Councillors
who were not peers and which Emily Cowper had expected
'to convulse the whole of Westminster Abbey with laughter'
appeared perfectly in keeping. 'Separately so gay a garb had
an odd effect on the persons of elderly or ill-made men,'
admitted Walter Scott, who had been induced to travel down
for the occasion by the newly invented steamships which
could make the journey from Leith within sixty hours. 'But
when the whole was thrown into one general body all these
discrepancies disappeared.'

The procession to the Abbey was led by the King's Herb-
Woman and her six young attendants who, in accordance
with a centuries-old tradition, strewed the way with herbs
and heavily scented flowers as a precaution against the
plague. The King walked in front of a canopy of cloth of
gold which the barons of the Cinque Ports had been instructed not to hold over his head so that he could be seen
by the people in the garrets and on the rooftops. He was
preceded by three bishops, carrying respectively a paten, a
chalice and a Bible. In front of the bishops were the officers
of state with the crown, the orb, the sceptre, and the sword of
state, regalia for which Messrs Rundell, Bridge & Company
were still owed £33,000 the following year. The peers
marched along in their state robes, in order of seniority; the
dignitaries of the City of London followed in their own no
less remarkable attire with their chains and emblems of
office. The King stopped for a moment to give his pages time
to unfold and display his crimson velvet gold-embroidered
train. He said to them twice in a clearly audible tone, 'Hold
it wider.'

The procession reached the West door of the Abbey at
about eleven o'clock. As the King stepped inside the building the choir began to sing the 'Hallelujah Chorus', and
the congregation stood and cheered. 'It was fearfully hot in
the Abbey and the King appeared distressed, almost to
fainting' as he made his way up the aisle with uneven

steps and evident difficulty. A lady in one of the galleries actually did faint and had to be carried out of the building.

The ceremony lasted for almost five hours; and the King, very pale, seemed at any moment likely to collapse, weighed down as he was by his heavy, cumbrous robes. 'Several times he was at the last gasp,' Lady Cowper noticed, 'he looked more like the victim than the hero of the fête. I really pitied him from my heart.' But, revived by sal volatile, he behaved on occasions in the most improper fashion, according to the Duke of Wellington, 'even in the most important and solemn' parts of the ceremony – 'soft eyes, kisses given on rings which everyone observed'. Fortunately these 'follies' and '*oëillades*' – which were noticed also by Lady Cowper who, being 'in the line of fire had a full view' – were abandoned during the sternly admonitory sermon of the Archbishop of York who spoke of a Sovereign's duty to 'encourage morality and religion', to preserve the morals of the people from the 'contagion of vice', and from a 'general depravity' which was 'the last calamity' that could befall a state. Nor did the King falter or make any ambiguous gestures during the crowning ceremony; and when this was over the congregation showed their enthusiasm once more by waving their caps and coronets, their purses and handkerchiefs, and by shouting at the tops of their voices, 'God Bless the King!' His Majesty was clearly 'much gratified', and, some thought, rather astonished by the vociferousness and evident sincerity of their acclamations.

As the premier earl present, the Earl of Denbigh performed homage to the King by repeating the oath of allegiance, kissing his hand and left cheek and touching with a finger the crown on his head. Then, the long and exhausting ceremony at last over, the King withdrew; and as soon as he had gone the peers and peeresses, the foreign ministers and their wives, the musicians and singers rushed out of the Abbey as though it had been on fire. So that when his Majesty reappeared he was greeted by the sight of 'empty benches covered with dirt and litter and the backs of his courtiers expediting their exits with a "sauve qui peut"-like rapidity'.

Soon after four o'clock the King, having had further recourse to sal volatile, proceeded to Westminster Hall to join his guests for the last coronation banquet ever to be given in England. The three hundred guests and the spectators in the tiered galleries above them were already there awaiting him.

'Of the splendour of the whole spectacle it is impossible for me to give you the *slightest* idea,' Lord Denbigh told his mother. 'It exceeded all imagination and conception. Picture to yourself Westminster Hall lined beneath with the peers in their robes and coronets, the Privy Councillors, Knights of the Bath and a multitude of different attendants and chief officers of state in most magnificent dresses, and with a double row of galleries on each side above, filled with all the beauty of London, the ladies vying with each other in the magnificence of their apparel and the splendour of their head-dresses. Some of them being literally a blaze of diamonds. Prince Esterhazy is said to have had jewels on his person estimated at *eighty thousand* pounds and the rest of the foreign ministers and their ladies were as splendid as jewels and fine clothes could make them.'

Before the King's arrival flower girls entered the Hall, strewing petals over the floor. 'The grace of their action, their slow movement, their white dresses, were indescribably touching,' Haydon recalled. 'Their light, milky colour contrasted with the dark shadow of the archway, which, though dark, was full of rich crimson dresses that gave the shadow a tone as of deep blood. ... The distant trumpets and shouts of the people, the slow march, and at last the appearance of the King himself crowned and under a golden canopy, and the universal burst of the assembly at seeing him, affected everybody. ... We were all huzzaing, and the King was smiling.'

Once he had settled himself down in his appointed place, the meal was brought in by a procession of Household officials, Gentlemen Pensioners, and – on horseback – the Lord High Constable, the Lord High Steward, and the Deputy Earl Marshal, the last of whom unfortunately found it necessary to swear at his horse in a voice that resounded around the Hall.

The next horse to appear was more easily managed, however, the rider having taken the precaution of borrowing from Astley's circus a white charger thoroughly accustomed to confined spaces and cheering crowds. The rider was the son of the King's Champion whose father, the Rev. John Dymoke, a Lincolnshire parson, had decided that his cloth was not compatible with the hereditary office which had descended to him from his ancestor, Sir John Dymoke, Champion of King Richard II. Young Dymoke, in full armour, a 'helmet on his head, adorned with a plume of feathers', trotted through the Gothic arch, rode up to the King, and flung a gauntlet down in front of the royal dais, challenging all comers to impugn his Majesty's title. No one presumed to pick the gauntlet up; and the King contentedly drank his Champion's health out of a cup of gold.

It was now the turn of the peers and bishops at the long tables in the centre of the Hall to drink his Majesty's health which they did with the customary rounds of cheering. The King stood up to thank them for their good wishes and to do them 'the honour of drinking their health and that of his good people'.

The censorious Mrs Arbuthnot, who – having, no doubt, discussed the King's behaviour with her friend the Duke of Wellington – accused him of kissing a diamond brooch to a lady admirer in the Abbey, recorded in her diary that he was 'continually nodding and winking' at this same lady in the Hall. But the Earl of Denbigh, who was standing near him, recalled no such improprieties. 'The King was very gracious to me at the banquet and called me to him,' Lord Denbigh said. 'He gave me his hand to kiss, and desired me to stand opposite to him at table and help him to some turtle soup to which I also helped the rest of the royal dukes. ... I also

helped a dish of quails, and carved a slice out of a capon for
the Duke of York. I had not a very arduous office as the
royal dukes had dined previously. Lord Chichester was my
assistant carver and cut up a pine-apple weighing eleven
pounds.'

At about half past seven the King retired from the Hall –
to which the Queen had unsuccessfully attempted to gain
admittance – and returned to Carlton House, leaving his
guests to enjoy the banquet. There were soups and salmon,
turbot and trout, venison and veal, mutton and beef, braised
ham and savoury pies, daubed geese and braised capon,
lobster and crayfish, cold roast fowl and cold lamb, potatoes,
peas and cauliflower. There were dishes of mounted pastry,
dishes of jellies and creams, over a thousand side dishes,
nearly five hundred sauce boats brimming with lobster
sauce, butter sauce and mint. The peers and the bishops,
having had nothing to eat since breakfast, turned to their
plates with relish, while their wives and children looked on
hungrily from the rows of seats above them. One peer at
least, taking pity on his famished family, tied a cold capon
in his handkerchief and tossed it up to them.

While fireworks exploded in Hyde Park, rockets hissed
past coloured balloons, church bells rang and guns thundered, the King could content himself with the knowledge
that he really had received, as Walter Scott put it, a 'general
welcome from his subjects'. 'The people were all in good
humour,' Lord Denbigh confirmed to his mother. 'The King
was *excitedly* and most enthusiastically cheered, and seemed
in the highest spirits.' Lord Colchester was also told that the
people were in good humour and that the few disloyal voices
were 'overpowered by bursts of loyalty'.

It was hard to believe that, so short a time before, the
King had been execrated wherever he went, that the hatred
he had inspired at the time of the Queen's trial was now sub-
merged if not in love at least in tolerance, that the enthusiasm with which, to Mme de Lieven's astonishment, he had

been greeted at a performance of the opera *Artaxerxes* at Drury Lane on 6 February, was not a misleading indication of the state of public opinion. Public opinion *had* changed unmistakably and steadily in recent months, so much so, indeed, that Grenville thought there was arising in the country enough 'of a royalist spirit and feeling to have enabled such a man as Pitt ... to avail himself of it'. It was now the Queen and her noisy supporters who were more likely to be greeted with groans than the King. She was denounced in the pages of Theodore Hook's new Sunday paper, *John Bull*; she was ridiculed in caricatures which depicted her in quite as unfavourable a light as that in which the King had been shown before the proceedings against her. Even *The Times* agreed that the King's visit to Drury Lane, the first of his reign, had been a success. He was received with 'immense acclamations'. There had been a few cat-calls from the galleries; Grenville reported that a few people called out 'The Queen!' and that one man shouted, 'Where's your wife, Georgey?' But most of the audience had 'testified their respect by rising immediately; all the gentlemen took off their hats, while numbers, particularly in the pit, waved them in the air with loud acclamations. The ladies in the boxes waved their handkerchiefs. ... His Majesty looked much paler than usual, but in good health. He bowed repeatedly to the audience, and continued to do so, remaining standing while the acclamations lasted.' He was obviously delighted. On the way downstairs he told Lady Bessborough that he had never been more gratified; and he later made a similar comment to Lord Castlereagh. During the performance of the farce *Who's Who?* which had followed the opera he had been seen to throw himself back in his chair, 'convulsed with laughter'.

After the Bill of Pains and Penalties had been thrown out of the House of Lords, various public meetings had been held for the purpose of 'congratulating her Majesty on the rejection of the Bill'. But they had not been very enthusiastically attended. Lord Althorp had expressed a wide-

spread opinion when he told Lord Milton, 'I have no doubt
in common prudence that the Queen ought to be restored to
all the rights and distinctions to which she has a legal
claim, but I cannot say that with my opinion of her general
conduct I should be inclined to take so strong a step in her
favour as to originate a county meeting for the purpose of
asking this of the King. I hope most sincerely that there will
be no meeting in Northamptonshire.'

A public meeting held at Leeds had been very poorly
attended by 'the more respectable part' of the population,
'considering how generally the proceedings against the
Queen had been disapproved amongst that class in this
town'. The general feeling had been overwhelmingly against
the two radicals who had spoken at the meeting. Lord Fitzwilliam was assured that the 'influence of these demagogues'
was certainly declining.

In London when the Queen had gone to St Paul's to give
thanks for the abandonment of the Bill – although *The
Times* reported the crowds in the streets as being enormous
– the entire proceedings had been 'a contemptible burlesque',
the Earl of Donoughmore had assured Sir Benjamin Bloomfield. Alderman Wood 'had talked of the necessity of having
seats set apart for the peers and peeresses, and the Members
of Parliament who would attend'. But, in fact, the congregation had been limited to the Lord Mayor, two Aldermen,
two Sheriffs, Sir Robert Wilson, Samuel Whitbread's son –
Whitbread himself had committed suicide in 1815 – two
other Members of Parliament, William Austin, Keppel
Craven and three Italians. The only female attendant had
been Lady Anne Hamilton.

In March 1821 the farce *Tom Thumb* had been performed
at Covent Garden. When a character had come on stage to
announce, 'Sire, the Queen is drunk,' the reply, 'Damn the
Queen!' had been applauded with 'frenzied enthusiasm' by
the 'entire audience'. Some time later during a performance
at Drury Lane, a man dashed up to Queen Caroline, and, to
the evident satisfaction of the audience, called her a 'damned

whore'. At another performance 'a set of radicals' demanded 'God save the Queen' instead of 'God save the King'; but the stage manager's refusal to comply with the request obviously met with the approval of the majority of the audience: 'The shouts [of the radicals] from the pit were by no means general.' Her popularity was now 'much on the wane'. Emily Cowper reported. 'And the King is as popular as possible. Not only in the theatres he is received with the greatest applause, but also in the avenues to the theatres where he has been hissed before.'

In June at Astley's circus, the Queen 'took an odd mode of procuring applause. At one moment there happened to be a profound silence in the house, of which she took advantage to stand up and curtsey all round. This was answered by some applause, but the majority was against her.'

The Queen still had her supporters, of course, as the King well knew from the secret reports he received from those who were employed to keep a watch on her movements and on the arrival and departure of her guests. The Duke of Sussex was a frequent visitor at her house; so was his messenger who delivered letters at her house sealed with black wax. Alderman Wood, his wife and his little granddaughter, of whom she had grown as passionately fond as she had been of Pergami's daughter, were often there too. Sir Robert Wilson called occasionally, as did Lord and Lady Milton and the Duke of Bedford. One day Lord and Lady Jersey appeared 'in a sedan accompanied by Mr Whitbread on foot'. But she did not have many callers. 'On Saturday two carriages arrived,' ran one of these reports of 'Secret Intelligence' which were regularly sent to Carlton House, 'one with 2 Ladys and the other with a Lady and Gentleman on a visite to her M— but could not be informed who they was. ... Her M— went this morning to town accumpend by Lord and Lady Wood [*sic*] with young Austin they Returned to Dinner – and at 6 this Evening the Carriage of young Austin took him and an Italian Count and [her Steward, John] Hieronimus surposed to go the play. There is no foreign courier arrived ... there has not bin many visitors for these Last few days.' Lady Hood, her Lady of the Bedchamber; Lady Anne Hamilton, her Mistress of the Robes; Lord Hood, her Chamberlain; and the Hon Keppel Craven, her Vice-Chamberlain, all still remained in attendance upon her. But it was reported that several members of her Household and most of her servants were growing restless and disaffected.

'The Queen has become very mistrustful', according to a characteristic message of 'Secret Intelligence'. 'The upper servants are quite in despair. They seem to say it's all over, that it is feared the Queen will remain in the discarded state that she is in as long as she remains in England. All the establishment wishes her Majesty would leave England. ... The Queen has not it appears the highest opinion of Lady Jersey although it is said her Ladyship, as well as Lady Grey, have pledged themselves to use all their exertions in supporting the honour and dignity of her Majesty. On the whole the Queen is very dull and appears to be dissatisfied.'

This report was dated 6 April. A later report of 10 May had it that the Queen was 'in excellent health and spirits'. But she was submitted to 'fresh insults' every day. 'Yesterday again two country-looking men stopped opposite the gate and made use of the most disrespectful language about her Majesty. They said amongst other things, "How does Mrs Innocence get on? How long does she mean to carry on the farce?" "I suppose," says one, "she is at this time of day tippling with some of the humbug Italians."'

A few weeks later a deputation of people arrived to present the Queen with an address. But they were a very different sort of supporter from the people who had cheered her on her way to the House of Lords the year before. Those triumphant days had passed for ever. As early as 22 January, when sixty-five addresses were presented to her at Brandenburg House to the accompaniment of loud music and waving banners, a 'very small proportion' of the spectators 'betrayed an interest in the Queen as formerly by the exhibition of laurel leaves or white favours'. The delegation that arrived at the Queen's house on 15 July were 'of the most miserable appearance' and seemed not in the least disposed to take their mission seriously. 'Their appearance was so truly ridiculous that servants in livery and many others turned them into ridicule. One of them asked one of the deputation what their white favours was for. The other answered, "For Caroline because she knows how to hold up her petticoats to a man".'

By this time the Queen had moved from Brandenburg House. She had allowed it to fall into such disrepair and neglect that she had received fourteen days' notice to quit. 'Indeed,' so the King's spies were informed by various of the Queen's servants who frequented the Swan at Hammersmith, 'Brandenburgh House is now in that state that it is not habitable.' Her Household had prevailed upon her to take another house; and in January, to the King's horror, she had entered into negotiations with Prince Leopold for the purchase of the lease of Marlborough House, which was only a short distance from Carlton House; but eventually, shortly before the coronation, she moved into Cambridge House in South Audley Street, while retaining Brandenburg House as a country retreat.*

* The Queen is going to take Cambridge House,' Lady Cowper recorded. 'Leopold having at last refused her Marlborough House. He has kept her in suspense three months, and now writes her word that it would offend a certain Personage, as if he cared about that when he went to see her. That's the shabbiest Ass!!' (Lever, 72). When she quit Lady Francis's house in St James's Square, which she had occupied during the trial, the Queen left it in a filthy state. The carpets were so discoloured 'with wax, ink, oil and other things thrown over them' that they were past cleaning. The tassels had been ripped off the curtains; the curtains themselves were badly torn; so were the covers to the drawing-room furniture. The blinds had never been drawn during the day, so the blue silk furniture was all faded. Ornaments and furniture had been broken, lustres smashed, keys lost. The silver was 'much bruized and damaged from the servants always throwing them down on the stone floors when done with'. The bedding and blankets had all to be 'sent to the scourers from

Her servants had not looked forward to the coronation with any pleasure. Alderman Wood had been overheard telling Lady Hood that there would be 'violent riots', that the people would 'never suffer the ceremony to take place without the Queen'. Fearful of these riots the servants had been reluctant to go out to watch the coronation procession. They had protested that 'they would not for any sum be spectators on any of the platforms', that during the riots which were to take place, the people, far from welcoming them as friends of the Queen, would 'have no mercy on them'.

The Queen herself, however, had been determined to attend the coronation and had written to Stephen Lushington to ask him 'by what means and measures' she could 'obtain her perogatif and privilege to assist as Queen Consort equally as the reste of the royal family to have a place allotted to her sole use'. She had also instructed her solicitor to ask permission of the Dean and Chapter of Westminster 'to inspect any ancient manuscripts amongst the archives of the Chapter relative to the Coronations of Kings or Queens'. Finally she had written to Lord Liverpool informing him that she would be present: she considered it 'as one of her rights and privileges which her Majesty [was] resolved ever to maintain'; she wished to be accompanied by 'those ladies of the first rank' whom his Majesty might 'think the most proper to attend' her. 'The Queen, being particularly anxious to submit to the good taste of his Majesty,' she had concluded, 'most earnestly entreate the King to informe the Queen in what dresse the King wishes the Queen to appear in, on that day, at the coronation.'

Lord Liverpool had considered that her threat to attend

---

total neglect' (RA Geo. IV, Box 11). A rumour that the Queen was interested in buying the house next door to the Lord Chancellor's so alarmed Lord Eldon that he bought it himself for £3,000 more than it was worth (RA Coutts Papers, 56/40, 5 September 1820).

the coronation was 'wholly undeserving of notice or attention'; but the King, who knew her so much better, had felt
sure that she must be taken seriously, and had issued instructions that she must be told that she could not *under
any circumstances appear*. He had returned the Queen's
letter to her unopened, 'in uniformity with a resolution
adopted *more than* twenty years ago, *and since invariably
adhered to by the King*'. Despite the King's apprehension,
Lord Liverpool had still been inclined to take the Queen's
letters more lightly, believing that her threats were made
'solely with a view of extorting money'. All the same, to
satisfy his Majesty, who had become 'excessively exasperated' on the subject, he had thought it advisable to write to
her to inform her categorically that the King 'having determined that the Queen [should] form no part of the ceremonial of his coronation, it was his royal pleasure that the
Queen [should] not attend the said ceremony'.

This firm rejection of her demands to be present had
made the Queen more determined than ever to go to the
Abbey, and not as a mere spectator. She could have obtained
a spectator's ticket without difficulty; but she would not
submit to sitting tamely in the stands as though she were a
foreign visitor. The King's spies had reported that they had
been told by Mrs Brown, her Majesty's porter's wife, that 'all
the Queen's establishment was in one opinion that the Queen
would certainly go to the coronation', that the Queen's
dressmaker had been to her house very often during the past
ten days.

'It appears by the Steward's account that her Majesty is
determined on going to the coronation,' another report had
confirmed. 'She is to be at Westminster Hall by half past
eight o'clock. Heronimus further said that he was quite
certain that the Queen would not change her mind – as he
had been with her seven years and never knew of one
instance of her Majesty's altering her resolution when once
she had made up her mind if even it would have cost her her

life. But many persons imagine in reality the Queen will not attempt to appear at the coronation, especially the Queen's coach maker. ... All the persons about the house are strictly forbid any intercourse with their neighbours. It is therefore most difficult to obtain any information about her future intention.'

36

Death of Queen Caroline
1821

'I am going to die, Mr Brougham; but it does not signify'

THE Queen had set out for the Abbey as planned in her coach of state, drawn by six bays. Lady Hood and Lady Anne Hamilton sat opposite her; Lord Hood and Keppel Craven followed in another carriage. *The Times* reported that 'the soldiers everywhere presented arms with the utmost promptitude and respect, and a thousand voices kept up a constant cry of "The Queen! The Queen for ever!"' Brougham also reported much applause and the waving of handkerchiefs, accompanied by 'hooting and cursing the King'. But less partial observers recorded that the Queen's reception was far from enthusiastic, that most of the spectators in the stands watched her in silence, and that the scattered shouts of 'The Queen for ever!' were drowned by 'loud whistling'. Lord Colchester was reliably informed that 'one attempt to raise a cry of Queen at the corner of a street ... totally failed'.

As though unsure of herself and discouraged by the attitude of the crowd, the Queen stopped her carriage and looked about her. In a moment or two the carriage moved forward again, and stopped close to the door of Westminster Hall which was 'closed amidst much confusion'. The Queen stepped down and, leaning on Lord Hood's arm, approached two other doors which were also shut in her face and guarded by hefty prize-fighters. She then went up to a door-keeper who requested to see their tickets. The subsequent conversation was recorded in the *Courier*:

Lord Hood:	'I present to you your Queen. Surely it is not necessary for her to have a ticket.'
Door-Keeper:	'Our orders are to admit no person without a peer's ticket.'
Lord Hood:	'This is your Queen. She is entitled to admission without such a form.'
The Queen:	(*smiling, but still in some agitation*): 'Yes, I am your Queen. Will you not admit me?'
Door-Keeper:	'My orders are specific, and I feel myself bound to obey them.' (*The Queen laughed.*)
Lord Hood:	'I have a ticket.'
Door-Keeper:	'Then, my Lord, we will let you pass upon producing it. This will let one person pass but no more.'
Lord Hood:	'Will your Majesty go in alone?' (*Her Majesty at first assented, but did not persevere.*)
Lord Hood:	'Am I to understand that you refuse her Majesty admission?'
Door-Keeper:	'We only act in conformity with our orders.' (*Her Majesty again laughed.*)

At this point there appeared on the scene one of the Gold Staffs, Sir Robert Harry Inglis, who had been warned by the Home Secretary that the Queen would attempt to get into the Hall or the Abbey and had been told to do all he could to prevent her.

'I was obliged to squeeze between Lady Anne Hamilton and the wall to get before the party,' he afterwards reported. 'I then turned and stood in the doorway. I found her Majesty accompanied by Lord Hood, presenting herself for admission. I said to her, respectfully, I hope, "Madam, it is my duty to inform your Majesty that there is no place for your Majesty in the Royal box, or with the royal family." (I forget which.) The Queen replied, "I am sorry for it." Some further conversation took place. Her Majesty then said,

"How can I get in my carriage?" I answered that I would give directions.'

As the Queen drove away, the roof of her landau open 'by way of exciting the mob', there were a few shouts and hisses from the crowd, a little cruel laughter; a voice here and there called out, 'Shame!' or 'Go away!' or 'Back to Como!' 'Back to Bergami!' But that was all. The incident passed without any of the violence which Alderman Wood had predicted; and the only person to have suffered by it was the Queen herself, that 'Bedlam Bitch of a Queen', as Walter Scott now called her.

It was obvious that her spirit was broken; and it was impossible not to feel pity for her now, not to regret that she had ever left Italy where she had been 'a merry soul', painted and preposterous but happy in her way. 'Nobody cared for *me* in this business,' she lamented. 'This business has been more cared for as a political business, than as the cause of a poor forlorn woman.' In her distress she fell ill, yet having doctored herself with 'laudanum and nervous medicines' without consulting her physicians, she insisted on going to Drury Lane where Robert Elliston had staged a magnificent pageant of the coronation with himself impersonating the King so well it was 'like a portrait'. He took the King's manner 'so exactly' that you could have supposed yourself at the ceremony.

After the performance was over, she 'got up and curtsied to the manager, to the pit, galleries and boxes in a manner so marked – so wild – with a countenance so haggard' that Lady Anne Barnard, who had never liked her, 'burst into tears to see royalty and pride so broken down and humbled'.

On her return home she began to vomit and her pulse grew fast and erratic. It was announced that she had 'an obstruction of the bowels attended with inflammation'. The pain in her stomach was intense, and she continued to be excessively sick. She was bled profusely and given large doses of opium and immersed in a warm bath. But, despite the opium, she could not sleep and the pain increased in vio-

lence. The doctors prescribed further bleeding, further doses
of opium, calomel and so much castor oil that Henry
Brougham thought it 'would have turned the stomach of a
horse'.

She was quite certain that she was going to die. 'Her will
and certain deeds had been got all ready by Friday night
according to her own instructions. Brougham asked her if it
was her pleasure then to execute them; to which she said,
"Yes, Mr Brougham; where is Mr Denman?" in a tone of a
person in perfect health.' Denman opened the curtain of the
bed; and she saw that he was there with Stephen Lushington. 'The will and papers being read to her, she put her hand
out of bed, and signed her name four different times in the
steadiest manner possible. In doing so she said with great
firmness, "I am going to die, Mr Brougham; but it does not
signify." Brougham said, "Your Majesty's physicians were
quite of a different opinion." "Ah," she said. "I know better
than them. I tell you I shall die, but I don't mind it." ' *'Je ne
mourrai sans douleur,'* she repeated to Lord Hood, *'mais je
mourrai sans regret.'*

Stephen Lushington, who went to see her on 7 August,
told Brougham that she 'talked incessantly on every subject
for three hours; and it [was] very remarkable that the only
persons she mentioned were the 'Petite Victorine, Bergami's
child and the child of Parson Wood', Alderman Wood's
granddaughter.

On 8 August, after yet another sleepless night, the pain
became more excruciating than ever, and she became delirious, then comatose. Finally she went into convulsions, her
eyes became fixed and her muscles paralysed. Her breathing
'stopped just before half past ten'.

Stephen Lushington, who had been appointed one of the
Queen's executors, immediately wrote to Lord Liverpool
informing him of her death; he spent much of the night
securing 'all the repositories' at Brandenburg House, a task
which occupied him until three o'clock the next morning.
Then, after lying down for two hours, he rushed to Hamp-

stead where that very day he was to be married. As soon as
the ceremony was over he returned to London to meet Lord
Liverpool who 'behaved extremely well – said the Government would defray the expense of the funeral'.

Lord Liverpool had already written to the King to advise
him that the funeral would take place 'as soon as decency
would permit'. 'With respect to the place of interment,'
Liverpool continued, 'it appeared to [those few members of
the Cabinet who happened to be in town] that Windsor or
Westminster Abbey must be selected for the purpose.' And
as regards a period of mourning this would be indispensably
necessary, 'as in no private family, whatever might have
been the faults or sins of the individual [was] mourning
dispensed with'. The next day, however, Liverpool was at
least able to relieve the King 'from all difficulties' as to the
Queen's funeral. For he had now learned that she had asked
for the burial to take place in Brunswick and for her body
to be transported there 'within three days if possible after
her demise'. She had also asked that the following inscription should be placed upon her coffin: 'Caroline of Brunswick, the injured Queen of England.' Such an inscription
could obviously not be approved, Lord Liverpool commented, 'by authority or consent of government, nor whilst
[the coffin was] in the charge of any officers of government'.

The King entirely agreed, and added that the Hanoverian
government, under whose immediate orders the interment
was to be conducted, 'could not be parties to such a measure'
either. The coffin must be removed quietly from Brandenburg House and transported down the Thames to the war-
ship which was to convey it to the Elbe. 'Moving the body
through any part of the country, or even through the town'
was to be avoided. As for mourning, that was to be for as
short a time as decorum demanded: the King considered
that three weeks would suffice and that the Earl Marshal
'should not give any orders for a general mourning' as his
Majesty felt 'an objection to render the mourning otherwise
than voluntary'.

Despite the King's anxiety about demonstrations and disturbances if the coffin were to be transported overland, orders were nevertheless issued for it to be taken from Hammersmith through Chelmsford to Harwich. Anticipating trouble from 'a considerable cavalcade of blackguards, male and female of all ranks', the Home Department did however direct 'the Life Guards at both barracks to be on the alert'. Instructions were also given to Sir Robert Baker, the chief Magistrate at Bow Street, to form a plan 'for stationing police along the line of march'; while 'the whole of the 1st Life Guards and the Blues, not otherwise on duty, were to be on the alert at their respective barracks'.

The precautions were well advised, for when it became known that the Queen's coffin was not to pass through the City 'a large concourse of people, on foot and on horseback, assembled at Hammersmith' with the evident intention of forcing the *cortège* to follow the road to Temple Bar. They succeeded in doing so; for Sir Robert Baker, certain that 'lives would be lost if it was persisted in not to go through the City', declined to give orders to remove the obstacles that the mob had put across the prescribed route. So the demonstrators, encouraged by Sir Robert Wilson and accompanied towards the end of their journey by the Lord Mayor, aldermen and members of the City's Common Council, had the satisfaction of celebrating their 'triumph over the government and the military' by escorting the funeral *cortège* through Temple Bar, across Ludgate Hill and down towards the Essex Road.

The *cortège*, so the Mail Coach Department reported, slowly proceeded to Chelmsford where the church bells were tolling 'as at all the other towns through which it passed'. The coffin was taken off its carriage and placed on the communion table in the church at Chelmsford where, to the 'astonishment of the spectators', Lady Anne Hamilton and Lord Hood suddenly burst out laughing. For Alderman Wood, who had been carefully hiding under his coat a silver plate, dropped it on the floor. On the plate was written, in accordance with the Queen's instructions, CAROLINE OF BRUNSWICK: THE INJURED QUEEN OF ENGLAND. It was quickly retrieved and, surrounded by mourners, a cabinet-maker 'very dextrously' screwed it onto the coffin. But, after a great deal of argument, Sir George Taylor, a representative of the King, persuaded the churchwarden to prohibit the coffin's removal with the silver plate still fixed to it. So the plate was removed before the coffin continued its interrupted journey to Harwich.

'On arriving at Harwich,' Henry Brougham recorded, 'we found everything ready prepared for immediate embarkation. The scene was such as I never can forget or reflect upon without emotion. The multitudes assembled from all parts of the country were immense, and the pier crowded with them as the sea was covered with boats of every size and kind, and the colours of the vessels were half-masted high, as on days of mourning. The contrast of a bright sun and the gloom on every face was striking, and the guns firing at intervals made a solemn impression. ... The crimson coffin slowly descended from the pier.'

On the day of the Queen's death, the yacht *Royal George* had arrived off Holyhead. One of the passengers, Major-General Sir Andrew Barnard, a Groom of the Bedchamber, reported that his Majesty had been 'in the best health and spirits during the whole passage' from Portsmouth. The sea air agreed with him, and he was obviously looking forward to his forthcoming visit to Ireland.

The following morning, however, he received the first accounts of the Queen's illness; and it was considered advisable for him not to sail straight across to Dublin Bay as had been planned, but to land at Holyhead, to go to stay with the Marquess of Anglesey at Plas Newydd and 'to postpone his public entry till something more decisive should be known as to the Queen's state'. The next bulletin from Hammersmith suggested that she was expected to recover, and the King returned to the yacht only to receive the news of her sudden death. 'Though it would be absurd to think that he was afflicted, he certainly was affected. ... He walked about the cabin the greater part of the night.' 'He had all the masts of the squadron lowered as a sign of mourning.'

The following day he received a copy of the Queen's will by which William Austin was to receive the whole of her estate on reaching the age of twenty-one; but there were so many demands on the estate that her combined assets in England and Italy were insufficient to satisfy the claims. She was, in fact, insolvent.* William Austin was not left destitute as she had instructed Messrs Coutts in 1818 to invest £200 a year (the rent she received from her house in Blackheath) on his behalf in government stock.† But the members of her Household to whom she had wished to give pensions were obliged to look for their money to the King.

---

* The Queen had evidently wanted to bequeath some diamonds to Pergami's child, Victorine; but Brougham and the other lawyers had thought it better to omit this from the will though they planned to send the jewels to her (*Creevey Papers*, 336). The Queen's furniture and effects, which were sold by auction at Cambridge House on 20 February 1822, realized no more than £8,085. According to a marked catalogue of sale the most expensive items of furniture were her billiard table (£42) and 'superb ebonized frame state bedstead' (£45 3s.). A portrait of her by Lawrence fetched no more than £56, a wooden sculpture of the Last Supper £29. The only valuable things in the house were the curtains, the pier glasses, chimney glasses and lustres (R A Geo. IV, Box 10).

† William Austin died in a lunatic asylum in Chelsea in 1849. As recorded in Part Two, the Queen had told James Brougham that Austin was not the child of the dockyard worker, Samuel Austin, and of his wife Sophia Austin, as the Commissioners who conducted the Delicate Investigation of 1806 had concluded. The Queen had said she had 'humbugged' the Commissioners and that William was really the natural son of Prince Louis Ferdinand of Prussia. She repeated the substance of this story to Dr Stephen Lushington on her deathbed (Brougham MSS, 19, 268). Austin himself, however, seems not to have doubted that Samuel and Sophia Austin were his parents. From 1810 to 1821 he wrote regularly to Sophia as his mother, giving her news of his activities on the Continent and making arrangements to see her when he was in England (Goulding Papers, Lincoln).

The King agreed to pay these pensions; but he asked Lord Liverpool to confer with the Lord Chancellor, the Attorney-General and the Solicitor-General as to the best way of re-claiming the jewels which were his property, not hers.

The King, who, when Napoleon had died, was said to have responded to the intelligence that his 'greatest enemy' was dead with the words, 'Is she, by God!', was not expected to display any prolonged grief at his bereavement or to feel less than a profound sense of relief after the first shock was passed. And on his fifty-ninth birthday, 12 August 1821, as he crossed the Irish Sea in the steam-boat he was certainly 'in great spirits'.

'We drank his health in sight of Irish land,' General Barnard told his sister-in-law, 'but although in mid-channel and much elated by the occasion we were not quite half seas over.' The Countess of Glengall, however, reported the King as being far more than half seas over. Indeed according to her he was 'dead DRUNK' when he landed and could hardly stand up. This, too, was what Lord Temple heard from William Fremantle. 'The passage to Dublin,' Temple was assured, 'was occupied in eating goose-pie and drinking whiskey in which his Majesty took most abundantly, singing many joyous songs, and being in a state, on his arrival, to double in number even the numbers of his gracious subjects assembled on the pier to receive him. The fact was that they were in the last stages of intoxication.' If this were so, he managed to disguise the worst effects of the wine and whisky punch from the Irish spectators on his arrival with some credit.

He landed at Howth at about half past four in the afternoon. Because of the Queen's death, his landing had not been announced, and there were less than two hundred people on the pier; but as the ship approached the landing place the crowds grew and excitement mounted. He stepped ashore, 'a little browned from the weather', in a plain blue coat with a black cravat and a foraging cap trimmed with gold lace, shook hands with several men who approached him, and greeted the Earl of Kingston with the words, 'Kingston, Kingston, you black-whiskered, good-natured fellow! I am happy to see you in this friendly country.' He then drove off to the Viceregal Lodge in Phoenix Park, escorted by a ragged procession of enthusiastic Irishmen, 'dozens of farmers and gentlemen on horseback, and nearly two thousand pedestrians'. At the gates of the Park the King invited them all into the grounds, told them not to trouble to keep off the grass, and asked them to accompany him to the house where he made them what General Barnard described as a 'short but hearty speech which completely won not only their hearts but has had the same effect wherever it has been repeated'.

He reminded them that he had made a long and rough sea voyage and that 'particular circumstances' had occurred of which it was 'better at present not to speak'. But, all the same, this was one of the happiest days of his life. He had long wished to visit Ireland. His heart had always been Irish; he had loved the country since the 'day it first beat'.

This was a little extravagant; but there was a good deal of truth behind the highflown phrases. He had always felt at ease in the company of most Irishmen, had always professed to a sympathetic understanding of most of Ireland's problems, and had consequently been more popular with most of the Irish people than he had ever been at home. At the time of the Regency Crisis in 1788–9 Irish commissioners had invited the Prince to exercise 'all legal powers, jurisdictions and prerogatives'; and in later years the Carlton House group of Members of Parliament derived much of its strength from its dozen or more Irish members. In 1821, the King's popularity in Ireland remained largely unabated, and his visit during the summer undeniably increased it. He charmed the people with his friendliness and approachability, with the easy, natural way he shook them by the hand, talked to them, smiled at them and gave numerous proofs of his generosity. It was easy enough, of course, to present a few peasants with pigs and chickens, to provide orphan children with new clothing, to distribute handfuls of guineas to needy labourers, to urge absentee landlords to live on their estates, to praise and to wear Irish wool and Irish cloth. But the fact was that Ireland was the first place he had chosen to visit now that he was King, and no reigning English sovereign had ever paid a state visit there since the time of Richard II. 'I was a rebel to old King George in '98,' said one old man, voicing a common sentiment, 'but by God I'd die a hundred deaths for his son, because he's a real King, and asks us how we are.' Another former Irish rebel, Lord Cloncurry, who had served a term of imprisonment in the Tower of London, wrote of the 'strange madness' that came over all Irishmen during the King's visit. He himself was affected by it; and gave 'a pledge of the sincerity' of his 'waiver of all bygones' by inviting the King to his house.

For the first few days of his visit, the King remained quietly 'in seclusion at the Park' as a mark of respect to his wife, though he made it clear that this was the only notice of his bereavement that he felt inclined to take. Bloomfield, himself an Irishman, had some difficulty in persuading him to wear mourning and to put a crape band round his arm. He remained in excellent spirits, though, and gave way in the end good-naturedly.

John Wilson Croker, another Irishman, who was in Dublin at the time and was a guest at the 'very hot and very dull' dinner party given in the Castle to celebrate the King's birthday, recorded in his journal an example of his good humour. Lord Castlereagh – who had become Marquess of Londonderry on his father's death in April – was reading aloud in the King's presence a letter that had arrived in Holyhead from England. When he came to the words, 'the Duke of York', Castlereagh 'looked horrorstruck and stopped short. "Come, Come," said the King. "You must now go on with it, or I shall think it worse than I dare say it will turn out to be." Castlereagh was then obliged to stammer on, *"The Duke of York is in despair at an event* [the Queen's death] *which so much diminishes his chance of the crown."*

The King, however, laughed very good-humouredly at it, and afterwards repeated the story with equal good humour.'

On 17 August his Majesty, wearing the Order of St Patrick on his field-marshal's uniform, and a mourning crape on his arm, made his public entry into Dublin, escorted by hundreds of carriages and thousands of 'gentlemen on horseback'. It was a lovely sunny day and as he stood up in his open carriage, waving his hat, pointing significantly to the big bunch of shamrock attached to its brim, and then laying his hand on his heart, the immense crowds roared their welcome. For almost an hour his carriage was halted by the dense throng that pressed around it, swaying it about so violently that the King was prevented from falling over only by one of his attendants who held him up under the arms. 'The people shouted,' Croker recalled. 'The Irish, it seems, do not know how to *hurrah* or *cheer*; they have not had much practice in the expression of public joy. After the King had received the addresses on the throne, he sent for me into his private room. He was walking about greatly agitated between pleasure at his reception in Ireland and dissatisfaction at what has occurred in London when the Queen's coffin was taken from Hammersmith. ... He kept me full half an hour, and talked the whole time, alternately at the triumph of Dublin and the horrors of London. Bloomfield tells me that the King sat up the greater part of the night fretting about this latter affair; it affects him certainly more deeply than I should have expected.' *

* General Barnard confirmed how angry the King was when he heard of the disturbances over the Queen's funeral procession during which, although the military had behaved 'with infinite temperance', two demonstrators had been killed (*Barnard Letters*, 295). The government felt obliged to ask Admiral Sir George Cockburn and John Wilson Croker, as Secretary to the Admiralty, 'to draw up a *mémoire justificatif*' of the reasons for taking the coffin overland to Harwich and not by water as the King had suggested. Cockburn justified the Admiralty's decision in a lengthy memorandum which pleaded the difficulties of getting a suitable frigate round to the Nore from Spithead in 'a gale of wind at *west*', as well as the possibility of

The events of the next few busy days, however, restored the King's spirits. There was a splendid review in the Park on 18 August, another 'wonderfully fine' day; there was a crowded levee on the 20th before which the King received addresses from the Presbyterian clergy, Catholic bishops and the Quakers, answering them all in a manner 'impressive and kind beyond description'. Then there was a Drawing-Room on the 21st when 'above a thousand ladies were presented, and really they were (with a very few and very inconsiderable exceptions), all ladies who might have very properly attended at St James's, and their dresses were both rich and in good taste. ... By some interruption, about one-third of the company were cut off and prevented coming up with the stream. The attendants thought there were no more to be presented, so the door of the presence chamber was shut, and the King made his bows and retired. In a few minutes it was found that the ante-rooms were again full. ... What was to be done? The King had retired and was undressed. On the other hand, the ladies were dressed and had no mind to retire; after a good deal of *pourparlers*, the King was told of the circumstances, and with great good nature he put on his fine coat, came back to the presence chamber, and went through the ceremony of kissing those hundred ladies more.'

After this Drawing-Room there was an 'extremely splendid' banquet given by the Dublin Corporation in a room specially built for the occasion and representing 'the interior circular court of a Moorish palace open to the sky; the battlements were a gallery filled with ladies, music and a company of halberdiers, in Spanish dresses of light blue silk, as a guard of honour to the King. It was lighted by a vast circle of lamps, hung by invisible wires, which had a

---

'greater mischiefs' if the coffin had been moved down the Thames and under London Bridge than had, in fact, been experienced in conducting it across country (Asp/K, ii, 458–64). The King accepted the excuses; but Sir Robert Baker, the Bow Street magistrate, was dismissed from his office.

wonderfully fine and curious effect.' The loud cheers that
greeted all references to the merits of the guest of honour
were echoed by the crowds of people in the streets outside.

This banquet was followed by another at Trinity College,
where at the singing of 'Rule Britannia' 'the royal countenance glowed with pleasure'; he beat the time with his hand
and vigorously struck the table in front of him 'at every
word'. This, in turn, was followed by a public breakfast at
Leinster House given by the Dublin Society, by visits to the
theatre and the Curragh, by the installation of new Knights
of the Order of St Patrick, and by a grand ball at the Castle.
And everywhere the King went he was greeted with the
same enthusiasm and was made to feel as welcome as he had
been on the day of his arrival. 'Were you here you would
imagine Ireland to be the richest country in the world,'
General Barnard told his sister-in-law, 'such exertions have
these poor people made to testify their attachment to George
the Fourth.'

His cheerful response to these exertions was considered
rather vulgar in some quarters in England. He 'seems to have
behaved not like a sovereign coming in state and pomp to
visit a part of his dominions,' Lord Dudley commented disapprovingly. 'But like a popular candidate come down upon
an electioneering trip.'

So far as the Irish were concerned, however, the single
disappointment he caused during the entire visit was at the
Dublin Society's breakfast which was held on the day that
the Queen was buried in her family tomb in Brunswick. The
King did his duty by going 'minutely through the museum'
at Leinster House but then left the breakfast abruptly,
spending no more than three or four minutes on the lawn
where there were tents and 'bands of music in all directions'.
Barnard thought that the walk through the museum had
tired him out; but Croker considered it just as likely that he
had left in a hurry because he was so anxious to get to Slane
Castle, the home of the Marquess and Marchioness of
Conyngham.

37

Lady Conyngham and William Knighton
1820–1821

'The King desires Lord Liverpool distinctly to understand that whatever appointments the King may think proper to make in his own family, they are to be considered as quite independent of the control of any Minister whatever'

LADY Conyngham was a fat, kindly, religious, rich and rapacious woman of fifty-two, the daughter of Joseph Denison, a city banker from a modest home in Yorkshire, who had come down to London where he had amassed, by industry and parsimony, a fortune of astonishing magnitude. She had been married for twenty-seven years and had four grown-up children. Her beauty was beginning to fade, and she had never been amusing or particularly intelligent, though she was much more shrewd than people supposed. The King adored her. For some time past he had been seeing less and less of Lady Hertford whose grandson, Lord Beauchamp, seeing the King riding with Lady Conyngham in the Park one day, burst out, 'By God, grandmother must learn to ride, or it is all over with us.'

Lady Hertford herself took the King's neglect very badly, pouring out her tearful, angry complaints to Mme de Lieven, protesting that she found 'the new love ridiculous in view of the age of the contracting parties'. In less emotional moods, Lady Hertford would haughtily protest that she took no interest in her rival – on being asked about her she would reply coldly that 'intimately as she had known the king … he had never ventured to speak to her upon the subject of his mistresses'.

Most people who knew them both well, however, doubted
that Lady Conyngham was in fact the King's mistress,
though she had rather a conspiratorial manner and was reported to have had lovers in the past. She was excessively
fond of clothes, money, and, above all, jewellery – one of her
proudest possessions being a sapphire surrounded by bril-
liants, which had belonged to the Stuarts and had been
given by the Cardinal of York to the King. The King had
given it to Princess Charlotte and, on her death, had asked
Prince Leopold to give it back to him as it was a crown
jewel.*

* 'Never were such jewels,' commented Emily Cowper after seeing
Lady Conyngham at a 'very brilliant and very dull' ball at Carlton
House in May 1821. 'The family pearls which she talked of last year
have increased greatly. The string is twice as long as it was and such
a diamond belt three inches wide with such a sapphire in the centre.
By the way I must tell you the history of it. The Cardinal York left
it to the King to be added to the jewels of the crown. The King in a
fit of parental fondness gave it to Princess Charlotte. When she died
he sent to Leopold for her jewels, saying they belonged to the crown.
Leopold, *qui n'aime pas rendre les bijoux*, as Mme de Lieven says,
murmured that he could not bear to part with anything which had
belonged to her. The King insisted, upon which Leo gave in and said
he would present them *au roi comme un homage*. The King saying in
particular he must have this stone for his coronation as it was to go
in the crown – when lo and behold here it has appeared in Lady
Conyngham's waist' (Palmerston Papers, C IV/4/3, 3 May 1821;
Lever, 79). Payments made to Messrs Rundell, Bridge & Co. alone
between January 1821 and January 1829 amounted to £105,618
(RA 32696). This sum included £3,150 for a pearl necklace with
'thirty-seven remarkably large oriental pearls' (RA 26161). In two
previous months, February and March 1820, the King paid £400 for
a pair of diamond ear-rings, £437 for a pair of pearl bracelets, £530
for an emerald necklace and £740 for a pearl necklace (RA 25997).
Lady Conyngham was certainly responsible for a fairly large proportion of this expenditure. Sir Benjamin Bloomfield, Keeper of the
Privy Purse, said that he thought the King would go mad such was
his infatuation for Lady Conyngham. He told Charles Arbuthnot
that it was 'quite shameful the way in which she [was] covered with
jewels and that he really [believed] the King [had] given her a
100,000 £s worth!!' (*Arbuthnot Journal*, i, 38). It should be added,
though, that after the King's death, Lady Conygnham returned to

Some pamphleteers described the King snoring in bed with his 'prime bit of stuff', his 'Vice-Queen'. But others who portrayed them

> Quaffing their claret, then mingling their lips,
> Or tickling the fat about each other's hips

were drawing an equally cruel but no doubt more realistic picture of their relationship which seems to have been warmly domestic rather than hotly passionate, to have fulfilled the King's needs for a motherly, affectionate woman to fuss over and fondle and be fussed over and fondled by. In its early flowering the relationship was also highly flirtatious. Lord Burghersh, indeed, thought it 'the most laughable thing that ever was'. The King 'never drank wine without touching her glass with his, holding her hand under the table all the time he was drinking'. As with the Hertfords, it was a relationship that embraced husband and children as well as wife, and most of the Conynghams seemed content with it. Mrs Arbuthnot heard that the King and Lady Conyngham spent their evenings 'sitting on a sofa together, holding each other's hands, whispering and kissing, Lord Conyngham being present'. Less complaisant than her husband was Lady Conyngham's brother, William Denison, senior partner of Messrs Denison, Heywood and Kennard, bankers of Lombard Street, who had vastly increased his father's immense fortune and who, dying unmarried and childless, left most of his own to his nephew, Lord Albert Conyngham, on condition that he took the unsullied name of Denison.*

---

the Keeper of the Privy Purse various jewels, including the Stuart sapphire, which she had reason to doubt 'his late Majesty ought to have given away' (Wellington Papers, 21 November 1830, 4 December 1830).

* William Denison had been offered a seat in the Commons by the Regent in 1812 but declined it on the grounds that 'he had no intention of coming into publick life' (RA 20071, 27 September 1812). He had been a Whig member for Camelford from 1796 to 1802,

   While William Denison felt his sister's virtue to have been
outraged by her association with the King, many others considered the liaison more absurd than scandalous. 'The King
made himself very ridiculous with Lady Conyngham,' Mrs
Arbuthnot commented disapprovingly after a great ball at
Carlton House in May 1821. He 'was devoted to her the
whole night and at last retired to one of the rooms with her
and placed a page at the door to prevent anyone going in.
[Various guests] were going in when the page stopped them
and, laughing, told them nobody could be allowed to go in.
As the King can see Lady Conyngham every day and all
day long, I really think he might control his passion and not
behave so indecently in public.'
   Charles Greville was equally disapproving. He described
the King, who was said to have gone on a strict diet to make
himself more attractive to his loved one, going up to her at
Brighton when she had given orders for the saloon to be
illuminated, and saying effusively, 'Thank you, thank you,
my dear; you always do what is right; you cannot please
me so much as by doing everything you please, everything
to show that you are mistress here.' Mme de Lieven, who had
'never seen a man more in love', gave Wellington 'a very
ridiculous account of a scene that she had had with the King
and Lady Conyngham. The King had made her sit by him
in the evening, Lady Conyngham being on the other side of
him, and had told her that he had never known what it was
to be in love before, that he was himself quite surprised at

represented Kingston-upon-Hull in 1806–7, and was Member for
Surrey from 1818 to 1849. His nephew, Lord Albert Conyngham,
who changed his name to Denison in 1849 in accordance with the
terms of his uncle's will, and who was created first Baron Londes-
borough in 1850, was widely rumoured to be King George IV's son,
unlikely as this seemed to judge from his lank form and toothy face,
which were much more like those of the Marquess of Conyngham.
He was born in 1805. Although it is not known for certain that the
King knew Lady Conyngham well at this time, she was already by
then a conspicuous figure in Brighton society (Musgrave, *Brighton*,
167).

the degree to which he was in love, that he did nothing from morning to night but think what he could do to please Lady Conyngham and make her happy, that he would do anything upon earth for her for that he owed his life to her ... and that she was an angel sent from heaven for him. *He cried*, Lady Conyngham cried and Mme de Lieven said that, being nervous and easily agitated, she had cried also; and all this passed in a crowded drawing room.' Mme de Lieven also told Metternich how he had had Lady Conyngham – 'a nice enough woman' – and all her family to stay with him at the Royal Lodge, how he used to visit her every afternoon at Brighton, where she had a house at the end of Marlborough Row, and how, in the evenings, he would sit down to dinner with her on his right, her eldest daughter, Lady Elizabeth on his left, her second son, Lord Francis Conyngham – 'dearest Frank' – at one end of the table, and the Marquess himself at the other.*

He loved the Conyngham children dearly. When nominating Lord Francis a Grand Cross of the Guelphic Order, he did so, he said, because he wished not only to remind Lord Francis himself but also to convey to others how much he 'loved and distinguished' him. His attentions to Lady Elizabeth were so marked that it was sometimes said that it was really she with whom he was in love and not her mother. And he wrote to the younger daughter, Maria, his 'most beloved and darling Maria', in the most affectionate way imaginable. 'You are ever present in my thoughts,' he told her. 'Believe me, my sweet child, when I tell you, that not only a day does not pass without my thinking of you, but that you are constantly before me, in my imagination and thoughts and you cannot imagine what a relief it is to me: in the midst of the many painful and anxious moments to which I

---

* Lady Conyngham's eldest son, the Earl of Mount Charles, disapproved of his mother's liaison with the King and so was rarely of the company. The King did all he could to placate him, sending him presents and using his influence to obtain for him desired appointments.

am doomed, when your dear little self ... darts before my mind's eye. ... Dearest Mater mentioned to me, the day before yesterday, that you complained of being tormented to the greatest degree with chilblains. I instantly sent off to our little friend Barrett at Brighton for his lotion. ... I need not say how much I have missed you and how long I have wished to see you ... and it is therefore with a delight I have not words to express that I announce to you that upon the arrival of a Knight Errant, who will suddenly arrive, seize upon you, and as suddenly convey you to the Old Castle at Windsor when you may be sure, my beloved child, you will be received with open arms by its old Possessor.'

He told her about the 'pretty little pranks' of a favourite puppy which caressed him with delight, ran about the room from him to Maria's Pater and back, sat up on her hind legs, and 'did everything but speak': 'After she had drank she came instantly back, lay down by the side of my bed, began crying for a moment or two ... walked to the door, whining piteously as if to say, "Let me out for I want to go and look after my kind mistress." We watched her and the moment the door was opened, she bolted, poor little thing, as fast as she could fly to your dearest Mater's rooms.'

Maria wrote to him in similar vein: 'How can I express my delight and thanks for your affectionate letter. I kissed it as I could not kiss the dear person that wrote it. I am over-joyed at the thought of seeing you soon.'

The whole correspondence shows how important to him was the family life which the Conynghams were able to share with him, how deeply he regretted never having had such a family of his own.*

---

* 'He always was fond of children,' Lord Melbourne told Queen Victoria, 'and took notice of them, etc.' The Queen replied, 'He took notice of me' (RA, Queen Victoria's Journal, entry for August 1838). He bought an enormous amount of playthings to give away as presents. His accounts are replete with bills for dolls and lead soldiers, boxes of ninepins, miniature farm yards, play houses, mechanical animals (rocking-horses, games and toys of every description (RA 29111–29204).

The influence of the Conynghams had already been strongly demonstrated when, without consulting the government, the King promised to promote to a vacant canonry at Windsor, the Rev. Charles Richard Sumner, curate of Highclere in Hampshire, who had been tutor to Lady Conyngham's three sons. The Prime Minister protested to Bloomfield that the stalls at Windsor had in the past, 'with scarcely any exception', been given to 'some clergyman of known character and merit, who had already filled some conspicuous situation in the Church, or to persons of family and connection'. Lord Liverpool thought that 'serious inconveniences' might result from the 'intended arrangement'. Lord Castlereagh also wrote to Bloomfield to emphisize how dangerous and 'prejudicial' was the step which the King had taken. And Lord Sidmouth added his warnings to the others by declaring that nothing had given him so much uneasiness since he had the 'honor of becoming a member of the present government'. The King, having taken a strong liking to the handsome and suave Charles Sumner was, however, insistent. He felt bound 'to recall to Lord Liverpool the communication made through Sir Benjamin Bloomfield which expressed "that the nomination of the Rev. Mr Sumner to the vacant Canonry at Windsor would be very acceptable to the King's wishes". The absence of Church preferment in this gentleman does not in the King's mind form a just ground of objection on this occasion; the more particularly as Mr Sumner's strict piety, exemplary conduct and great learning peculiarly recommended him for this mark of royal favour.'

For a time the problem appeared so intractable that it was thought that the government might be forced to resign. 'I left the Brighton Pavilion in a great state of excitement over a little affair which may become a big one,' Mme de Lieven wrote on 17 April 1821. 'The King wants to bestow the Canonry of Windsor on the tutor of Lady Conyngham's children. The Ministers will not tolerate this infringement of their privileges; for they alone have these places in their gift.

Within three days Bloomfield made the trip from Brighton
to London five times. The King is obstinate, and so are his
Ministers; and finally Liverpool went to Brighton yesterday
to tell the King that, as long as he is Minister, he will not
give way. I do not know what has been decided. The Duke of
Wellington said to me this morning: "Perhaps at this very
moment, we have already been turned out." It is certain that
there are more difficulties ahead. An extraordinary state of
affairs – the constant hostility between master and servants.'

Eventually, after Sumner had written to Bloomfield to say
that he did not wish to cause the King 'the uneasiness of a
single instant', a compromise was reached. The Windsor
canonry was given to the King's librarian and chaplain at
Carlton House, Dr James Stanier Clarke, whose appointments, together with the private chaplaincy at Windsor, a
salary of £300 a year, and 'a capital house opposite the Park
gates' were given to Sumner. Soon afterwards Sumner was
found a canonry at Worcester, and then, having refused the
bishopric of Jamaica and accepted a Deputy Clerkship of the
Closet, was consecrated Bishop of Llandaff before becoming
Bishop of Winchester. But the way in which his wishes had
at first been thwarted by Lord Liverpool 'mortally wounded'
the King who felt that he could never forget it.

Scarcely had the crisis over the Windsor canonry been resolved when the King's friendship with the Conynghams
involved him in another quarrel with the government. The
new disagreement was over the vacancy occasioned by the
resignation of the Marquess of Hertford who, in July 1821,
handed in his resignation as Lord Chamberlain of the King's
Household. Lord Liverpool assured the King that with
regard to a successor he was 'earnestly desirous' to meet his
personal wishes so far as he could do so 'consistently with the
responsibility which necessarily belonged to his situation as
his Majesty's First Minister'.

This suggestion that he was not entirely free to choose
whomsoever he pleased provoked the King into making an
angry response: 'The King desires Lord Liverpool distinctly

to understand that whatever appointments the King may think proper to make in his own family, they are to be considered as quite independent of the control of any Minister whatever; and Lord Liverpool must be aware that the present government was framed on that basis alone under him.'

The King, as Lord Liverpool feared, was determined to appoint Lord Conyngham to the vacant post in his Household; and the government was equally determined to prevent him, for Lady Conyngham was known to be intriguing with the opposition and was suspected of exacerbating his differences with his Ministers. It was intimated to the King that the only Household appointment to which the government would agree to Lord Conyngham's being appointed was Groom of the Stole. At a dinner party at the Duke of Wellington's, the King – still incensed with the government over their mismanagement of the Queen's funeral procession as well as the Conyngham appointment – 'behaved with pointed rudeness to Lord Liverpool in the presence of the foreign ministers'; and with Wellington himself he was seen to be no longer on friendly terms. He had recently much annoyed the Duke not only by declining a previous invitation to dinner and then going to dine with the Duke of Devonshire (to whom Lady Conyngham hoped to marry her elder daughter), but also by failing to consult him when the King had authorized a statement that he was going to do so. Thus provoked, Wellington said to him 'in his brusque manner, "If you do not like us, why do you not turn us out?" The King made no answer, and the Duke, after a short pause, made his bow.'

Although irritated at finding himself unable to gratify Lady Conyngham's wishes to the extent that he would have liked, the King was 'in excellent tone and spirits' when he came to visit her at Slane Castle in August. He found life there so enjoyable, he said, that he would like to stay in Ireland and have Lord Talbot, the Lord Lieutenant, sent over to London as his representative in England. The three

days he spent at Slane seemed to have been amongst the
happiest of his life. Indeed the whole of his visit to Ireland
afforded him the greatest pleasure. Lord Sidmouth, who had
accompanied him 'with a determination to hold the scales
even between all parties', had 'not heard an unpleasant word
nor seen a sullen look'. The King returned home more ready
than ever to protest that he was 'a most determined Irishman'. The Irish themselves had been delighted with him;
they had been 'out of their wits with joy', and had 'already
voted to build him a royal palace in *Dublin*'; he was 'very
likely to be now christened *Paddy* the 1st'. Orangemen and
Catholics, temporarily forgetting their differences, had been
united in their welcome, and there seemed good grounds to
hope that a more promising period in the troubled history of
their country had begun. Henry Hobhouse, Under-Secretary
of State for the Home Department, concluded that 'nothing
could have gone off better than the King's visit to Ireland'.
Even Daniel O'Connell, convinced that the spirit of reconciliation should be encouraged by every possible means,
went so far as to present the King of England with a laurel
crown upon his departure. The King accepted the tribute,
shook O'Connell cordially by the hand and declared to the
crowds gathered at the edge of the shore, 'My friends!
When I arrived in this beautiful country my heart over-
flowed with joy – it is now depressed with sincere sorrow. I
never felt sensations of more delight than since I came to
Ireland – I cannot expect to feel any superior nor many
equal till I have the happiness of seeing you again. Whenever an opportunity offers wherein I can serve Ireland, I shall
seize on it with eagerness. I am a man of few words. Short
adieux are best. God bless you, my friends. God bless you
all.'

'The scene was grand and affecting,' wrote General Barnard, who believed that his Majesty's visit would be 'productive of the best consequences' and that it had 'already tended
much to sooth those political animosities which so long [had]
been the destruction of the country'. 'The shores were

covered with people of all descriptions who expressed their
feelings on the occasion strongly, several who were nearest
the spot followed his barge up to their necks in water.' One
particularly enthusiastic supporter who had followed him
everywhere 'would have been drowned – for he could
not swim – had not the King sent a boat to his
assistance'.

As his band played 'St Patrick's Day', and cannon fired in
salute, as the crowds cheered and the flags fluttered from the
masts of the royal squadron, the King stood waving his hat
in the gathering darkness. Then he sat down on a sofa which
had been placed for him on deck; and the *Royal George*
sailed out to sea.

The voyage home was a fearful ordeal. Soon after the
squadron's departure, a gale forced it back to Dunleary; and
when at last the ships did get out into the Irish Sea a howling
storm tossed the *Royal George* away from the escorts, and it
was forty-eight hours before land was reached again at Mil-
ford Haven. 'Most even of our crew and company were
deadly sick,' the King wrote; 'but the very worst of all was
my poor self; and I am now on 10th September for the first
time, since we are again at anchor in smooth water, risen
from my bed, and not without considerable exertion. ... I
am ... completely shattered and torn to pieces.'

There was worse yet to come. The roads through Wales
and parts of the West Country to London were so primitive
and bumpy that it was considered advisable, now that the
wind had dropped, to continue the journey by sea round
Land's End to Portsmouth. But after a few hours' sailing
with 'a most promising breeze', 'a violent hurricane and tempest suddenly arose'. The King, who appears to have displayed an admirable fortitude at such times of physical
danger, dramatically recorded the consequences: 'The most
dreadful possible of nights and of scenes ensued, the sea
breaking everywhere over the ship. We lost the tiller, and
the vessel was for some minutes down on her beam-ends;
and nothing, I believe, but the undaunted presence of mind,

perseverance, experience and courage of Paget [Captain the Hon. Sir Charles Paget, commander of the *Royal George*] preserved us from a watery grave. The oldest and most experienced of our sailors were petrified and paralysed; you may judge somewhat, then, of what was the state of most of the passengers; every one almost flew up in their shirts upon deck in terrors that are not to be described.'

It was not until 16 September that the King arrived home. On his way through Hampshire to London he met Lord and Lady Harcourt on the road. He stopped his carriage, got out 'and sat with them in theirs, on the public highway, recounting all his perils at sea'. Lady Harcourt, so she told her friends, was 'quite edified at his pious acknowledgments of his escape, and there was quite a change to be noticed in his conduct'.

He would have liked to have gone down to Brighton for a while to recuperate; but there was no time, for within eight days he was due to leave for Hanover. Proud of being a Brunswicker as well as a patriotic Englishman, he had been looking forward to this trip. In the early summer he had discussed it enthusiastically and at length with Mme de Lieven who had found him at Carlton House 'lying at full length in a lilac silk dressing-gown, a velvet nightcap on his head, his huge bare feet (for he had gout) covered with a pink silk net'. She had 'spent an hour and a half *tête à tête* with this get-up', talking of 'love, religion, tittle-tattle, politics, plans for the journey'; and, having described to her his itinerary, he gave her 'two smacking kisses'. He was less excited now, though. It was not only that he was not yet feeling up to another long journey, but it had been decided that the Conynghams should not go with him. It was some comfort, however, that he was to be accompanied instead by Sir William Knighton.

Sir William Knighton was a remarkable man, industrious, conscientious, understanding and discreet, yet so affected,

irritating, staid and touchy that it was a cause of some astonishment in the King's Household that his Majesty was evidently so attached to him. Born in Devon, the son of an
impoverished country gentleman who had been disinherited
and died young, Knighton had been sent by his widowed
mother to a small school at Newton Bushell and then to
study medicine under an uncle at Tavistock. Having qualified at an early age he became an assistant-surgeon at the
Royal Naval Hospital at Plymouth, but, after marrying the
daughter of a captain in the Royal Navy, he moved to London and by 1806 had established himself in practice as a
fashionable *accoucheur* in Hanover Square. An occasional
patient of his was Moll Raffles, one of Lord Wellesley's
several mistresses; and when Lord Wellesley was asked to
lead an embassy to Spain in 1809 and decided to take Moll
with him, she persuaded her lover to ask Dr Knighton to
accompany them. Knighton agreed to go on the understanding that he would receive £5,000 in consideration for a two-
years' absence from London; and, on Wellesley returning to
England unexpectedly, having paid Knighton only a part of
that sum, he strongly recommended him to the Prince of
Wales as compensation for the loss of the remainder. Knighton had gone to see the Prince who had struck him then as
'very intelligent ... proud and overbearing, but with a most
fascinating complacency of manner'. The Prince had been
suffering from 'a lameness in his hand', caused either from
an accident 'or from the use of laudanum'. But Knighton
had not felt able to prescribe anything, since the complaint
was already being treated by Sir Everard Howe, Sir Walter
Farquhar and Henry Cline, the surgeon. All the same, the
Prince had been much impressed by Knighton, had kept
him talking for twenty minutes, and had afterwards told
Farquhar that he was 'the best-mannered medical man' he
had ever met. Some time later Knighton had been appointed
one of the Prince's physicians-in-ordinary, and within two
years he had been created a baronet. Sir William had be-

come by then far more than a doctor. The Regent had grown
accustomed to consulting him upon all manner of private
concerns, and clearly saw in him a worthy successor to that
faithful servant, the wily *débrouillard*, Colonel McMahon,
who had died in 1817.

Shortly before McMahon's death, Knighton, it seems, had
been sent down to McMahon's country cottage near Blackheath to retrieve from him any incriminating papers
concerning the King's past that he might still have in his possession there. Knighton claimed to have found McMahon
extremely feeble in both body and mind. His wife had just
died. She was 'an ill-educated woman', in Knighton's
opinion, 'with but two objects, that of making money and
the adoration of her husband'. She took every possible
opportunity of profiting from her husband's position and
was able to leave him a surprisingly large amount of money.
He was shattered by her death, began to drink to excess, and
to lose his reason. On arrival at his cottage Knighton gave
him some brandy which revived him sufficiently to hand
over 'all the King's private letters, early correspondence and
other documents'. In reporting his success to the King,
Knighton added, 'Nothing can have been more secret or
more satisfactory than the accomplishment of this desirable
object for no second person has been or need be, unless it
shall be your royal Highness's pleasure, brought acquainted
with any part of your early correspondence or early documents of any description.'

The discretion with which this confidential duty had been
performed evidently increased the King's respect for Knighton, who soon afterwards became Auditor of the Duchy of
Cornwall, and Secretary and Keeper of his Royal Highness's
Privy Seal and Council Seal. By the time of the visit to Ireland, Knighton, who was then forty-five, was undoubtedly his
most trusted confidant, though Sir Benjamin Bloomfield – on
Lady Hertford's recommendation – had actually succeeded
to the office of Private Secretary on McMahon's death four
years before. So heavily had the King begun to rely upon

Knighton, indeed, that he felt uneasy when he was not readily at hand, and was in the habit of summoning him to his presence in the most affectionate, not to say effusive terms.

'My dearest and best of friends,' he wrote in one characteristic letter in March 1821, when thanking him for a poem which Knighton, an inveterate poetaster, had written and sent to him for his approval. 'I have at length secured a moment to acknowledge your last kind letter, with the poem which accompanied it.' It was a 'very, very, very *wonderful* poem', he assured him with a wild, incoherent hyperbole – induced, no doubt, by drunkenness – a 'most *beautiful production* of the human mind, perhaps, if not the most grand one certainly of the very grandest and *most elegant* at the same time, that any pen produced, either in our language or in any other. You know I put but little value upon my taste and judgement in these matters, but as far as my opinion goes, dear friend, I never . . .' He never, in fact, had read such a poem; it demanded comparison with Shakespeare, Milton, and Dante; he had read it aloud and wept over it.

'I suppose you have seen Astley Cooper [the surgeon],' he continued in more sober mood, 'and therefore I shall leave everything upon that head till I see you next, which I trust *will be at latest four o'clock* on Tuesday next; when we will get our usual tete a tete together, before I am *condemned* to go to the Opera in *state*. I have much to say to you *then*.'

The King's correspondence is full of such summonses, nearly all of them highly urgent, addressed to his 'dear, very dear friend, his *very* dear and *best* friend'. 'For God's sake come down to me tomorrow morning, at latest by ten o'clock,' he begged Knighton on receipt of the news that the baby daughter of the Duke and Duchess of Clarence had died. 'You will be a *great consolation to me*. Ever your most affectionate friend.' 'Nothing but the most *pressing urgency* would induce me, indisposed as you are at the moment, to entreat you to come to me for a few instants,' he wrote after receiving an invitation from the Emperor of Austria to attend a conference in Vienna. 'I have *much, and that too of great importance, as well publicly as privately, and as it relates to myself, which I must with the shortest lapse of time possible discuss and talk over with you.'* 'Come to me here, *be it only for an hour, early* tomorrow morning, *if possible ... See you I must ... a very early* visit *tomorrow morning ...,'* run other injunctions. 'There certainly seems as if there were some sort of fatality that inevitably attends upon your leaving London, be it only for a single day, for your back is no sooner turned than some disagreeable and unforeseen *something* is sure almost instantly to start up. ... Come *immediately* ... I *must* see you. ... Always affectionately yours.'

Be it family matters, or foreign affairs, or bishoprics, or threats of blackmail, or negotiations with the Press, Knighton's presence and reassurance seems to have been deemed indispensable. His advice was readily given, and, when in the form of a written communication, usually couched in the fondest terms. 'There are no means within my reach that can adequately convey how much and how truly I am impressed with everything relative to your Majesty,' Knighton assured him in one typical letter. 'I trust that the Almighty will give you peace, and that your afflicted mind will cease to be tortured by the overwhelming inquietudes which have of late made such painful inroads on your health. I feel assured that all will be well. In the meantime let me implore your Majesty to *guard your health and to use every means to protect it in your power.* ... If you knew, Sir, what I really and sincerely felt, your Majesty would scarcely believe the *extent of my anxiety and misery respecting you. Burn this if you please.* I have the honour to be, Sir, your Majesty's most dutiful and most *affectionately attached devoted servant, Secret.'*

Knighton was careful to cultivate the Conynghams and one of his principal duties in the early days of his appointment, when Lady Conyngham did not wish to appear with the King in public, was to conduct her clandestinely in a hired carriage to Carlton House at times when Bloomfield was out of the way and consequently would not hear of her visit.

Many of Knighton's own visits to the King's bedroom were made with the same utmost secrecy. 'I hope to be in your Majesty's bedroom by half past twelve to-night,' he once wrote. 'Your Majesty had better let *no one* (with the exception of *the one*) *know that I am coming* – Pray remember this; and it may be as well that every person should be in bed – Be pleased to destroy this letter.'

The longer Knighton remained in his service, the greater was the King's dependence on him. In November 1820, when quarrelling with his Ministers, he submitted to him for his 'dear consideration' his memoranda upon the 'Advantages to be gained by a new government', and went so far as to say that he would do whatever Knighton desired.

While waiting off the Welsh coast to sail to Ireland, the King assured Knighton that it was 'utterly impossible' for him to tell him how *all abroad, how uncomfortable, and how miserable* he always felt when he did not have him 'immediately at his elbow'. And on the day after he arrived home the protestations were again repeated. The King had suffered the exhaustion and inconvenience of rising from the bed where he had been so sick 'soley for the purpose' of writing to his 'dearest friend'. 'For I too gratefully feel the warmth of your affectionate heart towards me at all times not only not to neglect you but to prove to you that you are always present in my mind.' *

* Henry Hobhouse had 'very much doubted' that the King would go to Ireland at all, since Knighton, who had 'great weight with Lady Conyngham', was very averse to his leaving the country. The King's journey, so Hobhouse recorded in his diary, 'would reduce Knighton to the alternative of declining to accompany his Majesty and thus endangering his influence on him, or going with him and thereby losing the profits (to which he is far from inattentive) of his intermediate practice in London'. Knighton was extremely 'fond of lucre', Hobhouse later recorded and quoted an observation made to him by Lord Lauderdale: 'Knighton's a damned clever fellow, but it is very odd, I have had four conversations with him, and each one

of them has ended with his asking me what I thought of the price of
stocks' (*Hobhouse Diary*, 75, 76, 94). After he had retired from medical practice Knighton told Canning that he had sacrificed £10,000 a
year by doing so (Stapleton MSS – quoted by Aspinall, 'George IV
and Sir William Knighton', *English Historical Review*, LV, January
1940, 64).

38

A Continental Journey
1821

'At table we heard of nothing but Hannover'

ON his visit to Hanover the King was to have the company
not only of Knighton but also of the Foreign Secretary, Lord
Castlereagh, who was given an excellent opportunity for a
meeting with Metternich for talks about a recently erupted
quarrel between Russia and the Turks. Declining to pass
through Dover, where the Queen had been cheered on landing the year before and where the witnesses who had been
sent to give evidence against her were stoned by the mob,
the King chose to embark at Ramsgate, where he was
greeted with almost as much enthusiasm as he had been in
Ireland. He spent the night in Ramsgate at Cliff House, the
commodious residence of a rich, genial sea-biscuit manufacturer, banker, former Lord Mayor of London and diehard
Tory Member of Parliament, Sir William Curtis, a great
favourite with the King, who was often a guest aboard his
lavishly fitted yacht. Fortified by Curtis's sumptuous hospi-
tality and rough warm company, the King sailed for Calais
where landing was 'effected with great difficulty' owing to
the wind.

He was welcomed by the Duc d'Angoulême at the Hotel
d'Angleterre, usually known as Dessin's after the proprietor
who had made it one of the most celebrated hotels in France.
Here at Dessin's, the chosen resting place of thousands of
English travellers, the King was presented with some 'excellent Maraschino', a liqueur to which his Majesty was known
to be 'extremely partial', by Beau Brummell's valet whose
master had settled in Calais as a means of escape from his

creditors. But the King was reluctant to renew his friendship
with a man who had been so rude to him – and to whom he
in turn had been so rude. So, ignoring the signature which
Brummell had inscribed in the book at Dessin's by way of
emphasizing his contrition, the King left Calais for Brussels
without seeing him.

At Brussels he recovered the spirits he had enjoyed in
Ireland, evidently enjoying himself immensely at a dinner
party given by the King and Queen of the Netherlands at
their palace at Laecken. Unfortunately the Prince of Orange
was there with the wife he had married after his rejection
by Princess Charlotte, the rather flamboyant former Grand
Duchess Anna Paulowna, who was glittering with diamonds.
The King exchanged a few polite words with the Prince, but
to his Russian wife he said abruptly, 'Madame, vous êtes
très brillante' and that began and ended the conversation.
However, on turning to her parents-in-law, he entertained
them delightfully with imitations of an eccentric member of
their family, whose voice and gestures he mimicked so well
that 'at every moment' they broke out into 'violent convulsions of laughter'. He was, thought the Duke of Wellington,
one of the other guests, 'very blackguard and entertaining'.

From Brussels the King went on to Waterloo where Wellington conducted him over the battlefield in pouring rain,
indicating the positions of the armies, the farmhouse at La
Haye Sainte, Hougoumont and Mont St Jean, the direction
of Ney's attack, the place where the Imperial Guard recoiled
as Maitland's guardsmen charged into them, the point where
Ziethen's Prussia Corps had appeared through the swirling
smoke. The King 'took it all very coolly', Wellington dis-
gruntledly told Lady Shelley; 'indeed, never asked me a
single question, nor said one word, till I showed him where
Lord Anglesey's leg was buried, and then he burst into
tears.' Recovering himself, he pottered about for some time,
picking at the ground with his stick, hoping to find the
bones. Failing to do so he gave orders that a tree whose
branches had been shattered by gunfire should be cut down,

made into a chair for Carlton House and inscribed with the glorious legend: GEORGIO AUGUSTO EUROPAE LIBERA-TORI.

Leaving Brussels for Hanover at the beginning of October, the King passed through Düsseldorf – where the garrison received him by torchlight as the band played 'God save the King' – and then took the rutted jolting road to Osnaburgh. It was more than sixty years since Osnaburgh had been honoured with a visit from a King of Hanover, and its citizens were determined to give an even more hospitable welcome to King George IV than they had given to his great-grandfather. They had illuminated their buildings, thrown arches of leaves and flowers across the roads, hung flags and streamers from the windows, and when his Majesty drove through the gates they appeared 'almost mad with joy'. So did the people of Hanover, which he entered on the evening of 7 October as a hundred and one guns roared their salute and the people cheered him as though he were a hero returning triumphant from the wars. They crowded round the cathedral where he was crowned a second time; they watched him review the army; they listened to him delightedly as he spoke to them in German, happy to disregard the foreign accent of which his father had complained; they noticed, with satisfaction, the insignia of the recently instituted Royal Hanoverian Guelphic Order which he wore prominently on his coat, to the exclusion of all other decorations; they observed, with sympathy, the tears that fell down his cheeks as he listened to the address made in his honour at the University of Göttingen where young girls in white, bearing flowers, presented him with a poem on a scarlet cushion. All in all the King's reception had been 'very cordial', Lord Castlereagh thought, and Knighton had also been deeply impressed by it. The 'dearest King' was truly 'beloved' here, if not in England; and apart from a sharp attack of gout which had seized him after spraining his knee as he clambered onto a ceremonial horse, he had stood up to the journey very well.

He had, however, been much displeased by the numbers of rich English people he had found living on the Continent, rejecting their own country in a manner he deemed highly unpatriotic. Lady Charlotte Goold told Lady Bedingfield that when one of these rich expatriates called on him attended by servants in white liveries, he rebuffed him with the comment that since he was able to go about in such splendid style he had much better do so in England. He subsequently indignantly refused to receive an address from a group of English residents on the grounds that 'he could not do so from English persons *on the Continent*'. Perhaps he was particularly cross with them because the gout was 'pinching him' so painfully that he was only too anxious now to get home.

The journey from Berlin to Carlsbad and Vienna, which the King had discussed with Mme de Lieven, was postponed. He had, however, seen Metternich in Hanover and was evidently well pleased to have done so. He liked and admired Metternich who, in London in 1814, had delighted him by conferring upon him, in the Emperor's name, the Order of the Golden Fleece and by creating him honorary colonel of a Hungarian regiment with a particularly splendid uniform. He had hoped to gratify Metternich in turn by asking Mme de Lieven to come out to Hanover to entertain them, by talking to him in the frankest, not to say indiscreet, manner, and by the most extreme forms of flattery, declaring that his greatest achievements stood comparison with those of Minos, Themistocles and Cato, Caesar, Gustavus Adolphus and Marlborough, not to mention – though he did mention – Pitt and Wellington. Although Metternich seemed rather embarrassed by these attentions, the King's well-publicized journey to Hanover and his friendly meeting there with the Austrian Emperor's representative undoubtedly did much to thwart Russia's designs on Turkey, and Castlereagh gave him due credit for its success.

His homeward voyage started at the beginning of November and a month later he was back at Brighton, his gout somewhat improved, 'cheerful and happy and good humoured with all the world', so pleased to be back in Lady Conyngham's company that he adopted the eccentric habit of taking snuff from her shoulder. He talked endlessly about his journey. 'Ah, my dear friend, I was longing to embrace you,' he called out one evening at the Pavilion to Mme de Lieven who thereupon received 'three great smacking kisses'. 'At table we heard of nothing but Hannover,' she reported to Metternich. 'He talked to me without stopping, and I hardly had a chance to exchange two words with my neighbour on my right. As for Castlereagh, he had a member of the Opposition next to him, someone who hardly speaks even to his friends; so that poor Castlereagh was reduced to falling on two enormous helpings of roast mutton. ... He had informed [Castlereagh] that I should be here; that means he thinks there is something between us. He informed me the day before that you were the lover of the Duchess of Cambridge [Princess Augusta of Hesse-Cassel]. At table he told [Castlereagh] to come and sit by me. He has a passion for encouraging the affairs he suspects.'

The next time Mme de Lieven was a guest at the Pavilion, the King was 'in a more talkative mood than ever', mostly upon 'the subject of high politics'. She wished that she could remember 'his ideas and the order in which he gave them'. 'I know that three times I bit my lip so as not to laugh,' she told Metternich, 'and that I ended up by eating all the orange-peel I could find, so as to give my mouth something to do to hide its twitching if the danger grew too great. Everything you had said to him was in his oration – I recognized the substance, I even recognized a few phrases; but everything was plunged in such confusion that it was impossible to disentangle the real text of his speech. We had Poland, mystery-mongers, M. de la Harpe, the Don Cossacks, a great deal about gold, my wit, the Hanoverian sappers, who wear green aprons with gold fringes, Benjamin Constant, and Madame de Deken, the Hungarian infantry and the prophecies of the King in 1814, Jesus Christ and the

Emperor Alexander who now sees things more clearly, for Prince Metternich says so, and finally the importance of remaining openly united. The end was the best part. The whole speech was addressed to me; but in a tone of voice which obliged everyone else to listen in silence. We should be there still if Admiral Nagle ['a bold, weatherbeaten tar' who was Groom of the Bedchamber] had not begun to snore so loudly that the King lost patience and broke up the meeting.'

For Prince Metternich's amusement, Mme de Lieven provided an overcoloured, but no doubt far from fanciful example of the King's conversation when in one of these expansive talkative moods:

His Majesty: My dear I'm no ordinary man; and – as for you – you've more intelligence in your little finger than all my subjects put together. I said 'little finger' because I did not want to say 'thumb'. Now you, my dear, who are so intelligent, you must admit I am not a fool.

Myself: Indeed, Sir, I wish I could tell you what I think without descending to commonplace flattery. Obviously your Majesty is a very remarkable man.

His Majesty: That's true. You have no conception of the ideas which sometimes go through my head. I have seen everything in a flash. I'm no mystery-monger (*in the King's vocabulary this word is equivalent to mystic*); but I am a philosopher. Nesselrode [Russian Secretary for Foreign Affairs] is an honest fellow; but Capo d'Istria [Russian statesman from Corfu and Nesselrode's colleague] is a rascal ... Lieven, I've just been saying that Capo d'Istria is a rascal; but (*sotto voce to me*) one of these days soon I shall be sending the Emperor a certain document – something really memorable – quite unprecedented – a document that will make a tremendous effect. I composed it myself; but I shall not tell you what it is. No good making those charming eyes at me. You won't discover. My dear, if I had a difficult negotiation on hand, I should entrust it to you in preference to anybody else. (*To the Princess Augusta*) Sister, I drink to your health. Long live wine. I say, long live women. 'Long live wine, long live men', you will retort. Gentlemen (*addressing the whole company*), the finest supporter of the throne the one man ... (*Here the King stops short, joins his hands, lifts his eyes to heaven and moves his lips as if he were reciting a prayer.*) (*Then to Princess Esterhazy*) My dear child, do you know the story of the tailor who was perpetually dropping his wife into the Seine? Very well, I'm the tailor. You don't understand me, but Madame de Lieven does – I can see that from the corner of her mouth.

Myself:	I understand the moral of the story, Sir. (*What story or what moral, I had no idea. But it didn't matter; he had no more idea than I had.*)
His Majesty:	That's right – the moral of the story (*Angrily*) *Damn it she takes the words out of my mouth!* My dear, as I have already told you, you're more intelligent than anybody else at table. ... What's that you're saying, my dear?
Myself:	Sir, I am comparing your Majesty to Pyrrhus.
His Majesty:	Yes, indeed, he was a great man; but, personally I prefer Henry IV, whom I admire almost to the point of extravagance. He shouldn't have kept Sully though. Sully was a rascal, wasn't he?
Myself:	I am sorry to disagree with you, Sir; but I should never have thought that of Sully.
His Majesty:	My dear, I assure you that I'm well up in the subject; I have read the memoirs of the period, M. de la Fayette, Mme de Sevigné, Mme de Bavière (*At this juncture he nods at me and we get up from the table.*)

Charles Greville, Clerk-in-Ordinary to the Privy Council and the Duke of York's horse-trainer, was also a guest at Brighton in December 1821. He, too, found the loquacious

King in excellent humour, but he found life at the Pavilion tedious. 'The gaudy splendour of the place amused me for a little and then bored me,' wrote this acute, prejudiced, fastidious and observant diarist. 'The dinner was cold and the evening dull beyond all dullness. They say the King is anxious that form and ceremony should be banished, and if so it only proves how impossible it is that form and cere- mony should not always inhabit a palace. ... The King was in good looks and spirits, and after dinner cut his jokes with all the coarse merriment which is his characteristic. Lord Wellesley did not seem to like it, but of course he bowed and smiled like the rest. I saw nothing very particular in the King's manner to Lady Conyngham. He sat by her on the couch almost the whole evening playing at patience, and he took her into dinner; but Madame de Lieven and Lady Cowper were also there and he seemed equally civil to all of them.'

It was not only his gratifying reception by the peoples of Ireland and Hanover which had helped to put the King in so cheerful and talkative a mood this winter. He had tem- porarily settled his differences with his irritable Prime Minister. As recently as two months before, this had seemed too much to hope for. Indeed, in his dissatisfaction with the government, he followed the example of Lady Conyngham and was actually civil to the Whigs, much to the alarm of Brougham who dreaded a change being 'operated by such means'. At Herrenhausen on 12 October the King had com- plained to Castlereagh that Liverpool's conduct had 'upon very many occasions been so monstrous' that he could 'not consent to a continuance of a system' which rendered his 'life full of inquietude and vexation'. He had again con- sidered the possibility of ridding himself of his difficult Prime Minister; and had reviewed the relative merits of Sidmouth, Wellington and Castlereagh as replacements. Castlereagh he had particularly favoured. There had been a coolness between the King and Castlereagh in the recent past, since not only were Lady Castlereagh and Lady Conyngham not on speaking terms, but the Foreign Secretary was Lady Hertford's nephew. The trip to Hanover, however, had brought them together in a friendship as warm as could be expected between two characters so totally incompatible. Yet, in the end, the King had reluctantly been forced to conclude that Liverpool, with a wider measure of support than Castlereagh or any other member of the Cabinet could command, was indispensable. His indispensability made him all the more objectionable to the King, who was constantly finding fault with him.

The trouble over Liverpool's refusal to agree to the appointment of Sumner to the Windsor canonry, the ill-managed affair of the Queen's funeral *cortège*, and the opposition to Lord Conyngham's being appointed Lord Chamberlain of the Household, had been followed by complaints about the King's creating Knights of the Thistle without taking the Cabinet's advice, and about the difficulties and delays in obtaining the royal signature to state papers.* There had also been a quarrel over the King's determination to appoint the sons of two friends of his to studentships at Christ Church, despite the protests of the Dean – supported by Liverpool – that the appointments ought to be made solely on the grounds of merit. More recently the King had been exasperated by Liverpool's resolve to re-admit to the government the Queen's former intimate friend, George Canning, whom he had not forgiven for leaving the country and resigning from the government at the time of the proceedings against the Queen in the House of Lords. Grudgingly the King allowed that he might

* Lord Lauderdale told Creevey that when Ministers had papers to sign they had 'to write a letter to Bloomfield begging him to get the King's signature'; and Bloomfield, in turn, had 'to solicit Du Paquier, the King's valet, to seize a favourable opportunity. . . . The operation [was] the most difficult possible to get accomplished' (*Creevey Papers*, 368).

perhaps be prepared to make up his mind to this 'painful arrangement' if, 'upon further reflection', the government desired it. It must be understood, though, that Canning must not be given an office which would expose the King to 'personal communication' with him, and that as soon as the Governor-Generalship of India was vacant he should be sent out there. The King added that the government must never deceive itself into supposing that any expediency would ever induce him 'to give up the sacred privilege of naming the personal servants of the Crown'. Lord Liverpool gloomily concluded that the King was determined to keep Canning out of any important post in the government 'for the purpose of the more easily oversetting it when he [thought] fit'.

Hoping to come to a better understanding with the King at a personal interview, Lord Liverpool had humbly solicited his 'Majesty to do him the honour of dining and sleeping at Walmer Castle, which is only seven miles from Dover', on his return from Hanover. But his invitation had met with this cold reply: 'The King cannot avail himself of Lord Liverpool's polite invitation, as it is the King's present intention to proceed either to Ramsgate, or, what is more probable, to pass up the river at once in the steam-boat. It is the King's fixed determination to shew as often as the occasion may offer, the thorough disgust he feels at the unpardonable conduct of such part of his subjects as reside in the town of Dover.'

Since then, however, there had been a *rapprochement*. A compromise, which well satisfied the Conynghams, had been reached over the disputed appointment to the vacant office in the Royal Household. Lord Conyngham was not appointed Lord Chamberlain, but he did not have to content himself with being a mere Groom of the Stole. He was made Lord Steward of the Household, and was also sworn in as a Privy Councillor and Constable of Windsor Castle. Lord Cholmondeley, the former Lord Steward, was compensated for vacating the office by the promise of a Blue Ribbon for himself and a peerage for his son. 'The two awkward offices of Chamberlain and Master of the Horse are thus avoided,' Castlereagh told his brother. 'The office of Groom of the Stole would have been a more prudent measure, but the King's objections were insuperable. The present arrangement has been productive of *unmixed satisfaction*, and I am sure the difference between the two offices, assuming confidence in all other matters re-established, could not in the mind of a statesman be a motive for giving the King a sentiment of either power or humiliation. The Duke of Montrose will be Chamberlain. The Duke of Dorset, Master of the Horse.'

Castlereagh had never seen 'his Majesty *apparently* in better humour', after these arrangements in his Household had been made. 'Complete harmony' had been restored between the King and the government and he received Liverpool at Brighton *'with cordiality'*. He said he had *'never* felt *so* happy'. 'Canning will probably go to India,' Castlereagh went on, 'but such is the harmony of the day that nothing deemed necessary upon political arrangements will now be refused. Such a changed man as the King you never saw. He is in the highest spirits and says he, Liverpool, is again! entitled to all his confidence.' The day of his reconciliaton with his Prime Minister was, he said, the 'happiest of his life'. When Canning was offered and accepted the Governor-Generalship of India, all the King's troubles seemed over.

The King's cheerful mood continued well into the New Year, the first few weeks of which he spent very quietly at Brighton, rarely leaving his room except to walk across to Lady Conyngham's house about half past three or four o'clock in the afternoon, and to stroll back at six when he dressed for dinner at half past. On 11 January 1822, Croker, a guest at the Pavilion, found him 'looking remarkably well and stout on his legs; he went round the circle as usual' before dinner.

'The King made us all eat some roast wild boar from

Hanover,' Croker recalled. 'It was very good, like pork with a game flavour; he asked me what I thought of it. I said it was to pork what pheasant was to fowl. "There I differ from you," said the King. "Nothing is as good as fowl; if they were as scarce as pheasants, and pheasants as plenty as fowl, no one would eat a pheasant."

'When his Majesty took a glass of wine with Lady Conyngham, he *touched glasses* with her in the old-fashioned way.'

He talked of his journey to Hanover and of a play he had seen at Calais where Admiral Nagle was mightily taken with one of the dancers who 'held her leg *square with her shoulder* in a wonderful manner'. 'But the best of all,' Croker thought, 'was the King's mimicry of the old Duc de la Chartre, explaining to him that these actors and dancers at Calais were second-rate performers. I never heard anything so perfect in the way of imitation of voice, matter, and manner, as his representation of the old mumbling Duke.'

The next evening at dinner, the King was as contented as ever. The conversation turned on Lady Hervey's letters which Croker had edited, using in his notes some anecdotes which the King had told him. 'He was very gracious on this point,' Croker recorded, 'and said that if I had consulted him and let him into my secret, he would have afforded me still more. He was, he said, a great *reservoir* of anecdote, for he had lived not only with all the eminent persons of the last fifty years, but he had had an early acquaintance with several eminent persons of the preceding half-century.'

After dinner they had 'a musical night. He never left the pianoforte; he sang in "Glorious Apollo", "Mighty Conqueror", "Lord Mornington's Waterfall" (encored), "Non nobis, Domini", and several other glees and catches.' Croker did not think his voice was a very good one; and he did not 'sing so much from the notes as from recollection'. Even so he gave 'the force, gaiety and spirit of the glees in a superior style to the professional men' who were of the party. One of these professional men was old Michael Kelly, the former lover of the King's one-time mistress, Mrs Crouch. Kelly was 'wheeled in, in a gouty chair, and sang the solo of "Sleep you or Wake you", with all the force of a broken voice. ... Lady Conyngham and [her daughter] Lady Elizabeth did not conceal their dissatisfaction at all this music. ... The King, indeed, left his music but one moment the whole evening.'

Later on in the month Mme de Lieven came down to stay at the Pavilion and she, too, found the King still 'in high good humour'. Although far from being in that 'perfect' state of health which he had been seen to be enjoying three months before, his gout showed no signs of lowering his spirits. The undoubted success of his visits to Ireland and the Continent had not, of course, silenced his critics. In one of several caricatures ridiculing his visit to Germany, William Heath depicted him in a red coat of foreign cut and a round Teutonic cap, smoking a meerschaum pipe and carelessly tossing coins to excited Hanoverian subjects, one of whom says, 'He is indeed a Hanoverian at heart', to which another replies, 'No, he is an Irishman, he says', whereupon a third comments, 'Why some years ago he said he and his brother William were the only ones in the family who were *not Germans*.' Behind the cart in which he sits staggers John Bull, a weeping, lame and bony animal, weighed down by huge bundles of taxes.

But most of his critics were much quieter than of late; and, though not many of his champions were prepared to go so far as Thomas Moore who – a monarchist since the visit to Ireland – declared that if he occupied himself about the King at all it would be to praise him with all his heart, most of them seemed prepared to admit that he might, after all, prove to be a better monarch than they had expected.

Before the end of January, however, his gout had grown very much worse and he was becoming increasingly cantankerous. He could scarcely manage to walk to the dining-room table; and when he did get there he ate very little, and could eat nothing at all without previously imbibing cherry brandy in quantities 'not to be believed'. He still sang in the evenings, but with only a shadow of his former verve and force. The Duke of Wellington was a guest at the Pavilion for the first time this winter, and he did not like it there. The rooms were so infernally hot; the air reeked of scent; the lights were dazzling; the guests spent their evening half-lying on cushions listening to music, or playing patience and sipping liqueurs. 'Devil take me,' he exclaimed to Mme de Lieven, 'I think I must have got into bad company.' He behaved, she thought, 'in a lordly way with his master' who nevertheless pressed him to stay when he wanted to leave. Wellington made the excuse that he had to go back for a meeting of the Privy Council. '*Damn the Council*,' was all the King said. The Duke grumbled to Mme de Lieven that he would now have to write a long letter of excuse to his colleagues; so she undertook to do this for him and wrote, '*By his Majesty's command, Damn the Council.*' He signed the note and sent it off.

On the last day of the month Wellington, Mme de Lieven and the other guests returned to London. 'We left the King very ill,' Mme de Lieven recorded. 'He is tortured by gout and employs the most violent remedies to be rid of it. He looks ghastly; he is plunged in gloom; he talks about nothing but dying. I have never seen him so wretched; he did everything he could to pull himself together, but in vain. The favourite is in despair, especially over his temper, which is as sour as can be. ... The least thing gets on his nerves – and a crooked candle produces a storm of abuse. He treated the Duke of York very badly; I do not think he addressed two words to him. He is always very nice to me.'

Mme de Lieven was trying hard to persuade him not to give up his postponed plans for going to Vienna. But he kept making excuses – 'if I am well, if I live, if European politics permit'. Then he refused to budge unless Lady Conyngham went with him; and she absolutely refused to go. She complained to Mme de Lieven of his growing arrogance and despotism; her son, Lord Francis, was threatening to leave the Household because he could not 'stand it any longer'. 'But she drags the King into every sentence, as if she were a parvenue,' Mme de Lieven told Metternich. 'You cannot imagine what idiocies go on in that household; it is like being in a mad-house.'

One of the King's main causes of irritation was Sir Benjamin Bloomfield, whose sulky moods, bossy behaviour and repeated complaints had become intolerable. His management of the King's financial affairs was far from satisfactory, and his presumption in bowing to the audience in his box at a theatre in Ireland when 'God save the King' was being played had caused the greatest offence. The King had also heard, so Henry Hobhouse recorded, that Bloomfield had been spending up to £100,000 on land in Ireland and he wondered where on earth he had managed to get hold of so much money. So, under pressure from Lady Conyngham, whose dislike of Bloomfield was much increased by his persistent claim that the Privy Purse was exhausted by paying for her diamonds, and under equal though more wily pressure from Knighton, who wanted Bloomfield's appointment for himself, the King wrote to Lord Liverpool to suggest that as the government was now hopefully 'fixed on a settled and firm basis', he was desirous that there should be 'no impediment or interruption' to their 'permanent tranquility'. It had, therefore, occurred to the King that 'it might be desirable to get rid of the office of Private Secretary. This office had always been looked upon 'with a jealous eye, both by the government and the country', and it would, in his opinion, be highly popular if they were 'to break up the *thing altogether*'. 'This, however, cannot be done without making an extended provision for Sir Benjamin Bloomfield,' the King continued, 'because I think it is desirable that he should quit the Privy Purse also, for by thus retiring entirely from my family, it would be the means of saving both himself and the government much inconvenience, arising from the natural consequence of mistaken power and patronage.'

Lord Liverpool agreed with the King that Bloomfield

should relinquish the offices of Private Secretary and Privy
Purse, and that, as compensation, he should be offered the
Governorship of Ceylon. So the King wrote Bloomfield a
kind letter, thanking him for the 'attachment, zeal and integrity' he had always displayed in the 'very laborious and
confidential duties' which had been imposed upon him, and
explaining that it was 'not from preference to any other individual, nor from want of any personal confidence' that made
his resignation advisable. 'But many circumstances have
occurred which induce the King to think it highly desirable
to place the office of his Private Secretary upon a different
footing from that on which it has hitherto existed in the
hands of Sir John McMahon and Sir Benjamin Bloomfield.
The King, in short, wishes to restore it, as nearly as possible,
to what it was when held by Sir Herbert Taylor under the
King, his father, and to limit the functions of the situation
to the arrangement of his papers, the copying of his letters
and the occasional writing what he may think proper to dic-
tate, and afterwards sign, but that in future no communication should be made to the King upon publick affairs except
through his Ministers, unless in those cases when the individuals making them are entitled to apply directly to the
King.'

Having thus written to Bloomfield, the King wrote to
Liverpool again to say that his 'own feelings of affection towards the individual in question' were 'not sufficiently relieved', and that whilst he was fully aware of the prudence
of the step which he was about to take for the sake of his
government there were 'many painful regrets mixed with it'.
He, therefore, wanted Bloomfield to be offered a Red Ribbon
as well as an Irish peerage. Liverpool had no objection to
Bloomfield having a Red Ribbon, and he was accordingly
awarded the Grand Cross of the Order of the Bath on
1 April; but the Prime Minister did object to the grant of an
Irish peerage, an honour usually conferred for 'services and
personal consequence in Ireland'.

In any case, Bloomfield refused to be content with an Irish peerage; and declined 'altogether the proposition respecting Ceylon', preferring to remain 'at home with his present allowances', that was to say 'the salary of both his offices of the Privy Purse and the Secretaryship, his pension, and the Park at Hampton Court'. He also demanded a British peerage, and, when Liverpool informed him that that was 'absolutely impracticable', he continued to demand it 'with increased pertinacity', though the King agreed with Liverpool as to its 'impropriety'.

Faced with Bloomfield's rejection of employment in Ceylon, the King repeated the suggestion that the Private Secretaryship ought to be abolished not only because of the 'inordinate power' of the office, but also because of the 'embarrassment and painful distress' he suffered in consequence of Sir Benjamin Bloomfield's 'unhappy, uncertain and oppressive temper', and the change that had been 'gradually taking place for the last two years, in his general demeanor'. If, therefore, he did not want to go to Ceylon, it would be very welcome if some other foreign mission could be found for him. He had by now been excluded from the small glass-walled sitting room in the Pavilion, known as the 'Magic Lantern', where the King's most intimate circle were accustomed to meet; and it was embarrassing to have him in Brighton or London at all. The King indeed had conceived a detestation of Bloomfield since the plan to get rid of him was proving so difficult to accomplish because of the man's exasperating obstinacy. He 'loathed and detested' him so much that he could not bring himself even to write his name, and was 'furious' with anybody who was even 'commonly civil' to him.

Fortunately another foreign mission which Bloomfield deemed acceptable was found for him. Having first of all secured the Governorship of Fort Charles in Port Royal, Jamaica – a sinecure worth £650 a year which Lord Stewart generously relinquished upon Bloomfield's resignation of the Privy Purse – he agreed to go as Minister to Stockholm, provided that when a vacancy occurred in a more southerly capital he would be offered it.

Despite the King's protestations of wishing to abolish the office of Private Secretary once Bloomfield had given up the post, he made it clear that he wanted Knighton to succeed him, if not in name at least to take over most of his duties. Lord Liverpool strongly urged him to do nothing 'in this way at the moment', emphasizing that the appointment 'would very much augment all the difficulties attendant upon the removal' of Bloomfield and 'would create a prejudice very inconvenient to Sir Wm. Knighton himself'. The King was determined to have his way, however, and before the end of the year Knighton was appointed Keeper of the King's Privy Purse, and was given instructions 'to undertake the entire management' of the King's 'private affairs'. Knighton accepted the charge, and entirely gave up his profitable practice as a physician.

His influence now became more pronounced than ever; and it was soon clear that although not Private Secretary in name, that was what in fact he was. The King openly admitted it, asking the Foreign Office to let Knighton have a key to the F.F.F. boxes as he was under the necessity of calling upon him 'to fulfil those duties that would naturally attach to the office of the King's Private Secretary'. The keys were sent. But when the King demanded that Knighton should be appointed to the Privy Council, Lord Liverpool objected. The King was insistent: 'You are already acquainted with my feelings relative to the admission of my invaluable friend Sir William Knighton into the Privy Council. The thing is so proper and just that I wish to have no conversation on the subject; as my first Minister I wish to do nothing but what is in unison with your feelings, as far as I can; nevertheless, there are occasions in which I must use my own judgment.'

Although he thought it might be necessary in the end to give way 'to avoid ill humour and other inconveniences',

Lord Liverpool reminded the King that no monarch had ever had a Private Secretary until King George III went blind; and when Sir Herbert Taylor was appointed to the situation, 'the late King, who understood these matters better than anyone', decided he ought to be put on exactly the same footing as an Under-Secretary of State; it was certainly never suggested that Taylor should become a Privy Councillor. Wellington was inclined to allow the King to have his way. But sensing perhaps that his Majesty was not as firm on the point as his letters suggested, Liverpool, supported by Bathurst and Peel, decided to hold firm. Knighton was thoroughly indignant. He disliked Liverpool intensely and was excessively put out by the slight to which he fancied himself subjected. 'The truth is Lord Liverpool and I ought to be like *man and wife*,' he complained to Charles Arbuthnot. 'It may be very improper that there should be any person in my situation; the King perhaps ought not to have a favourite, but he cannot do without me.'

When the King appeared to accept, with perfect equanimity, Liverpool's decision that he should not be a Privy Councillor, Knighton was more annoyed than ever, and went about complaining of his Majesty's ingratitude and selfishness, his changed attitude towards him.

There was certainly a strange ambiguity in the relationship between the two men that intrigued and mystified observers. It was said that what had really attracted the King to Knighton in the first place was the *accoucheur*'s willingness to gossip about 'all the complaints of all the ladies that consult him', and that there was some sort of 'secret chain' which bound them unwillingly together. Lord Francis Conyngham told Charles Greville that, despite the reliance the King placed upon Knighton and the affectionate nature of their correspondence, in reality he regarded him with 'a detestation that could hardly be described'. He was afraid of him and that was the reason why he hated him so much. He took a peculiar delight in saying mortifying things about him. Once he cried out, 'I wish to God somebody would assassinate Knighton!' Greville himself had heard the King say at a particularly boisterous party when some Tyrolese singers whom Esterhazy had brought down were kissing him, 'I would give ten guineas to see Knighton walk into the room now.'

Thomas Bachelor, a Page of the Backstairs, agreed that the King hated Knighton, whose influence over him was without any limit. He told Greville, whispering 'as if the walls had ears', that Knighton 'could do anything and without him nothing could be done; that, after him, Lady Conyngham was all powerful, but in entire subservience to him; that she did not dare have anyone dine there without previously ascertaining that Knighton would not disapprove of it'.

Another fascinated observer, Charles Arbuthnot, who, as Joint Secretary to the Treasury and Patronage Secretary, had many opportunities of seeing them together, also thought that the King feared and hated Knighton, 'as a madman hates his keeper'. He was 'perpetually talking at him' and at dinner one afternoon 'jeered at him for not understanding French, which nettled Knighton extremely'. In indignant revolt against such treatment, Knighton evidently declared that the King was 'a great beast who liked nothing so much as indecent conversation and that, in that respect, Lady Conyngham managed him well for he dared not do it in her presence. He said he had no regard for anybody but himself.'

The King afterwards told Arbuthnot that Knighton had actually blackmailed him over the secret papers which McMahon had accumulated, and that he had succeeded in extracting £50,000 from him, not to mention £12,000 which had had to be paid in compensation to the holder of 'a place in the Duchy of Cornwall' which Knighton had wanted for himself.

In retailing this extraordinary story – which, in a rather

different form, Henry Hobhouse also heard – the King added that, although 'very absurd', very ambitious and 'with no idea of how to behave himself in good company', Knighton was admittedly very clever and organized his affairs 'excessively well'. This at least was true. Knighton was, indeed, a highly capable and conscientious servant, who managed the King's finances with exemplary skill. Bloomfield had estimated that his Majesty's income might 'be averaged at £90,000 as applicable to his private expenditure'. To keep his expenditure within the limit of this income was a severely demanding and not always possible task; but Knighton arranged it as well as anyone could have been expected to do. Knighton, of course, was a man whose peculiar and privileged position naturally made him an object of suspicion and jealousy, particularly to those who had formerly enjoyed a small part of his influence. A typical enemy was Sir Thomas Tyrwhitt, who had himself for several years been Private Secretary to the King when he was Prince of Wales. Tyrwhitt thought Knighton the 'greatest villain as well as the lowest blackguard' that ever lived, and was deeply affronted when this 'most vindictive man, eternally upon the watch', came into the King's room without knocking and 'planted himself at the bottom of the bed', while he, Sir Thomas Tyrwhitt, was enjoying a private tête-à-tête with his Majesty.

Yet for all his faults and affectations, his irritating assumption of privileges, his constant hints at secret knowledge, his 'mysterious way of talking', his undoubted love of intrigue and evident desire for advancement, Knighton was undeniably astute, patient and persevering. Even Mme de Lieven, who spoke of him derisively as 'the man midwife', who thought that everyone was afraid of him, 'from the King downwards', considered him a 'very clever man', one 'who really [had] to be reckoned with.' She never knew what he was thinking: when one day he smiled in his silent mysterious way at several compliments she had paid the

King, she could not make out 'if that meant he was laughing at [her] or that he thought [she] was laughing at the King'.

Knighton's supreme usefulness in Greville's opinion was that he was the 'only man who could prevail upon the King to sign papers, etc', and bring his mind to bear on tiresome questions which he would otherwise have chosen to avoid. In this, rather than in blackmail, lay the cause of the King's sudden vituperative attacks. As Knighton himself admitted to George Canning, it was 'a most painful part of his duty to press business upon his Majesty ... and that his doing so sometimes produced unpleasant scenes'. 'I believe he has as great an esteem and affection for me as anybody living,' Knighton went on; 'but he is uncertain, the creature of impulse. ... When he has got a particular notion into his head, there is no eradicating it.' Knighton 'could not imagine how business would get on at all' were he not there to press the King to attend to it.

The relationship between the two men resembled more that of an exasperated governess and a wayward charge than that of servant and master. Reliance led to resentment, resentment to outbursts of angry abuse against the person without whose help unwelcome and distasteful duties could not be done. They quarrelled; Knighton complained of the King's ingratitude; the King, peevish and resentful, insulted Knighton and told lies about him; the ill-used servant went away to sulk. But then there would come a cry for help from his 'ever most truly attached and affectionate friend', the King, who insisted that whatever his *very* dear and *best* friend might chuse to think', they still *were* friends. Rather huffily the servant would return; and all would be quiet again until the next eruption.

39

A New Foreign Secretary
1822–1823

'The damnedest fellow in the world'

THE disagreements and tiresome correspondence first about Bloomfield and then about Knighton had endangered but not entirely broken the King's continuing more friendly association with his Ministers, particularly with Castlereagh, even though Lady Castlereagh and Lady Conyngham were still not speaking to each other. Indeed, it was whispered that he behaved in a particularly affectionate way towards Castlereagh merely to pique Lady Conyngham whom he appeared now to be finding exceptionally irritating and with whom he frequently quarrelled.

Mme de Lieven recorded his behaviour at the opening of Parliament at the begining of February 1822 when there were 'indescribable oglings'. Mme de Lieven had gone to the House of Lords being, as she confessed, a good courtier and having heard that the King liked 'people to go to look at him with his crown on his head'. 'When he came in, he seemed quite crushed. His heavy robes, his crown slipping down on to his nose, his great train making his fat neck look still fatter – everything conspired to heighten the comic effect. He avoided the steps in mounting; when he was finally seated on the throne, he looked prostrate. A moment later, he caught sight of me – a smile. A row higher, his eyes fell on Lady Cowper – another smile. Higher still, Lady Morley – he beamed. He began letting his glance wander down the rows; but more often he looked up, with his eyelids going hard at it. ... The signalling never stopped for a second.'

A few weeks later, when Wellington went to stay at the Pavilion, the King was still on poor terms with Lady Conyngham; and Wellington was told that he was 'terribly out of spirits'. For this reason, when the Cabinet apprehensively approached him with a proposal to reduce the Civil List they expected bitter opposition. They were, therefore, the more delighted to meet with a reception 'exactly the opposite of all they had anticipated. ... He came to meet them and said that he knew the reason of their visit, that he approved it completely, and that he thought it right and proper that he should accept the sacrifice' since they, too, were taking a cut in their official salaries. The result was 'general good-humour and keen disappointment on the part of the opposition'.

He readily agreed to a cut in the Civil List of £30,000 a year; and he made the gesture 'with more feeling' than the Duke had 'ever known him shew'. But he soon afterwards relapsed into despondency.

By the end of April his quarrel with Lady Conyngham had still not been made up; she did 'not go near him' and did 'nothing but yawn'; and he, for his part, was 'in a frightful state of melancholy', 'bored to death', avoiding people, talking intermittently of his approaching end. There appeared to be a temporary *rapprochement* between the King and Lady Conyngham in May, according to Lady Cowper, who thought that Lady Conyngham was now behaving rather more kindly to him; but there were squabbles still. When the Prince and Princess of Denmark came to London, the King felt obliged to give them a large dinner-party and made out a list of names on which were naturally included those of Lord and Lady Castlereagh. Lady Conyngham declared that if Lady Castlereagh were to be invited, she herself could not possibly attend. The King sulkily replied that if she refused to attend he would cancel the dinner altogether. Eventually he persuaded her to talk the matter over with Mme de Lieven who, with great difficulty, persuaded her to let him have the Castlereaghs.

After this, relations between the King and Lady Conyngham improved. One day in June, on a visit to the Royal Lodge, Lady Cowper saw them driving together in a pony-chaise at Windsor; he seemed in excellent humour, and behaved towards her with unprecedented tenderness. Another day he pointed at Lady Conyngham and sighed, 'Ah, heavens, if she were what I am! ... If she were a widow, as I am a widower, she would not be one for long.'

'Ah, my dear King how good you are.'

'Yes, I have taken an oath.' Then turning to Mme de Lieven, he added in a low voice, 'Patience; everything in good time.'

But despite his reconciliation with Lady Conyngham, he soon fell back into gloom once more, seeming to Mme de Lieven not to know what to do with his summer, looking like a man on the point of suicide. One evening he quarrelled bitterly with the Duke of Wellington about the relative merits of the British and French cavalry. Wellington thought the French were the better; the King, insisting that the English could beat them any day, eventually rose from the table with the angry comment, 'Well, it is not for me to dispute on such a subject with your Grace.'

He succeeded in appearing with a more cheerful face on 20 June at the annual children's ball at Carlton House to which Croker's adopted daughter, his wife's little sister, had been invited. The King was 'much amused with the children. He walked about, except for about an hour and a half that he sat in the conservatory with Lady Conyngham and Mme de Lieven, while the children – including his niece Princess Victoria – danced before him and the company stood around him.'

At every opportunity the indefatigable Mme de Lieven pursued her endeavours to persuade the King to go to Vienna, where she hoped to contrive another meeting between herself and Metternich; but she found it impossible to tie the King down; he was like a weathercock; the last person to speak to him carried the day. The government

were as anxious that he should not go to Vienna, as Mme de
Lieven was that he should. They were afraid, as Wellington
told Lady Cowper, that he would again be condemned, as he
had been on his return from Hanover, for throwing money
about recklessly on the Continent. They also feared the consequences of further meetings with Metternich and of the
King's becoming even more deeply identified with Metternich's policies. Lord Liverpool strongly urged him not to go
to the Continent again, but to bring forward his visit to
Scotland which had been planned for 1823. By the beginning of July, Lord Liverpool had won him over: he would
go to Scotland instead of to Vienna.

Having made up his mind to go to Scotland, the King
called in his tailors and jewellers to fit him out with an
appropriate array of fine costumes. This was a task he
always enjoyed to the full, and his accounts reveal that he
spent quite as much on clothes as he had done in the days
when he had been, as Prince of Wales, one of the young
arbiters of fashion. Opera pelisses, astrakhan Polish caps,
silk bathing gowns, white beaver morning gowns made
'extra wide and very long', 'rich gold marmalouk sword
belts', 'rich Muscovy sable muffs', 'super printed blue striped
long cloth shirts with full bosoms' by the score, white long
gloves by the dozen, prime doe pantaloons, 'superfine scarlet
flannel underwaistcoats lined with fine callico', gloves, boots,
stockings and black silk drawers were delivered to him in
enormous quantities, and at enormous expense. One of his
pages told Thomas Raikes that a plain coat would cost £300
before it met with his approbation. And Maria Edgeworth
learned that one particular blue silk coat, the repeated
alterations to which kept a tailor and two assistants busy at
Windsor for three weeks, eventually cost £600. It was
scarcely an exaggeration. He was constantly returning
clothes to his tailors for alterations, and ordering new clothes
while waiting for the work to be done. He bought well over
five hundred shirts during the nine years of the Regency,

and subsequently ordered at least eight field-marshal's full-dress uniforms.*

For his visit to Scotland, George Hunter of Tokenhouse Yard and Edinburgh supplied the King with a magnificent equipage – a pair of fine gold 'shoe rosettes studded all over with variegated gems', 'a goatskin Highland purse with massive gold spring top'; three black morocco belts; a fine gold head ornament for his bonnet 'consisting of the Royal Scots crown in miniature set with diamonds, pearls, rubies and emeralds'; a 'large gold brooch pin with variegated Scotch gems'; 'a powder horn richly mounted in fine gold'; 'a fine basket hilt Highland sword of polished steel'; 'a pair of fine polished steel Highland pistols'; 'sixty-one yards of royal satin plaid; thirty-one yards of royal plaid velvet; seventeen and a half yards of royal plaid cashmere'. The total cost, including £32 for 'twelve phial cases of eau de Cologne', was £1,354 18s.

His Highland attire and his other clothes packed in a variety of trunks, the King left London for Greenwich on 10 August 1822, making a detour around the City to empha-

---

* Uniforms delighted him, as they did the rest of the family, and his knowledge of them was remarkable. His fastidious eye immediately spotted the slightest mistake. 'Good evening, sir,' he once called out to Lord Charles Russell, who was negligent enough to appear at a ball in the uniform of the Royal Horse Guards without the regulation aiguillette. 'Good evening, sir, I suppose that you are the regimental doctor.' Breaches of etiquette in civilian dress were equally painful to his eye. One evening at Manchester House, Captain Gronow, who had recently been living in Paris where 'knee-breeches were only worn by a few old fogies', was surprised to be tapped on the shoulder by Horace Seymour. 'The "great man",' Seymour told him, 'is very much surprised that you should have ventured to appear in his presence without knee-breeches. He considers it as a want of proper respect for him.' The next morning Gronow 'mentioned what had occurred, with some chagrin', to his Colonel, Lord Frederick Bentinck, who told him not to take it to heart. 'Depend upon it, Gronow,' Lord Frederick said, 'the Prince, who is a lover of novelty, will wear trousers himself before the year is out.' And so he did (*Gronow Reminiscences*, ii, 148).

size his displeasure at the disturbances which had taken place there when the Queen's coffin was on its way to Harwich. At Greenwich he stepped aboard the *Royal George* wearing a blue coat very much plainer than the extremely expensive outfits in the trunks that were loaded in the hold.

To the firing of guns, the cheering of the crowds on the bank, and the strains of a band playing 'God save the King', the *Royal George* was towed down river to Gravesend by the steam-packet, *Comet*, attended by the Lord Mayor's barge, drawn by another steam-boat. The King stood on deck for a time, acknowledging the cheers of the crowd and then retiring to his cabin with his favourite valediction, 'God bless you all!' Four days later, in pouring rain at about two o'clock in the afternoon, the *Royal George*'s anchor was dropped off Leith.

Despite the efforts of the *Scotsman* and other newspapers to persuade their readers not to emulate the conduct of the Irish, the King's welcome was noisy and ebullient. All afternoon boats sailed around the *Royal George*, and their crews and passengers stood up, ignoring the rain, waving their hats and cheering. The King appeared on deck from time to time, bowing and smiling, the first King to have visited Scotland since the time of Charles II. During the afternoon Sir Walter Scott, who had been asked to supervise the arrangements for the King's reception, came aboard to welcome him to Scotland, to apologize for the appalling weather, of which he was 'perfectly ashamed', and to present him with a silver St Andrew's cross from the ladies of Edinburgh. The King greeting Scott as 'the man in Scotland' he 'most wished to see', accepted the cross gratefully, told Scott he would wear it in his hat, and offered him a glass of cherry brandy. Having drunk the King's health, Scott asked if he could keep the glass in memory of the occasion, and, the request being granted, he put it in his back pocket. He forgot all about it when he got home, sat down in a chair, and suddenly screamed so loudly that his wife thought he had cut his bottom on a pair of her scissors.

Next morning the King, wearing as promised the St Andrew's cross in his hat – together with a big thistle and a small sprig of heather – was brought to the landing stage in the royal barge. He was then driven in state to Holyroodhouse, attended by detachments of the Royal Company of Archers and the Scots Greys. He passed through streets magnificently decorated with crowns and stars, streamers and thistles and placards of welcome, past crowds of cheering people waving plumed and feathered hats and wearing buttons inscribed with some such legend as, 'You Are Welcome, King!' Obviously delighted by his reception and by the garlanded beauty of Edinburgh, he smiled and nodded engagingly as the open carriage rolled along the streets, making an occasional flattering remark, observing more than once, 'They are a nation of gentlemen.'

He stayed at Dalkeith Palace with the sixteen-year-old Duke of Buccleuch whose staff were asked to leave the kitchen and cellars in the more expert care of the royal cooks and butlers. The Duke's table was consequently much improved during the visit, but the King kept a careful and solicitous eye on his host. 'No! No!' he once protested when the Duke was offered a glass of the King's liqueur. 'No! No! It is too strong for his Grace to drink.'

From Dalkeith Castle the King drove out, with remarkable zest for a gouty man of sixty, to drawing-rooms and levees, to a command performance of *Rob Roy*, to the Caledonian Ball where he asked for Scottish reels – 'None of your foreign dances!' – to a civic banquet at which he made one of his adroit and pleasant speeches: 'I am quite unable to express my sense of the gratitude which I owe to the people of this country; but I beg to assure them that I shall ever remember as one of the proudest moments of my life the day I came among them, and the gratifying reception which they gave me. I return you, my Lord Provost, my lords and gentlemen, my warmest thanks for your attention this day; and I can assure you with truth, with earnestness and sincerity that I shall never forget your dutiful attention to me on my visit to Scotland and particularly the pleasure I have derived from dining in your hall this day.'

He proceeded in state, in his field-marshal's uniform, from Holyrood to Edinburgh Castle, as the cannon boomed in the fog. It was raining and windy as well as foggy, but he manfully stood beneath the Royal Standard on the Castle's highest battery smiling and waving his hat.

The only event during the visit which was not entirely successful was the levee at Holyroodhouse on 19 August. The King, though still very proud of his legs, did not really look his best in Highland costume; and the flesh-coloured pantaloons which – according to Sir David Wilkie who painted him in this attire – he wore under his kilt, did not improve the effect. Far stranger than the King's appearance, though, was that of his jovial, loud and uninhibited friend, the sea-biscuit manufacturer, Sir William Curtis, who appeared, 'a portentous figure', wearing full Highland uniform complete with a kilt of the Stuart tartan.

But although the appearance of these 'gallant Highlandmen' was widely ridiculed, the success of the King's visit was not impaired. When he left Edinburgh at the end of the month, having ensured that a suitably grateful letter was written to Sir Walter Scott and having knighted that other fine Scottish artist, Henry Raeburn, President of the Scottish Academy, he had cause to feel satisfied that the duties of yet another state visit had been well performed.

Lord Melville, the Scottish First Lord of the Admiralty, who was 'firmly persuaded' that his visit would be attended with 'important public benefit', wrote to congratulate him warmly upon 'the determined and deep rooted monarchical feeling which evidently pervaded the great body of the people'. And Sir Walter Scott at Abbotsford told Knighton on 12 September that 'ground for congratulation on the King's visit to Scotland continued to increase daily. It was impossible for anyone to have foreseen its extent among a people who are tenacious to a proverb of the opinion which they adopt.' Scott had no doubt that the good effects of the visit would be long felt after he was 'dead and gone'; he was particularly pleased, he said, that the people had been able to see for themselves that his Majesty was far from being as 'overgrown' as 'lying newspapers and caricatures' had suggested. 'Their delight was extreme at seeing a portly handsome man looking and moving every inch a King.'

The pleasures of the visit had been overcast at the outset by distressing news that had reached Edinburgh on 14 August. Two days before, at nine o'clock in the morning, the King's sixtieth birthday, Lord Castlereagh had killed himself. The King was 'horribly upset', 'bitterly lamented his loss', spoke of Castlereagh in the 'warmest terms'; and told Peel that it was the 'greatest loss he had ever sustained'. He had, however, been 'almost prepared' for the news. He had seen Castlereagh the day before he had left London, and had then been so appalled and alarmed by his behaviour that he had been unable to get to sleep that night. Castlereagh had displayed every sign of being deranged, gripping the King by the arm, accusing himself of all sorts of crimes, kissing his Majesty's hands, weeping, telling him that he was being accused of homosexual practices, that he was going to fly away to Portsmouth 'and from there to the ends of the earth'.

As soon as the King had managed to calm him down and to persuade him to go home, he sent for Lord Liverpool, asking him to come to him 'directly'. 'Either I am mad or Lord [Castlereagh] is mad,' he assured Liverpool. 'I am the more apprehensive on account of the strength of his mind. There is greater danger in these cases from strong minds than from weak ones.'

There had been indications of a possible collapse for some time. Castlereagh had been displaying inordinate suspicion of his colleagues, particularly of Wellington. His brother, Lord Stewart, had declared that he 'had never seen a man in such a state' and had burst into tears at the thought of it. And Mme de Lieven had reported him as looking 'ghastly' in June, as having aged five years in a week, of being a 'broken man'.

As a precaution, all his razors and pistols had been removed from his dressing-room; but, making use of 'a little nail-knife which he carried in his pocket book', he had cut his carotid artery with 'anatomical accuracy'.

The King, who had grown accustomed to Castlereagh and appreciated his skill as a mediator between the Crown and the rest of the Cabinet, now gloomily faced the prospect of having to agree to the appointment of a new Foreign Secretary. On his return to London he asked Croker if Lord Liverpool were in a good humour or not, 'almost as a boy after holidays asks in what temper "Dr Bury may be" '. Well aware that Liverpool would probably suggest Canning, who had not yet sailed for India, as a suitable candidate for the vacant office, the King made it clear that his previous objections still remained, that almost any other candidate would be preferable, and that Canning's 'departure for India should not be interrupted'. Wellington would have been the King's choice, with the Home Secretary, Robert Peel, also a strong candidate, promoted to the Chancellorship of the Exchequer with the leadership of the House of Commons. But Liverpool was convinced that Canning would have to come into the Cabinet as Foreign Secretary if his government were to survive. He would, indeed, have brought him in long before had not grief at Lady Liverpool's death made him feel incapable of coping with the King's intransigence so often and so forcibly expressed to him. Now the King must be overruled. Although opinion in the Cabinet was far from unanimous in Canning's favour, several members had threatened to resign if he were not readmitted; and there was danger of losing much support in Parliament. The Tory government desperately needed bolstering by the kind of liberal support which only Canning could supply. Canning himself had expressed a wish to go to India rather than to accept anything less than Castlereagh's 'whole heritage';

Peel had said that he did not wish to be considered in any sense a rival to Canning.

Having listened to Liverpool's arguments, the King consulted Peel, Wellington, Sidmouth, and other members of the Cabinet. He remained sulky, reluctant and unconvinced, complaining of the difficulty in being reconciled with a man whom 'he had said he never wanted to see again in his life'. Lady Conyngham, who had 'conceived a great antipathy to Canning', urged him to stand firm; but he was beginning to recognize the impossibility of this and burst out irritably, 'Very well, if you like. I will not appoint him; I will change the government and put in the Whigs.'

Wellington's advice was more realistic than Lady Conyngham's: his Majesty would have to forgive Canning, and agree to his appointment. The King protested that his 'honour as a gentleman' prevented him from doing any such thing whereupon Wellington, who disliked the clever, self-confident upstart Canning even more than the King did, replied that his duty as a monarch made it essential for him to take the best man available. On 8 September the King gave way. 'Very well, gentlemen,' he said. 'Since you are determined to have him, take him in God's name, but remember I tell you he will throw you all overboard.' When confirming this decision to Liverpool, he insisted that, in sacrificing his 'private feelings', he was making the greatest sacrifice he had ever made in his life. Without mentioning the Foreign Office, he said in a subsequent letter that he would agree to 'Mr Canning's re-admission into the government'; but he wanted him to be told that the King was aware that the 'brightest ornament of his crown' was the power of extending 'grace and favour to a subject who may have incurred his displeasure'.

This phrase deeply offended Canning who, at first, refused to accept the Foreign Office when it was formally offered to him. It was, he complained, just as though he had been given a ticket to Almack's and found written on the back:

'*Admit the rogue.*' Liverpool, however, thought the letter unexceptionable, and assured Peel that he considered it to be 'expressed with as much delicacy as, considering the King's strong personal feelings, could reasonably be expected'. In the end Canning decided to ignore the King's rebuke and to accept office.

As Canning took up his duties the King fell ill again, fretfully apprehensive as to the effect of the new Foreign Secretary's ideas on the kind of conservative monarchical Europe which Castlereagh had favoured, worrying continually about the attacks that were made on him in public and the importunities to which he was subjected in private. In May he had been delighted and astonished, on going to Drury Lane, to be greeted with the greatest enthusiasm, and by the National Anthem being repeated no less than six times. The Duke of Wellington had arrived just before him and had acknowledged the loud cheers of the audience 'with two little nods, as if to say, "how do you do", and then left them to clap their hands sore without giving another look'. The King, by contrast, had spent 'a good quarter of an hour bowing to the audience, as politely and respectfully as if it had been composed of Kings and Queens'. But the people so rarely behaved in this gratifying way in England. Far more often he had cause to complain of the assaults made on him in the Press, particularly in the Sunday papers, and of the 'obscene prints in the form of caricatures' that were still displayed in almost every shop window in London, exposing him 'in some indecent ridiculous manner'.

At the beginning of January 1823 Mme de Lieven 'found the King changed', 'aged a great deal in the last three months', and limping 'noticeably'. Emily Cowper was also much disturbed about him. 'The King is in a strange state of health now,' she reported to Frederick Lamb. 'He suffers dreadfully from rheumatic gout so as hardly to be able to turn in bed without screaming ... I cannot help feeling that his life is very precarious – one thing after another always starting up and keeping him so weak and ill.' He was, indeed, by then in a 'wretched state of health', suffering from 'irregularity of the pulse, occasional pain about the praecordia, sensation in the left arm and sudden breathlessness'. He was 'bled copiously' as usual; but the doctors feared that his heart was affected. If he adhered to the rules of conduct which they had laid down, they considered that 'his constitution, naturally so good', would 'continue to preserve his invaluable life for years'; but they felt it their duty to record in a 'most confidential private' document that it did sometimes happen that life was 'extinguished suddenly' where such symptoms existed as prevailed 'at present in his Majesty'.

Towards the end of March 1823 Croker reported him as being 'much weakened' by his attacks of gout. A few days later he took to his bed, refusing to see anybody but his doctors. He was still in bed at the beginning of May, and the newspapers were 'trying to make out' that he was going the same way as his father. He got up towards the middle of the month but by the fifteenth he had suffered a relapse, had erysipelas on one foot and a high temperature. Wellington confided in Mme de Lieven that he thought he would be dead in eight months, a verdict with which she was inclined to agree. It was 'a fact that since January 6 [he had] not enjoyed an hour's health, and often, for three or four weeks at a time, he had been very ill indeed'. At his age, it was not easy to recover from such attacks, 'especially with a complete lack of air and exercise'. All eyes were, therefore, on the Duke of York who was concerning himself much with public affairs, though the opposition derived little comfort from that as they had 'nothing to hope for from his reign'.

People were also watching Lady Conyngham who seemed to be 'taking precautions'. According to Mme de Lieven, whose comments upon her were always coloured by resentment at her influence over the King, Lady Conyngham had recently observed, 'What a pity now if all this were to end; for you must admit that it is charming.' As she spoke she looked around her drawing-room which was 'like a fairy's

boudoir'. That was the sort of thing she wanted from the
King, Mme de Lieven commented. If the King died, what
she would regret would be 'his diamonds, pearls, handsome
furniture and good dinners', and his ability to advance her
family. The King was well aware of this himself, so Mme de
Lieven claimed. He once observed to her, 'You see how she
takes advantage of her position to push her family. Oh she
knows very well when she is well off.' If the King saw
through her as clearly as that, Mme de Lieven could not
understand how his love for her could last so long. 'But it
does last,' she wrote, 'simply because he needs a habit.'

Annoyed to have the habit of Castlereagh broken, he
could not get used to Canning, although he had received
him politely enough when he had first taken up his appointment. 'I do not like him any better than I did,' he complained in the spring of 1823 to Mme de Lieven, who passed
on to Metternich the kind of conversation most pleasing to
him. 'I recognize his talent, and I believe we need him in the
Commons; but he is no more capable of conducting foreign
affairs than your baby. He doesn't know the first thing about
his job: no tact, no judgement, no idea of decorum. But
what is to be done? Can I change my Minister? No, for I
should only get someone worse. That is the fix I am in. The
best is bad; but the worst would be hateful, and there is nothing in between.' He was still talking of Canning in similar
terms to Wellington in May 1824, saying that he was 'the
damnedest fellow in the world and that he could not bear
him', while admitting that it 'would not do to turn him out'.
'Think of that damned fellow wanting me to have the King
and Queen of the Sandwich Islands to dinner,' he expostu-
lated the next month, 'as if I would sit at table with such a
pair of damned cannibals.' It was all made much worse, he
complained to Wellington, by the 'absurd, weak and disgusting conduct' of the Prime Minister, to whom he had
'always had an aversion' and whom, if Wellington had been
willing to succeed him, he would have endeavoured to replace: 'Depend upon it that Lord Liverpool, if he lives till

Doomsday, will never be corrected, or made fit for the high office, to which I raised him.' *

The King talked endlessly about foreign affairs to Mme de Lieven, to the Duke of York, to Wellington, who agreed that Canning 'knew no more of foreign politics than a child', to foreign ambassadors – notably Prince Esterhazy, the Austrian Ambassador, and Count Münster, the Hanoverian Minister – and to anyone else to whom he cared to elaborate his opinions. Lady Charlotte Greville, after sitting next to him at dinner, was forced to conclude that he really was becoming 'the greatest bore she ever saw'.

He took no trouble to disguise his dislike of Canning, or his regret that Castlereagh was dead. Castlereagh had understood the problems of Europe, and had artfully assured the King that the only other person who understood foreign affairs was his Majesty himself. He had known most of its sovereigns and leading statesmen personally; he had been controlled, patrician, well-mannered, faithful in defence of the monarchical system, whereas Canning, caustically witty and overtly ambitious, seemed to the King to take a view of foreign policy more in line with the Whigs than that of the Tories.

Of course, Castlereagh, while sympathizing with suppression of revolution in Europe, had been prevented by public opinion from interfering in the affairs of other states, even had he approved of the general right of intervention, which he did not. When revolution broke out in the Kingdom of the Two Sicilies, for example, he recognized Austria's right to crush it before it threatened the Emperor's interests in Italy;

---

* Wellington thought that it was as much Lord Liverpool's fault as the King's that they could not get on together (*Wellington and his Friends*, 40). As Mrs Arbuthnot said, Liverpool had a 'disagreeable, cold manner and a most querulous temper' which rendered it 'a difficult and unpleasant task to act in public life with him'. He must have been 'a very bad manager', she thought to be 'so perpetually getting into scrapes' with the King who was quite easily 'managed by those who took the trouble to please him when they could' (*Arbuthnot Journal*, i, 126).

but Austria must put down the uprising on her own since it did not endanger the general security of Europe. Castlereagh was 'like a great lover of music who is at church', the Austrian Ambassador in London declared. 'He wishes to applaud, but he dare not.'

Canning continued this policy of non-intervention, but he did not fully share Castlereagh's views of the monarchical principle and he wholly disagreed with his methods. He did not approve of conferences: even had he been able to meet foreign rulers and ministers in the way and on the terms that Castlereagh had done, he recognized the danger of conducting foreign policy over the heads of Parliament and people in the way that the King preferred.

The King firmly believed that the monarchs of Europe shared a common interest, that they ought to support each other in their struggle against the revolutionary movements now once more threatening to engulf them. He told the French *chargé d'affaires*, the Vicomte de Marcellus, that he wholeheartedly supported Marcellus's royal master whose troops intervened in Spain on behalf of the tottering Bourbon, King Ferdinand VII. And when *The Times* reported his indiscreet remarks, commenting that they were scarcely sentiments to be expected from a former disciple of Charles James Fox, the King riposted that he was now a royalist by trade and despised the 'shameful uncertainty' of his Cabinet.

He was extremely well-informed – often, indeed, he was better informed than his Ministers, for he did not hesitate to use his position as King of Hanover to obtain information not available to them through the diplomatic channels of that country. Nor did he hesitate to correspond freely with foreign courts until Canning threatened to expose his letters in Parliament. He even sent Knighton to the Continent on confidential missions necessarily out of tune with Canning's policies; and, encouraged by Mme de Lieven and Wellington, he went so far as to invite Metternich to stay at the Royal Lodge where, as King of Hanover, he could talk to him about affairs without the intervention of his Ministers. Metternich, warned by Canning of the consequences of a visit to England for such a purpose, thought it prudent to decline the invitation.

Thereafter the King took an increasingly perverse pleasure in using his acquired knowledge to discomfit Canning, to make him ill at ease in his presence. He delighted in contradicting him, in making outrageous comments he knew would annoy him. One day in June 1823 at the Royal Lodge where – despite his earlier avowal that he would never receive him – he sometimes included Canning amongst his guests, the conversation turned to Spain and her autocratic ruler. The King was in cheerful and confident mood, having been received at Ascot races that morning 'with a good deal of enthusiasm', and when Canning spoke apprehensively about King Ferdinand's policies, he retorted airily that there was 'nothing to be afraid of. Canning insisted that Prince Metternich wanted to rule the whole world, to wipe out every constitution from the surface of the globe. "No harm in that," said the King, "as long as our constitution is among them." '

The next month, at a ball at Carlton House, the King went out of his way to annoy Canning in front of the French *chargé d'affaires*. On this occasion, too, Canning refused to rise to the provocation; but after the King had moved away he said to Marcellus, 'Representative government has still one advantage that his Majesty has forgotten. Ministers have to endure without answering back the epigrams by which a King seeks to avenge himself for his impotence.'

Later on that summer the King led the after-dinner conversation round to Fouché. 'Instead of taking him for my Minister, as the King of France has done,' he said to Prince Polignac, 'I should have hanged him, and eighty other rascals with him; that is what I should have done with those Jacobins.' Prince Polignac 'pretended to look embarrassed, but was really delighted. He was much more so when the King said. "What an admirable speech M. de Chateaubriand

made in reply to all the nonsense that was talked here!
What good taste! We admired it greatly ..." Canning made
no movement.'

The differences between the King and Canning were
strongly emphasized the following year when the Cabinet
proposed negotiating a commercial treaty with Buenos Aires
which had ceased to acknowledge the sovereignty of the
King of Spain. Encouraged by Wellington, the King informed the Cabinet that he very much regretted this move
which would 'carry with it the appearance and promise of an
early recognition to the different insurrectionary States of
South America'. In a long and forceful letter to Lord Liverpool he roundly condemned the 'new political liberalism'
which he considered so dangerous a policy that for a time he
refused to talk about it personally to Canning who was required to communicate with him in writing. He reminded
the Prime Minister that 'the line of policy pursued by the
government ... at the close of the late war ... was *unanimity*
of cooperation with the great Continental Powers not only
for the purpose of putting an end to the existing hostilities,
but for preserving the future tranquility and peace of
Europe'. Lord Castlereagh, in conjunction with the Duke of
Wellington, had 'so effectually accomplished this desirable
and great object that the country had taken a position, in
relation to her continental policy, that she had never before
held'.

'The King supposes it will not be denied,' he continued,
'that the anarchy produced throughout the world by the
French Revolution has left a record so instructive that the
Councils of the British government should never fail to be
regulated by the wholesome remembrance of that terrible
event! That we should therefore regard with the utmost suspicion every attempt to revive the example of British
America which unhappily for Great Britain ended in a separation from the mother country. France treacherously assisted that successful enterprise and by her fatal policy gave
the first impulse to that revolution which entailed, for a

quarter of a century, such complicated misery on the whole of Europe.

'The revolutionary spirit of those days, although lulled and suspended, is by no means extinguished; and it would be wisdom to look to the ultimate consequences which the result of our recognition of the independence of the South American provinces may probably produce on the evil and discontented who are even at this moment controlled with difficulty by the established power of regular governments.'

The King concluded by saying that he had long been aware that the principles of his early friends, the Whigs, were 'the bane that threatened the destruction of our happy Constitution and the peace of the world', and that since he had abandoned them – for the good of the country – on his coming to power as Regent, could the present government suppose that he would permit 'any individuals now to force upon him measures of which he entirely disapproved', particularly when 'many members' of the present Cabinet (Wellington, Bathurst, Eldon and Westmorland among them) held the same opinion 'respecting the new political liberalism' as he did himself? 'No such thing! If the present line of policy [were] to be *further* pursued, the King [would] feel himself justified in taking such measures as the government [would] be the least prepared to accept.'

But the threat was an empty one. Commercial and other pressures were too strong to prevent recognition of the independence of Spain's South American colonies. Trade with them had increased fourteen times since the end of the Spanish monopoly. Even Castlereagh had declared that recognition of the new republics was more 'a matter of time than of principle'; and the President of the United States, James Monroe, knowing that Britain would oppose any move by the European powers to help King Ferdinand to recover his Empire, had announced in a statement which Canning described as 'a new doctrine', that an attempt by Europe to impose an unwelcome 'political system' on any part of the Western Hemisphere would be considered as dangerous to America's 'peace and safety'. So, on 31 December 1824, Buenos Aires, Mexico and Colombia – and shortly afterwards Brazil – were all recognized as independent countries.

The King was so annoyed by the government's action that he resolutely refused to read the speech announcing it at the opening of Parliament. He let it be known that his gout was so bad that he could not walk. He could not speak either, so he said, because he had lost his false teeth.

40

Palace and Castle
1823–1826

*'England ought to pride herself on her plainness
and simplicity'*

As often as he could the King escaped from London to the
privacy of the Royal Lodge, where he surrounded himself
with 'the Cottage clique' – Esterhazy and Esterhazy's *chargé
d'affaires*, Baron Neumann, Count Münster, Prince Polignac, the French Ambassador, and the Lievens – lamenting
with them the new liberalism, the sympathetic attitudes towards self-determination, that were spreading so fast across
the world and were destroying the hopes of the men who
had redrawn Napoleon's map of Europe at the Congress of
Vienna. Mme de Lieven, a guest during August 1823, told
Metternich how drearily the days passed in contrast with
the 'exceedingly agreeable' time that the Duke of Dorset
had spent there three years before. The suite which Mme de
Lieven and her husband occupied was below the level of the
garden from which the field mice came in to run about the
rooms. The King was miserable and limped through the
house, sometimes in tears. 'Yesterday evening the King began to sing,' she reported on the 12th, his sixty-first birthday. 'In order to produce the sole musical sound of which
his throat is capable, he closed his eyes, shed tears. ... I
stifled my laughter ... I really thought I should die, especially when I saw how affected the courtiers looked at the
sight of the royal tears.'

Sometimes Mme de Lieven was so bored that she felt close
to tears herself. She got up at nine, went straight out into
the garden and returned to her room at eleven to dress for
luncheon with the King. After luncheon she and the other

guests went out for a drive or on the river, returning half an hour before dinner. Dinner was followed by music, then by a game of écarté. The conversation was occasionally interesting, but usually 'so stupid' that she began to doubt her own intelligence. Once her mind wandered to a far more exciting evening spent with Metternich. She woke from her reverie to find the King 'gazing' at Lady Conyngham with an expression in which somnolence battled against love; Lady Conyngham was staring at a beautiful emerald on her arm; her daughter was toying with a ruby hanging round her neck.

On another occasion Mme de Lieven's unbearable boredom during the customary silence after grace led to her being seized with 'an uncontrollable fit of laughter'. First Lady Elizabeth Conyngham was infected by it, then Admiral Nagle, who upset a bottle which gave them all an excuse 'to go on laughing' and even get worse. The King was angry, Mme de Lieven said. 'He thought we were laughing at him. I did not mind; for the moment I was beyond caring. He could not scold me, so he scolded the daughter. Afterwards we played fourteen games of écarté and thirty-three games of patience.'

Frustrated in his efforts to control Canning's policies, the King could at least comfort himself with the knowledge that he was able to use his influence to more effect in the world of art and letters, that his opinions there did carry some weight, and that artists and writers were deeply grateful for his munificent patronage.

By this time the most important items in his collection had already been assembled. Since his purchase in 1814 of eighty-six splendid pictures from the collection of Sir Thomas Baring, he had been less and less inclined to buy paintings *en bloc*. In 1819 Sir Charles Long – who, with Lord Yarmouth and William Seguier, was one of his principal advisers – had heard that the famous Aynard collection would probably come on to the market in Paris. But the

King had decided that it was 'too general'; he was now limiting himself to what he 'actually wanted'; and he purchased only the *Farm at Laeken* by Rubens.

Yet though the quantity of the King's purchases had declined, their quality had not. He had paid a thousand guineas for Dou's *Interior of a Grocer's Shop*; he had bought Mieris's *Fruiterer's Shop*, Schalcken's *Candle-light*, Steen's *Morning Toilet*, De Hooch's *The Card-Players* and *A Courtyard in Delft*. In 1819 Lord Yarmouth had purchased for him Rembrandt's *Lady with a Fan*, a superb companion for Rembrandt's *Shipbuilder and his Wife* which he had acquired, together with fine paintings by Adriaen van de Velde, Wouwermans and Ostades at the Lafontaine sale at Christie's some years before.

The King's collection of pictures by contemporary artists, mostly English, had also continued to grow apace. He had year by year placed more and more commissions for portraits of his family and friends, his distinguished contemporaries and his beloved animals. Portraits by Beechey and Stroehling were added to those by Hoppner, Copley, Gainsborough and Reynolds. Pictures by Schwanfelder, Cooper, Doyle and Ward came to join the Sawreys, Gilpins, Garrards, Marshalls and Stubbses. Military subjects were as welcome as ever; so were genre scenes by artists like William Mulready and William Collins.

No artist was kept so busy as Thomas Lawrence who painted Lady Conyngham's daughters, Sir William Curtis, the Duke of Devonshire, Wellington, Lord Eldon, Canning, Bathurst, Liverpool and Walter Scott, as well as numerous other British and foreign notables, almost all the members of the King's immediate family, and on more than one occasion the King himself. Lawrence was eventually to receive well over £25,000 from the Privy Purse.

Nor were painters alone grateful for his patronage and generosity. The sculptors, John Flaxman and Richard Westmacott, as well as Chantrey, received satisfying commissions. Scott was always pleased to know that his latest work appeared on the King's table; Southey was gratified to learn that his Majesty esteemed his 'distinguished talents' and the usefulness and importance of his 'literary labours'. The Trustees of the British Museum were delighted when his father's library of some 65,000 volumes came into their possession and they received from Parliament a generous grant of £120,000 to build a suitable extension to the Museum in which they could be housed. On making this gift to the nation, the King told Lord Liverpool that as well as 'paying a just tribute' to the memory of his father, he had 'the satisfaction by this means of advancing the literature of the country'.* The advancement of literature was, indeed, a pursuit that the King continued to follow with credit. His

---

* The details of this transference of King George III's library to Bloomsbury are a mystery on which the Royal Archives throw no light. In 1850 an article appeared in the *Quarterly Review* which suggested that the King had originally intended to sell the library to the highest bidder. Richard Heber, the book collector, hearing that the Tsar was interested in buying it, approached Lord Sidmouth who arranged for the money which the King had hoped to receive from the Tsar to be paid to him out of the Droits of Admiralty (*Quarterly Review*, clxxv, 143). The Duke of York, who was very annoyed with his brother for having parted with their father's property, told Charles Greville that the King 'even had a design of selling the Library collected by the late King, but this he was obliged to abandon' (*Greville Diary*, 8 January 1823). The Duke of Clarence was also 'much vexed' by his brother's action and would never visit the King's Library at the British Museum (Macaulay's Journal, Trinity College, Cambridge, entry for 29 November 1849).

Antonio Panizzi, who was Keeper of Printed Books (1837–56) and Principal Librarian (1856–66) said in his evidence before the Select Committee of the House of Commons in 1836, when he was Assistant Librarian, that it was due to the personal influence of the Trustees that the King's Library came to the Museum. The Trustees 'worked very hard, to get that Library,' Panizzi declared, 'and exerted all their influence, both public and private' (Para. 4901).

Peel, however, who was one of the Trustees and had much to do with the disposal of the King's Library, confirmed in his correspondence with W. R. Hamilton that it was King George IV's personal wish that it should go to Bloomsbury as his father had always been so interested in the Museum (BM Peel MSS).

interest in the Stuarts which had led to the publication in 1816 of *The Life of James II ... Collected out of Materials by his own Hand*, was followed by the formation of a commission, headed by Sir Walter Scott, to edit the Stuart papers. The biography of Nelson, which the King had encouraged his librarian, James Stanier Clarke, to help to write, formed the basis for Robert Southey's classic *Life* and several later works. In 1820 the King readily and enthusiastically took up a proposal of Thomas Burgess, Bishop of St David's, for the establishment, under royal patronage, of a Society of Literature. He agreed to contribute the sum of a thousand guineas towards its establishment, and to make an annual grant of a hundred guineas. The Bishop mistook the King's meaning, and announced that the entire sum would be given annually. The King did not correct the mistake, and it was therefore settled that he would give a thousand guineas a year from the Privy Purse as pensions to ten Associates of the Society – the first of the ten names on the list being that of Samuel Taylor Coleridge – and to donate an annual prize of 'two medals of fifty guineas each'. A few years later the Society obtained from the Commissioners of Woods and Forests the lease of a site in St Martin's Place, Trafalgar Square, on which to build a house for their headquarters.*

Many other organizations also profited from the King's spontaneous generosity. The Royal Academy received ten more 'casts of statues from the antique'; Trinity College, Cambridge, received a grant of £1,000 towards the building of a new quadrangle to be known as The King's Court; £200 was contributed from the Privy Purse 'for the professional use of the English students at Rome'; £500 went towards a statue of James Watt; a suggestion from Peel that his Majesty should command 'two gold medals to be in future

---

* The house, designed by Decimus Burton, was demolished when the National Gallery was enlarged in the 1890s. The Society then moved to Hanover Square, then to Bloomsbury Square before settling in Hyde Park Gardens (Records of the Royal Society of Literature).

annually given as honorary rewards for the best papers sent
in to the Council of the Royal Society on Scientific Subjects'
was immediately accepted with the proviso that the medals
should be of the value of fifty guineas each and not twenty
as Peel had proposed. Numerous presents were given to
artists, writers and musicians whom the King asked to be
presented to him. One of these was Gioachino Rossini who
visited England in December 1823, 'a fat, sallow squab of a
man', in Lady Granville's opinion. 'The courtiers and the
rest of the society were indignant at his familiarity. Being
fat and lazy, and consequently averse to standing, he took
a chair and sat by the King, who, however, gave him the
kindest reception, and, less *petit* than his suite, understood
the man, and treated him as his enthusiasm for music disposed him to do.' He insisted on accompanying him, and,
though still a pretty good performer, he constantly put the
maestro out owing to his idiosyncratic notions of keeping
time. 'He at last offered an apology which Rossini accepted
with civility, and good-naturedly said, "There are few in
your Royal Highness's position who could play so well."'
Rossini afterwards professed himself much taken with his
royal accompanist. He had, he said, met no other monarch,
apart from the Tsar Alexander I, nearly so amiable: it was
'scarcely possible to form an idea ... of the charm of George
IV's personal appearance and demeanour'.

A project as dear to the King as any other was the formation of a national collection of pictures to rival those of Italy
and France. He had contrived to restore the Royal Collection to the eminent position it had held among the great
collections of the world before the Commonwealth government had sold off so many of the valuable paintings collected by Charles I; and he was always happy for the public
to see it. 'I have not formed it for my own pleasure alone,'
he commented when lending his Carlton House pictures for
an exhibition in 1826, 'but to gratify the public taste.' Yet
there was nothing in London to compare with the fine galleries in Paris, Florence, or, indeed, in several other lesser

Continental towns. So, with the idea of forming the nucleus of a national collection, the King urged the government to buy the thirty-eight splendid pictures of his friend John Julius Angerstein, who died in 1823. The government accepted his advice, bought Angerstein's collection for £57,000; added to it sixteen pictures donated by Sir George Beaumont, and housed them all in Angerstein's house in Pall Mall until a more suitable gallery could be built. The site eventually chosen for the national collection was on the north side of Trafalgar Square where William Wilkins's domed and turreted building was to be finished in 1828.

Trafalgar Square had already been planned by Nash as part of that ambitious scheme for the redevelopment of London which was being executed under the King's keenly interested eye. For more years than anyone could then remember the old Royal Mews had stood here, row upon row of stables, harness rooms and grooms' quarters surrounding Hubert Le Sueur's statue of Charles I. Nash envisaged the new square as forming the centrepiece of a fine road extending from the southern end of Regent Street across the bottom of Haymarket and linking up with another road to be built from Whitehall as far as the growing developments in Bloomsbury. Originally Nash had seen Carlton House as an integral part of this design. Carriages would come down Regent Street towards Henry Holland's imposing colonnade, would there turn left and rattle away across Haymarket through Trafalgar Square to Whitehall. But Nash was never able to realize this vision, for his patron decided that Carlton House, splendid as it was, was no longer a suitable residence for a King of England. He complained that its rooms were too small for large receptions, as indeed they were, and that, despite the immense sums which had been spent on it, it was antiquated and decrepit. It certainly appeared so now from the outside. Canova described it as 'blackened with dust and soot', and looking like 'an ugly barn'.

The King would have to have something new. Carlton House would have to be pulled down, terraces of houses

built on its site and in its garden, and a fine palace built to
replace Buckingham House, the far more modest London
home of his parents, known since his mother's death as the
King's House, Pimlico. He had had this plan in mind since
1819 when he had estimated that the new palace could be
built for £500,000, which was £350,000 more than the 'utmost
sum' that the government had in mind. At that time Lord
Liverpool had told him that 'in the present circumstances of
the country ... it would be quite impracticable to look to
any grant of public money' for the ambitious scheme which
his Majesty had in view. 'The only measure which could be
resorted to would be to sell or lease' part of the site of St
James's Palace; but this would 'not produce any considerable
sum' and Parliament would have to be consulted. So the
project had had to be dropped, but it was now revived again.
The King protested that he was now 'too old to build a
palace'; but a palace was what he wanted all the same.

Sir John Soane, Professor of Architecture at the Royal
Academy – who had rebuilt the Bank of England, enlarged
and enriched the Houses of Parliament, and designed many
fine houses in Regency London, including his own in Lincoln's Inn Fields – had hoped to be given the commission
as an attached architect to the Board of Works; and, believing that Buckingham House ought to be preserved, he
had prepared plans for the new palace in Green Park. But
the King did not want to live in Green Park. Pleading that
'early associations' endeared him to the spot, he insisted on
the palace being built on the site of Buckingham House, an
admirable site for a palace with gardens of forty acres
originally laid out by 'Capability' Brown. The King also
insisted that the architect must be Nash.

Nash went to work immediately and soon all manner of
building materials, including five hundred massive blocks of
veined Carrara marble, were unloaded at the site. By the
time the original estimate of £252,690 had been increased to
£331,973 the work was far from completed. Whole wings
had been torn down and rebuilt because they had not struck

the right note at their first appearance. Yet even in February 1827 when Creevey 'sallied forth to see the alterations' they still remained in his opinion the 'devil's own'. Other critics complained of the 'square towers at the side and wretched inverted egg-cup at the top', 'a common slop pail turned upside down'. Joseph Hume protested that the Crown of England did not require such splendour: 'Foreign countries might indulge in frippery, but England ought to pride herself on her plainness and simplicity.' How could the Chancellor of the Exchequer justify such extravagance? The Chancellor certainly found it hard to justify; but the work, once begun, could not very well be abandoned. Month after month it went on, the expenditure mounting towards an ultimate total of £700,000, excluding the cost of the Marble Arch, proposed by the King and designed by Nash as the main gateway into the forecourt.* People began to doubt that the King would live long enough to see it finished. His mordant friend, Joseph Jekyll, was reminded of a mausoleum.

Sternly criticized for his expenditure on Buckingham Palace, the King was just as severely censured for spending so much on Windsor Castle which was being simultaneously transformed at even greater cost and which, so Wellington complained, absorbed the King's attention to such a degree that he appeared 'not to be the least interested in public affairs'. The King had moved into the Castle in the autumn of 1823 for two months to see what living there was like. He

---

* The Marble Arch – constructed of marble from Seravezza – was ornamented with sculptures by Richard Westmacott and E. H. Baily whose friezes, extolling military and naval glories, were intended for the attic storey. These friezes were placed instead on the face of Buckingham Palace. It was originally proposed that a statue of Victory should surmount the Arch; but this idea was abandoned in favour of an equestrian statue of King George IV by Chantrey and Earle. In 1851, to make way for the construction of the east wing of Buckingham Palace, the Arch was removed to its present position at the top of Park Lane; and the statue of the King was taken to Trafalgar Square (Pevsner, *London*, i, 347, 556).

chose to occupy the rooms which his mother and sisters had
used rather than the gloomier rooms on the ground floor of
the north front where his father had spent his last years.
The State Apartments on the first floor of the northern
front, rebuilt by Charles II, would henceforward, he decided, be used for the state visits of foreign sovereigns.

Already he had given orders for the demolition of the
barracks-like Queen's Lodge which King George III had
built for his large family less than half a century before.
This would open up a fine view down Charles II's avenue,
known as the Long Walk, at the far end of which he
planned to place an equestrian statue of his father, commissioned from Richard Westmacott. He had also already
given orders for the Terrace to be closed to the public,
except on Sundays. Ever since George III's death, the Terrace had been used as a promenade, the people peering
through the windows while the children whipped tops and
flew kites. His order had caused a good deal of resentment,
particularly from the Canons of Windsor who claimed that
they had had a '*legal right*' to walk upon the Terrace since
the time of Charles II. The King had had to be firm with
the Canons, and to insist that he 'would never have chosen
Windsor Castle for his royal residence unless the privacy of
the Terrace could have been secured, and his Majesty
thereby not exposed to be overlooked and interrupted at all
periods of the day'. The local newspaper regarded the
closure of the Terrace in a more favourable light than the
Canons: the inhabitants of Windsor might 'at first feel this
measure as a privation', but at the same time they would
'cheerfully acknowledge' that the Castle was 'entirely wanting in privacy' and would hail the closure as an assurance
that the King was 'about to make this glorious palace of his
ancestors once more the seat of royalty'.

This, indeed, was what the King decided to do after his
brief sojourn in the Castle in the autumn of 1823; but, just
as Carlton House was considered unsuitable as a London
palace for the King of England, so Windsor Castle was at

present far from being an appropriate 'seat of royalty'. So, once again an approach had to be made to Parliament; and Parliament obligingly agreed that the work should be done. Eight commissioners were appointed to supervise it.

The commissioners decided to hold a competition and invited various architects, including Robert Smirke, John Nash and John Soane, to submit plans and estimates. Soane declined to compete, but the others agreed to do so. The winner, however, was a man not as well known as they – Jeffry Wyatt, the fifty-eight-year-old Derbyshire-born nephew of James Wyatt who had already provided a few romantic Gothic details to the buildings of the Upper Ward. Jeffry Wyatt had done work for the Dukes of Bedford, Beaufort and Devonshire and had built a large country house in Surrey for Samuel Farmer in the style of Henry VIII's palace of Nonesuch. He was an inventive and versatile architect, and the fact that he was rather careless in the matter of costing was not of the slightest interest to George IV who shared his enthusiasm for turning the Castle into a magnificently Gothic structure. Indeed, before Wyatt had been selected for the work, the King asked him to make a few drawings to illustrate his ideas on the subject. Wyatt estimated that the work would cost £122,500; but having arrived at this figure – so he later maintained – he was told by the Chancellor of the Exchequer, one of the Commissioners, that the government were thinking in terms of £150,000; so he adjusted his estimate accordingly.

On 12 August 1824, his sixty-second birthday, the King drove up to the Castle from the Royal Lodge to lay the foundation stone of a new archway on the southern side of the Upper Ward which was to bear his name and was to lead out into Charles II's elm-lined Long Walk. He was met by Wyatt, 'a busy-bustling, vain little man', who had already moved into Winchester Tower which he was to occupy until his death in 1840. Wyatt asked the King there and then, so it is said, if he could change his name to Wyatville, to avoid confusion with other members of his family, some of whom

were mere builders. 'Ville or mutton,' the King is supposed
to have replied cheerfully, 'call yourself what you like.' Later
the King, well pleased with his diminutive architect's work,
added a view of King George IV Gate to Wyatville's coat of
arms, allowed him to use the word 'Windsor' as a motto, had
his portrait painted by Lawrence, and knighted him.

In hopeful anticipation of such honours, Wyatville had
set to work with a will. Five hundred workmen had been
immediately employed; and two years later the numbers
had risen to 709 men regularly occupied on full-time work
at Windsor, with thirty-six men doing occasional work, and
fifty joiners and twenty plasterers preparing woodwork and
ornaments in London, making a total force of 815 men.

On the approach of the King's birthday in 1824, Wyatville
had hoped 'a treat might be given to the men' in celebration.
His Majesty had suggested sitting them all down to dinner
in the Castle grounds, but Wyatville, not trusting the
weather, had thought that it would be better to give all the
men five shillings each so that they could buy good dinners
for themselves 'at the various public houses in Windsor'. 'I
proposed to man the towers for a general Huzza! at precisely one o'clock,' he had told Knighton, 'but reflecting on
the chance of accident, and that the men would be lost
behind the battlements, I decide for assembling them either
along the south front or on the new Terrace for that purpose.'

He had chosen the new Terrace, and on the appointed day
the men, having been 'provided with dinners at the different
inns', had responded to Wyatville's signal by hailing the
occasion 'with repeated cheers'. A local journalist thought
that 'the effect of this assemblage of happy and industrious
artisans was most exhilarating'.

Gradually these industrious artisans transformed the
Castle. Walls and towers were demolished; apartments were
stripped and rotten timbers torn out; roofs were removed;
old towers were rebuilt; new towers were erected; Charles II's
windows were replaced by Gothic ones; courts vanished, a

state staircase and, eventually, the Waterloo Chamber took their place; a garden was made on the eastern side, an orangery to face the south; the Round Tower was raised by a stone crown 30 feet higher than the former structure; the Grand Corridor, 550 feet in length, provided a magnificent picture gallery as well as a covered way between the north front and the east.

Some observers were appalled by Wyatville's architectural contrivances, the imitation portcullis grooves in his gates, the bogus mortar joints in his freestone blocks, the picturesque machicolations of his new towers. But others – Sir Walter Scott among them – thought that the Gothicization, for all its whimsical extravagance, was successful and impressive. An essentially Gothic structure demanded Gothic treatment; and Wyatville was turning Windsor Castle into one of the most distinctive Gothic monuments in the world. The King himself warmly approved. He was later moodily to grumble about the smallness of the rooms, too cramped for their furniture; and about the lack of privacy, despite the closure of the Terrace. But he never grumbled about the grand design of the Castle's external appearance which he had inspired and which Wyatville had so efficiently executed. It was left to others, of course, to grumble about the cost.

The first £150,000 was soon spent; another £150,000 was as quickly disposed of; the cost soared to £600,000, as more extensive improvements were carried out and more furniture was bought, much of it in Paris. Even then the work was not finished. At times, indeed, it seemed that it never would be finished; for lack of funds more than once brought Wyatville to a standstill. When the total cost reached £800,000, and Parliament was asked to grant a further £100,000, the House of Commons rebelled. Was there to be no 'limit to such extravagance'? Who could say that next year there would not be another demand for £300,000 or £400,000? The Chancellor of the Exchequer protested that leaving the building unfinished would be 'a disgrace to the country'; but he was obliged to withdraw his motion in order to prevent 'a most painful discussion'. And Wellington, for one, was not surprised. 'The question is a bad one,' he told Knighton. 'We are in the wrong for bringing forward for the third or fourth time a vote for a fresh grant without an estimate of the whole expence.'

The proposal was therefore referred to a Select Committee which, while deploring the evident disregard of economy, recommended that the money should be provided since 'the complete repair of this ancient and royal residence' had now become an 'object of national concern'. It was also recommended that Wyatville, a rather harassed witness before the Committee, should remain in charge of the operations, 'for the sake of uniformity of character and design'. The members of the Commitee added that they entertained 'a favourable opinion' of his work. So did Mrs Arbuthnot who was 'quite delighted' with the Castle after going over it for the first time. She thought the new apartments would be 'quite beautiful'.

Other visitors to the Castle at the time of its reconstruction were not so complimentary. Lady Holland, who was shown over it in the summer of 1826, while admiring the 'glory of the architecture', thought that the state rooms were 'not spacious enough nor sufficiently numerous'. Charles Greville, after a visit in the summer of 1827, considered that not enough had been 'effected for the enormous sums expended'. It was a 'fine house', to be sure; but it was not a palace to stand comparison with 'Versailles, St Cloud and the other palaces in France'. Croker, who was taken over it by Wyatville early the following year, was inclined to agree with Greville. The 'new works' were 'in many respects handsome, and not inconvenient'; but the rooms were by no means 'what they ought to be'; 'they were 'neither in number and size what might have been produced for much less expense'.

Creevey was of the same opinion, though he thought the Grand Corridor 'above all price'. 'Mr Wyat-*ville* himself did

us the honour of conducting us through all the new apartments,' he told his stepdaughter. 'All the new living-rooms
make a very good gentleman's or nobleman's house, nothing
more.'

The crotchety and eccentric Lord Dudley thought that it
would have been a great deal better if it *had* been more of a
house and less of a castle. As one of the earliest guests there
after its completion, he angrily scolded Wyatville because
he felt so cold. The food was cold, too. Why, he had recently
dined with a lady where the soup was *hot*, and there was a
decent woodcock on the table! 'Look,' he exclaimed in protest at the Castle fare, 'Look at this wretched snipe.' As for
the Castle itself, a large house would have been much
better. Why had Wyatville had to make such a damned
great fortress of it? The Vikings weren't coming over again,
were they?

Wyatville himself was not altogether satisfied with the
finished interior which was far more to the King's taste than
to his own. He was inclined to agree with Croker who
thought it too much in the Louis XIV style to accord with
the general character of Windsor; it was altogether too
'French'. But the King, who had driven over regularly to see
the works, and to supervise the decorations and the furnish-
ing, had been insistent. He liked his woodwork and plaster
sumptuously gilded, his walls richly brocaded; he did not
want his beautiful fireplaces and doors from Carlton House
to disappear with the rest of the building; those that were
not required at Buckingham Palace must be found a place
at Windsor. One day the King asked Wyatville to incor-
porate some armorial stained glass from the conservatory at
Carlton House in the windows at Windsor. 'Wyatville
hummed and hawed at first a good deal,' the King told
Knighton. But eventually he was brought round to say in
his still strong Derbyshire accent – which his Majesty could
imitate to perfection – that he 'thought he cud pleace soom
of't to advantage, though 'e 'ad not joust thin fix'd where'.

41

The Windsor Recluse
1826–1827

'It is unpleasant for him to see a strange face'

'THE King,' wrote Lady Shelley in 1826, 'never thinks of anything but building.' As well as in London and at the Castle in Windsor, work was also now in progress at Virginia Water where ornamental temples were being built to decorate the shores of an artificial lake.

This lake had been made by his godfather, William Augustus, Duke of Cumberland, who, as Ranger of Windsor Great Park, had employed gangs of discharged soldiers on such works of improvement on the royal estate. The Duke's Deputy Ranger had been Thomas Sandby, brother of the artist, Paul; and it was to the designs of Thomas Sandby that a Chinese temple had been built at Virginia Water on an island in the middle of the lake.

This temple had suggested to the King the idea of building other decorative Moorish and Chinese pavilions on the shores of the lake; and on the bank in front of one of these, the King was often to be found with Lady Conyngham fishing on summer afternoons – though after the appearance in June 1826 of a popular caricature, 'A King-Fisher', which ridiculed this practice, he all but abandoned it. Still, an afternoon's drive down to Virginia Water became a regular feature of life at the Royal Lodge. 'They meet at three o'clock,' Lady Shelley recorded, 'at which hour five or six phaetons come to the door, each to receive a lady and gentleman who drive about the country until five. At that hour the whole party dine in a hut on the shore of Virginia Water. ... The party sit at table until between nine and ten o'clock, then they return to the Cottage, dress *presto*, and go into the saloon where they play at écarté and other games until midnight. It is every day the same: Oh! monotony!'

Sometimes, if the weather were fine, the guests would stay down by the lake for supper which was served either in one of the temples or in the shade of a folly, built by Wyatville from a selection of classical remains found in a courtyard in the British Museum and from Greek statues captured in a French frigate during the Napoleonic wars.

On special occasions the appearance of his Majesty would be greeted by 'God save the King' played by his band seated in a boat by the shore; and after a visit to *The Mandarin*, a junk that had been moored in the lake since the Duke of Cumberland's time, dinner would be served in tents erected on the lawns by the water's edge. Dinner usually lasted a long time, for the King still 'ate very heartily' when he was well and could still get through two or three bottles of claret before rising from the table.

Wellington was desperately bored by these parties, this perpetual '*junke thing*' which lasted 'from morning till night'. 'We embarked yesterday at three, and were upon the lake of Como, either in the boat or dining, till nine,' he complained one summer day in 1824 to Mrs Arbuthnot. 'We then returned, dressed as quickly as possible and passed the night at Ecarte and supper from which we broke up about one, thus passing ten hours in company! In my life I never heard so much nonsense and folly or so many lies in the same space of time. ... One is obliged to listen to [them] with a certain degree of complacency if one does not intend to offend. ... We are to have a repetition of the same today, as I see that unfortunately it is a fine day. ... I am not astonished that Lady C[onyngham] is tired out of her life.'

Wellington continued to be a regular visitor at Windsor, however, as he prided himself upon being able to settle differences as well as any man and loved being consulted, as Charles Greville said, and 'mixed up in messes'. He was particularly needed this summer because Lady Conyngham's eldest son, Mount Charles, was dying on the Continent; she wanted to go out to see him, and the King insisted on accompanying her. If he followed her, Wellington protested, the public would have the impression that 'it was neither more nor less than abdication of his high duties'. But the King remained adamant: if she went, he would go too. It appeared to Wellington that he was more in love with her than ever, a state of mind that the Duke found incomprehensible, for he had never seen so vulgar a woman as Lady Conyngham, though he recognized her shrewdness and the advisability of consulting her before approaching the King on matters of importance. She gave him the feeling that he thought he would have if he were ever 'to experience a revulsion of blood'; 'every time she spoke [he] trembled lest [he] should hear some fresh vulgarity'. He could not conceive why the King wanted to go abroad with her. By the beginning of September the crisis was over; Lady Conyngham had agreed to remain in England, and Knighton had left for France to take Lord Mount Charles to Italy.

The 'more tranquil state' in which Wellington left the King and Lady Conyngham after this matter had been settled did not last long. By the summer of 1826 Wellington felt sure that the King's love for Lady Conyngham was 'at an end'. The King still assured Knighton, with tears in his eyes, that he was 'more in love with her beauty than ever', but neither Knighton nor Wellington believed 'one word of it'. Mme de Lieven was convinced by now that Lady Conyngham did not love him at all, and that the King was aware of this and would certainly have replaced her had he not felt himself too old to contract fresh habits. He admitted as much himself to Wellington. 'With my age and infirmities,' he said, 'it is not worth while looking out for another.'

In fact, Wellington thought, complain though he constantly did of his infirmities, there was nothing the matter with him excepting 'what was caused by the effects of strong liquors taken too frequently and in too large quantities'. 'He drinks spirits morning, noon and night,' the Duke told Mrs Arbuthnot; 'and he is obliged to take laudanum to calm the irritation which the use of spirits occasions. ... The Accoucheur [Knighton] and Halford don't agree about the use of laudanum by the King. The former says it will drive him mad. Halford says spirits will drive him mad if laudanum is not given; and that he will take it in larger doses if it is not administered in smaller.' After an enormous dose of spirits on 2 August, the King exasperated Wellington by being 'very drunk, very blackguard, very much out of temper at times, and a very great bore'.

This was at the time of the visit to Windsor of his little niece, Victoria, the Duchess of Kent's child. Princess Victoria, then aged seven, and a 'clever, pretty, winning child' in Lady Shelley's opinion, was staying with her aunt Mary, the Duchess of Gloucester, at Cumberland Lodge. She was driven over to the Royal Lodge by her mother to see her uncle. 'Give me your little paw,' he said, affectionately taking her hand in his, and then pulled her on to his stout knee so that she could kiss him. It was 'too disgusting', she recalled more than half a century later, 'because his face was covered with grease-paint'. But at the time she had responded to his 'wonderful dignity and charm of manner': he never lost his way of pleasing young children. 'He wore the wig which was so much worn in those days,' she remembered clearly. 'Then he said he would give me something to wear, and that was his picture set in diamonds, which was worn by the Princesses as an order to a blue ribbon on the left shoulder. I was very proud of this – and Lady Conyngham pinned it on my shoulder.'

Next day, while she was out walking with her mother, the King, who was driving along in his phaeton with the Duchess of Gloucester, overtook her. As his horses were brought to a halt, the King called out cheerfully, 'Pop her in!' So she was lifted up and placed between him and her aunt Mary, who held her round the waist as the horses trotted off. She was 'greatly pleased', though her mother

appeared 'much frightened', fearful that her daughter would
either fall out on the road or be kidnapped.

The King drove her 'round the nicest part of Virginia
Water', and stopped at the Fishing Temple. Here 'there was
a large barge and everyone went on board and fished, while
a band played in another!' Afterwards he had her conducted
around his menagerie at Sandpit Gate where she inspected
his wapitis, his chamois and his gazelles.*

In the evenings Princess Victoria was invited to watch the
Tyrolese dancers creating a 'gay uproar' or listen to 'Uncle
King's' band playing in the conservatory at the Royal Lodge
by the light of coloured lamps. He asked her what tune she
would like the band to play next. With precocious tact she
immediately asked – as Rossini had done – for 'God save the
King!' 'Tell me,' he asked her later, 'what you enjoyed most
of your visit?' 'The drive with you,' she said. He was clearly
very much taken with her.

* The animals in the King's menagerie, superintended by Edward
Cross, grew in numbers year by year. By 1826 they included gnus
and monkeys, roebucks and kangaroos, musk deer and elks, Mandarin horses and Brahmin bulls, a zebra, a leopard, a llama, an
'enormous tortoise' and all manner of birds, including ostriches,
parrots, hawks, cranes, eagles, Chinese partridges and Greenland
geese, macaws, German hook-bill ducks, Siberian wild swans and an
orange-crested talking cockatoo (RA 25583–624). In August 1827,
accompanied by two Nubian attendants, there arrived a giraffe, a
present from the Pasha of Egypt. This giraffe so took the public's
fancy that 'nothing else seemed to be thought of' that summer
(WDNS iv, 94, 14 August 1827). It was depicted frequently in caricatures of the King and Lady Conyngham (BM *Sat*, x and xi, 15425,
15521, 15845, 16143). It was a beautiful creature: 'nothing could give
an idea of the beauty of her eyes,' a contemporary observer recorded.
'Imagine something midway between the eye of the finest Arab horse
and the loveliest southern girl, with long and coal-black lashes, and
the most exquisite beaming expression of tenderness and softness,
united to volcanic fire' (L. S. Lambourne, 'A Giraffe for George IV',
Country Life, vol. cxxxviii, 1965). The King was devoted to the
animal and one of his last acts of patronage was to commission (for
200 guineas) a portrait of her and her attendants, supervised by
Edward Cross, from Jacques-Laurent Agasse (*Animal Painting*,
The Queen's Gallery, Buckingham Palace 1966–67, 10, 21–2).

As Lady Shelley said, she paid her court extremely well. When giving him a bunch of flowers, she said, 'As I shall not see my dear uncle on his birthday I wish to give him this nosegay now'; and when wishing him goodbye she said with appealing gravity, 'I am coming to bid you adieu, sire, but as I know you do not like fine speeches I shall certainly not trouble you by attempting one.' Upon her return home she was most anxious that her mother should send 'her best love and duty to her "dear Uncle King" '.

Later that year, Sir Walter Scott was a guest at Royal Lodge, and he found the King as gracious and kind as Princess Victoria had done. He had recently assumed the debts of a partner in a printing business, and was rather cast down by worry. The King did all he could to make him feel at ease. He 'made me sit beside him and talk a great deal – *too much* perhaps', Scott recorded in his diary. 'For he has the art of raising one's spirits and making you forget the *retenue* which is prudent everywhere, especially at court. But he converses himself with so much ease and elegance that you lose thought of the prince in admiring the well-bred accomplished gentleman. . . . Educated as a prince he has nevertheless as true and kind a heart as any subject in his dominions. . . . He is in many respects the model of a British monarch . . . sincerely, I believe, desires the good of his subjects – is kind towards the distressed, and moves and speaks "every inch a King". I am sure that such a man is fitter for us than one who would long to lead armies, or be perpetually intermeddling with *la grande politique*. A sort of reserve, which creeps on him daily and prevents his going to places of public resort, is a disadvantage, and prevents his being so generally popular as is earnestly to be desired.'

The King's reluctance to show himself in public was, in fact, becoming almost obsessive. Rather than risk the cruel gibes that were unfailingly directed at his stout body and swollen legs, his now hobbling gait and the face whose ageing appearance grease-paint could only partially disguise, he chose to remain in secluded retirement as much as

he possibly could. He moved from London to the country
and back again with a secrecy that was hardly less than
furtive. He rarely now visited Brighton at all as he felt so
exposed there and as Lady Conyngham knew that Brighton
people disapproved of her.

As early as 1824 people attending his Drawing-Rooms
were forbidden to assemble in the antechambers to watch
him pass; and Captain Gronow, when on guard duty at
Carlton House, heard him angrily exclaim, 'I will not allow
those maid-servants to look at me when I go in and out.' The
next day while riding in Hyde Park, Gronow was told by
one of the Carlton House staff that the King 'constantly
complained of the servants staring at him, and that strict
orders had been given to discharge any one caught repeating
the offence'.

At Windsor when visitors were being conducted over the
Castle they were forbidden 'to turn their eyes to the window,
lest the King should be passing under it'; and throughout
his reign it had been his practice when driving out in the
Park to have a groom ride out in advance 'ordering everybody to retire'. He was reluctant even to attend the Royal
Academy before the opening of the exhibitions, pleading
that his gout made it so difficult for him to get up all the
stairs. He still went to Ascot, where he was invariably
greeted with applause as he bowled along the course in his
carriage and four, nodding and winking and kissing his
hand, just as he had done twenty years before on the
Brighton racecourse; but even at Ascot when he got into his
stand he was apt to sit in a darkened corner with a plain
brown hat cocked over one eye.

If only he would show himself more, Mrs Arbuthnot believed, he would be far more popular. As it was, on the rare
occasions when he did appear in public, he seemed now to
be offended rather than pleased by the welcome accorded
him, however flattering. In December 1826 he was 'excessively well received' when he made one of his rare appearances at Drury Lane where 'the shouts of applause were

quite deafening and "God Save the King" was sung again and again'; yet he looked 'very cross and very much bored'.

When, in 1827, his knees, legs and ankles swelled 'more formidably and terribly than ever', and he had to be carried up and down stairs and 'in general to be wheeled about everywhere', he became more of a recluse than ever. At the end of February 1828 the open-railed gate to the garden of St James's Palace was replaced by a close-boarded gate so that the public could not witness the King being carried to and from his carriage. At Windsor, in the relative privacy of the Park or the fields at Virginia Water, servants were constantly instructed to ensure that his Majesty was neither disturbed nor seen.

Prince Pückler-Muskau recorded how nervous his English host was when driving him through the Park to the royal stables. The Englishman, fearing that they might unexpectedly come upon the King, noticed with dismay that his carriages stood already harnessed in the yard. There were seven of them altogether, 'all with very low wheels, almost as light as children's carriages, and drawn by little poneys', the King's with four ponies, the others with two each. 'It is unpleasant for him to see a strange face, or indeed a human being of any kind whatsoever, within his domain,' Pückler-Muskau wrote, explaining his friend's fear of being caught at the stables when the King arrived. 'The Park is consequently (with the exception of the high road which crosses it) a perfect solitude. The King's favourite spots are, for further security, thickly surrounded by screens of wood, and plantations are daily laid out to add to the privacy and concealment. In many places, where the lay of the ground would enable you to get a glimpse of the sanctuary within, three stages of fences are planted one behind the other. ... My venerable host climbed up on the seat of the carriage and stood there, supported by his wife and me, to look about whether the King might not be somewhere in sight; nor was he perfectly tranquil till the gate ... closed upon us.'

Living in such seclusion at Windsor, the King, like his

guests, was often bored, and, in his boredom, endeavoured, to dramatize his life, making up stories about himself and his entourage, affecting to believe that the most unlikely people were in love with one another. He confessed to Mme de Lieven that, bored with Lady Conyngham, he would like her as his mistress instead; he showed her a portrait of herself by Lawrence hanging over his bed, and 'with gestures and passionate looks' begged to be allowed into her room. To Wellington and Knighton he confided the manifold faults of Lady Conyngham of whom he nevertheless pretended to be jealous, while affecting at the same time to be jealous of Wellington's friendship with Mme de Lieven.

'The King of England has been very ill,' Mme de Lieven told Prince Metternich in the spring of 1826. 'But bleeding does him no good; it merely gives him an excuse for staying in bed a little longer, which he likes better than anything *. .... The public of all classes and all opinions have been greatly alarmed; they are afraid of his successor. He is pig-headed and narrow-minded.'

It was Mme de Lieven's ill-founded opinion that the King was just as much afraid of the Duke as were the public. He was also 'very jealous' of him, she thought, and the realization that he would have to appoint him Regent if he went abroad with Lady Conyngham was one of the main reasons which had persuaded him not to go. 'Their relations are strange,' she wrote. 'They have no affection for one another, no esteem; and yet they are always making up to one another. The Duke of York attaches importance to the King's favour, the King, to his brother's moral support. They make fun of one another; they confide in me on this, as on many other equally delicate subjects.'

---

* Knighton told Canning that 'he verily believed that if it were not for the society of Lady C[onyngham] which made it necessary for HM to get up and dress himself for dinner, HM would lay the whole day in bed ... such was his indolence' (Canning Papers, 103b, 27 April 1825).

In fact, though they had quarrelled often enough in the past, and had never been as close to each other as they had been as children at Kew, the King and the Duke of York had been on the best of terms for some time past, even if they did make fun of one another and even if the Duke was fond of telling stories against his brother to his racing friends. The Duke was always welcome to stay at Brighton for as long as he pleased and to bring with him any society he chose; and when the Duchess died the King, in writing a letter of sympathy, assured his brother how much it meant to him that for so long there had been 'the most unvarying, the steadiest affection between them'. 'Believe me,' the King wrote, 'that from the very bottom of my soul, I do participate and enter into the whole extent of your distress.' They were not empty phrases; he had not got on so well with the eccentric, dog-loving Duchess during the last years of her life as he had done in the early days of her marriage, but his affection for his brother was deeply felt. In December 1823 the King had helped to pay the Duke's debts, mainly incurred through his continuing extravagance on the turf, by presenting him with £50,000 which Knighton had raised through the Rothschilds on the King's income from Hanover. And thereafter, although the King did not feel justified in trying to settle fresh debts of about £200,000 incurred by the Duke – mainly in the building of a huge new house to suit the grandiose ideas of his friend the Duchess of Rutland – the two brothers had seen a good deal of each other and their past differences seemed to have been entirely forgotten. There had been a certain coolness between them in 1825 after the death of Lord Mount Charles, when Lady Conyngham had left Windsor for a time. For the Duke, who the King supposed had once been attracted to Lady Conyngham himself, had written a letter to her and she had replied to it, thus renewing the King's jealousy. But the trouble had not lasted long.

When the Duke fell seriously ill with dropsy at the end of 1826, the King's concern was unfeigned. He was 'in great anxiety and uneasiness about him', Mrs Arbuthnot noted in her journal. Notwithstanding his jealousy of the Duke's popularity, he loved him 'more than any of his family'. He was grieved beyond measure by his death on 5 January, so 'much depressed in health and spirits', in fact, that he was not expected to be well enough to attend the funeral. No one could conceive the extent of his sorrow, he professed; he 'felt it every instant'. Even Charles Greville, who rarely recorded a word in the King's favour in the malicious pages of his early diaries, agreed that he 'showed great feeling about his brother and exceeding kindness in providing for his servants. ... He gave £6,000 to pay immediate expenses and took many of the old servants into his own service.' He asked Knighton to go down into the vault beneath St George's Chapel to select a place for the coffin as close as possible to their father who had liked the Duke better than himself.

On 20 January, ignoring the advice of his doctors, the King went down for the funeral to Windsor where it was reported that he was 'most grievously affected' and that 'every minute gun was like a nail driven into his heart'. It was a bitterly cold day, and the congregation which included most members of the Cabinet and of the Royal Family stood shivering in the gloom. There was no matting or carpeting on the floor, and Canning presumed that whoever had filched it had had bets on the duration of their lives. Lord Eldon sensibly followed Canning's advice and stood on his cocked hat and then 'in a niche of carved work where he was able to stand on wood'. But the Duke of Wellington caught a severe cold; so did the Duke of Sussex; so did the Lord Chamberlain of the Household, the Duke of Montrose. Canning contracted rheumatic fever, the Bishop of Lincoln subsequently died, and it was alleged that the soldiers who had made up the guard of honour expired at the rate of half a dozen a day.

Lord Liverpool, at the age of fifty-seven, was already chronically ill. Worried that the widespread distress and the industrial depression must lead to a relaxation of the Corn Laws, and that concessions would have to be made to Roman Catholics, he felt himself unable to cope with the difficulties that faced his government. On the morning of 17 February he had a stroke, and, though he did not die until the end of the following year, he was thereafter totally incapable of continuing in office.

42

The Tory Revolt
1827

'There never was anything like the bitterness of the
ultras against Mr Canning'

ALTHOUGH he had never been able to like Lord Liverpool,
the King was agitated beyond measure when he heard of
his fatal stroke. William Denison heard from his sister, Lady
Conyngham, that he would 'not permit any one whatever to
speak to him upon the subject of Lord Liverpool's illness',
or upon the subject of his successor as Prime Minister. For
fifteen days he did not leave his dressing-room at Brighton,
where he had gone for the therapy of 'warm bathing', refusing to see 'the face of a single human being – servants,
tailors and doctors excepted'. 'What the devil is it to come
to?' Creevey wondered. 'Was there ever such a child or
Bedlamite? Or were there ever such a set of lickspittles as his
Ministers to endure such conduct.... He is a poor devil.'

The government, already divided on the issues of the
Corn Laws, Catholic emancipation and Canning's foreign
policy, were now in total disarray. There seemed no possible
candidate for the office of Prime Minister who could hold
the two wings of the Tory party together as Liverpool had
succeeded in doing. Of the likely contenders for the office
Peel, who was only just thirty, was considered to be too inexperienced, though he had been Home Secretary for five
years and was, in Canning's opinion, the best one that the
country had ever had. He was also considered to be rather
too advanced in his views, except on the Catholic question.
Moreover, the King, whose dislike of him was fostered by
Knighton, found his *gauche* mannerisms extremely irri-

tating, particularly his awkward habit of suddenly thrusting out his hands while he talked. 'Mr Peel,' he said to him one night as he imitated the gesture, 'it is no use going on so, thrusting out your arms. The question is who is to be my Minister?'

Wellington, who had succeeded the Duke of York as Commander-in-Chief while retaining, at the King's request, the Master-Generalship of the Ordnance, was not at first supposed to be in the running for such high political office from which, in any case, he was believed to have disqualified himself by accepting command of the Army. Furthermore Canning could not be expected to serve under a Tory of the Duke's persuasion, particularly one who had consistently opposed his foreign policy and had endeavoured to contrive his dismissal. Yet Canning would have to be included in the government somehow, despite the opposition of many influential Tories and of the Duke of Buckingham who had been disappointed in his hopes of becoming Governor-General of India and who now recommended 'a balanced government without Mr Canning's assistance'.

Creevey thought that it was Canning who *'ultimately'* would win. Certainly the King was not nearly so averse to Canning now as he had been a few years before. There had been a sharp disagreement between them in the spring of 1824 when Canning caused the gravest offence by attending a banquet at the Mansion House given by Robert Waithman, the Lord Mayor, a strong supporter of Queen Caroline.* But that seemed now to have been overlooked.

---

* Wellington thought that the King had every reason to feel annoyed about Canning's dining 'with Lord Mayor Waithman, his speech, and his apology for the absence of his noble friend, Lord Liverpool. ... The Corporation of the City of London, or rather a party in the Corporation at the head of which is this very Lord Mayor, have more than once in my presence and in that of Lord L[iverpool] insulted the King. HM cannot visit the Corporation on account of a gross insult wantonly persevered in: their sticking up Queen Caroline's picture in the place of honour in the Common Council Room. ... Yet these Ministers go to these dinners and court

Canning bought a house near the Pavilion at Brighton, and he and his wife sought and obtained permission to take their morning walk under the trees in the Pavilion grounds.

From the end of April 1825 onwards, so Canning's private secretary said, 'nothing could surpass the good faith and kindness which the King manifested in the whole of his conduct towards him'. The gossips noted how Canning, at the King's request, had tactfully appointed Lord Francis Conyngham his Under-Secretary of State – a gesture which placated Lady Conyngham who had 'conceived a great antipathy to the Foreign Secretary'. It was an appointment, however, which Canning had not found difficult to make since the office had already been declined by four other men to whom he had previously offered it.* It was also noted

---

this very Lord Mayor.' Wellington did not 'think any King was ever so ill-treated by his two principal Ministers' (*Wellington and his Friends*, 40). The King himself steadfastly refused to dine in the City, even though assured that the picture of Queen Caroline would be 'hidden from view by scarlet hangings' if the invitation were to be accepted (Parker, i, 317). Wellington also thought that Liverpool had behaved very badly over the Windsor Canons' claim to walk on the Terrace. How could the King be expected to live there with Dean and Canons, wives and children and maids staring in at the windows at all hours of the day and night? Yet instead of refusing their claim, Liverpool had left it to the King to do so, saying that 'the late King had allowed everybody to walk upon the Terrace at all hours'. 'He won't see that the present King is not the late King,' the Duke had commented. 'This is not the way a King ought to be treated by his Minister' (*Wellington and his Friends*, 43).

* Lord Francis was naturally abused for accepting the offer. Lord Alvanley now called him '*Canningham*' (*Creevey Papers*, 401). And Mrs Arbuthnot referred to him as 'a regular spy' at Court. He certainly kept closely in touch with Sir William Knighton after his appointment. 'Mr C is at present confined to his bed with gout,' Conyngham reported to Knighton in a typical note on 13 December 1823; 'this has prevented him speaking much on the subject; besides, you are aware how irritable such an attack always makes such a person, more especially Mr C. who is never over cool in his mind' (RA 23084–5). 'They call F[rancis] Conyngham "Canning-game" – wit of White's, such as it is!' commented Emily Cowper. 'I don't think he much likes the appointment. Lady C[onyngham] writes to

how skilfully Canning had dealt with the problem of the
extremely handsome Lord Ponsonby, formerly one of Harriette Wilson's numerous lovers, and a man with whom Lady
Conyngham had once been very much in love. Harriette
Wilson had got hold of some letters written by Lady
Conyngham to Ponsonby and was threatening to publish
them. The King had evidently bought the letters to protect
Lady Conyngham's name; but no sooner had he done so
than Lord Ponsonby had returned to England from Corfu
where he had been living on a strictly limited income. Lady
Conyngham had met him unexpectedly in Lady Jersey's
drawing-room and had displayed signs of still being unduly
fond of him. The King had immediately consulted Canning
and asked him if he had any suitable foreign posts to offer
Ponsonby who, though 'he never in his life had thought of
adopting a diplomatic career', readily agreed to become
Envoy Extraordinary in Buenos Aires when Canning suggested it. According to Mme de Lieven – who thoroughly
disliked Canning, though she later courted him 'for political
objects' – the King had 'nearly swooned with gratitude. And
from that moment everything had been peace and love between them.'

It was also noticed by the gossips how close the relationship was between Canning and Knighton; for years Knighton had been intriguing against Lord Liverpool, having
never forgiven him for refusing him both the title of Private
Secretary and the office of Privy Councillor.

But there were other reasons for the King's more friendly
attitude towards the Foreign Secretary. Much as he had disapproved of Canning's foreign policy in the early stages of
its development, he had come to recognize that it had raised

---

me that they are all grieved to lose him and that at first they were all
against his taking it but then considering that he is a younger brother,
that it was originally his profession ... and so forth they had made
up their minds to it. He is to live in the Red House next to Carlton
House. I think it has a very bad effect for the C[onyngham]s with
the public' (Palmerston Papers, C/IV/4/3, 7 January 1823).

rather than lowered the standing of Britain in Europe, that
his own reputation had been enhanced in consequence, and
that the Foreign Secretary was succeeding in his professed
endeavours of making him 'comfortable and happy by placing him at the head of Europe, instead of being reckoned
fifth in the great confederacy'. Canning had also succeeded
in making him less unpopular in his own country than he
had been in the past, and the King was naturally drawn to
Ministers who could do that.

By the end of April 1825 the 'continental gossipings' at the
Royal Lodge had come to an end and 'the effects of all that
system', so Knighton assured Canning, 'were gradually passing away'. In November that year the King was prepared to
receive the Minister of the new South American republic of
Colombia with charm and courtesy. His Majesty's behaviour on that occasion, Canning assured Granville, was all
that he could have desired. Having made a short speech,
'extraordinarily well worded and pronounced', he listened
politely to a long response in the most atrocious French.
'Peace, peace, by all means and above all things,' the King
declared with relief and enthusiasm when the Minister had
at last finished. 'We have had thirty years of convulsions –
let us all now conspire to keep the peace.'

'And so the audience ended,' Canning contentedly concluded his letter to Granville. 'And so, behold! The New
World established, and, if we do not throw it away, ours!'

Canning owed his success with the King not only to his
successful policies and his cultivation of Knighton and the
Conynghams. He had gone out of his way to attract the
King, who was always susceptible to the charm of Irishmen
and always as ready to admire talent as to abhor mediocrity.
Canning alleviated his boredom, entertained him with witty
accounts of the proceedings in the Commons, artfully gave
him credit for the success of policies he had formerly opposed, respectfully asked him if he had anyone to recommend when there was some such appointment as foreign
messenger to fill, and never displayed those flashes of irri-

tation to which he was always liable particularly when his gout was troubling him.*

Yet for weeks the King recoiled from making any irrevocable decision regarding a new Prime Minister, hoping that the various contestants would wear themselves out in their conflicting efforts to achieve office, as they had done in 1812, and that a victor – preferably Canning whose claims were insistently pressed by Knighton – would emerge apparently *faute de mieux*. By the end of March it was obvious that the right-wing Tories were failing in their endeavours to form a government and that the path was becoming clearer for Canning. On 28 March the King invited him to come to stay at the Royal Lodge at the same time as Wellington. First he interviewed Wellington, on whose behalf Charles Arbuthnot had written an urgent letter to Sir William Knighton begging him to use his influence on the Duke's behalf. And as the morning wore on and his rival did not reappear, Canning grew more and more gloomy. At luncheon the King continued to show particular attention to Wellington; and after luncheon Canning feared that his hopes were sure to be disappointed when arrangements were made for the guests to drive out in the Park in the little two-seater pony carriages which were brought up from the stables. All the seats were allocated to the satisfaction of the King who, ignoring Canning's presence, said to Mme de Lieven, 'I am sure you and the Duke would like to go out together.' Just as everyone was ready to drive off, and the King was expected as usual to seat himself beside Lady Conyngham, he went up to Canning, took him by the arm, and said, 'I want to talk with you. I shan't go out.'

The talk mainly concerned the Roman Catholic question,

---

* 'Mr Canning, although quite ashamed to trouble your Majesty with a third letter on the same day,' runs a characteristic communication, 'cannot forbear humbly requesting of your Majesty that you would be graciously pleased to let him know if there be any person in whom your Majesty takes an interest, whom your Majesty would wish to be appointed to a Consulship in Spanish America' (Canning Papers, 100, 25 September 1823).

about which the King had been gradually changing his mind ever since the death of Fox. So long as his father was alive, he had been able to plead that he could do nothing against the well-known and constantly reiterated wishes of King George III, an attitude in which he was strongly encouraged by his friend the Duke of Northumberland, who deprecated the speeches in favour of Catholic Relief made by Lord Moira. In 1811 the King had assured Lord Wellesley that he still shared his views about the justice of Catholic Relief; but by 1813 the Duke of Richmond was 'delighted to find [his Majesty] as steady a Protestant as the Attorney-General' with the 'decided opinion that the Catholics [were] further than ever from their object'.

After his father's death he began to profess that he entertained precisely the same opinion as King George III had done as to the binding injunctions of the Coronation Oath. And when informed that there was no possibility of the Oath's being modified, he had said to Castlereagh, 'Remember, once I take that oath, I am for ever a Protestant King, a Protestant upholder, a Protestant adherent.' 'The sentiments of the King upon Catholic Emancipation,' he had informed Peel, 'are those of his revered and excellent father.'

To Knighton he had written, the 'emancipation of the Catholics [is] a measure entirely opposite to my own conscientious feelings which [have] been strengthened, if I may use the expression, by the pure and exalted spirit of my ever revered father.' He had been relieved when William Plunket's Roman Catholic Disability Removal Bill had been thrown out by the Lords in April 1821 after having been read for a third time in the Commons. And he had been further comforted in May 1825 when Sir Francis Burdett's Catholic Relief Bill had met a similar fate in the Lords after a firm speech by the Duke of York who had said that he considered, and always would consider, that the King was bound by his Coronation Oath to defend the Established Church. Yet the King was well aware that further attempts to emancipate the Catholics were bound to be made, and that the rapidly deteriorating situation in Ireland was rendering emancipation an issue of the utmost importance. Even Lord Eldon, who had formerly advocated postponing the issue, was coming to the view that the time had come when 'some decisive measures ought to be adopted'.* Nevertheless the King was anxious that Canning, a supporter of Catholic emancipation, should be in no doubt that his own views on the matter were as firm as ever. Canning advised him to form a government of men known to share his Majesty's views; but the King replied, as Canning doubtless expected, 'I cannot part with you.' In that case, Canning countered, if an entirely 'Protestant' government were not to be formed, he himself must either be Prime Minister or be recognized as the leader of the government with a titular Prime Minister in the House of Lords.

After this interview, choosing to suppose that he had induced Canning not to press the Catholic question in the event of his being asked to form a government, the King assured Peel that he need have no qualms about serving under Canning's leadership.

Peel did have qualms, however; so did Wellington; so did the Duke of Newcastle and Lords Mansfield and Falmouth; and so did the Duke of Rutland who went down to Windsor to protest in person 'on behalf of himself and brother Tories at Canning being cock of the walk'. The King, who quickly turned the Duke of Rutland away from Canning and on to race-horses, was now in as agitated a state as he had been at the beginning of the crisis. 'I am jaded and quite worn out, and writing from my bed, where I have laid down for a little rest,' he told Knighton on 6 April. 'Little or no advance has

---

* In a 'Private Minute respecting the Coronation Oath', Eldon reminded the King that he had sworn to the utmost of his power to 'maintain the laws of God, the true profession of the Gospel, and the Protestant Reformed religion established by law'. A king could not therefore, in consistency with his Coronation Oath, sign a Bill of concession to the Roman Catholics; but, Eldon added, a question worthy of consideration was whether he could sign a Bill enabling his successor to do so (RA 23347–52, undated).

as yet been made amidst perhaps almost unravelable per-
plexities.' In an attempt to escape responsibility he suggested that the Cabinet should decide the matter for him;
but the Cabinet declined to do so.

Peel now suggesed to Canning that the appointment of
Wellington might 'solve all difficulty'. But Canning felt
'obliged in frankness and honesty to say that it [did] not in
his mind afford any such solution'. The next day, 10 April,
the King again talked to Peel, but no satisfactory arrangement could be made with him; and, now thoroughly annoyed with both Wellington and Peel for what he took to be
their unreasonable and dictatorial manner, he at last told
Canning 'to prepare with as little delay as possible a plan for
the reconstruction of the Administration', a rather vague
instruction which Canning supposed to mean that he was to
be entrusted with its leadership.

As they had already indicated, neither Peel nor Wellington would serve in a government under Canning; nor would
any of the right-wing Tories join it. As Lord Howard de
Walden observed, 'there never was anything like the bitterness of the ultras against Mr Canning'. So Canning, unable
to form an exclusively Tory government, was forced to turn
to the Whigs. The King did all he could to set the Tories'
minds at rest. He sent for the Archbishop of Canterbury
and the Bishop of London and assured them that his views
on the Catholic question remained precisely those of his
father, and he authorized a public declaration to this effect.
But the 'Protestants' were unconvinced. In the House of
Lords, the Earl of Mansfield suggested that, had King
George III still been King, he would never have consented to
the formation of a government which was to contain a preponderance of 'Catholics' like Canning. This so provoked
the King that he wrote to the Archbishop of Canterbury to
ask him to tell Mansfield that he did not choose to 'pass un-
noticed' this direct calumny on his Protestant faith and
honour and that he did not deserve, 'as King of this country,
this wicked attempt to misrepresent and falsify them to his

Protestant subjects'. Before despatching the letter, the King showed it to Canning who agreed that it should go. Later, however, Canning had second thoughts, and wrote to the King warning him that it might be 'represented in Parliament as an interference with the freedom of parliamentary debate'. He ventured humbly to submit that, if the Archbishop had not already read or shown the letter to Mansfield, it might be better to convey the admonition it contained '*verbally*'. He humbly trusted that his Majesty would not mistake the motives of the advice which he presumed to offer nor doubt of his readiness to '*stand*' by his Majesty, if any such attack should ever be '*made*'.

Warmed by this and subsequent assurances of his Minister's 'most humble and *affectionate* duty', the King soon lost all his previous reservations about Canning. Indeed, he grew extremely fond of him, while relations between the King and Wellington grew worse and worse. Canning's past offences were overlooked; and the King settled down to work contentedly with a man whose great gifts were universally acknowledged and whose respectful treatment of his Sovereign was all the more welcome because it was imbued with a genuine affection, a warmth of feeling quite outside the King's normal experience of relations with his Ministers. He said that he had never had 'any Minister he liked half so well' as he liked Canning. Knighton, who shared Canning's ambition to break the hold of the aristocratic establishment on public life – and who also hoped that Canning might help him to become Chancellor of the Duchy of Lancaster – encouraged the King in his affection and did all he could to gain royal approval for Canning's policies.

The King's regard for Canning made the behaviour of his Tory colleagues all the harder for the King to accept, particularly as the resignations of Wellington, Peel, Westmorland, Bathurst, Eldon and Melville were followed by those of the Duke of Montrose, the Duke of Dorset, and several other members of his Household, including the Marquess of Graham and the Marquess of Londonderry, Castlereagh's

brother, a Lord of the Bedchamber. When Wellington resigned as Commander-in-Chief, which was not a political
appointment, the King showed his displeasure in the briefest
of replies:

'The King assures the Duke of Wellington that the King
receives the Duke's resignation of the offices of Commander-
in-Chief and Master-General of the Ordnance with the same
sentiments of deep regret with which the Duke states himself to offer it. The King abstains from any further expression of his feelings.'

He privately commented that he would keep the command of the army in his own hands until Arthur recovered
his temper. Intensely annoyed that the intransigent attitude
of Wellington and Peel and the other 'Protestant' Tories
had forced Canning to appoint a decidedly Whiggish cabinet, the King nevertheless was anxious not to remain permanently estranged from Wellington. He had always
admired him if he had not always liked him and he had
recently given him the first Duke of Marlborough's insignia
of the Order of the Garter 'as the only person worthy to wear
it'. He expressed his surprise to Wellington's brother, Lord
Maryborough, that the Duke had not been to see him all
summer. The Duke, having got his friend, Charles Arbuthnot, to write to Knighton asking for a *'command'* to attend
so that it could not be imputed against him 'that he had
gone to the King without being sent for', then rode over to
the Royal Lodge on the anniversary of the King's coronation. He did not stay long, and the conversation was 'for the
most part on general topics'; but the King could 'easily perceive, from little expressions which now and then dropped,'
so he told Canning, 'that the most assiduous pains had been
taken, and are still actively employed to give the strongest
jaundiced complexion to the past, as well as the present
state of things, and to keep up if not to widen as much as
malice and wickedness can contrive it, the breach which
exists between [Wellington] and my government'.

Although the Duke was highly gratified by his reception

at the Royal Lodge, the interview did little to improve the strained relationship. A few weeks later Lady Cowper found the King 'as bitter as ever against the Tories', and in no mood yet to forgive Wellington. While the Duke, for his part, was 'convinced that no man ever had such a hold upon the King' as that 'charlatan' Canning, whom he now disliked more than ever and whom he constantly denigrated. He was certain that 'Canning and all the present men' had got their hold upon the King by 'indulging him in all his expenses and whims'. Consequently, for the remainder of his life, he would 'be more difficult than ever to manage'.

Canning's hold, however, was soon broken. He had been ill in bed at the time of Liverpool's stroke, and during the first few months of his premiership he had never recovered his strength. The tasks that confronted him were appalling: not only had half the Cabinet resigned but the majority of the Tory party were against Catholic emancipation. Yet he knew that the Catholic question would have to be faced soon, and he had been obliged to tell the King that he 'must be free as air with respect to the question'. He had undertaken to ensure that it was put to sleep for a time, and could only hope that the King might eventually be induced to change his mind. In the meantime his relationship with the Whigs was a very wary one. Although a majority of them were prepared to accept a coalition against the ultra-Tories, there were many who were not, and and these included the followers of Grey who viewed Canning – as the son of an actress – with supercilious disdain. It was widely supposed, in fact, that Canning's government could only be considered as a stopgap. They were known as the 'warming pans'. As Lady Cowper remarked, 'The *Morning Chronicle* says it is like people going to keep places for the first act of a play.'

For the King, indeed for the monarchy, the crisis provoked by Canning's appointment proved cataclysmic. Throughout his reign the power of the crown had been declining, not so much because of the King's indolent character and aversion to uncongenial work as because of the increasing political consciousness of the people. In the past the crown had been sustained by the support of the Tories; but the King's dislike of Liverpool and some of his colleagues, his indiscreet talk about their principles and measures, his brilliant and heedlessly wounding mimicry of their idiosyncrasies and mannerisms, his discussions with advisers beyond their control and influence, all served to undermine their confidence in him. By turning to Canning and the Whigs who supported him, the King lost for good the confidence of the Tories who now abused him, so Lady Cowper said, 'a thousand times worse than the Whigs ever did'. Yet, by spurning the Tories in 1827, he did not regain the trust of the Whigs whom he had rejected in 1812. On both occasions the choice, hesitatingly and painfully made, was forced upon him largely by circumstances. But they were choices which left him in the end without influence in either camp.

In July the Duke of Devonshire invited the new Prime Minister to Chiswick for a change of air. But Canning felt no better there; and on 29 July he told the King that he did not know what was the matter with him; he felt 'ill all over'. The next week he died in the room where Fox had died twenty-one years before. 'This may be hard upon me,' he murmured towards the end, 'but it is harder upon the King.'

[43]

Protestants and Catholics
1827–1829

'The most Protestant man in his dominions'

THE King, as Canning had expected, heard the news of his death with the utmost sorrow and dismay. He felt he had lost a friend as well as an able and agreeable Prime Minister, and he immediately set about doing all he could for his family and friends. He arranged for Canning's private secretary, Augustus Granville Stapleton, an illegitimate son of their mutual friend, Lord Morley, to become a Commissioner of Customs; he pressed a bishopric upon Canning's old tutor, the Rev. Phineas Pett; he proposed that his widow should be created a viscountess with remainder to his heirs male, telling her that he could only show through her what his opinion was of 'Mr Canning's splendid talents'; he suggested that her brother-in-law, the Duke of Portland, should succeed Lord Harrowby as Lord President of the Council; he arranged for Canning's friend, the Foreign Secretary, Viscount Dudley and Ward, to be granted an earldom; and he sent for two of Canning's closest colleagues, Lord Goderich, Secretary of State for War and Leader of the House of Lords, and William Sturges-Bourne, until recently Home Secretary and now First Commissioner of Woods and Forests, telling them that he wanted the present government to remain in office with a reshuffled Cabinet under Lord Goderich's leadership. It was the King, however, rather than Goderich whose leadership was more evident in the selection of the Cabinet over which the Prime Minister was so ineffectively to preside.

When informing Lord Goderich of his choice, the King,

so excited by the arrival at Windsor of the beautiful giraffe
which had been sent to him by the Pasha of Egypt, did not
trouble to talk about much else. He afterwards thought it
as well, however, to make the offer of the premiership condi-
tional upon the new Cabinet agreeing to those principles of
governing the country upon which he claimed to have acted
from the time he had undertaken the Regency and 'from
that hour to the present':

The King distinctly stated to poor Mr Canning (on his becoming Minister) that the King had no desire of forming what is
termed an exclusive Tory government, as in that case it would
have deprived the King of the distinguished talents of many
members of the present Cabinet. Nevertheless there was a distinct understanding between the King and his late lamented
Minister (Mr Canning) on many very important points.

The King will begin, for example, by mentioning the question
of Parliamentary Reform. The King joined with Mr Canning in
giving his decided negative to that destructive project.

The King could not of course require of Mr Canning to adjure
his strong and settled opinions upon the subject of Catholic
emancipation : but there was a distinct understanding that the
King's conscientious feelings should not be disturbed upon that
painful question, upon which the King's opinions are unalterably fixed : and moreover if at any time this question was to be
forced upon Mr Canning, from that moment the Cabinet was to
be considered as dissolved.

To this communication Goderich replied, in the name of
the Cabinet, that, as to parliamentary reform, they did not
entertain the thought of bringing it forward or supporting it
as a measure of government; and, as to Catholic emancipation, they felt the 'deepest anxiety to avoid disturbing' his
Majesty's feelings 'upon a question of so much delicacy and
importance'. But although they did not consider themselves
'called upon at any time to propound that question in the
Cabinet without a conviction of the most urgent necessity',
they humbly observed that they thought the matter ought
still to remain, as in Mr Canning's day, 'an open question,

upon which each member of the Cabinet should be at liberty to exercise his own judgement, either in supporting that question if brought forward by others, or in propounding it'.

These assurances did not go nearly far enough for the King's satisfaction; but as he was 'very desirous of preserving the present government', he agreed to 'accept the note ... without entering into further detail'. In a subsequent message he suggested to Lord Goderich 'the best and safest mode of filling up the different offices'; and he made it clear that he considered it 'impossible, with any degree of security to the stability of the present government, to admit any further Whig member in the present Cabinet without its being at once designated a *Whig Administration*'. He had 'quite *made up his mind not* to extend the Cabinet with any more members belonging to the Whig Party', he reiterated two days later. He had 'no personal objections to Lord Holland', for whom Lord Dudley was prepared to resign as Foreign Secretary; but he had 'the very strongest objections to run any risk that the present government should bear either the name or even the semblance of a Whig administration : he could not consent 'to recognize the government except with persons already filling offices'.

To secure a Tory preponderance in the Cabinet he pressed William Sturges-Bourne to return to the Home Office, 'an appointment peculiarly agreeable to the King's feelings'; and, when Sturges-Bourne declined both this office and the Chancellorship of the Exchequer, he insisted that John Charles Herries, Financial Secretary to the Treasury and a friend of Knighton, should become Chancellor.

It was a highly unfortunate choice, for although Herries had proved himself an efficient and talented Treasury official, he was also one of the Commissioners for supervising the reconstruction of Windsor Castle, and it was naturally alleged that the King had selected him in order to use him for extracting more money for building from the government. Herries himself did not want the appointment.

He had already submitted his resignation as Financial
Secretary to the Treasury on account of ill-health and had
been persuaded by Canning to remain in that appointment
only until a suitable successor could be found. He felt himself 'placed in a very embarrassing situation by this sudden
call to an office which had been at no time an object of [his]
thoughts or wishes, and which in the present condition of
[his] health and strength [he] could not contemplate without
dismay'. He entreated Goderich to appoint instead William
Huskisson, Canning's President of the Board of Trade.

The Whig supporters of the government were even more
strongly opposed to Herries's appointment than he was himself. So firmly opposed were they, in fact, that Goderich, who
had agreed with the King that Herries should be Chancellor, felt obliged to submit that his Majesty's service would
be 'best promoted by placing in that situation Lord Palmerston', the Secretary at War, and that Herries should be
asked to take Palmerston's place without a seat in the
Cabinet.

To this arrangement the King fervently objected. He did
not like Palmerston; he did like Herries; and his personal
feelings had a powerful influence over his actions on all such
occasions. Besides, he would have those that were 'proper
for their business'; aristocratic 'ornaments' might follow
later, if the Cabinet wanted them. 'The office requires
ability and not aristocracy,' he wrote in a letter drafted by
Knighton as though the ghost of Canning were sitting by
their side. 'Only yesterday Mr Huskisson [concurred] that
Mr Herries was the fittest man. ... Is the King therefore
to be debarred from fulfilling a duty to the country because
it does not suit the fancy or the temper of particular individuals?'

The King summoned Herries to the Royal Lodge, and unsuccessfully endeavoured to force upon him the seals of
office. He then sent for the leading opponents to the appointment, explained that there had been a series of blunders
which were neither his fault nor theirs, and insisted that

they accept Herries as Chancellor. He informed Lord Goderich that 'one of the many agreeable qualities that Mr Canning possessed as the King's First Minister was – that Mr Canning never kept any thing back from the King'. His Majesty was, therefore, well aware of the high opinion Mr Canning had entertained of Mr Herries's talents, and supposed that Lord Goderich must also be sensible of having 'reaped so largely from his services'.

In face of the King's determination, and provoked by an attack on his personal integrity in the Whig newspapers, Herries reluctantly decided that he had 'no choice but to go to Windsor to accept the seals'. He made the journey on 3 September. He was not to remain Chancellor for long.

It was soon evident to everyone, including Goderich himself, that the Prime Minister was hopelessly ill-equipped for the task that faced him. He was an attractive, good-natured, businesslike man, but easy-going, hesitant and indecisive, incapable of controlling the disparate forces in the Cabinet and so little recovered from the death the year before of a beloved daughter that his problems often reduced him to tears. By the beginning of November the King had decided that the government would have to be strengthened by the admission of Lord Wellesley, who had recently been succeeded by the Marquess of Anglesey as Lord-Lieutenant of Ireland. But Lord Lansdowne, the Home Secretary, threatened to resign if Wellesley were admitted without Lord Holland. Goderich agreed that both Lord Holland and Wellesley would have to come in together, and he was persuaded by Lansdowne and by Huskisson, now at the Colonial Office, to write a letter to the King threatening to resign if his Majesty deemed this arrangement 'altogether inadmissible'.

Goderich showed the draft of this letter to Huskisson and Lansdowne, but afterwards, 'quite unnerved and in a most pitiful state', added that he could not conclude his statement without venturing to add how deeply he felt his own inadequacy to discharge the great duties to which his

Majesty's 'far too favourable opinion called him'. 'His own natural infirmities have been aggravated by a protracted state of anxiety during the last two years,' he pitifully went on; 'his health is enfeebled, and above all he fears that the health of one dependent upon him for support and strength, is still in a state of such feebleness and uncertainty as to keep alive that anxiety to a degree not easily compatible with the due discharge of duties which require the exertion of all the energies of the strongest mind.'

The King in his reply could 'only regret that Lord Goderich's domestic calamities' unfitted him for his present situation, but over this 'he unhappily [had] no control'. He suggested that the Duke of Wellington might be appointed to a seat in the Cabinet as a counterweight to Lord Holland.

While Goderich was apprehensively considering the implications of this proposal, the King discussed the whole problem with Huskisson. He 'spoke very kindly' of Goderich; but he was clearly of the opinion that he would have to be replaced. He considered replacing him by Lord Harrowby; but Harrowby refused the office and said that Goderich must be compelled to stay, at any rate at present. On hearing a rumour that Lord Grey was endeavouring to come to terms with the extreme Tories in order to turn the government out, the King decided that he must follow Harrowby's advice and keep Goderich in office for the moment.

But eventually a more capable leader would have to be found. Lord Lowther told Knighton that the King would have to form a government 'either exclusively Tory or exclusively Whig'. Englishmen liked a 'plain downright straightforward course' and were now 'quite nauseated with the twistings and patchings of the middle party'. There was no force or energy in the government all of whose plans were 'weakened and drivelled away by the necessity of compromise and accommodation of conflicting opinions'. The King had tried a mixed government in 1812 and it had failed; Canning's character had enabled him to 'amalgamate parties into a phalanx of some strength', but now that he had gone the government would inevitably fall to pieces 'from the discordant nature of its own material'. Knighton himself was already doing his best to hasten the disintegration of Goderich's government by revealing to *The Times* exactly how discordant its material was and how incompetent was its leader. He did not have long to wait before his wishes were fulfilled.

Two days after Lowther's letter was written, on 8 January 1828, Goderich went to Windsor to tell the King that his government was collapsing. Herries, deeply offended that Goderich and Huskisson had agreed to the nomination of Lord Althorp as chairman of the Finance Committee of the House of Commons without his being consulted, threatened to resign if the nomination were confirmed. Huskisson said *he* would resign if it were not. Goderich felt unable to carry on without either. He broke down and wept when explaining his dilemma to the King. The King offered him his pocket handkerchief and soon afterwards sent for the Duke of Wellington.

Wellington found him in bed wearing a dirty silk jacket and an equally grubby turban night cap. He had not been well for some time, suffering from gout and rheumatism, 'very acute pain in the back and loins and one arm'. His appetite was not what it was; and he rarely managed to enjoy a good night's sleep. Since Christmas he had been suffering from the after effects of 'a general cold and feverish attack, attended with great tightness and oppression upon the chest' for which Halford had bled him without producing 'such entire relief' as to allow him to leave his room. In the middle of February he had still 'not regained sufficient strength' to stand on his legs, 'much less to walk'. He had been asked to give away Princess Victoria's half-sister Feodore at her marriage to Count Hohenlohe-Langenburg, but he was not even able to attend the wedding. He confessed to Knighton that the anxieties that beset him on every side tore his 'poor feelings almost to shreds and drove him for a time almost distracted'. 'To you and to you alone, dear friend, it is that I can and I do look therefore for my relief,' he had written to Knighton from the Royal Lodge on 30 December in a scarcely coherent letter, '*as it is you and you alone who can and who I am sure will (from your real affection and attachment to me) entirely put an end to* [*my worries*], *and by your powerful exertions and means, crush and put the extinguisher upon that host of vipers and hornets which seems in particular at this moment to have congregated itself together and purposely to sting me personally.*'

It was not only the political crisis that worried him. Harriette Wilson, now living in Belgium as Mrs Rochfort, was renewing her efforts to extort money from her former lovers. Her *Memoirs* had appeared in four small volumes in 1825 and although they created such a sensation that they had been reprinted over thirty times within the year, the King had been able to ensure that, as Prince of Wales, he appeared in them but fleetingly. She was now making further allegations; and this entirely knocked him up and 'destroyed almost all the little amount of strength' he had. Knighton had already been over to the Continent in the autumn when he had decided the wisest course was to defy 'the enemy to do her worst'. He was to make another journey in March, and in the meantime the King was in perpetual anxiety that sooner or later, Mme Rochfort and her hellish gang' would publicize some most unsavoury stories.

In addition to this distress, there was the continuing worry about politics. When Wellington, who was now to become Prime Minister, went to discuss the new government with him, however, he seemed momentarily quite cheerful. 'Arthur,' he said, sitting up against the pillows, 'the Cabinet is defunct.' He then entertained the Duke with some hilarious imitations of his former Ministers, not merely catching their voices exactly but even contriving to make himself look like them. The Duke had 'never seen anything like it'. But the King's resurgence of spirits did not last long.

Wellington's refusal of office under Canning and his resignation from the Horse Guards still rankled; so did the behaviour at that time of Peel, for whom the King had now conceived a profound distaste and whom Wellington wished to reappoint Home Secretary. Indeed, the King viewed most of Wellington's proposed Cabinet with misgivings, though he had given him *carte blanche* to choose any Ministers he liked, with one exception – Grey. Herries was to be replaced by Henry Goulburn. Lord Carlisle, whom the King considered to be a 'personal and attached' friend, declined to accept office unless Lord Lansdowne was also invited to join the government; and Lord Lansdowne refused to serve under a Prime Minister who was not in favour of Catholic emancipation. The Duke of Devonshire, another 'attached and personal friend', followed Lansdowne's lead in refusing to continue in office under men who had behaved so badly towards Canning, though the King told him that his resignation would 'break his heart and drive him out of his senses'.

Moreover, the King soon realized that the freedom in the exercise of patronage which he had enjoyed in the days of Canning and Goderich was now to be severely curtailed. For the Duke of Wellington seemed even more determined to restrict the King's power than Liverpool had been. Never again was he to be allowed such enjoyable freedom to influence appointments on behalf of his friends and their relations and dependants.

While the King grew increasingly peevish and fretful, constantly disputing with the government about his rights of patronage, and threatening to dismiss them from office as though they were his footmen, Wellington decided that he wished he had never agreed to form a government in the first place: he might have avoided 'loads of misery'. As it was he spent his time, so he complained, 'in assuaging what gentlemen call their feelings'. At the first meeting of the Cabinet, one of his Ministers thought that they all displayed towards each other 'the courtesy of men who had just fought a duel'; at subsequent meetings the Cabinet met to debate, to dispute and to separate without coming to any decision. The Duke was particularly saddened that his colleagues considered the office of Prime Minister to be incompatible with that of Commander-in-Chief which he was induced unwillingly to relinquish. His colleagues in turn found him domineering. For his part, the King, who had once complained that Wellington was 'incapable of flexibility', that he 'set about a question like a battery of cannon', now insisted that either 'King Arthur must go to the Devil, or King George to Hanover'.

So far as the King was concerned, the Duke's worst offence was what he took to be his softening attitude towards Catholic emancipation. In July Daniel O'Connell, though disqualified as a Roman Catholic, was elected Member of Parliament for Clare. Wellington, whom Creevey rightly believed to have long been aware of the need 'to do something for the Catholics of Ireland', realized that the question of emancipation could now no longer be shelved. The King, on the contrary, became 'the most Protestant man in his dominions'.

He had been encouraged to remain so by the Duke of Cumberland, whose prejudice against Catholics verged on fanaticism. Writing from Berlin, the Duke had urged him never to 'lose sight of that great question on which the safety and wellfare of the British Monarch and Empire must stand or fall' to show 'publicly, the purity and *staunchness* of your sentiments on the *great* question'. He had told him that their brother William – for whom the office of Lord High Admiral had lately been revived – must have 'done great good' by asserting at an anniversary dinner that he was 'unalterably attached' to the 'sound and strict principles of the Church of England'. He had reminded him of the opinions of their 'late revered father'; and had emphasized the necessity of filling up any vacancies in the Cabinet with staunch Protestants.

Thus encouraged by Cumberland the King's views became more and more intransigent. Wellington believed he had now convinced himself that he held these views sincerely, though he also believed that the King was influenced by his knowledge that they were popular views and that his father and the Duke of York had been widely praised in the country for holding them so firmly. Wellington did not attempt to argue for emancipation other than as a matter of urgent expediency; but the King declined to listen to arguments of any kind. 'God bless you!' he had said to Anglesey upon his departure to Ireland as Lord-Lieutenant. 'I know you are a true protestant.' And now that Anglesey was proving far from being a true protestant by favouring concessions, he would have to be withdrawn. Wellington advocated a less drastic approach, a letter of remonstrance. But the King persisted: Anglesey's reply in which he attempted to justify himself was 'a proud and pompous *farrago* of the most *outré* bombast'. So eventually the Lord-Lieutenant was brought home.

The Duke, too, was persistent. If inclined to be dictatorial in the Cabinet, as though he were once again a general laying down a plan of operations for his staff, he was far too astute to adopt such tactics with the King. 'I make it a rule never to interrupt him,' he told Charles Greville, 'and when in this way he tries to get rid of a subject in the way of business which he does not like, I let him talk himself out, and then quietly put before him the matter in question so that he cannot escape from it.' It was, even so, extremely difficult to get him to stick to the point for he was 'extraordinarily ingenious in turning the conversation from any subject he did not like'. Also he was becoming increasingly, exhaustingly garrulous. He would begin a conversation with 'a long history of his own life, of his political sentiments, of what his father had said of him, of his honesty, his uprightness, his good temper, his firmness, etc., etc.', and would talk in this strain 'for an hour and a half till he was out of breath' before asking, 'Now what have you got to say to me?'

Throughout the late summer and autumn of 1828 Wellington persisted in his endeavours to bring the King round to a less rigid view of the Catholic question; while the King avoided him as often as he could, pleading severe illness. Indeed, he frequently was very ill, although, as Joseph Jekyll remarked, not so desperately so as the newspapers, which gave him 'a mortal disease once a week', liked to make out. His right hand, as Knighton said, was 'full of gouty inflammation and as large as two hands'; his arm, too, was so swollen that his valet could not get it into the sleeve of his coat; he was also suffering from 'attacks of spasms' – which the Duke of Cumberland warned him were caused by *'worry of mind'* – from piles, from inflammation of the bladder, from symptoms of dropsy and from various other ailments for which he took such huge doses of laudanum that Cumberland – who seems to have considered himself something of a medical authority – warned Knighton that he would 'kill himself but, previous to that, palsy himself'.

All the same he was well enough to attend the Jockey Club dinner at St James's towards the end of June. Charles Greville – to whom the King always found time to whisper a few remarks about racing at Privy Council meetings – was there and reported the King as being in very good form. He 'made one or two little speeches' and 'nothing could [have gone] off better'. He was also able to attend Egham Races at the end of August, and, a month later, to welcome to England Donna Maria de Gloria, the nine-year-old *de jure* Queen of Portugal. He greeted her with what Wellington considered to be far too much warmth and affection, for it was the government's view that she had been brought over to England in order to commit public opinion to support her against those who wished to deprive her of her inheritance. The King, to whom personalities were always more important than politics, to whom little girls were always attractive, and to whom Donna Maria particularly appealed as a fellow-royal in distress, took her to his heart. In December, attended by a sovereign's escort of Life Guards, he made his formal entry into Windsor Castle, accepted the keys in a crimson bag from Wyatville, and later conducted the Queen of Portugal round the apartments as though she were a beloved niece as well as an honoured guest. He assured her as he said goodbye that he would 'do all in his power to re-instate her in her rights. The child burst out into a fit of crying, and threw her little arms round his neck.'

As 1828 drew to a close, Wellington gradually began to make ground with the King on the Catholic question. His Majesty still insisted that he had the right to refuse his consent to any Bill which might be passed through Parliament, but by January 1829 he had at least been persuaded to agree that the Cabinet should consider and discuss the problem.

Having got so far, Wellington was dismayed to learn that the Duke of Cumberland, the 'most mischievous fellow' he knew, intended to come home from Berlin. He urged him not to come; he persuaded the King to allow Knighton to go over to Germany to stop him; and the King himself, while assuring Cumberland that he loved and valued him above all his other brothers, begged him to stay in Germany. 'The Duke of Wellington has given me some sensible reasons. ... I must say that it is a great disappointment to me. But I look forward to the happiness of seeing you, the dearest Duchess and my beloved George [their son, aged nine] in the spring. In the Duke of Wellington's ability to administer the affairs of this country I have every reason to place the greatest reliance.'

The next day the Duke of Wellington wrote to Cumberland to tell him that a Catholic Relief Bill was to be introduced, that there was no doubt that the Duke would be put forward as a leader in the cause against it, and that he would be held responsible for 'all the consequences of the violence of others'.

But Cumberland was not to be dissuaded. Before he received Wellington's letter he told Knighton that he proposed to sacrifice his comfort by coming over on 14 or 15 January and that there was no need to do anything other than order '*good fires*' in his rooms; he would drive down to

Windsor as soon as he arrived. Supporters of the Bill dreaded
his coming for he was, so Brougham told Grey, 'fuller of
spirits and all mischief than ever'. Lord Ellenborough, who
thought him a 'Mephistopheles' sure to do all the harm he
could, was appalled by the news of his imminent arrival.
'The King is afraid of him,' he wrote in his diary. 'God
knows what mischief he may do.'

Ignoring Wellington's advice, Cumberland arrived in England on 14 January welcomed by crowds of cheering Protestants. He drove down as planned to Windsor and was soon
as inseparable a companion of the King as he had been in
1811.

His influence over his brother was immediately apparent.
All the work that Wellington had done over a period of
months was undone in a few days. Cumberland knew just
how to work on the King's emotional feelings and how to
provoke him to make stands against his better judgement.
Wellington explained this by saying that, although the King
was afraid of nothing which was 'hazardous, perilous or
uncertain', he dreaded ridicule; and the Duke's powers of
ridicule were unsurpassed.

As well as being cruelly sarcastic, Cumberland was clever,
insinuating and plausible. He succeeded in deepening all the
King's prejudices about the Catholic Relief Bill, in persuading him that his Coronation Oath made it impossible
for him to countenance it, that emancipation was not a
policy that evoked any enthusiasm amongst the great majority of people in the country, and that feeling against it in
some quarters was very strong. Dr Sumner, now Bishop of
Winchester, wrote to the King putting forward a well-
reasoned case for Catholic relief; but his brother's arguments carried far more weight.

Before the end of the month the King seemed on the
verge of becoming as fanatical an anti-Catholic as Cumberland himself. He talked for hours on end on the subject and
once he had got to it there was 'no stopping him'. Lady
Holland heard that he 'worked himself up into a fury when-

ever the subject was mentioned'; and Lord Francis Conyngham, who had now succeeded his brother as Lord Mount
Charles, 'verily believed he would go mad'. * The King told
Lord Eldon that if he were ever made to give way he 'would
go to the Baths abroad, and from there to Hanover', would
never return to England, and that his subjects might then
get a 'Catholic' King in the shape of the Duke of Clarence
who had come round to declaring himself in sympathy with
the Bill. The King's agitation became even more extreme
when it became clear that the Conynghams and his Household generally did not support him in the stand he was
taking.

Wellington, knowing that Cumberland was intriguing to
bring down the government, went down to Windsor on 26
February to give Knighton a letter to hand to the King as
soon as he was awake. If the Duke of Cumberland were to
stay in the country, Wellington wrote, the King would do
well to recommend an immediate change of government,
for if matters were delayed and allowed to remain in their
present state the prospect was nothing 'but chaos'. The Duke
had heard a rumour that Cumberland was planning to get
together a mob of 20,000 Protestants to march on Windsor
to petition the King and to frighten him into refusing any
concessions. Wellington rather hoped that the rumours were
true, for if they were he would have sent Cumberland 'to the
Tower as soon as look at him'. It was suggested that a more
reliable method of getting rid of Cumberland would have
been to appoint him Governor of Hanover and bring home
the Duke of Cambridge as Commander-in-Chief. But Wellington could not approve of this idea, as Cambridge was
'as mad as Bedlam'.

On 27 February Wellington again went down to Windsor
where he found the King 'in a very agitated state'. The audi-

* Some years before Sir William Knighton had told Canning that
he had known the King talk himself into such a state when sober
as to appear utterly drunk ('Most Secret Memorandum', 27 April
1825, quoted in Stapleton, 440).

ence lasted for over five hours, during which tears were shed and there were renewed threats of abdication. Wellington, firm and unyielding, made a little headway against the King's intransigence and received a kiss upon leaving.

The battle, though, was not yet won. Cumberland was still at Windsor; and Peel, having changed his views about emancipation, honourably offered himself for re-election as Member for Oxford University and was defeated by a concourse of rampantly Protestant Masters of Arts. The King was encouraged by this not to give way, though he would have dearly liked to escape from the problem altogether by going abroad to take the baths at Wiesbaden, a suggestion that alarmed Wellington who knew that he would spend 'such sums of money'. Wearily the Duke went down to Windsor yet again on 2 March.

By then the King was worried to distraction not only by the crisis over the Relief Bill but also by Harriette Wilson's furtive activities and, so Lord Kensington told Creevey, by the fear that Captain Thomas Garth, who was rumoured to be Princess Sophia's son either by old General Garth or even by the Duke of Cumberland, was intent on making further trouble now that Cumberland was in England again. The King became so ill with worry that Ellenborough was told he was in danger of going mad; 'nothing but the removal of the Duke of Cumberland from his presence' would restore him to peace.

Wellington, who was really upset to see 'the poor old man's distress and agitation', also sometimes thought that the King would go mad, if indeed he was not mad already. Several years before, he had baldly stated in a letter to Mme de Lieven that he considered the King to be insane. Since then the Duke and others had been astonished by a habit that his Majesty had developed of pretending that he had taken part in events or had felt emotions that were quite outside his experience. He once said, for example, that when he was a young man Lord Chesterfield had told him, 'Sir, you are the fourth Prince of Wales I have known, and I must give your Royal Highness a piece of advice: stick to your father; as long as you adhere to your father you will be a great and a happy man, but if you separate yourself from him, you will be nothing but an unhappy one.' 'And by God,' the King commented with what appeared to be quite passionate sincerity, 'I never forgot that advice and acted upon it all my life.'

He even, so it was said, took a perverse pleasure in astounding his Ministers by pretending that he had fought at Waterloo and had helped to win the Battle of Salamanca, 'when things were looking very black indeed', by leading a magnificent charge of dragoons disguised as General Bock. He had also, so he claimed, ridden 'Fleur-de-Lis' for the Goodwood Cup. When recalling these stirring events the tears would often start to his eyes, and no one was quite sure whether or not he was making some elaborate joke. Sometimes it seemed that he had succeeded in persuading himself that he had actually participated in the sagas he so vividly described. When Wellington called on him on 2 March he found him in one of these strange moods and was much exhausted by an inconclusive interview which lasted for three hours.

The next audience which Wellington, Peel and Lyndhurst all attended on 4 March was even more exhausting, and after it the Duke was more than ever convinced that the King was mad. He had talked almost continuously for five and three quarter hours, constantly sipping brandy and water, threatening to retire to Hanover, explaining that he must consult the Archbishop of Canterbury and the Bishop of London, breaking down and weeping, rambling on about the Coronation Oath which he now appeared 'to confuse with the oath of Supremacy'. Ultimately, in face of his Ministers' unyielding attitude, he asked for their resignation. They gave it and left the room, where Knighton and Lady Conyngham later found him, in a 'deplorable state', lying on a sofa, utterly worn out. Before he went to bed, however, having discussed the matter at length with Knighton and the Conynghams, and having eaten a good dinner, he had accepted the fact that he could not do without Wellington and must accept Catholic emancipation. The ultra-Tory opponents of the Bill were not strong enough to form an alternative government. He would have to recall him. 'My dear Friend,' he wrote wearily. 'As I find the country would be left without an administration, I have decided to yield my opinion to *that* which is considered by the cabinet to be for the immediate interests of the country. Under the circumstances you have my consent to proceed as you propose with the measure. God knows what pain it causes me to write these words. G.R.'

Arthur had won. He really was 'King Arthur' now, the King commented bitterly; O'Connell was 'King of Ireland'; as for himself, he was merely 'Canon of Windsor'. But even so, Wellington's troubles were not over, for he feared that the King would change the government as soon as the Bill was passed or even before it was passed, and he was tempted to resign immediately. He was 'so overworked and so indignant' that he 'abused the King most furiously', saying that he was 'the worst man he ever fell in with in his whole life, the most selfish, the most false, the most ill-natured, the most entirely without one redeeming quality'. Mrs Arbuthnot tried to calm him down, to persuade him not to do anything from temper, that he owed a public duty to the country to remain at his post. But he was 'so angry he did not say much except that he would *be damned* if he would stay'.

Grenville, however, considered the Duke's fears were groundless. The King 'is fonder of abusing his Ministers than of changing them', he told the Duke of Buckingham. 'For a few hard words cost him nothing; but a great political change could not be made, if at all, without much more trouble, fatigue, and worry to the King than he will like to expose himself to.'

Grenville was right. Wellington remained in office; and on 10 April, after much grumbling and muttering, the King gave his consent to the Roman Catholic Relief Act. A week later he received Wellington at Windsor where he was 'sitting for his picture *in a Highland dress*'. The Duke was kept waiting for twenty minutes before the King appeared, still wearing plaid stockings. He 'was not in bad humour but cold', and the Duke remained with him for less than half an hour.

After he had returned to London, Wellington reported: 'I saw Lady Conyngham who was very much alarmed at the prospect of having the Duke of Cumberland there so long. But she told me nothing excepting that the King was more easy since he had given the royal consent to the Bill. I have seen different persons since who have been there.' One of these persons was Sir Henry Halford who told him on 23 April that his Majesty was 'more composed and in pretty good spirits'. Unfortunately, however, the atmosphere in the Castle was bound to be rather unpleasant so long as the Duke of Cumberland remained. Lady Conyngham was 'dreadfully afraid of him and perhaps not without reason'.

'The Duke of Cumberland keeps the whole house in awe, particularly the Lady,' Wellington confirmed. 'She appears to be in perpetual alarm lest he should say something to alarm her; and the King sees the whole. Under these circumstances they say that the residence at the Castle is not the pleasantest that could be found.' Certainly Maria Conyngham found it tiresome enough; and though the King disliked emerging from the seclusion which the Castle afforded him, rather than disappoint her, he went to London in April for the parties which she wanted to attend.

44

The Final Years
1829–1830

*'A bold man, afraid of nothing if his Ministers
would stand by him, and certainly neither afraid
of pain or death'*

CATHOLIC emancipation was not the only issue which
divided the King and the Cabinet. There were also differences over the royal prerogative of mercy, differences which
showed the King's character in a more attractive and liberal
light. He had always taken particular pleasure in using this
prerogative, in doing what lay in his power to ameliorate the
harshness of the criminal code, as Lord Sidmouth, Home
Secretary between 1812 and 1821, had known well enough.
One of the first acts of his reign had been to abolish the
legal use of torture in Hanover; and on arriving there in
October 1821 he had immediately pardoned a man serving
a prison sentence whose destitute wife, the mother of his
'eight little children', had appealed to him for mercy.

He had afterwards been frequently in touch with Peel,
Sidmouth's successor, on behalf of some unfortunate felon
whose history had excited his compassion or that of Lady
Conyngham. It was her influence over the King, so it is tradi-
tionally supposed by her descendants, which led to the abo-
lition of the flogging of female prisoners; and it is certain
that he himself warmly encouraged other measures taken in
his reign to lessen the severity of legal punishment. He was
also interested in the protection of animals from cruelty and
was a personal friend of Richard Martin – whom he nick-
named 'Humanity Dick' – the Irish Member of Parliament
responsible for the first legislation anywhere in the world for

the prevention of cruelty to animals and one of the founders of the Royal Society for the Prevention of Cruelty to Animals which was established in 1824.

The King's correspondence with Peel is replete with such requests as these: 'to make every possible enquiry into the case of the boy Henry Newbury, aged thirteen, and to commute his sentence from transportation, in consideration of his youth, to confinement in the House of Correction. . . . The King quite approves of Mr Peel's humane recommendations respecting Davis; but what is to be done concerning Desmond, who is of the same age? Is there any opening for the other poor young man Ward? The King would be truly glad if such could be found. . . . The King has received Mr Peel's note, and he must say, after the deepest reflection, that the executions of to-morrow, from their unusual numbers, weigh most heavily and painfully on his mind. . . . The King therefore desires that . . . four may only suffer . . . for the same crime . . . in the place of eight.'

Peel did not always feel able to accede to the King's requests; and on one occasion, believing that the plea for mercy originated with Lady Conyngham, resolved to resign if the King persisted in it. Nor could Peel agree to a reprieve in the case of Joseph Hunton, a Quaker with ten children who was sentenced to hanging for forgery. The King strongly pressed for a mitigation of the capital sentence and urged Peel to confer with the Lord Chancellor and the Lord Chief Justice whose joint opinion was that 'it would be very difficult hereafter to enforce the capital sentence of the law in any case of forgery if mercy [were to be] extended in this case'.

When he did persuade Peel to pardon a man his delight was endearing. Once when Peel was staying at the Pavilion he received a sudden summons in the middle of the night to go to the King's room. Having induced Peel to believe that mercy was justified in a case that was troubling him, the King kissed him, and then, noticing what a poor dressing-gown he was wearing, he said to him, 'Peel, where did you get your dressing-gown? I'll show you what a dressing-gown ought to be.' And he handed him one of his own.

No one who knew the King well could doubt that his concern for condemned criminals was prompted by a genuine humanity. His servants acknowledged him to be a most considerate master. One of them, a valet on his deathbed, told Count Boruwlaski 'that his Majesty during the course of his ... illness had never omitted to visit his bedside *twice every day*, not for a moment merely, but long enough to soothe and comfort him, and to see that he had everything necessary and desirable, telling him all particulars of himself that were interesting to an old and attached servant and humble friend'.

Sir Andrew Barnard, who served the King as equerry, was equally attached to him. 'I feel proud and gratified at being one of his servants,' Sir Andrew once declared. 'I trust ... that the whole people of England will appreciate his great and good qualities in the same manner that those do who have had the happiness of seeing them more closely.' Lady Anne Lindsay, who had married Barnard in 1793, and who had so deeply sympathized with the King in his relationship with the difficult and short-tempered Mrs Fitzherbert, was quite as devoted to him as her husband. She loved him, she confessed, 'very much ... God bless him!' Although now estranged from him, Lady Holland, too, thought of him with affection: there was 'more good in him than [fell] to the lot of most princes; and had he not been a prince, he would', she was sure, 'have been a most amiable man'.

A characteristic story of the lengths to which he would go to serve his friends was related by Lord Eldon who was constantly badgered by the King, when Regent, to make Joseph Jekyll a Master in Chancery. Eldon admired Jekyll more as a wit than as a lawyer and was reluctant to make the appointment, though the King assured him that Jekyll would make a first-class Master if given the chance. For months Eldon resisted the King's importunities until one day he received a call from him at his house in Bedford Square. The servants informed the King that Eldon was ill with gout and could see no one; but the King stepped inside, walked up the staircase, and knocked at all the bedroom doors until he found the one where Eldon was hiding from him. The King sat down by the bed and embarked upon a long eulogy of his friend Jekyll, his talents and integrity. Eldon remained obdurate.

At last the King threw himself back in his chair exclaiming, 'How I do pity Lady Eldon!'

'Good God!' said the Chancellor. 'What is the matter?'

'Oh, nothing, except that she will never see you again. For here I remain until you promise to make Jekyll a Master in Chancery.'

'Well I was obliged at last to give in,' Eldon recorded. 'I could not help it.' And in the end Jekyll 'got on capitally'.

Artists and writers had particular reason to be grateful for the interest which the King continued to take in them. At a time when he was poor and unhappy and his reputation was overcast, Benjamin Robert Haydon submitted for the King's inspection his canvas *The Mock Election* based on a scene he had witnessed in a debtor's prison. The King bought it for five hundred guineas, a much higher price than most of Haydon's pictures were then commanding. 'We drank the King's health in the large goblet I had painted in his picture,' Haydon told his friend Mary Russell Mitford in high excitement. 'God save the King!'

'A thousand and a thousand congratulations to you and your loveliest and sweetest wife,' Miss Mitford replied no less happily. 'I have always liked the King, God bless him. He is a gentleman – and now my loyalty will be warmer than ever.'

David Wilkie was similarly indebted to the King for his generous support and affectionate concern at a time of adversity. 'Go to Wilkie,' the King instructed Knighton on hearing that Wilkie was ill and worried about some pictures that he was unable to finish. 'He is proud and shy – he may

not want money at all, and it would not do to offer him that.
Say to him, however, that ... I entertain [so] confident [an]
expectation of his recovery ... that he has my permission to
consider me as his banker. ... He may draw for what he
wants, and repay me ... at his leisure, in the shape of pictures. I can never have too many Wilkies in my collection.' *

   Wilkie did not accept the money, but when he was better
and had returned from the Continent, the King, who, as an
admirer of Teniers and Ostade was naturally attracted to
Wilkie's work, asked him to come and see him. He afterwards bought several of his pictures, including *The Spanish
Posada* and *The Defence of Saragossa*. The King's kindness
to Wilkie, so the sculptor, Francis Legatt Chantrey said, was
'beautiful'.

   Chantrey, who sculpted numerous statues of the King, was
himself full of gratitude and affection. He recalled how pleasantly the King had put him at his ease when he sat for him
for the first time. 'Now, Mr Chantrey,' he had said with the
utmost friendliness, 'I insist on your laying aside everything
like restraint, both for your own sake and for mine; do here,
if you please, just as you would if you were at home. ... Now
Mr Chantrey,' he had added, holding out his wig as the
sculptor prepared the clay. 'Which way shall it be? With the
wig or without it?'

   He had behaved in the same easy, friendly way when he
had first met Scott, whose work he so much admired and
whose presence was always welcome in his library. 'Let us
have just a few friends of his own, and the more Scotch the

---

   * In 1811 the King had asked Benjamin West to commission on
his behalf a picture from Wilkie as a companion piece to Edward
Bird's *The Country Choristers* which he had bought the year before
for 250 guineas. 'Let Wilkie make choice of the subject,' he had said
to West, 'take his time in painting it and fix his own price' (RA
20499: Asp/K, i, 235). This commission resulted in *Blind Man's Buff*
with which the King was so pleased that he asked Wilkie for 'a
companion picture of the same size'. So Wilkie painted *The Penny
Wedding* for which the King paid £545 in 1820 (RA27039, 10 February 1820; Millar, *Later Georgian Pictures*, 12, 138).

better,' he had suggested to their mutual friend, William Adam, when arranging to have Scott invited to a small dinner party. It was a highly successful party, Adam remembered. The King, then Regent, had been 'particularly delighted with the poet's anecdotes of the old Scotch judges and lawyers, which his Royal Highness sometimes *capped*'. Croker, who was also of the party, said afterwards that the King had been enchanted with Scott, 'as Scott with him; and on all his subsequent visits to London, he was a frequent guest at the royal table'. The King was 'the first gentleman he had seen – certainly the first *English* gentleman of the day,' Scott decided. 'There was something about him which, independently of the *prestige*, the "divinity", which hedges a King, marked him as standing by himself.'

On later occasions when they met, Scott was always deeply gratified to note with what cordiality, with what 'great distinction', the King treated him, how he shook hands with him 'before the whole company'. 'No subject was ever more graciously received by a Sovereign,' Scott proudly recalled, remembering the day he had been created a baronet, 'for he scarce would permit me to kneel, shook hands with me repeatedly, and said more civil and kind things than I care to repeat.'

From that day onward it was 'impossible to conceive a more friendly manner' than the King always used towards Scott, whose books, like those of Jane Austen, he so warmly recommended.

As flattered as Scott by the place of honour accorded to him at the King's table was Thomas Lawrence, who, up till the time of his death in 1830, continued to paint for the King as vigorously as ever.

Exceptionally generous towards artists, the King, indeed, gave liberally to countless other people who succeeded in arousing his admiration or pity. His 'private benevolence', as Knighton wrote in a 'secret and confidential' letter to the Duke of Wellington, stood unrivalled. His family were particularly fortunate. In addition to the £50,000 he provided for the Duke of York, he found £10,000 in 1826 for the Duke of Clarence, and several lesser sums for Princess Elizabeth. Upon hearing that the affairs of Charles Arbuthnot, who had had to resign the Secretaryship of the Treasury on account of ill-health, were in a 'most desperate and wretched state', he borrowed £15,000 on his behalf and gave it to him with the words, 'Take this and never let the subject be mentioned again and, above all, do not let it cause any shyness or embarrassment between us.' As Mrs Arbuthnot said, it showed 'how really kind and good-natured' the King was when he acted 'upon the first impulse' and when he had 'no ill-natured person to check him.'

In the theatre, Michael Kelly, John O'Keefe and Charles Mathews were three of many performers who had occasion to be grateful to him when they were in straitened circumstances. He had only to hear of an actor or indeed of anyone in distress, so Knighton said, and he wished to help them; he had but to hear of a worthy cause, and he was anxious to support it. As well as such outright gifts as £1,000 towards the building of St David's College, Lampeter, a theological college for poor Welshmen, 'a most laudable effort' which he could not praise in 'terms of sufficient commendation', and larger sums to the distressed weavers of Spitalfields, he regularly supported year by year numerous charities from foundling hospitals to orphanages, old people's homes to lunatic asylums, from the British and Foreign School Society to the Royal Infirmary for Diseases of the Eye. Even his adversary, Henry Brougham, praised him for his staunch and generous support of popular education.

Once he had given his reluctant consent to the Catholic Relief Bill, the King's relations with his Ministers began to grow less antipathetic, though the improvement was certainly slow. At a ball on 11 June he ignored several members of the Cabinet; and at Ascot he had a 'whole party of Canningites in his house and not one Minister'. He 'gave a bad reception to all the friends of government who went into his stand, and said to Mr Peel that he should have as soon expected to see *a pig in a church* as him at a race! Mr Peel was invited to dine at the Lodge, but he pretended he had no clothes and refused to go.'

As the year progressed, however, relations became almost cordial. The King could not forgive Lord Ellenborough, the Lord Privy Seal, for having opposed the third reading of the King's Property Bill in a speech which caused great offence to Lady Conyngham by questioning the Sovereign's rights to leave property to others apart from his successor. And when he invited the Ministers to dinner, Ellenborough was pointedly omitted from the list of guests. But with the other Ministers, even with Peel, he was now on quite friendly terms. With Wellington, indeed, he was once more on the same footing as he had been in 1823 when he had expressed the opinion that 'it would be difficult to find a man of such consummate integrity, possessing such straightforward, *true* political wisdom, or such unsullied principles that comprehend everything that is noble, everything that is great'. The King still lamented Canning's death, of course, and regretted the passing of those days when he had enjoyed more sense of power than the stern Wellington allowed him; but Arthur was a friend once more, and a great man after all.

Wellington was conscious of the King's attachment to him, and regarded him in turn now with a kind of affection. He told Ellenborough that he would be 'very sorry to hurt him'; he could not 'bear to see the King in distress'. Also he had a genuine respect for his undoubted gifts. He had a 'wonderful knowledge of character', and was 'a bold man, afraid of nothing if his Ministers would stand by him, and certainly neither afraid of pain or death'. To be sure he could on occasions still be so utterly exasperating that the Duke felt like giving him up 'as a bad job'. He was the 'greatest *vagabond* that ever existed', he was once driven to conclude, 'he was always acting a part to himself'.

'He is not happy unless he is ill,' Mme de Lieven com-

mented sardonically; and it was only too true that he was
thankful to have an excuse to retreat to his bedroom when
some unpalatable duty faced him or some unpleasant decision had to be made. Even when he was well he allowed
documents to remain unsigned until there was serious talk
of the 'necessity of appointing an officer to affix some kind
of signet which should be equivalent to, and supersede, the
royal signature'. Peel mentioned at a Cabinet dinner 'the
circumstance of the King having signed no commissions for
more than two years'. 'He will not sign parchment,' Lord
Ellenborough noted. 'There can be no reason why the commissions should not be on thick paper; but they say the King
would sign them for the first few days, and then give it up.'

The time that Ministers wasted at Windsor was incal-
culable. As Wellington reproachfully put it in a letter to
Knighton, 'When one goes to Windsor no person can answer
for the hour of return.' The accomplished and fastidious
Charles Greville was far more explicit in his condemnation.
'His greatest delight,' Greville complained, 'is to make those
who have business to transact with him, or to lay papers
before him, wait for hours in the ante-room while he is
lounging with Mount Charles or anybody, talking of horses
or any trivial matter; and when Mount Charles has said,
"Sir, there is Watson [Sir Frederick Beilby Watson, Master
of the Household] waiting etc.," he replies, "Damn Watson,
let him wait." He does it on purpose and likes it. ... A more
contemptible, cowardly, selfish, unfeeling dog does not exist
than the King, on whom much flattery is constantly
lavished. He has a sort of capricious good nature, arising,
however, out of no good principle or good feeling, but which
is of use to him, as it cancels often in a moment and at small
cost a long score of misconduct. ... There never was such a
man or behaviour so atrocious.'

Although most Ministers did not share this harsh and
aggravated judgement, few of them were not on occasion
infuriated by the King's conduct, incensed to discover, when

they called at the Castle to discuss business with him, that he was incapacitated from doing so by laudanum or cherry brandy. When he emerged from the effects of these over-doses he was in such 'a state of excessive irritation' that it was considered advisable not to see him. Lord Aberdeen, the Foreign Secretary, had experience of this when he went to Windsor to discuss the offer of the throne of Greece which had been made to Prince Leopold.

Prince Leopold had continued to live at Claremont Park after Princess Charlotte's death on the splendid annuity of £50,000 which the government continued to provide for him. He had been a constant source of irritation to the King who had been deeply offended by his having called on the Queen after her 'trial' and having allowed his house in London, Marlborough House, to be illuminated in celebration of her 'acquittal'. The Hon. George Agar-Ellis, Member of Parliament for Seaford, had noticed how cross the King had looked at a party at the Duke of Wellington's when, sitting 'in full blown dignity on a sopha between Lady Conyngham and Madam Lieven', his eye had alighted upon the young and handsome features of his son-in-law.

The King was appalled by the offer of the Greek throne to the suave, calculating 'Marquis Peu-à-Peu', and his dislike of him grew more intense than ever. How could the government be 'such fools as to think he could be of any use'? His Majesty could not 'but *deeply regret* the selection made by France and Russia of Prince Leopold as the Prince to be placed at the head of the Greek Kingdom', he wrote to the Duke of Wellington. 'Without entering into a detail of reasoning, the King considers Prince Leopold *not qualified* for this peculiar station.'

He prepared himself for the interview with Lord Aberdeen by taking a hundred drops of laudanum, and was after-wards so much agitated that his barber 'thought he should have cut him twenty times'. Once more there were rumours that the government were to be dismissed; but when the

King saw that further resistance was useless he gave way to
Prince Leopold's nomination 'in deference to the desire of
the two great Powers', though he did so very 'grumpily'.

He was all the more grumpy and agitated because he had
been constantly badgered not to agree to the appointment
by the Duke of Cumberland who urged him in the strongest
terms not to give way 'to the over-bearing and dictatorial
spirit of the Duke of Wellington'.

Three days after he had given way – evidently without
daring to tell his brother that he had done so – he received
a characteristic letter from him, a letter that shows how fully
justified were the government's suspicions of Cumberland:

> You must remember that ... yesterday sennight ... you stated
> to me in the clearest and most positive manner that in an audi-
> ence which you had given to Lord Aberdeen ... you had gone
> through the whole matter of the Grecian case, that you had
> expressed your *astonishment* and at the same time your *dis-
> pleasure* that negotiations should have gone on for upwards of
> four months without either the Duke of Wellington or Lord
> Aberdeen having ever mentioned one word to you on the subject.
> Lord Aberdeen replied that Prince Leopold was not the nomina-
> tion of England but of France; this naturally made you feel
> outrageous, and your reply to Lord Aberdeen was, 'Whether the
> King of France would not be amazingly astonished if Prince
> Polignac [now Charles X's foreign minister] had without the
> King of France's knowledge, intrigued through the Duke of
> Wellington to have a son of the Duke of Orleans named as a
> candidate by the King of England.' Lord Aberdeen admitted the
> truth of this, and, on talking over the personal merits of Prince
> Leopold, Lord Aberdeen took pretty good care to say that it was
> not his choice but the Duke of Wellington's. I do not think it is
> worth while to call your attention upon the *contradiction, false-
> hood* and *absurdity* of this excuse; but I have seen enough of
> Lord Aberdeen in this whole transaction and know enough of
> his conduct herein to be fully convinced that he is become a
> most apt scholar of the Duke of Wellington, who, you as well as
> myself know, will stick at nothing to make good his point. ...

Now the question stands thus, whether in the eyes of all
Europe, and in great parts of this country, George the IVth is to

be considered as King and *Master*, having a right to be *consulted* and *informed* upon all great matters of importance, of which there is no doubt the formation of Greece and her sovereign must be a most weighty question, or whether the Duke of Wellington is to proclaim to all Europe that *he* is the *master* and that you must give way to his arrogance whenever he thinks it proper; and I am perfectly convinced that the Duke of Wellington has contributed through his friends to have this whole thing made as public as possible to show *his power* to the world which he makes no disguise in proclaiming.

Cumberland went on to assure the King that Wellington was 'fully determined to show the world' that he did 'not care a farthing' about him or any of his commands. 'If you give way on this point,' Cumberland warned him, 'you are completely ruined for not only it must shake you in the opinion of all Europe, but your giving way on this occasion is neither more nor less than signing and sealing the Duke of Wellington not only as your Minister for the rest of your reign, but as Dictator in the country.' The King had missed his opportunity to get rid of the Duke over the Catholic question; now Providence had furnished him 'with another opportunity' which it was his duty to take.*

Although the King never went nearly so far in his opposition to the Duke of Wellington as Cumberland urged him to do, there were scenes similar to those provoked by Prince Leopold and the Greek question when Wellington refused to allow the King to create Nash a baronet, on the grounds that it was a step which would 'be attended with the greatest inconvenience' in view of the other numerous 'pressing applications' and the public's attitude towards the enormous and continuing expenses of Buckingham Palace. The King

* The Duke of Cumberland's assertions that Wellington was endeavouring to assume dictatorial powers were reflected in numerous contemporary caricatures. A typical one by Heath portrayed Wellington trying on the royal crown in front of a looking-glass while the King, sucking his thumb in a cradle, is rocked to sleep by Lady Conyngham, believed to be one of the Prime Minister's closest allies (BM *Sat*, xi, 15521).

was outraged: Nash was being most 'infamously used'. He should be created a baronet *'forthwith'*, not only as an act of justice to himself but to the King's *'own dignity'*. Once again his Majesty was overruled; he took to his bed again.

There were pleasant days though, even in that summer of 1829 when his eyesight was failing and he could scarcely write any more by candlelight. In May he gave his annual children's ball which was attended by his 'little friend', the Queen of Portugal, who fell down, cutting her nose on one of her diamonds; she cried a great deal, and he was 'very kind to' her. The next month there was a concert at St James's Palace where he listened with evident satisfaction to the singing of Maria Malibran. Later there was the Jockey Club dinner at which he did not speak much and seemed to be in pain; but the next week Mme du Cayla, formerly the mistress of Louis XVIII, thought him handsome still with a pair of beautiful legs.

At Windsor, where he spent the summer in the Royal Lodge, he still drove out occasionally in his little pony-chaise to visit the animals in his menagerie at Sandpit Gate and to address a few words of comfort to his ailing giraffe; his affection for it and his grief at its death in August were cruelly ridiculed by Heath and Doyle who caricatured him and Lady Conyngham weeping over it sentimentally. Sometimes, when he had inspected the menagerie, he would sit for a time in his chaise with his favourite cockatoo on his arm, sipping a glass of cherry-gin which 'was always kept in preparation for him'.

He now spent the greater part of his time at Windsor, though in bed, remaining there often until dinner-time, after which, enlivened by punch, he would still occasionally sing songs and 'relate anecdotes of his youth'.

The curtains of his room were opened between six and seven in the morning when the newspapers were brought to him.* Sometimes he had a book read to him, or called upon the pretty actress, Eliza Chester, whom he had appointed his reader, to entertain him with a play. His favourite novelists were still Scott and Jane Austen, but he also enjoyed the works of Lady Morgan and called Croker a 'damn black-guard' for making some adverse comments on her novel, *Florence Macarthy*. He also read a great deal of history, memoirs and travel books, and had 'an extraordinary memory' for the information he gleaned from them, and 'liked to talk of them', so Sir Astley Cooper said. His accounts reveal his catholicity of taste as a book-collector, and his concern to buy almost every book that was published about Napoleon. When Napoleon died, and the library which was sent out to St Helena was returned to London, he asked his librarian to go through it and show him any books which had been annotated. From an inspection of these he came to the conclusion that Napoleon's favourite author was Ossian.

When the King's reading was finished, and after attending to what business he could bring his mind to dwell upon, he would doze and then order something to eat or drink, a glass of chocolate perhaps or a chicken and a goblet of soda water, or sometimes, after several glasses of cherry brandy or punch, he would eat an astonishingly heavy meal with quantities of pastry and vegetables. During the meal he would talk to his pages and *valets de chambre*, to his stud groom, Jack Redford, or to whichever doctor happened to be available. One morning in November 1829 he was to be

* When his sight was capable of it he 'read every newspaper quite through', so Mount Charles said; and Lord Howick was 'rather surprised to hear from Huskisson', so he noted in his journal in March 1829, 'that the King is in the habit of reading every newspaper that is published' (MS Journal of 3rd Earl Grey, 10 March 1829). Certainly throughout his life his Household had taken deliveries of enormous quantities of newspapers: at Carlton House no less than 546 copies of eight different newspapers were delivered every day (RA 28398–915).

seen 'in a white cotton night cap and a rather dirty flannel
jacket, propped up with pillows, and sipping his chocolate',
as he talked alternately to Chantrey about some statues he
was making for Windsor, to James Wardrop, his surgeon
in ordinary, about the stuffing of the giraffe, and to the Duke
of Cumberland and a tailor about the possibility of providing the Guards, and later all the infantry, with new uniforms. A servant interrupted this divan to announce the
Duke of Wellington, whereupon he put on a black velvet
cap with a gold tassel and a grand blue silk *douillette* and
limped into the next room to receive him in the character of
King George IV. After half an hour's official talk he returned to his bedroom, and tumbled into bed again to resume the discussion on the army's coats and breeches.

He was evidently in fairly good spirits that day, but his
health was deteriorating fast. He was quite blind now in one
eye, and the fear of blindness in the other, upon which an
operation for cataract had been proposed, made him 'nervous, sad and troubled', although when Wellington called
he put on a brave face and displayed not the least concern.
At Christmas he complained to Knighton of being already
'blind as a beetle'. He bought a great number of magnifying
glasses and pairs of spectacles with pebble lenses; but they
do not appear to have been of much use.

He was also having trouble with his remaining teeth.
Years before he had complained of discomfort from his
false teeth, as a cure for which Lord Lauderdale had recommended him to place a piece of lint steeped in tincture of
myrrh between the gum and the gold on the inside of the
plate. Since then his dentist, Samuel Cartwright, had been
repeatedly called in to treat him: in 1829, Cartwright was
obliged to attend his patient thirty-seven times, charging
twenty guineas for each visit to Windsor and three guineas
an hour at St James's; his total bill for the period, including
mechanical work, came to over £700.

In November 1829 Lady Conyngham also fell ill with
what began as 'a bad bilious fever' and then culminated in

fainting fits so persistent that she thought she was dying. The King, whose practice it had long been to visit her room for an hour or so's desultory conversation each evening, appeared to be much more concerned about her health than she had been in the past about his. When he seemed really unwell she devoted herself to prayer, and once, on being told that he was 'very ill', she burst into tears; but usually she appeared to have little patience with his various complaints and to believe that his sufferings, apart from his obvious gout and failing sight, were more imagined than real.

She still talked of leaving him as she had done intermittently for years. In June 1823, when the King had grumbled to Wellington that her temper was really 'beyond bearing', she in turn had impatiently complained of being so bored that she could not possibly stand it any longer; and, in October that same year, the Duke had told Mrs Arbuthnot that her conduct was 'shocking', that the King 'was full of attention and quite *aux petits soins* with her and that she shrugged her shoulders at him and seemed quite to loathe him; so much so that everybody observed it. She told the Duke that the whole thing bored her to death and that she would go away and have done with it.'

In March 1825, when she had been in deep affliction because of the death of her eldest son, she did leave Windsor for a time and was 'disposed to give up the thing altogether'. 'It has always been known that the late Lord [Mount Charles] detested and remonstrated against the connection,' Fremantle commented, 'and it is whispered that he left her a written exhortation. Whether this be true or not, I cannot pretend to say; but I can answer for her having resisted all application' to return. Eventually she did so only on condition that she would be allowed to dine alone in her own apartment whenever she chose. 'Considering [the King's] extreme kindness to her,' Mrs Arbuthnot commented, 'she really does make him a most ungrateful return. She detests him, shows it plainly, yet continues to accept all his presents which are of enormous value.'

In the summer of 1825 she had again become 'very restless
and impatient' under what she called her 'terrible restraint
and confinement'. She had then announced 'her fixed determination to go abroad', and had been prevented from doing
so only by the efforts of Lord Lauderdale who persuaded her
that 'however blameable it was in her to get into her present
situation', now that she *was* in it, it was her 'bounden duty to
submit and go through with it'. The same advice was given
to her by the Duke of Wellington. In the winter of 1826,
more bored than ever, she had thrown herself back on her
sofa, declining to speak. It had been the general opinion at
that time, so Lady Grey said – though Lady Grey herself
did not believe the reports – that she hated 'Kingy'. Now, at
the beginning of 1830, recovered from her illness and looking 'twenty years younger', she was once again 'bored to
death' and was really thinking of 'removing'.

When she was in this kind of mood the King relied on
Knighton to keep her at bay. He was finding Knighton more
tiresome than ever, and displayed 'great irritability' in his
manner when there was business to discuss. Yet, as Knighton noted in his diary on 6 February 1830, 'the King seemed
embarrassed at the thoughts of my absence, not from any
feelings towards myself, I am satisfied, but from the contention His Majesty would have with Lady Conyngham. ...
The King talked to me at dinner because I was opposite –
but at night on his going to bed there was no desire to talk
to me in preference to his eating his supper.'

45

The Last Illness
1830

'We have an Herculean constitution to work upon'

IN the spring of 1830 the King began to suffer from severe attacks of breathlessness and found it impossible to get to sleep except 'by a good contrivance of pillows and a bed chair'. Throughout the night he would wake up periodically and then, in need of company and reassurance, he would ring his bell and ask a valet to pour him a glass of water, although there was a jug on the table beside his chair. The pains in his bladder were also growing worse, and to alleviate them he took increasingly enormous doses of laudanum.* Laudanum, however, was having less and less effect. In the past he had been known to spend 'the greater part of the twenty-four hours in a state of stupor'; now he could take over 250 drops in a period of thirty-six hours and remain quite capable of conducting a rational conversation with the Duke of Wellington.

His doctors found him an appallingly difficult patient, combining a nervous apprehension as to his condition with a refusal to adopt a way of life which might improve it. They themselves, though, were far from being in agreement as to how he should be treated. Sir Henry Halford, Sir Wathen Waller, Sir Matthew Tierney, as well as James Wardrop and

---

* 'Nothing can exceed the pain of such attacks,' Knighton had told Canning four years before, when Wellington had dismissed all the King's ills as imaginary. As a cure for the complaint – diagnosed as 'gout, principally confined to the neck of the bladder and all along the course of the urethra' – leeches were applied around the King's pelvis (Canning Papers, 103b).

Benjamin Brodie, the surgeons, and O'Reilly, the apothe-
cary, were all in attendance at different times and seem
rarely to have agreed with each other's diagnoses and treat-
ments. The King was sceptical about the skills of all of them,
particularly of those of O'Reilly, 'the damnedest liar in the
world', whom he appears to have considered more as an
amusing purveyor of gossip than as a medical attendant to
be taken seriously. When he was really apprehensive about
himself he sent for Knighton who, though he had not practised for many years, had not forgotten his medical knowledge: when Halford and O'Reilly advocated the use of a
bougie for the King's urethral complaint, Knighton was
proved right in objecting to it for it made the condition
more painful than ever. Knighton also rightly continued to
condemn Sir Henry Halford for allowing the King far too
much laudanum. But neither Knighton nor any of the other
doctors had the least control over their difficult patient, who
alarmed them all exceedingly by his dreadful spasms of
breathlessness. At first there would be a gurgling in his
throat, then not only his face but even the ends of his fingers
would turn black as he tried to get his breath. Yet as soon as
he felt better he would drink a large glass of brandy, get up
and go for a ride round the park.

His mode of living now was 'really beyond belief', so Mrs
Arbuthnot learned. One day in April 'at the hour of the servants' dinner, he called the page in and said, "Now you are
going to dinner. Go downstairs and cut me off just such a
piece of beef as you would like to have yourself, cut from the
part you like the best yourself, and bring it me up." The
page accordingly went and fetched an enormous quantity of
roast beef, all of which he ate, and then slept for five hours.'

'One night he drank two glasses of hot ale and toast, three
glasses of claret, some strawberries!! and a glass of brandy.
Last night they gave him some physic and, after it, he drank
three glasses of port wine and a glass of brandy. No wonder
he is likely to die. But they say he will have all these things
and nobody can prevent him.' For breakfast on 9 April,

Wellington said that he had 'a pidgeon and beef steak pie of which he eat two pigeons and three beef-steaks, three parts of a bottle of Mozelle, a glass of dry champagne, two glasses of port [and] a glass of brandy! He had taken laudanum the night before, again before this breakfast, again last night and again this morning.'

On 14 April he was taking a ride in his pony-chaise when he decided to stop and have a look at his hounds. As he was inspecting them he was seized with a very severe attack of breathlessness. That evening the Duke of Wellington reported him as being 'very unwell', though in 'very good humour', and heavily dosed with laudanum.

'We regret to state,' Halford and Tierney reported next morning in an official bulletin, 'that the King has had a bilious attack. His Majesty, although free from fever, is languid and weak.' Subsequent bulletins, issued at intervals during the following three weeks, were equally vague and non-committal but rather more reassuring: 'His Majesty has passed two good nights and continues better. ... The King continued as well as his Majesty has been for several days past, until this morning when his Majesty experienced a return of the embarrassment of his breathing. His Majesty is now again better. ... The King has suffered less from the attacks of embarrassment in his breathing. ... His Majesty has passed a good night. His Majesty's symptoms are somewhat alleviated. ... The King's symptoms have not varied. ... The King's symptoms remain the same....'

In his private reports to Wellington, however, Halford expressed a far deeper concern. The King was greatly alarmed by his attacks of breathlessness, and did not like to be left alone for a moment, clinging anxiously to Halford's hand until the doctor was 'completely knocked up'.

There were occasions when, after large doses of laudanum, massive quantities of ether, and a few hours' sleep, the King professed himself much refreshed; but 'the instant he called upon himself for an exertion, all his difficulties were renewed'; and then 'it was hardly possible to be more distressed than he was'. On 1 May there was a 'gigantic struggle' for breath, after which the doctors' 'whole thoughts' were 'devoted to procuring rest'.

The King began to dread the appearance of documents, since the effort of signing them brought on spasms of extreme agitation and breathlessness. He asked if Parliament could pass an Act for saving him the trouble, particularly as he could scarcely see the papers which he was expected to sign. But when Halford told him that Parliament 'would not agree without ascertaining previously from the physicians the cause and extent of this disability', all his habitual fears of making such information public were reawakened and he 'withdrew his proposal instantly and said he would take the earliest opportunity of affixing his royal signature'. Afraid of displaying his weakness in front of the Duke of Cumberland, he signed papers valiantly and without complaint when the Duke was present; but he begged Halford not to leave him on these occasions for fear lest he should become involved in some exhausting political discussion, or better still, not to allow the Duke into his room at all.

So the month wore on. On some days, after Brodie had made punctures in his swollen legs, and 'his Majesty had been able to take such a posture as permitted him to sleep uninterrupted a few hours', there would be a marked improvement. Although he did not ask to have the newspapers read to him – a sure sign of weakness – he did manage to eat a reasonable meal; and when not beset by fears of suffocation he behaved with a courage that Halford profoundly admired.

Others, besides Halford, were much impressed by the King's fortitude in his sufferings, by the way he would speak cheerfully of a speedy recovery between prognostications of his imminent demise. He assured Lady Conyngham that he was about to die at any moment; but that, the Duke of Wellington thought, was merely to 'try and vex' her; and certainly such dire prophecies were in keeping with his practised methods of eliciting concern and sympathy. To the

Duke he expressed not the least apprehension, and the Duke admired him for it. So did Croker, who reported that he was contemplating the situation 'boldly'. Even Lord Ellenborough wrote, 'in constitution and mind he is certainly a wonderful man. I have no doubt that the feeling that he is always in representation makes him behave in the face of death as a man would on the field of battle.' Yet although they admired his courage, most of his Ministers regarded his approaching death with little sympathy and less regret. As for his heir, he could not conceal his excitement at the prospect before him. The Duke of Clarence and his brothers wrote suitably dutiful letters to Knighton expressing their anxious wishes for his amendment; but the King well knew that the devotion they all expressed did not go very deep. His sisters really did love him, and always had. The Duke of Cambridge, with whom he had been on the best of terms for twenty years, was also concerned, perhaps. But Clarence and Cumberland were thinking of their own future now, not of his; and Sussex he presumed to be indifferent, even though he did send 'affectionate messages'. The Duke of York might have sincerely grieved for him, and might, too, have made a worthy successor; but the King could not conceive that Clarence would be one. 'Look at that idiot!' he had once whispered in Mme de Lieven's ear at the dinner table, indicating his brother whose red-thatched face – 'like a frog's head carved on a coconut' – could be seen at the other end of the table. 'They will remember me, if he is ever in my place.'

Nearly all those whom he had once thought of as his real friends were dead. Fox was gone and Canning, Gerard Lake and John McMahon, Payne and Moira, the Duke of Northumberland and the Duchess of Devonshire, Lady Bessborough and Lady Lade. Sheridan, too, was dead; and he could not but deeply regret that they had quarrelled at the end over money which the King had sent to him.*

* Thomas Moore, in his *Life of Sheridan*, gave a highly tendentious account of this transaction and of the King's offer to Sheridan of

Mrs Fitzherbert was still alive but when she heard that he was ill she had not at first been sympathetic. She remembered, as she told her adopted daughter the Hon. Mrs Dawson-Damer, 'that the King always liked to make himself out worse to excite compassion, and that he always wished everyone to think him dangerously ill when little was the matter with him'. She had supposed that this was now the case. Later, however, she heard from Sir Henry Halford, an old friend, that the King was, in fact, 'excessively ill'. His constitution was 'a gigantic one', and his 'elasticity under the most severe pressure' exceeded everything Halford had witnessed in thirty-eight years' experience. But the worst circumstances in which he had ever witnessed the Dukes of Clarence and Sussex, 'under their attacks of spasmodic asthma', hardly approached the King's distress at times. What the final result would be, Halford could hardly venture to say.

Having received this letter, Mrs Fitzherbert overcame her former reluctance and wrote to him for the last time: 'After many repeated struggles with myself, from the apprehension of appearing troublesome or intruding upon your Majesty, after so many years of continual silence, my anxiety respecting your Majesty has got the better of my scruples, and I trust your Majesty will believe me most sincere when I assure you how truly I have grieved to hear of your sufferings. . . . No one can feel more rejoiced to learn your Majesty

---

£500 when he lay dying, supposedly in great distress. Lockhart, who reviewed the book unfavourably, thought that Moore's treatment of the King was more 'unpardonable than anybody knows – for Croker took care to put him in possession of all the facts of the case long before the book was printed. First and last old Sherry (besides his sinecure) received from the Privy Purse upwards of £30,000 in cash' (*Scott Letter-Books*, 146). Certainly the King had been very patient with Sheridan's vagaries, and there can be little doubt that Sheridan misappropriated the £3,000 which the King had given him to buy a seat in Parliament from the Duke of Norfolk, using the money instead to settle some pressing debts (*Croker Papers*, i, 86–7; Bingham, 351–3).

is returned to complete convalescence, which I pray you may long enjoy, accompanied by every degree of happiness you may wish for or desire. I have enclosed this letter to Sir H[enry] H[alford],' she concluded, emphasizing her disapproval of Sir William Knighton whom she had always disliked and distrusted, 'as your Majesty must be aware there is no person about him through whom I could make a communication of so private a nature accorded with the perfect conviction of its never being divulged.'

Halford noticed how eagerly the King seized the letter when it was given to him, and with what emotion he read it before placing it under his pillow. But the will which he had made in her favour in 1796 he wished now to alter. In 1823 when his life had been threatened by a man named Griffith, he had asked Lord Eldon to go to see him 'upon the subject of a will'. He had then told Eldon that he thought Mrs Fitzherbert ought to have £10,000 a year for life, rather than the £6,000 a year which was already granted to her on the security of the Brighton Pavilion. He had also mentioned the 'natural son, an officer in the East Indies, to whom he thought himself bound to give a legacy of £30,000. ... He then spoke of a residuary legatee. He said the Duke of York would succeed to a station which made it unnecessary to make him residuary legatee.' In any case, he went on, the Duke had had £50,000 from him; the Duke of Clarence had had £30,000; it 'could not be expected that he should look to the family of the Duke of Kent', nor to the Duke of Sussex. The Duke of Cambridge 'wanted nothing'; and 'he added, naming his several sisters, that he did not think there was a necessity to attend to them as residuary legatees. ... He then said he should make *a friend* residuary legatee, *not naming the person*, but he certainly meant Lady C[onyngham].'

He repeated his wishes now to Knighton who was desired to inform Lady Conyngham of them. When Knighton had delivered the message, the King asked him, 'Well, how did she receive it?'

'She was very much affected, Sir, and burst into tears.'

'Oh, she did, did she?'

Later, so Agar-Ellis was informed 'in the greatest secrecy' by Lady Lyndhurst whose husband was consulted in the matter, the King formally declared his wishes again 'before three witnesses who were Sir Henry Halford, Sir [Matthew] Tierney and Sir William Knighton: His wishes were that everything he stood possessed of should become the property of Lady C[onyngham]. When this declaration was made about a fortnight before the King died the D[uke] of W[ellington] was told of it and came down to Windsor and threatened Lady C[onyngham] if she took advantage of it. He told her among other *gentlemanlike* speeches that she was like Madame du Barri, and that Madame du B's conduct brought about the French Revolution.' Agar-Ellis added that they did not mean to execute the will, if they could possibly avoid it.

In spite of his weakness and sleeplessness, the pain in his limbs, his rapidly decreasing appetite and his frightening attacks of breathlessness, the King continued to endure his sufferings without undue complaint. He looked 'wasted and wasting'; yet, as the Duke of Wellington noticed, his hand was 'cool and healthy, his eye was lively, and his mind as clear and active as ever, and even his spirits were good; in fact he showed strong vitality'. He asked for the *Racing Calendar*, enquired how work was getting on with the new dining-room at the Royal Lodge which Wyatville had been instructed to begin the previous September, and insisted that it must be finished in time for Ascot races. On 12 May Wellington saw him again and found him 'good humoured and alive, his eyes as brilliant as ever', though 'several quarts of water' had been taken from his feet the day before and his colour was now 'dark and sodden'. He was still talking of going to Ascot on 26 May and of convalescing at Aix-la-Chapelle; he remained in 'very good humour'.

But by now, as the Duchess of Gloucester reported, he was

'enormous, like a feather bed', while the dropsied swelling in his legs had made them 'hard as stone'. His face was drawn, his features pinched. He had attacks of choking, and in speaking of Leopold – against whom he was 'furious' for deciding not to go to Greece after all now that the King's approaching death brought their niece Victoria closer to the throne – he 'had a seizure which threatened to be fatal'. The remedies he had been given for dropsy had upset 'the functions of the stomach', and on 15 May he had eaten nothing for three days.

Yet on the 17 May when Peel went to visit him, he appeared 'lively, intelligent and strong'. At this and at a subsequent, and final, meeting early in June all their past differences were forgotten and they spoke as friends. The King asked Peel to push his day-bed towards the window, saying that he had little time left now in which to enjoy the view over the garden, which, in fact, he could only vaguely discern. Peel's old father had died that month, and the King said, 'You are just returned from your father's funeral. You will soon have to pay the like ceremony to me.' Peel attempted to take his mind from such thoughts by talking about the Royal Lodge, but the King said, 'Ah, poor Cottage, I shall never see it again.'

On 21 May, after a very bad night, the King's condition rapidly deteriorated, though Halford continued to write admiringly of his patience and bravery. There was 'still power left' in the King's 'extraordinary constitution'; on 15 June he was actually reported to be in 'very good spirits'.

The King's Signature Bill had now been passed, allowing documents to be stamped not signed; yet he still liked to suppose that this was only a temporary measure, even that he was well on the way to recovery. And when he did talk of his expected demise he was more likely to do so with a kind of reckless cheerfulness than in the mournful tone he thought it appropriate to adopt in discussing the painful subject with Peel. 'You know,' he announced carelessly one day, 'I shall be dead by Saturday.' He was 'as amusing as

ever', so Knighton said; and Croker heard that he was 'as
clear, as communicative, as agreeable, nay as *facetious* in his
conversation as he had ever been'.

Knighton, to whom he was now 'particularly affectionate',
had put a Bible on the table beside his bed, and he was seen
often to pick it up and look into it. Although in the past he
had dutifully attended church on Sunday mornings, had
taken the Sacrament at Easter and Christmas and had had a
little chapel built in the grounds of the Royal Lodge, he had
never been a particularly religious man and had always disliked sermons, except those that gave him 'pleasure and
satisfaction'. But in recent years he had seemed to take his
religious duties more seriously and had attended Holy Communion more often. He now appeared really to derive comfort from the Sacrament which, administered to him by the
Bishop of Chichester, Dr Robert Carr, a former Vicar of
Brighton, he took in his room with Knighton and Lady
Conyngham. He also seemed comforted by the prayers for
his recovery which were being said in the churches. These
prayers, which the Bishop repeated to him, kneeling by his
bed, ended with the words, 'Finally grant, O heavenly
Father, that when it shall be Thy good pleasure to call him
from this world unto Thee, he may receive a glory in Thy
everlasting Kingdom; through the merits and mediation of
our Lord and Saviour, Jesus Christ. Amen.' '*Amen, Amen,
Amen!*' the King repeated fervently when the Bishop had
finished.

He later talked of this prayer to a visitor who assured him
that the public took a great interest in his state. 'He seemed
much pleased, and expressed his own conviction that it
ought to be so, for he "had always endeavoured to do his
duty", and had never willingly done harm to anyone.' As for
the prayer, he added with a touching appreciation of its
literary rather than its spiritual merits, it was 'in very good
taste'.

Although the public were asked to pray for the King's
recovery, they had been given very little information as to

what was the matter with him. 'The King's symptoms remain the same', a typical bulletin had stated on 22 May. 'His Majesty has passed a better night.' The *Lancet* was highly critical of the 'vague, unsatisfactory and mysterious' bulletins that emanated from Windsor. The King was clearly suffering from a disease from which there was 'no instance of recovery upon record'; yet his medical attendants seemed unaware 'of the precarious situation of their royal patient'. His death had been predicted 'eight or nine years ago when Sir Henry Halford, Sir William Knighton and Sir Matthew Tierney stated under their hands that the King laboured under an organic disease of the heart which might terminate in sudden death'.

In subsequent issues both the *Lancet* and the *London Medical Gazette* were even more critical of the doctors at Windsor whose methods they deplored. Powerful diuretics, morphia, ether and laudanum had all 'failed to produce the desired effects'.

On 12 June *The Times* quoted the *Lancet*'s criticism of the bulletins which were 'so scandalous, so ambiguously framed'. 'His Majesty', the *Lancet* regretted to say, 'is in as alarming a state as ever. The integuments have been again punctured, but his body and his extremities from the immense collection of water, are still enormously swollen. In the management of the royal sufferer, the attendants experience considerable difficulty in inducing him to take proper medicines, food, and drink. The King does not consider that his case is hopeless. From private information, however, we can only say that although in our opinion ultimate recovery is impossible, immediate dissolution is not inevitable. The medicines which have been administered for some time past have consisted chiefly of *aether* and the *sedative tincture of opium*.'

The King himself declined to accept the fact that ultimate recovery was impossible. As though anxious to show Wellington and Lord Farnborough that he was not to be easily defeated, he paid particular attention to the official papers that were brought to him on 16 June and 'all the arrears, about four hundred documents' were stamped. But thereafter the King grew increasingly weak, 'more languid and poorly'. He continued to see as little as possible of Cumberland whose recent alleged affair with Lady Graves had 'horribly annoyed' him; and did not appear to relish the visits of Clarence, but he looked forward to his sisters' visits 'with the greatest pleasure'.

Towards the end of the third week in June, his doctors expressed their unanimous opinion that his system was now 'giving way at all points'. Yet, as Halford reported to Wellington, almost taking for granted now the resilience of his astonishing patient, he was 'easily satisfied that he would get the better of this illness'. On the day that he saw Wellington for the last time, 'he said he was getting quite well and should be able to move soon'.

At half past eleven the following Friday night, 25 June, the King dismissed Sir Henry Halford and sent him to bed; the pages too retired to the outer room. Soon he fell asleep in his chair, leaning on the table which was customarily placed in front of him, his forehead resting on one hand, his other hand in that of Sir Wathen Waller, who was sitting up with him. At a quarter to two he woke up, asked for his medicine, and then drank a little clove tea. After drinking the tea he fell asleep again, and remained asleep until just before three when he sent for the pages to bring in his nightchair. 'He had instantly a purgative motion,' Waller reported, 'but observed, "I do not think all is right," and then added, a common expression of his, "What shall we do next?" I answered, "Return as soon as possible to your chair."' The King did so and then, feeling faint, he ordered the windows to be opened. He tried without success to drink some sal volatile, whereupon Sir Henry Halford was summoned. He was still holding Waller's hand, 'more strongly than usual', when suddenly he looked him full in the face and, 'with an eager eye', exclaimed, 'My dear boy! This is death!'

He then closed his eyes and lay back in his chair. At that moment Halford entered the room. 'His Majesty gave him his hand but never spoke afterwards and, with a very few short breathings, expired exactly as the clock struck the quarter after three, June 26, 1830.'

'I am truly brokenhearted,' Sir Wathen Waller told his son, 'and have lost one of the most affectionate friends man ever possessed. At my age I can ill spare a friend whose eye ever beamed with pleasure on me for nearly forty long years, but I must not go on, for at this moment I can ill bear it.'

[46]

Post Mortem

'Un roi grand seigneur'

THE doctors who conducted the post mortem concluded that the King had been suffering for many years from arteriosclerosis. They also found that many of his internal organs were in an unhealthy condition; but that 'the immediate cause of his Majesty's dissolution was the rupture of a blood vessel in the stomach'.

In a private letter to his son, Wathen Waller added that a contributory cause of death was 'over excitement and high living. There was also a small stone found in the bladder which accounts for the pain he felt all last winter. ... His will was opened and there is nothing in it to annoy the present King. ... He is to be buried the Wednesday after next.'*

The funeral took place, in fact, on Thursday 15 July at Windsor where, though the town was full of visitors, 'the only sign of mourning which [was] visible [was] in their dress'. For six hours the day before, the King's body lay in state in the Castle, attended by various members of his Household, Gentlemen Pensioners and Yeomen of the Guard. Yeomen of the Guard also lined the Grand Staircase which – like the rooms through which the public passed on their way to the State Apartment where the coffin lay – was draped in black. A sheet covered all but the King's face. He

* The King's will was never proved. Wellington paid off all outstanding debts from the estate and handed over the residue to King William IV. On condition that she continued to receive her allowance of £10,000 a year, Mrs Fitzherbert signed a release of her claims on all the King's personal estate and effects (Wellington Papers, Miscellaneous 31).

'looked well, as though asleep, but his cheeks were sunken and the abdomen much raised'.

At nine o'clock on the evening of 15 July, the coffin was carried to St George's Chapel between lines of Grenadier Guardsmen, every fifth one of whom bore a burning flambeau. Its pall was held by six dukes and four eldest sons of dukes. In front of them, leading the procession, were the trumpeters, drummers and fifers of the Guards. These were followed by peers bearing banners, Blanc Coursier King of Arms with the crown of Hanover, and Clarenceux King of Arms with the crown of England. The Duke of Wellington carried the Sword of State. Behind him walked King William IV, in a 'magnificent velvet purple cloak', with the collars of the Order of the Garter, the Bath, the Thistle, St Patrick and the Royal Hanoverian Guelphic Order around his ample neck.

It was an impressive spectacle. But the scene inside the chapel, so far as it could be discerned in the smoke from the Guardsmen's guttering flambeaux, was far from dignified.

The Times reporters, who could see 'not a single mark of sympathy' amongst the congregation, thought that nothing could have been worse managed. 'It seemed as if the servants of the household, the friends of the carpenters and upholsterers, the petty tradesmen of the town had been admitted to the exclusion of all those who, for public character or official situation, ought to have been allowed free access to the funeral of the Sovereign. We never saw so motley, so rude, so ill-managed a body of persons. They who first entered not only seized the best places, but prevented others from taking any.'

To add to the confusion in the chapel, during the singing of a hymn, a piece of the carved work which hung over one of the stalls, crashed to the ground, striking Sir Astley Cooper on the forehead. The wound bled profusely; but Sir Astley clasped a handkerchief to his head and manfully remained in his place.

To Agar-Ellis, who thought that there was 'too much

tinsel magnificence' about the Earl Marshal's ceremonial for it to be moving, nothing seemed more indecorous than the new King's behaviour. Bustling with excitement, he 'talked to the people on both sides of him while coming up the aisle, and afterwards when sitting at the head of the coffin'. He 'talked incessantly and loudly to all about him,' Joseph Jekyll confirmed, 'so that the most frivolous things were overheard.'

King William IV's behaviour was not all that was incongruous, Agar-Ellis thought. 'Sussex and Cumberland looked awfully fierce in their black cloaks. . . . Some of the figures in the chapel were incomparably absurd. The Duke of Buckingham squatting down in a stall exhausted (for he had held a corner of the pall) looked exactly like a giant tortoise, then the vulgar, insolent air of Lord Ellenborough in a coat covered with gold – the greasy importance of Verulam carrying a banner, and old Cathcart with another which he could hardly support – the horrid nervous grimaces of the Duke of Norfolk and the awkward gestures of Lord Conyngham were all in their different ways most ludicrous. . . . Mount Charles was much affected and I think no-one else.' Lord Ellenborough agreed that no one appeared much affected: 'It was considered a mere pageant, even by his household who had lived so intimately with him for years.'

After two hours King William could wait no longer. While the anthem was being sung, he rose from his seat, thanked the Earl Marshal for making all the arrangements and left the chapel.

In the absence of the King, while minute guns boomed in the Long Walk, the body of King George IV was lowered into the grave. He had earnestly asked Wellington, whom he had appointed one of his executors, to ensure that he was buried in his night clothes and 'with whatever ornaments might be upon his person at the time of his death'. Wellington had assured him that this would be done. Afterwards he realized what lay behind the King's request, for noticing a black ribbon around the neck in the open coffin, he had been driven by curiosity to see what was suspended from it. He had drawn aside the collar of the nightshirt to reveal a diamond locket containing a miniature portrait of Mrs Fitzherbert. The Duke blushed deeply as, with some hesitation, he told Mrs Dawson-Damer what his inquisitiveness had led him to discover. When Mrs Dawson-Damer, in turn, told Mrs Fitzherbert that the King had been buried with her picture round his neck, she listened without a word. But presently it was seen 'that some large tears fell from her eyes'.*

If Mrs Fitzherbert and his sisters wept, if Waller and Mount Charles and many of his servants grieved for him, and if Mme de Lieven heard the news of his death with 'real sorrow', there were few others amongst the public at large who sincerely mourned their loss. During his protracted illness, a few prints had been issued suggesting that John Bull had 'always liked G[eor]ge' – though he had once had a bit of a quarrel with him – and heartily hoped that he would recover. But these were not truly reflective of the state of public feeling. Most people had seemed indifferent, and the rich principally concerned that his expected death would interfere with their arrangements for the summer. At Brooks's, of course, bets had been lightheartedly laid upon the duration of his life.

When the Privy Council met for the first time after his death, 'there was no grief in the room. ... It was like an *ordinary levee.*' And after his funeral, 'all Windsor' was drunk, so Joseph Jekyll said. 'Suppers and champagne for parties who remained there, and everything but grief or regret.' Gangs of pickpockets roamed the streets, and the 'quantity of watches, money, etc., that fell into the hands of

---

* John Whiting, the King's Page of the Backstairs, told Queen Victoria that the portrait was of Lady Conyngham; but Sir George Seymour, Mrs Dawson-Damer's brother and one of Mrs Fitzherbert's executors, had 'no doubt it was Mrs Fitzherbert's portrait'. Sir Wathen Waller and Sir Frederick Watson both assured him that they had seen it (Sir George Seymour's annotations of Langdale's *Memoirs of Mrs Fitzherbert*, Seymour of Ragley MSS, CR 114/A/536/7).

the marauders [was] of an immense amount in value, almost
to surpass belief'.

The crowded London streets had 'more the appearance of
rejoicing than mourning'. On the day of the funeral the
shops were shut and 'in a great number of instances the
shutters even of the private dwellings were up'; the church
bells tolled; minute guns fired from the Tower and in St
James's Park; but there was no 'solemn expression of feeling
nor much decorum of behaviour'. The young Lord Howick,
driving between Brooks's Club and the Travellers' and 'all
about that part of the town' a few days after the funeral,
found the streets still 'excessively crowded'; the people were
not in mourning and there was 'no sign of sorrow to be
seen except a single shutter before the windows of the shops.
It looked much more as if some good news had arrived than
anything else.'

The King had 'never sincerely inspired anyone with attachment,' Mme de Lieven thought, 'and had hardly been
susceptible to attachment himself'. 'No one trusted him. ...
He was full of vanity and could be flattered at will.' Yet 'unquestionably he had some wit and great penetration; he
quickly summed up persons and things; he was educated
and had much tact, easy, animated and varied conversation,
not at all pedantic. He adorned the subjects he touched, he
knew how to listen; he was very polished. For my part I had
never known a person like him, who was also affectionate,
sympathetic and galant.'

Sir Astley Cooper, the surgeon, who had also known him
well, emphasized this fundamental kindness in a man who
was, however, 'violent in his temper'. Cooper had been called
in to carry out an operation for the removal of a wen on the
King's head in 1821, an operation which was much more
dangerous than had been expected and which, as Wellington and Henry Hobhouse confirmed, the King had undergone without the least fuss or trouble. Over the subsequent
years Cooper had formed a high opinion of the attainments
of his extraordinary and contradictory patient. He was 'in-

dolent', he had to admit, 'and, therefore, disposed to yield, to avoid trouble; nervous, and therefore anxious to throw every onus from his own shoulders. Yet he was the most perfect gentleman in his manners and address – possessing the finest person, with the most dignified and gracious condescension, though excessively proud; familiar himself but shocked at it in others. ... He would sometimes be coarse in his conversation, but again nobody could be more refined and polished when he chose. Every story of a character about town, every humorous anecdote, he was perfectly acquainted with, and was constantly seeking means of adding to his stock, and then took the greatest pleasure in relating them to others. He was himself witty, but the points of his conversation consisted principally in anecdote, and the relation of jokes. ... If I had wanted to decide upon what I ought to do, nobody would have given me better advice; but he very likely would have practised just the contrary himself, for with respect to himself he was too often guided by prejudice.'

Cooper was particularly impressed by his wide knowledge, especially of history and literature, his 'ability to recount anecdotes of everybody'. He 'had an extraordinary memory – he recollected all that he had read or seen – and had the faculty of quickly comprehending everything. If he saw a steam-engine, he would describe not only its principles of action, but enter minutely into its construction. ... If [he] observed any medicine that was new to him, he immediately asked its object and was not satisfied until he knew all its properties. He was also fond of inquiring into the uses of the various instruments employed in surgery.' Upon being introduced to a manufacturer of surgical instruments who had invented a new form of saddlebag for army surgeons, he amazed the inventor by his detailed knowledge of his craft and not only pointed out something that was lacking – a large sponge – but showed him where it could be accommodated. The King, Cooper concluded, would have made 'the first physician or surgeon of his time, the first speaker in the House of Commons or Lords, though, perhaps, not the best divine'.

Those who had known the King less well spoke of him less generously. A few people who had cause to be grateful for his generosity or patronage confessed to lamenting the King's death – Benjamin Haydon and Joseph Jekyll amongst them. A few others – like Creevey – remembering past kindnesses, mourned 'poor Prinney'. Mrs Arbuthnot wrote of the 'strange creature's' occasionally doing 'remarkably good natured things'. A few dutiful sermons were preached, associating the King with the advances, improvements, reforms and brilliant successes of his age. A few dutiful letters were written: Scott expressed to Knighton his 'deep sorrow for the loss of a sovereign whose gentle and generous disposition, and singular manner and captivating conversation, rendered him as much the darling of private society, as his heartfelt interest in the general welfare of the country, and the constant and steady course of wise measures by which he raised his reign to such a state of triumphal prosperity, made him justly delighted in by his subjects'.

A few public men delivered tedious eulogies, emphasizing – as, indeed, was his due – 'his late Majesty's munificence as patron and collector'. A few newspapers recorded 'the triumphs of his Regency and reign', and endeavoured to draw a parallel between these triumphs and the late King's character and attainments. The *Morning Post* went so far as to mourn the 'loss of a monarch so conspicuously endowed with all the qualities calculated to endear him to the hearts of his subjects', 'one of the best and most popular monarchs that ever swayed the sceptre of Britain', 'so good and excellent a King'.

But such effusively extravagant praise was wholly out of tune with the general mood of the country. This mood was more accurately reflected by *The Times* which roundly attacked the King's 'most reckless, unceasing and unbounded prodigality', and his 'indifference to the feelings of others'.

'In the tawdry childishness of Carlton House and the montebank Pavilion, or cluster of pagodas at Brighton,' *The Times*'s merciless obituary continued, 'His Royal Highness afforded an infallible earnest of what might one day be expected from His Majesty when the appetite for profusion and the contempt for all that deserves the name of architecture, should have reached their full maturity. ... Princess Caroline's reception in her husband's house was a stain to manhood. A fashionable strumpet usurped the apartments of the Princess – her rights – the honours due to her – everything but the name she bore. ... The heroine has now at least nothing to fear from her destroyer. ... The late King had many generations of intimates with whom he led a course of life, the character of which rose little higher than that of animal indulgence.'

Three weeks later, after the harshness of these judgements had been compared with the almost fawning tributes which the paper had paid to King William IV, *The Times* returned to the attack, making full amends for the thick black mourning bands which surrounded its columns: 'There never was an individual less regretted by his fellow-creatures than this deceased King,' an editorial insisted the day after the funeral. 'What eye has wept for him? What heart has heaved one throb of unmercenary sorrow ... for that Leviathan of the *haut ton*, George IV. ... If he ever had a friend – a devoted friend in any rank of life – we protest that the name of him or her never reached us. An inveterate voluptuary, especially if he be an artificial person, is of all known beings the most selfish. Selfishness is the true repellant of human sympathy. Selfishness feels no attachment, and invites none; it is the charnel house of the affections. Nothing more remains to be said about George IV but to pay – as pay we must – for his profusion; and to turn his bad conduct to some account by tying up the hands of those who come after him in what concerns the public money.'

King William IV, on the other hand, had already 'gained more upon the English tastes and prepossessions of his sub-

jects by the blunt and unaffected – even should it be grotesque – cordiality of his demeanour' than King George IV
had ever done during the sixty-seven years of his existence.
The excessive cordiality of King William IV was not to
everyone's taste, of course. At his first Privy Council he
shortsightedly did his best to make out the face of every
Councillor who knelt before him to kiss his hand, greeting one he recognized with a genial, 'How d'ye do?', obviously restraining himself with difficulty from shaking hands
with them all. 'Poor Prinney,' Creevey wrote, noting the
contrast, 'put on a dramatic, royal, distant dignity to all.'

It was certainly true that the new King was popular, all
the more so because of the contrast between his familiar,
gregarious manner and the seclusion in which his prede-
cessor had chosen to spend the last years of his life. So
obviously delighted to be King, William IV strode about the
London streets, nodding cheerfully to left and right. One
day in St James's Street the mob followed him and 'one of
the common women threw her arms round him and kissed
him'. 'The mob adores him,' Mme de Lieven thought. 'He
goes about openly and treats everyone familiarly – that is
enough for John Bull. England is quite a new world, and
Wellington said to me quite truly, "This is not a new reign,
it is a new dynasty."' All the glories of the past reign were
forgotten and the vices of the King who had presided over
them were maliciously 'exaggerated'.

As though he wished to emphasize the difference between
himself and his brother, and to show that he was quite the
bluff, simple, economical Englishman, King William IV
pulled down most of the Royal Lodge; he replaced the German band with a smaller English one; he pruned the
Windsor Castle staff and dismissed the French cooks; he had
the recently installed gas installation pulled out; he sent the
animals in the royal menagerie to the London Zoo; he made
over a miscellaneous collection of treasures and objects of
art to the nation. His brother had been very fond of such
'knicknackery', he explained when inspecting one of his

pictures, but he couldn't see much in it himself. Aye, it might be pretty. 'Damned expensive taste, though.'

His brother had not only collected this particular sort of knicknackery. His wardrobes and chests of drawers were found to be crammed with all manner of articles, new and old, with which he had been unable to bring himself to part. As well as his immense collection of coats and suits, waistcoats, and shirts, boots and breeches, gloves and hats and walking sticks, there were, so Charles Greville learned, 'five hundred pocketbooks, of different dates, and in every one of them money'.* There were vast numbers of wigs, dirty handkerchiefs and faded nosegays; there were three hundred whips, 'canes without number, every sort of uniform, the costumes of all the orders in Europe, splendid furs, pelisses, etc.' and, among countless other pieces of clothing, a dozen pairs of new corduroy riding-breeches ordered from his tailor long after he had given up riding. There were quantities of women's gloves, and locks of women's hair 'of all colours and lengths, some having the powder and pomatum yet sticking to them', and huge packets of love letters, including copies of his own, 'descriptive of the most furious passion'.†

* In 1829 the King spent £228 on a huge variety of pocket-books (RA 28915).

† The bulk of this correspondence, including letters 'expressive of ardent attachment' that had passed between the King and Mrs Fitzherbert, were burned by Knighton and Wellington as the King's executors. Letters which the King had written 'in great abundance' to Lady Jersey had already been burned by her executor, Lord Clarendon, in the presence of her son (*Creevey Papers*, 368). Mrs Fitzherbert, who did not trust Knighton, at first declined to hand over the King's letters in her possession; and it was not until August 1833 that she gave her formal consent to their destruction (Wellington Papers, Miscellaneous 31, 24 August 1833). Soon afterwards nearly all of these letters were burned by Wellington in the drawing-room of her house in the presence of her friend, Lord Albemarle. There were so many of them that after several hours' work Wellington said to Albemarle, 'I think, my Lord, we had better hold our hand for a while, or we shall set the old woman's chimney on fire' (Albemarle, ii, 71). Mrs

Even more might have been discovered had not Knighton already taken it upon himself to destroy the most heated and compromising of the letters, and had not Lady Conyngham removed various trinkets to which she felt herself entitled. According to current gossip, indeed, she took more than a few trinkets. She was alleged to have taken whole wagonloads of treasure into the obscurity which thereafter surrounded her until her death in 1861, a widow of ninety-one, at her country house in Kent. Contemporary cartoons portrayed her standing in the Castle between curtains framing shelves of money bags and jewels, and, assisted by her husband and daughter, vigorously packing up her loot. When, soon after the King's death, she and her family left the Castle, Miss Margaretta Brown, sister-in-law of one of the Windsor canons, celebrated her departure by writing in her diary, underlining each word with heavy strokes, 'GOOD RIDDANCE. I am glad we are going to have a QUEEN.'

The departure of the Conynghams was not regretted. But, despite *The Times*'s vilification of their former patron and protector, despite the general public's indifference to his death, there were still those who, years later, were reduced to tears by their affectionate memories of him. Riding out with Sir John Cope's hounds in 1833, Wellington galloped past 'skeletons of the tents' near the late King's fishing temples at Virginia Water. The sight of the ruins made him 'quite unhappy'. 'Alas!' he said to Charles Davis, Huntsman of the

---

Fitzherbert insisted on keeping some papers, including those which established her marriage to the King, and these were preserved in Messrs Coutts's vaults until 1905 when they passed into the Royal Archives. Wellington was always determined that they should never be opened, and threatened to move for an injunction from Chancery if any attempt were made to publish them. He told John Gurwood, his private secretary, that 'the publication would be mischievous, as the Prince by marrying a Catholic had by law forfeited the crown' (Sir George Seymour's annotations to Langdale's *Memoirs of Mrs Fitzherbert*, Seymour of Ragley MSS, CR 114/A/536/7). The King's marriage to Mrs Fitzherbert was not made public until after Wellington's death.

Royal Buckhounds, 'The poor King! Many a day have I passed with him in those tents!'

Davis 'burst out crying and was obliged to pull up his horse'.

Some years before, Wellington had referred to the King as 'a man of universal accomplishments'; and at the time of his death he had spoken in the House of Lords of his being acknowledged by all to be 'the most accomplished man of his age'. 'My Lords,' the Duke had declared, 'his Majesty's manners ... received a polish, his understanding acquired a degree of cultivation, almost unknown in any individual. ... No man ever approached him without having evidence of his dignity, his condescension, his ability, and his fitness for the exalted station which he occupied. ... Upon every occasion [he evinced] a degree of knowledge and of talent much beyond that which could reasonably be expected of an individual holding his high station.'

In lapidary inscriptions a man is not on oath; and on listening to these extravagant tributes Lord Grey was observed to 'smile a little'. But Wellington's eulogy was not wholly insincere. He recognized that the nation would always have cause to be grateful to a man who had been 'a most magnificent patron of the arts in this country, and in the world', that with the King's acknowledged faults went many varied virtues. 'He was, indeed,' he eventually decided, 'the most extraordinary compound of talent, wit, buffoonery, obstinacy and good feeling – in short a medley of the most opposite qualities, with a great preponderance of good – that I ever saw in any character in my life.'

It is a fitting epitaph. Prince Talleyrand provided a shorter one, no less apt: 'Kings nowadays are always seeking popularity, a pointless pursuit. King George IV was *un roi grand seigneur*. There are no others left.'

Sources

So that this edition of *George IV*, which was first published in two volumes, might conveniently be reissued in one, the references to sources, originally indicated by numerals in the text, have been omitted.

Abbreviations:

RA	– Royal Archives
BM	– British Museum
BM *Sat*	– *British Museum Catalogue of Political and Personal Satires*
PRO	– Public Record Office
HMCR	– Historical Manuscripts Commission Reports
WSD	– Wellington Supplementary Despatches
WDCM	– Wellington Despatches Correspondence and Memoranda
Asp/P	– Aspinall, ed., *Correspondence of George, Prince of Wales*
Asp/K	– Aspinall, ed., *Letters of King George IV*
Asp (*Charlotte*)	– Aspinall, ed., *Letters of the Princess Charlotte*

MANUSCRIPT

Royal Archives (Windsor Castle); British Museum – Fox MSS; Holland House MSS; Hickleton Papers; Add. MSS, 13714, 28063, 29179, 29764, 29915, 33132–3, 33629, 34453, 34992, 37062, 37282, 37296, 37297, 37414, 37728, 37847, 38191, 38242, 38264, 38278, 38285, 38564, 38565, 38574, 38716, 38742, 38752, 38760, 40306, 40344, 41857, 43727, 47560, 47570, 47579, 51520, 51457; Brighton Pavilion MSS; Hurd MSS (Hartlebury Castle); Mary Robinson MS Memoirs and Letters (Chequers); Chatsworth MSS; Wentworth Woodhouse Muniments (Sheffield); Finch MSS (Bodleian); Crawford Muniments (Balcarres); Fremantle Collection (Aylesbury); Goderich Papers (Aylesbury); Earl Grey Papers (Durham); Fitzwilliam Papers, Brook Records and Lord Dover's Papers (Delapre Abbey); Palmerston Papers (Winchester); Petworth House Archives (Chichester); Ragley MSS (Warwick); Pretyman Papers (Ipswich); Markham Papers (York); Capell Manuscripts (Hertford); Goulding Papers (Lincoln);

Harrowby Papers (Sandon Hall); Wellington Papers (Stratfield Saye); Farquhar Correspondence and Hook MSS (Bucklebury); Denbigh MSS (Pailton House); Canning Papers (Leeds); Brougham MSS (University College, London); Lord Chamberlain's MSS (Public Record Office); Brooks's Club Archives; Coutts & Co. Archives

NEWSPAPERS AND JOURNALS

Adam's Weekly Courant, Brighton Gazette, Brighton Herald, Courier, Daily Advertiser, The Diary, European Magazine, Evening Mail, Examiner, The Gazeteer and New Daily Advertiser, General Advertiser, General Evening Post, Gentleman's Magazine, John Bull, Lloyd's Evening Post, London Advertiser, London Chronicle, London Evening Post, London Gazette, London Packet, London Recorder or Sunday Gazette, Morning Chronicle and London Advertiser, Morning Post, Morning Herald, Morning Star, Oracle, Parker's General Advertiser, Public Advertiser, St James's Chronicle, Sun, Sussex Advertiser, The Times, True Briton, The World

HISTORICAL MANUSCRIPT COMMISSION REPORTS

The Manuscripts of the Earl of Lonsdale (13th Report, Appendix, Part VII); The Manuscripts and Correspondence of James, 1st Earl of Charlemont (13th Report, Appendix, Part VIII); The Manuscripts of the Earl of Carlisle (15th Report, Appendix, Part VI); The Manuscripts of the Duke of Rutland (14th Report, Appendix, Part I); The Manuscripts of J. B. Fortescue preserved at Dropmore (13th Report, Appendix, Part III; 14th Report, Appendix, Part V); The Manuscripts of the Marquess of Ailesbury (15th Report, Part VII)

PRINTED

Abbot Diary: Colchester, Charles, Lord, ed., *The Diary and Correspondence of Charles Abbot, Lord Colchester* (3 vols., 1861)

Account of the Visit of HRH the Prince Regent to the Corporation of London in June 1814 (1815)

Account of the Visit of HRH the Prince Regent to the University of Oxford in June [1814] (1815)

ADEANE, J. H., ed., *The Girlhood of Maria Josepha Holroyd, Lady Stanley of Alderley* (1896)

ADEANE, J. H., ed., *The Early Married Life of Maria Josepha Holroyd, Lady Stanley of Alderley* (1899)

AIRLIE, Mabel, Countess of, *In Whig Society* (1921)
Lady Palmerston and her Times (2 vols., 1922)

ALBEMARLE: George Thomas, Earl of Albemarle, *Fifty Years of my Life* (2 vols., 1876)

ANGELO, Henry [Domenico Angelo Malevolti Tremanondo], *Reminiscences of Henry Angelo with Memoirs of his Late Father and Friends* (2 vols., 1830)

ANGLESEY, Marquess of, *One-Leg, The Life and Letters of Henry William Paget, 1st Marquess of Anglesey* (Cape, 1961)

Arbuthnot Journal: Wellington, Duke of, and Francis Bamford, eds., *The Journal of Mrs Arbuthnot* (2 vols., 1950)

ASPINALL (*George III Correspondence*): Aspinall, A., ed., *The Later Correspondence of George III* (5 vols., Cambridge University Press, 1962–70)

ASPINALL (*George IV Correspondence*): Aspinall, A., ed., *The Letters of King George IV, 1812–30* (3 vols., Cambridge University Press, 1938)

ASPINALL (*Prince's Correspondence*): Aspinall, A., ed., *The Correspondence of George, Prince of Wales 1770–1812* (8 vols., Cassell, 1963–71)

ASPINALL (*Princess Charlotte's Letters*): Aspinall, A., ed., Letters of the Princess Charlotte (Home & Van Thal, 1949)

ASPINALL and SMITH: Aspinall, A., and Smith, E. Anthony, eds., *English Historical Documents 1783–1832* (Eyre & Spottiswoode, 1959)

ASPINALL, A., ed., *The Correspondence of Charles Arbuthnot* (Camden Third Series, vol. lxv, Royal Historical Society, 1941)

ASPINALL, A., *Politics and the Press, c. 1780–1850* (Home & Van Thal, 1949)
The Formation of Canning's Ministry, February to August 1827 (Camden Third Series, vol. lix, Royal Historical Society, 1937)
'George IV and Sir William Knighton' (*English Historical Review, 1940*)
Lord Brougham and the Whig Party (1927)

Auckland Correspondence: Bath and Wells, Bishop of, ed., *Journal and Correspondence of William, Lord Auckland* (4 vols., 1861–2)

AUSTEN-LEIGH, J. E., *A Memoir of Jane Austen* (1870)

Authentic Account of the Visit of HRH the Prince Regent to Oxford (1814)

AYLING, S. E., *George III* (Collins, 1972)

BAGOT, Josceline, ed., *George Canning and his Friends* (1909)

BAKER, Herschel, *John Phillip Kemble* (Harvard University Press, 1942)

Barnard Letters: Powell, Anthony, ed., *Barnard Letters 1778–1824* (Duckworth, 1928)

BARTLETT, C. J., *Castlereagh* (Macmillan, 1966)

BAYNE, William, *Sir David Wilkie* (1903)

BELL, Robert, *The Life of the Right Honourable George Canning* (1846)

Berry Journals: Lewis, Lady Theresa, ed., *Extracts of the Journals and Correspondence of Miss Berry* (3 vols., 1865)

BINGHAM, Madeleine, *Sheridan: The Track of a Comet* (Allen & Unwin, 1972)

BIRKENHEAD, Sheila, *Peace in Piccadilly: The Story of Albany* (Hamish Hamilton, 1958)

BLAKISTON, Georgiana, *Lord William Russell and his Wife, 1815–1846* (Murray, 1972)

Bland Burges Letters: Hutton, James, ed., *Selections from the Letters and Correspondence of Sir James Bland Burges* (1885)

BLOOMFIELD, Georgina, Lady, *Memoir of Benjamin, Lord Bloomfield* (2 vols., 1884)

Book, or the Proceedings and Correspondence upon the Subject of the Inquiry into the Conduct of the Princess of Wales, The (edition printed by Richard Edwards, 1813)

BOULTON, William B., *Thomas Gainsborough: His Life, Work, Friends and Sitters* (1905)

BRAYBROOK, Edward W., *The Royal Society of Literature of the United Kingdom* (1897)

BRAYLEY, Edward Wedlake, *Illustrations of His Majesty's Palace at Brighton: formerly the Pavilion* (1838)

British Museum Catalogue of Satires, see George, M.D.

BROCK, M. G., 'George Canning' (*History Today*, August 1951)

BROCK, W. R., *Lord Liverpool and Liberal Toryism, 1820–27* (Frank Cass, 1967)

BROOKE, John, *King George III* (Constable, 1972)

BROUGHAM *(Statesmen)*: Brougham, Henry, *Historical Sketches of Statesmen who Flourished in the Time of George III* (3 vols., 1845)

BROUGHAM *(Memoirs)*: Brougham, Henry, *The Life and Times of Henry Lord Brougham written by Himself* (3 vols., 1871)

BRYANT, Arthur, *The Age of Elegance* (Collins, 1950)

Buckingham Memoirs: Buckingham and Chandos, The Duke of, *Memoirs of the Court and Cabinets of George the Third* (2 vols., 1855)

BUCKINGHAM *(George IV)*: Buckingham and Chandos, Duke of, *Memoirs of the Court of George IV* (1859)

BUCKINGHAM *(Regency)*: Buckingham and Chandos, Duke of, *Memoirs of the Court of England during the Regency* (1856)

Buckingham Palace: John Russell, John Harris, Geoffrey de Bellaigue, Oliver Millar, *Buckingham Palace* (Nelson, 1968)

BURKE, S. Hubert, *Ireland Sixty Years Ago* (1885)

Burke Correspondence: Copeland, Thomas W., gen. ed., *The Correspondence of Edmund Burke* (9 vols, Cambridge University Press, 1958–70)

Bury Diary: Steuart, A. Francis, ed., *The Diary of a Lady in Waiting by Lady Charlotte Bury: Being the Diary Illustrative of the times of George IV* (2 vols., 1808)

Byron Letters: Prothero, R. E., ed., *The Works of Lord Byron. Letters and Journals* (1898)

CALVERT: *An Irish Beauty of the Regency* (1911)

CAMPBELL: Campbell, Lord, *Lives of the Lord Chancellors and Keepers of the Great Seal of England* (1846)

Candid Enquiry into the Case of the Prince of Wales, A (1786)

CANNON, John, *The Fox-North Coalition* (Cambridge University Press, 1970)

Castlereagh Correspondence: Londonderry, 3rd Marquess of, ed., *Memoirs and Correspondence of Viscount Castlereagh* (1848–53)

CECIL, Lord David, *The Young Melbourne* (Constable, 1939)

CHAPMAN, R. W., ed., *Jane Austen's Letters to her Sister Cassandra and others* (Oxford University Press, 1952)

CHENEVIX TRENCH, Charles, *The Royal Malady* (Longmans, 1964)

CHIFFNEY, Samuel, *Genius Genuine* (1804)

CHILDE-PEMBERTON, W. S., *The Romance of Princess Amelia ... Including Extracts from Private and Unpublished Papers* (1910)

CHRISTIE, Ian R., *Myth and Reality in Late Eighteenth Century Politics* (Macmillan, 1970)
The End of North's Ministry, 1780–82 (Macmillan, 1958)

CLARK, Mrs Godfrey, ed., *Gleanings from an Old Portfolio* (3 vols., 1896)

CLARKE, Mary Anne, *The Rival Princes* (2 vols., 1810)

CLONCURRY, Lord, *Personal Recollections* (1849)

COBBETT, William, *History of the Regency and Reign of King George the Fourth* (1830)

COLERIDGE, Ernest Hartley, *The Life of Thomas Coutts, Banker* (2 vols., 1920)

COLERIDGE, S. T., *Letters, Conversations and Recollections* (1836)

COLVIN, Christina, ed., *Maria Edgeworth: Letters from England* (Clarendon Press, 1971)

COLVIN, H. M., *A Biographical Dictionary of English Architects, 1660–1840* (John Murray, 1954)

CONNELL, Brian, *Portrait of a Whig Peer* (Deutsch, 1957)

COOPER, Bransby Blake, *The Life of Sir Astley Cooper, Bt.* (2 vols., 1843)

Cornwallis Correspondence: Ross, Charles, ed., *Correspondence of Charles, first Marquess Cornwallis* (3 vols., 1859)

Creevey Papers: Maxwell, Sir Herbert, ed., *The Creevey Papers: A Selection from the Correspondence and Diaries of the Late Thomas Creevey, M.P.* (1905)

CRESTON: Creston, Dormer, *The Regent and his Daughter* (Eyre & Spottiswoode, 1952)

Croker Papers: Jennings, Louis, J., ed., *The Croker Papers* (3 vols., 1884)

CROLY, George, *The Personal History of His Late Majesty King George the Fourth* (2 vols., 1841)

DALLING, Lord, *Life of Lord Palmerston* (2 vols., 1870)

D'Arblay Diary: Barrett, Charlotte, ed., *Diary and Letters of Madame D'Arblay* (4 vols., 1876)

D'ARBLAY, Mme, *Memoirs of Dr Burney* (1832)

DARVALL, F. O., *Popular Disturbances and Public Order in Regency England* (1934)

DERRY, John W., *The Regency Crisis and the Whigs, 1788-9* (Cambridge University Press, 1963)
Charles James Fox (Batsford, 1972)

Devonshire Diary: The Diary of Georgiana, Duchess of Devonshire [printed in Walter Sichel's *Sheridan*, 399-426 (1909)]

Dutch Pictures from the Royal Collection (The Queen's Gallery, Buckingham Palace, Lund Humphries, 1971)

Edgeworth Letters: Hare, Augustus, ed., *The Life and Letters of Maria Edgeworth* (1894)

EDWARDS, H. S., *The Life of Rossini* (1869)

EHRMAN, John, *The Younger Pitt* (Constable, 1969)

Ellenborough Diary: Colchester, Lord, ed., *A Political Diary, 1828-50 by Edward Law, Lord Ellenborough* (2 vols., 1881)

Elliot Letters: Minto, the Countess of, ed., *Life and Letters of Sir Gilbert Elliot, First Earl of Minto* (3 vols., 1874)

ELWIN, Malcolm, see *Noels and Milbankes*

ERREDGE, John Ackerson, *History of Brightelmston* (1862)

Farington Diary: Grieg, James, ed., *The Farington Diary by Joseph Farington RA* (8 vols., Hutchinson, 1922-28)

FITZGERALD, Percy, *The Life of George the Fourth* (2 vols., 1881)

FOORD, Archibald, S., *His Majesty's Opposition, 1714-1830* (Clarendon Press, 1964)

FORTESCUE *(George III Correspondence)*: Fortescue, Sir John, ed., *The Correspondence of King George the Third, 1760-83* (6 vols., 1927-28)

FOSTER, VERE, ed., *The Two Duchesses* (1898)

FOTHERGILL, Brian, *Sir William Hamilton* (Harcourt, Brace and World, 1969)

Fox Correspondence: Russell, Lord John, ed., *Memorials and Correspondence of Charles James Fox* (4 vols., 1853-57)

Fox Journal: Ilchester, Earl of, ed., *Journal of Henry Edward Fox, afterwards 4th Earl Holland* (2 vols., 1923)

Frampton Journal: Mundy, Harriot Georgiana, ed., *The Journal of Mary Frampton* (1885)

Francis Letters: Francis, Beata and Eliza Keary, eds., *The Fran-*

cis Letters by Sir Philip Francis and Other Members of the Family (n.d.)

Francis Memoirs: Merivale, Herman, ed., *Memoirs of Sir Philip Francis* (2 vols., 1867)

FULFORD, Roger, *George the Fourth* (Duckworth, 1935)
Royal Dukes: The Father and Uncles of Queen Victoria (Duckworth, 1933)
Samuel Whitbread, 1764-1815: A Study in Opposition (Macmillan, 1967)

Fulke Greville Diaries: Bladon, F. McKno, ed., *The Diaries of Colonel the Hon. Robert Fulke Greville* (Lane, 1930)

GALT, J., *George III, His Court and Family* (1820)

GARLICK, Kenneth, *Sir Thomas Lawrence* (Routledge & Kegan Paul, 1954)

GASH, Norman, *Mr Secretary Peel* (Longmans, 1961)

GEORGE, M. Dorothy, *Catalogue of Personal and Political Satires* (vols. v–xi, British Museum, 1935–54)
English Political Caricature to 1792 (Clarendon Press, 1959)
English Political Caricature 1793–1832 (Clarendon Press, 1959)

Georgiana: Bessborough, Earl of, ed., *Georgiana* (John Murray, 1955)

GILLEN, Mollie, *The Prince and His Lady* (Sidgwick & Jackson, 1970)

Glenbervie Journals: Bickley, Francis, ed., *The Diaries of Sylvester Douglas (Lord Glenbervie)* (Constable, 1928)

GORE, John, *Creevey's Life and Times* (1934)

Granville Leveson Gower Correspondence: Granville, Castalia Countess, ed., *Lord Granville Leveson Gower (First Earl of Granville) Private Correspondence 1781–1821* (2 vols., 1916)

GRATTAN, Henry, *Memoirs of the Life and Times of Henry Grattan* (1839–46)

GRAY, Denis, *Spencer Perceval* (Manchester University Press, 1963)

GREENWOOD, Λ ice Drayton, *Lives of the Hanoverian Queens of England* (vol. ii, 1911)

Greville Memoirs: Strachey, Lytton, and Fulford, Roger, eds., *The Greville Memoirs, 1814–1860* (Macmillan, 1938)

Gronow Reminiscences: The Reminiscences and Recollections of Captain Gronow (2 vols., 1892)

HAMILTON, Edwin, *A Record of the Life and Death of HRH the Princess Charlotte* (1817)

Hamilton Letters: Anson, Elizabeth and Florence, eds., *Mary Hamilton ... At Court and at Home ... 1756–1816* (1925)

Harcourt Papers: Harcourt, Edward William, ed., *The Harcourt Papers* (14 vols., 1880–1905)

HAWES, Frances, *Henry Brougham* (Jonathan Cape, 1957)

Hawkins Memoirs: Hawkins, Laetitia, *Anecdotes, Biographical Sketches and Memoirs* (2 vols., 1822)

HAYDON, B. R., *Correspondence and Table-Talk* (1876)

Haydon Diary: Pope, Willard Bissel, ed., *The Diary of Benjamin Robert Haydon* (Harvard University Press, 1960)

HAYTER, John, *The Herculanean and Pompeian Manuscripts* (n.d.)
A Report upon the Herculanean Manuscripts (1811)

HAYWARD, A., *Diaries of a Lady of Quality from 1797 to 1844* (1864)

HERRIES, Edward, *Memoir of the Public Life of J. C. Herries* (1880)

Historical Account of his Majesty's Visit to Scotland, An (1822)

Historical Account of the Public and Domestic Life and Reign of George IV, An (1830)

History of the Life and Reign of George the Fourth, The (3 vols., 1831)

Hobhouse Diary: Aspinall, A., ed., *The Diary of Henry Hobhouse, 1820–1827* (Home & Van Thal, 1947)

HOBHOUSE, Christopher, *Fox* (John Murray, 1934)

HOLLAND *(Further Memoirs)*: Stavordale, Lord, ed., Holland, Henry Richard, Lord, *Further Memoirs of the Whig Party, 1807–1821* (1905)

HOLLAND *(Journal)*: Ilchester, Earl of, ed., *Journal of Elizabeth, Lady Holland 1791–1811* (2 vols., 1908)

HOLLAND *(Letters)*: Ilchester, Earl of, ed., *Elizabeth, Lady Holland to her Son, 1821–1845* (Murray, 1946)

HOLLAND *(Memoirs)*: Holland, Henry Edward, Lord, ed., Holland, Henry Richard, Lord, *Memoirs of the Whig Party During my Time* (2 vols., 1852–1854)

HORN, D. B., and RANSOME, Mary, eds., *English Historical Documents, 1714–83* (Eyre & Spottiswoode, 1957)

HUISH, Robert, *Memoirs of George the Fourth* (2 vols., 1831)

HUNT, James Henry Leigh, *Autobiography* (1885)

HUNTER, Richard, see Macalpine

ILCHESTER, Countess of (with Lord Stavordale), *The Life and Letters of Lady Sarah Lennox* (2 vols., 1901)

JACKSON, G. A., ed., *Brougham and his Early Friends* (1908)

JEFFREYS, Nathaniel, *A Review of the Conduct of His Royal Highness, the Prince of Wales* (1806)
A Letter Addressed to Mrs Fitzherbert in Answer to a Complaint that her Feelings have been Hurt by the mention of her Name in the Review of the Conduct of the Prince of Wales (1787)

Jekyll Correspondence: Bourke, Algernon, ed., *Correspondence of Mr Joseph Jekyll . . . 1818–38* (1894)

Jerningham Letters: Castle, Egerton, ed., *The Jerningham Letters: Being Excerpts from the Correspondence and Diaries of the Hon. Lady Jerningham and of her Daughter Lady Bedingfield* (2 vols., 1896)

JESSE, Captain, *The Life of Beau Brummell* (1854)

JESSE, J. H., *Memoirs of the Life and Reign of King George III* (5 vols., 1901)

JONES, George, *Sir Francis Chantrey* (1849)

JONES, Wilbur Devereux, *'Prosperity Robinson': The Life of Viscount Goderich* (Macmillan, 1967)

Journal of an English Traveller or Memoirs and Anecdotes of HRH Caroline of Brunswick Princess of Wales (1817)

KILVERT, Rev. Francis, *Memoirs of the life and Writings of the Rt Rev Richard Hurd* (1860)

King's Visit to Scotland, The (British Museum, 1876, e, 24)

Knight Autobiography: Kaye, Sir J. W., and Hulton, J., eds., *The Autobiography of Miss Cornelia Knight* (2 vols., 1861)

KNIGHTON, Lady, *Memoirs of Sir William Knighton* (2 vols., 1838)

Lamb Letters: Lamb, Charles, *Letters* (1945)

LANDON, H. C. Robbins, ed., *The Collected Correspondence and London Notebooks of Joseph Haydn* (Barrie & Rockcliff, (1959)

LANGDALE, Hon. Charles, *Memoirs of Mrs Fitzherbert* (1856)

Leadbeater Papers, The (1862)

LEAN, E. Tangye, *The Napoleonists: A Study in Political Disaffection, 1760–1960* (Oxford University Press, 1970)

Leeds Memoranda: Browning, Oscar, ed., *The Political Memoranda of Francis Fifth Duke of Leeds* (1884)

LENNOX, Lord William Pitt, *Fifty Years' Biographical Reminiscences* (1863)
My Recollections from 1806–1873 (1874)
The Story of my Life (1854)

LESLIE, Anita, *Mrs Fitzherbert* (Hutchinson, 1960)

LESLIE, Shane, *George the Fourth* (Ernest Benn, 1926)
The Life and Letters of Mrs Fitzherbert (2 vols., Burns & Oates, 1939–40)

Letter to the House of Peers on the Present Bill, depending in Parliament, relative to the Prince of Wales' debts by A Hanoverian (1795)

Letter to the Prince of Wales on a Second Application to Parliament to discharge Debts Wantonly Contracted since May 1787, A (1795)

LEVER, Sir Tresham, *The Letters of Lady Palmerston* (John Murray, 1957)

Lieven (Grey Correspondence): Le Strange, G., ed., *The Correspondence of Princess Lieven and Earl Grey* (3 vols., 1890)

Lieven (London Letters): Robinson, Lionel G., ed., *Letters of Dorothea, Princess Lieven during her Residence in London, 1812–1834* (1902)

Lieven (Metternich Letters): Quennell, Peter, ed., *The Private Letters of Princess Lieven to Prince Metternich 1820–26* (1948)

Lieven (Palmerston Correspondence): Sudley, Lord, ed., *The Lieven-Palmerston Correspondence, 1828–1856* (Murray, 1943)

LINDSTRUM, Derek, *Sir Jeffry Wyatville: Architect to the King* (Clarendon Press, 1973)

LLOYD, H. E., *George IV, Memoirs of his Life and Reign* (1830)

LOCKHART, J. G., *Memoirs of the Life of Sir Walter Scott* (1837–38)

LONGFORD, Elizabeth, *Victoria R.I.* (Weidenfeld & Nicholson, 1964)
Wellington: Pillar of State (Weidenfeld & Nicholson, 1972)

LUTTRELL, Barbara, *The Prim Romantic: A Biography of Cornelia Knight, 1758–1837* (Chatto & Windus, 1965)

Lyttelton Correspondence: Wyndham, Hon. Mrs Hugh, ed., *Correspondence of Sarah Spencer Lady Lyttelton, 1787–1870* (1912)

MACALPINE, Ida, and HUNTER, Richard, *George III and the Mad-Business* (Allen Lane The Penguin Press, 1969)

MACFARLANE, Charles, *Reminiscences of a Literary Life* (1917)

MACKAY, William, and ROBERTS, W., *John Hoppner R.A.* (1909)

Malmesbury Diaries: Malmesbury, 3rd Earl of, ed., *The Diaries and Correspondence of James Harris First Earl of Malmesbury* (4 vols., 1844)

Markham Memoir: Markham, Sir Clements, *A Memoir of Archbishop Markham, 1719–1807* (1906)

MARPLES, Morris, *Six Royal Sisters: Daughters of George III* (Michael Joseph, 1969)

MARSHALL, Dorothy, *The Rise of George Canning* (Longmans, 1938)

MARTIN, Sir Theodore, *Life of Lord Lyndhurst* (1883)

MATHEWS, Anne, *A Continuation of the Memoirs of Charles Mathews* (1839)

MELVILLE, Lewis, *Beau Brummel, His Life and Letters* (1924)

MEMES, J. S., *Memoirs of Antonio Canova* (1825)

Memoirs of His Royal Highness the Prince of Wales (1808)

MILES, W. A., *A Letter to his Royal Highness the Prince of Wales with a Sketch of the Prospect before him* (1808)

MILLAR, Oliver, *The Tudor, Stuart and Early Georgian Pictures in the Collection of her Majesty the Queen* (Phaidon Press, 1963)
Later Georgian Pictures in the Collection of her Majesty the Queen (Phaidon Press, 1969)

MITCHELL, L. B. G., *Charles James Fox and the Disintegration of the Whig Party, 1782–1794* (Oxford University Press, 1970)

Mitford Letters: Chorley, Henry, ed., *Letters of Mary Russell Mitford* (1872)

MOLLOY, J. Fitzgerald, ed., *Memoirs of Mrs Robinson* (1894)

Moore Journals: Russell, Lord John, ed., *Memoirs, Journal and Correspondence of Thomas Moore* (1853)

MOORE, Thomas, *Intercepted Letters; or The Twopenny Post-Bag* (1813)

MOORE (*Sheridan*): Moore, Thomas, *Memoirs of the Life of the Right Honourable Richard Brinsley Sheridan* (2 vols., 1825)

MORSHEAD, Owen, *George IV and Royal Lodge* (Regency Society of Brighton and Hove, 1965)
Windsor Castle (Phaidon Press, 1957)
MUNK, William, *The Life of Sir Henry Halford, Bt* (1895)
MURRAY, Hon. Amelia, *Recollections of the Early Years of the Present Century* (1868)
MURRAY, Robert H., *Edmund Burke* (Oxford University Press, 1931)
MUSGRAVE, Clifford, *Life in Brighton* (Faber, 1970)
The Royal Pavilion: An Episode in the Romantic (Leonard Hill, 1964)

NAMIER, Sir Lewis, *Crossroads of Power* (Hamish Hamilton, 1962)
NEW, Chester W., *The Life of Henry Brougham to 1830* (Clarendon Press, 1961)
NICHOLLS, John, *Observations on the Situation of His Royal Highness the Prince of Wales* (1795)
NICOLSON, Sir Harold, *The Congress of Vienna* (Constable, 1940)
NIGHTINGALE, J., *Memoir of the Public and Private Life of . . . Caroline, Queen of Great Britain* (1820)
Noels and Milbankes: Elwin, Malcolm, ed., *The Noels and Milbankes*, (Macdonald, 1967)
Northumberland Diaries: Greig, James, ed., *The Diaries of a Duchess: Extracts from the Diaries of the First Duchess of Northumberland, 1716–1776* (1926)

OLIVER, J. W., *The Life of William Beckford* (Oxford University Press, 1932)
OMAN, Carola, *The Gascoyne Heiress: The Life and Diaries of Frances Mary Gascoyne-Cecil* (Hodder & Stoughton, 1968)

Paget Papers: Paget, Sir Augustus B., ed., *The Paget Papers: Diplomatic and other Correspondence of the Rt Hon. Sir Arthur Paget* (2 vols., 1896)
PALMER, Alan, *Metternich* (Weidenfeld & Nicolson, 1972)
Papendiek Journals: Delves Broughton, Mrs Vernon, ed., *Court and Private Life in the Time of Queen Charlotte: Being the Journals of Mrs Papendiek* (2 vols., 1887)

PARKER, Charles Stuart, *Sir Robert Peel, from his Private Papers* (3 vols., 1891–1899)

Parliamentary History of England, The

PARRY, Edward, *Queen Caroline* (Benn, 1930)

Peel Memoirs: Stanhope, Earl, and E. Cardwell, eds., *The Memoirs of Sir Robert Peel* (2 vols., 1857)

PELLEW, George, *The Life and Correspondence of the Right Honourable Henry Addington, First Viscount Sidmouth* (3 vols., 1847)

PETRIE, Sir Charles, *Canning* (revised edition, 1946)

The Four Georges: A Revaluation (1935)

Lord Liverpool and his Times (1954)

PEVSNER, Nikolaus, *The Buildings of England: London* (2 vols., Penguin Books, 1962)

PLUMB, J. H., *The First Four Georges* (Batsford, 1956)

Plumer Ward: Phipps, Hon. Edmund, *Memoirs of the Political and Literary Life of Robert Plumer Ward* (1850)

Porphyria – A Royal Malady: Articles published in or commissioned by the British Medical Journal (British Medical Association, 1968)

PÜCKLER-MUSKAU, Prince, *Tour in England, Ireland and France, 1826–8* (1832)

PYNE, W. H., *The History of the Royal Residences* (1819)

RAE, William Fraser, *Wilkes, Sheridan, Fox: the Opposition under George the Third* (1927)

RAIKES, Thomas, *A Portion of the Journal Kept by Thomas Raikes Esq. from 1831 to 1847* (4 vols., 1856–1857)

RANDOLPH, Herbert, *Life of Sir Robert Wilson* (2 vols., 1862)

REID, Loren, *Charles James Fox: A Man for the People* (Longmans, 1969)

Report of the Proceedings: Nightingale, J., ed., *Report of the Proceedings before the House of Lords on a Bill of Pains and Penalties* (3 vols., 1821)

RICHARDSON, Joanna, *George IV: A Portrait* (Sidgwick & Jackson, 1966)

'George IV, Patron of Literature' in *Essays by Divers Hands*, vol. xxxv (Oxford University Press, 1969)

The Disastrous Marriage: A Study of George IV and Caroline of Brunswick (Jonathan Cape, 1960)

RICKWORD, Edgell, *Radical Squibs and Loyal Ripostes* (Adams & Dart, 1971)

RIDLEY, Jasper, *Lord Palmerston* (Constable, 1970)

ROBERTS, Henry D., *A History of the Royal Pavilion, Brighton* (Country Life, 1939)

ROBERTS, Michael, *The Whig Party, 1807–1812* (Frank Cass, 1965)

ROBERTS, W., *Sir William Beechey, R.A.* (1901)

Robinson Correspondence: Morley, Edith J., ed., *The Correspondence of Henry Crabb Robinson with the Wordsworth Circle* (1927)

ROGERS *(Table-Talk)*: Bishop, Morchard, ed., *Recollections of the Table-Talk of Samuel Rogers* (Richards Press, 1952)

ROLO, P. J. V., *George Canning: Three Biographical Studies* (Macmillan, 1965)

Romilly Memoirs: Memoirs of Sir Samuel Romilly (3 vols., 1840)

ROSE, John Holland, *Life of William Pitt* (2 vols., 1924)

Rose Diaries: Harcourt, Rev. Leveson Vernon, ed., *The Diaries and Correspondence of the Rt Hon. George Rose* (2 vols., 1860)

RUSH, Richard, *Memoranda of a Residence at the Court of London* (1933)

RUSSELL, Lord John, *The Life and Times of Charles James Fox* (3 vols., 1859–66)

Scott Journal: J. G. Tait, ed., *The Journal of Sir Walter Scott* (1939–50)

Scott Letter-Books: Partington, Wilfred, ed., *The Private Letter-Books of Sir Walter Scott* (1930)

Scott Letters: Grierson, H. J. C., ed., *The Letters of Sir Walter Scott* (Constable, 1923–37)

Shelley Diary: Edgcumbe, Richard, ed., *The Diary of Frances, Lady Shelley* (2 vols., 1912–13)

Shelley Letters: Ingpen, R., ed., The Letters of Percy Bysshe Shelley (1912)

SHERIDAN *(Journal)*: Le Fanu, William, ed., *Betsy Sheridan's Journal: Letters from Sheridan's Sister* (Eyre & Spottiswoode, 1960)

SHERIDAN *(Letters)*: Price, Cecil, ed., *The Letters of Richard Brinsley Sheridan* (Clarendon Press, 1960)

SICHEL, Walter, *Sheridan* (2 vols., 1909)

SITWELL, Osbert, *Left Hand, Right Hand* (Macmillan, 1945)

Slight Reminiscences of a Septuagenarian from 1802 to 1815 by Emma Sophia, Countess Brownlow (1867)

SMILES, Samuel, *A Publisher and his Friends* (1911)

Southey Correspondence: Southey, Rev. C. C., ed., *The Life and Correspondence of the late Robert Southey* (1849)

Spencer-Stanhope Letter-Bag: Stirling, A. M. W., ed., *The Letter-Bag of Lady Louisa Spencer-Stanhope* (1913)

STANHOPE, Earl, *Life of the Rt Hon. William Pitt* (4 vols., 1867)

Stanhope Memoirs: Memoirs of the Lady Hester Stanhope as related by herself in conversation with her physician (3 vols., 1845)

STAPLETON, A. G., *Political Life of George Canning* (2 vols., 1831)

STEEGMAN, John, *The Rule of Taste from George I to George IV* (Macmillan, 1968)

STOCKDALE, J., *The History and Proceedings of the Lords and Commons ... with Regard to the Regency* (1789)

STOCKMAR, E. von, ed., *Memoirs of Baron Stockmar* (Trans. Max Müller, 2 vols., 1872–1873)

STOKES, Hugh, *The Devonshire House Circle* (1917)

STROUD, Dorothy, *Henry Holland* (Country Life, 1966)

STUART *(Daughters of George III)*: Stuart, Dorothy Margaret, *The Daughters of George III* (Macmillan, 1939)

STUART *(Foster)*: Stuart, Dorothy Margaret, *Dearest Bess: The Life and Times of Lady Elizabeth Foster, afterwards Duchess of Devonshire from her Unpublished Journals and Correspondence* (Methuen, 1955)

Stuart Letters: Johnson, B. B., ed., *The Letters of Lady Louisa Stuart* (1926)

SUMMERSON, John, *John Nash, Architect to King George IV* (Allen & Unwin, 1935)

SUMNER, George Henry, *Life of Charles Richard Sumner* (1876)

TAYLOR, Thomas, *Life of Benjamin Robert Haydon* (2 vols., 1853)

TEMPERLEY, Harold, ed., *The Unpublished Diary and Political Sketches of Princess Lieven* (Cape, 1935)

The Foreign Policy of Canning, 1822–7 (1925)

THOMPSON, E. P., *The Making of the English Working Class* (Gollancz, 1963; Penguin Books, 1968)

TOOKE, Horne, *A Letter to a Friend on the Reported Marriage of His Royal Highness, the Prince of Wales* (1787)

Tour to York, A Circumstantial Account of His Royal Highness the Prince of Wales's visit to that City (1789)

TOYE, Francis, *Rossini* (Arthur Barker, 1954)

TROTTER, J. B., *Memoirs of the Later Years of the Rt Hon. Charles James Fox* (1811)

TWISS, Horace, *The Public and Private Life of Lord Chancellor Eldon* (3 vols., 1844)

Two Words of Counsel, and one of Comfort. Addressed to His Royal Highness the Prince of Wales by an old Englishman (1795)

Vindication of the Conduct of Lady Douglas during her Intercourse with the Princess of Wales ... etc. (1814)

VULLIAMY, C. E., *Aspasia: The Life and Letters of Mary Granville, Mrs Delany, 1700–1788* (Bles, 1937)

Walpole Correspondence: Lewis, W. S., ed., *The Yale Edition of Horace Walpole's Correspondence* (34 vols., Oxford University Press, 1937–65)

WALPOLE *(George III)*: Barker, G. F. Russel, ed., Walpole, Horace, *Memoirs of the Reign of King George the Third* (4 vols., 1894)

WALPOLE *(Last Journals)*: Steuart, A. Francis, ed., *The Last Journals of Horace Walpole During the Reign of George III* (2 vols., 1910)

WATSON, J. Steven, *The Reign of George III, 1760–1815* (Oxford University Press, 1959)

WEBSTER, Sir Charles, *The Foreign Policy of Castlereagh 1815–22* (2nd edn, 1934)

WEIGALL, Lady Rose, *A Brief Memoir of Princess Charlotte of Wales* (1874)

Wellington and his Friends: Wellington, 7th Duke of, ed., *Wellington and his Friends: Letters of the 1st Duke of Wellington* (Macmillan, 1965)

Wellington Despatches, Correspondence and Memoranda, 1819–32 (8 vols., 1867–80)

Wellington Supplementary Despatches: Wellington, Duke of, ed., *Supplementary Despatches 1794–1818* (15 vols., 1858–72)

WHALLEY, George, 'Coleridge and the Royal Society of Literature' in *Essays by Divers Hands*, vol. xxxv (Oxford University Press, 1969)

WHITE, R. J., *The Age of George III* (History Book Club, 1968)
From Waterloo to Peterloo (Heinemann, 1957)

WILBERFORCE, Robert Isaac, and Wilberforce, Samuel, *The Life of William Wilberforce* (5 vols., 1838)

WILKINS, W. H., *Mrs Fitzherbert and George IV* (2 vols., 1905)

WILKS, John, *Memoirs of Her Majesty, Queen Caroline* (1822)

WILLIAMS, D. E., *The Life and Correspondence of Sir Thomas Lawrence* (1831)

Williams Wyn Correspondence: Layard, G. S., ed., *Correspondence of Charlotte Grenville, Lady Williams Wyn and her Three Sons* (1920)

WILLIAMSON, G. C., *Richard Cosway, R.A., and his Wife and Pupils* (1897)

WILLIS, G. M., *Ernest Augustus, Duke of Cumberland and King of Hanover* (Arthur Barker, 1954)

WILSON, Harriette, *Memoirs of Harriette Wilson Written by Herself* (4 vols., 1825)

Windham Papers: Windham, Rt Hon. William, *The Windham Papers* (2 vols., 1913)

WOODHAM-SMITH, Cecil, *Queen Victoria: Her Life and Times* (vol. 1, Hamish Hamilton, 1972)

WOODWARD, Sir Llewellyn, *The Age of Reform 1815–1870* (Oxford University Press, 1961)

WRAXALL: Wheatley, Henry B., ed., *The Historical and Posthumous Memoirs of Sir Nathaniel William Wraxall, 1772–1784* (5 vols., 1884)

YONGE, C. D., *Life and Administration of Robert Banks Jenkinson, 2nd Earl of Liverpool* (3 vols., 1868)

ZIEGLER, Philip, *Addington: A Life of Henry Addington, First Viscount Sidmouth* (Collins, 1965)
King William IV (Collins, 1972)

Index